Turbo Pascal ® 6 DiskTutor,
Second Edition

Werner Feibel

Berkeley   New York   St. Louis   San Francisco
Auckland   Bogotá   Hamburg   London   Madrid
Mexico City   Milan   Montreal   New Delhi   Panama City
Paris   São Paulo   Singapore   Sydney
Tokyo   Toronto

Osborne **McGraw-Hill**
2600 Tenth Street
Berkeley, California 94710
U.S.A.

Osborne **McGraw-Hill** offers software for sale.For information on software, translations, and book distributors outside of the U.S.A., write to Osborne **McGraw-Hill** at the above address.

Turbo Pascal® 6 DiskTutor, Second Edition

Copyright © 1991 by McGraw-Hill, Inc. All rights reserved. Printed in the United States of America. Except as permitted under the Copyright Act of 1976, no part of this publication may be reproduced or distributed in any form or by any means, or stored in a database or retrieval system, without the prior written permission of the publisher, with the exception that the program listings may be entered, stored, and executed in a computer system, but they may not be reproduced for publication.

1234567890 DOC 9987654321

ISBN 0-07-881738-2

Turbo Pascal is a registered trademark of Borland International, Inc.

Information has been obtained by Osborne **McGraw-Hill** from sources believed to be reliable. However, because of the possibility of human or mechanical error by our sources, Osborne **McGraw-Hill**, or others, Osborne **McGraw-Hill** does not guarantee the accuracy, adequacy, or completeness of any information and is not responsible for any errors or omissions or the results obtained from use of such information.

To the next generation of programmers

Contents

Acknowledgments

As always, the folks at Osborne/McGraw-Hill—Emily Rader, Judith Brown, Vicki Van Ausdall, and Jeff Pepper—deserve thanks and recognition for their helpfulness and competence. They provided me with the materials I needed to complete this revision, took changes over the telephone when time was at a premium, and basically turned the material I sent them into a finished product. Working with them hardly seems like work.

Ann Kameoka, the copy editor, deserves special credit for working with a manuscript that arrived in no apparent order. Despite that, Ann did an excellent job of finding errors and inconsistencies.

Steven Nameroff again deserves thanks for his technical reviewing and his suggestions. I am also very grateful to him for allowing me to adapt an excellent chapter he wrote on Turbo Vision for this book.

Finally, my love to my wife Luanne, who always makes everything more enjoyable and interesting.

Preface

Turbo Pascal 6 DiskTutor introduces you to Turbo Pascal, which has served to define the Pascal language for over 1.5 million users. Many of these people learned to program using the Turbo Pascal compiler. Many others have used Turbo Pascal to create major applications programs that are in use all over the world.

Turbo Pascal 6 DiskTutor provides thorough coverage of the Pascal language, including object-oriented programming—a technique that has been available in specialized languages for several years and is now available in the most recent versions of Turbo Pascal.

The book's format is informal and easy to follow. It does not assume that you've had any programming experience. However, it does include advanced topics (such as linked lists and the use of operating system services) that are often omitted from introductory programming books.

The presentation is illustrated through hundreds of listings, with over 200 example programs included on disk.

You can use the programming facilities in Turbo Pascal's integrated development environment (IDE) to explore the 10,000-plus lines of code in the example programs and also to create your own programs.

The example programs are designed to make it easy to continue exploring the topics on your own, either by modifying the programs or by trying various values in the programs.

You'll find the programs most valuable if you study the code. Most of the procedures and functions in the programs are discussed in detail, and you'll find lots of suggestions for changes and extensions to make.

Once you've finished this book, you'll know the syntax of the Pascal language, and you'll have enough experience and guides (in the form of example programs), to create programs for solving problems of interest to you. You will have learned enough to design and write sizeable programs on your own — using either object-oriented or traditional programming techniques.

If you work with the example programs, you'll find numerous procedures and functions that you can use directly in your own programs or that you can adapt easily to suit your particular needs. Similarly, if you explore enough, you will develop a sense of when object-oriented methods are most appropriate and when other approaches make more sense.

For example, once you've worked through the entire book, you'll have learned enough concepts to write a game program in which players compete against each other or against a clock and in which you can use graphics and sound.

How This Book Is Organized

The book's 14 chapters are in two major sections. The first section (Chapters 1 through 10) covers the core of the Pascal language; the second section (Chapters 11 through 14) covers extensions to the language provided in Turbo Pascal. These extensions make your programming task easier and make the language implementation even more powerful. Turbo Pascal's very powerful object-oriented features are covered in this second section.

Topics in later chapters generally build upon earlier concepts. This has made it easier to organize the material to present to you; it also makes it easier for you to understand and organize the concepts as you learn Pascal.

Chapter 1 introduces the language and the implementation in general terms. Chapter 2 provides an informal introduction to Pascal and to the IDE through several examples. In Chapter 3 you'll learn how to represent simple types of information in Pascal and also how to declare and use variables in your programs. In this chapter, you'll learn how to give simple instructions, such as assigning values to variables.

Chapters 4 and 6 describe how to create procedures and functions — the building blocks of an organized Pascal program. Grouping individual statements, or instructions, into procedures and functions enables you to organize your programs and also to reuse your code in other programs. Because procedures and functions are so important to good programming, they are introduced early; because there are many things to learn about procedures and functions, they are discussed again later—after you've had a chance to learn (in Chapter 5) about the looping and selection constructs Pascal provides for controlling your program's execution.

Chapter 7 shows you how to represent and use more complex information (such as records, which can contain various types of information; and arrays, or collections, of values). As you'll find, Turbo Pascal offers a wide variety of data types, and even allows you to create your own types so you can tailor the program to your particular task.

In Chapter 8, you'll learn about files and about saving your program's output to disk or getting information into your program from the disk. Pointers—very powerful programming tools—are discussed in Chapter 9. As you'll see, the concept of pointers makes it possible for you to create even more powerful and efficient ways of storing information than those built into the language.

Chapter 10 actually represents a transition between the first and second sections. This chapter discusses units, a feature of Turbo Pascal that enables you to create and compile collections of procedures and functions for use in your programs. Although units are not a feature of the original Pascal as defined by Niklaus Wirth (the language's creator), they have become available in almost every implementation of the language. Because Turbo Pascal has become such a predominant version, units have become more or less standard features of the language. In Chapter 10, you'll learn about procedures and functions available through several Turbo Pascal units. For example, you'll learn how to control activity on the screen and how to do simple graphics.

Chapters 11 through 13 provide an introduction to object-oriented programming. You'll learn what objects are and how to define objects that inherit features from other objects. You'll learn how to associate methods, or actions, with objects, and how to let the program decide which method should be used in a particular situation in a program. Chapter 13 introduces Turbo Vision, an object-oriented tool collection that was used to create the IDE and which you can use in your own programs. Once you've had a taste of object-oriented programming, you'll find yourself using these techniques for many of your programs.

Finally, Chapter 14 covers several miscellaneous topics. Among other things, you'll learn how to manipulate individual bits in your programs and how to use services provided by the operating system. For example, you'll learn how to time parts of a program and how to check the current date and time.

Once you've covered all these topics, you'll be set to continue your programming education on your own!

Conventions

It may make your task a bit easier if you're aware of certain typographical and stylistic conventions that are used in this book.

In the text, new terms are written in *italic* type when they are defined or explained.

Keypresses are represented by small capital letters; for example, ENTER.

Words that are used in Pascal programs (such as variable names, type names, and so forth) are written in boldface type when these words appear in the text—that is, when they appear outside of program listings. Certain words are reserved as part of the Pascal language definition and may not be used for other purposes. For example, the word **PROCEDURE** has a special meaning in Pascal and may be used in only one way in a program. Other words are predefined in Turbo Pascal (for example, the names of simple data types). Such reserved and predefined words are represented in boldface type, in all uppercase letters.

Other books will use different conventions for such words. For example, the documentation for the Turbo Pascal compiler uses a monospace font to represent reserved and predefined words. Similarly, Borland's documentation for Turbo Pascal uses only lowercase letters when specifying such words.

Pascal allows you to use meaningful names, or identifiers, for your variables, procedures, and functions. Thus, you can name a variable **MonthlyMortgagePayment** instead of **X**. The former is much more descriptive and is easy to remember and understand. The example programs use meaningful names for variables both because it is good programming practice and because it makes your learning task easier. You can concentrate on the principles involved or illustrated in a program instead of having to worry about what a particular variable represents. Such identifiers are written with mixed-case letters, using a technique in which the initial letter of each "word" in an identifier is capitalized, as in the example, **MonthlyMortgagePayment**.

You can put comments in your Pascal programs. In the program listings, comments begin with (* and end with *). Pascal also lets you use { and } as the start and end of comment markers. This book uses the first format, and the Turbo Pascal documentation uses the curly braces.

Conventions When Running Programs

One of the nice features of Turbo Pascal is that programs run very quickly. In the IDE, this speed is even more apparent because everything takes place in memory. In fact, a program executes so quickly in the IDE that you'll be back in the editor before you've even had a chance to see what the program did.

NOTE To enable you to see the program's output, the example programs are written so that they wait until you press ENTER at the end of the program. In the first few chapters, you'll be prompted to press ENTER; in later chapters, you'll have to remember to do this yourself.

Certain programs let you enter values repeatedly. In some cases, a program will continue until you enter a specified value. At that point, either the program will terminate immediately (because no more output is needed) or the program will show you the result from your last value and then wait for you to press ENTER.

Language Core

Part One

1 *Introduction*

Welcome to the Turbo Pascal DiskTutor!

If this is your first experience with a programming language, you'll find that Pascal is an excellent language to learn, and the DiskTutor should make your task easier and more pleasant. If you've programmed before, but you're new to Pascal, you'll find it a clean and simple, but powerful language. If you're familiar with Pascal and are just curious, you'll find much to satisfy your curiosity in Borland's implementation of the language.

Pascal

Pascal differs from most programming languages in that it was designed to *teach* programming, rather than to do programming. However, it has turned out to be very useful, and has been used to write all types of programs, even very large ones.

Pascal was created by Niklaus Wirth about 20 years ago. Wirth had been on the committee that designed ALGOL, a very important language in the history of programming. As the ALGOL language became increasingly complex due to the committee's work, Wirth became frustrated, and he decided to develop a language on his own.

Wirth wanted to develop a language that was simple enough to teach as a first language, but powerful enough to make it possible to teach programming as a systematic discipline. Pascal fulfills both of these criteria very well.

As you'll see, Pascal is a small language that is easy to learn and easy to read. It is a *high-level* language, which means that its commands and data structures work at a level close to the one at which you would solve a problem, as you'll see in the following example. Thus, you can create a data structure to represent a collection of information that belongs together. (A *data structure* is simply a template for storing a body of information in a particular way.)

In Pascal, this information can be all of the same type (whole numbers, for instance) or of different types. Suppose you wanted to represent the following information about a recipe ingredient:

■ Ingredient's name

■ Amount of the ingredient

■ Food group

■ Number of calories

■ Cholesterol

■ Fat content

■ Protein content

■ Sodium content

You could create a data structure to represent this information. Pascal lets you specify such a data structure in a way that makes it easy to understand the representation.

The following Pascal code would describe a way of representing information concerning 20 ingredients. By reading the listing you should get a good idea of what is being represented. (Don't worry about the details of the syntax for now; you'll have plenty of opportunity to concern yourself with that later.)

```
TYPE FoodGroup = ( Unknown, EggsAndDairy, FruitsAndVegetables,
                   Grains, MeatAndFish);

     FoodUnit = ( Number, Ounce, Cup, Teaspoon, Tablespoon,
                  FluidOunce, Pinch, Gram, Dash);

     (* Describe a template for information
        about a single ingredient
     *)
     Ingredient = RECORD
                    Name : STRING;
                    Amount : REAL;
                    AmountUnit : FoodUnit;
                    Group : FoodGroup;
                    Calories : INTEGER;
                    Cholesterol, Fat, Protein : REAL;
                    Sodium : INTEGER;
                  END;

     (* Describe a template for info about 20 ingredients *)
     IngredList = ARRAY [ 1 .. 20] OF Ingredient;
```

The first part of the listing creates a new type of information known as a **FoodGroup**. This type can take on only a small number of possible values, namely, the ones listed. Notice that you can use meaningful names for the values; you don't have to specify the values in numerical terms.

The next part of the listing creates another new type: **FoodUnit**. Variables of this type can contain values that represent commonly used units when discussing ingredient quantities.

The third part of the listing describes a data structure named **Ingredient** for storing information about a recipe ingredient. This structure contains several different items of information about the ingredient. For example, there is a slot in this ingredient record to store a name for the ingredient. There are also slots to store other types of information including **FoodUnit** and **FoodGroup** values. You'll see how to create such data structures when you learn about Pascal's **RECORD** type.

Finally, there is a description of an **ARRAY**, a data structure for storing multiple items of the same kind. In this case, the items, or elements, are **Ingredient** records. As you can tell from the syntax, an **IngredList** array will store information about 20 ingredients.

The more you can represent a problem in terms familiar to you, the easier your task will be. You should always try to use the language to solve your problem, rather than modifying your problem to fit the language. Pascal makes it possible for you to make the language fit your problem.

Turbo Pascal

Turbo Pascal provides a very powerful programming environment and is a very solid implementation of Pascal. The environment integrates several of the most important resources for creating and testing a program so that they work together smoothly. This makes your life easier. These components include an easy-to-use editor, a compiler, a debugger, numerous windows, and very extensive on-line help.

Borland's Turbo Pascal language definition has long been the standard for implementations on personal computers. Turbo Pascal provides several extensions to standard Pascal that make the language more powerful and also easier to use. For example, Turbo Pascal makes it very easy to manipulate strings, which will come in handy when writing your programs.

Turbo Pascal gives you access to Pascal's small but thorough and well thought out collection of predefined procedures and functions. In addition, Turbo Pascal provides dozens of other procedures and functions, which have been defined for the implementation.

Borland's language implementation includes the *integrated development environment* (IDE), which provides a total programming environment. If you're used to different tools (editors, and so forth), Borland provides a command-line compiler, **tpc**. Appendix D, "Command-line Compiler Options," summarizes the commands and options for this compiler. For the most part, discussion in this book will concern the IDE.

With version 5.5, Turbo Pascal introduced object-oriented capabilities for the language. These represent a major alternative to structured programming methods, which have guided programmers for the past few decades. If you're not familiar with structured or object-oriented programming, don't worry. You'll learn a bit about the former in various parts of the book, and a good deal about the latter in Chapters 11 through 13.

Version 6 of Turbo Pascal includes a very useful collection of object-based resources. These are powerful enough to create the Turbo Pascal IDE. *Turbo Vision,* as this resource collection is called, enables you to create and manage windows, dialog boxes, and menus. You'll learn about Turbo Vision in Chapter 13.

The Turbo Pascal Integrated Development Environment

The Turbo Pascal IDE makes it very easy for you to edit, compile, run, and debug your programs. All these capabilities are available within the integrated environment. One consequence of this is that these components can communicate with each other. For example, if the compiler finds an error in your program, the location of this error is marked. The editor can find this error in your text file, and there is a command that lets you move directly to the error.

Within the IDE, there are dozens of commands available to you. The editor alone understands over 50 commands. The IDE also includes a *menu bar* with 10 menus from which you can select commands. Figure 1-1 contains a screen showing a program source file (program P2-3.PAS, which is used in Chapter 2, "Pascal: An Overview").

Note the menu bar at the top containing nine labelled menus, from File to Help. Each of these is accessible by pressing the ALT key together with the first letter of the entry's name. For example, to access the File menu, you would press ALT-F.

The tenth menu is "named" ≡, and is accessible by pressing ALT-SPACEBAR. This menu is also known as the System menu. It contains three miscellaneous commands.

Figure 1-1 also shows several other features of an IDE screen. For example, the bottom part of the screen contains a *status line.* This line contains messages and hints about useful commands in the current context. As you perform functions in the IDE keep your eye on the status line; you'll see it change as you move from one menu or task to another.

The *close box* and the *scroll bars* are used with a mouse to close a window and to move around in a file, respectively. There are other features and components in IDE screens. You'll learn about these as they are used.

Setting Up the IDE

If you haven't already done so, you'll want to install Turbo Pascal and the example program files. To install Turbo Pascal, just follow the prompts of the INSTALL program. For the following discussion, let's assume you've installed your version in the TP directory on drive C; that is, in directory C:\TP.

In order to access the IDE from any directory, you need to add the location of the IDE files to your PATH statement. For the example, this would mean adding the following to your PATH statement:

```
c:\tp
```

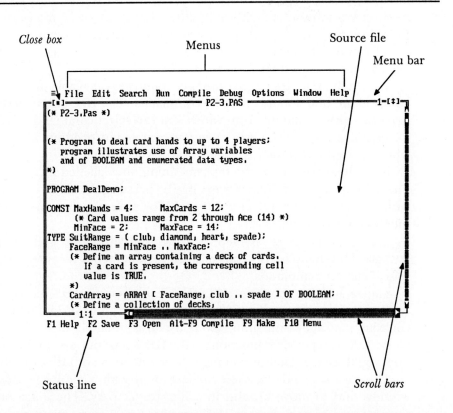

Close box   Menus   Source file   Menu bar

```
≡ File  Edit  Search  Run  Compile  Debug  Options  Window  Help      1═[↕]═
═[■]══════════════════════ P2-3.PAS ═══════════════════════
(* P2-3.Pas *)


(* Program to deal card hands to up to 4 players;
   program illustrates use of Array variables
   and of BOOLEAN and enumerated data types.
*)

PROGRAM DealDemo;

CONST MaxHands = 4;      MaxCards = 12;
      (* Card values range from 2 through Ace (14) *)
      MinFace = 2;       MaxFace = 14;
TYPE SuitRange = ( club, diamond, heart, spade);
     FaceRange = MinFace .. MaxFace;
     (* Define an array containing a deck of cards.
        If a card is present, the corresponding cell
        value is TRUE.
     *)
     CardArray = ARRAY [ FaceRange, club .. spade ] OF BOOLEAN;
     (* Define a collection of decks,
══ 1:1 ═══◄□
F1 Help  F2 Save  F3 Open  Alt-F9 Compile  F9 Make  F10 Menu
```

Status line   Scroll bars

Figure 1-1.   *Example IDE screen. Items with italicized names require a mouse.*

Preparing the Example Programs   This book includes over 200 source files with example programs. These are used to illustrate principles related to the Pascal language and to programming in general. You'll get much more out of this book if you run the programs and make suggested modifications.

Because you don't have to worry about typing them in, the programs can be longer (and therefore more interesting) than you'll usually find in books about programming. For example, in the next chapter you'll find a program that deals hands for card games, and one that alphabetizes lines of text. In Chapter 2, these programs are used primarily to entertain and to illustrate general features of Pascal. In Chapter 12, "Virtual Methods in Object-Oriented Programming," you'll find a program that lets you play anagrams with up to two other players. By then, you'll be able to understand even the smallest details of the program.

In order to fit the example programs on the disk, programs from each chapter have been combined into a single file for that chapter. This file has extension .CMB, for example, CH2.CMB. The EXTRACT program included on the disk creates a separate file for each example program in the .CMB file.

You can use any of the following command lines to extract the five example programs from CH2.CMB:

```
extract
extract ch2
extract ch2.cmb
```

The program will also save a list of the files created in EXTRACT .LOG. If the file doesn't exist when you execute EXTRACT, you'll be asked whether the program should create the log file.

You can work with the example programs anywhere you wish. To keep things more manageable, you will probably want to create a separate work directory for the example files. This makes it easier to keep track of the programs.

Running an Example Program

Let's compile and run program P2-3.PAS, just to see how it's done. If you haven't done so, move to the work directory for this book and extract the file from CH2.CMB. You may first need to copy the CH2.CMB file from the distribution disk to the work directory. If you've already done this, move to the directory containing this source file. You also need to make sure the IDE files are accessible.

To start working with P2-3.PAS in the IDE, type

```
turbo p2-3
```

You don't need the .PAS extension. Unless you specify otherwise, the compiler assumes the file name ends in .PAS. After this command, your screen will look like the one in Figure 1-1.

To run the program, you can use the **R**un command on the Run menu. You can specify this command in several ways:

■ Press ALT-R to access the Run menu and then press ENTER to select the highlighted command (which happens to be Run).

■ Press ALT-R to access the Run menu and then type **R** to select the command containing that letter in highlighted form.

■ Press CTRL-F9 — that is, the control key along with the F9 function key.

■ Use a mouse to select the menu entry by clicking on it.

The first three methods use the keyboard. The first two methods use the IDE menu structure to select available commands. These differ only because Borland has provided multiple ways to give the same command. This makes it easier for users to learn at least one form of the command.

The third method uses a shortcut keystroke for the desired command. Many of the IDE commands have such shortcuts associated with them. These *hot keys* enable you to bypass the menu. Any associated hot keys are shown next to a menu entry and may also be mentioned in the status line, as shown in Figure 1-2. In the figure, the CTRL-F9 hot key for the Run command is shown on the menu.

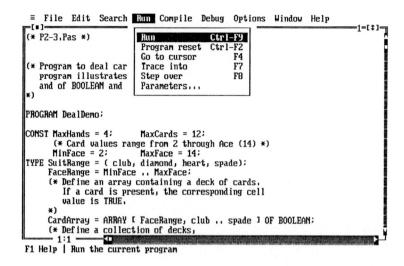

Figure 1-2. *Run menu showing hot keys on menu and on status line*

The Run command will compile and start executing the program. You'll be asked how many players are to be dealt hands, and how many cards each player should be dealt. After you enter your answers, the program will deal and display the hands.

To leave the IDE, press the ALT and X keys simultaneously (ALT-X). If you've made any changes to the source file, you'll be asked whether you want to save the changes. You'll learn more about the IDE in Chapter 2 and where relevant, throughout the book. See Appendix C, "IDE Commands," for a complete summary of these commands.

Troubleshooting

If things went as planned, you're all set to start on what should be a fun learning and exploration process. If things did not go quite as well, make sure the TURBO program and auxiliary files are stored in a directory that is on your path. To see what the current path is, just type **path** at the DOS command line.

You should also make sure you're working with extracted files—that is, with files that have names such as P2-3.PAS. If the file you're trying to compile has a .CMB extension, you need to run the EXTRACT program first.

Creating Programs in the IDE

Creating an executable Pascal program is actually a multistep process. The first step is to create a *source code* file (such as P2-3.PAS used in the example). This is a text file that you can create with an ordinary text editor or with the IDE's built-in editor. The source file will contain Pascal language statements.

Once you've created the Pascal source file, the compiler processes the source code and checks for spelling, typing, and syntax errors. If any errors are found, you need to correct them.

Once all the errors are corrected, the Turbo Pascal compiler builds a compiled version of your file in memory or on disk. You can then run this version of the file in the IDE.

You can save your corrected source file. Depending on certain internal settings, the compiler may only be compiling to memory so that no .EXE file is created. In the next chapter you'll learn how to set this option as well as learning about other IDE commands. Additional IDE commands are introduced only when relevant for an example or a discussion. Appendix C has a summary of the IDE and editor commands.

On-Line Help

You'll find that there is very extensive on-line help available in the IDE. In light of this, the discussion of IDE commands, options, and so forth has been kept fairly informal in this book. This (and the fact that the IDE is so easy to use anyway) made it possible to provide more information about Pascal and more example programs.

————————

In this chapter, you learned a bit about Pascal's heritage and goals, and also a few things about some of the language's features. In the next chapter, "Pascal: An Overview," you'll get an informal survey of some of Pascal's elements. You'll also learn the more common editor commands and how to invoke some of the IDE commands.

2 *Pascal: An Overview*

This chapter includes several example programs that illustrate some of Pascal's major constructs. These examples will give you a feel for Pascal's look and features. They also provide a general background for the remainder of the book.

Don't worry about the details of the programs for now. By running and modifying these programs, you'll get exposure to Pascal and an introduction to the Turbo Pascal environment. You'll learn about some of the more common editor commands, and about the capabilities of Turbo Pascal. The second part of the chapter is a more extensive discussion of the integrated development environment (IDE). You may want to skim that now, and refer to it as needed.

To get the most out of this chapter, you should run the programs and try making the suggested changes. You'll have to work with programs without knowing Pascal. Fortunately, in Pascal the source code can make it clear what the program does. This means that you should be able to guess what the program does just by reading it properly.

Starting the IDE

To start the IDE, simply type

```
turbo
```

and press ENTER. Unless you've already been editing files (so that you have a work file), your IDE screen should look something like Figure 2-1.

The screen shows an empty edit window in the IDE. Note that the menu bar and status line are the same as in the Chapter 1 example. There are a few other features to point out in the figure.

First, notice the NONAME00.PAS filename centered at the top of the edit window. This name is displayed in the *title bar,* which will be found at the top of every window.

Since you can have multiple windows open in the IDE, each window is identified by a number. The first window is number 1, the next is 2, and so forth. In Figure 2-1, the current edit window has number 1.

In the upper right-hand corner of the screen, you will find a *zoom box.* You can click on this with a mouse to make the window larger or smaller. Essentially, clicking will toggle the window between states in which the window takes the entire screen and those in which the screen is shared with other windows.

You can also change the window size using the *resize corner* at the lower right. This corner, accessible with a mouse, enables you to change the window size in smooth increments. This is in contrast to the zoom box, which makes drastic changes in window size.

Help!

Notice the bottom line on the screen, which lists several commands and the keys for invoking them. First is F1 for Help. You can press function key F1 to get help with the current environment. When you do this, you'll receive help about editing commands, as shown in Figure 2-2. Browse through these screens by pressing PGDN and PGUP to move toward the end and the beginning of the information, respectively.

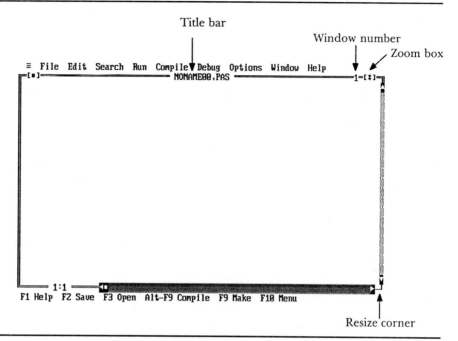

Figure 2-1. *Startup screen for Turbo Pascal IDE*

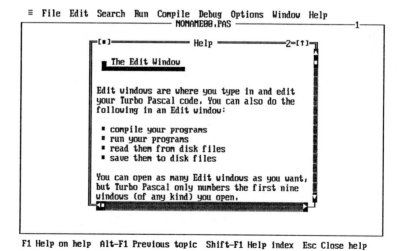

Figure 2-2. *Example Help screen for edit window*

Notice that the command list has changed. When you're in the help context, a different set of commands is available and is listed on the status line.

When you're finished exploring the information about editing, press ESC to return to the edit window.

New IDE Commands

Here are the commands you've learned so far:

ESC   End the Help session and return to the edit
                                 window

F1   Get help about the editor commands

Opening a File in the Edit Window

To load your first program file into the edit window, press ALT-F and then type **O** or press ENTER. Your screen will look like the one in Figure 2-3. Pressing ALT-F accesses the File menu, and typing **O** or pressing ENTER selects the first command on the menu, Open.

You're expected to type a file name in the box that contains *.PAS. To do this, just start typing. The contents of the box will disappear as soon as you start. The first example program on your program disk is in file P2-1.PAS. You can include or omit the .PAS extension, since the IDE assumes this extension unless you specify otherwise.

You can also press ENTER instead of typing a file name. This moves you to the Files box.

This list box displays any files in the current directory that have extension .PAS, and also includes a list of accessible directories. You can use the arrow keys to move to the desired file, and then press ENTER to select it.

Once you've specified or selected the file, the contents of P2-1.PAS are loaded into the edit window. To accomplish this, you pressed ALT-F and then ENTER. Notice, in Figure 2-3, that the entry for Open also specifies F3. This indicates that you can open a file simply by pressing function key F3. F3 is known as a *hot key* for the Open command, since F3 accomplishes the same thing as the ALT-F ENTER sequence. In general, you can use a hot key regardless of where you are in the IDE. Thus, you could have gotten the dialog box shown in Figure 2-3 directly from the edit window.

Running a Program

After you've given the appropriate commands, the following file should be in the edit window. This file illustrates the structure of a Pascal program and welcomes you to the IDE.

Files that are included on your program disk are identified by the file name in the margin. This is the name for the file on the disk. This name always begins with *P*, the chapter number, and a dash, and ends with the extension .PAS. Notice that the program itself has a different name.

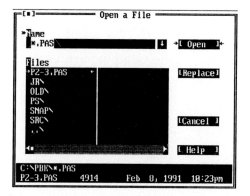

Figure 2-3. *Screen after selecting Open command from File menu*

Thus, file P2-1.PAS contains a program named **FirstExample**. The discussion uses either the program name or the file name to refer to a program, depending on the context.

```
P2-1    (* Write a greeting and a value to the screen. *)

        PROGRAM FirstExample;
        VAR   Name : STRING;

          PROCEDURE SayHello;
          BEGIN
            WRITE ( 'Hello there, and welcome to the IDE, ');
          END; (* SayHello *)

        BEGIN  (* Main program body *)
          Name := 'whoever you are'; (* Assign a value to Name *)
          SayHello;
          WRITELN ( NAME);
          WRITELN ( 'Press ENTER to end program.');
          READLN;
        END.
```

This program initializes a **STRING** variable with the value **whoever you are**, and then writes a greeting to the screen. To run the program, simply press ALT-R for the Run menu, and then type **R** or press ENTER to select the Run command. You can do the same thing by pressing CTRL-F9. Your program will be compiled to memory or to disk, and will then execute.

The target for the program depends on an IDE option setting. The setting is Destination on the Compile menu and is accessible through ALT-C D. This value toggles between disk and memory.

The specified value will remain in effect as long as your session lasts or until the value is changed. If you want to save the new value permanently, save the options information to disk.

To do this, use ALT-O S, which opens the Options menu and selects the Save command from there. The parting message tells you to press ENTER to end the program officially.

The window in which the program's output is displayed is called the *user,* or *output screen.* Once you've run the program, you can view the user screen any time by pressing ALT-F5. This command toggles (switches back and forth) between the user screen and the edit window.

On-Line Help About Pascal

The IDE has on-line help about the Pascal language. To learn about a reserved word or a predefined procedure or function, move the cursor to the word of interest and press CTRL-F1 to invoke the appropriate help.

For example, to find out about Turbo Pascal's **STRING** type, move the cursor to one of the letters in the word "STRING" and press CTRL-F1. You'll see a description of this information type. Pressing PGDN will let you read additional information about strings.

Notice the word "characters" in the first help screen about strings. The word is highlighted to indicate that it is a *keyword*, or cross-reference. This means that more information is available about the topic. If you press TAB to move to the highlighted word and then press ENTER, you'll find a new help screen that tells you about Pascal's **CHAR** type. This screen also has a cross-reference.

You can get more information about the highlighted keyword by pressing ENTER. When you're ready to return to earlier help screens, press ALT-F1. Each time you do this, you'll move back one screen. Press ESC to quit the on-line help and to return to the edit window.

Pascal Program Structure

The structure of program **FirstExample** illustrates the three main components of a Pascal program:

■ A *heading*, which specifies the program name and may include additional information. The heading must be the first part of a Pascal program. In the example, this is the line that begins with the reserved word **PROGRAM**. (Reserved words are part of the Pascal language definition and can't be used for other purposes in a Pascal program.)

■ Optional *declarations*, which may specify variables or constants. You can also declare "actions," by defining procedures or functions to carry out a specified task. Once included in a declaration section, these routines can be called at appropriate points in the program. Much of the

challenge of Pascal is learning how to write good procedures and functions. In the example, one variable (**Name**) is declared and one procedure (**SayHello**) is defined.

■ A *body*, which contains the actual program instructions, or statements.
The body is the last part of a Pascal program. In the example, the
program body contains five statements, including a call to **SayHello** and
calls to procedures **WRITE**, **WRITELN**, and **READLN**, which are predefined procedures in Pascal.

The declaration section of a program is very important. Part of the
secret of successful programming is determining the most appropriate
way to represent your problem. This means specifying data types to
store the problem's components and values; it also means specifying
procedures and functions to carry out the actions needed to produce the
solution.

A problem that uses the most appropriate data types is much easier
to solve than one that uses less appropriate ones. In fact, if you do the
declarations properly, the main program is sometimes a very simple
sequence of procedure and function calls.

A Pascal program body—that is, the *main program*—starts with the
reserved word **BEGIN** and finishes with the reserved word **END**. This
last word *must* be followed by a period in Pascal. The program body is
the last component in the source file.

REMEMBER   A program body must have a period (.) after the **END**
that terminates the main program.

Pascal Program Style

You can include comments—notes to yourself or to other readers—in
your Pascal source code by putting them between (* and *) or between
{ and }. (It's a good idea to be generous with comments in your programs.)

Pascal is quite flexible in letting you use space and indentation in
your programs. For example, Pascal compilers don't care whether you
leave spaces between a procedure name (such as **WRITE**) and the left
parenthesis that follows it. Nor does it matter whether you leave a space

between the left parenthesis and the material following it. (You can't put a space in the middle of a word, however.)

The examples use such spaces because it makes the source code more open and easier to read. You can also use indentation to differentiate various portions of a program. For example, in the file P2-1.PAS, statements in the program body and in procedure **SayHello** are indented two spaces more than the surrounding material.

You needn't imitate the comment, spacing, and indentation conventions used here; you should, however, develop your own style and use it consistently.

Pascal Program Execution

In a Pascal program, execution begins at the start of the program body and continues (generally with digressions) to the last statement in the body. Because of the way Pascal programs execute, the main program body is often a good place to start reading the source code. Remember, the program body comes at the end of the program source file.

The main program in **FirstExample** initializes **Name** to a specific value. The **:=** is Pascal's *assignment operator*. This operator stores the value to its right (**whoever you are** in the example) in the variable specified to the operator's left (**Name**).

After this, the program calls procedures **SayHello**, **WRITELN**, and **READLN**. These calls are *statements* — particular instructions to the system.

A *procedure call* or *function call* is an instruction to begin executing the routine (that is, procedure or function) named in the call. Thus, a call to **SayHello** transfers control (temporarily) to that procedure. The individual statements in the procedure are executed and control then reverts to the main program (in this case).

Execution will then continue from the point after the call. Thus, in **FirstExample**, after **SayHello** has finished, the value of **Name** is written by the call to **WRITELN**.

Statements

Within the **BEGIN** and **END** boundaries, a program or procedure body consists of statements. In Pascal, you can have *simple* or *compound* statements.

Simple Statements   A simple statement generally represents a single instruction and accomplishes a single task. For example, an assignment and a procedure call are both accomplished in simple statements. In the program, procedure **SayHello** consists of a single simple statement—a call to the predefined procedure **WRITE**. The calls to **SayHello** and to **WRITELN** and **READLN** in the main program are also simple statements.

Each of the following is a simple statement:

```
WRITE ( 'Hello');
MyValue := MyValue + 35;
SayHello;
```

The first statement says to write the word "Hello" (without the quotes) to the screen. The statement is a procedure call, which is effected by simply naming the procedure to be called. **WRITE** is a predefined procedure that is available for use in your program. This procedure is an instruction to write something to the standard output device (usually the screen).

The material to be written is specified as one or more arguments, or parameters, to **WRITE**. An *argument* is an item of information specified for use in a procedure or function. The information is passed into the routine (and may also be passed back out) and is used within the body of the routine.

In the call to **WRITE**, the material within the parentheses is a string argument. The single quotes around the argument identify the argument as a *string literal,* or *constant.* Chapter 3, "Turbo Pascal's Simple Data Types," contains more information about **WRITE** and related routines, as well as about strings.

The second statement adds 35 to the current value of a variable named **MyValue**. Recall that **:=** is Pascal's assignment operator. The value to the right of the operator is stored in the variable specified to the left of the operator. Thus, the new value of **MyValue** is 35 more than its old value.

The third line is simply a call to the procedure **SayHello**. When this statement is encountered, the current routine (which may be the main program or another routine) stops executing temporarily while procedure **SayHello** executes. Chapter 4, "Procedures and Functions," and Chapter 6, "Procedures and Functions Revisited," cover procedure calls and program execution.

Compound Statements A compound statement actually consists of multiple statements, which may themselves be either simple or compound. Compound statements in Pascal are bounded by a **BEGIN** and an **END**. Compound statements are particularly useful with Pascal's control constructs—for deciding what your program should do next. The first example program does not contain any compound statements.

Tracing Through a Program

To see how this program works, you can watch it execute step by step. The IDE Trace command lets you do this. The hot key for this command is F7, as shown on the Run menu. To step through the program, press F7.

If you keep pressing F7, the program switches from the program body to procedure **SayHello** when this procedure is called. The Trace command lets you step through each procedure as it executes. (Actually, you can't step through predefined procedures such as **WRITE**.)

Figure 2-4 shows the screen after you press F7 five times with the file P2-1.PAS in the edit window. The highlighted statement is always the one *just about* to execute.

At this point, the call to **WRITE** in **SayHello** will be the next statement to execute. Press ALT-F5 before pressing F7 again. This will switch you to the user's screen. You'll see that nothing has been written yet. Press F7 once more and then press ALT-F5 again. Your screen will look like the one in Figure 2-5.

After this instruction has been carried out, the program has written the general greeting but has not yet written any name information. You need to leave **SayHello** and then call **WRITELN** in the program body before you can see the "whoever you are" message. Press F7 a few more times and then press ENTER to terminate the program.

Changing the Program

If you read the program carefully, you may have noticed that it uses both **Name** and **NAME**. This discrepancy does not cause any problems be-

```
  ≡  File  Edit  Search  Run  Compile  Debug  Options  Window  Help
 ┌[■]════════════════════════ P2-1.PAS ═══════════════════════1═[‡]═┐
 │(* P2-1.Pas *)                                                    │
 │                                                                  │
 │(* Write a greeting and a value to the screen. *)                 │
 │                                                                  │
 │PROGRAM FirstExample;                                             │
 │                                                                  │
 │VAR   Name : STRING;                                              │
 │                                                                  │
 │  PROCEDURE SayHello;                                             │
 │  BEGIN                                                           │
 │    WRITE ( 'Hello there, and welcome to the IDE, ');             │
 │  END; (* SayHello *)                                             │
 │                                                                  │
 │BEGIN  (* Main program body *)                                    │
 │  Name := 'whoever you are'; (* Assign a value to Name *)         │
 │  SayHello;                                                       │
 │  WRITELN ( NAME);                                                │
 │  WRITELN ( 'Press ENTER to end program.');                       │
 │  READLN;                                                         │
 │END.                                                              │
 └── 12:1 ──◄█══════════════════════════════════════════════════►──┘
 F1 Help  F7 Trace  F8 Step  F9 Make  F10 Menu
```

Figure 2-4. *Screen just before executing highlighted line while tracing through program*

cause Pascal is not case sensitive. In Pascal, **Name** and **NAME** are considered equivalent. This book uses uppercase characters for words that are predefined in Turbo Pascal.

For consistency—and for a quick lesson on IDE editor commands—change **NAME** to **Name**. Since the file is small, you can easily move to the specified word by using the arrow keys on the numeric keypad. (Make sure NUMLOCK is OFF, however.)

```
C:\PBK>turbo
Turbo Pascal  Version 6.0  Copyright (c) 1983,90 Borland International
Hello there, and welcome to the IDE,
```

Figure 2-5. *Output screen from example program*

To make the desired change:

■ Use the arrow keys to move the cursor to the *A* in **NAME**.

■ Press INS on the numeric keypad or press CTRL-V.

■ Type **ame**.

■ Finally, press INS again.

Congratulations, you've made your first editing changes to a DiskTutor program.

The INS key lets you toggle between two editing modes: insert and overwrite. Pressing INS the first time put you in overwrite mode; pressing it again put you back in insert mode (the default).

In *overwrite mode,* the characters you type write over the existing characters. In *insert mode,* characters that have already been written are displaced but not erased.

Make some other changes in the program to learn additional editor commands. (Keep in mind that F1 displays help about the editor commands.) Substitute your name for the generic "whoever you are." Use the arrow keys to move the cursor until it is on top of the *w* in "whoever."

To delete the material within the single quotes, you can press the DEL key (on the numeric keypad) repeatedly, or you can press CTRL-T three times (in this case). The DEL key deletes the current character and slides the remainder of the material to the left to fill the vacated space. CTRL-T deletes from the current cursor position to the end of the current word or the next word if the cursor is between words.

Once you've deleted the generic name, type your own name. If you make a mistake while typing, press the BACKSPACE key to delete the preceding character, and then type the correct character.

Now run the program again by pressing CTRL-F9. Finally, trace through the program one more time. This time, however, execute **SayHello** without tracing through it step by step. Press F7 three times until the call to **SayHello** is highlighted. Instead of F7, press F8 (to Step

Over the procedure call). This tells the IDE to execute procedure **SayHello** but to spare you the details. After you press F8, the next line in the main program body will be highlighted. If you press ALT-F5, you'll see that **SayHello** has done its work.

To end the first session, simply press ALT-X to quit the IDE. This sequence is actually the hot key for the Exit command on the File menu (ALT-F X).

Because you've made changes to the program file, you'll be asked whether to save the changes. If you want to keep the program with your name in it, type **Y** or press ENTER to select the default choice. If you want to keep the original version of the program, type **N**.

New IDE Commands

Here are the IDE commands you learned in the preceding pages:

CTRL-FI	Provides help about the Pascal construct the cursor is on. If the cursor is not on a reserved word or a predefined routine, the help index is displayed.
ALT-F	Moves to the menu line and selects the File menu.
ALT-F O or F3	Loads a file to be specified into the edit window.
ALT-R	Moves to the menu line and selects the Run menu.
ALT-R R or CTRL-F9	Runs the program currently in the edit window. The program will be compiled if necessary.
ALT-F5	Toggles between the output and the edit windows when a program is executing.
ALT-R T or F7	Traces through a program step by step.

ALT-R S or F8	Steps over the procedure or function on the current line (that is, executes the routine, but doesn't trace through it step by step).
CTRL-V or INS	Toggles between insert and overwrite modes in the edit window.
DEL	Deletes the character at the current cursor position.
BACKSPACE	Deletes the character at the previous cursor position.
CTRL-T	Deletes the current word.
ALT-F X or ALT-X	Exits the IDE. If you've changed a file, you'll be asked whether you want to save the changed version.

Another Example Program

Another example program demonstrates some more of Pascal's features. Make sure that you're in the directory in which file P2-2.PAS is located, and that the directory containing the Turbo Pascal program files is in your PATH definition. At the DOS command line, type

```
turbo p2-2
```

This invokes the DiskTutor environment and immediately puts the file P2-2.PAS in the edit window. The following listing shows this file:

P2-2
```
(* Program to generate random values.
   Program illustrates some Pascal control constructs.
*)

PROGRAM LoopExample;

VAR   Count : INTEGER;

   (* Generate random integers, and check whether
```

```
      certain of them are even or odd.
  *)
  PROCEDURE HandleRandom ( Count : INTEGER);
  VAR Value : INTEGER;
  BEGIN
    (* Get a random integer between 0 and 25000 *)
    Value := RANDOM ( 25001);
    (* For every third value, tell whether it's even or odd *)
    IF Count MOD 3 = 0 THEN
    BEGIN
      WRITE ( Value : 5, ' is ');
      IF ODD ( Value) THEN
        WRITELN ( 'odd')
      ELSE
        WRITELN ( 'even');
    END
    ELSE (* for the other cases, just write the value *)
      WRITELN ( Value : 5);
  END; (* HandleRandom *)

BEGIN  (* Main program body *)
  (* The first assignment ensures that the same
     sequence of random values is generated each time.
  *)
  RandSeed := 1919;
  (* RANDOMIZE; *) (* can replace previous statement *)
  (* Call HandleRandom 9 times *)
  FOR Count := 1 TO 9 DO
    HandleRandom ( Count);
  WRITELN;
  WRITE ( 'Press ENTER to end program.');
  READLN;
END.
```

This program generates nine random integers from 0 to 25000. For every number generated, the program displays the value. In addition, for every third value, the program checks whether the value is even or odd, and tells you which it is.

The program illustrates two of Turbo Pascal's control structures:

■ The **IF** statement, which enables your program to do different things depending on what conditions hold at a particular point in your program.

■ The **FOR** statement, which enables your program to repeat an action or series of actions a specified number of times.

The program also contains a procedure with a parameter. A *parameter* is a means of passing information into and out of a procedure or function, in order to control how the routine (procedure or function) works on a particular call. You'll learn about parameters in Chapters 4 and 6.

Press CTRL-F9 to compile and run this program. Try to determine what parts of the program produced the different output lines. Then use some of the IDE's debugging capabilities to compare your guesses with the program's actual performance.

Among other things, in the IDE you can keep track of the values of variables as the program executes. For example, in the **LoopExample** program, several decisions depend on the values of **Count** and **Value**. You can specify these two variables as *watch variables*. In that case, the IDE keeps track of their values in the watches window as the program executes. To specify **Value** as a watch variable, press ALT-D W. This gives you access to the Watch submenu on the Debug menu. The first command on this submenu is to add a watch variable. To select this command, just press ENTER. (Notice that you could have accomplished the same thing with CTRL-F7.) You'll see a box on the screen. The contents of this box depend on the cursor's current position in the edit window. Type **Value** and press ENTER. You'll see this variable entered in the watches window, along with an "Unknown identifier" message.

After giving the Watch commands, you will actually be in a new window. Since this window was the most recent one, it will be active. To get back to the edit window, press F6. This command moves through the currently opened windows.

Once back in the edit window, you can use the arrow keys to put the cursor on the word **Count** and press CTRL-F7 again. You'll see **Count** in the resulting box. Press ENTER to add this word to the watch variable list. Press F6 to make the watches window available again. Now trace through the program by using F7. Keep an eye on the watches window as you step through the program to see how the values of the two watch variables change. Don't forget to check the user screen occasionally (press ALT-F5) to see what output the program has produced.

Trace through at least three values of **Count** to see how the logic changes when **Count** is divisible by 3. By tracing through the program, you can see how the **IF** and **FOR** structures work.

In its current version, the **LoopExample** program generates the same random sequence each time because a specific value has been assigned to **RandSeed** (a predefined variable that provides a starting value for the random number function). To generate a different value each time, put comments around the line in which **RandSeed** is assigned a value, and remove the comments from around the call to **RANDOM-IZE**. (This is a predefined procedure that generates a starting value for **RandSeed**.) The following lines show how to make this adjustment:

```
(* RandSeed := 1919; *)
RANDOMIZE;
```

The Edit Window Revisited

Notice the two numbers near the lower-left corner of the edit window. These numbers represent the row and column coordinates of the current cursor position. The two numbers tell you the line and column number of the current cursor position. The first line of the file is line 1, and the leftmost column is column 1. A line can be up to 249 characters long in the Turbo Pascal editor—as you will learn if you page through the help material about the edit window. To get this information, just press F1 while you're in the edit window, and press PGDN until you get to the screen about line lengths.

When you're editing a file, you can be in either of two modes: insert or overwrite. If the cursor is large, you're in overwrite mode. An example illustrates the difference between the two modes.

Suppose the cursor is on the letter *i* in the word "bit" and you type an **a**. In insert mode, the *a* is written at the current cursor position, and the material from that position to the end of the line is moved to the right by one space. The word "bit" becomes "bait." In overwrite mode, on the other hand, the new letter replaces the character at the current cursor position. Thus, "bit" becomes "bat."

Example: Using Complex Data Types

The next example illustrates more features of Pascal, including complex and specialized data types, and nested routines. Nested routines are defined inside another procedure or function rather than in the declaration section of the main program. The following program deals card hands to as many as four players, as you may recall from your practice session in Chapter 1. Each hand can have up to ten cards. To load the program while still in the IDE:

■ If you're currently working with P2-2.PAS, press ALT-F3 to close the current file.

■ Press F3 to call the open box, and type **P2-3** as the file you want.

If you're on the DOS command line (rather than in the IDE), you can work with the program directly by typing

```
turbo p2-3
```

First, run the program a few times. Try dealing five-card and seven-card hands. Vary the number of players being dealt cards. The following listing shows the contents of file P2-3.PAS:

P2-3
```
(* Program to deal card hands to up to 4 players;
   program illustrates use of Array variables
   and of BOOLEAN and enumerated data types.
*)

PROGRAM DealDemo;

CONST MaxHands = 4;        MaxCards = 12;
      (* Card values range from 2 through Ace (14) *)
      MinFace = 2;        MaxFace = 14;
TYPE SuitRange = ( club, diamond, heart, spade);
     FaceRange = MinFace .. MaxFace;
     (* Define an array containing a deck of cards.
        If a card is present, the corresponding cell
        value is TRUE.
     *)
     CardArray = ARRAY [ FaceRange, club .. spade ] OF BOOLEAN;
     (* Define a collection of decks,
        each corresponding to a player.
     *)
     Group = ARRAY [ 1 .. MaxHands] OF CardArray;
VAR Deck : CardArray;
    Players : Group;
    NrCards, NrHands, Index : INTEGER;
```

```
(* Initialize a deck to the specified value *)
PROCEDURE InitCards ( VAR Cards : CardArray;
                          Value : BOOLEAN);
VAR SuitCounter : SuitRange;
    FaceCounter : FaceRange;
BEGIN
  FOR SuitCounter := club TO spade DO
    FOR FaceCounter := MinFace TO MaxFace DO
      Cards [ FaceCounter, SuitCounter] := Value;
END; (* InitCards *)

(* Display the contents of a particular deck *)
PROCEDURE DispCards ( VAR Cards : CardArray);
VAR SuitCounter : SuitRange;
    FaceCounter : FaceRange;

  (* Write a card number or J Q K or A *)
  PROCEDURE ShowCard;
  BEGIN
    IF FaceCounter < 11 THEN
      WRITE ( FaceCounter : 4)
    ELSE
    BEGIN
      CASE FaceCounter OF
        11 : WRITE ( 'J' : 4);
        12 : WRITE ( 'Q' : 4);
        13 : WRITE ( 'K' : 4);
        14 : WRITE ( 'A' : 4);
      END; (* CASE OF FaceCounter *)
    END;
  END; (* ShowCard *)

BEGIN  (* DispCards *)
  FOR SuitCounter := club TO spade DO
  BEGIN
    CASE SuitCounter OF
      club : WRITE ( 'clubs   : ');
      diamond : WRITE ( 'diamonds: ');
      heart : WRITE ( 'hearts  : ');
      spade : WRITE ( 'spades  : ');
    END; (* CASE OF SuitCounter *)
    FOR FaceCounter := MinFace TO MaxFace DO
      IF Cards [ FaceCounter, SuitCounter] = TRUE THEN
        ShowCard;
    WRITELN;
  END;
END; (* DispCards *)

(* Deal the specified # of cards to the players *)
PROCEDURE Deal ( VAR Deck : CardArray;
                 VAR Players : Group;
```

```
                                  NrCards, NrHands : INTEGER);
            VAR CurrSuit : SuitRange;
                CurrFace : FaceRange;
                CIndex, HIndex : INTEGER;

              (* Determine the "next" card in the deck *)
              PROCEDURE GetCard ( VAR TheFace : FaceRange;
                                  VAR TheSuit : SuitRange);

                (* Determine the suit of the next card *)
                PROCEDURE GetSuit ( VAR TheSuit : SuitRange);
                VAR Result : INTEGER;
                BEGIN
                  Result := RANDOM ( 4);
                  CASE Result OF
                     0 : TheSuit := club;
                     1 : TheSuit := diamond;
                     2 : TheSuit := heart;
                     3 : TheSuit := spade;
                  END; (* CASE  OF Result *)
                END; (* GetSuit *)
              BEGIN  (* GetCard *)
                REPEAT
                  GetSuit ( TheSuit);
                  TheFace := RANDOM ( MaxFace - MinFace + 1) + MinFace;
                (* Keep looking until a card is selected that is
                   still in the deck.
                *)
                UNTIL Deck [ TheFace, TheSuit] = TRUE;
              END; (* GetCard *)

            BEGIN  (* Deal *)
              FOR CIndex := 1 TO NrCards DO
              BEGIN
                FOR HIndex := 1 TO NrHands DO
                BEGIN
                  GetCard ( CurrFace, CurrSuit);
                  Players [ HIndex, CurrFace, CurrSuit] := TRUE;
                  Deck [ CurrFace, CurrSuit] := FALSE;
                END; (* FOR Hindex *)
              END; (* FOR CIndex *)
            END;  (* Deal *)

          (* Determine # players and # of cards per hand *)
          PROCEDURE GetGameInfo ( VAR NrCards, NrHands : INTEGER);
          BEGIN
            REPEAT
              WRITE ( '# of players? (Max = ', MaxHands, ') ');
              READLN ( NrHands);
            UNTIL NrHands <= MaxHands;
            REPEAT
              WRITE ( '# of Cards? (Max = ', MaxCards, ') ');
```

```
      READLN ( NrCards);
    UNTIL NrCards <= MaxCards;
  END; (* GetGameInfo *)

BEGIN  (* Main program *)
  RANDOMIZE;  (* "shuffle" deck generator *)
  GetGameInfo ( NrCards, NrHands);
  InitCards ( Deck, TRUE);
  FOR Index := 1 TO MaxHands DO
    InitCards ( Players [ Index], FALSE);

  Deal ( Deck, Players, NrCards, NrHands);

  (* Display the hands *)
  FOR Index := 1 TO NrHands DO
  BEGIN
    WRITELN ( 'PLAYER ', Index, ': ');
    DispCards ( Players [ Index]);
    WRITELN;
  END;
  (* 4 hands fill the screen, so wait before showing deck *)
  IF NrHands = 4 THEN
  BEGIN
    WRITE ('Press ENTER to continue.');
    READLN;
  END;
  (* then display the remainder of the deck. *)
  WRITELN ( 'DECK: ');
  DispCards ( Deck);
  WRITE ( 'Press ENTER to end the program.');
  READLN;
END.
```

Seeing how the program is organized will help you understand it. The main program has three main sections:

■ The *setup* section, which initializes important variables and determines the constraints of the game (number of hands and players). This section consists of the first four statements, including the first **FOR** statement.

■ The *deal* section, which distributes the required number of cards to each player. The single call to **Deal** represents this section.

■ The *display* section, which shows the contents of each player's hands and the remaining cards in the deck. The remaining statements in the main program (except the **READLN**, which keeps you on the output screen) make up the display section.

This program has a relatively short body but a rather long declaration section. It defines numerous procedures and some useful data types.

First, notice the **CONST** declarations near the top of the file. These specify names for values used in the program. The first of these, for example, associates a meaningful name (**MaxHands**) with a special value in the program. This value is declared as a constant (rather than a variable) because it does not change throughout the program. Giving the value a name makes it easier to change the actual numerical value if necessary. For example, suppose you need to limit hands to five cards. You could simply change the value of **MaxHands** at the top of your file. No matter how often you refer to this value in your program, every such reference will automatically be modified the next time you compile the program.

In addition to these constants, the declaration section includes several type definitions in which you describe a type of information by listing its possible values or by describing a template for an item of such information. For example, the program defines a **SuitRange** type, which can take on **club**, **diamond**, **heart**, and **spade** as possible values. These values describe an *enumerated type*, in which you can use meaningful names to represent values, rather than having to use arbitrary numerical or letter codes to represent these values. You'll learn about enumerated types in Chapter 3.

FaceRange describes a type that can take on numerical values only within a certain range. These values are used as codes for card values. Values 2 through 10 are regular number cards, and higher values represent picture cards (14 is an ace).

The type definitions also include two templates. The first template describes a **CardArray** as a collection of every combination of four suits and 13 face values—that is, as something that could store information about a complete deck of cards. The description not only shows that you can use arrays in Pascal, but that you can use enumerated as well as numerical values to identify elements (cells) of an array. For example, you can refer to the cell corresponding to 7, **club** (which would be used to represent information about the seven of clubs).

In this program, the individual cells of such an array contain a value that can be either **TRUE** or **FALSE**. You'll learn about arrays in Chapter

7, "Turbo Pascal's Structured Data Types," and about **BOOLEAN**s (a data type that can take on only two possible values: **TRUE** and **FALSE**) in the next chapter. The description of a **Group** in the **DealDemo** program also says it is an array. However, the individual elements of this array are actually **CardArrays**.

The next part of the program's declaration section shows how to declare variables of the types just described, as well as of other, pre-defined, types. This is followed by definitions for several procedures. These procedures execute the work requested in the main program by carrying out the details involved in, for example, initializing a variable of type **CardArray.**

Procedure **GetGameInfo** determines how many players you want to have and how many cards each player will get. The procedure illustrates another Pascal control construct, the **REPEAT** loop. This loop is executed over and over until a certain condition becomes true.

The **InitCards** procedure initializes each cell in a **CardArray** variable to the specified initial value. For example, in the program, the **Deck** variable is initialized to **TRUE**. This means that, at the start of the program, all the cards are in the deck.

Each player's hand, conversely, is initialized to **FALSE**, since these hands start out empty. During the deal, cards are selected at random from **Deck** and assigned to a specified hand. As part of this process, the card is removed from the deck by setting its cell to **FALSE**. In contrast, the recipient's hand grows when a card is added. This is reflected in the fact that the appropriate cell is initialized to **TRUE**.

Procedure **InitCards** uses a nested **FOR** loop, in which the inner loop is executed once for each value the outer loop indicates. Thus, for each suit, the cards from 2 through ace are initialized.

Procedure **Deal** is actually responsible for getting the cards to the players in the correct order. The source code for this procedure illustrates that procedures (and functions) can have other routines defined inside them. In Chapter 6, you'll learn how to define routines within other routines.

Deal first selects a card that hasn't been dealt yet. This card is then added to the appropriate player's hand. This procedure illustrates nested **FOR** loops, which you'll study in more detail in Chapter 5, "Turbo Pascal's Control Structures." The card selection is done by **GetCard**, which is nested in **Deal**. **GetCard**, in turn, uses **GetSuit** for part of its work.

Procedure **DispCard** checks each cell of a **CardArray**. If the cell contains **TRUE**, the card is present, so the routine needs to indicate this. **DispCard** uses a nested routine, **ShowCards**, to indicate that a card is present. This nested procedure handles cards with values of 11 through 14 (that is, picture cards) differently.

Watching Selected Portions of a Program

In earlier examples, you learned how to follow a program's execution step by step. This is feasible for small programs; however, it would quickly become too time consuming to step through larger programs. With Turbo Pascal, you can use breakpoints to stop the program at selected points. A *breakpoint* is a marker that you insert into your program. During its execution, the program stops when it reaches a breakpoint. Until then, the program executes at full speed.

You can insert a breakpoint at the start of a program portion you're interested in. Then you can trace through that portion of the program. When you're finished, let the program continue executing at full speed until it finishes or until it reaches another breakpoint.

Let's watch how **CurrFace** and **CurrSuit** in **Deal** are assigned values. To do this, you'll do the following:

1. Use CTRL-F7 to specify **CurrFace** and **CurrSuit** as watch variables.

2. Set a breakpoint at the call to **GetCard** in **Deal**.

3. Trace through and step over the instructions involved in selecting a card.

To set the watch variables, press CTRL-F7 and then type **CurrFace** in the resulting box. After this variable has been added to the watches window, press CTRL-F7 again, and specify **CurrSuit** as the second watch variable.

To set the breakpoint, press F6 to return to the edit window, then move the cursor to the following line from the main body of the **Deal** procedure:

```
GetCard ( CurrFace, CurrSuit);
```

Once the cursor is on this line, press ALT-D T to set a breakpoint by selecting the Toggle breakpoint command. Note that the hot key for this command is CTRL-F8. After this command, the line will be highlighted to indicate that a breakpoint is set.

Press F6 to reopen the watches window. Then press CTRL-F9 to compile and run the program. The program will ask you to specify the number of players and the number of cards. To make things simple, you may want to pick two players and five cards. The program will immediately stop on the breakpoint line. (Actually, by the time it gets there it will already have initialized over 200 cells.)

Use F7 and F8 to trace through the call to **GetCard** and **GetSuit**. You may want to skip **GetSuit** (which means using F8 when you reach this call). Keep track of the values that are assigned so you know that these cards have actually been dealt. After you've traced through the call to **GetCard**, press CTRL-F9 again. This resumes program execution with the next statement. The program continues until it reaches the breakpoint again. You might want to explore one or two more calls to **GetCard**.

You can ask the DiskTutor to evaluate any expression or variable even while your program is executing. For example, trace into **GetSuit** until the **CASE** line is highlighted. Even if you haven't specified **Result** as a watch variable, you can still see its value.

Press ALT-D to access the Debug menu. The first choice on this menu is Evaluate/modify. . . (which has CTRL-F4 as its hot key). This command lets you specify a variable or expression whose value is to be determined. Type **Result** in the top box and press ENTER. You'll see a number in the middle box, which represents the current value of **Result**. Your screen will look like the one in Figure 2-6.

Notice that there is a box for "New value." You can assign a new value to **Result**. To do so, press the TAB key until you're in the third box. Enter the desired value (make sure it's a valid one—that is, between 0 and 3 in this case) and press ENTER. Then press ESC to close the Evaluate box. You'll be back in procedure **GetSuit**. Use F7 to trace through the **CASE** statement. Notice that the program searches until it reaches the new value that you've specified.

Continue tracing until the last line of **GetSuit** is highlighted. This is just before procedure **GetSuit** finishes and control is returned to procedure **GetCard**. Before you continue, think about what procedures have been called to get you to this point.

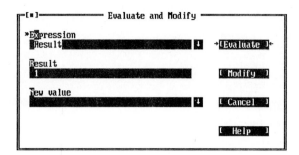

Figure 2-6. *The Evaluate and Modify dialog box*

You started in the main program (**DealDemo**), which called **Deal**. **Deal** called **GetCard**, and so forth. To check your guess, you can activate the *call stack*. Press ALT-W K or just press CTRL-F3 (which is the hot key for the Call Stack command). You'll see a box such as the one shown in Figure 2-7.

The Call Stack box lists all the procedures that are currently active or temporarily suspended. Recall that a program executes statements one after the other unless there is a procedure or function call. In such a case, the calling routine is suspended temporarily while the called routine does its work. This routine may, in turn, call another routine, which calls another, and so forth. The suspended routines and their parameter values are listed in the call stack. The currently executing routine is at the top of the call stack. Note that the call stack also includes information about the arguments with which the routines are called. Press ENTER to close the call stack.

When you've explored enough, press CTRL-F8 the next time the program stops at the breakpoint. Then press CTRL-F9. This time the program will run to completion because the CTRL-F8 removed the breakpoint. Now check whether the values you watched while tracing actually ended up in the players' hands.

Run the program and use the debugging features (evaluate, watch variables, breakpoints, and so forth) to deal each of three players'

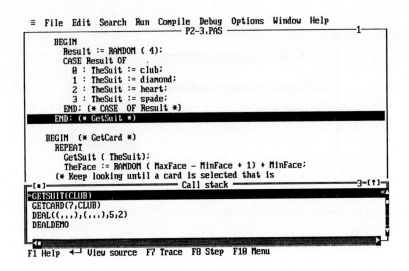

```
≡  File  Edit  Search  Run  Compile  Debug  Options  Window  Help
┌──────────────────────── P2-3.PAS ──────────────────────────1─┐
│     BEGIN                                                      │
│       Result := RANDOM ( 4);                                   │
│       CASE Result OF                    .                      │
│          0 : TheSuit := club;                                  │
│          1 : TheSuit := diamond;                               │
│          2 : TheSuit := heart;                                 │
│          3 : TheSuit := spade;                                 │
│       END; (* CASE  OF Result *)                               │
│█████END;█(*█GetSuit█*)█████████████████████████████████████████│
│                                                                │
│     BEGIN  (* GetCard *)                                       │
│       REPEAT                                                   │
│         GetSuit ( TheSuit);                                    │
│         TheFace := RANDOM ( MaxFace - MinFace + 1) + MinFace;  │
│         (* Keep looking until a card is selected that is       │
┌─[■]═══════════════════════ Call stack ══════════════════════3─[↑]─┐
│»GETSUIT(CLUB)                                                    «│
│ GETCARD(7,CLUB)                                                  │
│ DEAL((...),(...),5,2)                                            │
│ DEALDEMO                                                         │
│◄■                                                              ►│
└────────────────────────────────────────────────────────────────┘
F1 Help  ◄┘ View source  F7 Trace  F8 Step  F10 Menu
```

Figure 2-7. *Call stack during program execution*

straight flush poker hands. (A straight flush hand consists of 10, jack, queen, king, and ace, all in the same suit.) Each player will have a straight flush in a different suit.

Recycling Your Programs

You can write Pascal programs that are easy to adapt for other purposes. To learn this, and a few more IDE commands, you will create a new program based on file P2-3.PAS. The new program is designed to deal hands using a pinochle deck. Pinochle is played with a 48-card deck. Only face values from 9 through ace are used, and each card appears twice in the deck. Thus, there are two queens of hearts, two 10s of clubs, and so forth.

As you'll see, you need to make only a few changes to the **DealDemo** program. Put this new program in a file called PINOCH.PAS. From the DOS command line, type

```
turbo pinoch
```

You'll be in a new edit window, since file PINOCH.PAS doesn't exist yet. To simplify your task, copy the contents of P2-3.PAS into the edit window by pressing CTRL-K R. This command copies the contents of a specified file into the edit window at the current cursor position.

Specify P2-3 as the file (the .PAS extension is assumed). You'll see the contents of this file in inverse video. To restore the screen to its usual mode, press CTRL-K H, which hides special marking of a block of text.

The first two changes are near the top of the file, so you can easily use the arrow keys to reach them. Change the value of **MaxCards** to 16 and of **MinFace** to 9.

Instead of storing true or false values in the cells, this program needs to store the number of a particular card in the deck or hand. This value can be **0, 1,** or **2.** In the program, this will mean changing **BOOLEAN** to **INTEGER.** You can do this with Turbo Pascal's Find and Replace command. Press ALT-S R to activate the Find and Replace command. On the status line, you'll be asked to specify the text to find. For the first substitution, type **BOOLEAN,** but do not press ENTER. Instead press TAB to move to the New text box. Type **INTEGER** in this box, and press ENTER. This tells the IDE to use the default options when searching for text to be replaced. The default options were part of the dialog box in which you specified your command. This box is shown in Figure 2-8.

When the first occurrence of **BOOLEAN** is found, you'll be asked whether to make the substitution. There are three places where a reference to **BOOLEAN** occurs. Press CRTL-L to repeat the find-and-replace process at each of these locations. For simplicity, respond **Y** for each case. (If you're going to use this pinochle program, you should update the comments to bring them in line with the new program.)

To find and change the next string, move the cursor to the top of the file by pressing CTRL-PGUP. Now type ALT-S F to give the Find command. You'll be asked to specify the string to find. Type the following, and press ENTER.

```
Until Deck
```

Because the search mechanism is not case sensitive by default, the cursor will move to the following line:

```
UNTIL Deck [ TheFace, TheSuit] = TRUE;
```

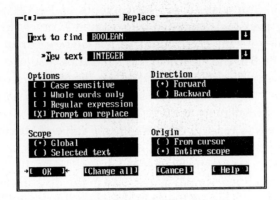

Figure 2-8.   *Dialog box for Search and Replace command*

Change the **= TRUE** to **> 0**.

Move to the two assignment statements in the center of **Deal**, and change these to the following:

```
INC ( Players [ HIndex, CurrFace, CurrSuit]);
INC ( Deck [ CurrFace, CurrSuit], -1);
```

The first statement increases the value representing a particular card. This means that the player has been dealt another of these cards. The second statement removes that card from the deck by decreasing the value in the cell corresponding to the card.

You need to add a new variable to procedure **DispCards**. Move the cursor to the top of the file and then search for

```
PROCEDURE DispCards
```

Once you're on this line, move the cursor to the line under the one that begins with **FaceCounter**. Add the following line:

```
Counter : INTEGER;
```

Then move to the **IF** statement near the end of this procedure. Replace the **IF** line with the following:

```
FOR Counter := 1 TO Cards [ FaceCounter, SuitCounter] DO
```

There are just two minor changes in the main program body. In the calls to **InitCards**, replace the **TRUE** with 2 in the first call, and the **FALSE** with 0 in the second call. These substitutions reflect the fact that a pinochle deck begins with two copies of each card, and a pinochle hand begins with no cards.

Congratulations; you're ready to run your program. The complete program (with minimal changes in the comments) is shown in the following listing. This program is not on the program disk, so save your copy if you plan to build an actual pinochle player.

Try dealing 15 cards to each of three players or 12 cards to each of four players.

```
(* Program to deal card hands to up to 4 players;
   program illustrates use of Array variables
   and of INTEGER and enumerated data types.
*)

PROGRAM DealDemo;

CONST MaxHands = 4;        MaxCards = 16;
      (* Card values range from 2 through Ace (14) *)
      MinFace = 9;         MaxFace = 14;
TYPE SuitRange = ( club, diamond, heart, spade);
     FaceRange = MinFace .. MaxFace;
     (* Define an array containing a deck of cards.
        If a card is present, the corresponding cell
        value is TRUE.
     *)
     CardArray = ARRAY [ FaceRange, club .. spade ] OF INTEGER;
     (* Define a collection of decks,
        each corresponding to a player.
     *)
     Group = ARRAY [ 1 .. MaxHands] OF CardArray;
VAR Deck : CardArray;
    Players : Group;
    NrCards, NrHands, Index : INTEGER;
```

```
(* Initialize a deck to the specified value *)
PROCEDURE InitCards ( VAR Cards : CardArray;
                          Value : INTEGER);
VAR SuitCounter : SuitRange;
    FaceCounter : FaceRange;
BEGIN
  FOR SuitCounter := club TO spade DO
    FOR FaceCounter := MinFace TO MaxFace DO
      Cards [ FaceCounter, SuitCounter] := Value;
END; (* InitCards *)

(* Display the contents of a particular deck *)
PROCEDURE DispCards ( VAR Cards : CardArray);
VAR SuitCounter : SuitRange;
    FaceCounter : FaceRange;
    Counter : INTEGER;

  (* Write a card number or J Q K or A *)
  PROCEDURE ShowCard;
  BEGIN
    IF FaceCounter < 11 THEN
      WRITE ( FaceCounter : 4)
    ELSE
    BEGIN
      CASE FaceCounter OF
        11 : WRITE ( 'J' : 4);
        12 : WRITE ( 'Q' : 4);
        13 : WRITE ( 'K' : 4);
        14 : WRITE ( 'A' : 4);
      END; (* CASE OF FaceCounter *)
    END;
  END; (* ShowCard *)

BEGIN  (* DispCards *)
  FOR SuitCounter := club TO spade DO
  BEGIN
    CASE SuitCounter OF
      club : WRITE ( 'clubs   : ');
      diamond : WRITE ( 'diamonds: ');
      heart : WRITE ( 'hearts  : ');
      spade : WRITE ( 'spades  : ');
    END; (* CASE OF SuitCounter *)
    FOR FaceCounter := MinFace TO MaxFace DO
      FOR Counter := 1 TO Cards [ FaceCounter, SuitCounter] DO
        ShowCard;
    WRITELN;
  END;
END; (* DispCards *)

(* Deal the specified # of cards to the players *)
PROCEDURE Deal ( VAR Deck : CardArray;
                 VAR Players : Group;
                 NrCards, NrHands : INTEGER);
```

```
    VAR CurrSuit : SuitRange;
        CurrFace : FaceRange;
        CIndex, HIndex : INTEGER;

      (* Determine the "next" card in the deck *)
      PROCEDURE GetCard ( VAR TheFace : FaceRange;
                          VAR TheSuit : SuitRange);

        (* Determine the suit of the next card *)
        PROCEDURE GetSuit ( VAR TheSuit : SuitRange);
        VAR Result : INTEGER;
        BEGIN
          Result := RANDOM ( 4);
          CASE Result OF
            0 : TheSuit := club;
            1 : TheSuit := diamond;
            2 : TheSuit := heart;
            3 : TheSuit := spade;
          END; (* CASE  OF Result *)
        END; (* GetSuit *)

      BEGIN  (* GetCard *)
        REPEAT
          GetSuit ( TheSuit);
          TheFace := RANDOM ( MaxFace - MinFace + 1) + MinFace;
        (* Keep looking until a card is selected that is
            still in the deck.
        *)
        UNTIL Deck [ TheFace, TheSuit] > 0;
      END; (* GetCard *)

  BEGIN  (* Deal *)
    FOR CIndex := 1 TO NrCards DO
    BEGIN
      FOR HIndex := 1 TO NrHands DO
      BEGIN
        GetCard ( CurrFace, CurrSuit);
        INC ( Players [ HIndex, CurrFace, CurrSuit]);
        INC ( Deck [ CurrFace, CurrSuit], -1);
      END; (* FOR HIndex *)
    END; (* FOR CIndex *)
  END;  (* Deal *)

(* Determine # players and # of cards per hand *)
PROCEDURE GetGameInfo ( VAR NrCards, NrHands : INTEGER);
BEGIN
  REPEAT
    WRITE ( '# of players? (Max = ', MaxHands, ') ');
    READLN ( NrHands);
  UNTIL NrHands <= MaxHands;
  REPEAT
    WRITE ( '# of Cards? (Max = ', MaxCards, ') ');
    READLN ( NrCards);
```

```
        UNTIL NrCards <= MaxCards;
     END; (* GetGameInfo *)

BEGIN  (* Main program *)
  RANDOMIZE;  (* "shuffle" deck generator *)
  GetGameInfo ( NrCards, NrHands);
  InitCards ( Deck, 2);
  FOR Index := 1 TO MaxHands DO
     InitCards ( Players [ Index], 0);
  Deal ( Deck, Players, NrCards, NrHands);

  (* Display the hands *)
  FOR Index := 1 TO NrHands DO
  BEGIN
     WRITELN ( 'PLAYER ', Index, ': ');
     DispCards ( Players [ Index]);
     WRITELN;
  END;
  (* 4 hands fill the screen, so wait before showing deck *)
  IF NrHands = 4 THEN
  BEGIN
     WRITE ( 'Press ENTER to continue.');
     READLN;
  END;
  (* then display the remainder of the deck. *)
  WRITELN ( 'DECK: ');
  DispCards ( Deck);
  WRITE ( 'Press ENTER to end program.');
  READLN;
END.
```

Now that you've managed that conversion, think about how to change either dealing program to work for blackjack. Perhaps when you've learned more about the language features used in the program (arrays, control structures, procedures, and functions) you'll want to build a blackjack program.

New Command Summary

In the card-dealing program examples, you've learned the following new IDE commands:

ALT-D	Moves to the menu line and selects the De-bug menu.
ALT-D W A or CTRL-F7	Adds to the watches window a watch variable to be specified.
ALT-D T or CTRL-F8	Toggles between setting and cancelling a breakpoint.
ALT-D E or CTRL-F4	Evaluates a specified expression or variable, or assigns a new value to a variable.
ALT-W K or CTRL-F3	Displays the call stack. This command works only if a program is currently executing.
ALT-S F or CTRL-Q F	Finds string to be specified. Options are described in the second part of the chapter.
ALT-S R or CTRL-Q A	Finds string to be specified and replaces it with another string to be specified. Options are described in the second part of the chapter.
ALT-F3	Closes the file currently being edited.
CTRL-K R	Reads contents of a file into the current file.
CTRL-K H	Toggles between hiding and displaying marked text.

Example: Command-Line Arguments and Files

The next example illustrates some of the more advanced features of Pascal—such as files. It also shows how to pass information to the program before it starts executing. The following program:

■ Reads up to 200 (**MaxSize**) lines from a specified file

■ Sorts these lines

■ Writes the sorted lines to another file

```
P2-4    (* Program to sort lines read from a file,
            and to write the sorted lines to another file.
        *)

        PROGRAM Bubble;

        CONST MaxSize = 200;
        TYPE  String80Array = ARRAY [ 1 .. MaxSize] OF STRING [ 80];
        VAR   Str : String80Array;
              NrVals, Count : INTEGER;
              Source, Log : Text;
              SourceOK, LogOK : BOOLEAN;
              SourceName, LogName : STRING;

          PROCEDURE GetString ( Message : STRING;
                                VAR Info : STRING);
          BEGIN
            WRITE ( Message, '? ');
            READLN ( Info);
          END; (* GetString *)

          (* Sort an array of strings by letting the "largest"
             remaining string work its way to the top of an
             array on each pass through the array.
          *)
          PROCEDURE BubbleSort ( VAR Info : String80Array;
                                 Size : INTEGER);
          VAR Temp : STRING [ 80];
              Low, High, Top : INTEGER;
          BEGIN
            Top := Size + 1;
            WHILE ( Top > 1) DO
            BEGIN
              Low := 1;
              High := 2;
              WHILE High < Top DO
              BEGIN
                (* if lower string needs to move upward in the array *)
                IF Info [ Low] > Info [ High] THEN
                BEGIN
                  Temp := Info [ Low];
                  Info [ Low] := Info [ High];
                  Info [ High] := Temp;
                END; (* If lower string needs to move upward *)
                Low := Low + 1;
                High := High + 1;
              END; (* WHILE High < Top *)
              Top := Top - 1;
            END; (* WHILE Top > 1 *)
          END;  (* BubbleSort *)
```

```
    (* Get file names, if necessary.
       Open the source file, and create a log file.
    *)
    PROCEDURE HandleFiles;
    BEGIN
      IF ParamCount = 2 THEN
      BEGIN
        SourceName := ParamStr ( 1);
        LogName := ParamStr ( 2);
      END
      ELSE
      BEGIN
        GetString ( 'Source file name', SourceName);
        GetString ( 'Log file name', LogName);
      END;
      ASSIGN ( Source, SourceName);
      (*$I-*)
      RESET ( Source);
      (*$I+*)
      IF IOResult = 0 THEN
        SourceOK := TRUE
      ELSE
        SourceOK := FALSE;
      ASSIGN ( Log, LogName);
      (*$I-*)
      REWRITE ( Log);
      (*$I+*)
      IF IOResult = 0 THEN
        LogOK := TRUE
      ELSE
        LogOK := FALSE;
    END; (* HandleFiles *)


    PROCEDURE GetLines;
    BEGIN
      (* Get the lines to be sorted *)
      Count := 0;
      WHILE ( NOT ( EOF ( Source)) AND ( Count < MaxSize)) DO
      BEGIN
        Count := Count + 1;
        READLN ( Source, Str [ Count]);
      END;
      NrVals := Count;
    END; (* GetLines *)

BEGIN  (* Main Program *)
  HandleFiles;

  IF SourceOK AND LogOK THEN
  BEGIN
    GetLines;
```

```
      BubbleSort ( Str, NrVals);    (* sort the lines *)

      (* Write the sorted lines to the log file *)
      FOR Count := 1 TO NrVals DO
        WRITELN ( Log, Str [ Count]);
      WRITELN ( 'Log file written. Press ENTER to end program');
      CLOSE ( Source);
      CLOSE ( Log);
    END
    ELSE
      WRITELN ( 'File Error. Press ENTER to end program');
    READLN;
  END.
```

The fundamental data type in this program is an array of strings, described in the following line from the program:

```
TYPE  String80Array = ARRAY [ 1 .. MaxSize] OF STRING [ 80];
```

This line describes a 200-element array. Each element in this array is a string of up to 80 characters. The string length limitation is indicated by the **[80]** at the end of the line. Recall that earlier programs used variables of type **STRING**. Such variables could be up to 255 characters long.

Since lines from text files are rarely longer than 80 characters, you can save a great deal of space by working with the 80-character strings. You'll see lots more uses for such strings throughout the book.

The two files used in the program are declared as variables of type **Text**. Before you can use these files, you must open or create them. This is done in procedure **HandleFiles**.

File **Source** must already exist, so the program can read from it. For this reason, you just need to open the file; **Log**, on the other hand, is created anew each time and old log files with the same name are lost. You'll learn more about the syntax of file opening and creation in Chapter 8, "Files."

After the files have been prepared in procedure **HandleFiles**, the program reads the lines from **Source**. This takes place within the **WHILE** loop in procedure **GetLines**. The **WHILE** loop executes as long as the end of the source file has not been reached and fewer than 200 lines have been read. If the file contains fewer than 200 lines, the end of the file will eventually be reached and the loop will stop.

After sorting the array, the lines are written to the log file. The last part of the program closes the files to save their contents.

The Bubblesort Algorithm

The core of the program is actually the single statement that calls **BubbleSort**. This procedure sorts the array of strings using what is known as a *bubblesort*, or *exchange*, algorithm. The sorting is based on the ASCII code of the letters with which each line begins. This is roughly an alphabetical ordering, except that all lines that begin with an uppercase letter precede those that begin with a lowercase letter.

Thus, a line that begins with *A* would be near the front of the sorted array, and one that begins with *z* would be near the end. Because of the way the ASCII character set is arranged, lines that begin with *Z* would precede those that begin with *a*. The discussion refers to strings that come later in a sorted list as *larger* strings.

The basic strategy behind the bubblesort algorithm is as follows:

■ Make repeated passes through the array.

■ On each pass, compare successive cells. For example, on the first pass the algorithm would compare cells 1 and 2, then cells 2 and 3, 3 and 4, and so forth, until all the remaining cells have been compared.

■ If necessary, exchange the strings in two cells so that the larger string ends up in the higher cell.

■ When all the cell pairs have been compared, the top cell will contain the string that comes last in the sorting. Thus, after the first pass through the array, cell 200 will contain the string that comes last in the sorted list. This string has "bubbled" to the top of the array—hence, the algorithm's name. (The highest cell may have an index less than 200 if fewer than 200 lines were read.)

■ The next time through the array, you need not look at the last cell (you know its string is in the proper place). That means you only need to examine at most 199 cells the second time through.

■ After this pass, the 199th cell will contain the last line from the 199 remaining lines.

■ Continue this process until there are no more passes to make.

You'll work more with the bubblesort algorithm in Chapter 7, "Turbo Pascal's Structured Data Types," and Chapter 12, "Virtual Methods in Object-Oriented Programming."

Providing Command-Line Information

The program needs two items of information from you: the names of the source and log files. In the IDE, you can specify this information as command-line parameters. For example, suppose you want to sort the lines in program P2-3.PAS and write the sorted lines to the file P2-3 .SRT.

Press ALT-R to access the Run menu. Then type **A** or use the arrow keys to move the cursor to the Parameters command. Then press ENTER. This gives you access to a Command-Line Parameters box. In the box, type

```
p2-3.pas p2-3.srt
```

You must include the extensions for the file names here. Press ENTER to save the contents of the box and return to the edit window.

If you run the program now, it won't ask you for file name information because it uses the two values you entered in the Command-Line Parameters box. You'll learn more about command-line arguments in Chapter 14, "Miscellaneous Topics."

CAUTION   Be very careful to specify the source and log file names in the correct order.

New IDE Commands

This example introduced only two new commands.

ALT-R	Moves to the menu line and selects the Run menu
ALT-R A	Selects Parameters command from the Run menu

The IDE: A More Detailed Look

The remainder of this chapter includes a more detailed summary of the commands available in the edit window and through the IDE menus. For the most part, lists summarize the commands. You may want to use this and Appendix C, "IDE Commands," primarily as references.

First, the editor commands are discussed. The most common simple movement commands are summarized in the following list. For a complete list of editor commands, see Appendix C or the on-line help accessible through F1.

Moving Around in Your File

You can use the arrow keys on the numeric keypad to move up and down, left and right. Pressing one of the arrow keys moves you by one character horizontally or by one line vertically. You can accomplish the same thing by pressing the keys E, D, X, and S in conjunction with the CTRL key, that is, CTRL-E, CTRL-X, and so forth. These four letters form a diamond on the keyboard. The relative position of a key among the four indicates the direction of movement. Thus, CTRL-E moves up one line (like the UP ARROW key) and CTRL-S moves one column to the left. The HOME key moves the cursor to the beginning of a line, and the END key moves it to the end of the line. (NUMLOCK must be OFF, or the numeric keypad keys will represent digits rather than movement keys.)

As you learn more commands, you'll find that many of them come in different "sizes." For example, you can move the cursor a single character at a time, or a single word at a time; you might move to the beginning of a word, a line, or a screen. The CTRL key can modify ordinary keys and reproduce the same command at a different level.

For example, the RIGHT ARROW key moves the cursor to the right by one character. Modifying the RIGHT ARROW key with CTRL—that is, pressing CTRL-RIGHT ARROW—moves the cursor to the next word. (You should press the CTRL key before the RIGHT ARROW to avoid moving the cursor as soon as you press RIGHT ARROW.)

Experiment with the other cursor movement keys. You can modify most of them by using CTRL. The following list summarizes what happens when you modify each of them with CTRL.

Finally, the PGUP and PGDN keys move you a screen at a time. PGUP moves you toward the start of the file and PGDN moves you toward the end of the file.

CTRL-E or UP ARROW	Moves the cursor one line toward the top of the screen.
CTRL-X or DOWN ARROW	Moves the cursor one line toward the bottom of the screen.
CTRL-S or LEFT ARROW	Moves the cursor one character to the left.
CTRL-D or RIGHT ARROW	Moves the cursor one character to the right.
CTRL-A or CTRL-LEFT ARROW	Moves the cursor to the start of the current or preceding word.
CTRL-F or CTRL-RIGHT ARROW	Moves the cursor to the start of the next word.
CTRL-Q S or HOME	Moves the cursor to the start of the current line.

CTRL-Q D or END	Moves the cursor to the end of the current line.
CTRL-R or PGUP	Moves the cursor to the top of the screen.
CTRL-C or PGDN	Moves the cursor to the bottom of the screen.
CTRL-PGUP	Moves the cursor to the start of the file.
CTRL-PGDN	Moves the cursor to the end of the file.
CTRL-HOME	Moves the cursor to the top line of the screen, remaining in the current column.
CTRL-END	Moves the cursor to the bottom line of the screen, remaining in the current column.

Inserting and Deleting Text

The following list summarizes the commands for inserting and deleting text:

CTRL-V or INS	Toggles between insert and overwrite mode.
CTRL-N	Inserts a blank line at the current cursor position, pushing lines downwards in the file.
CTRL-G or DEL	Deletes the character at the current cursor position. Characters to the right of the position move leftward to fill in the vacated spot.
CTRL-H or BACKSPACE	Deletes the character preceding the one at the current cursor position. Characters to the right of the deleted character move leftward to fill in the vacated spot.

CTRL-Y	Deletes (yanks) the current line.
CTRL-Q Y	Deletes from the current cursor position to the end of the current line.
CTRL-T	Deletes from the current cursor position to the end of the current word.

Manipulating Blocks of Text

In the Turbo Pascal editor, you can mark and manipulate entire blocks of text. Block commands all consist of a control key combination followed by another character. For example, CTRL-K B marks the beginning of a block of text; similarly, CTRL-K K marks the end of the desired block. On your screen, the marked text will be highlighted or a different color.

CTRL-K B	Marks the beginning of a block of text.
CTRL-K K	Marks the end of a block of text.
CTRL-K T	Marks a single word. If the cursor is in the middle of a word, the entire word is marked. If the cursor is between words, the word to the left of the cursor is marked.
CTRL-K Y	Deletes (yanks) the marked block from the file.
CTRL-K V	Moves the marked block from its current position to the cursor location.
CTRL-K C	Copies the block to a second location. After this command, the block will be in your file twice.

CTRL-K W	Writes the block to a new file whose name you must specify. The IDE assumes that this file has a .PAS extension unless you specify otherwise.
CTRL-K R	Reads a block from a file and inserts it at the current cursor position. You must specify the file whose contents you want to copy.
CTRL-K P	Prints a block.

If no block has been marked, nothing happens. The exception is the Print command, which prints the contents of the edit window.

When reading a block from a file, you can specify a file name with wildcard characters (such as *.PAS). (A *wildcard character* is one that can be replaced by one or more other characters. For example, the file name *.PAS specifies any file with the .PAS extension.) In that case, you'll get a list of file names with the extension .PAS in the current directory. You can then use the arrow keys to select a file from that list. This technique can be handy if you forget a file name.

Setting Place Markers

The Turbo Pascal editor also lets you mark up to ten locations in your file. Once they are marked, you can jump quickly to these locations. This can be convenient if you have a long file. For example, you might have to skip to various procedure or function definitions, and then back to the main program.

You can mark the start of the main program body by moving the cursor to that location and typing CTRL-K, followed by a number between 0 and 9. For example, suppose you mark this location with CTRL-K 0. To jump to this location, just press CTRL-Q 0.

CTRL-K n	Marks the current cursor position as location n, where n is a number in the range 0..9
CTRL-Q n	Moves to the marked location n, where n is a number in the range 0..9

Finding and Replacing Text

As you've seen, you can search for specified text and can replace it with other text. To find a specified string (of up to 30 characters in length), type CTRL-Q F. In the resulting dialog box, you'll be prompted for the text you want to find. Type the desired text and press ENTER. You can also specify search options in the dialog box. These options are identical to those in Figure 2-8, except that the Find dialog box lacks the Prompt on replace option.

The search process continues from the current cursor position to the end or the beginning of the file—depending on the direction in which you want to search. If you want to repeat the last search, press CTRL-L.

To replace specified text, use the Find and Replace command, which you can invoke by pressing ALT-S R or CTRL-Q A. You'll be asked for the string to find and then for the replacement text. Finally, you'll be asked to specify any options that will guide the search process.

By default, the IDE asks you to verify each substitution. If you simply want to replace all occurrences without verification, select the Change all command.

ALT-S F or CTRL-Q F	Searches for a string to be specified
ALT-S R or CTRL-Q A	Searches for a string to be specified and replaces it with a second string also to be specified
CTRL-L	Repeats the last Find or Find and Replace command

Miscellaneous Editor Commands

There are several other miscellaneous editor commands:

CTRL-P	Enables you to write control characters in your file. Generally, your files will consist of printable characters—letters,

digits, and various other symbols. Sometimes, however, you may want to include control characters in your file. You can do this by pressing CTRL-P and then the letter corresponding to the character you want to include. Such characters will appear in low-intensity mode or inverse video.

CTRL-Q] or CTRL-Q [Finds matching delimiter. If the cursor is on any of the following characters, you can find the right counterpart to the character:

{ [(* < " '

Similarly, if the cursor is on any of the following characters, you can find the left counterpart to the character:

' " > *)] }

To find the counterparts for (* and *), the cursor must be on the parenthesis element of the delimiter.

ALT-R or CTRL-Q L   Restores the current line to undo any changes since the cursor was moved to the line. This command works *provided that you haven't moved from the line.*

The remaining editor commands are summarized in Appendix C.

Using the IDE Menus

To pull down the menus in the IDE, you simply press ALT, along with the first letter of the menu name. For example, to access the File menu, press ALT-F. The one exception to this rule is the System menu, which is accessed with ALT-SPACEBAR.

Let's look briefly at the general features of the menus. Menus have several types of entries:

■ Commands that require no additional information and which are carried out immediately—for example, the New command on the File menu.

■ Commands that require additional information and involve a dialog box—for example, the Open command on the File menu. Such commands are identified by the ellipsis (. . .) following the command name.

■ Entries that open to another menu—for example, the Environment entry on the Options menu. Such entries are identified by a ▶ at the end of the entry box.

To select a menu entry, pull down the menu, then do either of the following:

■ Use the UP and DOWN ARROW keys to move to the desired entry, then press ENTER.

■ Press the highlighted letter in the entry you want. Any menu entry that is valid in a particular context will have a highlighted letter in that context.

Certain menu entries have hot keys associated with them—for example, F3 is associated with the Open command on the File menu. These are keystrokes that select the command directly. That is, hot keys allow you to bypass the menus.

You can get information about a menu entry by checking the status line when the menu entry is highlighted or by accessing Help when the entry is highlighted. To get help about the highlighted option, press F1.

The System Menu

The System menu contains three entries that are not associated with any particular part of the IDE. This menu is indicated by ≡ on the menu bar. The ALT-SPACEBAR command accesses this menu.

About (ALT-SPACEBAR A)   This command displays information about the version of Turbo Pascal.

Refresh Display (ALT-SPACEBAR R)   The Refresh Display command restores the screen in the IDE. You'll rarely need to use this command; however, it will be useful if a program has accidentally overwritten the screen.

Clear Desktop (ALT-SPACEBAR C)   The Clear Desktop command closes all windows and clears all history lists.

The File Menu

The File menu contains commands for creating, opening, closing, and printing files. To pull down the File menu, press ALT-F. Your screen will look like the one in Figure 2-9.

Open. . . (F3 **or** ALT-F O)   Use this command to open an existing file and load it into the edit window. You'll need to specify the file in a dialog box such as the one shown earlier in Figure 2-3.

You can either type the name of the file (with or without the .PAS extension) or press ENTER to see a listing of all the files in the current directory that have the extension .PAS. In such a listing, you can use the arrow keys to highlight the file you want to edit, then press ENTER. You'll be put back to the edit window, which will now contain the file you asked to load.

If you ask the IDE to load a nonexistent file, it will create a new file with that name, and will put you in the edit window.

Figure 2-9. *The File menu*

New (ALT-F N) Use this command to open a new file in an edit window. The file has a name such as NONAMExx.PAS, where xx is replaced by a pair of digits in the program.

Save (F2 or ALT-F S) Use this command to save the current file to disk. The file will be saved under the name the file had when you started editing it. New files — that is, files you haven't named yet — are given the name NONAMExx.PAS. If you try to save such a file, you'll first be asked for a file name.

If you were editing an existing file, the original version of the file — that is, the version with which you started the editing session — will be preserved with the extension .BAK.

Save as. . . (ALT-F A) This command lets you save the file in the active edit window under a new name. You must specify the file name in a dialog box.

Save all (ALT-F L) This command saves the contents of all files that have been modified since the last time they were saved.

Change Directory. . . (ALT-F C) You can change the current directory with this command. When you invoke Change Directory. . ., you'll be asked to specify a directory. The path name of the current directory will be shown. To change this, just start typing. The entire name will disappear and will be replaced by the path you type.

After you specify the name and press ENTER, all references to files are assumed to refer to the new current directory unless the file's path is specified. The new directory will remain the current directory after you leave the IDE.

Print (ALT-F P)   You can print the contents of the active edit window with this command. The entire file will be printed.

GetInfo. . . (ALT-F G)   This command displays information about the current file and environment, as shown in Figure 2-10.

DOS Shell (ALT-F D)   Use this command to exit from the IDE temporarily. You will be at a DOS command line, from which you can execute programs and carry out commands. When you're finished doing what you want, type

```
exit
```

to return to the IDE.

Be careful when you exit to a DOS shell. There are certain things you should not do in such a situation. Do not install memory-resident programs, because memory may be allocated incorrectly. You should also not delete or modify any files being modified in the IDE. Doing that is just asking for trouble.

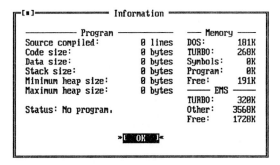

Figure 2-10.   *Information provided after selecting Get Information command on File menu*

Exit (ALT-X **or** ALT-F X)   Exit ends your session with the IDE and puts you
back in the DOS environment. If you've been editing a file and haven't
saved it yet, you're asked whether to save the changes you made before
leaving the IDE.

The Edit Menu

The Edit menu lets you move text around within a file and between files.
Text will often be stored in a *clipboard,* an intermediate location for text
being moved from one window to another.

The Edit menu commands are shown in Figure 2-11. Many of the
commands on the Edit menu work only for selected text. To select text,
you need to mark it, which you can do in several ways. In all cases, you
need to move to the start of the text you want to select.

■ On the keyboard, keep the SHIFT key pressed while defining the text
you want to mark. Use the arrow keys to move.

■ On the keyboard, press CTRL-K B to mark the beginning of the selected
block. Then move to the end of the block and press CTRL-K K. If you just
want to select single words, you can use CTRL-K T.

■ With a mouse, drag the pointer over the text you want to select. If you
want to select a single line, you can double click anywhere on the line.

Restore Line (ALT-E R)   Use this command to undo the last editing you
did on the current line. When you give this command, you must still be
on the line (or where the line used to be).

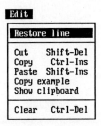

Figure 2-11.   *The Edit menu*

Cut (SHIFT-DEL **or** ALT-E T)   The Cut command removes the selected text from the current window and copies it to the clipboard. From there you can move the text to as many new windows as you want.

Copy (CTRL-INS **or** ALT-E C)   Use this command to copy the selected text to the clipboard, from which you can copy the text to other files. The command leaves the text in the current window.

Paste (SHIFT-INS **or** ALT-E P)   You can paste the selected text from the clipboard to the cursor location in the active edit window with this command.

Copy Example (ALT-E E)   This command copies an example from the IDE Help files to the current window.

Show Clipboard (ALT-E S)   Use this command to open the clipboard, so you can edit its contents. You can cut material from this window, just as from any other edit window.

   You may want to experiment with a short clipboard file, to see where text is stored when it is cut or copied from the clipboard. To do this, just cut some simple text from an edit window to the clipboard, then open the clipboard window.

Clear (CTRL-DEL **or** ALT-E L)   The Clear command deletes the selected text from the active window, but does not copy it to the clipboard. As a result, the deleted text is gone for good.

CAUTION   Be careful when using this command; you will not be able to retrieve the text.

The Search Menu

The Search menu contains commands for finding specific text, or certain types of text (such as run-time errors). There are also commands for moving to particular locations (such as a particular line number or to the start of a specified procedure).

Find . . . (ALT-S F)   You can search for specified text with the Find command. You can specify a variety of search instructions, as you can see in Figure 2-12. You can start the search from any of several places:

■ Current cursor position

■ Start of the file

■ End of the file

■ Start of a selected block of text

You can search forward or backward, and you can specify whether the search should cover only the selected block.

In addition to the search methods and scope, you can specify search criteria. If "Case sensitive" is selected, a search for **Thor** would match **Thor**, might match **Thoroughfare**, but would definitely not match **thoroughly.** If "Whole words only" is selected, the **Thor** does not match **Thoroughly**, but might match **thor**—depending on the case sensitivity setting.

If you select "Regular expression," then certain characters get special meaning in a block of text, and the IDE's search process becomes more

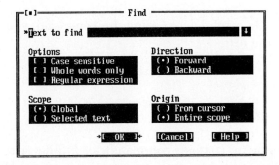

Figure 2-12.   *Dialog box for Find command on Search menu*

powerful. For example, a period (.) can be used to match any character. Thus, **b.t** matches **bat**, **bbt**, **b6t**, but not **beet** (too many characters) and not **bt** (no match for the **t** at the end of **b.t**).

An asterisk (*) or a plus sign (+) after a letter indicates that any number of occurrences of the preceding letter will match. With *, that number can be 0; with +, at least one occurrence of the character is needed. For example, **fur*y** matches **fuy**, **fury**, **furry**, and even **furrry**; **fur+y**, on the other hand, matches the last three, but does not match **fuy**.

The caret (^) and the dollar sign ($) are used to indicate that matches must occur at the beginning (^) or the end ($) of a line. For example, **^hello** matches in the first of the following lines but not the second (because leading blanks are characters too).

```
hello there

    hello there
```

Similarly, **hello$** would match in the first but not the second of the following lines (because there is text following the **hello**).

```
please say hello

please say hello to the girl
```

You can use brackets to specify a collection of characters that would constitute a match. For example, **[aeiouy]** would match any vowel, but no other letters. If the characters of interest are consecutive, you can save yourself some typing by using a dash (-) between the first and last character in the sequence. For example, **[3-7]** matches any of the characters 3, 4, 5, 6, or 7.

A third way you can specify a collection of letters is by specifying the letters you will *not* accept. For example, **[^aeiouy]** tells the IDE to look for any character *except* a vowel.

You can use all these capabilities within a single set of brackets. For example, **[^aeiouy1-5]** accepts any character except a vowel or a digit between 1 and 5. Thus, **w** and **6** would be matches, but neither **e** nor **3** would be.

If you need to search for one of the special characters, you can put a backslash in front of it. This tells the IDE that the character is being used as an ordinary character, not as a wildcard. For example, **hello\$** matches **hello$**, regardless of where the string occurs on a line.

Replace... (ALT-S R)   Use this command to replace specified text with other text. As with the Find command, you can specify search behavior. You can also specify whether the IDE should ask you to verify each replacement.

Search Again (CTRL-L or ALT-S S)   Search Again repeats the last search or replace command.

Go to Line Number... (ALT-S G)   Use this command to specify a line number to find.

Find Procedure... (ALT-S F)   Use this command to search for the definition of a procedure or function you specify. This command is available only when debugging.

Find Error... (ALT-S E)   You can search for the location of a run-time error with this command. You need to provide the segment and offset location of the error. This information is provided when the run-time error occurs.

The Run Menu

If you press ALT-R, you'll get access to the Run menu, the options for which are shown in Figure 2-13. From this menu, you can execute your program. If necessary, the program will be compiled automatically before executing. Programs execute very quickly in the IDE. This can be a disadvantage if you're trying to study the program's operation. To help with such problems, the IDE enables you to control program execution in various ways, as described in several commands from the Run menu.

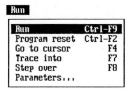

Figure 2-13. *Run menu selections*

Run (CTRL-F9 **or** ALT-R R) If you select this command, the IDE will execute your program. Invoking the Run command automatically invokes the compiler, if needed.

Program Reset (CTRL-F2 **or** ALT-R P) This command ends a debugging session, releasing any allocated memory and closing any files opened for the session.

Go to Cursor (F4 **or** ALT-R G) This command enables you to specify a location at which program execution will stop temporarily. The location is determined by the cursor position when you invoke the command.
     When invoked, the program will execute at full speed until it reaches the statement at the current cursor position. At that point the program stops, awaiting instructions from you.

Trace Into (F7 **or** ALT-R T) Use this command to execute your program step by step. When you invoke this command, the cursor will move to the next statement to be executed in the program. The current statement is actually executed. The next statement is always highlighted.
     If a statement is a procedure call, the cursor moves to the beginning of the routine called, and you can step through the procedure as it executes.

Step Over (F8 **or** ALT-R S) The Trace into command actually lets you step through any procedures your program calls (other than predefined routines). The Step over command, on the other hand, says to execute the routine, but not to do it step by step. Thus, you can get the results of a particular routine without having to watch it do its work.

Parameters. . . (ALT-R A) Use this command to specify command-line arguments for a program to be executed within the IDE.

The Compile Menu

The Compile menu lets you compile programs selectively — compiling only those files that need to be compiled. To pull down this menu, press ALT-C.

Compile (ALT-F9 or ALT-C C) Use this command to compile the file in the active window. The compiled program is written to disk (as an .EXE file) or is held in memory — depending on the value of Destination.

Make (F9 or ALT-C M) The Make command creates a compiled program by processing all files required for the program. However, the command compiles only those files that have changed since the last compilation and any files dependent on these changed files. The compilation begins with the file in the current edit window or with the file that has been specified as the *Primary file*.

Build (ALT-C B) The Build command recompiles all files required for a program, regardless of whether the files have changed since the last compilation.

Destination (ALT-C D) Use this command to specify whether the compiler should create a disk image of the executable program or whether the program should just be compiled to memory. Compiling to memory is considerably faster and is probably the best strategy during the early phases of program development. The command toggles between Disk and Memory.

Primary File. . . (ALT-C P) Use this command to specify which file is to be compiled if you invoke the Make or Build command.

The Debug Menu

The IDE comes with debugging facilities that you can use to examine the execution of your programs in very close detail. For example, you can set breakpoints, that is, mark certain statements in your program so execution will stop temporarily when such a statement is reached. You'll generally want to examine the value of specific variables at such break-points. The Debug menu contains commands for specifying these watch variables.

You can evaluate the values of variables you specify on the run, and you can even use this facility as a simple calculator. To pull down the Debug menu, press ALT-D.

Evaluate/Modify. . . (CTRL-F4 or ALT-D E)   Use this command to specify a variable or an expression for the debugger to evaluate. The debugger will indicate the current value in a box. You can change this value and then resume program execution with the new value included in the program.

You can even use the Evaluate command as a little calculator. For example, while you're editing a file, press CTRL-F4 to invoke the Evaluate command. Then type the following into the first box:

```
37 * 23.5 / 3.65 / 1.3
```

You'll get a result of 183.2455216 in the value box.

Watches (ALT-D W)   This entry represents a submenu through which you can specify watch variables to be added or removed in the debugging environment.

Add Watch Variable (CTRL-F7 or ALT-D W A)   Use this command to add a variable to the watches window, so you can observe its value as the program executes. After you give this command, you'll be asked to specify the name of the variable to watch.

Delete Watch Variable (ALT-D W D)   You can remove the specified variable from the watches window with this command.

Edit Watch. . . (ALT-D W E)   You can change the information in the current watch expression with this command.

Remove All Watch Variables (ALT-D W R)   This command clears the watches window and removes all watch variables from this list.

Toggle Breakpoint (CTRL-F8 **or** ALT-D T)   You can toggle between setting and removing a breakpoint at the current cursor position in the edit window with this command.

Breakpoints. . . (ALT-D B)   Use this command to edit the breakpoint list, which contains information about each breakpoint you have set in your program.

The Options Menu

The Options menu (ALT-O) lets you modify your working environment and lets you save and retrieve configuration information.

Compiler. . . (ALT-O C)   This entry lets you control details of how the compiler does its work. The options you can change in the dialog box for this command relate to

- The way the program is arranged in memory (code generation)
- Checking done by the compiler (run-time errors, syntax options)
- Additional information generated by the compiler (debugging)
- Mathematics (numeric processing)

   You may want to enable all the checking options during the early phases of program development. These make it easier to find errors, but they slow down program execution. When the program is running well, remove these checks to speed up the program.

Memory Sizes. . . (ALT-O M)   This entry lets you specify the stack and heap space for your program.

Linker. . . (ALT-O L)   This entry lets you control the behavior of the linker during the program creation process. In particular, you can specify what information is to be included in the map file. You can also specify whether the linker should use memory or the disk for storing intermediate values. Using memory is faster, but may cause problems when you try to build big programs—because you may run out of memory.

Debugger. . . (ALT-O B)   This entry lets you control the behavior of the debugger in the IDE. In particular, you can specify whether the debugger should swap between the output screen and the source code window during a debugging session. "Smart" swapping tells the debugger to swap only if something has been written to the output screen.

Directories. . . (ALT-O D)   Use this command to specify directories where various types of files will be found. In particular, you can specify where the main compiler and environment files are located, where precompiled units are to be found, and so forth.

Environment (ALT-O E)   This entry is actually a submenu, which you can use to set up your working environment to make it more useful to you.

Preferences. . . (ALT-O E P)   Use this entry to set various options relating to the screen and to the way the IDE handles your files. The dialog box for this entry is shown in Figure 2-14.

Editor. . . (ALT-O E E)   Use this entry to specify how the IDE editor is to behave. In particular, you can specify the indentation rules for the editor, whether to keep backup versions of your files, and so forth.

Mouse. . . (ALT-O E M)   Use this entry to specify the behavior of the mouse, if you're using one.

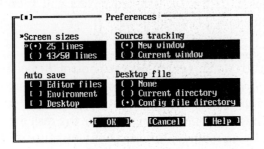

Figure 2-14. *Preferences dialog menu*

Startup. . . (ALT-O E S)   You can specify details of the working environment with this command. These settings relate to the screen, to memory, and to the IDE configuration. Figure 2-15 shows the options you can specify in the Startup dialog box.

Colors. . . (ALT-O E C)   Use this entry to select the combination of foreground and background colors most comfortable for you.

Save Options. . . (ALT-O S)   This command tells the IDE to save the setting values you've specified. You'll be asked to specify the name of the file in which to save the configuration. This command is useful if you have several different configurations that you use frequently.

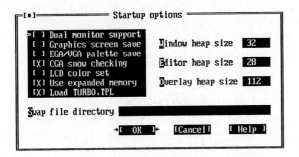

Figure 2-15. *Startup options dialog box*

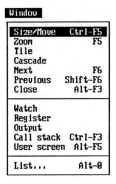

Figure 2-16. *The Window menu*

Retrieve Options. . . (ALT-O R) This command tells the IDE to read setting values from a file you specify. You'll be asked to specify the name of the file from which to read the configuration.

The Window Menu

The Window menu lets you control the way windows appear on the screen and also which windows are visible. To access this menu, press ALT-W. The Window menu is shown in Figure 2-16.

Size/Move (CTRL-F5 or ALT-W S) Use this command to move the current window and also resize it. Once you select the command, you can use the arrow keys to move the window according to your needs.

Zoom (F5 or ALT-W Z) Use Zoom to toggle between making the current window as large as possible and restoring the original size.

Tile (ALT-W T) The Tile command lays all open windows out in such a way that each is visible and none are overlapping. The consequence is that each window occupies only a small area on the screen, so you can't see much in any one window. Figure 2-17 shows several windows tiled. The active window is highlighted.

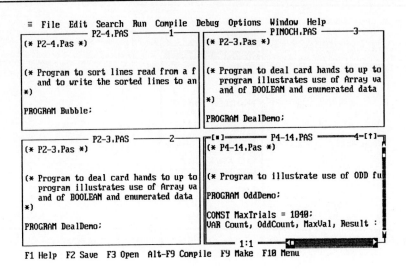

Figure 2-17. *Tiled (nonoverlapping) windows*

Cascade (ALT-W A)   The Cascade command lays all open windows out in such a way that, at any given time, the active window is visible and other windows are partially hidden. The only part of inactive windows that is visible is the title bar for the window.

Compare Figure 2-18, which shows cascaded windows, with Figure 2-17, which has tiled windows.

Next (F6 or ALT-W N)   Use this command to make the next window in the list of open windows the active one. Windows are stored in a circular list. If you have four windows open, and window 4 is currently active, the Next command makes window 1 active.

Previous (SHIFT-F6 or ALT-W P)   Use this command to make the previous window in the circular list of open windows the active one. If you have four windows open, and window 1 is currently active, the Previous command makes window 4 the active one.

Close (ALT-F3 or ALT-W C)   Use this command to close the current window.

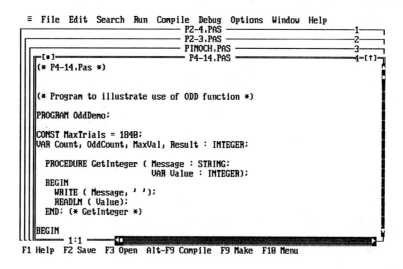

Figure 2-18. *Cascaded (overlapping) windows*

Watch (ALT-W W)   This command opens a watches window. This window displays the values of any watch variables or expressions you have set.

Register (ALT-W R)   This command opens a window in which the contents of the PC's registers are displayed.

Output (ALT-W O)   Use this command to make the program's output window the active one. Once opened, you need to close the window yourself—either by clicking on the close box (if you have a mouse) or by giving the Close command (ALT-W C).

Call Stack (CTRL-F3 **or** ALT-W K)   Use this command to open a window containing a list of the procedures and functions that have been called and are temporarily on hold while the topmost routine executes.

User Screen (ALT-F5 **or** ALT-W U)   The User screen command lets you see program output on a full screen. This is in contrast to the output window, which may only be on part of the screen.

List. . . (ALT-O or ALT-W L)   This command provides a list of the files in all open windows. You can select a file from this list, thereby making its window the active one.

Help Commands

The following help commands are available:

F1	Provides help relevant to the current context. For example, if you're in the edit window, F1 displays help about editor commands. If you're in a menu box, F1 displays help about the command or the topic in the box.
SHIFT-F1	Provides an index of topics from which you can select one for more help.
ALT-F1	Redisplays the help screen shown most recently before the current screen.
CTRL-F1	If the cursor is currently on a Pascal reserved word or on the name of a predefined procedure or function name, this command provides help about the concept or routine.

A Final Example

Let's look at one more example, to refresh and reinforce your mastery of the IDE editor. The following two programs will also give you a chance to test your recall of the editing commands.

The first program lets you determine the maximum of a set of values. To provide the values, simply enter them.

When you've finished entering your values, enter **0.0** as your last value. This value tells the program that you're finished. This last value *must* be included at the end of your data entry but is not included in any counts or computations.

P2-5

```
(* Program to compute the maximum of a set of values. *)

PROGRAM GetMaxValue;

CONST StopValue = 0.0;      (* value to indicate end of input *)
VAR CurrMax, CurrVal : REAL;
    Count : INTEGER;

  (* Return the larger of two values passed as parameters *)
  FUNCTION FindMax ( Val1, Val2 : REAL) : REAL;
  BEGIN
    IF Val1 > Val2 THEN
      FindMax :=Val1
    ELSE
        FindMax :=Val2;
  END; (* FindMax *)

BEGIN
  Count :=0
  CurrMax := -1000000.0;

  WRITELN ( 'Enter values, with ', StopValue: 3 : 1,
            ' as the last value.');
  (* Read values until the StopValue is encountered *)
  READ ( CurrVal);
  WHILE CurrVal <> StopValue DO
  BEGIN
    Count := Count + 1;
    CurrMax := FindMax ( CurrMax, CurrVal);
    READLN ( CurrVal);
  END; (* WHILE NOT StopValue *)

  (* Display results *)
  WRITELN ( Count, ' values read: Max = ', CurrMax : 10 : 3);
  WRITE ( 'Press ENTER to end program.');
  READLN;
END.
```

Now use the editing commands (such as Find and Replace) to modify the program to find the *minimum* of a set of values. When you're done, the program will look like the one in the following listing (which is not included on your example program disk).

```
(* Program to compute the minimum of a set of values. *)

PROGRAM GetMinValue;

CONST StopValue = 0.0;     (* value to indicate end of input *)
```

```
VAR CurrMin, CurrVal : REAL;
    Count : INTEGER;

  (* Return the larger of two values passed as parameters *)
  FUNCTION FindMin ( Val1, Val2 : REAL) : REAL;
  BEGIN

    IF Val1 < Val2 THEN
      FindMin :=Val1
    ELSE
      FindMin :=Val2;
  END; (* FindMin *)

BEGIN
  Count := 0;
  CurrMin := 1000000.0;

  WRITELN ( 'Enter values, with ', StopValue: 3 : 1,
            ' as the last value.');
  (* Read values until the StopValue is encountered *)
  READ ( CurrVal);
  WHILE CurrVal <> StopValue DO
  BEGIN
    Count := Count + 1;
    CurrMin := FindMin ( CurrMin, CurrVal);
    READLN ( CurrVal);
  END; (* WHILE NOT StopValue *)

  (* Display results *)
  WRITELN ( Count, ' values read: Min = ', CurrMin : 10 : 3);
  WRITE ( 'Press ENTER to end program.');
  READLN;
END.
```

This chapter provided an informal introduction to Pascal and the opportunity to use the IDE. You should be familiar with the most common editing commands now. You'll find more information about the IDE throughout the book; Appendix C, "IDE Commands," contains a summary of the commands.

The next chapter starts a more systematic introduction to Pascal's data types.

3 *Turbo Pascal's Simple Data Types*

Pascal includes a rich variety of data types to make it easier for you to represent different kinds of information in the most useful way. It also enables you to create your own data types.

A *data type* provides a template within which specific information will be stored. For example, an **INTEGER** is a data type that stores whole numbers and is allocated two bytes of storage. Similarly, an **ARRAY** is a data type that will hold multiple values, all with the same form. The storage allocated for such a type depends on the number and types of elements. For example, an array of 100 **INTEGER**s would be allocated 200 bytes, and could be used to store 100 whole numbers.

Turbo Pascal extends the standard version of Pascal, providing an even wider collection of data types and making the language more flexible and easier to use. A variable's type determines the amount of storage allocated for the variable and the kinds of operations you can carry out with the variable. Both of these are important for the compiler.

Pascal provides data types to represent both simple and complex information. This chapter presents some of the simple types that Turbo Pascal makes available to the programmer.

Before looking at data types, however, this book discusses some more general issues regarding the components of Pascal programs and the way programs are put together.

Throughout this book are various suggestions about using indentation, naming, and comments in your programs. You may want to do things differently than they're done here. The important thing is to develop your own programming style and to use it consistently.

Pascal Programs

Statements are the basic elements of a Pascal program. Programs are essentially executed statement by statement. Statements represent the individual instructions required to complete the task the program is designed to do. For example, you'll use assignment statements to store information in program variables. You'll also have statements that call procedures and functions to compute values and to do the required work.

You have considerable leeway in how you write your statements. You can leave as much space as you wish between elements of a statement; you can even put different elements on different lines. Just about the only thing you can't do when writing the source code is to break in the middle of a word or a string. For example, the following listing shows three versions of the same statement:

```
MyInt := 7      (* version 1 *)

MyInt:=7         (* version 2 *)

MyInt
:=
7                (* version 3 *)
```

Notice that a statement can be split over multiple lines, as in the third version.

On the other hand, the next version is invalid, since there is a space in the middle of a variable name:

```
My Int := 7     (* invalid statement *)
```

This flexibility can be useful, since it allows you to use spacing and indentation to organize your program. However, when processing your source file, the compiler needs to know where one statement ends and another begins. To provide this information, use semicolons (;) to separate statements. You don't need a semicolon after the last statement of a program, procedure, or function; however, you do need a semicolon if another statement follows in the program, procedure, or function.

The following listing includes three places where a semicolon is optional:

P3-1
```
(* Program to illustrate use, and non-use, of semicolons *)

PROGRAM SemiColons;

VAR IntVal : INTEGER;

   (* Wait for user to press ENTER, to keep output on screen *)
   PROCEDURE AwaitUser;
   VAR Ch : CHAR;
   BEGIN
     WRITE ( 'Press Enter to continue.');
     READ ( Ch)             (* ; can be omitted here, *)
                            (*   since no statements follow *)
   END; (* AwaitUser *)

   (* Gets an integer from the procedure. *)
   PROCEDURE GetInteger ( Message : STRING;
                          VAR Value : INTEGER);
   BEGIN
     WRITE ( Message, ' ');
     READLN ( Value)        (* ; can be omitted here, *)
   END;

BEGIN
  GetInteger ( 'Value?', IntVal);
  WRITELN ( IntVal);
  AwaitUser                 (* ; can be omitted here *)
END.
```

The semicolon is omitted before each of the **END**s—the ones that terminate **AwaitUser**, **GetInteger**, and the main program. A semicolon is also optional after the last statement in a compound statement. (Recall that compound statements are bounded by **BEGIN** and **END**.) That is, you can omit the semicolon before the **END** that terminates the compound statement. You may include a semicolon in any of these places. This book includes such semicolons for consistency.

There are also a few places where you *cannot* include a semicolon. These places are discussed as relevant.

Notice that you also use a semicolon after the procedure heading and after each variable declaration line.

REMEMBER   In Pascal, semicolons are used to separate statements.

Comments

You should include notes and comments in your source-code file. This information can help you if you need to change or fix the program.

In Pascal, there are two ways of specifying comments: You can put the material between (* and *) or between { and }. When the compiler sees a (* or a {, it ignores any text until it reaches the corresponding *) or }.

CAUTION   Be careful not to comment out lines of code accidentally.

The following program shows a mistake that can get you into trouble if you're not careful. Run the program to see its output. To see why this happens, use F7 to trace through the program.

P3-2
```
(* Program illustrating difficulties that can arise
     through incorrect use of comments.
     The middle line will not be displayed.
*)

PROGRAM CommentError;

BEGIN  (* Main Program *)
  WRITELN ( 'One');  (* Start a comment
  WRITELN ( 'Two');     finish a comment *)
  WRITELN ( 'Three');
  READLN;
END.
```

The comment in this program starts after the first call to **WRITELN** and ends on the next line. (Remember to press ENTER when you're finished looking at the output.)

In such a case, the intent may be to provide comments for the first and second statements. However, the compiler reads the entire second line as part of the comment. As a result, the output from the program displays **One** and **Three**, but not **Two**.

The following listing shows the correct way to include comments for the first two lines. Compare the output when you run this program with the output from the **CommentError** program.

P3-3
```
(* Program illustrating how to fix a faulty comment *)

PROGRAM CommentFix;

BEGIN
  WRITELN ( 'One');   (* Start and finish a comment *)
  WRITELN ( 'Two');   (* Start and finish another comment *)
  WRITELN ( 'Three');
  READLN;
END.
```

You can include comments anywhere in your program, except in the middle of a name (such as a procedure or variable name). You should get into the habit of documenting your programs by including generous and clear comments.

You cannot nest comments — that is, you can't have a comment inside another comment. For example, the following line would lead to an error:

```
(* You cannot have (* nested *) comments *)
```

While the compiler is moving through a comment, it simply checks for the appropriate end of comment symbols. That is, if the comment begins with (*, the compiler looks for a matching *); if the comment begins with {, the compiler looks for a matching }.

As soon as it finds this symbol, the compiler assumes that the comment is finished and resumes processing your program file. In the preceding listing, the compiler would process

```
comments *)
```

as part of the source file, causing a compiler error.

Actually, you can fool the compiler into accepting nested comments because you can use two different symbols around comments. To put one comment inside another—should you ever find a good reason for doing so—use one set of symbols for the outer comment and the other set for the nested comment. The following listing shows nested comments that the compiler would accept:

```
(* You can have { quasi-nested } comments *)
```

Variables

In your programs, you'll want to save various items of information. Since many of these items will change their values during the course of program execution, your program needs to provide some way of saving these values.

A *variable* is a named area of memory that is used to store such information. When writing a program, you set aside memory by declaring variables. When you declare a variable, you specify a name and a type for it. The compiler finds an available area of memory and associates the location of this memory with the name that you've provided.

The location of this memory is known only to the program; you needn't concern yourself with this. To read the information stored at that location or to write something there, you simply need to specify the variable name in the appropriate context. You'll learn how do this later in the chapter.

Naming Variables

When programming, you'll declare and use named constants and variables to represent particular values. You'll also name and define procedures and functions to carry out specific tasks. This section describes what constitutes a name in Pascal.

In Turbo Pascal, a *name*, or *identifier*, must begin with a letter (*a* through *z* or *A* through *Z*), or an underscore (_). This letter may be followed by any number of letters, digits (*0* through *9*), and underscores. (The original Pascal does not allow underscores in identifiers, but most of the common Pascal implementations do. If you plan to compile your programs in environments other than Turbo Pascal, don't use underscores in your identifiers, just to be on the safe side.) The identifier can be as long as you want. The compiler, however, will read only the first 63 characters.

The first seven identifiers in the following list are valid in Turbo Pascal; the remaining ones are not:

```
(* valid *)
AValidName
AlsoVALID
Likewise3
Tea4Two
Q
HARDTOREADBUTVALID
Valid_in_TurboPascal       (* not valid in standard Pascal *)

(* invalid *)
Not-Valid           (* dash (-) is not allowed *)
3Likewise           (* first character is a digit *)
Split Name          (* illegal space between words *)
```

In Pascal, the case (upper or lower) of the characters in a name is not significant; all characters are treated as if they were the same case. Thus, the following three names are all considered equivalent:

```
Version1
VERSION1
VeRsIoN1
```

REMEMBER In Turbo Pascal, valid identifiers begin with a letter or underscore. This letter may be followed by letters, digits, or underscores. The case of the letters does not matter.

Restrictions on Names

There are certain words that you can't use as identifiers, since these are *reserved keywords* of the Pascal language. For example, you can't use the word **PROCEDURE** as an identifier for a variable, because this word specifies the beginning of a procedure definition. Similarly, you can only employ the word **IF** in constructs used to make decisions in your program.

The following list contains the reserved keywords in standard Pascal:

AND	FUNCTION	PROGRAM
ARRAY	GOTO	RECORD
BEGIN	IF	REPEAT
CASE	IN	SET
CONST	LABEL	THEN
DIV	MOD	TO
DO	NIL	TYPE
DOWNTO	NOT	UNTIL
ELSE	OF	VAR
END	OR	WHILE
FILE	PACKED	WITH
FOR	PROCEDURE	

You've seen several of these words in the example programs in Chapter 2, "Pascal: An Overview." Turbo Pascal has several additional reserved words, shown in the following list:

ASM	INTERFACE	UNIT
CONSTRUCTOR	OBJECT	USES
DESTRUCTOR	SHL	XOR
IMPLEMENTATION	SHR	
INLINE	STRING	

Pascal also has some keywords that are *predefined identifiers* but are not reserved. This means that you can use these words as identifiers; however, it's a bad idea to do so. For example, consider the potential confusion if you used the word **INTEGER** as an identifier.

The following list shows standard Pascal's predefined identifiers and directives:

ABS	BOOLEAN	CHR
ARCTAN	CHAR	COS

DISPOSE	ODD	SIN
EOF	ORD	SQR
EOLN	OUTPUT	SQRT
EXP	PACK	SUCC
FALSE	PRED	TEXT
FORWARD	PUT	TRUE
GET	READ	TRUNK
INPUT	READLN	UNPACK
INTEGER	REAL	WRITE
LN	RESET	WRITELN
MAXINT	REWRITE	
NEW	ROUND	

Some of these identifiers (such as **REAL, CHAR**, and **INTEGER**) represent data types. Others (such as **FALSE, TRUE**, and **MAXINT**) represent predefined values. Still others (such as **ABS, WRITELN, READ**, and **NEW**) represent predefined procedures and functions. You'll learn about the entities that correspond to these identifiers in the appropriate places in the book.

The next list shows the most common predefined Turbo Pascal identifiers and directives:

ABSOLUTE	FILESIZE	MEM
ADDR	FILLCHAR	MEMAVAIL
APPEND	FLUSH	MOVE
ASSEMBLER	FRAC	NEAR
BLOCKREAD	FREEMEM	PARAMCOUNT
BLOCKWRITE	GETMEM	PARAMSTR
BUFLEN	HALT	PI
BYTE	HEAPPTR	PORT
CLOSE	HI	POS
CONCAT	INSERT	PRIVATE
COPY	INT	PTR
DELETE	INTERRUPT	RANDOM
ERASE	IORESULT	RANDOMIZE
EXIT	LENGTH	RELEASE
EXTERNAL	LO	RENAME
FAR	MARK	SEEK
FILEPOS	MAXAVAIL	SEEKEOF

SEEKEOLN	SWAP	UPCASE
SIZEOF	TRUNCATE	VAL
STR	TYPEOF	VIRTUAL

CAUTION It is very bad programming practice to use predefined identifiers as names for your variables.

You may use whatever identifiers you want in your programs. However, it is better to use meaningful names. Your program will be much easier to read (especially six months from now) if you use names such as **RunningTotal** rather than **X** for your variables.

This book uses only letters and digits in identifiers, which makes it easier to transport the programs to other environments. To distinguish individual words in an identifier, the first letter of each word will be in uppercase—for example,

```
ASampleNameWithMultipleWords
```

is used instead of

```
ASAMPLENAMEWITHMULTIPLEWORDS
asamplenamewithmultiplewords
```

or

```
a_sample_name_with_multiple_words
```

Reserved words and predefined identifiers will be written in all uppercase.

Variable Declarations

Pascal is an example of a *strongly typed language*. This means that the compiler must know the type of information being stored in a variable slot before the variable can be used. Furthermore, the compiler will enforce restrictions on the operations allowed with different types.

In order to specify the type of a variable, you must *declare* the variable. You've seen this in the example programs of Chapter 2. In a variable declaration, you specify a variable name and a type for the variable. You can have multiple variable declarations. The first line of declarations begins with the word **VAR**. Subsequent lines begin with identifiers. The name and type information are separated by a colon(:).

For example, the following two lines appeared in program P2-5 in Chapter 2:

```
VAR CurrMax, CurrVal : REAL;
    Count : INTEGER;
```

These two lines declare three variables. The first line declares two variables of type **REAL**. (You'll find information about this type later in this chapter.) If you declare two variables of the same type, you can list them together by separating the individual names with commas.

The second line declares **Count** to be a variable of type **INTEGER**. You'll also learn about integers in greater detail later in the chapter.

The syntax for a variable declaration is as follows:

<variable name>{, <variable name>}":" <type>

The material within angle brackets (< >) specifies the sort of value to include at that point. Material within curly braces ({ }) is optional, but may be repeated multiple times. Material within double quotes must appear exactly as stated. You'll generally include a semicolon after the declaration—to separate it from the next line.

You can leave as many spaces as you wish between variable names, but you cannot leave a space within a variable name. You can use multiple lines to list your variable declarations. For example, the following declarations are all valid ways to specify variables:

```
(* a variable list can be split over multiple lines *)
Val1, Val2, Val3,
Val4, Val5, Val6 : REAL;

(* each variable also can be declared separately *)
IVal1 : INTEGER;
IVal2 : INTEGER;
```

```
IVal3 : INTEGER;
IVal4 : INTEGER;
IVal5 : INTEGER;
```

When you declare a variable, the compiler allocates a memory location that will be used to store the variable's value. The amount of storage allocated depends on the variable's type.

Pascal does *not* initialize variables when you declare them. For this reason, you can't make any assumptions about the starting contents of program variables unless you assign them values in the program.

Failure to initialize a variable can lead to unpredictable results, as in the following program. Run the program in different sessions (for example, when you have been doing different things on the computer) to see what the output is.

P3-4
```
(* Program to illustrate what happens if you use
   an uninitialized variable.
*)

PROGRAM NoInitials;

VAR Value : INTEGER;

BEGIN
  Value := Value + 5;
  WRITELN ( Value);
  READLN;
END.
```

The output from this program depends on the bit pattern stored in the memory allocated for **Value** when the program starts.

CAUTION   Pascal does not initialize program variables. It's up to you to make sure that variables are initialized before you use them.

Operators

Pascal has a rich collection of data types and enables you to create your own data types. In contrast, Pascal has a relatively small collection of operations that you can carry out on variables. Other languages, such as C, have fewer data types but a greater number of operators.

An *operator* is something that can combine values to produce a new result, or that can produce a new value from an existing one. An operator generally takes information in one form and returns it in a different form.

For example, addition (**+**) takes information in the form of two values and returns it in the form of a sum. Such an operator—one that takes two values and returns one—is known as a *binary operator*.

The values associated with an operator are known as its *operands*. Operators and operands are combined in *expressions*. When you write an expression such as

```
7 + MyVal
```

the 7 is the *left operand* for the addition operator, and the variable **MyVal** is the *right operand*. Thus, a binary operator takes two operands and returns a single value.

There are also *unary* operators, which take one value and return another. For example, the **NOT** operator in Pascal takes an operand that is **TRUE** or **FALSE**, and returns the opposite value (that is, **FALSE** for **TRUE** and **TRUE** for **FALSE**). This operator takes a single operand (the original value) and returns a different value.

Certain operators are valid for all of the simple data types discussed in this chapter. However, in general, you cannot mix different types in the same expression. For example, you cannot directly compare an integer and a character.

Pascal compilers are very good at detecting such *type conflicts*. With a few exceptions, type conflicts are not allowed in Pascal.

Assignment Operator

As you learned in Chapter 2, the assignment operator (**:=**) takes one operand—a variable or value—and assigns the value of this operand to a variable. The left element of an assignment statement must be a variable, since there must be storage in which to save the value. In general, the operand and the variable must be of the same type. The exceptions to this restriction will be noted as they arise.

The following listing shows same sample assignment statements:

```
MyIntVariable := 37;

YourIntVariable := MyIntVariable;

MyString := 'hello';

MyValue := 7 * YourValue + 2 / TheirValue;
```

Notice that the operand for the assignment operator can be an extended expression. The entire expression is evaluated before the assignment operator is applied.

Comparison Operators

In programs, you often need to compare two values. For example, function **FindMax** in Chapter 2 compared **Val1** and **Val2**, to determine whether **Val1** was less than **Val2**. Similarly, you compared two strings in the **BubbleSort** procedure to determine whether one was "less" (came earlier in a sort) than another.

Such comparisons make sense for both numerical and nonnumerical information. In addition, the result of such a comparison is not a number. Rather, the result is a yes or no— more commonly called true or false in computer science. (In fact, **TRUE** and **FALSE** are predefined values in Pascal.)

Pascal has six comparison, or relational, operators, each of which takes two operands and returns a **TRUE** or **FALSE**. (Such values belong to a type known as **BOOLEAN**, which is discussed later in the chapter. Thus, comparison operators return **BOOLEAN** values.) While the comparison operators can handle both numeric and nonnumeric operands, the operands must be of the same type for any given comparison.

For instance, the first two comparisons in the following list are valid, but the last is not because the two operands are of different types:

```
(* valid comparisons *)
'Hello' = 'Good Bye'
7 >= 23
```

```
7 < 'Hello'   (* invalid comparison: type conflict *)
```

Pascal's comparison operators are

■ **Equality operator (=)** This operator returns **TRUE** if the two operands are equal to each other, **FALSE** otherwise. For example:

```
'hello' = 'hello'   (* TRUE *)
38 = 23             (* FALSE *)
```

■ **Inequality operator (< >)** This operator returns **TRUE** if the two operands are *not* equal to each other, **FALSE** otherwise. For example:

```
'hello' <> 'hello'   (* FALSE *)
38 <> 23             (* TRUE *)
```

■ **Greater than operator (>)** This operator returns **TRUE** if the left operand is greater than the right one, **FALSE** otherwise. For example:

```
'zebra' > 'aardvark'   (* TRUE *)
'gnu' > 'gnu'          (* FALSE *)
38.65 > 199.357        (* FALSE *)
```

■ **Greater than or equal to operator (>=)** This operator returns **TRUE** if the left operand is greater than *or equal to* the right one, **FALSE** otherwise. For example:

```
'zebra' >= 'aardvark'   (* TRUE *)
'gnu' >= 'gnu'          (* TRUE *)
38.65 >= 199.357        (* FALSE *)
```

■ **Less than operator (<)** This operator returns **TRUE** if the left operand is less than the right one, **FALSE** otherwise. For example:

```
'zebra' < 'aardvark'   (* FALSE *)
'gnu' < 'gnu'          (* FALSE *)
38.65 < 199.357        (* TRUE *)
```

■ **Less than or equal to operator (<=)** This operator returns **TRUE** if the left operand is less than *or equal to* the right one, **FALSE** otherwise. For example:

```
'zebra' <= 'aardvark'    (* FALSE *)
'gnu' <= 'gnu'           (* TRUE *)
38.65 <= 199.357         (* TRUE *)
```

REMEMBER   The assignment and comparison operators are available for all of Pascal's simple data types. The comparison operators all produce a **BOOLEAN** result (a **TRUE** or **FALSE**), regardless of the operands being compared.

Operator Precedence

When you use more than one operator, *operator precedence* determines the order in which operators are applied.

For example, you might recall from algebra that multiplication takes precedence over addition. You can see this rule of precedence in the following expression, which evaluates to 26 rather than 42.

```
8 + 6 * 3
```

The result is 26 because the 6 * 3 (= 18) is computed first, and the resulting product is added to 8.

To make the expression equal 42, you need to add parentheses to override the rule of multiplicative precedence. The expression in the following listing evaluates to 42:

```
(8 + 6) * 3
```

Beyond such precedence rules, operators will generally be evaluated in a fixed direction. For example, most people evaluate the following expression from left to right, since all the operators have the same precedence:

```
1 + 2 + 6 + 23 + 85 + 189
    3 + 6 + 23 + 85 + 189
        9 + 23 + 85 + 189
            32 + 85 + 189
               117 + 189
                  306
```

Pascal's operators also have an order of precedence, which you'll learn as the operators are introduced.

The assignment operator has the lowest precedence of any Pascal operator. For this reason, you need not put parentheses around expressions on its right. In other words, the low precedence ensures that a value for the entire expression will be computed before the value is assigned to the variable on the left.

The comparison operators all have the same precedence, which is just above that for the assignment operator.

Constant Definitions

Often you'll need to use specific values in your programs. For example, suppose you're writing a physics program in which you need to describe the motion of falling bodies. You will almost certainly need the value specifying the acceleration due to gravity (about 10 meters per second per second). This value will be the same wherever you use it in the program. That is, the value will be *constant*.

Pascal lets you associate names with such values. You can then refer to the values by name. Such constant definitions belong in the declaration section of your program.

The syntax for a constant definition is

```
<constant name> "=" <value>
```

As with variable declarations, you can define multiple constants. The first line of a constant definition must begin with the reserved word **CONST**. Subsequent lines begin with blank space or with identifiers.

Note that you use an equal sign rather than an assignment operator when defining a constant. This is deliberate. When you assign a value, you are carrying out an action—as implied by the term "assignment *operator*." In contrast, when defining a constant, you are equating a name and a value rather than storing a value in a particular memory location. Essentially, when processing your file the compiler simply substitutes the specified value for every occurrence of the constant's name.

If the compiler simply replaces the name with the value, why bother to define the constant in the first place? There are several reasons. First, your program will be much easier to understand if the reader sees something like **AccelerationConstant** instead of a value such as 9.8 in the source file. Second, using a constant definition makes it much easier to change the value if necessary. For example, suppose your physics program used the value of the acceleration constant in 50 different places. It would be very easy for you simply to type **9.8** in all of these places as you were writing your program.

However, suppose that you want to adapt the program to do computations about bodies falling on the moon. There, the acceleration due to gravity is only about 1.6 meters per second per second. To adapt your program for moon motion, you would need to change 9.8 to 1.6 everywhere in your program.

A global search and replace may not work, since you may have used the same value (9.8) for a different purpose. In such a situation, the only course is to check each occurrence of 9.8 and decide whether to change it to 1.6. This method will be tedious and error prone. Chances are good that you'll overlook an occurrence, or change one too many values.

On the other hand, if you define a constant to represent the acceleration due to gravity, you can adapt your program by changing the value in the constant's definition. Thereafter, the compiler will make the changes for you. Doesn't it seem better to let the compiler do the work for you?

In the original version of Pascal, constant definitions must come before variable declarations in your program. In Turbo Pascal, however, the relative order of constant definitions and variable declarations is not fixed.

In addition to constant values, you can define constant types in Turbo Pascal. You'll learn more about this capability in Chapter 7, "Turbo Pascal's Structured Data Types."

Predefined Procedures for Input and Output

Pascal provides procedures for reading and writing information. You've already used these procedures in the example programs in Chapter 2.

This section takes a closer look at what these procedures are and how to use them.

Output Procedures

Pascal provides the **WRITE** and **WRITELN** procedures for writing information to the screen or to a file. **WRITELN** displays the specified information and then moves the cursor to the start of the next line. (To move to the start of a new line, the procedure sends a combination of carriage return and linefeed commands, often denoted by CRLF. Thus, **WRITELN** sends a CRLF after it has displayed all of its arguments.) **WRITE** simply displays the specified information, but does not move the cursor to the next line (that is, does not send a CRLF). The following program shows how to call these two procedures:

P3-5
```
(* Program to illustrate use of WRITE and WRITELN procedures. *)
PROGRAM DisplayDemo;
VAR TestVal : INTEGER;

BEGIN
   TestVal := 22222;   (* Programmer must initialize variables *)
   WRITE ( 'Just a sentence, without CRLF.');
   WRITELN ( 'This continues on the same line.');
   WRITELN;
   WRITELN;
   WRITE ( 'There should be two blank lines above this one.');
   WRITELN;
   WRITE ( 'Eight = ', 8, '; nine = ', 9);
   WRITELN ( '; ten = ', 10);
   WRITELN ( 'TestVal = ', TestVal);
   READLN;
END.
```

Run the program and compare its output with the following:

```
Just a sentence, without CRLF.This continues on the same line.


There should be two blank lines above this one.

Eight = 8; nine = 9; ten = 10
TestVal = 22222
```

Notice that **WRITE** and **WRITELN** can take a variable number of arguments. If you call **WRITELN** with no arguments, it simply sends its CRLF. (Although it is syntactically correct, you would never call **WRITE** without arguments, since it would then do nothing.)

Not only do these procedures take a variable number of arguments, the arguments can be of different types. For example, several of the calls have string arguments (words, phrases, or sentences within single quotes). Two of the last three procedure calls also have numerical values — namely, the numbers 8, 9, and 10 — as arguments. You can also pass variable names as arguments, as in the final call to **WRITELN**. In this case, the procedure writes the value currently stored at the location set aside for the variable.

If you are passing multiple arguments to **WRITE** or **WRITELN**, use commas to separate the arguments. You *need* not leave space between arguments, but you can leave as much as you wish. You may not put a space in the middle of an identifier. The following valid calls with multiple arguments both display the same results:

```
WRITE ( Arg1,Arg2,Arg3);
WRITELN ( Arg1,           Arg2,            Arg3);
```

Note that the space between arguments in the second statement does not put any space in the output.

You can continue an argument list over multiple lines; however, you must break between two arguments when doing this. In particular, you cannot break a string value over two lines. For example, the first of the following calls is valid, but not the second. The third call shows one way of fixing the incorrect call. It breaks the long string into two shorter ones, making each of these a separate argument.

```
(* a valid call to WRITELN *)
WRITELN ( Arg1, Arg2, 'A string argument',
        Arg4,
        'Another string argument', Arg6);

(* an invalid call to WRITELN *)
WRITELN ( Arg1, Arg2, 'A string argument
        broken over two lines',
        Arg4,
        'Another string argument', Arg6);
```

```
(* a possible fix for the preceding call to WRITELN *)
WRITELN ( Arg1, Arg2, 'A string argument',
          ' broken over two lines',
          Arg4,
          'Another string argument', Arg6);
```

To make your program easier to read, you may want to use space and line breaks between arguments in your procedure calls.

In Chapter 2, you also used **WRITELN** to write information to a file (LOG) in the **Bubble** program. If the first argument to **WRITE** or **WRITELN** is a file variable, the information is written to the specified file; if no file variable is specified in the procedure call, the procedure writes to the standard output device, which is generally the screen. You'll learn more about writing to files in Chapter 8, "Files."

In the sections on individual data types, you'll learn how to use **WRITE** and **WRITELN** to control the format of the information display.

Input Procedures

Pascal provides **READ** and **READLN** for reading input from the keyboard or from a file. As with the output routines, **READ** and **READLN** can take a variable number of arguments. For example, the following are all valid calls to these input routines:

```
READLN ( FileArg, MyInt, YourInt);

READ ( FileArg, MyInt, YourInt);

READLN ( Val1);
```

The first call reads two values from the file specified by **FileArg**, assuming that **FileArg** has been declared as a file variable. In each call the first value read is assigned to the variable **MyInt** and the second is assigned to **YourInt**. After reading these two values, the procedure moves to the next line in the file.

The call to **READ** in the second example statement does the same thing as the first call, but it does not move to the next line in the file after reading the two values. This difference can have consequences.

For example, suppose the information in your file is stored on lines as follows:

```
39  27   293
54
```

What will be the result for the following pair of calls? In particular, what will be the value of **TheirInt**?

```
READLN ( FileArg, MyInt, YourInt);
READLN ( FileArg, TheirInt).
```

After reading 39 into **MyInt** and 27 into **YourInt**, the first call to **READLN** moves to the next line in the file. Thus, 54—the next integer value—is assigned to **TheirInt**. The value 293 is ignored in this example.

Suppose you had the following two calls instead:

```
READ ( FileArg, MyInt, YourInt);
READ ( FileArg, TheirInt).
```

In this case, 39 and 27 are assigned as before. This time, however, 293 is assigned to **TheirInt**, since the first call to **READ** did not move to the next line after reading its two values.

If your call to **READ** or **READLN** does not include a file variable as the first argument, the procedure assumes that the information is to come from the standard input, usually the keyboard. Thus, the following two calls each expect you to type in three values:

```
READ ( Arg1, Arg2, Arg3);
READLN ( Arg1, Arg2, Arg3);
```

If these are numeric values, you can enter some or all of the values on the same line—separated by spaces—or you can put the values on separate lines. You must press ENTER after putting the last value on each line.

If you simply call **READLN**, with no arguments, the program will stop when it gets to the procedure call, and will wait for you to press ENTER before continuing. This is a good way to have a program pause — for example, while you're examining output.

Most of the example programs on disk end with a call to **READLN**. This pause lets you see the output before you're returned to the editing environment.

If you tell **READ** or **READLN** to read a particular type of value, and then type a different kind of value, you may get a run-time error and crash your program. For example, if you tell the procedure to expect a number and it finds a string of characters instead, you'll get a run-time error.

Real Numbers

Sometimes you'll be able to do your work using just whole numbers. At other times, you'll need to work with numbers (such as 1.5 or 39.33) that have fractional components. Such fractional numbers are called *real numbers*.

Real numbers use a period (.) to separate the whole number from the fractional part. Ordinarily, this period is called a decimal point, because we generally represent numbers using 10 as the base. However, it is possible to use bases other than 10 to represent numbers. For example, most compilers represent values in binary form — using 2 as the numerical base.

This discussion uses decimal values, but the same concepts apply when you use other bases.

Pascal's REAL Type

Pascal has a predefined type, **REAL,** for representing real numbers. The Turbo Pascal compiler allocates six bytes for each **REAL** variable. Within this storage, the range of possible **REAL** values you can represent is

$2.9*10^{-39}$ through $1.7*10^{38}$ for positive numbers
$-2.9*10^{-39}$ through $-1.7*10^{38}$ for negative numbers

The following program shows how to declare and use variables of type **REAL**. Run the program several times. Enter some very small values and some extremely large values. You might also try entering a value with a large number of decimal digits.

P3-6
```
(* Program to illustrate declaration and use of REALs *)

PROGRAM RealTest;

VAR RValue : REAL;

   (* Get a REAL value from user. *)
   PROCEDURE GetReal ( Message : STRING;
                       VAR Value : REAL);
   BEGIN
     WRITE ( Message, '? ');
     READLN ( Value);
   END; (* GetReal *)

BEGIN   (* Main Program *)
  GetReal ( 'Value', RValue);
  WRITELN ( RValue);            (* use default output format *)
  WRITELN ( RValue : 10 : 5); (* use specified output format *)
  READLN;
END.
```

This program gets a **REAL** value from the user and then displays the value twice. The output format is discussed later in the chapter.

When it sees the declaration for the variable **RValue**, the compiler sets aside six bytes of storage because **RValue** is declared to be a **REAL**.

Procedure **GetReal** is modeled on **GetString**, which was used in Chapter 2, program P2-4.

Syntax for REAL Values

REAL values must have a particular format in Pascal. A **REAL** value may begin with an optional sign (**+** or **−**). For example, +35.35, −3.53, and 353.5 are all valid **REALs**.

A **REAL** value *must* contain at least one digit, and *may* contain one decimal point. If the number contains a decimal point, there must be *at least* one digit before (to the left of) the decimal point. (This digit can be 0 if necessary.) For example, the first six values in the following listing are valid, but the final three are invalid:

```
(* valid real numbers *)
35.47
+5.5
-6
399999
0.731
-3.

(* invalid real numbers *)
+.3             (* no digit before decimal point *)
3.+5            (* sign is not at start of value *)
3.5.7           (* only one decimal point allowed per number *)
```

You may use scientific notation to specify real numbers. In *scientific notation,* numbers are expressed as a value and an exponent. The *exponent* specifies the power of 10 by which you need to multiply the value in order to get the number. For example, the following listing represents 15 in several different ways using scientific notation, and illustrates the syntax for scientific notation in Pascal:

```
0.15E2
1.5E1
15e0
150e-1
1500E-2
```

The *e* (or *E,* since Pascal is not case sensitive) marks the beginning of the exponent. The value following this represents the power of 10 by which you need to multiply the number. Each positive power of 10 means another multiplication by 10. Thus, **0.15E2** means $0.15 * 10^2$, or $0.15 * 10 * 10$, or $0.15 * 100$.

Similarly, each *negative* power of 10 means to *divide* by 10. Thus, **1500E−2** means 1500/10/10 or 1500/100.

If you use scientific notation, the *e* may be followed by a sign (+ or −) and must be followed by a whole number.

REMEMBER The format for a valid **REAL** value is as follows:

■ Optional + or − sign

■ One or more digits (which may be 0)

■ Optional decimal point followed by zero or more digits

■ Optional *E* or *e*, followed by optional + or − sign, followed by a whole number

Displaying REAL Values

When displaying **REAL** values, you can control the output format or you can let the system use its default display format. The first call to **WRITE-LN** in the **RealTest** program uses the default output format for **REAL** values. By default, Turbo Pascal writes real numbers in scientific notation.

For example, for an input of **3579.987654**, the earlier program **RealTest** produces the following output:

```
3.5799876540E+03
3579.98765
```

The first line contains the scientific notation. Recall that the number following the *E* is the power of 10 by which the value needs to be multiplied. An exponent value of 3 means to multiply the number by 10^3, or 1000.

The second call to **WRITELN** in **RealTest** also displays the value of **RValue**, but uses a format you specify. In the call to **WRITELN**, the

```
: 10 : 5
```

after the variable name specify the field width and the precision for the output.

■ The *field width* specifies the number of columns to use when displaying the number. The field width for the output is set to ten columns.

■ The *precision* specifies the number of digits to include after the decimal point. The precision is set to five digits after the decimal point.

The decimal point and sign are included in the field width. Thus, when you specify a field width of ten columns, the decimal point and sign may use two of these. If so, you would get only eight digits.

If the value to be written is longer than the field width you've specified, **WRITELN** ignores your format instructions and uses as many columns as needed. If fewer columns are needed than you've specified, the output has blanks at the left; the rightmost digit is in the last column specified by the field width.

REAL Values as Approximations

You may recall from algebra that there are an infinite number of different real values. In fact, you can find as many values as you wish between any two real values. However, there are only a finite number of bit combinations possible in the space allocated for a **REAL** variable. This means that not all real numbers can be represented by a variable of type **REAL**. Such values are actually approximate values.

The approximations can be in error for any of several reasons. There may not be enough bits to represent the required number of digits. For example, a **REAL** in Turbo Pascal can accurately represent values having no more than about 11 digits.

Errors may be introduced because of rounding or truncation that takes place during computations. For example, suppose you want to add the following:

0.12345678901234567890 and 1.12345678901234567890

Since these values exceed the limits of precision (about 11 digits) for type **REAL**, your system will actually perform a computation involving fewer digits. The result will reflect these truncated computations.

This means that some computations involving **REAL** variables and values will be only approximately correct, particularly computations that involve an extreme range of values, values requiring extreme precision, or values requiring lots of computations.

Fortunately, such errors will be very small in magnitude, and generally will appear only in the extreme decimal places—at values smaller than the precision you'll need for most computations. For example, you'll rarely need a result to be accurate to more than five or six decimal places. Errors are more likely to occur in the ninth or tenth place. In such a case, your result won't even register the error.

When comparing two **REAL** values, it is generally better to check whether the two values differ only slightly, rather than whether they are exactly equal.

CAUTION   Be careful when using **REAL** variables, especially when looking for exact values. The representations for two apparently identical **REAL** values may actually be different because of the way the two values were computed.

Operators for REAL Values

In addition to specifying the amount of storage, a variable declaration determines the operations you can carry out on the variable. As you'll find, certain operators make sense only with certain variables. For example, you can add or multiply two numbers, but not two characters.

Assignment and Comparison Operators   You can use the assignment operator and the comparison operators with **REAL** variables and values, as shown here:

```
(* Program to illustrate use of
   assignment and comparison operators with REALs
*)

PROGRAM RealOps1;

CONST CutOff = 1000.0;
      TwiceCutOff = 2000.0;
```

P3-7

```
VAR Val1, Val2 : REAL;

  PROCEDURE GetReal ( Message : STRING;
                            VAR Value : REAL);
  BEGIN
    WRITE ( Message, ' ');
    READLN ( Value);
  END; (* GetReal *)

BEGIN    (* Main Program *)
  GetReal ( 'Value 1:', Val1);
  IF Val1 > CutOff THEN
    Val2 := Val1
  ELSE
    Val2 := CutOff;
  WRITELN ( 'Val1 = ', Val1 : 10 : 3,
            '        Val2 = ', Val2 : 10 : 3);
  IF Val1 <= TwiceCutOff THEN
    Val2 := TwiceCutoff;
  WRITELN ( 'Val1 = ', Val1 : 10 : 3,
            '        Val2 = ', Val2 : 10 : 3);
  READLN;
END.
```

The main program uses two comparison operators (both in **IF** clauses) and three assignment operators (all of which change the value of **Val2**). For inputs of **123.45**, **1234.5**, and **12345.0**, the program produced the outputs shown in the following listing:

```
(* for 123.45 *)
Val1 =      123.450     Val2 =     1000.000
Val1 =      123.450     Val2 =     2000.000
(* for 1234.5 *)
Val1 =     1234.500     Val2 =     1234.500
Val1 =     1234.500     Val2 =     2000.000

(* for 12345.0 *)
Val1 =    12345.000     Val2 =    12345.000
Val1 =    12345.000     Val2 =    12345.000
```

As mentioned, it can be dangerous to check whether two **REAL** values are exactly equal, as the following program shows:

```
P3-8    (* Program to illustrate dangers of comparing REALs
            for strict equality.
        *)
```

```
PROGRAM PrecisionDemo;

CONST Increment = 0.003;
VAR CompVal : REAL;

BEGIN
  CompVal := 0.9;
  (* Loop will keep executing, because
     the bit patterns for CompVal and 1.2 won't
     be identical. Press CTRL-C to end program.
  *)
  WHILE ( CompVal <> 1.2) DO
  BEGIN
    WRITELN ( 'CompVal = ', CompVal : 10 : 7);
    CompVal := CompVal + Increment;
    IF ( CompVal > 1.2) THEN
      READLN;
  END;
  WRITELN ( 'CompVal = ', CompVal : 10 : 7);
  READLN;
END.
```

This program executes a loop until you break out of the program, which you can do by pressing CTRL-C.

The program *apparently* reaches 1.2, the value that should stop the **WHILE** loop. The output indicates that **CompVal** is equal to 1.2—at least to six decimal places. However, the fact that the loop continues executing indicates that the two values are not exactly identical.

When checking for the equality (or inequality, as in this case) of two **REAL**s, Turbo Pascal compares their actual bit patterns. The value of **CompVal** is attained through repeated computations, which can introduce errors. Its bit pattern will almost certainly differ from the pattern for 1.2. This is why it's extremely unlikely that two **REAL**s will be exactly equal— especially if either or both values have been obtained through computations.

Arithmetic Operators   Not surprisingly, you can carry out the usual operations on **REAL** values: You can add, subtract, multiply, and divide them. The addition (+) and subtraction (−) operators enable you to combine two **REAL** values to produce a third value of the same type. The following program lets you add or subtract two values. Run the program and try several pairs of values.

P3-9
```
(* Program to illustrate use of
     addition and subtraction operators for REALs
 *)

PROGRAM RealOps2;

CONST EmptyString = '';    (* a blank string *)
      PlusOp = '+';
VAR Val1, Val2 : REAL;
    Operation : STRING;

   PROCEDURE GetString ( Message : STRING;
                               VAR Value : STRING);
   BEGIN
     WRITE ( Message, ' ');
     READLN ( Value);
   END; (* GetString *)

   PROCEDURE GetReal ( Message : STRING;
                             VAR Value : REAL);
   BEGIN
     WRITE ( Message, ' ');
     READLN ( Value);
   END; (* GetReal *)

BEGIN    (* Main Program *)
  (* Find out what operator user wants *)
  GetString ( '+ or - (ENTER to stop)', Operation);
  (* While user wants to continue ... *)
  WHILE Operation <> EmptyString DO
  BEGIN
    GetReal ( 'Value 1: ', Val1);
    GetReal ( 'Value 2: ', Val2);
    IF Operation = PlusOp THEN
      WRITELN ( Val1 + Val2 : 10 : 3)
    ELSE
      WRITELN ( Val1 - Val2 : 10 : 3);
    GetString ( '+ or - (ENTER to stop)', Operation);
  END; (* WHILE Operation <> EmptyString *)
  WRITELN ( 'Press ENTER to leave program.');
  READLN;
END.
```

Notice the arguments in the calls to **WRITELN** in the main program. Despite the length of the material within parentheses, these calls have just one argument. The expressions

```
Val1 + Val2
```

```
Val1 - Val2
```

each evaluate to a **REAL**, which is substituted for the expression before the writing occurs. The remaining material within parentheses specifies the format.

Note the constant, **EmptyString**. This is defined as a string with no characters—as when you press ENTER without typing something first.

The multiplication (*) and division (/) operators also work as they do in algebra. Recall that division by 0 is not defined in algebra. In Pascal, it produces a run-time error and crashes your program.

The following program lets you multiply or divide two values:

P3-10
```
(* Program to illustrate use of
    multiplication and division operators for REALs
*)

PROGRAM RealOps2;

CONST EmptyString = '';
      TimesOp = '*';
VAR Val1, Val2 : REAL;
    Operation : STRING;

  PROCEDURE GetString ( Message : STRING;
                        VAR Value : STRING);
  BEGIN
    WRITE ( Message, ' ');
    READLN ( Value);
  END; (* GetString *)

  PROCEDURE GetReal ( Message : STRING;
                      VAR Value : REAL);
  BEGIN
    WRITE ( Message, ' ');
    READLN ( Value);
  END; (* GetReal *)

BEGIN   (* Main Program *)
  (* Find out what operator user wants *)
  GetString ( '* or / (ENTER to stop)', Operation);
  (* While user wants to continue ... *)
  WHILE Operation <> EmptyString DO
  BEGIN
    GetReal ( 'Value 1: ', Val1);
    GetReal ( 'Value 2: ', Val2);
    IF Operation = TimesOp THEN
      WRITELN ( Val1 * Val2 : 10 : 3)
    ELSE
      WRITELN ( Val1 / Val2 : 10 : 3);
```

```
    GetString ( '* or / (ENTER to stop)', Operation);
  END; (* WHILE Operation <> EmptyString *)
  WRITELN ( 'Press ENTER to leave program.');
  READLN;
END.
```

This program is actually identical to the preceding one, with the following exceptions:

■ The constant **PlusOp** has been replaced by **TimesOp**.

■ The operators in the message for both calls to **GetString** have been changed (from **+** to **∗** and from **−** to **/**).

■ The operators in the two calls to **WRITELN** in the main program have been changed.

Precedence of Operators for REALs

The arithmetic operators actually fall into two levels of precedence. Multiplication and division—both known as *multiplicative operators* (division is the inverse of multiplication)—have the same precedence. This precedence is higher than that for the *additive operators* (addition and subtraction).

The precedence of all arithmetic operators is higher than that of the comparison operators and, therefore, of the assignment operator. Later sections extend this order of precedence to include other operators.

Miscellaneous Issues Concerning REALs

If you accidentally type a nonnumeric value when the program is expecting a **REAL**, the program will crash with a run-time error.

Although Turbo Pascal lets you represent a large range of **REAL** values, you can still exceed these limits. This is known as *overflow*. In case of overflow involving **REAL** values, the program will crash with a run-time error.

Whole Number Types

Turbo Pascal provides several data types for storing whole numbers. For the most part, these types differ in the amount of storage allocated for the type, and in whether the type allows negative numbers.

The INTEGER Type

The **INTEGER** type is defined for all versions of Pascal. This type is used to represent whole numbers from $-32{,}768$ to $32{,}767$. The compiler allocates two bytes, or 16 bits, for values of type **INTEGER**. Within this representation, you can store values ranging from -2^{15} through $2^{15} -1$. (The leftmost, sixteenth, bit represents the value's sign. If this bit is 1, the value is negative.)

Pascal includes a predefined constant, **MAXINT**, whose value is the maximum integer value for the implementation. In Turbo Pascal, this value is 32,767.

The following program shows how to declare, initialize, and display **INTEGER** variables:

```
(* Program to illustrate use of integer values *)

PROGRAM IntExample;

VAR Int1, Int2 : INTEGER;

   (* Get an integer value from the user. *)
   PROCEDURE GetInteger ( Message : STRING;
                          VAR Value : INTEGER);
   BEGIN
     WRITE ( Message, '? ');      (* prompt user *)
     READLN ( Value);             (* read response *)
```

P3-11

```
    END; (* GetInteger *)

BEGIN
  GetInteger ( 'Value 1', Int1);
  GetInteger ( 'Value 2', Int2);
  WRITELN ( 'The sum of ', Int1, ' and ', Int2,
           ' is ', Int1 + Int2);
  WRITELN·( 'MAXINT = ', MAXINT);
  READLN;
END.
```

As usual, the variable declarations are made in the declaration section of the program. In this case, two integer variables are declared, and the compiler sets aside four bytes of storage for these two variables.

Like **GetReal**, procedure **GetInteger** is modeled on **GetString** in Chapter 2. You'll build an improved version of this procedure in Chapter 6, "Procedures and Functions Revisited."

When specifying integers, you cannot use commas between digits; you may use only digits and an optional sign at the start of the number. For example, −32500 and +28400 are valid, but −32,500 and +28,400 are not.

Controlling Output Format

By default, Turbo Pascal uses as many columns as needed to write your whole number value. This is convenient, but can also have unexpected consequences. For example, run the following program and look at its output:

P3-12
```
(* Program to illustrate what happens when you don't
   leave any space between values when writing them.
*)

PROGRAM NoSpace;

VAR Val1, Val2, Val3 : INTEGER;

  PROCEDURE GetInteger ( Message : STRING;
                         VAR Value : INTEGER);
  BEGIN
    WRITE ( Message, ' ');
```

```
     READLN ( Value);
  END; (* GetInteger *)
BEGIN
  GetInteger ( 'Value 1', Val1);
  GetInteger ( 'Value 2', Val2);
  GetInteger ( 'Value 3', Val3);
  WRITELN ( Val1, Val2, Val3);
  READLN;
END.
```

The following listing shows the output for inputs of **33, 66,** and **99**:

```
336699
```

To avoid this error, you can put blanks between the values. The following version of the call to **WRITELN** will put space between the values:

```
WRITELN ( Val1, '   ', Val2, '    ', Val3);
```

You can also specify a different output format, if you wish. To change the format, you need to specify the number of columns the program should use when writing your value. For example, the following statement says to write the value of **ValToDisplay**, and specifies a field width of 15 columns:

```
WRITELN ( ValToDisplay : 15);
```

If the value being written is longer than the field width, the field width is ignored, and the entire value is written. If the value being written is shorter than the specified field width, the left part of the output is filled with blanks. Such an output format—in which the last digit of the value is in the last column specified by the field width — is said to be *right justified,* or *flush right.*

Operations on INTEGERs

In addition to the assignment and comparison operators (which are available for all types), you can use the following operators with **INTE-GER** operands.

Arithmetic Operators You can add, subtract, and multiply **INTEGER** values. These operators work just as they do for **REAL** operands.

To add two integers, use the addition operator (+). The examples in the following listing use this operator:

```
MySum := IntVal1 + IntVal2;

WRITELN ( MySum + YourSum);

Total := MySum + YourSum + TheirSum;
```

Similarly, the subtraction operator (−) lets you subtract one value from another, as you can see in the following listing:

```
MySum := IntVal1 - IntVal2;

WRITELN ( MySum - YourSum);

Total := MySum - YourSum + TheirSum;
```

The multiplication operator (*) produces a result that is the product of its two operands:

```
MyProduct := IntVal1 * IntVal2;

WRITELN ( MyProduct * YourProduct);
(* The following could be dangerous because the
   products may be too big for the integer range.
   See text for more on integer overflow.
*)
Total := MyProduct * YourProduct * TheirProduct;
```

What about division? For example, what's 17 divided by 3 when you're working with whole numbers? As you may recall, the result in such a case is generally expressed as a whole number value and a remainder. For example, when you divide 17 by 3 the result is 5 with a remainder of 2. That is, 3 goes into 17 five times, since $3 * 5 = 15$; the 2 left over after subtracting 15 from 17 is the remainder.

Pascal has two operators that produce the preceding results for integers. The division operator for **INTEGER** operands is **DIV**. This operator takes two integer operands—for instance, **Op1** and **Op2. Op1 DIV Op2** returns the number of times **Op2** goes into **Op1**, ignoring any remainder.

The following program demonstrates the **DIV** operator:

P3-13
```
(* Program to exercise INTEGER DIV operator *)

PROGRAM TestIntOps;

CONST IntError Value = -32768;
      Op = 'DIV';
VAR   IntResult, Val1, Val2 : INTEGER;
      Count : INTEGER;

  PROCEDURE GetInt ( Message : STRING;
                       VAR Value : INTEGER);
  BEGIN
    WRITE ( Message, '? ');
    READLN ( Value);
  END; (* GetInt *)

  (* Return result of applying DIV operator to arguments *)
  FUNCTION IntDiv ( Dividend, Divisor : INTEGER) : INTEGER;
  BEGIN
    IF Divisor = 0 THEN
      IntDiv := IntErrorValue
    ELSE
      IntDiv := Dividend DIV Divisor;
  END; (* IntDiv *)

BEGIN
  GetInt ( 'Value 1', Val1);
  GetInt ( 'Value 2', Val2);

  FOR Count := 1 TO 3 DO
  BEGIN
    IntResult := IntDiv (Val1, Val2);
    WRITELN ( Val1, ' ', Op, ' ', Val2, ' = ', IntResult);
    Val1 := IntResult;
  END; (* For count := 1 to 3 *)
  READLN;
END.
```

For inputs of **178** and **7** as **Val1** and **Val2**, respectively, the program produces the following output:

```
178 DIV 7 = 25
25 DIV 7 = 3
3 DIV 7 = 0
```

As you saw, integer division produces two results: a whole number quotient and a remainder. The **MOD** operator returns the remainder.

Given two **INTEGER** arguments, the **MOD** operator returns the whole number remainder when the first argument is divided by the second (using integer division). For example, when **LeftOperand** is 78 in the following listing, the expression

```
LeftOperand MOD 23
```

evaluates to 9, since $78 - 69 = 9$. Notice that the result from applying the **MOD** operator will range between 0 and one less than the second (right) operand. Thus, the result of the expression in the preceding listing will always be a value between 0 and 22, regardless of the value of **LeftOperand**.

The following program illustrates the **MOD** operator:

P3-14

```
(* Program to illustrate use of MOD operator *)

PROGRAM ExploreMod;

CONST MaxTrials = 500;
VAR Result, Count, HeadCount, RowCount : INTEGER;

BEGIN
  RANDOMIZE;
  HeadCount := 0;
  RowCount := 0;
  FOR Count := 1 TO MaxTrials DO
  BEGIN
    (* the following call returns a pseudorandom integer
       between 0 and MAXINT
    *)
    Result := RANDOM ( MAXINT);
    (* If result is even, count it as a head,
       and write a period.
    *)
    IF result MOD 2 = 0 THEN
    BEGIN
      WRITE ( '.');
      RowCount := RowCount + 1;
    END
```

```
    ELSE    (* if not even, write a space *)
      WRITE ( ' ');
    (* after 50 trials, move to a new line *)
    IF Count MOD 50 = 0 THEN
    BEGIN
      WRITELN ( RowCount : 3);
      HeadCount := RowCount + HeadCount;
      RowCount := 0;
    END;   (* IF count MOD 50 = 0 *)
  END;
  WRITELN ( HeadCount, ' heads');
  READLN;
END.
```

The call to the predefined procedure **RANDOM** with the argument **MAXINT** results in a pseudorandom integer in the range 0 through **MAXINT**.

If the value returned is even, the program writes a period and increments a counter. If the value is not even, the program writes a space. Every 50 trials, the program moves to a new line. This is determined by testing whether **Count** leaves a remainder of 0 when divided by 50.

For a sample run, the program produced the following output:

```
... .  .  .. ..  . .. ........  ... ..  ..... ....   33
.. . . ... .. ...  .  . .     .  . . . . ..          22
. .. . .. ..  . . .     .. . .. ..      ..... .      23
......         ...  .  .. .. . .      ... . .. .... . 26
.. . .. .     .  ... ..  . ... .. . ....... ..  ... . 28
.. . . .. . . .. .   .. . .. . . .. .  . . . . .. .   25
. .....  .    . .   ...   .... .. . . . . . ..        25
.. ..    . ....   .... .. .. ....  .    . ... .       26
.. .    . .. .. . . .  ..  .... .   .. ....           24
   . .   .. . .... .. ..... ........ ... . ..... .    32
264 heads
```

Precedence for the Arithmetic Operators

Since the addition, subtraction, and multiplication operators are the same ones as for **REAL**s, their precedence is the same as for that type.

Both the **DIV** and **MOD** operators involve division — a multiplicative operator. Not surprisingly, the precedence for the **DIV** and **MOD** operators is the same as for the multiplication and (**REAL**) division operators.

Hexadecimal Values

In everyday work, you deal with numbers in decimal form, using 10 as the numeric base. In base 10, you work with ten different digits: 0 through 9. In decimal values, each column represents a power of 10. In particular, each column represents values that are ten times the values to the right. Thus, the decimal value 4326 is composed of 6 ones, 2 tens, 3 hundreds, and 4 thousands.

In computer science, numbers are often represented in bases other than 10. The most common alternate representations are binary (base 2), octal (base 8), and hexadecimal (base 16).

In base 16, each column represents a different power of 16, rather than 10. Thus, the hexadecimal number 4326 represents 6 ones, 2 sixteens, 3 two hundred fifty-sixes (16 * 16), and 4 four thousand ninety-sixes (256 * 16). Converted to decimal form, this value is 6 + 32 + 768 + 16384, which equals 17190.

In base 10, you have ten different digits; you need 16 digits for base 16. To represent such values, use the digits 0 through 9 as usual; then use the letters a through f (or A through F) to represent the hexadecimal digits 10, 11, 12, 13, 14, and 15, respectively. Thus, the hexadecimal value CAFE is equivalent to 12 * 4096 + 10 * 256 + 15 * 16 + 14, or 51,966.

You can use hexadecimal values in your Turbo Pascal programs. To specify that a value is hexadecimal rather than decimal, put a dollar sign ($) before it. For example, $39 is equivalent to 57 in base 10 (3 * 16 + 9). The following program shows how to assign hexadecimal values:

P3-15
```
(* Program to illustrate use of hexadecimal constants. *)

PROGRAM HexDemo;

VAR HexInt : INTEGER;
```

```
BEGIN
  HexInt := $387d;
  WRITELN ( 'In decimal form, HexInt = ', HexInt);
  READLN;
END.
```

Miscellaneous Issues Concerning INTEGERs

Whole numbers are a special case of real numbers—they're simply real numbers without fractional parts. Therefore, you can assign an **INTEGER** value to a **REAL** variable without complaint from the compiler. You cannot do the reverse, however. That is, you can't assign a **REAL** to an **INTEGER** variable. The compiler will report a type conflict error.

What happens if you try to represent a value outside the range of possible values? For example, what happens if you add 1 to 32767? Recall that overflow with **REAL** values results in a run-time error.

Because of the way that **INTEGER** values are represented, **INTEGER** overflow does not produce a run-time error. However, such overflow will produce an incorrect result.

If you add 1 to 32767 in a Pascal program, you get −32768 rather than 32768. If you add 2 to 32767, you'll get −32767. Notice that you don't get -32769, which is outside the range of possible values for **INTEGER**s. Similarly, if you subtract 1 from −32768, you'll get 32767, rather than −32769. If you subtract 2 from −32768, you'll get 32766.

To understand how overflow is handled, imagine the range of possible integer values arranged in a giant circle, as in Figure 3-1.

0 is at the top of the circle, and the positive values go down the right side. The negative values go down the left side. At the bottom, you'll have 32767 as the extreme positive value and −32768 as the extreme negative value. On the circle, these two values will be next to each other.

You can think of addition and subtraction as operations that move you in a particular direction on the circle. To add two numbers, find the first one on the circle. In a clockwise direction, move the number of values specified by the second number. The value that you land on will be the sum. Thus, adding 1 to 32767 moves you to −32768.

Similarly, to subtract one value from another, start at the first value. Then move in a counterclockwise direction to reach the result. If you subtract 2 from −32768, you'll see why the "result" is 32766.

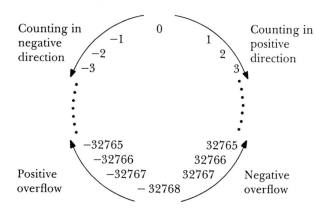

Figure 3-1. *Representation of overflow conditions*

The following program illustrates **INTEGER** overflow: Try adding and subtracting various values. What happens when you add values that are several times too large (for example, when you add 400000 to a value)?

P3-16
```
(* Program for exploring integer overflow *)

PROGRAM Test;

CONST Smallest = -32768;
      Largest = MAXINT;

VAR FromSmallest, ToLargest : INTEGER;

  PROCEDURE GetInteger ( Message : STRING;
                         VAR Value : INTEGER);
  BEGIN
    WRITE ( Message, ' ');
    READLN ( Value);
  END; (* GetInteger *)

BEGIN
  GetInteger ( 'Subtract what from smallest? (0 to stop)',
            FromSmallest);
  (* while user wants to explore,
     subtract from Smallest and add to Largest
  *)
```

```
  WHILE FromSmallest <> 0  DO
  BEGIN
     GetInteger ( 'Add what to largest?',
                 ToLargest);
     WRITE ( Smallest:7, ' - ', FromSmallest:7, ' = ');
     WRITELN ( Smallest - FromSmallest: 7);
     WRITE ( Largest:7, ' + ', ToLargest:7, ' = ');
     WRITELN ( Largest + ToLargest: 7);
     GetInteger ( 'Subtract what from smallest? (0 to stop)',
                 FromSmallest);
  END; (* WHILE FromSmallest <> 0 *)
END.
```

For inputs of **5** for both **FromSmallest** and **ToLargest**, the program produces the following:

```
Subtract what from smallest? (0 to stop) 5
Add what to largest? 5
  -32768 -       5 =   32763
   32767 +       5 =  -32764
```

You will not get any error messages when integer overflow occurs at run time, as part of a computation or through an assignment. Therefore, you need to be very careful when multiplying integers or adding large values. If such large values are likely to occur in your program, you should consider working with **REAL** variables or with one of the integer variants described in the next section.

You *will* get a compiler error message if you explicitly try to assign an actual value that is beyond the range for **INTEGER** values. For example, if you try to assign the value **35000** to an **INTEGER** variable, you'll get a compiler error that the constant is out of range.

Variants and Extensions of the INTEGER Type

In addition to type **INTEGER**, the only whole number type defined in standard Pascal, Turbo Pascal provides several other simple types for representing whole numbers. These types differ from **INTEGER**s in the range of values that can be represented.

The same operators are available for these types as for **INTEGER** variables. Any differences in the way overflow is handled are discussed in connection with the individual types.

Type LONGINT Turbo Pascal provides a **LONGINT** type for representing a larger range of values than that afforded by the **INTEGER** type. The compiler allocates four bytes (32 bits) for **LONGINT**s. This gives a range of values between -2^{31} and $2^{31}-1$, or between $-2,147,483,648$ and $2,147,483,647$, inclusive. (The commas in the numbers are for clarity. You can't use commas when writing **LONG-INT**s in your programs.)

The predefined constant, **MAXLONGINT**, is set equal to the maximum **LONGINT** value in the implementation.

The following listing shows how to declare a **LONGINT** variable. The syntax for using **LONGINT**s is the same as for **INTEGER**s.

```
VAR MyLong : LONGINT;
```

If you try to display or use a value that is larger than **MAXLONGINT**, the result will be an overflow value. Thus, **MAXLONGINT** + 1 is $-2,147,483,648$. Overflow handling works as it does for **INTEGER**s. You can think of **LONGINT**s as being arranged on a large circle, such as the one in Figure 3-1, but with a much larger range of values.

Type WORD Turbo Pascal's **WORD** type is allocated just as much storage as an **INTEGER** (two bytes), but can only be used to represent nonnegative values. The range for **WORD** variables is thus 0 through 65535 (that is, 0 through $2^{16}-1$), inclusive. Essentially, a **WORD** differs from an **INTEGER** in that the leftmost bit is used for computing the number in a **WORD**, rather than being used as a sign bit, as with **INTEGER**s.

WORD overflow is handled just like **INTEGER** overflow, except that, in the circle, there are no negative values. Also, 65535 and 0 are adjacent.

You can tell the compiler whether you want it to do *range checking*. When this option is on, the compiler checks whether variables are being assigned values that lie outside their valid ranges. By default, range checking is off in the IDE. To turn range checking on or off, put the appropriate line at the top of your program:

```
{$R+}       (* turn range-checking ON  *)

{$R-}       (* turn range-checking OFF *)
```

When range checking is off, the compiler will not complain if you assign **WORD** values to **INTEGER** variables, and vice versa. If the **WORD** value is greater than **MAXINT**, the overflow process will come into play. Similarly, if you assign a negative **INTEGER** value to a **WORD** variable, the result will be a different value, which uses all 16 bits to compute a magnitude.

The Turbo Pascal compiler will not complain if you assign a **LONGINT** value to a two-byte variable (that is, an **INTEGER** or a **WORD**). Only two of the bytes will be assigned to the variable. For example, if you assign **MAXLONGINT** to a **WORD** variable, the **WORD** will have the value **65535**. (This is because of the bit pattern in the two bytes assigned to the **WORD**.)

CAUTION   It's rarely a good idea to assign **LONGINT** values to shorter variables or to assign **WORD** values to **INTEGER** variables.

Types SHORTINT and BYTE   Turbo Pascal has two whole number types that are allocated only one byte of storage. The **SHORTINT** type can store values from −128 to 127. In this type, the leftmost bit represents the sign.

The **BYTE** type does not have a sign bit. As a result, it can represent values from 0 to 255. The **BYTE** type can be useful if you're reading a binary file, for example.

The compiler will not protest if you assign variables of these types to each other. Similarly, you can assign longer whole number values to one-byte variables. Keep in mind, however, that only one byte of the larger values will be assigned to the variables.

Table 3-1 summarizes Turbo Pascal's whole number types.

Character-Based Types

Pascal also allows you to represent nonnumerical information. For example, there is a predefined type for representing individual characters.

Type	Size	Minimum Value	Maximum Value
SHORTINT	1 byte	− 128	127
BYTE	1 byte	0	255
INTEGER	2 bytes	− 32768	32767
WORD	2 bytes	0	65535
LONGINT	4 bytes	− 2,147,483,648	2,147,483,647

Table 3-1. *Turbo Pascal's Whole Number Types*

In addition, Turbo Pascal includes a predefined type for representing strings of characters.

The CHAR Type

Pascal's **CHAR** type is used for storing individual characters. These are stored as ASCII codes in Turbo Pascal. **CHAR** variables are allocated one byte, which means that the character's code can be any value from 0 through 255.

To include a specific character in your program, enclose it in single quotes. For example, the following statement assigns the letter *Q* to the (**CHAR**) variable **MyChar**:

```
MyChar := 'Q';
```

The standard ASCII character set (see Appendix A, "ASCII Codes") contains 128 characters, with codes that range from 0 through 127. (Character codes 128 through 255 are often known as *extended ASCII* characters. You can also use such codes for special purposes in particular programs.)

In the ASCII character set, each alphabetic character is associated with a particular code. For example, *A* has ASCII code 65, and *a* has ASCII code 97. The ASCII codes for the letters are ordered and contiguous. Thus, the ASCII code for *A* is 65; for *B* it's 66; for *C* it's 67; and so on, through 90, the code for *Z*. Similarly, the lowercase letters have consecutive ASCII codes, beginning with 97 for *a*.

In addition to the upper- and lowercase letters, there are ASCII codes for digits (0 through 9), and special symbols (#, %, &, [, <blank space>, and so forth). The ASCII codes for the digits are also consecutive, beginning with 48, the code for the digit 0. (Note that digits as characters and digits as numerical values are different. For example, '3' and 3 are different. '3' is a **CHAR** value; 3 is an **INTEGER** value. You should also be careful not to confuse the zero character (0) with an uppercase version of the character before *P*—namely, *O*.)

These characters (letters, digits, and special characters) are known as *printable characters*. The printable characters have the ASCII codes from 32 through 126.

To specify a printable character, put the character between single quotes, as in the preceding listing. You can also specify such characters by using the ASCII code directly, preceded by #. For example, #67 represents *C* and #106 represents *j*. When using the # representation, do *not* put quotes around the value.

In addition to the printable characters, there are *control characters*. These carry out certain actions or send particular signals. For example, the TAB key is a control character, as are the carriage return (CR) and linefeed (LF) characters. In fact, all the characters with ASCII codes 0 through 31 are control characters.

You can also specify control characters by using # followed by the character's code. For example, #7 specifies the character with ASCII code 7, which sends a beep.

The control characters with ASCII codes 1 through 26 each have names that include a letter. For example, ASCII code 1 is known as CTRL-A, code 2 is CTRL-B, and so on through ASCII code 26, which is CTRL-Z. To specify any of these characters, you can precede the letter with a caret (^). For example, ^G also specifies character #7 (the beep character); ^I specifies #9 (the TAB character).

The following program shows how to specify various types of **CHAR** values. Run the program a few times. What happens if you enter a character such as CTRL-D or CTRL-G?

P3-17
```
(* Program to illustrate use of CHAR variables and constants *)

PROGRAM BeepTest;
(* the first two constants represent two ways
   to specify the same character.
*)
CONST BeepChar = #7;
      BeepChar2 = ^G;
      TabChar = ^I;  (* send a TAB -- to move cursor *)
                     (* to next tabstop *)
VAR ChVal : CHAR;
```

```
    (* Get a CHAR value from user *)
    PROCEDURE GetChar ( Message : STRING;
                          VAR Value : CHAR);
    BEGIN
      WRITE ( Message, ' ');
      READLN ( Value);
    END; (* GetChar *)

BEGIN
  GetChar ( 'Enter a Character please.', ChVal);
  WRITELN ( BeepChar, TabChar, ChVal,
            TabChar, ChVal, BeepChar2);
  READLN;
END.
```

In standard Pascal, the only operators available for **CHAR**s are the assignment and comparison operators. ASCII codes are used when comparing two **CHAR** values. Thus,

```
'H' < 'h'
```

is **TRUE** because the ASCII code for *H* (72) is less than the code for *h* (104).

In Turbo Pascal, you can also "add" two characters. Such addition is known as *concatenation,* and involves putting elements together to form another element. When you concatenate two characters, the result is a string.

Thus, the following expression assigns the value **'yz'** to the string variable (**StrResult**) on the left-hand side of the assignment:

```
StrResult := 'y' + 'z';  (* StrResult becomes 'yz' *)
```

The STRING Type

Unlike standard Pascal, Turbo Pascal has a predefined **STRING** type. Variables of this type are used to store character sequences. You can either declare strings with no length specified or you can declare strings that have a maximum length.

The following listing illustrates how to define three different string variables. The first variable (**DefaultStr**) has an unspecified length. In Turbo Pascal, this means that it can have up to 255 characters. The second type (**STRING [30]**) can have at most 30 characters, and the third declaration (**STRING [75]**) specifies a string variable (**Str75**) with up to 75 characters.

```
VAR DefaultStr : STRING;     (* Maximum length = 255 chars *)
    Str30 : STRING [ 30];    (* Maximum length =  30 chars *)
    Str75 : STRING [75];     (* Maximum length =  75 chars *)
```

To specify a string value, put the character sequence within single quotes, as in the following examples:

```
DefaultStr := 'This string can have up to 255 chars';
Str30 := 'This one can have <= 30 chars';
Str75 := 'This string can have up to 75 chars';
```

If you try to assign a string that is longer than the allotted storage, as many characters as possible are assigned and the extra characters are ignored. Because characters that would make a string too long are ignored, the compiler will not complain if you try to assign the value of **DefaultStr** to **Str30**. A maximum of 30 characters will be copied, and any remaining characters in **DefaultStr** will be ignored.

The compiler is stricter when you're passing a string parameter. By default, the compiler insists that strings passed as **VAR** parameters be identical to the parameter as defined. Thus, the following program ends in an error when the compiler reaches the call to **StrParTest**, because the second actual parameter (**STR**) and the second formal parameter (**Incoming**) are not of the same type:

P3-18
```
(* Program to illustrate VAR-string type checking.
   With string type checking on, the call to StrParTest
   in the main program produces a compiler error.

   Remove space between * and $ to activate the
   $V- directive, which turns off VAR-string type checking.
*)

(* $V-*)
PROGRAM StrParamDemo;
```

```
TYPE Str30 = STRING [ 30];
VAR Str : STRING;
    ShrtStr : Str30;

  PROCEDURE StrParTest ( VAR NewVal, Incoming : Str30);
  BEGIN
    NewVal := Incoming;
    WRITELN ( 'Incoming: ', Incoming);
    WRITELN ( 'New     : ', NewVal);
  END; (* StrParTest *)

BEGIN
  Str := '123456789012345678901234567890123 4567890';
  (* This assignment works regardless of whether
     $V- or $V+ hold.
  *)
  ShrtStr := Str;
  WRITELN ( 'Str     : ', Str);
  WRITELN ( 'ShrtStr : ', ShrtStr);
  (* Pass a STRING when a Str30 should be passed;
     works only if $V- is set.
  *)
  StrParTest ( ShrtStr, Str);
  WRITELN ( 'After calling StrParTest:');
  WRITELN ( 'Str     : ', Str);
  WRITELN ( 'ShrtStr : ', ShrtStr);
  READLN;
END.
```

To get the program to compile, you need to turn **VAR**-string type checking off. To do this, remove the space to the left of the **$V-** near the start of the program. This invokes the directive to turn **VAR**-string type checking off.

Strictly speaking, the type underlying a string is not a simple type; however, you can treat it as such. This is convenient, since you'll be using strings in lots of applications throughout the book. In Chapter 7, "Turbo Pascal's Structured Data Types" you'll learn how strings are implemented in Turbo Pascal.

As with **CHAR** values, the assignment and comparison operators are available for the **STRING** type. Again, ASCII codes are used when comparing two strings. The strings are compared character by character until the codes for corresponding characters in the two strings differ. For example,

```
'helpful' > 'hello'
```

is **TRUE** because the *p* in **helpful** has a higher ASCII code than the second *l* in **hello**. Up to that point, the two strings are identical.

You can also combine two strings to produce a longer string. This concatenation process is like the one described for characters. The result is a string, as the following listing shows. After the assignment, **LongerStr** has the value **a longer string**.

```
(* After the assignment, LongerStr = 'a longer string' *)
LongerStr := 'a longer' + ' string';
```

While there are few operators available for strings, there are several predefined procedures and functions for manipulating strings. You'll learn about these in the next chapter.

Controlling Output Format for Strings

As with real numbers and integers, you can specify the output format for character and string variables. To specify a field width, indicate the information to be written, write a colon (:), and then specify the field width. If the value to be output is longer than the field width, the field width specifier is ignored. If the string value being written is shorter than the specified field width, the string is right justified.

Logical Types

In addition to numerical and character information, Pascal has a pre-defined type for storing logical truth values. Such values can be either true or false.

As you saw in Chapter 2, "Pascal: An Overview" Pascal has two predefined constants, **TRUE** and **FALSE**. These two values belong to Pascal's **BOOLEAN** type. In fact, they are the *only* two values possible for

BOOLEAN variables. (Note that there are no quotes around the Boolean values. These values are not strings; they are predefined logical values.)

A **BOOLEAN** variable is one that can have either of two values: **TRUE** or **FALSE**. The following program shows how to declare and use **BOOLEAN** variables. (**BOOLEAN** variables are named after George Boole, who developed algebraic methods for solving logic problems.)

P3-19

```
(* Program to explore use of Boolean variables *)

PROGRAM ExploreBool;

CONST MaxTrials = 10;
VAR Bool1, Bool2 : BOOLEAN;
    Count, Val1, Val2 : INTEGER;

BEGIN
  RANDOMIZE;
  FOR Count := 1 TO MaxTrials DO
  BEGIN
    Val1 := RANDOM ( MAXINT);
    Val2 := RANDOM ( MAXINT);
    IF Val1 > Val2 THEN
      Bool1 := TRUE
    ELSE
      Bool1 := FALSE;
    (* If both values are odd or both are even ... *)
    IF (Val1 - Val2) MOD 2 = 0 THEN
      Bool2 := TRUE
    ELSE
      Bool2 := FALSE;
    (* You can write the value of BOOLEAN variables *)
    WRITELN ( Val1, ' ', Val2, ';   ', Bool1, ' ', Bool2);
  END;
  READLN;

END.
```

Run this program a few times, and work through a few of the results yourself. If you run the program, you'll get output such as the following. Try modifying the program to produce aligned output.

```
21009  19020;   TRUE FALSE
14691  20014;   FALSE FALSE
28667  20844;   TRUE FALSE
1893  26083;   FALSE TRUE
```

```
29578  11268;   TRUE TRUE
24378  15671;   TRUE FALSE
4553   16152;   FALSE FALSE
17525  23100;   FALSE FALSE
28166  5061;    TRUE FALSE
24590  13053;   TRUE FALSE
```

Notice that you can display the value of a **BOOLEAN** variable. You cannot, however, input the value of a **BOOLEAN** with a **READ** or **READLN** statement.

One way to assign a value to a **BOOLEAN** variable is to put a *Boolean expression* on the right side of the assignment operator. Such an expression evaluates to **TRUE** or **FALSE**. An expression involving a comparison operator is a commonly used Boolean expression. For example, the following statements all assign (the values of) Boolean expressions to variables:

```
Bool1 := 7.5 > 13          (* assign FALSE to Bool1 *)
Bool2 := 'a' = 'a'         (* assign TRUE to Bool2 *)
Bool3 := 'z' = 'Z'         (* assign FALSE to Bool3 *)
Bool4 := TRUE <> FALSE     (* assign TRUE to Bool4 *)
Bool5 := MAXINT < MAXLONGINT  (* assign TRUE to Bool5 *)
```

Notice that a Boolean expression need not involve **BOOLEAN** operands. Of the five examples, only the fourth involves **BOOLEAN** elements. However, *all* Boolean expressions evaluate to a **BOOLEAN** value.

Boolean expressions are crucial for defining Pascal's looping constructs (such as the **IF** and **WHILE** statements you saw in Chapter 2). You'll see much more of Boolean expressions and of **BOOLEAN** values when you learn about Pascal's control constructs.

REMEMBER   You can display the value of a **BOOLEAN**; however, you cannot read the value of a **BOOLEAN** from the keyboard or from a file.

Operators for BOOLEAN Variables

You can use the assignment operator and the comparison operators with **BOOLEAN** values. When comparing two **BOOLEAN**s, you are

Value of Left Operand (A)	Value of Right Operand (B)	Value of A AND B
FALSE	FALSE	FALSE
FALSE	TRUE	FALSE
TRUE	FALSE	FALSE
TRUE	TRUE	TRUE

Table 3-2. *Truth Table for AND Operator*

comparing **TRUE** and **FALSE** values. For reasons that will be explained later in the chapter, **TRUE** < **FALSE**. Thus, the expression

```
TRUE < FALSE     (* evaluates to TRUE *)
```

evaluates to **TRUE**. (Such a direct comparison between two **BOOLEAN** constants should never be necessary.) In addition to these operators, there are several operators that work only with **BOOLEAN** operands. The **BOOLEAN** operators are **AND, OR, XOR,** and **NOT.**

The AND Operator   The **AND** operator takes two **BOOLEAN** operands and produces a **BOOLEAN** result. This operator returns **TRUE** only if *both* the left and the right operands are **TRUE**. The behavior of the **AND** operator can be summarized in a *truth table,* which shows the outcome for every possible pairing of two **BOOLEAN** variables. Table 3-2 provides the truth table for the **AND** operator. Notice that only the bottom combination results in a **TRUE.**

The following program illustrates the **AND** operator:

```
P3-20   (* Program to illustrate use of Boolean AND Operator *)

        PROGRAM AndDemo;

        CONST EvenDivisor = 6;
              OddDivisor = 7;
        VAR Val1, Val2 : INTEGER;

          (* Get an integer value from the user. *)
          PROCEDURE GetInteger ( Message : STRING;
                                  VAR Value : INTEGER);
          BEGIN
            WRITE ( Message, ' ');    (* prompt user *)
            READLN ( Value);          (* read response *)
          END; (* GetInteger *)
```

```
BEGIN
  GetInteger ( 'Value 1? ', Val1);
  GetInteger ( 'Value 2? ', Val2);
  IF ( Val1 MOD EvenDivisor = 0) AND
     ( Val2 MOD OddDivisor = 0) THEN
    WRITELN ( 'Both divisors work')
  ELSE
    WRITELN ( 'Sorry, but no go.');
  READLN;
END.
```

This program writes "Both divisors work" if **Val1** leaves no remainder when divided by **EvenDivisor** *and* **Val2** leaves no remainder when divided by **OddDivisor**. If either of these tests evaluates to **FALSE**, the program writes the "sorry, but no go" message.

Notice the parentheses around each Boolean expression. These are necessary because the **AND** operator has a higher precedence than the comparison operators. If there were no parentheses around the expressions, the **AND** operator would try to combine 0 and **Val2**. This would lead to a type conflict error, since the **AND** operator needs two **BOOLEAN** operands.

The OR Operator   The **OR** operator also takes two **BOOLEAN** operands and produces a **BOOLEAN** result. The outcome from the **OR** operator is **FALSE** only if *both* operands are **FALSE**, and **TRUE** otherwise. Thus, the **OR** operator produces a **TRUE** if *either or both* of the operands are **TRUE**. Table 3-3 shows the truth table for the **OR** operator.

The difference between this table and the truth table for **AND** lies in the middle two cases, where the operands have different values. Whereas the **AND** operator yields **FALSE** in those cases, the **OR** operator produces **TRUE**.

Value of Left Operand (A)	Value of Right Operand (B)	Value of A OR B
FALSE	FALSE	FALSE
FALSE	TRUE	TRUE
TRUE	FALSE	TRUE
TRUE	TRUE	TRUE

Table 3-3. *Truth Table for OR Operator*

The following program illustrates the **OR** operator:

P3-21
```
(* Program to illustrate use of Boolean OR Operator *)

PROGRAM OrDemo;

CONST EvenDivisor = 8;
      OddDivisor = 5;
VAR Val1, Val2 : INTEGER;

  (* Get an integer value from the user. *)
  PROCEDURE GetInteger ( Message : STRING;
                         VAR Value : INTEGER);
  BEGIN
    WRITE ( Message, ' ');   (* prompt user *)
    READLN ( Value);           (* read response *)
  END; (* GetInteger *)

BEGIN
  GetInteger ( 'Value 1? ', Val1);
  GetInteger ( 'Value 2? ', Val2);
  IF ( Val1 MOD EvenDivisor = 0) OR
     ( Val2 MOD OddDivisor = 0) THEN
    WRITELN ( 'At least one divisor works')
  ELSE
    WRITELN ( 'Sorry, but neither divisor works.');
  READLN;
END.
```

This program indicates that "At least one divisor works" if either of the Boolean expressions is **TRUE**—that is, if either 8 or 5 divides its respective **Val***x* variable.

The **OR** operator also has a higher precedence than the comparison operators, so the parentheses are needed around the Boolean expressions. It's a good idea to use parentheses generously—just to be sure that you and the compiler interpret statements in the same way.

The XOR Operator   The preceding **BOOLEAN** operators are defined in standard Pascal. In addition, Turbo Pascal has an **XOR** operator, which yields **TRUE** if exactly one of the two operands is **TRUE**. For this operator, *only* the mixed cases yield **TRUE**, as you can see in Table 3-4.

This operator differs from the **OR** operator only in the last line of the truth table. Whereas the **OR** operator allows both operands to be **TRUE**, the **XOR** (for e**X**clusive **OR**) operator will not allow both operands to be **TRUE**.

Value of Left Operand (A)	Value of Right Operand (B)	Value of A XOR B
FALSE	FALSE	FALSE
FALSE	TRUE	TRUE
TRUE	FALSE	TRUE
TRUE	TRUE	FALSE

Table 3-4. *Truth Table for XOR Operator*

The following program illustrates how to use the **XOR** operator, as well as the other two Boolean operators you've seen so far:

P3-22

```
(* Program to illustrate use of Boolean XOR Operator *)

PROGRAM BoolOpsDemo;
CONST EvenDivisor = 6;
      OddDivisor = 7;
      MaxCount = 50;
VAR Count : INTEGER;

BEGIN
  WRITELN ( 'AND' : 10, 'OR' : 10, 'XOR' : 10);
  WRITELN;
  FOR Count := 1 TO MaxCount DO
  BEGIN
    IF ( Count MOD EvenDivisor = 0) AND
       ( Count MOD OddDivisor = 0) THEN
      WRITELN ( Count : 10);
    IF ( Count MOD EvenDivisor = 0) OR
       ( Count MOD OddDivisor = 0) THEN
      WRITELN ( Count : 20);
    IF ( Count MOD EvenDivisor = 0) XOR
       ( Count MOD OddDivisor = 0) THEN
      WRITELN ( Count : 30);
  END; (* FOR Count ... *)
  READLN;
END.
```

The preceding program displays values between 1 and **MaxCount** that have certain properties—as tested in the Boolean expressions.

The NOT Operator The remaining Boolean operator is the unary operator **NOT**. The **NOT** operator takes a **BOOLEAN** operand and yields a **BOOLEAN** whose value is the opposite of the operand's value. Thus, if the operand is **TRUE**, the **NOT** operator yields **FALSE**.

You can apply the **NOT** operator to any **BOOLEAN** value or variable or to a Boolean expression. The first five statements in the following listing are valid applications of the **NOT** operator; the remaining three are invalid:

```
(* valid *)
NOT NOT FALSE                (* returns FALSE *)
NOT TRUE                     (* returns FALSE *)
NOT ( 3 > 5)                 (* returns TRUE *)
NOT (( 3 > 5) AND ( 5 < 7))  (* returns TRUE *)
NOT ( 3 < 5) AND ( 5 < 7)    (* returns FALSE *)

(* invalid *)
NOT ( 3)        (* can't use NOT with INTEGER *)
NOT ( 'g')      (* can't use NOT with CHAR *)
NOT ( 'goodbye')  (* can't use NOT with STRING *)
```

Notice that you don't need parentheses around the operand for the **NOT** operator. Also, compare the last two valid statements. These differ in that the fourth has parentheses around the entire Boolean expression involving the **AND** operator. The two statements produce different results because the **NOT** operator has higher precedence than the **AND** operator. Therefore, in the last statement, the expression

```
NOT ( 3 < 5)
```

is evaluated to **FALSE** and this result becomes the left operand for the **AND** operator.

The following program illustrates the **NOT** operator:

```
P3-23    (* Program to explore use of Boolean NOT operator *)

         PROGRAM ExploreNot;

         CONST MaxTrials = 10;
         VAR Bool1, Bool2 : BOOLEAN;
             Count, Val1, Val2 : INTEGER;

         BEGIN
           RANDOMIZE;
           FOR Count := 1 TO MaxTrials DO
           BEGIN
             Val1 := RANDOM ( MAXINT);
             Val2 := RANDOM ( MAXINT);
```

```
      (* The following Boolean expression is TRUE if
         Val1 is LESS than Val2
      *)
      IF NOT ( Val1 > Val2) THEN
        Bool1 := TRUE
      ELSE
        Bool1 := FALSE;
      (* If both values are odd or both ar even ... *)
      IF (Val1 - Val2) MOD 2 = 0 THEN
        Bool2 := TRUE
      ELSE
        Bool2 := FALSE;
      (* You can write the value of BOOLEAN variables *)
      WRITELN ( Bool1, ' ', Bool2);
    END;
    READLN;
  END.
```

Precedence for the BOOLEAN Operators

All of the Boolean operators have a higher precedence than the comparison operators. Table 3-5 shows the order of precedence for all of the operators that you've seen so far, including the Boolean operators.

Enumerated Types

Pascal enables you to create your own simple type by listing, or enumerating, the possible values this type can take. Once you've done this, you can declare variables of the new type. Because you list the individual

Operators	Comments
NOT	Boolean negation
*, /, DIV, MOD, AND	Multiplicative operators
+, −, OR, XOR	Additive operators
=, <>, >, >=, <, <=	Comparison operators
:=	Assignment operator

Table 3-5.   *Precedence Hierarchy for Pascal Operators*

values, such types are known as *enumerated* types.

For example, suppose you want to represent a deck of cards. To represent a card, you need the card's suit and its face value. The following program shows how to create variables to represent both of these items of information—without resorting to arbitrary numerical codes for these values. Note that the program doesn't do anything observable; it simply shows the syntax for assigning enumerated values to variables. Once you've learned more about Pascal's syntax, you may want to expand this program—for example, to deal poker or gin rummy hands.

P3-24
```
(* Program illustrating how to define, declare and
   use enumerated types.
*)
PROGRAM Cards;

(* Define a type by listing the possible values
   variables of this type can take.
*)
TYPE CardSuit = ( club, diamond, heart, spade);
     FaceValue = ( two, three, four, five, six, seven, eight,
                   nine, ten, jack, queen, king, ace);

VAR Suit : CardSuit;
    Face : FaceValue;

BEGIN

  Suit := club;
  Face := ten;
END.
```

The preceding program defines the appropriate variables, and then makes the assignments for a ten of clubs.

Using a TYPE Definition to Create the Type

The first step in working with enumerated types is to create a **TYPE** definition. You must do this in the declaration section, and must specify a name for the type and a list of the values that the type can have. This list of values appears in parentheses, with individual values separated by commas.

The syntax for a **TYPE** definition to create an enumerated type is

```
<type name> "= (" <value>{, <value>}")"
```

The equal sign and the parentheses are fixed; the remaining elements will vary with each definition. Notice that the type values are not within quotes. These values are not strings; rather, they are names to be associated with internal codes.

Internally, Turbo Pascal simply associates the numerical codes 0 through <*number of values* − 1> with the values you've listed. This makes it easy for the compiler to use your new type; the meaningful value names make it easier for you to read the program.

One consequence of using such a representation is that values are actually ordered. For example,

```
hearts > club
```

because the internal code (2) for **heart** is larger than the code (0) for **club**. Similarly, an **ace** value is higher than a **jack**.

This ordering may be useful in a program. For example, to compare two cards you could use a comparison operator to determine which value was "larger." The assignment and comparison operators are the only operators available for enumerated types.

You can define multiple types. The first type definition line begins with the word **TYPE**; subsequent type definition lines begin with an identifier or with blank space.

The example program defined two enumerated types: **CardSuit** and **FaceValue**. The first of these can take on four different values, the second can take on 13.

A **TYPE** definition is simply a description. Such a definition does not create any variables of the specified type, nor is any storage allocated to store variables of that type.

The amount of storage allocated for such variables depends on the possible values that the type can have. For types that have fewer than 256 different values, one byte is allocated; for types with more values, two bytes are allocated.

Declaring Enumerated Variables

No **CardSuit** variables exist until the declaration of **Suit**; similarly, no storage is allocated for any **FaceValue** variables until **Face** is declared.

Once you've defined a type, you can declare variables of this type. To do so, use the same syntax as in the variable declarations for other types. In the examples, two separate variables are used to represent the suit and face value information. In Chapter 7, you'll learn about a more complex type that you can use to represent both of these items of information in the same variable.

Using Enumerated Variables

Once you have declared the appropriate variables, you can do what you wish. The assignment operator and the comparison operators are the only operators that work with enumerated types.

Assignments to enumerated variables have the same format as other assignments.

Note that the enumerated type values are not within quotes in the assignment statements. Again, this is because these are not strings.

You'll find lots of uses for enumerated types in your programs. Since you can use meaningful names for the values (instead of using arbitrary numerical codes) it is easier to keep an overview of your actions with such variables.

Unfortunately, you can't write the value of an enumerated type variable directly to the screen or a file. Nor can you read the value of such a variable directly.

This chapter covered Turbo Pascal's simple data types. As you saw, there are many types to choose from, and you can even create your own types if you need to.

In the next chapter, you'll learn about some of the predefined procedures and functions available for use with these simple types. You'll also start learning how to define your own procedures and functions.

4 Procedures and Functions

In the last chapter, you learned about Pascal's simple types. You also learned about various components of a Pascal program, such as statements, comments, constant definitions, and variable declarations. This chapter introduces two other important program elements: procedures and functions.

Whereas statements (individual instructions) are the fundamental elements of Pascal programs, a program is really built out of procedures and functions, which consist of statements. The main program calls these procedures and functions to do its work. (This chapter refers to both procedures and functions as *routines*.)

Before discussing how to define your own routines, this book looks briefly at what procedures are and how they work. You'll also learn how Pascal's functions differ from procedures.

Procedures: General Features

A *procedure* is a collection of statements grouped together to accomplish a particular task. The procedure's name refers to this collection of statements. In many ways, a procedure is really a miniature program. As you'll find, a procedure can have its own declaration section and procedure body. Procedures are designed to carry out some task, such as clearing the screen, sorting a collection of values, beeping at the user, and so forth. Sometimes a procedure will need to perform a general task with variations each time. For example, a procedure may add a collection of numbers. Each time the procedure is called, the values and the number of values to add will be different. To work properly, the procedure must be able to handle such differences.

To determine what the variants are, procedures need to be able to communicate with the caller (the main program or another routine). Procedures can communicate with callers in two ways:

- By using global variables, which are accessible to other routines

- By using parameters to pass information into and out of the procedure

These alternatives are described later in the chapter.

Procedure Definitions and Calls

It's important to distinguish between procedure definitions and procedure calls. To use a procedure, just call it in your program. Before you can use a procedure, however, you must define it.

A *procedure definition* specifies the variables used by the procedure and the sequence of instructions to be executed in accomplishing the procedure's task. Such a definition appears in the declaration section of your program or, as you'll see in Chapter 6, "Procedures and Functions Revisited," of another routine.

Once you've defined a procedure, you can use it in your program. To accomplish the task for which the procedure was defined, you just call the procedure. A *procedure call* is a mechanism by which program control is passed temporarily to the called procedure.

REMEMBER   In Pascal, you need to define a procedure before you can call it.

When a procedure is called, the instructions contained in the procedure definition are carried out. After the procedure finishes executing, control reverts to a point in the calling routine that is immediately after the procedure call.

The following listing shows how this process works.

```
P4-1    PROGRAM ProcedureShell;

        VAR Val1, Val2 : INTEGER;

                        PROCEDURE ChangeInfo;
                        BEGIN
(* 7 *)                     Val1 := Val1 * Val2;
(* 8 *)                     Val2 := Val1 + Val2;
(* 9 *)                     Val1 := Val1 * Val2;
                        END;   (* ChangeInfo *)
        BEGIN
(* 1 *)    Val1 := 1;
(* 2 *)    Val2 := 2;
(* 3 *)    ChangeInfo;
(* 4 *)    WRITELN ( Val1);
(* 5 *)    WRITELN ( Val2);
(* 6 *)    READLN;
        END.
```

The flow of control in the program is as follows:

1. The program starts executing at the top of the program body—line 1 in the example. The assignments in lines 1 and 2 are carried out.

2. When the main program reaches line 3, it stops executing temporarily.

3. Control is transferred to procedure **ChangeInfo**. The next statement to execute will be the assignment in line 7.

4. The statements in **ChangeInfo** are executed in sequence—that is, lines 7, 8, and 9.

5. After line 9 has finished executing, control transfers back to the main program, continuing at line 4.

6. The main program resumes execution with the statement corresponding to line 4.

7. Lines 5 and 6 are executed, and the program is finished.

The calls to **WRITELN** have the same results as the call to **Change-Info**. That is, the main program is suspended temporarily while procedure **WRITELN** executes. Although **WRITELN** is predefined, it isn't very different from procedures that you write.

The preceding example program provides the simplest scenario of how the flow of control changes as the program executes. All of these procedure calls are made from the main program. However, procedures can also call each other, and the flow of control through the program can get quite involved.

For example, one of the statements in **ChangeInfo** might have been a call to another procedure (say **VerifyChanges**). At that call, **Change-Info** stops executing temporarily while control is transferred to **VerifyChanges**.

At this point, both the main program *and* procedure **ChangeInfo** are suspended. **VerifyChanges** executes its statements until it finishes its task. When **VerifyChanges** is finished, control is returned to **Change-Info**, which resumes executing with *its* next statement.

Of course, **VerifyChanges** may have called **MakeMoreChanges**, in which case. . .well, you get the picture.

When a procedure is called, a temporary environment is set up for it. This environment includes temporary storage, which is allocated for any variables that are declared in the procedure. This environment and storage will "disappear" once the procedure finishes. That is, the memory locations allocated for the procedure's variables will be returned to a common pool of available memory for use by the program. One consequence of this is that you won't be able to access the storage allocated for a procedure's variable once you leave the procedure.

Pascal Procedures

In Pascal, the structure of a procedure is very similar to that of a program. In particular, a procedure consists of

- A procedure heading
- An optional declaration section
- A procedure body

The Procedure Heading

The procedure heading—also known as the *interface*—consists of the reserved word **PROCEDURE**, followed by a procedure name. The procedure name can be any valid identifier, and may be followed by a parameter list (discussed shortly). The heading will be followed by a semicolon to separate it from subsequent source code.

   The following are all examples of procedure headings. The first two have no parameter lists and the rest do. **GetDate** has three parameters, all of the same type.

```
PROCEDURE BeepUser;

PROCEDURE Wait;

PROCEDURE Count ( HowHigh : INTEGER);

PROCEDURE BubbleSort ( VAR Info : String80Array;
                           Size : INTEGER);

PROCEDURE GetString ( Message : STRING;
                      VAR Value : STRING);

PROCEDURE GetDate ( VAR Month, Date, Year : INTEGER);
```

The Declaration Section

Procedures can have their own declaration sections—in which you can define constants and types and can declare variables. You can even define other procedures and functions in a procedure's declaration section. The syntax for these definitions and declarations is the same as for the program's declaration section. However, there are differences in the accessibility of the objects defined and declared in this declaration section, as you'll see later.

The Procedure Body

The procedure body contains the statements that accomplish the task for which the procedure was defined. The procedure body starts with

BEGIN and terminates with **END**. Unlike the **END** that terminates a program body, however, the **END** after a procedure body is followed by a semicolon.

When control transfers to a procedure, it begins executing with the first statement in the procedure body and continues executing until the last statement has been carried out. After the last statement, control returns to the calling routine.

REMEMBER   The **END** that terminates a procedure body is followed by a semicolon, not a period.

Global and Local Variables

Earlier, you learned that a procedure can communicate with a caller using either global variables or parameters. This section describes global variables and their counterparts, local variables.

A *global variable* is one that is accessible to the main program and to routines defined within the main program. In Chapter 3, "Turbo Pascal's Simple Data Types," you learned how to declare variables in the program body. Such declarations allocate memory for global variables. For now, think of a global variable as one that is declared in the main program.

You can also declare variables in the declaration section for a procedure or function. Such declarations are known as *local variables*. For example, the following program contains several procedures with local declarations. Notice that you can specify constants as well as declare variables. In fact, you can also create types and define routines.

P4-2
```
(* Program to illustrate declaration and use of
   local and global variables.
*)

PROGRAM LocalDemo;

(* Global Declarations *)
CONST MaxTrials = 10000;
VAR Qtile1, Qtile2, Qtile3, Qtile4 : REAL;

   (* Generate random values between 0.0 and 1.0,
      classifying result into one of four groups.
      Procedure contains local declarations,
      but also uses several global variables.
```

```
*)
PROCEDURE RandomSamples;
(* Specify 3 local constants and 2 local variables *)
CONST Cutoff1 = 0.25;
      Cutoff2 = 0.50;
      Cutoff3 = 0.75;
VAR   Result : REAL;
      Count : INTEGER;
BEGIN
  WRITELN ( '  Starting RandomSamples');
  RANDOMIZE;
  (* MaxTrials is a global constant *)
  FOR Count := 1 TO MaxTrials DO
  BEGIN
    Result := RANDOM;
    (* Classify resulting value into the following groups:
        0.0 <= value < Cutoff1 (0.25)
        Cutoff1 <= value < Cutoff2 (0.50)
        Cutoff2 <= value < Cutoff3 (0.75)
        Cutoff3 <= value < 1.0.
        The QtileX variables are all global.
    *)
    IF Result < Cutoff1 THEN
      QTile1 := QTile1 + 1
    ELSE IF Result < Cutoff2 THEN
      QTile2 := QTile2 + 1
    ELSE IF Result < Cutoff3 THEN
      QTile3 := QTile3 + 1
    ELSE
      QTile4 := QTile4 + 1;
  END; (* FOR Count := 1 TO MaxTrials *)
  WRITELN ( '  Ending RandomSamples');
END; (* RandomSamples *)

(* Display values of four global variables.
   Procedure also shows that you can use identifiers
   to specify output format.
*)
PROCEDURE DisplayResults;
CONST FWidth = 8;
      Precision = 4;
BEGIN
  WRITELN ( '  Starting DisplayResults');
  WRITELN ( '  Qtile1 = ', Qtile1 : FWidth : Precision);
  WRITELN ( '  Qtile2 = ', Qtile2 : FWidth : Precision);
  WRITELN ( '  Qtile3 = ', Qtile3 : FWidth : Precision);
  WRITELN ( '  Qtile4 = ', Qtile4 : FWidth : Precision);
  WRITELN ( '  Ending DisplayResults');
END; (* DisplayResults *)

(* Write a Beep Character *)
PROCEDURE BeepUser;
```

```
    CONST BeepChar = ^G; (* ASCII 7 *)
    BEGIN
      WRITELN ( '  Starting BeepUser');
      WRITE ( BeepChar);
      WRITELN ( '  Ending BeepUser');
    END;  (* BeepUser *)

BEGIN (* Main program *)
  WRITELN ( 'Starting Main program');
  Qtile1 := 0;
  Qtile2 := 0;
  Qtile3 := 0;
  Qtile4 := 0;
  RandomSamples;
  DisplayResults;
  BeepUser;
  WRITELN ( 'Ending Main program');
  READLN;
END.
```

This program generates 10,000 random values between 0.0 and 1.0. Depending on the value of each trial, a counter for one of four groups is incremented. After generating these values, a second procedure displays the results of the sampling. Finally, the program beeps and waits for the user to press ENTER.

The preceding program contains both global and local variables. The declarations and constant specifications in the main program (four **REAL**s and one **CONST**) represent the global variables. The declarations within each of the procedures represent local variables and constants.

What's the difference between local and global variables? For one thing, you can use global variables anywhere in the program. Thus, both **RandomSamples** and **DisplayResults** use the global **QtileX** variables. Local variables, on the other hand, can be used, and are recognized, only in the procedure in which they were declared. Essentially, a procedure creates a miniature environment for its declarations and definitions, and for the procedure body. Local variables are a part of this environment, and cannot exist outside of it.

For example, the constants **FWidth** and **Precision** are recognized only within **DisplayResults**. If you try to refer to these constants in the main program or in one of the other procedures, you'll get an "undeclared identifier" compiler error. This is because these constants don't exist when **DisplayResults** is not activated. Similarly, only **RandomSamples** can use **Result** in this program.

Chapter 6 describes how to define routines within other routines and contains more on local and global environments.

Parameters

So far, you've been calling procedures and passing arguments to these procedures. The arguments provide information that the procedures need to carry out their tasks. For example, a sorting procedure needs to know what values you want to sort, and may need to know how many values are to be sorted. You can pass this information to the procedure as arguments.

How do you define a procedure that takes an argument when called? Earlier you learned that a procedure heading might have a parameter list. This is where you would prepare the procedure's environment for the information that will be passed as arguments.

A *parameter* is a slot through which information can be passed. In Pascal, such a slot will be of a particular size—depending on the type of information being passed. Parameters can represent either one-way or two-way slots for information transfer. When you define a procedure, you have to provide slots for every argument that will be passed to the procedure in a call. For example, the procedure in the following program counts to a number specified in an argument. Look at the definition of **CountVals** to see how the parameter is handled.

```
P4-3     PROGRAM ProcExample;

         VAR NrTimes : INTEGER;

           PROCEDURE CountVals ( HowHigh : INTEGER);
           VAR Index : INTEGER;
           BEGIN
             FOR Index := 1 TO HowHigh DO
               WRITELN ( Index);
           END; (* CountVals *)

         BEGIN
           CountVals ( 30);
           NrTimes := 95;
           CountVals ( NrTimes);
           READLN;
         END.
```

Procedure **CountVals** takes one argument: the value to which the procedure should count. When you call **CountVals**, this value is specified within the parentheses after the procedure name. In the two calls to **CountVals**, the arguments are 30 and **NrTimes** (which evaluates to 95), respectively.

When defining the **CountVals** procedure, you need to indicate that this procedure will get an item of information when called. You do this by including a *formal parameter* declaration within the parentheses in the procedure heading. This parameter declaration specifies a name and a type for each slot through which information is being passed to or from the procedure.

Multiple Parameters

You can declare multiple parameters for a procedure. These parameters can be of the same or different types. The following listing contains several procedure headings to illustrate the various aspects of procedure declaration syntax:

```
PROCEDURE CountVals ( HowHigh : INTEGER);

PROCEDURE BubbleSort ( VAR Info : String80Array;
                           Size : INTEGER);

PROCEDURE GetString ( Message : STRING;
                    VAR Value : STRING);

PROCEDURE GetDate ( VAR Month, Date, Year : INTEGER);
```

The syntax for a single parameter list entry—which declares a parameter for use in the procedure—is as follows:

{"**VAR**"} < identifier > ":" < type specifier >

Note that the interface for **CountVals** in the previous listing illustrates this format. The identifier may be preceded by the reserved word **VAR**.

If you have multiple parameters of the same type, you can list them all as part of the same declaration. You need to separate the individual parameter names by commas, as in the interface for **GetDate** in the preceding listing. If you have multiple parameters of different types, the individual parameter declarations must be separated by a semicolon, as in the headings for **BubbleSort** and **GetString**. The parameters need not be listed on separate lines, although such a style makes them easier to read.

Formal Parameters and Arguments

When you specify formal parameters in a procedure heading, you're defining slots through which information will be passed for use by the procedure. When you *call* the procedure, you put information into these slots by specifying, or *passing*, arguments. Whereas formal parameters represent slots, arguments represent actual information. (In fact, arguments are often known as *actual parameters*.)

For each formal parameter you specify, you must pass an argument when you call the procedure. Thus, you must specify two arguments when calling **GetInteger**, whereas you only need to specify one when calling **CountVals**. You also need to pass the arguments in the correct order. Each formal parameter will have a type associated with it, and the formal parameters will be specified in some order. Each actual parameter must also have a type associated with it, and the type for each argument must match the type for the corresponding formal parameter. (Certain predefined routines are exceptions to these restrictions. For example, **WRITELN** can take a variable number of arguments, and these may be of different types each time the procedure is called.)

For example, the first five calls in the following listing are valid, but the next four are not:

```
                (* Valid Calls *)
(* Assume MyInt is an initialized INTEGER variable *)
(* Assume MyStr is an initialized STRING variable *)
CountVals ( MyInt);      (* can pass a variable as a parameter *)
CountVals ( 30);         (* can pass an integer value *)
CountVals ( 2 * 15);     (* can pass an integer expression *)

(* After each of the following calls,
   MyInt will have a new value.
*)
GetInteger ( MyStrVal, MyInt);  (* STRING variable is OK *)
GetInteger ( 'Value?', MyInt);  (* STRING constant is OK *)
```

```
                        (* Invalid Calls *)
CountVals ( MyInt, 30);          (* too many arguments *)
CountVals ( 20.3);               (* argument must be INTEGER *)
GetInteger ( MyInt);             (* first argument's missing *)
GetInteger ( MyInt, 'Value?');   (* arguments are in
                                    the wrong order *)
```

Declaring and Using Parameters

What happens when you declare a parameter for a procedure? Such a declaration is essentially an instruction to allocate storage whenever the procedure is called. The storage should be of the size required to represent a value of the type specified for the parameter. For example, when you declare **HowHigh** as a formal parameter of type **INTEGER** for **CountVals**, two bytes of temporary storage will be allocated whenever **CountVals** is called. This storage will be freed for reuse when the procedure has finished.

What happens when you pass an argument in a procedure call? When you call **CountVals** with an argument of 30, the program copies this value into the storage allocated temporarily for **HowHigh**. Similarly, when the program calls **CountVals** with **NrTimes** as the argument, the current value of **NrTimes** is copied to **HowHigh**—that is, to the storage allocated for **HowHigh**. Once this value is copied, nothing further is done with **NrTimes**. Its value does not change as a result of the procedure call.

When calling a procedure such as **CountVals** with an argument, only the argument's value is of interest; the source of that value is not. Because only values count, such parameters are said to be *passed by value.* Shortly, you'll learn an alternate way to pass parameters. Because the value of such an argument is copied to the procedure's local environment, you must be certain that your argument has a value—that is, that it has at least been initialized. Otherwise, the procedure is working with gibberish and will give you incorrect results.

You can pass information by value in various forms:

- As a constant value (for example, 30 or 'A string constant')

- As a variable (for example, **NrTimes** or **GreetingStr**)

- As an expression (for example, 3 + 5 or 7 < 5)

When you declare a parameter, temporary storage is allocated for it. In addition, the parameter's name is associated with the allocated storage. This name was specified within the procedure's environment (in particular, in the parameter list for the procedure) and is, therefore, a local name. Thus, when procedure **GetInteger** is executing, there will be areas of memory associated with the identifiers **Message** and **Value**. These names will *not* be recognized outside the procedure's environment.

Similarly, the storage allocated for an **INTEGER** in **CountVal**'s local environment is known as **HowHigh** while **CountVal** is executing. Once the procedure is finished, the name disappears, as does the storage. Like the storage, the name is local to the procedure: The main program does not know that the identifier **HowHigh** exists.

The calling environment does not know the local names for the parameters. It knows only the number and kinds of slots that will need to be passed information. For example, when **GetInteger** is called, whatever value is in the first slot will be referred to as **Message**, and whatever value is in the second slot will be referred to as **Value**. To the calling environment, the information in such slots has different names. For example, in the main program the first argument might be a string variable (such as **StrVariable**) or constant, and the second might be an **INTEGER** variable (such as **MyInt**).

Two-Way Parameters

You've been using parameters to pass information into your procedures. The procedure may need an item of information to do its work, but this information is not changed for the calling routine. However, sometimes you'll need to pass information back out from a procedure to the calling routine. For example, procedure **GetInteger** needs to provide an **INTEGER** value to the calling routine. In the case of **GetInteger**, this is accomplished by returning the desired value in the second parameter. **GetInteger**'s second parameter declaration begins with the reserved word **VAR**. This word indicates that the parameter (**Value**) will be used differently than the **Message** parameter.

A parameter whose declaration begins with **VAR** is intended for passing information back from a procedure to the calling routine. When the procedure finishes executing, the **VAR** parameter will have a particular value. The argument that was originally passed from the calling routine to the procedure will have this same new value. (As it turns out, this is because both identifiers—argument and formal parameter names—refer to the same memory location for a **VAR** parameter.)

The following example examines two-way parameter passing more closely. It contains two versions of the same procedure. Each version is supposed to swap the values in two variables.

P4-4
```
(* Program to illustrate two different uses of parameters *)

PROGRAM ParamTest;

VAR Val1, Val2 : INTEGER;

   (* Ostensibly swaps contents of First and Second;
      DOES NOT DO ITS TASK.
      Works with copies, so the changes disappear
      when the procedure finishes executing.
   *)
   PROCEDURE BadIntSwap ( First : INTEGER;
                          Second : INTEGER);
   VAR Temp : INTEGER;
   BEGIN
      Temp := First;
      First := Second;
      Second := Temp;
   END; (* BadIntSwap *)

   (* Correctly swaps contents of First and Second;
      Procedure works with storage allocated for arguments, so
      the changes are made to the variables passed as arguments.
      This means the changes endure once the procedure finishes.
   *)
   PROCEDURE GoodIntSwap ( VAR First : INTEGER;
                           VAR Second : INTEGER);
   VAR Temp : INTEGER;
   BEGIN
      Temp := First;
      First := Second;
      Second := Temp;
   END; (* GooodIntSwap *)

   PROCEDURE GetInteger ( Message : STRING;
                          VAR Value : INTEGER);
   BEGIN
      WRITE ( Message, ' ');
```

```
      READLN ( Value);
    END; (* GetInteger *)

BEGIN  (* Main program *)
  GetInteger ( 'Value 1?', Val1);
  GetInteger ( 'Value 2?', Val2);
  WRITELN ( 'Original Val1 = ', Val1:5, ';  Val2 = ', Val2:5);
  BadIntSwap ( Val1, Val2);
  WRITELN ( 'After BadIntSwap');
  (* The following line will be identical to first display *)
  WRITELN ( '         Val1 = ', Val1:5, ';  Val2 = ', Val2:5);
  GoodIntSwap ( Val1, Val2);
  WRITELN ( 'After GoodIntSwap');
  WRITELN ( '         Val1 = ', Val1:5, ';  Val2 = ', Val2:5);
  READLN;
END.
```

Run the program and compare the output from the two versions. This program produces the following output, for inputs of 12 and 13.

```
Original Val1 =    12;  Val2 =    13
After BadIntSwap
        Val1 =    12;  Val2 =    13
After GoodIntSwap
        Val1 =    13;  Val2 =    12
```

First, notice that nothing changed when **BadIntSwap** did its work; the two values were exchanged by **GoodIntSwap**, however. The interfaces for the two procedures indicate that the difference lies in the **VAR**s preceding the parameter names in **GoodIntSwap**.

There were no changes in the values of **Val1** and **Val2** after they were passed to **BadIntSwap**. When the arguments were passed to **BadIntSwap**, their values were copied to **First** and **Second**. Since only copies were involved in **BadIntSwap**, it should come as no surprise that the values were not exchanged in the main program.

In contrast, when **GoodIntSwap** finishes, the values of the two parameters—**Val1** and **Val2** in the main program—have been exchanged. Somehow, the procedure knew where the two arguments were located, and could make the exchanges. Essentially, procedure **GoodIntSwap** had access to variables **Val1** and **Val2**, even though these names are not mentioned in the body of the procedure. The procedure refers to the memory locations at which it does its work as **First** and **Second**.

These locations correspond to the locations of **Val1** and **Val2**. This means that changes to **First** and **Second** are also changes to **Val1** and **Val2**.

Based on the changes in their values after **GoodIntSwap** has finished, you might think that **Val1** and **Val2** were passed directly rather than in the form of copies. Such parameters are said to be *passed by reference*. Parameters that are passed by reference can be changed in the called procedure. Rather than allocating temporary storage for such parameters when the procedure is called, the compiler allocates enough storage to represent the location of the variables in the calling routine.

Because parameters that are passed by reference must be associated with a memory location (in which the changes will be made), you cannot pass specific values (such as 30) or expressions (such as 3 + 5) to such parameters. You can only pass variables by reference—so that a memory location known to the calling routine can be changed.

You'll learn more about local and global names and variables, and about parameter passing in Chapter 6. For now, another example will illustrate the difference between passing by value and by reference.

Examples of Parameter Passing

The following program calls three procedures that are identical except for their parameter lists. Each routine has two parameters but a different number of **VAR** parameters. For example, **AllValues** has no **VAR** parameters, so both arguments are passed by value. This means that copies of the arguments are passed to the procedure. None of the changes to these copies will affect the original arguments.

ValueVar has one parameter (the first) that is passed by value, and a second that is passed by reference. In this case, one of the parameters is associated with storage accessible through the calling routine. Changes made at this location will remain in effect even when **ValueVar** has finished executing. Finally, for **AllVars** both parameters are passed by reference. This means that both of the parameters will affect values in the calling routine.

P4-5

```
(* Program to illustrate passing by value and by reference.
   Program also shows that same identifiers can be used
   in multiple places in a program.
*)

PROGRAM ParamDemo;
VAR G1, G2 : INTEGER;

   (* Both arguments are passed by value, so no changes
      endure after procedure finishes.
   *)
   PROCEDURE AllValues ( X, Y: INTEGER);
   BEGIN
     WRITELN ( '    Entering AllValues   : X = ', X,
               ';  Y = ', Y);
     X := X * 2;
     Y := Y * 4;
     WRITELN ( '    Leaving AllValues    : X = ', X,
               ';  Y = ', Y);
   END;  (* AllValues .. 2 *)

   (* First argument is passed by value; second by reference.
      Only second parameter's value remains -- as the new
      value for the second argument when ValuVar was called.
   *)
   PROCEDURE ValueVar ( X : INTEGER; VAR Y: INTEGER);
   BEGIN
     WRITELN ( '    Entering ValueVar    : X = ', X,
               ';  Y = ', Y);
     X := X * 2;
     Y := Y * 4;
     WRITELN ( '    Leaving ValueVar     : X = ', X,
               ';  Y = ', Y);
   END;  (* ValueVar .. 2 *)

   (* Both arguments are passed by reference,
      so both arguments passed in the call to AllVars
      will have new values.
   *)
   PROCEDURE AllVars ( VAR X, Y: INTEGER);
   BEGIN
     WRITELN ( '    Entering AllVars     : X = ', X,
               ';  Y = ', Y);
     X := X * 2;
     Y := Y * 4;
     WRITELN ( '    Leaving AllVars      : X = ', X,
               ';  Y = ', Y);
   END;  (* AllVars .. 2 *)

BEGIN (* Main Program *)
  G1 := 10;    G2 := 20;
```

```
     WRITELN ( 'Calling AllValues        : G1 = ', G1,
             '; G2 = ', G2);
     AllValues ( G1, G2);
     WRITELN ( 'Returning from AllValues : G1 = ', G1,
             '; G2 = ', G2);
     WRITELN;

     WRITELN ( 'Calling ValueVar         : G1 = ', G1,
             '; G2 = ', G2);
     ValueVar ( G1, G2);
     WRITELN ( 'Returning from ValueVar  : G1 = ', G1,
             '; G2 = ', G2);
     WRITELN;

     WRITELN ( 'Calling AllVars          : G1 = ', G1,
             '; G2 = ', G2);
     AllVars ( G1, G2);
     WRITELN ( 'Returning from AllVars   : G1 = ', G1,
             '; G2 = ', G2);
     READLN;
   END.
```

The following listing shows the output from this program. **X** and **Y** are the local names for **G1** and **G2**, respectively. Compare the values while in each routine with the values in the main program when the routine has finished executing.

```
Calling AllValues        : G1 = 10; G2 = 20
    Entering AllValues   :  X = 10;  Y = 20
    Leaving AllValues    :  X = 20;  Y = 80
Returning from AllValues : G1 = 10; G2 = 20

Calling ValueVar         : G1 = 10; G2 = 20
    Entering ValueVar    :  X = 10;  Y = 20
    Leaving ValueVar     :  X = 20;  Y = 80
Returning from ValueVar  : G1 = 10; G2 = 80

Calling AllVars          : G1 = 10; G2 = 80
    Entering AllVars     :  X = 10;  Y = 80
    Leaving AllVars      :  X = 20;  Y = 320
Returning from AllVars   : G1 = 20; G2 = 320
```

Functions

Procedures are designed to do something for you. In contrast, functions are designed to *find* or *compute* something for you. Procedures may or may not report on what they do, or return a particular result. Functions, on the other hand, always return a result.

You may recall from algebra that a function is something that can be evaluated for particular starting values, or arguments. In simple cases, such an evaluation returns a single value. For example, the function

$$y = x^2$$

returns a value for any value of x — namely, the square of x. Thus,

$$2.25 = 1.5^2$$

This result is said to be the value of the function at the starting value (1.5, in this case).

Similarly, suppose you have a function (**SQRT**) that computes the square root of values that you pass the function. When you call **SQRT** with an argument, the function will return a single value — the square root of the argument you passed. For example,

```
SQRT ( 81.0)
```

yields 9.0 as the value of the function for a starting value of 81.0. Similarly,

```
SQRT ( 6.25)
```

yields 2.5 as the value.

In Pascal, a *function* is a routine that always returns a specific value. Functions have the same components as procedures: a heading (or interface), a declaration section, and a body. The syntax for defining and for calling functions is different from the syntax for procedures, especially the syntax for the interface. Fortunately, the rules and principles involving parameters are the same for both types of routines.

Defining Functions in Turbo Pascal

The following function definitions illustrate the syntax for functions. This listing is included on your disk, but it is not a program.

```
P4-6    (* Return the larger of One, Two *)
        FUNCTION Max ( One, Two : REAL) : REAL;
        BEGIN
          IF One > Two THEN
            Max := One
          ELSE
            Max := Two;
        END; (* FUNCTION Max : REAL *)

        (* Return the smaller of One, Two *)
        FUNCTION Min ( One, Two : REAL) : REAL;
        BEGIN
          IF One > Two THEN
            Min := Two
          ELSE
            Min := One;
        END; (* FUNCTION Min : REAL *)
```

The interface for a function is similar to a procedure heading, but differs in some important ways:

■ The heading begins with the reserved word **FUNCTION** rather than **PROCEDURE**.

■ Following the name and the (optional) parameter list, the function heading ends with a return type—for example, **REAL**.

In Turbo Pascal, a function can return any simple type, as well as strings and some types not discussed yet. A function's return type is specified after a colon (:) in the heading.

A function body also differs from a procedure body in one important way. Recall that a function returns its value. The function must get its value through an assignment statement somewhere in the function body. Such an assignment sets the function equal to the value of some variable, value, or expression of the appropriate type. The function name can be on the left side of an assignment statement only within the function's body. For example, in **Max**, the function would be finished and would return to the calling routine after either of the two assignment statements executed.

REMEMBER A function heading must begin with the reserved word **FUNCTION** and must end with a return type, specified following a colon. The function body must contain a statement in which a value of the return type is assigned to the function.

Calling a Function

As you've seen, to call a procedure, you just specify its name and the appropriate argument list. Function calls work a bit differently. Keep in mind that a function is simply a way of generating a specific value — namely, the value of the function. In fact, Pascal treats a function call as a value. For this reason, a function call can appear anywhere a value of its return type can appear. The following program illustrates several places where you might have a function call:

P4-7
```
(* Program to illustrate function definitions and calls *)

PROGRAM FnCalls;

VAR Smaller, Larger, Val1, Val2 : REAL;

  (* Return the larger of One, Two *)
  FUNCTION Max ( One, Two : REAL) : REAL;
  BEGIN
    IF One > Two THEN
      Max := One
    ELSE
      Max := Two;
  END; (* FUNCTION Max : REAL *)

  (* Return the smaller of One, Two *)
  FUNCTION Min ( One, Two : REAL) : REAL;
  BEGIN
    IF One > Two THEN
      Min := Two
    ELSE
      Min := One;
  END; (* FUNCTION Min : REAL *)
```

```
     PROCEDURE GetReal ( Message : STRING;
                         VAR Value : REAL);
     BEGIN
       WRITE ( Message, ' ');
       READLN ( Value);
     END; (* GetReal *)

BEGIN (* Main program *)
  GetReal ( 'Value 1?', Val1);
  GetReal ( 'Value 2?', Val2);
  (* right side of an assignment statement can have a REAL;
     therefore, a function call is allowed.
  *)
  Smaller := Min ( Val1, Val2);
  Larger := Max ( Val1, Val2);
  WRITELN ( 'Val1 = ', Val1 : 10 : 3,
            '; Val2 = ', Val2 : 10 : 3);
  WRITELN ( 'Smaller = ', Smaller : 10 : 3,
            '; Larger  = ', Larger : 10 : 3);
  (* You can write REAL values, so Min and Max can be
     arguments to another routine.
  *)
  WRITELN ( 'Min      = ', Min ( Val1, Val2) : 10 : 3,
            '; Max      = ', Max ( Val1, Val2) : 10 : 3);
  (* You can even put function calls into expressions
     in arguments.
  *)
  WRITELN ( 'Sum      = ',
            Min ( Val1, Val2)  + Max ( Val1, Val2) : 10 : 3);
  READLN;
END.
```

Function calls are either on the right side of an assignment statement or arguments to other procedures or functions. When the program is executing and a function call is reached:

■ The calling routine is suspended temporarily and control is switched to the function, which begins executing.

■ The function executes in sequence, beginning at the top of the function body, and continues through the body until an appropriate value can be computed and assigned to the function.

■ After the function has been assigned a value, this value is returned to the calling routine, which resumes execution with the new value at the appropriate point in the program.

Because a function is simply a value, a function call can never appear as a statement by itself. That is, a function call cannot have the same format as a procedure call. For example, consider that the following two statements would be equivalent if such a function call were allowed:

```
Min ( 39.0, 45.5);    (* a fancy way of saying 39 *)

39.0;                 (* a value is not a statement *)
```

Since a value by itself is not a statement, a function call (which is equivalent to a value) can't be a statement.

Parameters to Functions

Parameter passing works the same way for functions as it does for procedures. That is, you can pass by value or by reference. Because a function generally returns its main result directly, you'll have less need to change arguments. As a result, you're more likely to pass arguments by value to functions.

Predefined Procedures and Functions

Pascal includes about a dozen predefined routines that you can use in your programs; Turbo Pascal adds several dozen more routines to this collection. The rest of this chapter contains brief descriptions of some of the simpler predefined routines. These routines will enable you to achieve a variety of results in programs until you've learned about control constructs and more advanced data types. Appendix B, "Turbo Pascal Procedures and Functions," contains a more complete list of predefined routines.

Predefined Routines in Standard Pascal

This section contains descriptions of the routines that are predefined in standard Pascal. These routines are also available in Turbo Pascal. Even when a routine has been predefined in both standard Pascal and in Turbo Pascal, there may still be differences in what the routine can do. For example, many of the predefined routines can take any whole number argument. In Turbo Pascal, this means that you can pass any of five different types (**BYTE, SHORTINT, INTEGER, WORD,** or **LONG-INT**). In standard Pascal, such arguments can only be **INTEGER**s, since none of the other whole number types is predefined.

FUNCTION ABS (IntVal : **SHORTINT**) : **SHORTINT**;
FUNCTION ABS (IntVal : **INTEGER**) : **INTEGER**;
FUNCTION ABS (IntVal : **LONGINT**) : **LONGINT**;
FUNCTION ABS (RVal : **REAL**) : **REAL**;

This routine returns the *absolute value* of its argument, which must be a signed whole number type or a **REAL**. The return type is the same type as the argument. Essentially, the absolute value of a number is its positive form. For example, the following two statements produce the same result:

```
Result1 := ABS ( -39.0);   (* returns 39.0 *)
Result2 := ABS ( 39.0);    (* returns 39.0 *)
```

The following program illustrates the **ABS** function:

P4-8

```
(* Program to illustrate use of ABS function *)

PROGRAM AbsDemo;

VAR RVal, Result : REAL;

  PROCEDURE GetReal ( Message : STRING;
                          VAR Value : REAL);
  BEGIN
    WRITE ( Message, ' ');
    READLN ( Value);
  END; (* GetReal *)
```

```
BEGIN  (* Main Program *)
  REPEAT
    GetReal ( 'Value (> 500 to stop)? ', RVal);
    Result := ABS ( RVal);
    WRITELN ( 'ABS ( ', RVal : 8:3, ') = ', Result : 8 : 3);
  UNTIL RVal > 500.0;
  READLN;
END.
```

FUNCTION ARCTAN (Value : **REAL**) : **REAL**;

This routine returns a trigonometric value—namely, the angle that corresponds to a particular *tangent* value. Both the argument and the return type are **REAL**s. The following program illustrates the **ARCTAN** function:

P4-9

```
(* Program to illustrate use of ARCTAN function *)

PROGRAM ArctanDemo;

VAR RVal, Result : REAL;

  PROCEDURE GetReal ( Message : STRING;
                        VAR Value : REAL);
  BEGIN
    WRITE ( Message, ' ');
    READLN ( Value);
  END; (* GetReal *)

BEGIN  (* Main Program *)
  REPEAT
    GetReal ( 'Value (> 10.0 to stop)? ', RVal);
    Result := ArcTan ( RVal);
    WRITELN ( 'ArcTan ( ', RVal : 8:3, ') = ', Result : 8 : 3);
  UNTIL RVal > 10.0;
  READLN;
END.
```

FUNCTION CHR (OrdValue : **BYTE**) : **CHAR;**

This routine returns the character with the specified ordinal value. The ordinal value represents an ASCII code in Turbo Pascal. For example, the following program writes several things on the same line:

P4-10

```
(* Program to illustrate use of CHR function *)

PROGRAM CHRDemo;

CONST CarriageReturn = 13;
      BackSpace = 8;
VAR Result : INTEGER;

BEGIN
  Result := 100;
  WRITE ( Result : 30);
  (* send a backspace, to move back one column,
     then write a new digit at the end of the number
     -- which is where the cursor is after the Backspace.
  *)
  WRITE ( CHR ( BackSpace), 1);
  (* send a carriage return but no linefeed,
     so cursor moves to start of same line.
  *)
  WRITE ( CHR ( CarriageReturn));
  WRITE ( Result : 20);
  WRITE ( CHR ( BackSpace), 2);
  WRITE ( CHR ( CarriageReturn));
  WRITE ( Result : 10);
  WRITE ( CHR ( BackSpace), 3);
  WRITE ( CHR ( CarriageReturn));
  READLN;
END.
```

The preceding program:

■ Writes **100** using a large field width but without moving the cursor to the next line. The field width is smaller each time this action is carried out.

■ Writes a backspace character (ASCII 8), which moves the cursor back over the last digit in the **100**.

■ Writes a new digit to replace the last digit. This digit changes each time the action is carried out.

■ Writes a carriage return character (ASCII 13), which moves the cursor to the leftmost column of the current line. (You would need a linefeed to also move to the next line.)

The middle two actions are performed with a single call to **WRITE**. This sequence of actions is repeated three times. Each time, the value (100) is written in a smaller field width, and each time the last digit in the number is replaced by a different digit.

ORD is a related function.

FUNCTION COS (Angle : **REAL**) : **REAL**;

This routine returns the cosine of the angle specified in the (**REAL**) argument. This will be a **REAL** value from −1.0 to 1.0. The angle is specified in radians rather than degrees. Radian measures express angles as fractions or multiples of π ($\approx$ 3.14159265). For example, 180 degrees is equivalent to π radians; 1 radian is about 57 degrees.

The following program lets you explore the **COS** function. Run it to see how this trigonometric function behaves.

```
P4-11   (* Program to illustrate use of COS function *)

        PROGRAM CosDemo;

        VAR Cosine, Angle : REAL;

          PROCEDURE GetReal ( Message : STRING;
                                VAR Value : REAL);
          BEGIN
            WRITE ( Message, ' ');
            READLN ( Value);
          END; (* GetReal *)
```

```
BEGIN
  REPEAT
    GetReal ( 'Angle (in radians; > 100.0 to stop)?', Angle);
    Cosine := COS ( Angle);
    WRITELN ( 'Cosine of ', Angle : 6 : 4,
              ' radians = ', Cosine : 6 : 4);
  UNTIL Angle > 100.0;
  READLN;
END.
```

SIN and **PI** are other trigonometric functions.

FUNCTION EXP (ValToRaise : **REAL**) : **REAL**;

This routine returns the result of raising e ($\approx$ 2.7181828) to the specified power. For example, the following program computes **EXP (Val)** for values that the user enters:

P4-12
```
(* Program to illustrate use of EXP function *)

PROGRAM ExpDemo;

VAR Val, Result : REAL;

  PROCEDURE GetReal ( Message : STRING;
                      VAR Value : REAL);
  BEGIN
    WRITE ( Message, ' ');
    READLN ( Value);
  END; (* GetReal *)

BEGIN
  REPEAT
    GetReal ( 'Value? (> 10 to stop) ', Val);
    Result := EXP ( Val);
    WRITELN ( 'EXP (', Val : 10 : 3, ') = ', Result : 10 : 3);
  UNTIL Val > 10.0;
  READLN;
END.
```

FUNCTION LN (Val : REAL) : REAL;

This routine returns the *natural logarithm* (logarithm to base e) of **Val**, which must be greater than 0.0. The natural logarithm of a value is the power to which e must be raised in order to get the number. For example, $e^2 \approx 7.389056$. This means that **LN** (7.389056) is 2, since e must be raised to this power to yield 7.389056.

The following program extends the program for **EXP** to include the **LN** function. The results indicate that **EXP** and **LN** are inverse functions.

P4-13

```
(* Program to illustrate use of EXP and LN functions *)

PROGRAM ExpAndLnDemo;

VAR Val, Result, LResult : REAL;

   PROCEDURE GetReal ( Message : STRING;
                       VAR Value : REAL);
   BEGIN
     WRITE ( Message, ' ');
     READLN ( Value);
   END; (* GetReal *)

BEGIN
  REPEAT
    GetReal ( 'Value? (< 0 to quit)', Val);
    Result := Exp ( Val);
    WRITELN ( 'EXP (', Val : 10 : 3, ') = ', Result : 10 : 3);
    LResult := LN ( Result);
    WRITELN ( 'LN  (', Result : 10 : 3, ') = ', LResult:10:3);
  UNTIL Val < 0.0;
  READLN;
END.
```

FUNCTION ODD (Val : LONGINT) : BOOLEAN;

This routine returns **TRUE** if **Val** is an odd number (leaves a remainder of 1 when divided by 2) and **FALSE** otherwise. The argument is a whole number type.

The following program illustrates how to use **ODD**. The program generates random **INTEGER** values. If the value is odd, the program writes a period; if the value is even, the program writes a space.

Run the program several times. Try setting different large values (for example, values over 5000) for the maximum value to generate (**MaxVal**). The proportion of odd values is generally close to 50 percent. That is, about half of the random **INTEGER** values generated will be odd and the other half will be even.

Then run the program using different small values (for example, less than 20). Try some cases in which **MaxVal** is odd, and others in which **MaxVal** is even. Notice that the proportion of odd values fluctuates much more when you have a smaller range of values.

P4-14

```
(* Program to illustrate use of ODD function *)

PROGRAM OddDemo;

CONST MaxTrials = 1840;
VAR Count, OddCount, MaxVal, Result : INTEGER;

   PROCEDURE GetInteger ( Message : STRING;
                                VAR Value : INTEGER);
   BEGIN
     WRITE ( Message, ' ');
     READLN ( Value);
   END; (* GetInteger *)

BEGIN
  OddCount := 0;
  RANDOMIZE;
  GetInteger ( 'Largest value to generate? (< 0 for MAXINT)',
            MaxVal);
  IF MaxVal < 0 THEN
    MaxVal := MAXINT;
  FOR Count := 1 TO MaxTrials DO
  BEGIN
    Result := RANDOM ( MaxVal);
    (* Note that function can be used
       wherever a BOOLEAN is valid.
    *)
    IF ODD ( Result) THEN
    BEGIN
      WRITE ( '.');
      (* Increment the odd value counter by 1 *)
```

```
      INC ( OddCount);
    END
    ELSE
      WRITE ( ' ');
  END;
  (* determine and display the proportion of odd values *)
  WRITE ( OddCount, ' odd values out of ', MaxTrials);
  WRITELN ( '; (', (OddCount / MaxTrials) * 100 :5:2, '%)');
  READLN;
END.
```

FUNCTION ORD (Val : **BYTE**) : **LONGINT**;
FUNCTION ORD (Val : **SHORTINT**) : **LONGINT**;
FUNCTION ORD (Val : **INTEGER**) : **LONGINT**;
FUNCTION ORD (Val : **WORD**) : **LONGINT**;
FUNCTION ORD (Val : **LONGINT**) : **LONGINT**;
FUNCTION ORD (Val : **CHAR**) : **LONGINT**;
FUNCTION ORD (Val : **BOOLEAN**) : **LONGINT**;

This routine returns the ordinal value of the argument, which can be of any ordinal type, that is, a whole number type, or a **CHAR**, **BOOLEAN**, or enumerated type. For **CHAR**s, this value is the ASCII code. For whole number types, the result is simply the value. For **BOOLEAN**s, the result is 0 for **FALSE** or 1 for **TRUE**. For enumerated types, the result is one less than the value's position in the list of values. That is, for enumerated types, the first element has value 0, the second has value 1, and so forth.

The following program illustrates the use of the **ORD** function:

P4-15

```
(* Program to illustrate use of ORD function *)

PROGRAM OrdTest;

TYPE MyType = ( vala, valb, valc);
VAR I1 : INTEGER;
    C1 : CHAR;
    B1 : BOOLEAN;
    M1 : MyType;

BEGIN
```

```
  I1 := -1;
  C1 := 'a';
  B1 := FALSE;
  (* for enumerated types, first element has ordinal value 0,
     second element has ordinal value 1, etc.
  *)
  M1 := valc;
  WRITELN ( 'ORD ( I1) = ', ORD ( I1));  (* returns -1 *)
  WRITELN ( 'ORD ( C1) = ', ORD ( C1));  (* returns 97 *)
  WRITELN ( 'ORD ( B1) = ', ORD ( B1));  (* returns 0 *)
  WRITELN ( 'ORD ( M1) = ', ORD ( M1));  (* returns 2 *)
  READLN;
END.
```

CHR is a related function.

FUNCTION PRED (Val : **BYTE**) : **BYTE**;
FUNCTION PRED (Val : **SHORTINT**) : **SHORTINT**;
FUNCTION PRED (Val : **INTEGER**) : **INTEGER**;
FUNCTION PRED (Val : **WORD**) : **WORD**;
FUNCTION PRED (Val : **LONGINT**) : **LONGINT**;
FUNCTION PRED (Val : **CHAR**) : **CHAR**;
FUNCTION PRED (Val : **BOOLEAN**) : **BOOLEAN**;

This routine returns the value preceding the one passed as an argument. The argument can be of any ordinal type. The result is undefined if you ask for the predecessor of the minimum value for the argument type.

The following program illustrates the use of the predecessor function:

P4-16
```
(* Program to illustrate use of PRED function *)

PROGRAM PredDemo;

TYPE MyType = ( vala, valb, valc);
VAR I1 : INTEGER;
    C1 : CHAR;
    B1 : BOOLEAN;
    M1 : MyType;
```

```
BEGIN
  I1 := -32768;
  C1 := 'q';
  B1 := FALSE;
  (* for user defined types, first element has ordinal value 0,
     second element has ordinal value 1, etc.
  *)
  M1 := valc;
  WRITELN ( 'PRED ( I1) = ', PRED ( I1));
  WRITELN ( 'PRED ( C1) = ', PRED ( C1));
  WRITELN ( 'PRED ( B1) = ', PRED ( B1));
  (* You can't write the value of an enumerated type;
     one way to determine whether the PRED did anything
     is to write the new ordinal value.
     Since ORD ( valc) = 2, the new value should be 1.
  *)
  WRITELN ( 'PRED ( M1) = ', ORD ( PRED ( M1)));
  READLN;
END.
```

SUCC is a related function.

> ## PROCEDURE READ;
> ## PROCEDURE READLN;

READ and **READLN** are the procedures for doing input from files or from the standard input (keyboard). You've already learned about these two routines in Chapter 3, "Turbo Pascal's Simple Data Types."

> ## FUNCTION ROUND (Val : REAL) : LONGINT;

This routine converts a **REAL** to a **LONGINT** by rounding the number's fractional part. The function rounds downward if the fractional part is less than 0.5, and rounds upward otherwise. In Turbo Pascal, the result is a **LONGINT**; in standard Pascal, the result is an **INTEGER**. For example, the first statement in the following listing assigns the value 39 to **Result**; the second assigns the value 40:

```
Result := ROUND ( 39.46);   (* assigns 39 *)

Result := ROUND ( 39.86);   (* assigns 40 *)
```

This function lets you get a value of one type (**LONGINT**) from a value of a different type (**REAL**).

You can use the following program to experiment with the **ROUND** function. Try entering several positive and negative values. What happens to a value such as 3.5? With that information, try to predict what will happen to −3.5.

P4-17
```
(* Program to illustrate use of ROUND function *)

PROGRAM RoundDemo;

VAR RVal, Result : REAL;

   PROCEDURE GetReal ( Message : STRING;
                       VAR Value : REAL);
   BEGIN
     WRITE ( Message, ' ');
     READLN ( Value);
   END; (* GetReal *)

BEGIN  (* Main Program *)
   REPEAT
     GetReal ( 'Value (> 500 to stop)? ', RVal);
     Result := ROUND ( RVal);
     WRITELN ( 'ROUND ( ', RVal : 8:3, ') = ', Result : 8 : 3);
   UNTIL RVal > 500.0;
   READLN;
END.
```

FUNCTION SIN (Radians : REAL) : REAL;

This routine returns the sine of the angle specified in the (**REAL**) argument. This will be a **REAL** value from −1.0 and 1.0. The angle is specified using radians rather than degrees. Radian measures express angles as fractions or multiples of π (≈ 3.14159265). For example, 180 degrees is equivalent to π radians; 1 radian is about 57 degrees.

The following program illustrates the **SIN** function. Run the program for various radian values between 0 and 2π (≈ 6.2831853). Can you determine the behavior of the sine function within this range of values? See the discussion of the **SQR** function for another program involving **SIN**.

P4-18
```
(* Program to illustrate use of SIN function *)

PROGRAM SinDemo;

VAR Sine, Angle : REAL;

    PROCEDURE GetReal ( Message : STRING;
                            VAR Value : REAL);
    BEGIN
      WRITE ( Message, ' ');
      READLN ( Value);
    END; (* GetReal *)

BEGIN
  REPEAT
    GetReal ( 'Angle (in radians; > 100 to stop)?', Angle);
    Sine := SIN ( Angle);
    WRITELN ( 'Sine of ', Angle : 6 : 4,
             ' radians = ', Sine : 6 : 4);
  UNTIL Angle > 100;
  READLN;
END.
```

COS and **PI** are other trigonometric functions.

FUNCTION SQR (Val : SHORTINT) : SHORTINT;
FUNCTION SQR (Val : INTEGER) : INTEGER;
FUNCTION SQR (Val : LONGINT) : LONGINT;
FUNCTION SQR (Val : REAL) : REAL;

This routine returns the square of the argument—that is **Val** * **Val**. The returned value is of the same type as the argument, which must be a whole number type or a **REAL**. Thus, if you pass in an **INTEGER** argument, the returned value will also be an **INTEGER**. With a function such as **SQR**, you'll need to be careful of overflow when using whole numbers.

The following program demonstrates the **SQR** function. The program uses **LONGINT** values. What's the largest value that you can enter without overflow?

P4-19
```
(* Program to illustrate use of SQR function *)

PROGRAM SqrDemo;

VAR LVal, Result : LONGINT;

  PROCEDURE GetLongInt ( Message : STRING;
                            VAR Value : LONGINT);
  BEGIN
    WRITE ( Message, ' ');
    READLN ( Value);
  END; (* GetLongInt *)

BEGIN  (* Main Program *)
  REPEAT
    GetLongInt ( 'Value (< -500 to stop)? ', LVal);
    Result := SQR ( LVal);
    WRITELN ( 'SQR ( ', LVal:10, ') = ', Result : 15);
  UNTIL LVal < -500.0;
  READLN;
END.
```

The following program uses the **SQR** function to illustrate a relationship between the sine and cosine values for a particular value:

P4-20
```
(* Program to illustrate use of SQR function,
   and a relationship between the SIN and COS functions.
*)

PROGRAM SqrAndTrigDemo;

VAR Sine, Cosine, Angle : REAL;

  PROCEDURE GetReal ( Message : STRING;
                         VAR Value : REAL);
  BEGIN
    WRITE ( Message, ' ');
    READLN ( Value);
```

```
    END; (* GetReal *)

BEGIN
  WRITELN ( '  SIN(x)  ', '  COS(X)  ',
              'SQR(Sine) + SQR(Cosine)');
  WRITELN;
  REPEAT
    GetReal ( 'Angle (> 100 to stop)?', Angle);
    Sine := SIN ( Angle);
    Cosine := COS ( Angle);
    WRITELN ( Sine : 10 : 4, Cosine : 10 : 4,
              SQR ( Sine) + SQR ( Cosine) : 17 : 4);
  UNTIL Angle > 100;
  READLN;
END.
```

FUNCTION SQRT (Val : SHORTINT) : REAL;
FUNCTION SQRT (Val : INTEGER) : REAL;
FUNCTION SQRT (Val : LONGINT) : REAL;
FUNCTION SQRT (Val : REAL) : REAL;

This routine returns the square root of the argument, which must be a nonnegative value. The argument can be any whole number type or a **REAL**. The returned value is always a **REAL**.

The following program lets you see the **SQRT** function in action:

P4-21
```
(* Program to illustrate use of SQRT function *)

PROGRAM SqrtDemo;

VAR RVal, Result : REAL;

  PROCEDURE GetReal ( Message : STRING;
                      VAR Value : REAL);
  BEGIN
    WRITE ( Message, ' ');
    READLN ( Value);
  END; (* GetReal *)

BEGIN  (* Main Program *)
  GetReal ( 'Value (< 0 to stop)? ', RVal);
  WHILE RVal > 0 DO
```

```
   BEGIN
     Result := SQRT ( RVal);
     WRITELN ( 'SQRT ( ', RVal : 8:3, ') = ', Result : 8 : 3);
     GetReal ( 'Value (< 0 to stop)? ', RVal);
   END; (* WHILE RVal > 0 *)
END.
```

```
FUNCTION SUCC ( Val : BYTE) : BYTE;
FUNCTION SUCC ( Val : SHORTINT) : SHORTINT;
FUNCTION SUCC ( Val : INTEGER) : INTEGER;
FUNCTION SUCC ( Val : WORD) : WORD;
FUNCTION SUCC ( Val : LONGINT) : LONGINT;
FUNCTION SUCC ( Val : CHAR) : CHAR;
FUNCTION SUCC ( Val : BOOLEAN) : BOOLEAN;
```

This routine returns the value following the one passed as an argument. The argument can be of any ordinal type. The result is undefined if you ask for the successor of the maximum value.

The following program illustrates the successor function:

P4-22

```
(* Program to illustrate use of SUCC function *)

PROGRAM SuccDemo;

TYPE MyType = ( vala, valb, valc);
VAR I1 : INTEGER;
    C1 : CHAR;
    B1 : BOOLEAN;
    M1 : MyType;

BEGIN
  I1 := 32767;
  C1 := 'q';
  B1 := TRUE;
  (* for user defined types, first element has ordinal value 0,
     second element has ordinal value 1, etc.
  *)
  M1 := valc;
  WRITELN ( 'SUCC ( I1) = ', SUCC ( I1));
```

```
    WRITELN ( 'SUCC ( C1) = ', SUCC ( C1));
    WRITELN ( 'SUCC ( B1) = ', SUCC ( B1));
    (* You can't write the value of an enumerated type;
       one way to determine whether the SUCC did anything
       is to write the new ordinal value.
       Since ORD ( valc) = 2, the new value should be 3,
       although there is no enumerated value with this
       ordinal value.
    *)
    WRITELN ( 'SUCC ( M1) = ', ORD ( SUCC ( M1)));
    READLN;
END.
```

PRED is a related function.

FUNCTION TRUNC (Val : REAL) : LONGINT;

This routine converts a **REAL** to a **LONGINT** by dropping the number's fractional part. The result is a **LONGINT** in Turbo Pascal and an **INTEGER** in standard Pascal. This function always rounds downward. Thus, both of the assignments in the following listing assign 39 to **Result**:

```
Result := TRUNC ( 39.46);   (* assigns 39 *)

Result := TRUNC ( 39.86);   (* assigns 39 *)
```

Like **ROUND**, the **TRUNC** function enables you to convert a value from **REAL** to a whole number type. The following program lets you compare the behavior of **TRUNC** and **ROUND**. How do these two functions differ for values such as 3.5? 3.8? −3.8?

P4-23
```
(* Program to illustrate use of TRUNC function *)

PROGRAM TruncDemo;

VAR RVal, Result : REAL;

   PROCEDURE GetReal ( Message : STRING;
                       VAR Value : REAL);
   BEGIN
```

```
      WRITE ( Message, ' ');
      READLN ( Value);
   END; (* GetReal *)

BEGIN   (* Main Program *)
  REPEAT
    GetReal ( 'Value (> 500 to stop)? ', RVal);
    Result := TRUNC ( RVal);
    WRITELN ( 'TRUNC ( ', RVal : 8:3, ') = ', Result : 8 : 3);
    Result := ROUND ( RVal);
    WRITELN ( 'ROUND ( ', RVal : 8:3, ') = ', Result : 8 : 3);
  UNTIL RVal > 500.0;
  READLN;
END.
```

PROCEDURE WRITE;
PROCEDURE WRITELN;

These are the routines for writing material to the screen or to a file. You've already learned about them in Chapter 2, "Pascal: An Overview."

Routines Predefined in Turbo Pascal

The remaining routines in this chapter are predefined in Turbo Pascal but not in standard Pascal. Many of them involve strings.

FUNCTION CONCAT (Str1, StrX : **STRING**) : **STRING**;

This routine creates a larger string by combining individual string arguments. The larger string is returned. When concatenating two strings (say **Str1** and **Str2**), the result is a longer string that contains both strings, with **Str1** first. This function can take two or more string arguments.

The following program illustrates the **CONCAT** function:

```
P4-24   (* Program to illustrate use of CONCAT function *)

        PROGRAM ConcatDemo;

        VAR Str1, Str2, Str3, Str4, LargeStr : STRING;
            Result : INTEGER;

          PROCEDURE GetString ( Message : STRING;
                                VAR Value : STRING);
          BEGIN
            WRITE ( Message, ' ');
            READLN ( Value);
          END; (* GetString *)

        BEGIN
          RANDOMIZE;
          Result := RANDOM ( MAXINT);
          GetString ( 'Str1?', Str1);
          GetString ( 'Str2?', Str2);
          GetString ( 'Str3?', Str3);
          GetString ( 'Str4?', Str4);
          IF ODD ( Result) THEN
          BEGIN
            WRITELN ( 'Concatenating Str1 through Str4');
            LargeStr:= CONCAT ( Str1, Str2, Str3, Str4);
          END
          ELSE
          BEGIN
            WRITELN ( 'Concatenating Str4 through Str1');
            LargeStr := CONCAT ( Str4, Str3, Str2, Str1);
          END;
          WRITELN ( LargeStr);
          READLN;
        END.
```

The program gets strings from the user, and, after reading the strings, it gets a random value. If this value is odd, the program concatenates the strings in order; if the value is even, the program concatenates them in reverse order. In the latter case, the resulting string consists of **Str4**, **Str3**, **Str2**, and **Str1**, in that order.

FUNCTION COPY (AStr : **STRING**;

Start, NrChars : **INTEGER**) : **STRING**;

This routine returns a substring copied from **Str**. The copied substring begins with character **Start** of **Str**. At most, **NrChars** characters are copied from **Str**. For example, the following call copies the first seven characters of **Str** to **ResultStr**:

```
ResultStr := COPY ( Str, 1, 7);
```

If the end of **Str** is reached before enough characters have been copied, **COPY** returns a shorter substring. If **Start** is larger than the length of **Str**, the function returns an empty string.

Run the following program to copy various substrings from strings that you specify. Try to copy more characters than you have in your string. For example, if **SVal** is ten characters, tell the program that you want to copy 12 characters. Similarly, try to start copying from a point beyond the end of the string. For example, if **SVal** is ten characters, try to copy from position 11. To end this program, you have to press ENTER twice. The first keypress stops the **WHILE** loop; the second one puts you back in the Turbo Pascal editor.

P4-25
```
(* Program to illustrate use of COPY function *)

PROGRAM CopyDemo;

CONST EmptyString = '';
VAR SVal, Result : STRING;
    StartIndex, NrCh : INTEGER;

  PROCEDURE GetInteger ( Message : STRING;
                         VAR Value : INTEGER);
  BEGIN
    WRITE ( Message, ' ');
    READLN ( Value);
  END; (* GetInteger *)

  PROCEDURE GetString ( Message : STRING;
                        VAR Value : STRING);
```

```
      BEGIN
        WRITE ( Message, ' ');
        READLN ( Value);
      END; (* GetString *)

BEGIN  (* Main Program *)
  GetString ( 'String (ENTER to stop)? ', SVal);
  WHILE SVal <> EmptyString DO
  BEGIN
    GetInteger ( 'Starting position? ', StartIndex);
    GetInteger ( '# chars to copy? ', NrCh);
    Result := COPY ( SVal, StartIndex, NrCh);
    WRITELN ( 'Substring ', StartIndex : 2, ' .. ',
            NrCh : 2, ' = ', Result);
    GetString ( 'String (ENTER to stop)? ', SVal);
  END;  (* WHILE SVal <> EmptyString *)
END.
```

PROCEDURE DEC (**VAR** ValToDec : **INTEGER**{;
Amount : **LONGINT**});

This routine decrements the first argument by the amount specified in the optional second argument. If there is no second argument, the procedure decrements **ValToDec** by 1. The first argument must be an ordinal type.

The following program illustrates the **DEC** procedure:

P4-26   `(* Program to illustrate use of DEC procedure *)`

```
PROGRAM DecDemo;
(*$R-*)
VAR I1 : INTEGER;
    L1 : LONGINT;
    C1 : CHAR;
    B1 : BOOLEAN;

  (* Display one value of each of four types *)
  PROCEDURE DispTypes ( IVal : INTEGER;
                        LVal : LONGINT;
                        CVal : CHAR;
```

```
                          BVal : BOOLEAN);
    BEGIN
      WRITELN ( 'Integer value = ', IVal);
      WRITELN ( 'LongInt value = ', LVal);
      WRITELN ( 'Char value    = ', CVal);
      WRITELN ( 'Boolean value = ', BVal);
    END;  (* DispTypes *)

  BEGIN
    (* Initialize values *)
    (* You can have more than one statement per line *)
    I1 := 30;            L1 := 55000;
    C1 := 'g';           B1 := TRUE;
    (* Decrement each value by 1 *)
    DEC ( I1);           DEC ( L1);
    DEC ( C1);           DEC ( B1);
    DispTypes ( I1, L1, C1, B1);
    (* Decrement each value by 3;
       Note what happens to the BOOLEAN;
       Is this consistent with overflow handling?
    *)
    DEC ( I1, 3);        DEC ( L1, 3);
    DEC ( C1, 3);        DEC ( B1, 3);
    DispTypes ( I1, L1, C1, B1);
    READLN;
  END.
```

As you can see from this listing, you can have more than one statement on a single line. Lines with multiple statements are more difficult to read, so this book avoids them.

The following listing contains the output from the previous example program:

```
Integer value = 29
LongInt value = 54999
Char value    = f
Boolean value = FALSE
Integer value = 26
LongInt value = 54996
Char value    = c
Boolean value = TRUE
```

This program works only if you have the range-checking compiler option set to off. When range checking is set to on, the compiler does not let you decrease the value of a variable below the minimum value for that type. For example,

```
DEC ( B1, 3);
```

will cause an error. Because **BOOLEAN**s have only two possible values, you can't legally decrease a **BOOLEAN** value by 2.

To turn range checking on or off for a particular program, put one of the following two statements at the top of your program:

```
{$R+}    (* turn range checking ON  *)

{$R-}    (* turn range checking OFF *)
```

PROCEDURE DELETE (VAR Str : **STRING**;
StartingIndex,
NrToDelete : **INTEGER**);

This procedure deletes a substring from **AStr**. The substring begins at character **StartingIndex** and continues for **NrToDelete** characters altogether.

If there are not enough characters in the string to delete, the procedure deletes from character **StartingIndex** to the end of the string. If **StartingIndex** is greater than the length of **AStr**, nothing is deleted. For example, the following statement deletes the first nine characters from **StrToShorten**:

```
Delete ( StrToShorten, 1, 9);
```

The following program presents the **DELETE** procedure. Try deleting past the end of your **SVal** string. For example, start deleting at a position past the end of the string or start somewhere within **SVal** and delete more characters than **SVal** between the starting position and the end of the string.

```
P4-27   (* Program to illustrate use of DELETE function *)

PROGRAM DeleteDemo;
```

```
CONST EmptyString = '';
VAR SVal : STRING;
    StartIndex, NrCh : INTEGER;

  PROCEDURE GetInteger ( Message : STRING;
                             VAR Value : INTEGER);
  BEGIN
    WRITE ( Message, ' ');
    READLN ( Value);
  END; (* GetInteger *)

  PROCEDURE GetString ( Message : STRING;
                            VAR Value : STRING);
  BEGIN
    WRITE ( Message, ' ');
    READLN ( Value);
  END; (* GetString *)

BEGIN  (* Main Program *)
  GetString ( 'String (ENTER to stop)? ', SVal);
  WHILE SVal <> EmptyString DO
  BEGIN
    GetInteger ( 'Starting position? ', StartIndex);
    GetInteger ( '# chars to delete? ', NrCh);
    DELETE ( SVal, StartIndex, NrCh);
    WRITELN ( 'Remaining string = ', SVal);
    GetString ( 'String (ENTER to stop)? ', SVal);
  END;  (* WHILE SVal <> EmptyString *)
END.
```

FUNCTION FRAC (Val : **REAL**) : **REAL**;

This routine returns the fractional part of **Val**. Both argument and return type are **REAL**. For example, if **MyReal** is 97.454545, then

```
Result := FRAC ( MyReal);
```

assigns the value **0.454545** to **Result**.

The following program demonstrates the **FRAC** function:

```
P4-28    (* Program to illustrate use of FRAC function *)

         PROGRAM FracDemo;

         VAR RVal, Result : REAL;

           PROCEDURE GetReal ( Message : STRING;
                                 VAR Value : REAL);
           BEGIN
             WRITE ( Message, ' ');
             READLN ( Value);
           END; (* GetReal *)

         BEGIN  (* Main Program *)
           REPEAT
             GetReal ( 'Value (> 500 to stop)? ', RVal);
             Result := FRAC ( RVal);
             WRITELN ( 'FRAC ( ', RVal : 8:3, ') = ', Result : 8 : 3);
           UNTIL RVal > 500.0;
           READLN;
         END.
```

INT is a related function.

PROCEDURE INC (VAR ValToInc : **INTEGER**{;
Amount : **LONGINT**});

This routine increments the first argument by the amount specified in the optional second argument. If there is no second argument, the procedure increments **ValToInc** by 1. The first argument must be an ordinal type.

The following program illustrates the **INC** procedure. (This is the same program as for **DEC**, except that all references to **DEC** have been changed to **INC**.)

```
P4-29    (* Program to illustrate use of INC procedure *)

         PROGRAM IncDemo;
         (*$-*)
         VAR I1 : INTEGER;
```

```
   L1 : LONGINT;
   C1 : CHAR;
   B1 : BOOLEAN;

(* Display one value of each of four types *)
PROCEDURE DispTypes ( IVal : INTEGER;
                      LVal : LONGINT;
                      CVal : CHAR;
                      BVal : BOOLEAN);
BEGIN
   WRITELN ( 'Integer value = ', IVal);
   WRITELN ( 'LongInt value = ', LVal);
   WRITELN ( 'Char value    = ', CVal);
   WRITELN ( 'Boolean value = ', BVal);
END;  (* DispTypes *)

BEGIN
   (* Initialize values *)
   (* You can have more than one statement per line *)
   I1 := 30;           L1 := 55000;
   C1 := 'g';          B1 := TRUE;
   (* Increment each value by 1 *)
   INC ( I1);          INC ( L1);
   INC ( C1);          INC ( B1);
   DispTypes ( I1, L1, C1, B1);
   (* Increment each value by 3;
      Note what happens to the BOOLEAN;
      Is this consistent with overflow handling?
   *)
   INC ( I1, 3);          INC ( L1, 3);
   INC ( C1, 3);          INC ( B1, 3);
   DispTypes ( I1, L1, C1, B1);
   READLN;
END.
```

The following listing contains the output from the preceding program. Compare this output with that from the program **DecDemo**, which illustrated the use of the **DEC** procedure.

```
Integer value = 31
LongInt value = 55001
Char value    = h
Boolean value = TRUE
Integer value = 34
LongInt value = 55004
Char value    = k
Boolean value = TRUE
```

As with the **DEC** procedure, this program only works if range checking is set to off.

PROCEDURE INSERT(StrToAdd : **STRING**;
            VAR WhereToAdd : **STRING**;
            StartingPos : **INTEGER**);

This routine inserts **StrToAdd** into **WhereToAdd**, beginning at position **StartingPos**. If the resulting string is longer than 255 characters, only the first 255 characters are saved. For example, if **MyString** has the value 'there, duckies', the statement

```
(* Assume MyString = 'there, duckies' *)
INSERT ( 'Hello ', MyString, 1);
```

makes **MyString** equal to "Hello there, duckies" after the call.

You can use the following program to investigate the **INSERT** procedure:

P4-30
```
(* Program to illustrate use of INSERT function *)

PROGRAM InsertDemo;

CONST EmptyString = '';
VAR SVal, ToAdd : STRING;
    StartIndex : INTEGER;

  PROCEDURE GetInteger ( Message : STRING;
                         VAR Value : INTEGER);
  BEGIN
    WRITE ( Message, ' ');
    READLN ( Value);
  END; (* GetInteger *)

  PROCEDURE GetString ( Message : STRING;
                        VAR Value : STRING);
  BEGIN
    WRITE ( Message, ' ');
    READLN ( Value);
```

```
  END; (* GetString *)

BEGIN  (* Main Program *)
  GetString ( 'String (ENTER to stop)? ', SVal);
  WHILE SVal <> EmptyString DO
  BEGIN
    GetString ( 'String to add? ', ToAdd);
    GetInteger ( 'Starting Position? ', StartIndex);
    INSERT ( ToAdd, SVal, StartIndex);
    WRITELN ( 'Result = ', SVal);
    GetString ( 'String (ENTER to stop)? ', SVal);
  END;   (* WHILE SVal <> EmptyString *)
END.
```

FUNCTION INT (Val : **REAL**) : **REAL**;

This routine returns the integer part of **Val**—but expressed as a **REAL**. Both argument and return type are **REAL**s. For example, if **MyReal** is 97.565656, then

```
Result := INT ( MyReal);
```

assigns 97.0 to **Result**.

Run the following program to compare the results of **FRAC** and **INT**:

P4-31

```
(* Program to illustrate use of INT function *)

PROGRAM IntDemo;

VAR RVal, Result : REAL;

  PROCEDURE GetReal ( Message : STRING;
                      VAR Value : REAL);
  BEGIN
    WRITE ( Message, ' ');
    READLN ( Value);
  END; (* GetReal *)

BEGIN  (* Main Program *)
```

```
    REPEAT
      GetReal ( 'Value (> 500 to stop)? ', RVal);
      Result := INT ( RVal);
      WRITELN ( 'INT  ( ', RVal : 8:3, ') = ', Result : 8 : 3);
      Result := FRAC ( RVal);
      WRITELN ( 'FRAC ( ', RVal : 8:3, ') = ', Result : 8 : 3);
    UNTIL RVal > 500.0;
    READLN;
END.
```

FRAC is a related function.

FUNCTION LENGTH (Str : **STRING**) : **INTEGER**;

This routine returns the length of string **Str**. For example, if **MyStr** is 'this long', then

```
Result := LENGTH ( MyStr);
```

assigns 9 to **Result**.

The following program illustrates the **LENGTH** function:

P4-32
```
(* Program to illustrate use of LENGTH function *)

PROGRAM LengthDemo;

CONST EmptyString = '';
VAR SVal : STRING;
    Result : INTEGER;

  PROCEDURE GetString ( Message : STRING;
                        VAR Value : STRING);
  BEGIN
    WRITE ( Message, ' ');
    READLN ( Value);
  END; (* GetString *)

BEGIN  (* Main Program *)
  GetString ( 'String (ENTER to stop)? ', SVal);
  WHILE SVal <> EmptyString DO
```

```
BEGIN
  Result := LENGTH ( SVal);
  WRITELN ( SVal, ' is ', Result:2, ' characters long');
  GetString ( 'String (ENTER to stop)? ', SVal);
END;  (* WHILE SVal <> EmptyString *)
END.
```

FUNCTION PI : REAL;

This routine returns the value of π ($\approx$ 3.14159265). This is useful if you're working with the trigonometric functions (**COS** and **SIN**).

FUNCTION POS (StrToFind, StrToSearch : **STRING**) : **INTEGER**;

This routine searches for **StrToFind** in **StrToSearch**. If the substring is found in **StrToSearch**, the function returns the starting position of the substring's first occurrence. If the substring is not found in **StrToSearch**, the function returns 0.

For example, if **Pattern** is 'for' and **Source** is 'California', the statement

```
(* Assume Pattern = 'for' and Source = 'California' *)
Result := POS ( Pattern, Source);
```

assigns 5 to **Result**.

You can use the following program to examine the **POS** function:

```
P4-33    (* Program to illustrate use of POS function *)

         PROGRAM PosDemo;

         CONST EmptyString = '';
         VAR SVal, ToFind : STRING;
            Result : INTEGER;

           PROCEDURE GetString ( Message : STRING;
                                    VAR Value : STRING);
           BEGIN
             WRITE ( Message, ' ');
             READLN ( Value);
           END; (* GetString *)

         BEGIN  (* Main Program *)
           GetString ( 'String (ENTER to stop)? ', SVal);
           WHILE SVal <> EmptyString DO
           BEGIN
             GetString ( 'String to find? ', ToFind);
             Result := POS ( ToFind, SVal);
             WRITELN ( 'Starting position = ', Result);
             GetString ( 'String (ENTER to stop)? ', SVal);
           END;  (* WHILE SVal <> EmptyString *)
         END.
```

FUNCTION RANDOM : REAL;
FUNCTION RANDOM (MaxVal : WORD) : WORD;

This routine returns a pseudorandom value. The function may be called with zero or one argument. If the function is called without an argument, it returns a pseudorandom **REAL** between 0.0 and 1.0. If a **WORD** argument is included, the function returns a **WORD** between 0 and the maximum value specified.

PROCEDURE RANDOMIZE;

This routine initializes the random number generator with a random seed value. This seed is stored in the predefined variable **RandSeed**. You should call this procedure at the start of any program that will be used to generate random values by using **RANDOM**.

If you don't call this procedure, the random sequence generated will depend on whatever is stored in the (uninitialized) **RandSeed**. If you want to generate the same sequence each time, initialize **RandSeed** to the same value, instead of calling **RANDOMIZE**.

FUNCTION SIZEOF(<type or variable name>) : **WORD**;

This routine returns the amount of storage allocated to the variable or type specified. The result represents the number of bytes allocated for the argument. The argument can be a type specifier or a variable name.

The following program displays the storage allocated for the types you've seen so far:

P4-34
```
PROGRAM SizeDemo;

VAR I1 : INTEGER;
    By1 : BYTE;
    S1 : SHORTINT;
    L1 : LONGINT;
    W1 : WORD;
    C1 : CHAR;
    Bo1 : BOOLEAN;
    Stg : STRING;
    R1 : REAL;

BEGIN
    WRITELN ( 'INTEGER : ', SIZEOF ( INTEGER) : 3, ' bytes; ',
             '  I1 : ', SIZEOF ( I1) : 3, ' bytes');
    WRITELN ( 'BYTE    : ', SIZEOF ( BYTE) : 3, ' bytes; ',
             '  By1: ', SIZEOF ( By1) : 3, ' bytes');
    WRITELN ( 'SHORTINT: ', SIZEOF ( SHORTINT) : 3, ' bytes; ',
             '  S1 : ', SIZEOF ( S1) : 3, ' bytes');
    WRITELN ( 'LONGINT : ', SIZEOF ( LONGINT) : 3, ' bytes; ',
             '  L1 : ', SIZEOF ( L1) : 3, ' bytes');
```

```
      WRITELN ( 'WORD    : ', SIZEOF ( WORD) : 3, ' bytes; ',
                '    Wl : ', SIZEOF ( Wl) : 3, ' bytes');
      WRITELN ( 'CHAR    : ', SIZEOF ( CHAR) : 3, ' bytes; ',
                '    Cl : ', SIZEOF ( Cl) : 3, ' bytes');
      WRITELN ( 'BOOLEAN : ', SIZEOF ( BOOLEAN) : 3, ' bytes; ',
                '    Bol: ', SIZEOF ( Bol) : 3, ' bytes');
      WRITELN ( 'STRING  : ', SIZEOF ( STRING) : 3, ' bytes; ',
                '    Stg: ', SIZEOF ( Stg) : 3, ' bytes');
      WRITELN ( 'REAL    : ', SIZEOF ( REAL) : 3, ' bytes; ',
                '    Rl : ', SIZEOF ( Rl) : 3, ' bytes');
      READLN;
END.
```

Notice that the program produces the same result, whether you ask about a type or a variable of that type. In Chapter 8, "Files," you'll see why a **STRING** is allocated 256 bytes but can only have 255 characters.

This program produces the following output:

```
INTEGER :    2 bytes;    Il :    2 bytes
BYTE    :    1 bytes;    Byl:    1 bytes
SHORTINT:    1 bytes;    Sl :    1 bytes
LONGINT :    4 bytes;    Ll :    4 bytes
WORD    :    2 bytes;    Wl :    2 bytes
CHAR    :    1 bytes;    Cl :    1 bytes
BOOLEAN :    1 bytes;    Bol:    1 bytes
STRING  : 256 bytes;    Stg: 256 bytes
REAL    :    6 bytes;    Rl :    6 bytes
```

FUNCTION UPCASE (Ch : CHAR) : CHAR;

This routine returns the uppercase version of the character passed as an argument. Note that the argument itself is passed by value, so that it is not changed in the calling routine.

The following program demonstrates the **UPCASE** function:

P4-35   (* Program to illustrate use of UPCASE function *)

         PROGRAM UpcaseDemo;

```
CONST EmptyString = '';
VAR SVal : STRING;
    Index, Lgth : INTEGER;

  PROCEDURE GetString ( Message : STRING;
                        VAR Value : STRING);
  BEGIN
    WRITE ( Message, ' ');
    READLN ( Value);
  END; (* GetString *)
BEGIN  (* Main Program *)
  GetString ( 'String (ENTER to stop)? ', SVal);
  WHILE SVal <> EmptyString DO
  BEGIN
    WRITE ( SVal, ' : ');
    Lgth := LENGTH ( SVal);
    FOR Index := 1 TO Lgth DO
      SVal [ Index] := UPCASE ( SVal [ Index]);
    WRITELN ( SVal);
    GetString ( 'String (ENTER to stop)? ', SVal);
  END;  (* WHILE SVal <> EmptyString *)
END.
```

In this chapter, you learned about procedures and functions. In particular, you learned how to define and call routines and how to pass parameters by value and by reference. As you create more example programs, you'll become more comfortable with each of these methods.

The chapter also included a whirlwind tour of some of Turbo Pascal's predefined routines. You'll soon see more of these functions and learn about other predefined routines.

In the next chapter, you'll learn about the structures that Pascal provides for controlling the sequence in which your program executes.

5 *Turbo Pascal's Control Structures*

This chapter describes the structures that Pascal provides for controlling what your routines and programs do at various points in their execution. You'll learn about Pascal's constructs for selection (taking conditional actions) and iteration (repeating, or looping, actions). An *iteration* is a trial or a repetition.

Pascal provides two types of statements for making selections during execution, and three types of iteration statements. In a *selection construct,* a particular action may be taken if a condition holds; otherwise, either a different action or no action may be taken. In an *iteration construct,* an action may be repeated (possibly with variation). This repetition may continue for a fixed number of times, or it may continue while a condition holds or until some specified condition becomes true.

You'll learn about one of the iteration structures first. This will enable you to work with example programs that do more interesting things. Then you'll learn about Pascal's selection constructs and its other iteration constructs.

Simple Repetition:
The FOR Statement

In Chapter 4, "Procedures and Functions," you created the procedure
CountVals to count to a specified value. To accomplish its task, the
procedure uses a **FOR** loop, which repeats as often as specified in the
parameter. This loop is one of the three iteration constructs provided in
Pascal.

In Pascal, the **FOR** loop is used when you know how often something
needs to be done. For example, the following program repeats the same
sequence of actions **MaxVals** times. This repetition is controlled by a
FOR loop. In addition, the procedures defined in the program have
their own **FOR** loops, which control various actions taken by these
routines.

P5-1

```
(* Program to illustrate use of FOR loops *)

PROGRAM ForDemo1;

CONST MaxVals = 10;
      MaxItems = 5;
VAR Index, Result :INTEGER;

  (* Generate and display values based on random integers *)
  PROCEDURE DispVariants ( Value : INTEGER);
  CONST MaxVariants = 15;
  VAR Count : INTEGER;
  BEGIN
    (* Value is the value generated by the main program *)
    WRITE ( Value : 5);
    (* Write MaxVariants values *)
    FOR Count := 11 TO MaxVariants DO
      WRITE ( Value + RANDOM ( Count * 100) : 5);
    WRITELN;
  END; (* DispVariants *)

  PROCEDURE PutHeadings;
  VAR Count : INTEGER;
  BEGIN
    WRITE ( ' ' :  5, ' Val ');
    FOR Count := 1 TO MaxItems DO
      WRITE ( Count * 100 + 1000 : 5);
    WRITELN;
    (* write 60 dashes, to make a line *)
    FOR Count := 1 TO MaxItems * 7 DO
      WRITE ( '-');
```

```
    WRITELN;
  END; (* PutHeadings *)

BEGIN (* Main *)
  RANDOMIZE;
  PutHeadings;
  (* Generate MaxVals random integers *)
  FOR Index := 1 TO MaxVals DO
  BEGIN
    WRITE ( Index * 100 : 4, ':');
    Result := RANDOM ( Index * 100);
    DispVariants ( Result);
  END; (* FOR Index := 1 TO MaxVals *)
  READLN;
END.
```

The main program generates ten pseudorandom **INTEGER**s. The first value is between 0 and 99, the second between 0 and 199, and so on up to the last value, which is between 0 and 999. Output based on each of these values will be placed on a separate line.

In the main program, notice that the loop contains only one compound statement. In fact, the **FOR** loop applies to the statement immediately after the **FOR** loop specification. This can be a simple or compound statement. If it's a compound statement, the loop may carry out multiple instructions each time it executes. Together, the loop formulation and the statement following it make up the **FOR** statement.

The **FOR** loop in the main program consists of three actions grouped as a compound statement. Each time through the loop, the program carries out all three actions.

On each of the lines created in the main program, **DispVariants** writes five variants on the original pseudorandom value. Each variant is the sum of the starting value for the line and another pseudorandom integer. The first of these is between 0 and 1099, the second between 0 and 1199, and so on, until the last one, which is between 0 and 1499.

The **FOR** loop in **DispVariants** is followed by a simple statement—the only statement that is repeated in the procedure. The call to procedure **WRITELN** is made only after the **FOR** loop has repeated the required number of times.

Procedure **PutHeading** also contains two **FOR** loops. The first of these writes some headings for the table that the program generates. The second **FOR** loop draws a line by writing a single character over and over.

This program produces output such as:

```
    Val  1100 1200 1300 1400 1500
 ---------------------------------
 100:    28  277  383  858  461  235
 200:    59  583 1205  754 1012 1212
 300:   268  873 1457 1506 1142  957
 400:   212 1174  932 1032  772  290
 500:    22  561  159 1085  541  536
 600:   196 1288 1317  932  672 1213
 700:   429 1093 1331  751  708  931
 800:   513  641  761 1080 1303 1212
 900:   352  837  773  488 1303 1702
1000:   449  721  463 1587 1461  893
```

The **FOR** loop has the following syntax:

```
" FOR" <loop variable> " :=" <starting value> " TO"
                              <ending value> " DO"
```

The *loop variable,* also called the *control variable,* keeps track of the repetitions. It serves as a counter for the loop. This variable can be of any ordinal type. In the example program, all loop variables happen to be **INTEGER**s; however, you'll see other types of loop variables later in the chapter and throughout the book.

The starting and ending values can be variables, values, or expressions, but must be of the same type as the loop variable. Thus, the **FOR** loop in the main program repeats as **Index** takes the values from 1 through **MaxValues** (10). The loop variable in **DispVariants** takes on values from 11 through **MaxVariants** (15).

There are no instructions that explicitly change the value of the loop variable. With a **FOR** loop, the program automatically adjusts the value of the loop variable. You don't need to change this value in your source code. In fact, it is very dangerous to do so. While the **FOR** loop is executing, you should not explicitly change the value of the loop variable. Doing so will lead to problems. For example, a **FOR** loop such as the one in the following listing will lead to surprising results. Substitute the following listing for the loop in program **ForDemo1**, and compare the output with that from the original version of the program.

```
FOR Index := 1 TO MaxVals DO
BEGIN
   WRITE ( Index * 100 : 4, ':');
   Result := RANDOM ( Index * 100);
   DispVariants ( Result);
   INC ( Index);
END; (* FOR Index := 1 TO MaxVals *)
```

The value of the looping variable is undefined after the loop has finished. If you want to use the variable, you need to initialize it again.

If the ending value for a loop is smaller than the starting value, the loop does not execute. If the ending value is equal to the starting value, the loop executes once.

Do not put a semicolon after the **DO**. This would execute a null statement—that is, do nothing—and end the **FOR** statement. Compile and run the following program to see what would happen. Watch the value of **Count** as you trace through the program.

P5-2
```
(* Program to illustrate consequences of putting
   ; after DO
*)

PROGRAM BadForDemo;

VAR Count : INTEGER;
BEGIN
   FOR Count := 1 TO 10 DO;
      WRITELN ( Count);
   WRITELN ( 'Done with FOR loop.');
   READLN;
END.
```

This program writes only a single value of **Count**. The **WRITELN** statement is only executed once. The **FOR** loop, on the other hand, does nothing ten times.

Looping Backwards

Suppose you want to write a sequence of letters in a reverse order—for instance, you may want to write a line such as

```
t    s    r    q    p    o    n    m    l    k    j
```

Is there an easy way to accomplish this? In fact, there is another version of the **FOR** loop in which the loop variable counts backwards. The following program illustrates this version of the **FOR** loop. You may need to run the program a few times before it generates random values suitable for looping backwards.

P5-3
```
(* Program to illustrate how to loop backwards with a
      FOR loop.
*)

PROGRAM ReverseLoop;

VAR ChIndex, StartCh, EndCh : CHAR;

    (* Generate a random character between 'a' and 'z' *)
    PROCEDURE  RandomCh ( VAR TheCh : CHAR);
    (* Note that you can have an expression as the
        "value" of a constant.
    *)
    CONST Offset = ORD ( 'a');
    VAR Val : INTEGER;
    BEGIN
      (* Val will be between 97 ('a') and 122 ('z') *)
      Val := RANDOM ( 26) + Offset;
      TheCh := CHR ( Val);
    END;  (* RandomCh *)

BEGIN
  RANDOMIZE;
  RandomCh ( StartCh);
  RandomCh ( EndCh);
  WRITE ( StartCh, ' to ', EndCh, ': ');
  (* Display a sequence of characters --
      from last down to first.
  *)
  FOR ChIndex := StartCh DOWNTO EndCh DO
    WRITE ( ChIndex : 2);
  WRITELN;
  READLN;
END.
```

The program generates two random characters. The first is used as the starting character and the second as the ending character. The program then displays the letters between these two characters—from starting to ending character. If the starting character comes earlier than the ending character, the loop does not execute. (Note in **RandomCh** that you can have an expression (**ORD('a')**) as the value of a constant.)

The only syntactic difference between the **FOR** loop in the **Reverse-Loop** program and earlier **FOR** loops is the reserved word **DOWNTO** instead of **TO**. As a consequence, however, the value before the **DOWNTO** should be *greater* than the value after it.

If the final value is larger than the initial one, the **DOWNTO** version of the loop does not execute; if the two values are equal, the loop executes once.

Nested FOR Loops

You can put whatever kind of statement you want after a **FOR** loop specification, including a **FOR** statement. For example, suppose you want to write a display such as the following:

```
a.1   a.2   a.3   a.4   a.5   a.6   a.7   a.8   a.9
b.1   b.2   b.3   b.4   b.5   b.6   b.7   b.8   b.9
c.1   c.2   c.3   c.4   c.5   c.6   c.7   c.8   c.9
d.1   d.2   d.3   d.4   d.5   d.6   d.7   d.8   d.9
e.1   e.2   e.3   e.4   e.5   e.6   e.7   e.8   e.9
f.1   f.2   f.3   f.4   f.5   f.6   f.7   f.8   f.9
g.1   g.2   g.3   g.4   g.5   g.6   g.7   g.8   g.9
h.1   h.2   h.3   h.4   h.5   h.6   h.7   h.8   h.9
i.1   i.2   i.3   i.4   i.5   i.6   i.7   i.8   i.9
j.1   j.2   j.3   j.4   j.5   j.6   j.7   j.8   j.9
k.1   k.2   k.3   k.4   k.5   k.6   k.7   k.8   k.9
```

To get this display, you need to

1. Write a line in which the same letter is repeated several times.

2. For each repetition of the letter, pair a different digit with the letter and display this pair separated by a period.

3. After the desired number of digits have been paired with the letter, move to the next line and the next letter.

The following program produces the output. Run it to see what this output looks like. You might also want to trace through the two loops, with **Outer** and **Inner** as watch variables.

P5-4

```
(* Program to illustrate use of nested FOR loops *)

PROGRAM NestedForDemo1;

CONST MaxSize = 9;
VAR Outer : CHAR;
    Inner : INTEGER;

BEGIN
  FOR Outer := 'a' TO 'k' DO
  BEGIN
    FOR Inner := 1 TO MaxSize  DO
      WRITE  ( Outer:3, '.', Inner);
    WRITELN;
  END;
  READLN;
END.
```

The **FOR** loop controlled by **Inner** is said to be *nested* within the loop controlled by **Outer**. This means that the loop controlled by **Inner** is executed for every value of **Outer**.

To understand how nested **FOR** loops behave, try varying the preceding program. For example, try making **WRITELN** part of the inner loop. You can do this in either of two ways, both of which will produce the same result:

P5-5

```
(* combine WRITELN with WRITE *)
FOR Outer := 'a' TO 'k' DO
BEGIN
  FOR Inner := 1 TO MaxSize DO
    WRITELN  ( Outer:3, '.', Inner);
END;

(* make WRITELN part of the compound statement associated with
   inner loop.
*)
FOR Outer := 'a' TO 'k' DO
BEGIN
  FOR Inner := 1 TO MaxSize DO
  BEGIN
    WRITE  ( Outer:3, '.', Inner);
```

```
        WRITELN;
    END;
END;
```

Try using each of these loops in the **NestedForDemo1** program to see how they alter the original version of the program.

You can also try switching the specifications for the inner and outer loops. That is, you can try the **FOR** loop in the following program. Before you run the program, however, try to guess its outcome.

P5-6

```
(* Program to illustrate use of nested FOR loops *)

PROGRAM NestedForDemo2;

CONST MaxSize = 9;
VAR Outer : CHAR;
    Inner : INTEGER;

BEGIN
  FOR Inner := 1 TO MaxSize DO
  BEGIN
    FOR Outer := 'a' TO 'k'  DO
      WRITE  ( Outer:3, '.', Inner);
    WRITELN;
  END;
  READLN;
END.
```

When you run this version of the program, the display will look as if the original output has been switched. That is, the first row of the original output will be the first column of the new output, and the first column of the original will be the first row of the modified output.

When you have nested **FOR** loops, the inner loop will execute more often than the outer one. In fact, the entire inner loop will execute once for each pass through the outer loop.

FOR loops are extremely useful; this book includes many more examples that use this construct.

Selection Constructs: The IF Statement

In your programs, you'll often want to carry out an action *if* a particular condition holds, but to proceed as usual if the condition does not hold.

For example, your program might search a collection of numbers to see how often a particular value appears in the collection. The program will read each number in the collection and compare it with the value sought. If the current number equals the value sought, the program reports this fact; otherwise, the program simply continues (gets and compares the next number, and so forth).

Pascal's **IF** statement lets you make such a decision, as shown in the following program. The program generates random integers. If the value is divisible by 10, the program writes a dot on the screen; after 50 dots, it sends a **WRITELN**.

P5-7
```
(* Program to illustrate use of IF construct.
   Program generates MaxTrials pseudorandom integers. If an
   integer is divisible by Divisor, the program writes a dot and
   increments a counter. After LineWidth dots have been written,
   the program writes the number of trials so far, and then
   moves to the next line.
*)

PROGRAM IfDemo;

CONST MaxTrials = 5000;
      LineWidth = 50;
      Divisor = 10;
VAR Result,  Index, NrHits, NrTrials : INTEGER;
BEGIN
  RANDOMIZE;
  NrHits := 0;
  NrTrials := 0;

  FOR Index := 1 TO MaxTrials DO
  BEGIN
    Result := RANDOM ( MAXINT);
    INC ( NrTrials);
    (* If number is divisible by 10, write a dot, etc. *)
    IF ( Result MOD Divisor = 0) THEN
    BEGIN
      WRITE ( '.');
      INC  ( NrHits);
      (* If there are enough dots on the line, ... *)
      IF ( NrHits MOD LineWidth = 0) THEN
        WRITELN ( NrTrials : 10);
    END; (*  IF Result is divisible by 10 *)
  END; (* FOR Index := 1 to  MaxTrials *)
  WRITELN;
  WRITELN ( MaxTrials, ' trials, ',
```

```
                   NrHits, ' divisible by 10');
      READLN;
  END.
```

As you can see, the syntax for an **IF** statement is

> *"IF"* <Boolean expression> *"THEN"*
> <simple or compound statement>

The expression in the **IF** statement must evaluate to a **BOOLEAN**. If this expression is **TRUE**, the action or actions in the next statement are carried out. If the expression is **FALSE**, the program skips the next statement. For example, the first **IF** statement in the preceding program tests whether the random value is divisible by 10. If so, the actions within the compound statement are carried out. If not, the program begins the next iteration of the **FOR** loop.

Note that the example contains a nested **IF** statement. This is allowed, just as nested **FOR** statements are allowed. In fact, notice that the first **IF** statement is nested inside the **FOR** loop. Any kind of control construct can be nested inside of any other kind of control construct. This simple property—known as *encapsulation*—is what enables you to build such varied and powerful programs.

REMEMBER The **IF** statement executes when the Boolean expression following the **IF** is **TRUE**. If so, the next simple or compound statement is executed; if not, the statement is bypassed.

Deciding Between Alternatives: The IF-ELSE Statement

Sometimes you'll want to decide between two alternative actions. If a particular condition holds, do one thing; otherwise, do something different. To accomplish this, Pascal allows you to add an **ELSE** clause to an **IF** statement. This **IF-ELSE** variant enables you to do much more in your programs than a simple **IF** would allow.

The following program shows how to use the **IF-ELSE** construct:

P5-8

```
(* Program to illustrate use of IF-ELSE construct *)

PROGRAM IfElseDemo;

CONST MaxTrials = 500;
VAR Result, Count, HeadCount, RowCount : INTEGER;

BEGIN
  RANDOMIZE;
  HeadCount := 0;
  RowCount := 0;
  FOR Count := 1 TO  MaxTrials DO
  BEGIN
    Result := RANDOM ( MAXINT);

    (* If result is even, count it as a head,
       and write a period.
    *)
    IF result MOD 2 = 0 THEN
    BEGIN
      WRITE ( '.');
      RowCount := RowCount + 1;
    END
    ELSE    (* if not even, write a space *)
      WRITE ( ' ');

    (* after 50 trials, move to a new line *)
    IF Count MOD 50 = 0  THEN
    BEGIN
      WRITELN ( RowCount : 3);
      HeadCount := RowCount + HeadCount;
      RowCount := 0;
    END;  (* IF count MOD 50 = 0 *)
  END; (*FOR Count := 1 TO MaxTrials DO*)
  WRITELN ( HeadCount, ' heads');
  READLN;
END.
```

The program generates random integers. If the value is even, the program writes a dot; otherwise, it writes a space. Every 50 trials, the program writes some summary information and then moves the cursor to the next line. The following listing shows output from a sample run:

```
 .  ..  .  . .     ... .. .    .. ...   .... ....  ...   30
 .  ..  .. .    .. . . ..  .     .. ....  .  .      ..   23
..  ..  .. . .. ...    .. ...    . .  . . ...  . .  26
  .  .  ..  . ..  .   .   . ...   ..  . ..  .   .    19
  ....        .   . .        .  . ..  .  .  .. .  ..    19
  ....  ..  ..........  .    ... . . ..      .  ...     .   28
  .... ...   .     .   .       . .  . .  . ....   ... .  22
  .  .  .  .. . ..... . ..  .     ..    .. .   .  .  .   20
  .  . ......  . .....   ...    .  .  ... ...   . .....30
    . .  ..  . ......      .... ...    ....... . . . 26
243 heads
```

The **ELSE** clause specifies the alternate action to take if the Boolean expression for the preceding **IF** clause is **FALSE**. The **ELSE** clause encompasses the simple or compound statement immediately after the **ELSE**.

Notice that there is no semicolon between the **END** that terminates the actions for the **IF** part and the **ELSE** that begins the alternate clause. This is one of the few places in Pascal where you may not have a semicolon. Notice that there are semicolons between the statements within the compound statement preceding the **ELSE**. There is also a semicolon to separate the end of the **ELSE** clause (and, therefore, the end of the entire **IF-ELSE** statement) from subsequent source code.

REMEMBER   You may not put a semicolon before an **ELSE** clause.

Syntactically, the entire **IF-ELSE** construct is treated as one statement by the compiler. Putting a semicolon before the **ELSE** would separate it from the **IF**, making the **ELSE** clause a statement on its own. This is not possible, since the **ELSE** clause must have a preceding **IF** clause.

Working Through Alternatives: An Extended IF-ELSE Statement

Sometimes you may have a whole sequence of decisions to make, with each decision depending on the answer to the previous one. The general format for such a series of decisions is shown here.

> **IF A THEN** \<statement\>
> **ELSE IF B THEN** \<statement\>
> **ELSE IF . . . THEN** \<statement\>
> **ELSE** \<statement\>

You can have as many **IF-ELSE** clauses as you need.

For example, consider the following simple problem, known as the *3A + 1 Problem*. The problem is defined in terms of the algorithm used to solve it. (For our purposes, an *algorithm* is simply a well-defined sequence of actions.)

1. Start with an arbitrary whole number, A.

2. If A = 1, stop.

3. Otherwise, if A is even, replace A with A **DIV** 2 and go back to step 2.

4. Otherwise, if A is odd, replace A with 3A + 1 and go back to step 2.

Interestingly enough, it's not known whether this algorithm will always end at 1 for any starting value. It is known that the algorithm stops for all values less than 536,870,912, or 2^{29}. The algorithm's behavior varies widely—even for numbers that are close to each other. For example, it takes 115 iterations to reach 1 when starting with 73, but only 22 iterations when starting with 74 and only 14 when starting with 75.

The following program applies the 3A + 1 algorithm to a value you specify and also illustrates an extended **IF-ELSE** statement. Run the program with a starting value of 13.

P5-9
```
(* Program to illustrate use of extended IF-ELSE statement.
   Program carries out 3A + 1 algorithm.
*)

PROGRAM ThreeADemo;

VAR Val, Count, Even, Odd : LONGINT;

   PROCEDURE GetLongInt ( Message : STRING;
```

```
                              VAR Value : LONGINT);
    BEGIN
      WRITE ( Message, ' ');
      READLN ( Value);
    END; (* GetLongInt  *)


    (* If a multiple of 20 lines have been written to the screen,
        pause to let user read them.
    *)
    PROCEDURE CheckForFullScreen (  NrLines : LONGINT);
    CONST FullPage = 20;
    BEGIN
      IF NrLines MOD FullPage = 0 THEN
      BEGIN
        WRITE ( 'Press ENTER to go on. ');
        READLN;
      END;
    END;  (* CheckForFullScreen *)

BEGIN
  WRITELN ( 'CTRL-C ends the program anytime.');
  Count := 0;
  Even := 0;
  Odd := 0;
  (* step 1 of the algorithm: get a starting  value *)
  GetLongInt ( 'Value?', Val);
  (* the core of the algorithm *)
  REPEAT
    INC ( Count);
    (* step 2 in the algorithm *)
    IF ( Val = 1) THEN
      INC ( Odd)
    (* step 3 in the algorithm *)
    ELSE IF ( Val MOD 2 = 0) THEN
    BEGIN
      INC ( Even);
      Val := Val DIV 2;
    END

    (* if neither step 2 nor 3 applies, step 4 must apply *)
    ELSE  (* if Val is odd *)
    BEGIN
      INC ( Odd);
      Val := 3 * Val + 1;
    END; (*  IF-ELSE IF-ELSE Statement *)

    WRITELN ( 'Val = ', Val:8, '; Odd = ', Odd:8,
            '; Even = ',  Even:8);
    CheckForFullScreen ( Count);
  UNTIL Val = 1;
  WRITELN ( 'After ', Count:8, ' iterations, result = 1.');
```

```
    WRITELN ( Even:8,    ' even values; ', Odd:8, ' odd values');
    READLN;
END.
```

You may want to work through an example to get some experience with the extended **IF-ELSE** found in the program. The following listing shows the program's output for a starting value of 13. Execute the program by hand to see how each intermediate value is computed.

```
Value? 13
Val =        40; Odd =        1; Even =           0
Val =        20; Odd =        1; Even =           1
Val =        10; Odd =        1; Even =           2
Val =         5; Odd =        1; Even =           3
Val =        16; Odd =        2; Even =           3
Val =         8; Odd =        2; Even =           4
Val =         4; Odd =        2; Even =           5
Val =         2; Odd =        2; Even =           6
Val =         1; Odd =        2; Even ▪           7
After         9 iterations, result = 1.
          7 even values;         2 odd values
```

You might also want to try some values of your own. If you pick a value that never seems to reach 1, press CTRL-C to break out of the program. Some values that end fairly quickly include 5, 10, 13, 16, and 21.

You should keep in mind several things about this extended **IF-ELSE** statement. First, notice that there are no semicolons before any of the **ELSE**s. This is because the entire sequence (beginning with the first **IF** and ending after the action for the last **ELSE**) is considered a single statement. In addition, all of the alternatives processed in this sequence are mutually exclusive— at least as far as the program is concerned. This means that *exactly one* of the clauses will be executed.

This exclusivity is the key to the extended **IF-ELSE** construct. Run the following version of the program and then look at its source code. This version has removed the **ELSE** clauses but has left the **IF** clauses. This version of the program will never terminate. To see why, consider what happens if a 1 reaches the third **IF**. You'll need to press CTRL-C when you are ready to stop this version of the program.

```
P5-10    (* INCORRECT version of 3A + 1 algorithm.
             Extended IF-ELSE  replaced by IF clauses.
         *)

         PROGRAM ThreeADemo;

         VAR Val, Count, Even, Odd : LONGINT;
```

```
    PROCEDURE GetLongInt ( Message : STRING;
                           VAR Value : LONGINT);
  BEGIN
    WRITE ( Message, ' ');
    READLN ( Value);
  END; (* GetLongInt  *)


  (* If a multiple of 20 lines have been written to the screen,
     pause to let user read them.
  *)
  PROCEDURE CheckForFullScreen (  NrLines : LONGINT);
  CONST FullPage = 20;
  BEGIN
    IF NrLines MOD  FullPage = 0 THEN
    BEGIN
      WRITE ( 'ENTER to go on CTRL-C to stop ');
      READLN;
    END;
  END;  (* CheckForFullScreen *)

BEGIN
  WRITELN ( 'CTRL-C ends the program anytime.');
  Count := 0;
  Even := 0;
  Odd := 0;
  GetLongInt ( 'Value?', Val);
  (* the core of the algorithm *)
  REPEAT
    INC ( Count);
    IF ( Val = 1) THEN
      INC ( Odd);
    IF ( Val MOD 2 = 0) THEN
    BEGIN
      INC ( Even);
      Val := Val DIV 2;
    END;
    IF ( Val MOD 2 = 1) THEN
    BEGIN
      INC ( Odd);
      Val := 3 * Val + 1;
    END;

    WRITELN ( 'Val = ', Val:8, '; Odd = ', Odd:8,
              '; Even = ',  Even:8);
    CheckForFullScreen ( Count);
  UNTIL Val = 1;
  WRITELN ( 'After ', Count:8, ' iterations, result = 1.');
  WRITELN ( Even:8,  ' even values; ', Odd:8, ' odd values');
  READLN;
END.
```

Notice that semicolons have been added after each of the **IF** clauses. These are necessary, since each **IF** clause in this program represents a different statement.

What follows is one more example that compares an extended **IF-ELSE** statement with several independent **IF** statements. The following program checks whether each in a series of numbers is divisible by 2, 3, 5, or 7. As soon as one of these values is found to divide the number, the program writes this information and moves on to the next number.

P5-11
```
(* Program to illustrate extended IF-ELSE construct *)

PROGRAM DivisibilityDemo;

CONST Prime1 = 2;
      Prime2 = 3;
      Prime3 = 5;
      Prime4 = 7;
VAR Count, MaxTrials, StartValue, Result : INTEGER;

  PROCEDURE GetInteger ( Message : STRING;
                            VAR Value : INTEGER);
  BEGIN
    WRITE ( Message, ' ');
    READLN ( Value);
  END; (* GetInteger *)

BEGIN
  GetInteger ( 'Starting value?', StartValue);
  GetInteger ( 'Maximum value? (> starting value)', MaxTrials);
  FOR Count := StartValue TO MaxTrials DO
  BEGIN
    WRITE ( Count:3, ': ');
    (* If divisible by Prime1 ... *)
    IF Count MOD Prime1 = 0 THEN
      WRITE ( Prime1:4)
    (* Else if divisible by Prime2 ... *)
    ELSE IF Count MOD Prime2 = 0 THEN
      WRITE ( Prime2:4)
    (* Else if divisible by Prime3 ... *)
    ELSE IF Count MOD Prime3 = 0 THEN
      WRITE ( Prime3:4)
    (* Else if divisible by Prime4 ... *)
    ELSE IF Count MOD Prime4 = 0 THEN
      WRITE ( Prime4:4)
    (* Else if not divisible by any of the previous values *)
    ELSE
      WRITE ( '**');
```

```
    WRITELN;
  END;
  READLN;
END.
```

Because of the way the extended **IF-ELSE** works, exactly one of the clauses can be **TRUE**. As soon as one of the clauses satisfies its condition, the program stops processing the **IF-ELSE** statement. One result is that each number has exactly one divisor (or **) associated with it in the output, as in the following listing, which covers values from 2 through 25:

```
 2:     2
 3:     3
 4:     2
 5:     5
 6:     2
 7:     7
 8:     2
 9:     3
10:     2
11:  **
12:     2
13:  **
14:     2
15:     3
16:     2
17:  **
18:     2
19:  **
20:     2
21:     3
22:     2
23:  **
24:     2
25:     5
```

Contrast this with the output from the following program, which converts the series of **IF-ELSE** clauses into separate **IF** statements:

P5-12
```
(* Program to illustrate separate IF statements.
   Compare program and output with DivisibiltiyDemo1.
*)

PROGRAM DivisibilityDemo2;
```

```
CONST Prime1 = 2;
      Prime2 = 3;
      Prime3 = 5;
      Prime4 = 7;
VAR Count, StartValue, MaxTrials, Result : INTEGER;

   PROCEDURE GetInteger ( Message : STRING;
                              VAR Value : INTEGER);
   BEGIN
     WRITE ( Message, ' ');
     READLN ( Value);
   END; (* GetInteger *)

BEGIN
   GetInteger ( 'Starting value?', StartValue);
   GetInteger ( 'Maximum value? (> starting value)', MaxTrials);
   FOR Count := StartValue TO MaxTrials DO
   BEGIN
     WRITE ( Count:3, ': ');
     (* If divisible by Prime1 ... *)
     IF Count MOD Prime1 = 0 THEN
       WRITE ( Prime1:4);
     (* if divisible by Prime2 ... *)
     IF Count MOD Prime2 = 0 THEN
       WRITE ( Prime2:4);
     (* if divisible by Prime3 ... *)
     IF Count MOD Prime3 = 0 THEN
       WRITE ( Prime3:4);
     (* if divisible by Prime4 ... *)
     IF Count MOD Prime4 = 0 THEN
       WRITE ( Prime4:4);
     (* Notice that the ELSE at the end has disappeared *)
     WRITE ( '**');
     WRITELN;
   END;
   READLN;
END.
```

In this version, a particular value can have more than one prime divisor since the divisors are checked independently of each other. This program produces the following output or values 2 through 25:

```
2:    2**
3:    3**
4:    2**
5:    5**
6:    2   3**
7:    7**
```

```
 8:     2**
 9:     3**
10:     2   5**
11: **
12:     2   3**
13: **
14:     2   7**
15:     3   5**
16:     2**
17: **
18:     2   3**
19: **
20:     2   5**
21:     3   7**
22:     2**
23: **
24:     2   3**
25:     5**
```

Beware of the Missing ELSE

Look at the following program before you run it. Try to determine what the output will be for an input of 0 and for an input of 5. Run the program for several different values — negative, 0, and positive. Remember which values you used, because you should run a related program with the same values. Trace through this program for these three values.

P5-13

```
(* Program to illustrate dangling IFs *)

PROGRAM ElseTest;

VAR Val : INTEGER;

  PROCEDURE GetInteger ( Message : STRING;
                         VAR Value : INTEGER);
  BEGIN
    WRITE ( Message, ' ');
    READLN ( Value);
  END; (* GetInteger *)

BEGIN
  GetInteger ( 'Value?', Val);
  IF Val <> 0 THEN
```

```
   IF ( Val < 0) THEN
     WRITELN ( 'Negative')
(* according to indentation, this ELSE should be
   paired with the first IF.
   According to Pascal's syntax, however,
   it is paired with the inner IF.
*)
ELSE
  WRITELN ( 'Val = zero');
WRITELN ( 'Done. Press ENTER to terminate program');
READLN;
END.
```

The program reads an integer value and then responds differently, depending on whether **Val** is positive, negative, or 0. The program's indentation indicates the *intended* flow of control. According to the indentation, the program tests whether **Val** is nonzero. If this is **TRUE**, the program should then test whether **Val** is negative and write "Negative" if it is. If **Val** is positive, the program is not supposed to do anything because no **ELSE** construct is intended after the inner **IF**. According to the indentation, the **IF** portion of the *outer* construct (**Val <> 0**) ends here. If the original test is **FALSE**—that is, if **Val** is 0—the program was intended to write "Val = zero" on the screen.

Unfortunately, the compiler sees this construct somewhat differently. It matches an **ELSE** with the nearest **IF** that does not have an **ELSE** associated with it. In practice, this is the innermost **IF** without an **ELSE**. In this case, the inner **IF** has no **ELSE** portion. Therefore, the compiler associates the **ELSE** with this **IF**. The result is that the program writes "Val = zero" when **Val** has the value 5. Because the **ELSE** is associated with the inner **IF**, there is no alternative action for the outer **IF**. This means that the program does nothing when **Val** has the value 0.

There are two ways around this difficulty. First, you can include an inner **ELSE** that simply tells the program to do nothing, as in the next program. Run this program, using the input for the previous program. Compare the output from the two programs.

```
P5-14    (* Program to illustrate a fix for dangling IFs *)

         PROGRAM ElseTest2;

         VAR Val : INTEGER;

           PROCEDURE GetInteger ( Message : STRING;
```

```
                                   VAR Value : INTEGER);
   BEGIN
     WRITE ( Message, ' ');
     READLN ( Value);
   END; (* GetInteger *)

BEGIN
  GetInteger ( 'Value?', Val);
  IF Val <> 0 THEN
    IF ( Val < 0) THEN
      WRITELN ( 'Negative')
    (* The following ELSE is an instruction to do
       nothing, but serves to close up the inner IF.
       Note that no semicolon follows the new ELSE.
    *)
    ELSE (* Do nothing *)
  ELSE
      WRITELN ( 'Val = zero');
  WRITELN ( 'Done. Press ENTER to terminate program');
  READLN;
END.
```

The second way of dealing with the missing **ELSE** problem is to use **BEGIN** and **END** to create a compound statement—thereby grouping the statements the way you want them. The following listing shows how to do this:

P5-15

```
(* Program to illustrate a fix for dangling IFs *)

PROGRAM ElseTest3;

VAR Val : INTEGER;

  PROCEDURE GetInteger ( Message : STRING;
                             VAR Value : INTEGER);
  BEGIN
    WRITE ( Message, ' ');
    READLN ( Value);
  END; (* GetInteger *)

BEGIN
  GetInteger ( 'Value?', Val);
  IF Val <> 0 THEN
  (* Put the inner IF within a compound statement *)
  BEGIN
    IF ( Val < 0) THEN
      WRITELN ( 'Negative')
  END  (*  compound statement that's executed if Val <> 0 *)
```

```
    ELSE
      WRITELN ( 'Val = zero');
    WRITELN ( 'Done. Press ENTER to terminate program');
    READLN;
END.
```

In this version, the first **IF** is followed by a compound statement that contains the inner **IF**. The **END** that terminates the compound statement also separates the inner **IF** from the **ELSE**. In this way, the **ELSE** is grouped with the starting **IF**, as intended.

The three versions of the **IF** construct—**IF**, **IF-ELSE**, and extended **IF-ELSE**—represent the first type of selection construct. There are **IF** statements of various sorts throughout the book. In fact, you'll rarely write a program in which you don't use at least one **IF** statement.

Selecting from Among Several Possibilities: The CASE Statement

Pascal has another selection construct that is particularly useful when you have numerous things to test for, or when a test involves many possibilities. For example, to test whether a particular character is a vowel, you might be tempted to use the following (very long) Boolean expression:

```
IF ( TestCh = 'a') OR ( TestCh = 'e') OR ( TestCh = 'i') OR
   ( TestCh = 'o') OR ( TestCh = 'u') OR ( TestCh = 'A') OR
   ( TestCh = 'E') OR ( TestCh = 'I') OR ( TestCh = 'O') OR
   ( TestCh = 'U') THEN
```

Or, suppose that you want to test whether a character is a vowel, a consonant, an even digit, an odd digit, or another printable character. One approach to this would be to use an extended **IF-ELSE** statement. The structure of such a test would be

---

IF TestCh is a consonant **THEN** . . .
ELSE IF TestCh is a vowel **THEN** . . .
ELSE IF TestCh is an even digit **THEN** . . .
ELSE IF TestCh is an odd digit **THEN** . . .
ELSE . . .

Each of the individual tests—such as whether **TestCh** is a consonant or whether it's an even digit—can be long Boolean expressions.

Pascal's **CASE** statement simplifies testing for conditions such as these, and Turbo Pascal's extensions of the **CASE** statement make your job even easier. The **CASE** statement provides selection criteria based on the value of a particular test variable or expression, which must be of an ordinal type. Essentially, the **CASE** statement allows you to group and list all the values of the variable or expression that lead to each of your possible actions.

For example, the following program lets you test whether a particular character falls into any of the groups discussed previously—consonant, vowel, even or odd digit, or another printable character:

P5-16
```
(* Program to illustrate use of CASE statement *)

PROGRAM CaseDemo;
VAR TestStr : STRING;
    Index, HowLong, NrConsonants, NrVowels,
    NrEven, NrOdd, NrPrintable : INTEGER;
    Ch : CHAR;

  PROCEDURE GetString ( Message : STRING;
                          VAR Value : STRING);
  BEGIN
    WRITE ( Message, ' ');
    READLN ( Value);
  END; (* GetString *)


BEGIN
  GetString ( 'String to process?', TestStr);
  HowLong := LENGTH ( TestStr);
  NrConsonants := 0;
  NrVowels := 0;
```

```
    NrEven := 0;
    NrOdd := 0;
    NrPrintable := 0;
    FOR Index := 1 TO HowLong DO
    BEGIN
      Ch := UPCASE ( TestStr [ Index]);
      (* Use Ch as the basis for decision making *)
      CASE Ch OF
        'A', 'E', 'I', 'O', 'U' : INC ( NrVowels);
        'B' .. 'D', 'F' .. 'H',
        'J' .. 'N', 'P' .. 'T', 'V' .. 'Z' : INC ( NrConsonants);
        '0', '2', '4', '6', '8' : INC ( NrEven);
        '1', '3', '5', '7', '9' : INC ( NrOdd);
        ELSE  INC ( NrPrintable);
      END; (* CASE of TestStr [ Index] *)
    END; (* FOR Index := 1 TO HowLong *)
    WRITELN ( 'NrVowels    = ', NrVowels:3,
              '; NrConsonants = ', NrConsonants:3);
    WRITELN ( 'NrEven      = ', NrEven:3,
              '; NrOdd        = ', NrOdd:3);
    WRITELN ( 'NrPrintable = ', NrPrintable:3);
    READLN;
END.
```

The program reads a string and then looks at each character. Depending on the category to which the character belongs, a particular counter is incremented.

LENGTH is a predefined Turbo Pascal function that returns the number of characters in the string argument. **TestStr [Index]** specifies the **Index**th character in the string. The **UPCASE** function converts its character argument to uppercase—if the character is a letter—and returns the uppercase version.

The **CASE** statement works as follows:

■ Each time through the **CASE** statement, the value of **Ch** is checked.

■ If this value is a vowel—that is, has one of the five values listed (*A* through *U*)—**NrVowels** is increased by 1. The statement (simple or compound) following the colon (:) is executed. If this happens, processing of the **CASE** statement is complete and the program continues with the next iteration of the **FOR** loop.

■ If the value is not a vowel, the program checks the next set of candidate values, which represent the consonants. These are specified as characters in several consecutive clusters. For example, all characters between *B* and *D* (that is, *B*, *C*, and *D*) are consonants, as are all characters between *J* and *N*. Such a range of characters is indicated by two dots (..) between the starting and ending values. If the value of **Ch** is one of these, **NrConsonants** is increased by 1 and the **CASE** statement is finished.

■ If the character is neither vowel nor consonant, the program checks whether it is an even digit, and then whether it is an odd digit.

■ If the value of **Ch** still has not been characterized at this point, the **ELSE** clause of the **CASE** statement is applied. In this case, **NrPrintable** is increased by 1. Notice that there is no colon between the **ELSE** and the statement executed. Notice also that an **END** terminates the **CASE** statement. This is one of three places in Pascal where you find an **END** without a corresponding **BEGIN**.

The syntax for a **CASE** statement is as follows :

```
"CASE" <ordinal variable or expression> "OF"
    <value list> ":" <simple or compound statement>";"
    <value list> ":" <simple or compound statement>";"
    . . .
    <value list> ":" <simple or compound statement>";"
    {"ELSE" <simple or compound statement>";"}
"END"
```

The line beginning with **ELSE** is optional and is allowed in Turbo Pascal but not in standard Pascal. You can have at most one **ELSE** clause in a **CASE** statement.

The **CASE** statement is controlled by the variable or expression following the word **CASE**. This will generally be a variable that can take on the values covered in the individual components of the **CASE** statement. It may also be an expression (such as **MyInt** + 7) that will evaluate to one of the values. It could even be an actual value (such as 7), but you wouldn't really need a **CASE** statement in such a situation.

A *value list* may consist of a single value, several values separated by commas, or a range of values indicated by a starting value, two dots, and an ending value. The ability to specify a range of values is an extension to standard Pascal, and is available in Turbo Pascal.

When the program encounters a **CASE** statement, the value lists are searched until a match is found or until the end of the **CASE** statement. When a match is found, the statement associated with the appropriate value list is executed. After this, processing of the **CASE** statement is finished. If none of the specified values match and you have an **ELSE** clause in the **CASE** statement, the statement associated with the **ELSE** is executed. If there are no matches and you do not have an **ELSE** clause, a Turbo Pascal program does nothing inside the **CASE** statement and execution continues with the statement following the **CASE** statement. If such a situation arises in standard Pascal, the program's behavior is undefined.

The statement associated with a value list can be a simple or a compound one. In fact, you can even have another **CASE** statement associated with a value list—that is, you can have a **CASE** statement nested inside the specification for another such statement.

The following program illustrates a nested **CASE** statement. Before running the program, work through an iteration of the **FOR** loop in the main program for **Count** values of 8 and 9. You should trace through at least one example involving a **CASE** statement. This is a good candidate.

P5-17
```
(* Program to illustrate nested CASE statements *)

PROGRAM NestedCaseDemo;

CONST MaxTrials = 10;
VAR Count, Value : INTEGER;

BEGIN
  RANDOMIZE;
  FOR Count := 1 TO MaxTrials DO
  BEGIN
    Value := RANDOM ( MAXINT);
    (* Notice that the CASE statement also can be controlled
       by an expression.
    *)
```

```
      CASE  Value MOD 4 OF
         0 :
           BEGIN
             WRITELN ( Value:5, ' is divisible by 4');
             Value := RANDOM ( MAXINT);
             (* A nested CASE statement -- fired only if the outer
                result was 0. Notice that the same variable can
                be involved in both CASE statements.
             *)
             CASE Value MOD 2 OF
                0 : WRITELN ( Value:15, ' is even');
                1 : WRITELN ( Value:15, ' is odd');
             END; (* Nested CASE of Value *)
           END;
         1 : WRITELN ( Value:5, ': Remainder is 1');
         2 : WRITELN ( Value:5, ': Remainder is 2');
         3 : WRITELN ( Value:5, ': Remainder is 3');
         (* ELSE clause is optional, and is not needed here *)
      END;    (* CASE of Value MOD 4 *)
    END; (* FOR Count := 1 TO MaxVals *)
    READLN;
END.
```

The program generates at least ten random integer values and displays some information about these values. If a generated value is divisible by 4, the program generates another random value and checks whether this value is odd or even. This second test is done in a **CASE** statement that is nested within one of the possible values for the outer **CASE** statement. The first **END** under the 0 case terminates the nested **CASE** statement; the second one terminates the compound statement associated with the 0.

For a sample run, the program produced the following output:

```
16382: Remainder is 2
18067: Remainder is 3
27128 is divisible by 4
         21344 is even
  726: Remainder is 2
 1340 is divisible by 4
         11832 is even
15911: Remainder is 3
21374: Remainder is 2
 6027: Remainder is 3
 6816 is divisible by 4
         11935 is odd
17031: Remainder is 3
```

Notice that both of the **CASE** statements in this program are controlled by expressions (rather than variables) that evaluate to a small range of possible integer values.

Iteration Constructs

Earlier in this chapter, you learned about the **FOR** loop, which repeats something a specified number of times. The loop is controlled by a counter that is updated automatically by the program. When the counter reaches the specified ending value, the loop stops executing.

More commonly, your program loops will need to execute an indeterminate number of times. The criterion for stopping or continuing the loop will be some condition, which will be tested before or after each iteration of the loop. For example, suppose that you want to determine how long it would take you, on the average, to generate a random value divisible by 17. You might start generating random integers and counting the number of values generated up to that point. You would continue generating values until you got one that was divisible by 17.

The Impulsive Iteration Construct: The REPEAT Statement

The following program lets you run multiple trials of this sort, and introduces an iteration construct for controlling such a loop. Run the program a few times. Do the results seem to be clustered within a particular range? If so, can you think of an explanation for this result?

P5-18

```
(* Program to illustrate use of REPEAT construct *)

PROGRAM RepeatDemo;

CONST Divisor = 17;
      MaxTrials = 1000;
VAR Value, Count, NrTries,
    RunningSum, ShortestRun, LongestRun : LONGINT;

   PROCEDURE CheckExtremes ( Value : LONGINT;
                             VAR Shortest, Longest : LONGINT);
```

```
    BEGIN
      IF Value > Longest THEN
        Longest := Value;
      IF Value < Shortest THEN
        Shortest := Value;
    END; (** CheckExtremes *)

    PROCEDURE DisplaySummary ( NrTrials, Total,
                                Shortest, Longest : LONGINT);
    BEGIN
      WRITELN ( 'Longest Run = ', Longest:3);
      WRITELN ( 'Shortest Run = ', Shortest:3);
      WRITELN ( 'Average Run Length = ',
                Total / NrTrials : 10 : 3);
    END; (* DisplaySummary *)

BEGIN
  RANDOMIZE;
  RunningSum := 0;
  ShortestRun := MAXINT;
  LongestRun := 0;

  WRITELN ( 'Generating values...');
  FOR Count := 1 TO MaxTrials DO
  BEGIN
    NrTries := 0;
    (* Repeat the following loop until program
       generates a number that's divisible by Divisor.
       This loop executes AT LEAST once.
       The REPEAT loop ends with the UNTIL line.
    *)
    REPEAT
      Value := RANDOM ( MAXINT);
      INC ( NrTries);
    UNTIL ( Value MOD Divisor = 0);

    CheckExtremes ( NrTries, ShortestRun, LongestRun);
    INC ( RunningSum, NrTries);
  END; (* FOR Count := 1 TO MaxTrials *)

  DisplaySummary ( MaxTrials, RunningSum,
                   ShortestRun, LongestRun);
  READLN;
END.
```

This program is controlled by the **REPEAT** loop nested inside the **FOR** loop. Such a loop keeps executing a series of statements until some condition becomes **TRUE**. This test condition is known as the *termination condition,* since the loop must repeat until the termination condition becomes **TRUE**.

For a few sample runs, this program produced the following results:

```
Longest Run = 100
Shortest Run = 1
Average Run Length =        17.451

Longest Run = 124
Shortest Run = 1
Average Run Length =        17.112

Longest Run = 99
Shortest Run = 1
Average Run Length =        16.428

Longest Run = 134
Shortest Run = 1
Average Run Length =        17.055

Longest Run = 153
Shortest Run = 1
Average Run Length =        16.833
```

Change the value of **MaxTrials** to 100 in program **RepeatDemo**. Then run several new samples. Do the results from the second series of runs differ more dramatically from each other than when you ran 1000 trials each time? This increased variability (range of values) in the outcome occurs because a smaller number of trials gives you a less stable result.

Finally, change the value of **Divisor** and run the program again. Do the results cluster around a different value this time? The average run length is directly related to the divisor. For example, if the divisor were 2, you would expect to get an even number about every other time. On the average, it would take a run length of 2 to give you the desired result.

The syntax for a **REPEAT** loop is simple.

```
"REPEAT"
    <any sequence of simple and/or compound statements>
"UNTIL" <Boolean expression>
```

The Boolean expression is the termination condition.

Notice that you don't need a **BEGIN** and **END** to delimit the statements that make up the **REPEAT** loop. This is accomplished by the **REPEAT** at the start and the **UNTIL** at the end of the loop.

A **REPEAT** loop does its work first, and then tests whether it can stop. This execution format—act, then test—means that the loop will execute at least once, since it doesn't test until after it has done its work.

The termination condition will generally involve a particular variable whose value determines whether the Boolean expression is **TRUE** or **FALSE**. This variable is called the *loop variable*. In order for the loop to terminate eventually, the value of the loop variable needs to change over iterations. If the loop variable stays constant, and its initial value doesn't make the termination condition **TRUE**, the loop never stops executing.

For example, **RepeatDemo** presumes that you'll eventually generate a random number divisible by **Divisor**. While there is no absolute guarantee of this, you can be confident that such a number will be generated.

In a **REPEAT** loop, it's your responsibility to make sure that the value of the loop variable changes. You can accomplish this by generating values (as in the example program) or by assigning different values to the loop variable. The **REPEAT** loop differs from the **FOR** loop in that you must make such changes or must tell your program to make them. (Recall that in a **FOR** loop, the program updates the loop variable automatically.)

REMEMBER   A **REPEAT** loop carries out its task and *then* checks whether it can stop. For this reason, such a loop executes at least once. It's your responsibility to ensure that the value of the loop variable changes over iterations, so that the termination condition can eventually become **TRUE**.

The Cautious Iteration Construct: The WHILE Statement

In contrast to the **REPEAT** statement—which acts first and asks questions later—Pascal's **WHILE** construct checks first and acts only if certain conditions are fulfilled (that is, are **TRUE**). You've seen the **WHILE** construct in earlier programs. Its syntax is

---

"**WHILE**" < Boolean expression > "**DO**"
< simple or compound statement >

The Boolean expression in this statement is called the *continuation condition*. A **WHILE** statement executes *while* the continuation condition is **TRUE**. Thus, a **WHILE** loop stops when a condition no longer holds—that is, becomes **FALSE**. In contrast, a **REPEAT** loop stops when a condition becomes **TRUE**.

The next program also looks for a number divisible by 17, but uses a **WHILE** statement:

P5-19
```
(* Program to illustrate use of WHILE construct *)

PROGRAM WhileDemo;

CONST Divisor = 17;
      MaxTrials = 1000;
VAR Value, Count, NrTries,
    RunningSum, ShortestRun, LongestRun : LONGINT;

  PROCEDURE CheckExtremes ( Value : LONGINT;
                            VAR Shortest, Longest : LONGINT);
  BEGIN
    IF Value > Longest THEN
      Longest := Value;
    IF Value < Shortest THEN
      Shortest := Value;
  END; (* CheckExtremes *)

  PROCEDURE DisplaySummary ( NrTrials, Total,
                             Shortest, Longest : LONGINT);
  BEGIN
    WRITELN ( 'Longest Run = ', Longest:3);
    WRITELN ( 'Shortest Run = ', Shortest:3);
    WRITELN ( 'Average Run Length = ',
              Total / NrTrials : 10 : 3);
  END; (* DisplaySummary *)

BEGIN
  RANDOMIZE;
  RunningSum := 0;
  ShortestRun := MAXINT;
  LongestRun := 0;
  WRITELN ( 'Generating values...');
  FOR Count := 1 TO MaxTrials DO
  BEGIN
    Value := RANDOM ( MAXINT);
    NrTries := 1;
    (* As long as the most recently generated value
       is NOT divisible by Divisor, execute the loop.
       If the first value generated is divisible by Divisor,
       this loop will never execute.
```

```
        Compare the Boolean expression with the one for the
        REPEAT loop.
    *)
    WHILE ( Value MOD Divisor <> 0) DO
    BEGIN
      Value := RANDOM ( MAXINT);
      INC ( NrTries);
    END;
    CheckExtremes ( NrTries, ShortestRun, LongestRun);
    INC ( RunningSum, NrTries);
  END; (* FOR Count := 1 TO MaxTrials *)
  DisplaySummary ( MaxTrials, RunningSum,
                   ShortestRun, LongestRun);
  READLN;
END.
```

This program does exactly the same things as the previous one. However, the inner looping is controlled by a **WHILE** instead of a **REPEAT** loop. This has several consequences.

Because the **WHILE** loop tests before doing anything, it's necessary to generate a value outside the loop. This value primes the loop, so that the loop variable in the continuation condition has been initialized. This is not necessary with the **REPEAT** loop because it initializes the loop variable in the body of the loop, which comes before the test.

Because you're looking for a **FALSE** result in a **WHILE** loop, the Boolean expression in the program looks for values that are *not* divisible by **Divisor**. This test is essentially the opposite of the test made in the **REPEAT** loop in an earlier example.

As it turns out, the **REPEAT** and **WHILE** statements can be made equivalent to each other. In principle, this means that the constructs are interchangeable; wherever you can use one type of loop, you can also use the other. However, in particular situations, one or the other type of loop will generally be more convenient.

Because the continuation condition could be **FALSE** on the very first test, the body of the **WHILE** loop may never execute. As do the other control constructs—except for the **REPEAT** construct—the **WHILE** loop applies to the next statement, simple or compound.

The program will not change a **WHILE** statement's loop variable automatically. As a consequence, you need to change this variable, either explicitly through assignment or through procedure or function calls. In practice, you'll almost always have a compound statement for a **WHILE** statement. For a **WHILE** loop, you will need a **BEGIN** and **END** to mark the boundaries of the statement.

REMEMBER   A **WHILE** loop checks whether it can continue, and carries out its task only if it can. For this reason, such a loop may never execute. You must make sure that the value of the loop variable changes over iterations so that the continuation condition can eventually become **FALSE**.

The following program generates a table of the printable ASCII characters and also illustrates the importance of changing the loop variable:

P5-20
```
(* Program to illustrate WHILE loop, and
   importance of changing value of loop variable.
*)

PROGRAM ASCIIDisplay;

VAR Count : INTEGER;
    CurrCh : CHAR;

   (* Display the current character;
      Move to a new line after every 5 values.
   *)
   PROCEDURE Display;
   BEGIN
      WRITE ( '    ', ORD ( CurrCh) : 3, '  ', CurrCh);
      INC ( Count);
      IF Count MOD 5 = 0 THEN
         WRITELN;
   END;

BEGIN
   Count := 0;
   (* space -- #32 -- is the first printable CHAR *)
   CurrCh := #32;
   (* #126 is the last printable character *)
   WHILE ORD ( CurrCh) < 127 DO
   BEGIN
      Display;
      (* get the next character *)
      INC ( CurrCh);
   END;
   READLN;
END.
```

The program does two things as long as **CurrCh** is less than 127: it displays the character and increases the value of **CurrCh** within the loop. This program produces the following output:

32		33	!	34	"	35	#	36	$
37	%	38	&	39	'	40	(	41	)
42	*	43	+	44	,	45	-	46	.
47	/	48	0	49	1	50	2	51	3
52	4	53	5	54	6	55	7	56	8
57	9	58	:	59	;	60	<	61	=
62	>	63	?	64	@	65	A	66	B
67	C	68	D	69	E	70	F	71	G
72	H	73	I	74	J	75	K	76	L
77	M	78	N	79	O	80	P	81	Q
82	R	83	S	84	T	85	U	86	V
87	W	88	X	89	Y	90	Z	91	[
92	\	93	]	94	^	95	_	96	'
97	a	98	b	99	c	100	d	101	e
102	f	103	g	104	h	105	i	106	j
107	k	108	l	109	m	110	n	111	o
112	p	113	q	114	r	115	s	116	t
117	u	118	v	119	w	120	x	121	y
122	z	123	{	124	¦	125	}	126	~

If you remove the line

```
INC ( CurrCh);
```

the program will never terminate, since it will display a space (ASCII 32) over and over.

The Structure of Iteration Statements

Although their syntax is quite simple, iteration statements can have subtle effects. The output from a **WHILE** or **REPEAT** loop can vary quite a bit, depending on the details of the Boolean expression that controls the loop. In particular, three things affect the way in which an iteration loop does its work:

■ The boundary (starting and ending) values for the loop variable

■ The actual test being done in the Boolean expression (continuation or termination condition)

■ Where in the loop body the loop variable is changed

The following example illustrates how these factors affect a loop. The program computes and displays some numerical values. Read the program and then run it to see what its routines do.

P5-21
```
(* Program to illustrate effects of varying details
   of a WHILE loop.
*)

PROGRAM LoopDemo;

CONST MaxValue = 10;

  (* Return the cube of the argument *)
  FUNCTION Cube ( Val : INTEGER) : INTEGER;
  BEGIN
    Cube := Val * Val * Val;
  END; (* FN Cube *)

  (* Compute and display a series of cubes;
     change loop variable BEFORE computing and
     displaying results.
  *)
  PROCEDURE WChangeAtTop;
  VAR Count, RunningSum, Result : INTEGER;
  BEGIN
    Count := 1;
    RunningSum := 0;
    WHILE Count <= MaxValue DO
    BEGIN
      INC ( Count);
      Result := Cube ( Count);
      INC ( RunningSum, Result);
      WRITELN ( Count:2, ': Cube = ', Result:4,
                '; RunningSum = ', RunningSum:4);
    END; (* WHILE Count <= MaxValue *)
  END; (* WChangeAtTop *)

  (* Compute and display a series of cubes;
     change loop variable AFTER computing and
     displaying results.
  *)
  PROCEDURE WChangeAtBottom;
  VAR Count, RunningSum, Result : INTEGER;
  BEGIN
    Count := 1;
    RunningSum := 0;
    WHILE Count <= MaxValue DO
    BEGIN
      Result := Cube ( Count);
```

```
        INC ( RunningSum, Result);
        WRITELN ( Count:2, ': Cube = ', Result:4,
                  '; RunningSum = ', RunningSum:4);
        INC ( Count);
      END; (* WHILE Count <= MaxValue *)
    END; (* WChangeAtBottom *)

BEGIN
  WRITELN ( 'WHILE ChangeAtBottom:');
  WChangeAtBottom;
  WRITELN ( '------------------------------------------');
  WRITELN ( 'WHILE ChangeAtTop:');
  WChangeAtTop;
  READLN;
END.
```

This program produces the following output. You should work through these two procedures by hand to develop your understanding of how they behave. Then trace through the program to confirm your hand execution.

```
WHILE ChangeAtBottom:
 1: Cube =     1; RunningSum =     1
 2: Cube =     8; RunningSum =     9
 3: Cube =    27; RunningSum =    36
 4: Cube =    64; RunningSum =   100
 5: Cube =   125; RunningSum =   225
 6: Cube =   216; RunningSum =   441
 7: Cube =   343; RunningSum =   784
 8: Cube =   512; RunningSum =  1296
 9: Cube =   729; RunningSum =  2025
10: Cube =  1000; RunningSum =  3025
------------------------------------------
WHILE ChangeAtTop:
 2: Cube =     8; RunningSum =     8
 3: Cube =    27; RunningSum =    35
 4: Cube =    64; RunningSum =    99
 5: Cube =   125; RunningSum =   224
 6: Cube =   216; RunningSum =   440
 7: Cube =   343; RunningSum =   783
 8: Cube =   512; RunningSum =  1295
 9: Cube =   729; RunningSum =  2024
10: Cube =  1000; RunningSum =  3024
11: Cube =  1331; RunningSum =  4355
```

The only difference between **WChangeAtTop** and **WChangeAt-Bottom** is the location of the statement

```
INC ( Count);
```

In **WChangeAtTop,** the loop variable's value is changed before anything is done with it in the loop. In this case, the loop works with the values 2 through 11 instead of 1 through 10. On the other hand, by changing this variable at the end of the loop body—as in **WChangeAtBottom**—the procedure works with the values 1 through 10.

You could use **REPEAT** loops in the procedures. In that case, the termination condition corresponding to the continuation conditions in the current program would be

```
Val > MaxValue
```

To explore the effects of changes in the factors mentioned earlier on the behavior of a loop, display the sums of cubes information for the condition combinations summarized in Table 5-1.

A Comparison Example

The following program lets you compare the behavior of **WHILE** and **REPEAT** loops directly. In particular, you can see the consequences of testing before or after the loop.

Initial Looping Variable	Continuation Condition	Change in Looping Variable
1	Count <= MaxValue	Bottom
1	Count <= MaxValue	Top
1	Count < MaxValue	Bottom
1	Count < MaxValue	Top
0	Count <= MaxValue	Bottom
0	Count <= MaxValue	Top
0	Count < MaxValue	Bottom
0	Count < MaxValue	Top

Table 5-1. *Suggested Variants on the WHILE and REPEAT Loops*

```
P5-22    (* Program to enable direct comparison between
             WHILE and REPEAT loops.
         *)

         PROGRAM WhileAndRepeatDemo;

         VAR Value : INTEGER;

           PROCEDURE GetInteger ( Message : STRING;
                                  VAR Value : INTEGER);
           BEGIN
             WRITE ( Message, ' ');
             READLN ( Value);
           END; (* GetInteger *)

           PROCEDURE WhileTest ( Count : INTEGER);
           BEGIN
             WHILE ODD ( Count) DO
             BEGIN
               WRITE ( Count, ' : ');
               Count := Count DIV 2;
             END;
             WRITELN ( 'Done');
           END; (* WhileTest *)

           PROCEDURE RepeatTest ( Count : INTEGER);
           BEGIN
             REPEAT
               WRITE ( Count, ' : ');
               Count := Count DIV 2;
             UNTIL ( NOT ( ODD ( Count)));
             WRITELN ( 'Done');
           END; (* RepeatTest *)

         BEGIN
           REPEAT
             GetInteger ( 'Value? (0 to stop) ', Value);

             WRITELN ( 'WhileTest:');
             WhileTest ( Value);
             WRITELN ( '---------------------------');
             WRITELN ( 'RepeatTest:');
             RepeatTest ( Value);
           UNTIL ( Value = 0);
           READLN;
         END.
```

The following listing shows some sample outputs for selected starting values. Compare the behavior of the **WHILE** and the **REPEAT** loops.

```
Value? 14
WhileTest:
Done
--------------------------
RepeatTest:
14 : 7 : 3 : 1 : Done

Value? 37
WhileTest:
37 : Done
--------------------------
RepeatTest:
37 : Done

Value? 31
WhileTest:
31 : 15 : 7 : 3 : 1 : Done
--------------------------
RepeatTest:
31 : 15 : 7 : 3 : 1 : Done

Value? 64
WhileTest:
Done
--------------------------
RepeatTest:
64 : Done
```

Notice that, for certain values, the **WHILE** loop never computes any results, whereas the **REPEAT** loop always displays at least one value.

Congratulations, you've just mastered all of Pascal's control constructs! You'll be using these constructs extensively throughout the book and in the programs that you write on your own.

In this chapter, you learned about selection and iteration constructs. The selection constructs are: **IF**, **IF-ELSE**, extended **IF-ELSE**, and the **CASE** statement. The iteration constructs are the **FOR**, **REPEAT**, and **WHILE** loops.

In the next chapter, you'll start putting this knowledge to use as you learn how to define more complex procedures and functions.

6 *Procedures and Functions Revisited*

Chapter 4, "Procedures and Functions," described the general structure of procedures and functions (routines). You learned how to define routines and how to specify and use parameters with these routines. This chapter discusses various miscellaneous but important details about procedures and functions. You'll learn how to define procedures and functions inside of other routines. You'll also learn how to determine which routines can call which other ones. Finally, there is an introduction to recursion, a powerful programming technique in which a routine calls itself.

Calling Procedures and Functions

When the compiler processes your source file, it essentially processes the source code from start to finish, evaluating each statement to make sure it conforms to Pascal's syntax. Among other things, the compiler evaluates procedure and function calls.

Recall from Chapter 4 that the argument list in a procedure or function call must correspond to the parameter list in the called routine's interface. For the compiler to evaluate such a call, it must know the called routine's interface. Suppose, for example, that procedures **A** and **B** are both defined in the main program. If procedure **A** calls **B**, the compiler needs to know **B**'s interface to evaluate the syntactic correctness of the call. In practice, this would mean that procedure **B** must be defined before **A**. But suppose procedure **B** calls **A** as well? For this to work, **A** must be defined before **B**. Is there any way around these contradictory requirements?

Pascal allows you to use a **FORWARD** declaration to specify just the interface for a procedure or function while actually defining the routine later on. To do this, simply specify the procedure heading followed by a semicolon. After the heading, put the reserved word **FORWARD** followed by a semicolon. This tells the compiler not to expect the rest of the routine (that is, declarations and body).

```
PROCEDURE CheckValues ( Val1, Val2 : REAL); FORWARD;
```

Later in the declaration section, you must include the actual definition for this procedure. The definition will include a parameterless heading, the routine's declaration section, and the procedure body.

For example, the following listing represents the definition for procedure **CheckValues** after the **FORWARD** declaration in the previous listing:

```
(* no parameters, since they were listed in the FORWARD line *)
PROCEDURE CheckValues;

  (* Declarations go here, as always *)

BEGIN
  (* procedure body here, as always *)
END;
```

The parameter list is not specified because the compiler already has that information. You may find it useful, however, to include the parameter information as a comment, as in the following alternative to the heading in the definition for **CheckValues**:

```
PROCEDURE CheckValues; (* Val1, Val2 : REAL *)
```

REMEMBER In a **FORWARD** declaration, the procedure or function heading (with parameter list) is followed by the reserved word **FORWARD**. A semicolon must separate the procedure or function heading and the **FORWARD**, and a semicolon must separate the **FORWARD** from subsequent statements. The routine's declarations and body cannot be included with the **FORWARD** declaration. The parameters cannot be included with the actual procedure or function definition.

Nested Routines

In Chapter 4, you learned that procedures and functions have the same structure as a program: heading, declarations, and body. As in the main program, you can define procedures and functions in a routine's declaration section. A routine that is defined inside another is said to be nested in the outer routine.

The following program provides examples of nested routines. Trace through the program to see the sequence in which routines are called. Look at the call stack (CTRL-F3) at various points in the program—to see what routines have been started. Procedure **GetBoundedInt** uses two nested routines to get the desired value. Procedure **AdjustVals** makes any necessary adjustments so that the lower bound is less than the upper bound. This covers cases in which the **GetBoundedInt** procedure might be called with the middle two parameters reversed. Similarly, function **IsBetween** checks whether the value entered by the user falls within the specified bounds. If this function returns **TRUE**, the **REPEAT** loop can be terminated.

P6-1
```
(* Program to show definition and use of nested routines *)

PROGRAM NestedExamples;

VAR Value : INTEGER;

   (* Get an integer lying within the boundaries
      specified by MinVal and MaxVal
   *)
   PROCEDURE GetBoundedInt ( Message : STRING;
                             MinVal, MaxVal : INTEGER;
                             VAR Value : INTEGER);

      (* Fix boundary values if they are reversed --
```

```
                   that is, if Small > Large.
            *)
            PROCEDURE AdjustVals ( VAR Small, Large : INTEGER);
            VAR Temp : INTEGER;
            BEGIN
              WRITELN ( 'Start AdjustVals');
              IF Small > Large THEN
              BEGIN
                Temp := Small;
                Small := Large;
                Large := Temp;
              END;
              WRITELN ( 'Finish AdjustVals');
            END; (* AdjustVals *)

            (* Return TRUE if Small <= Val <= Large *)
            FUNCTION IsBetween ( Val, Small, Large : INTEGER) : BOOLEAN;
            BEGIN
              WRITELN ( 'Start IsBetween');
              IsBetween := ( Small <= Val) AND ( Large >= Val);
              WRITELN ( 'Finish IsBetween');
            END;   (* FN IsBetween *)

          BEGIN
            WRITELN ( 'Start GetBoundedInt');
            AdjustVals ( MinVal, MaxVal);
            REPEAT
              WRITE ( Message, ' ');
              READLN ( Value);
            UNTIL IsBetween ( Value, MinVal, MaxVal);
            WRITELN ( 'Finish GetBoundedInt');
          END; (* GetBoundedInt *)

        BEGIN
          WRITELN ( 'Start main program');
          GetBoundedInt ( 'Value between -5 and 39:',
                          -5, 39, Value);
          WRITELN ( Value);
          WRITELN ( 'Finish main program');
          READLN;
        END.
```

Procedure **AdjustVals** and function **IsBetween** are both nested in **GetBoundedInt**. This nesting routine provides the *immediate environment* for the two nested routines. Conversely, the two routines are said to be defined in **GetBoundedInt**'s *local environment*.

Such nested routines are accessible only while the nesting routine is executing. This restriction means that the main program cannot call either **AdjustVals** or **IsBetween**. (In fact, the main program doesn't even know that these routines exist.) This invisibility is a very useful property, since it makes it easier for you to isolate independent portions of your programs.

By limiting the number of routines that have access to a procedure or function, you can minimize the likelihood of bugs or errors resulting from improper use of that routine. Similarly, by limiting the contexts in which that procedure or function can be called, you can make it easier to identify the source of any errors involving the routine.

Using nested procedures also makes your source code easier to read. In the *parent* (that is, nesting) routine, you'll have a single procedure or function call instead of the code that carries out the work of the nested routine. This advantage will be particularly useful when you need to write more complex procedures and functions. This nesting process can be continued. That is, a nested routine can include nested routines of its own, and so forth. Later in this chapter, you'll see examples of multiple levels of nesting.

Program Design Issues

The ability to nest routines helps you to create procedures and functions that are independent of each other. It also enables you to hide the messy details of a task from the main program.

For example, suppose you're designing interactive software and would like to make your programs as robust as possible. You must make sure to handle input properly. If your program is expecting numerical input and the user accidentally types a string, an ordinary Pascal program will crash.

To avoid this, you need to include a routine that reads information as a string and then converts the string to a numerical value of the appropriate sort. Such a routine has to check for various types of values and also for invalid input. You can create a self-contained routine for doing this by nesting the subtasks within the routine. To keep things manageable, you will build an **INTEGER** as an example.

The basic strategy is to process the string, character by character, and to build a numerical value from these characters. The procedure stops when it finds an invalid character or reaches the end of the string. This procedure will perform the same sequence of actions repeatedly.

1. Check whether the next character is a digit.

2. If so, determine the numerical value of the digit; otherwise, exit from the loop.

3. If a digit was read, multiply the number so far by 10 and add the digit's value to this running total.

4. Update counters.

The procedure will also need to check a special case: whether the first character is a minus (−) or plus (+) sign.

The following listing includes a procedure, **MakeInt**, that implements such a strategy. Run the program, using valid and invalid values. For example, try the program with values such as **5, −35, 58g,** and **"hello"**.

The procedure contains three nested routines to carry out some of the tasks just described. To see how the procedure works, add some **WRITELN** statements that tell you where the program is at various points in its execution.

P6-2
```
(* Program to illustrate procedure nesting and
   to provide MakeInt -- a more robust input
   handler for integers.
*)

PROGRAM IntDemo;

VAR  StrVal : STRING;
     Result :INTEGER;

   (* Build an integer value from a string.
      The first character can be a + or -; after that, only
      digits are allowed. The procedure stops processing as
      soon as a non-digit is encountered.
   *)
   PROCEDURE MakeInt ( Str : STRING;
                       VAR Result : INTEGER);
   CONST ErrorVal = 0;
         Base = 10;
   VAR Index, HowLong : INTEGER;
       Negative : BOOLEAN;

      (* Returns TRUE if Ch is a digit character. *)
      FUNCTION IsDigit ( Ch : CHAR) : BOOLEAN;
      BEGIN
        IsDigit := ( Ch >= '0') AND  ( Ch <= '9');
```

```pascal
      END; (* IsDigit *)

    (* Returns the numerical value of the 'digit" Ch *)
    FUNCTION ToVal ( Ch : CHAR) : INTEGER;
    BEGIN
      ToVal := ORD ( Ch) - ORD ( '0');
    END; (* ToVal *)

    (* Set Negative if the number starts with a minus
       sign; skip the first character if it's a +
    *)
    PROCEDURE HandleFirstCh;
    BEGIN
      IF Str [ 1] = '-' THEN
      BEGIN
        Negative := TRUE;
        INC ( Index);
      END
      ELSE IF Str [ 1] = '+' THEN
        INC ( Index);
    END; (* HandleFirstCh *)

BEGIN  (* MakeInt *)
  Result := 0;
  Negative := False;
  HowLong := LENGTH ( Str);
  IF HowLong > 0 THEN
  BEGIN
    Index := 1;
    HandleFirstCh;
    WHILE ( Index <= HowLong) DO
    BEGIN
      IF IsDigit ( Str [ Index]) THEN
      BEGIN
        Result := Base * Result + ToVal ( Str [ Index]);
        INC ( Index);
      END
      ELSE
        Index := HowLong + 1;
    END;  (* WHILE HowLong > 0 *)
    IF Negative THEN
      Result := Result * -1;
  END
  ELSE  (* If a null string was passed, return ErrorVal *)
    Result := ErrorVal;
END; (* MakeInt *)

PROCEDURE GetString ( Message : STRING;
                      VAR Value : STRING);
BEGIN
  WRITE ( Message, ' ');
  READLN ( Value);
END; (* GetString *)
```

```
BEGIN
  REPEAT
    GetString ( 'Value? (> 500 to stop)', StrVal);
    MakeInt ( StrVal, Result);
    WRITELN ( StrVal, ' : ', Result);
  UNTIL Result > 500;
  READLN;
END.
```

By moving the code for these actions to nested procedures, you can simplify the code for the actual **MakeInteger** routine. A single-line call to **HandleFirstCh**, for example, is much easier to read and understand than the source code for the procedure. There is a price to pay for this improvement in code clarity: The routine executes a bit more slowly since it takes time to invoke a procedure or function.

By defining the utility functions **ToVal** and **IsDigit** within **MakeInt**, you make the procedure independent of anything but predefined routines (such as **ORD**). If the procedure doesn't work correctly, you know that the error must lie somewhere within the definition for **MakeInt**.

Reading Source Files During Compilation

The **MakeInt** routine is a more robust way of getting whole-number input from the user. Unlike **GetInteger**, this routine won't crash if the user accidentally types a letter instead of a number. This is a good routine to use in programs that need to get integer input.

So far, you've been copying **GetInteger** to each new source file, or perhaps even typing it in from scratch. This would become quite tedious with **MakeInt**, which is much longer than **GetInteger**.

You can keep the source code for **MakeInt** (and perhaps also for a modified version of **GetInteger**) in a separate file. If you want to use these routines in a program, you can tell the compiler to read the contents of the file at the appropriate point in the main program's declaration section.

To do this, you need to use a *compiler directive* — an instruction to the compiler to set certain flags or to carry out a particular action. For example, suppose you have the contents of **MakeInt** and **GetInteger** in a file named IO.PAS. The following listing shows the contents of this file. Notice the modification in **GetInteger** to get a numerical value by calling **MakeInt**.

```
P6-3      (* IO.PAS:
             Contains MakeInt and GetInteger.
             NOTE: This file is not a program; it does not compile.
          *)

             (* Build an integer value from a string.
                The first character can be a + or -; after that, only
                digits are allowed. The procedure stops processing as
                soon as a non-digit is encountered.
             *)
             PROCEDURE MakeInt ( Str : STRING;
                                    VAR Result : INTEGER);
             CONST ErrorVal = 0;
                   Base = 10;
             VAR Index, HowLong : INTEGER;
                 Negative : BOOLEAN;

               (* Returns TRUE if Ch is a digit character. *)
               FUNCTION IsDigit ( Ch : CHAR) : BOOLEAN;
               BEGIN
                 IsDigit := ( Ch >= '0') AND  ( Ch <= '9');
               END; (* IsDigit *)

               (* Returns the numerical value of the 'digit" Ch *)
               FUNCTION ToVal ( Ch : CHAR) : INTEGER;
               BEGIN
                 ToVal := ORD ( Ch) - ORD ( '0');
               END; (* ToVal *)

               (* Set Negative if the number starts with a minus
                  sign; skip the first character if it's a +
               *)
               PROCEDURE HandleFirstCh;
             BEGIN
               IF Str [ 1] = '-' THEN
               BEGIN
                  Negative := TRUE;
                  INC ( Index);
               END
               ELSE IF Str [ 1] = ''+' THEN
                  INC ( Index);
             END; (* HandleFirstCh *)

          BEGIN  (* MakeInt *)
            Result := 0;
            Negative := False;
            HowLong := LENGTH ( Str);
            IF HowLong > 0 THEN
            BEGIN
              Index := 1;
```

```
        HandleFirstCh;
        WHILE ( Index <= HowLong) DO
        BEGIN
          IF IsDigit ( Str [ Index]) THEN
          BEGIN
            Result := Base * Result + ToVal ( Str [ Index]);
            INC ( Index);
          END
          ELSE
            Index := HowLong + 1;
        END;  (* WHILE HowLong > 0 *)
        IF Negative THEN
          Result := Result * -1;
      END
      ELSE  (* If a null string was passed, return ErrorVal *)
        Result := ErrorVal;
    END; (* MakeInt *)


    (* Prompt user and read an INTEGER.
       Modified to call MakeInt.
    *)
    PROCEDURE GetInteger ( Message : STRING;
                            VAR Value : INTEGER);

    VAR TempStr : STRING;
    BEGIN
      WRITE ( Message, ' ');
      READLN ( TempStr);
      MakeInt ( TempStr, Value);
    END; (* GetInteger *)
```

Once you have created this file, you can include its contents in other files. The following program shows how to include one file in another one:

P6-4

```
    (* Program to illustrate use of INCLUDE $I directive. *)

    PROGRAM IncludeDemo;

    VAR IntVal : INTEGER;

    (* The following line tells compiler to read IO.PAS here *)
    (*$I IO.PAS *)

    BEGIN
      GetInteger ( 'Value?', IntVal);
      WRITELN ( 'You entered ', IntVal);
      READLN;
    END.
```

The compiler directive—the line beginning with **(*$I**—tells the compiler to read the contents of the specified file (IO.PAS) at that point in the file. The effect is the same as if the source text from that file were physically included in the program source file. The compiler includes the source code and compiles it, just as all other text in the program is compiled. The syntax for the include directive is

---

"(*$I " <file name> " *)"
or
"{$I " <file name> " }"

The **$I** must immediately follow the comment characters; otherwise, the directive will be interpreted as a comment rather than a compiler directive. Other directives will be mentioned where needed in the book. See the on-line help for a summary of the compiler directives.

Accessibility of Routines and Variables

Since routines can be nested, the rules that govern what can call what can get a bit involved. The same identifiers may be used in different places in a program, which further complicates the issue. This section and the next discuss Turbo Pascal's accessibility and naming rules.

Program **Shell1** is shown in the next listing and is extended in subsequent listings. You may want to fill in actual statements to test the assertions in this section with specific examples. The accessibility rules are marked with bullets in the text.

P6-5
```
(* Program shell to illustrate procedure and function
   nesting and accessibility.
   This version contains just two level 1 routines.
*)

PROGRAM Shell1;
  PROCEDURE G1; FORWARD; (* So A1 can call G1 *)

  PROCEDURE A1;
  BEGIN (* A1 *)
  END; (* A1 *)
```

```
      PROCEDURE G1;
      BEGIN (* G1 *)
      END; (* G1 *)

BEGIN (* Main program *)
    WRITELN ( 'Done with Shell1. Press ENTER to end program.');
    READLN;
END.
```

The preceding program provides a shell for procedure calls. In its current form, **Shell1** contains two empty procedures (**A1** and **G1**) and the main program. (Empty procedures are perfectly valid; they just don't do anything.)

The following discussion covers routines defined at different levels — that is, nested to varying depths. Think of the main program as level 0. Routines defined in the declaration section of the main program are at level 1.

■ In Pascal, the main program can call any procedure or function defined in the program's declaration section — in other words, it can call any level 1 routine. The main program is the immediate environment for these routines. For example, procedures **A1** and **G1** are level 1 procedures in the preceding program.

■ Level 1 routines can call each other, provided that the interface information is available. Thus, the **FORWARD** declaration for **G1** is necessary if **A1** is to call **G1**. (Notice the format for a parameterless **FORWARD** declaration.)

A level 1 routine can have level 2 procedures and functions defined in its local environment. For example, program **Shell2**, in the following listing, contains three level 2 routines: **B2** and **D2** are nested in **A1**, and **H2** is nested in **G1**. **H2** is defined in **G1**'s local environment; conversely, **G1** is the immediate environment for **H2**. Notice that **D2**'s **FORWARD** declaration is made in **D2**'s immediate environment (that is, in the declaration section of **A1**), not in the main program.

P6-6
```
(* Program shell to illustrate procedure and function
     nesting and accessibility.
     This version contains level 1 and level 2 routines.
*)
```

```
PROGRAM Shell2;
  PROCEDURE G1; FORWARD;

  PROCEDURE A1;              (* Level 1 *)
    (* Note that this FORWARD declaration is in
       A1 not in the main program -- because
       D2 is defined inside A1, and not in the main program.
    *)
    PROCEDURE D2; FORWARD;

    PROCEDURE B2;            (* Level 2 *)
    BEGIN  (* B2 *)
    END; (* B2 *)

    PROCEDURE D2;            (* Level 2 *)
    BEGIN  (* D2 *)
    END; (* D2 *)

  BEGIN (* A1 *)
  END; (* A1 *)

  PROCEDURE G1;              (* Level 1 *)

    PROCEDURE H2;
    BEGIN  (* H2 *)
    END; (* H2 *)

  BEGIN (* G1 *)
  END; (* G1 *)

BEGIN (* Main program *)
  WRITELN ( 'Done with Shell2. Press ENTER to end program.');
  READLN;
END.
```

■ A level 1 routine can call any level 2 routines nested within it, but cannot call any other level 2 routines. Thus, **A1** can call both **B2** and **D2** but cannot call **H2**. Similarly, **H2** is the only level 2 routine that **G1** can call.

■ The level 2 routines within a procedure or function can call each other—again, provided that the necessary interface information is available. Thus, **B2** and **D2** can call each other because **D2** has been **FORWARD** declared. On the other hand, level 2 routines nested within different routines cannot call each other. Thus, **H2** cannot call either **B2** or **D2**.

- Level 2 routines can call any level 1 routine—provided that the appropriate interface information is available to level 2's immediate environment.

- The main program *cannot* call any level 2 routines.

Level 2 routines can also have nested routines, which would be at level 3. In program **Shell3**, **C3** and **E3** are level 3 routines:

```
P6-7      (* Program shell to illustrate procedure and function
             nesting and accessibility.
             This version contains routines from levels 1, 2, and 3.
          *)

          PROGRAM Shell3;
            PROCEDURE G1; FORWARD;

            PROCEDURE A1;                 (* Level 1 *)
              PROCEDURE D2; FORWARD;

              PROCEDURE B2;               (* Level 2 *)

                PROCEDURE C3;             (* Level 3 *)
                BEGIN (* C3 *)
                END; (* C3 *)

              BEGIN  (* B2 *)
              END; (* B2 *)

              PROCEDURE D2;               (* Level 2 *)

                PROCEDURE E3;             (* Level 3 *)
                BEGIN (* E3 *)
                END; (* E3 *)

              BEGIN  (* D2 *)
              END; (* D2 *)

            BEGIN (* A1 *)
            END; (* A1 *)

            PROCEDURE G1;                 (* Level 1 *)

              PROCEDURE H2;               (* Level 2 *)
              BEGIN  (* H2 *)
              END; (* H2 *)

            BEGIN (* G1 *)
            END; (* G1 *)
```

```
BEGIN (* Main program *)
  WRITELN ( 'Done with Shell3. Press ENTER to end program.');
  READLN;
END.
```

■ Level 3 routines can call level 1 routines with a known interface, the level 2 routines that represent the level 3 routines' immediate environments, and any level 2 routines that their immediate environments can call. Thus, **C3** can call **A1** and **G1** because they are both level 1; **C3** can call **B2** because **B2** is the immediate environment for **C3**; and **C3** can call **D2** because this is a level 2 routine that **B2** can call. An interface is known to a level 3 routine if the interface is accessible to the routine's immediate environment.

■ Level 3 routines defined within the same routine can call each other, but they *cannot* call level 3 routines nested inside other routines. Thus, **C3** and **E3** cannot call each other.

■ Level 1 routines cannot call any level 3 routines.

■ A level 2 routine can call only the level 3 routines nested within it, but no other level 3 routines. Thus, **B2** can call **C3** but not **E3**. On the other hand, **D2** can call **E3** but not **C3**.

Such nesting can continue to arbitrary levels. For example, program **Shell4** shows a level 4 procedure, **F4**, nested within **E3**.

P6-8

```
(* Program shell to illustrate procedure and function
   nesting and accessibility.
   This version contains routines from levels 1, 2, 3, and 4.
*)

PROGRAM Shell4;
  PROCEDURE G1; FORWARD;

  PROCEDURE A1;                   (* Level 1 *)
    PROCEDURE D2; FORWARD;

    PROCEDURE B2;                 (* Level 2 *)

      PROCEDURE C3;               (* Level 3 *)
      BEGIN (* C3 *)    .
      END; (* C3 *)

    BEGIN  (* B2 *)
    END; (* B2 *)
```

```
    PROCEDURE D2;                  (* Level 2 *)

      PROCEDURE E3;                (* Level 3 *)

        PROCEDURE F4;              (* Level 4 *)
        BEGIN (* F4 *)
        END; (* F4 *)

      BEGIN (* E3 *)
      END; (* E3 *)

    BEGIN  (* D2 *)
    END; (* D2 *)

  BEGIN (* A1 *)
  END; (* A1 *)

  PROCEDURE G1;                    (* Level 1 *)

    PROCEDURE H2;                  (* Level 2 *)
    BEGIN  (* H2 *)
    END; (* H2 *)

  BEGIN (* G1 *)
  END; (* G1 *)

BEGIN (* Main program *)
  WRITELN ( 'Done with Shell4. Press ENTER to end program.');
  READLN;
END.
```

With this level, you can finally establish some general rules for accessibility. All statements assume that any necessary interface information is available—either through forward declarations or through the relative position of the routines.

■ A level 4 routine can access any level 5 routines defined in its local environment.

■ A level 4 routine can access any level 4 routines nested within the same immediate environment.

■ A level 4 routine can access its nesting routine—that is, the routine that constitutes the routine's immediate environment. Thus, **F4** can access **E3**.

■ A level 4 routine can access any level 3 and level 2 routines accessible to its nesting routine. Thus, **F4** could access any level 3 routines defined in **D2**, as well as any level 2 routines accessible to **E3**. In this case, the latter condition would make **B2** and **D2** accessible.

■ Like routines at all levels, a level 4 routine can access any level 1 routine.

The following list shows what is accessible to routines at various levels. The list assumes that any necessary **FORWARD** declarations have been made. Also keep in mind that a routine can, in principle, call itself.

Main Program	**All Level 1 Routines**
Level 1	All level 1 routines with known interface. Any level 2 routines defined in local environment.
Level 2	All level 1 routines with known interface. Any level 2 routines defined in the same immediate environment. Any level 3 routines defined in local environment.
Level 3	All level 1 routines with known interface. Any level 3 routines defined in the same immediate environment. The nesting routine. Any level 2 routines accessible to the nesting routine. Any level 4 routines defined in local environment.
Level n	All level 1 routines with known interface. Any level n routines defined in the same immediate environment. The nesting routine. Any level $n-1$, $n-2$, ..., 3, 2 routines accessible to the nesting routine. Any level $n+1$ routines defined in local environment.

No procedure can call any routine more than one level deeper than itself. For example, a level 6 routine cannot call a level 8 routine. It could, however, call any level 7 routines defined in its local environment.

Scope and Accessibility

As you've seen, you can't just call a procedure or function from anywhere in your program. The routine is accessible only in certain contexts. The contexts within which a routine is accessible represent its *scope*. A procedure or function is said to be *within scope* if that routine is accessible at a given point in a program.

The summary of accessibility in the previous section shows that level 1 routines are always within scope. This is why such routines are known as *global routines*. All other routines have a more limited scope, and are generally known as *local routines*.

The concept of scope also applies to constants, types, and variables. That is, there are rules concerning the accessibility of variables and other declarations in a program. The rules for constants and types are the same as for variables.

The sample program shell from **Shell4** shows these rules. Suppose that there is a reference to a variable in procedure **F4**. How does the program search for the memory that corresponds to the identifier?

First, the routine's local environment is checked—in this case, the declaration section of **F4**. If the variable is not found there, the declaration section of the immediate environment (**E3** in the example) is checked. If the variable is still not found, the declaration section of the immediate environment's immediate environment (**D2**, in the example) is searched. This process continues through successive immediate environments until the variable is found or the main program is reached. The main program (the global environment) is the last place searched.

REMEMBER   The local environment of the currently executed routine is checked first whenever the program needs to find the storage associated with a variable name or a procedure or function body.

If a routine can search a particular environment, it can "see" declarations and definitions in that environment. Thus, **F4** can see its local environment, as well as the declaration sections of **E3**, **D2**, **A1**, and the main program. **F4** cannot see **B2**, **G1**, and so forth. Note that there is a difference between being able to call a routine and being able to see that routine's local environment. For example, **F4** cannot see either **B2** or **G1**, but can call both of these routines.

In general, a routine may be able to call another one but will not necessarily be able to see it. For example, **E3** can call **F4**, but cannot see it. On the other hand, if a routine can see another routine, it can also call that routine. Thus, **F4** can both call and see **E3**.

A variable is within scope of any routine that can see the environment within which the variable is declared. For example, a variable declared in **A1** is within scope in **A1**, **B2**, **D2**, **C3**, **E3**, and **F4**, but *not* in **G1** or **H2**.

Visibility

You can use the same identifiers in more than one place in your programs. For example, the following program uses the same identifier (**Val**) in three different places. Three different memory locations are given the same name.

P6-9

```
(* Program to illustrate visibility of names *)

PROGRAM Visibility;

VAR Val : INTEGER;     (* Global declaration *)

  PROCEDURE GetInteger ( Message : STRING;
                             VAR Value : INTEGER);
  BEGIN
    WRITE ( Message, ' ');
    READLN ( Value);
  END; (* GetInteger *)

  PROCEDURE Change ( VAR Value : INTEGER);
  VAR Val : INTEGER;     (* Local declaration *)

    FUNCTION OKToChange ( Val : INTEGER) : BOOLEAN;
    BEGIN
      OKToChange := Val <= ( MAXINT DIV 2);
```

```
    END; (* FN OKToChange *)

  BEGIN
    GetInteger ( 'Value? (0 to stop)', Val);
    IF OKToChange ( Val) THEN
      Value := Val * 2
    ELSE
      Value := Val DIV 2;
    WRITELN ( 'In Change, Val = ', Val);
  END; (* Change *)
BEGIN (* Main program *)
  REPEAT
    Change ( Val);
    WRITELN ( 'In main, Val = ', Val);
  UNTIL Val = 0;
  READLN;
END.
```

In the example program, the global **Val** is within scope for all contexts—the main program, **Change**, and **OKToChange**. The local **Val**, declared within **Change**, is within scope only for that procedure and for **OKToChange**. Finally, **OKToChange**'s parameter **Val** is within scope only for the function.

What is referenced when **Val** is used in a particular location depends on the visibility of the identifier **Val**. An identifier's visibility determines the contexts in which the identifier refers to a specific object (that is, a memory location or a routine). If an object is out of scope, it has no visibility. If the object is within scope in a particular context, it may or may not be visible.

For two objects with the same name, the object with the greater visibility will be referenced if the identifier is used in a statement. For example, within function **OKToChange**, the formal parameter has a greater visibility than either the **Val** declared in **Change** or the global **Val**—even though all three are within scope.

An analogy might clarify the distinction between scope and visibility. Suppose you know a group of people who are somewhat familiar with programming and programming languages. For example, assume they have heard of Pascal and of Niklaus Wirth. Now, suppose that one of your friends is named Emma Wirth. Since both Niklaus and Emma Wirth are known to your group, both of these "objects" have scope among your friends.

What if someone asks "What's Wirth working on these days?" at a get-together with your friends. The assumption would probably be that the question is about Emma. In that context, Emma Wirth has greater visibility than Niklaus Wirth. Suppose the same question were asked at the Eidgenossische Technische Hochschule in Zürich (where Niklaus Wirth teaches). Emma Wirth is probably unknown there, so she would not be within scope. In that case, Niklaus Wirth would automatically have greater visibility than Emma Wirth.

To determine the relative visibility of two identical identifiers, you need to know how the program decides which object you mean when you use an identifier in the program. The basic strategy of the program is to search outward, beginning with the local environment. As soon as a match is found, the program stops searching. The first match that is found has the greatest visibility of all the candidates within scope.

When a reference is made to a variable or procedure in a routine, the following search strategy is implemented and continues until an object or routine with the appropriate name is found.

■ The local environment (which includes the routines's own interface) is checked first.

■ The immediate environment is checked next.

■ The immediate environment's immediate environment is checked.

■ Successive immediate environments are checked until the main program's declaration section is reached. This is the last place checked.

This is why the formal parameter **Val** is referenced in **OKToChange**, whereas the local variable declared in **Change** is used when that procedure is executing. The global **Val** is used only in the main program, since the level 1 and level 2 routines each have the same identifier.

Note that the storage allocated for the global variable, **Val**, is accessible in procedure **Change**, although the global identifier **Val** is visible only in the main program. In fact, this location is referenced by means of the **VAR** parameter, **Value**. Changes to the **Value** parameter in the procedure are also changes to the global **Val**.

Recursion

Earlier you learned about the flow of control when a program is executing and routines are called. Generally, a routine is temporarily suspended while another routine executes and is then reactivated when the called routine finishes its work.

For example, if the main program calls procedure **First**, the program is suspended temporarily and **First** begins executing. Suppose **First** calls **Second**. At that point, **First** is also suspended—so there are now two suspended routines. If **Second** calls **Third** during execution, **Second** will become another suspended routine—number three.

If **Third** doesn't call any new routines, it will eventually finish executing. When this happens, control will pass back to the caller—in this case, **Second**. If **Second** also calls no new routines, it will eventually finish; **First** will reactivate at that point. The last routine to be reactivated will be the main program, since it was the first to be suspended.

There is nothing strange about this process. Keep in mind that procedures and functions are reactivated backwards—the most recently suspended is the first to be reactivated, and so forth.

A special and powerful case of this process in action is a *recursive routine,* a routine that calls itself. This means that one version of the routine (the caller) is suspended, and a new version (the called) is activated. A recursive routine is given a task to do. If the task can be done in a single step, the routine does it and returns control to the caller. Otherwise, the procedure or function passes a simpler form of the task to a new version of the routine. Thus, each caller passes an easier version of the task to the new routine.

Eventually, the problem will be solvable in a single step. That version of the routine will thus finish its work and return control to the caller. The temporarily suspended versions of the routine will generally do their part of the problem after the result has come back from each called routine.

In the following example program, procedure **Count** is recursive. This version of **Count** displays information about the call's position in the recursion.

P6-10
```
(* Program to illustrate use of recursion in a procedure.
   Program counts to a specified number.
*)
PROGRAM RecurseDemo;

VAR Level, CountVal : INTEGER;
```

```
(* Prompt user and read an INTEGER. *)
PROCEDURE GetInteger ( Message : STRING;
                         VAR Value : INTEGER);
VAR TempStr : STRING;
BEGIN
  WRITE ( Message, ' ');
  READLN ( Value);
END; (* GetInteger *)

(* Recursive procedure to count to a specified value *)
PROCEDURE Count ( Val : INTEGER);
BEGIN  (* Count *)
  (* Display information about the procedure call *)
  Level := Level + 1;
  WRITELN ( ' ':Level * 2, 'Starting count, level = ',
            Level:2, '; val = ', Val);

  (* The actual Count routine is contained in the
     next three lines.
  *)
  IF ( Val > 1) THEN
    Count ( Val - 1);
  WRITELN ( ' ':Level * 2, Val);

  (* Display information about the procedure call *)
  WRITELN ( ' ':Level * 2, 'Leaving count, level  = ',
            Level:2, '; val = ', Val);
  Level := Level - 1;
END;  (* Count *)
BEGIN
  REPEAT
    Level := 0;
    GetInteger ( 'Count to what value? ( 0 to stop)', CountVal);
    Count ( CountVal);
  UNTIL CountVal = 0;
  READLN;
END.
```

The recursion in this program occurs in **Count**. When asked to count to six, this procedure produced the following output:

```
Count to what value? 6
  Starting count, Level =  1; Val = 6
    Starting count, Level =  2; Val = 5
      Starting count, Level =  3; Val = 4
        Starting count, Level =  4; Val = 3
          Starting count, Level =  5; Val = 2
            Starting count, Level =  6; Val = 1
```

```
    1
      Leaving count, Level  =  6; Val = 1
     2
      Leaving count, Level  =  5; Val = 2
    3
     Leaving count, Level  =  4; Val = 3
   4
   Leaving count, Level  =  3; Val = 4
  5
 Leaving count, Level  =  2; Val = 5
6
Leaving count, Level  =  1; Val = 6
```

The program displays the output in a manner that helps show what happened at various levels of recursion. Thus, the six lines beginning with **Starting** are all displayed in calls to **Count**. Each of these calls is with a different argument, indicated by the number written after the introductory message.

Figure 6-1 shows the action that produces each of these lines. In the figure, the word "main" refers to the main program.

Notice how each version of **Count** calls a copy of itself, but with a smaller argument (a simpler problem). This process stops when the program gets to **Count(1)**. At this point, the currently executing version of **Count** can perform its task—displaying the parameter's value—right away. Thus, **Count(1)** actually displays its result. In its current form, **Count(1)** also displays a "Leaving" message to make it easier to follow the flow of control. All these elements are written at the same level of indentation. After this message, the value of **Level** is decreased by one since the program is moving back up to the previous level of calls. **Level** is a variable that keeps track of the number of suspended procedures and functions.

The routine then returns control to its caller: **Count(2)**. This routine executes the statement after the call to **Count(1)**. This statement tells **Count(2)** to display the current value of **Val**, which is 2 in that version of **Count**.

Notice that this call to **WRITELN** is *not* in an **ELSE** clause. This action is carried out by each version of **Count**. Thus, the successively higher values of **Val** are written as control reverts back to the appropriate versions of **Count**. Figure 6-2 shows this return process.

The Flow of a Recursive Call

Notice the relationship between the order in which the routines are completed and the order in which they are called in the output from the previous program. As you saw earlier, the last routine to be called is the first one to be finished, and the first procedure or function to be

Call	Line	Suspended
Main		------
Count(6)	Starting ... Level = 1; Val = 6	Main
Count(5)	Starting ... Level = 2; Val = 5	Main Count(6)
Count(4)	Starting ... Level = 3; Val = 4	Main Count(6) Count(5)
Count(3)	Starting ... Level = 4; Val = 3	Main Count(6) Count(5) Count(4)
Count(2)	Starting ... Level = 5; Val = 2	Main Count(6) Count(5) Count(4) Count(3)
Count(1)	Starting ... Level = 6; Val = 1	Main Count(6) Count(5) Count(4) Count(3) Count(2)

Figure 6-1. *Calling and suspending sequence as* **Count** *executes*

suspended is the last one to finish. You can see this in the program's indentation pattern. The program begins and ends at the leftmost lines. The lines indented furthest are those in the middle of the program, and these lines are consecutive.

Because the procedure's parameter is passed by value, each version of **Count** keeps its own copy of **Val**. This makes it possible for the different versions to have different values.

Return to	**Line**		**Suspended**
			Main
			Count(6)
			Count(5)
			Count(4)
			Count(3)
Count(1)	Leaving . . . Level = 6; Val = 1		Count(2)
			Main
			Count(6)
			Count(5)
			Count(4)
Count(2)	Leaving . . . Level = 5; Val = 2		Count(3)
			Main
			Count(6)
			Count(5)
Count(3)	Leaving . . . Level = 4; Val = 3		Count(4)
			Main
			Count(6)
Count(4)	Leaving . . . Level = 3; Val = 4		Count(5)
			Main
Count(5)	Leaving . . . Level = 2; Val = 5		Count(6)
Count(6)	Leaving . . . Level = 1; Val = 6		Main
Main			------

Figure 6-2.   *Returning and reactivating sequence as **Count** executes*

Features of a Recursive Routine

What follows is the unembellished form of the recursive procedure in the preceding program. This listing, which is not a program, contains a clean version of **Count**. You can substitute this version for the annotated version in **RecurseDemo**.

P6-11
```
(* Recursive procedure to count to a specified value *)
PROCEDURE Count ( Val : INTEGER);
BEGIN  (* Count *)
  IF ( Val > 1) THEN
    Count ( Val - 1);
  WRITELN ( Val);
END;  (* Count *)
```

Without the statements that write information about the recursion level, this procedure turns out to be very simple. Nevertheless, **Count** has all the features a recursive routine needs. In particular, a recursive routine must include the following types of statements:

■ The statements needed to carry out the task of the routine. In the **Count** procedure, this is the call to **WRITELN**.

■ A test to determine whether the routine can avoid calling itself again — that is, to determine whether the routine can simply do its work and terminate. In the preceding procedure, this is the **IF** statement testing whether (**Val** > 1).

■ A statement that calls the routine itself. This call must be made with parameter values that will eventually make the test condition take on a value to bypass the recursive call. The preceding routine accomplishes this by calling the procedure with arguments that approach the termination value of 1.

The routine must test whether a recursive call is necessary *before* making such a call. If you write your routine so that the routine first calls itself and then tests whether it can stop, the routine will never end, as in the following version of the recursive procedure:

```
(* FAULTY recursive counting procedure.
   !! DO NOT USE this version, since it will not work.
*)
PROCEDURE Count ( Val : INTEGER);
BEGIN  (* Count *)
  (* Because the recursive call is made first,
     the procedure never tests whether the call is
     necessary. Instead, the routine just keeps calling.
  *)
  Count ( Val - 1);
  IF ( Val > 1) THEN
    WRITELN ( Val);
END;  (* Count *)
```

Similarly, the next version of the procedure is incorrect because the value of **Val** used in each call is moving away from the termination value of 1. This version will also end in a run-time error.

```
(* FAULTY recursive counting procedure.
   !! DO NOT USE this version, since it will not work.
*)
PROCEDURE Count ( Val : INTEGER);
BEGIN  (* Count *)
  IF ( Val > 1) THEN
    (* Val INCREASES, so it will never be 1;
       therefore the routine will never terminate.
    *)
    Count ( Val + 1);
  WRITELN ( Val);
END;  (* Count *)
```

REMEMBER A recursive routine must always test whether it can stop *before* calling another version of itself. If a recursive call is made, the parameters in some calls should eventually have values that will make further recursive calls unnecessary.

Another Example

In the next recursive routine, there are two recursive calls within the same routine. This procedure generates *Fibonacci numbers,* which show up in many contexts. Fibonacci numbers are named after Leonardo of Pisa (also known as Fibonacci). He discovered these numbers as the solution to the following problem about the rate at which rabbits reproduce. How many pairs of rabbits will be produced in one year, given these conditions:

■ You begin with a single pair.

■ Every month each pair begets a new pair.

■ A rabbit pair becomes productive from the second month on.

At the start, and after the first month, you have just the one pair of rabbits. Thus, the first two Fibonacci numbers—**Fib(1)** and **Fib(2)**—are 1. Subsequent Fibonacci numbers are formed by adding the two preceding Fibonacci numbers. Thus, in the third month, you will have two pairs: the original pair and the pair produced by them. In the fourth month, you will have these two pairs and another pair produced by the original rabbits. In other words, **Fib(3)** is 2 (1 + 1), and **Fib(4)** is 3 (1 + 2). In the fifth month, you'll have the three pairs, plus two new pairs: one from the original pair and one pair from the oldest pair of offspring: **Fib(5)** is 5 (3 + 2).

Fibonacci numbers show up in many other contexts. For example, the growth of leaves on a plant stem follows a Fibonacci sequence in many plants. To see this, locate three leaves that are directly above each other on the stem. Count the number of leaves on the stem between the lowest and the middle of the three leaves. Then count the number between the middle and the highest leaf. These two numbers will generally be successive terms in the Fibonacci sequence. (This, of course, assumes that leaves haven't fallen off or been removed for other reasons.)

Mathematically, a Fibonacci number is defined recursively—that is, in terms of itself. The definition is as follows:

■ The first two Fibonacci numbers—**Fib(1)** and **Fib(2)**—are defined to be 1.

■ Each successive Fibonacci number is the sum of the two preceding Fibonacci numbers. That is,

Fib(x) = Fib(x − 1) + Fib(x − 2)

Number	Value	Source
Fib(1)	1	definition
Fib(2)	1	definition
Fib(3)	2	Fib(1) + Fib(2)
Fib(4)	3	Fib(2) + Fib(3)
Fib(5)	5	Fib(3) + Fib(4)
Fib(6)	8	Fib(4) + Fib(5)
Fib(7)	13	Fib(5) + Fib(6)
Fib(8)	21	Fib(6) + Fib(7)
Fib(9)	34	Fib(7) + Fib(8)
Fib(10)	55	Fib(8) + Fib(9)
Fib(11)	89	Fib(9) + Fib(10)
Fib(12)	144	Fib(10) + Fib(11)
Fib(13)	233	Fib(11) + Fib(12)
Fib(14)	377	Fib(12) + Fib(13)
Fib(15)	610	Fib(13) + Fib(14)

Table 6-1. *The First 15 Fibonacci Numbers*

Table 6-1 shows the first 15 Fibonacci numbers.

The following program contains a recursive procedure for generating Fibonacci numbers:

P6-12
```
(* Program to illustrate recursion using
   Fibonacci number generation.
*)
PROGRAM FibonacciDemo;

VAR FibVal : INTEGER;

  (* Prompt user and read an INTEGER. *)
  PROCEDURE GetInteger ( Message : STRING;
                         VAR Value : INTEGER);
  VAR TempStr : STRING;
  BEGIN
    WRITE ( Message, ' ');
    READLN ( Value);
  END; (* GetInteger *)

  (* Compute the specified Fibonacci number.
     NOTE: Don't call this procedure for values larger than
           about 25 or 30; if you do, you'll be waiting a
           l o n g time for the routine to finish.
```

```
*)
FUNCTION Fib ( Val : INTEGER) : LONGINT;
BEGIN
  IF ( Val <= 2) THEN
    Fib := 1
  ELSE
    (* Two other Fibonacci numbers must be computed *)
    Fib := Fib ( Val - 2) + Fib ( Val - 1);
END;  (* FN Fib *)

BEGIN
  REPEAT
    GetInteger ( 'Compute what Fibonacci value? (1 to stop)',
              FibVal);
    WRITELN ( 'Fib ( ', FibVal, ') = ', Fib ( FibVal));
  UNTIL FibVal = 1;
  READLN;
END.
```

Procedure **Fib** computes the desired Fibonacci number using recursion. If the argument is small—1 or 2—the procedure immediately returns a value; otherwise, the routine ships the problem out to two different versions of itself. One version computes the preceding Fibonacci number (**Fib(*n* − 1)**), and the other version computes the Fibonacci number before that (**Fib(*n* − 2)**).

Each of these calls may, in turn, call other versions of **Fib**. Figure 6-3 shows the calls involved in computing **Fib(5)**. The actual results are computed at the very bottom of this tree. You can read off the answer by counting the 1's at the bottom of the figure.

As you might guess from the figure, the calls to **Fib** quickly proliferate. In other words, although recursion can be a very powerful technique in some situations, it can also be very inefficient. The following program shows how quickly the number of calls to **Fib** increases as you ask for larger Fibonacci numbers:

```
P6-13    (* Program to compute a specified Fibonacci number,
            and also to keep track of the number of recursive calls.
            Program also illustrates recursion.
         *)
         PROGRAM LoudFibonacciDemo;

         VAR FibVal : INTEGER;
             Calls : LONGINT;

            (* Prompt user and read an INTEGER. *)
```

```
   PROCEDURE GetInteger ( Message : STRING;
                          VAR Value : INTEGER);
VAR TempStr : STRING;
BEGIN
  WRITE ( Message, ' ');
  READLN ( Value);
END; (* GetInteger *)
FUNCTION LoudFib ( Val : INTEGER) : LONGINT;
BEGIN
  Calls := Calls + 1;
  IF ( Val <= 2) THEN
    LoudFib := 1
  ELSE
    LoudFib := LoudFib ( Val - 2) + LoudFib ( Val - 1);
  END;  (* FN LoudFib *)

BEGIN
  REPEAT
    Calls := 0;
    GetInteger ( 'Compute what Fibonacci value? (1 to stop)',
               FibVal);
    WRITE ( 'Fib ( ', FibVal:2, ') = ', LoudFib ( FibVal):10);
    WRITELN ( '; ', Calls:10, ' calls to Fib');
  UNTIL FibVal = 1;
  READLN;
END.
```

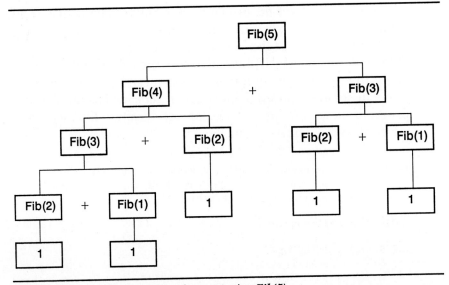

Figure 6-3. *Execution sequence when computing **Fib(5)***

This program produces the following results for a range of values:

```
Fib (  5) =           5;         9 calls to Fib
Fib ( 10) =          55;       109 calls to Fib
Fib ( 15) =         610;      1219 calls to Fib
Fib ( 20) =        6765;     13529 calls to Fib
Fib ( 25) =       75025;    150049 calls to Fib
Fib ( 26) =      121393;    242785 calls to Fib
Fib ( 27) =      196418;    392835 calls to Fib
Fib ( 28) =      317811;    635621 calls to Fib
Fib ( 29) =      514229;   1028457 calls to Fib
Fib ( 30) =      832040;   1664079 calls to Fib
```

Notice that the number of calls gets very high, even for relatively small values of **FibVal**.

Iterative Solutions to Recursive Problems

Sometimes a nonrecursive, or *iterative*, solution to a problem is much quicker. You can always find an iterative way to do a task. For example, the following listing contains an iterative Fibonacci function.

Add this function definition to either the **FibonacciDemo** or the **LoudFibonacciDemo** program. Then call both the recursive and the iterative functions. Compare how long it takes to find the desired Fibonacci number. Note how much faster the iterative version becomes (compared to the recursive version) as you ask for higher numbers.

P6-14
```
(* Iterative Fibonacci function. Function works by
   storing values of the two most recent Fibonacci numbers,
   since these are used to compute the next one.
*)
FUNCTION IterFib ( Val : INTEGER) : LONGINT;
VAR Smaller, Larger, RunningFib : LONGINT;
    Count : INTEGER;
BEGIN
  (* Fib ( 1) and Fib ( 2) = 1 *)
  IF Val < 3 THEN
    IterFib := 1
  (* Fib ( 3) = 2 *)
  ELSE IF Val = 3 THEN
    IterFib := 2
```

```
  ELSE    (* If Val > 3 *)
  BEGIN
    (* Smaller contains Fib ( n - 2);
       Larger contains Fib ( n - 1);
    *)
    Smaller := 1;
    Larger := 2;
    Count := 4;
    REPEAT
      (* RunningFib is the current Fibonacci number *)
      RunningFib := Smaller + Larger;
      (* After computing a new number, the values of
         Smaller and Larger change.
      *)
      Smaller := Larger;
      Larger := RunningFib;
      INC ( Count);
    UNTIL Count > Val;
    IterFib := RunningFib;
  END;    (* IF Val > 3 *)
END;  (* FN IterFib *)
```

This function works by storing the two most recent Fibonacci numbers as intermediate values, and using these to compute each successive Fibonacci number. As each new number is computed, that number becomes **Fib(*n* − 1)** for the next value to be computed. The listing itself is much longer than the recursive solution. However, it is also much faster. Whereas the recursive version takes almost two million calls to compute **Fib(30)**, the iterative version manages it in a few dozen additions.

Despite its inefficiencies, recursion is a very powerful technique. You'll use it in later chapters to build a data structure called a list.

This chapter covered miscellaneous information about procedures and functions. Some of this information (the scope and visibility rules, for example) is also useful for understanding other aspects of the language (such as the use of variable names in different parts of the program).

The chapter also discussed recursion, a programming technique in which a routine calls itself to accomplish part of its task.

In the next chapter, "Turbo Pascal's Structured Data Types," you'll learn about Turbo Pascal's more advanced data types.

7 *Turbo Pascal's Structured Data Types*

The data types you've learned about so far have been used to store various types of information. However, each variable could store only one item of information. (The one exception to this restriction is the **STRING** type, which you can view as a single string or as the individual characters that make up the string.)

In this chapter, you'll learn about some other data types, which are used for storing multiple items of information in the same variable. These data types—**ARRAY, RECORD**, and **SET**—are known as *structured types,* or *aggregate types*, since variables or values of these types are actually made up of components. (This chapter also includes a brief introduction to the **OBJECT** data type used in object-oriented programming. You'll learn more about this new and powerful programming technique in Chapter 11, "Object-Oriented Programming in Turbo Pascal.")

For example, an array consists of one or more components (cells), each of which contains the same type of information. A record also consists of one or more components (fields), each of which may contain the same or a different type of information. Finally, a set is an unordered collection of values (elements), all of the same type. You specify the details of these components when you define your types.

You can use these structured types as building blocks for creating data types that exactly suit the needs of your problem. For example,

■ If you need to store the grade point averages of an entire class, you can store them in an array of **REAL**s.

■ If you need to store a student profile (for example, name, grade point average, major, and so on), you can store this information in a record.

■ If you need to store profiles for an entire class, you can store them in an array, each of whose cells is a record.

■ If you need to keep track of the courses a student has taken, you can use a set to represent this list.

■ If you need to associate this information with a student's profile, you can create a record that has both a profile and a course set as components.

Definitions and Declarations

When you declare a variable as being of a simple type, the compiler knows exactly what you mean. For each simple type, the compiler knows the operations allowed and the storage to be allocated. Things are a bit different when you're working with structured types.

Structured types are really building blocks. There are several kinds of blocks, each of which can be of just about any data type.

■ Homogeneous blocks (arrays)

■ Heterogeneous blocks (records)

■ Blocks whose contents can increase or decrease, as needed (sets)

■ Record-like blocks that can inherit components from other blocks (objects)

Thus, when you create an aggregate type, you can vary many things in your description. For example, you can specify the number of elements the new type can hold as well as the type of elements to be stored in the cells.

Because these blocks are really generic components, you need to describe a particular structured type before you can declare variables of that type. You provide such descriptions as **TYPE** definitions in the declaration section of the program or routine.

The general format for such definitions is as follows:

```
<ArrayType>  =  "ARRAY ["<bounds>"] OF" <base type>
<RecordType>  =  "RECORD" <list of components> "END"
<SetType>  =  "SET OF" <base type>
<ObjectType>  =  "OBJECT" <list of components> "END"
```

You'll see specific examples in the next few sections.

REMEMBER   You need to describe a new structured data type before you can declare variables of that type.

The ARRAY Type

Suppose you want to test Turbo Pascal's random number generator to see whether all digit pairs are equally likely to end the integers generated. You could do this by counting the number of times each pair of digits (that is, 00 through 99) ends random integers.

To represent the 100 frequencies that result, you could declare 100 different variables, for example, **F0**, **F1**, **F2**, and so on, through **F99**—a tedious chore, to say the least.

After you declare these variables, you need to do just as much work to modify the frequencies after each integer is generated. For example, you need a **CASE** statement with 100 possible values to make the required changes. The following listing shows what the shell of such a statement would look like:

```
CASE Remainder OF
   0 : INC ( F0);
   1 : INC ( F1);
   2 : INC ( F2);
   (*
       and so on, to
   *)
  98 : INC ( F98);
  99 : INC ( F99);
END; (* CASE of Remainder *)
```

This looks like a lot of work, and it is! Fortunately, Pascal provides the **ARRAY** type to handle such situations. An *array* is an aggregate variable whose components are multiple values, all of the same type. These individual components are known as the *cells* of the array. Each cell has an *index* associated with it, to identify the cell.

In Pascal, an array must have a fixed number of elements. The cell indexes for these elements must have values between explicitly specified starting and ending indexes (bounds).

Defining and Declaring an Array

For example, the data for the random digits problem can be represented in a 100-element array, each of whose cells will contain an integer. The following program shows how to define, declare, and use such an array. Run the program to see a sample outcome.

P7-1

```
(* Program to illustrate use of ARRAYs. Program generates random
   integers, and counts the frequency with which each pair
   of digits terminates these numbers.
*)

PROGRAM TestDigits;
```

```
CONST MaxTrials = 5000;
(* Describe the data type to be used *)
TYPE Remainders = ARRAY [ 0 .. 99] OF INTEGER;
VAR Freqs : Remainders;
    Index, Result : INTEGER;

  (* Initialize the cells of Vals.
     Note: this is a call by reference.
  *)
  PROCEDURE InitRemainders ( VAR Vals : Remainders;
                                  InitValue : INTEGER);
  VAR Index : INTEGER;
  BEGIN
    FOR Index := 0 TO 99 DO
      (* Initialize the IndexTH cell *)
      Vals [ Index] := InitValue;
  END; (* InitRemainders *)

  (* Display Remainders array -- 4 cells per line.
     Note: this is a call by value.
  *)
  PROCEDURE DispRemainders ( Vals : Remainders);
  VAR Index : INTEGER;
  BEGIN
    (* all values are written, even though loop counter only
       goes to 24 -- because four values per line are written.
    *)
    FOR Index := 0 TO 24 DO
    BEGIN
      WRITE ( '[':5, Index:3, ']: ', Freqs [Index]:3);
      WRITE ( '[':5, Index + 25:3, ']: ', Freqs [Index + 25]:3);
      WRITE ( '[':5, Index + 50:3, ']: ', Freqs [Index + 50]:3);
      WRITE ( '[':5, Index + 75:3, ']: ', Freqs [Index + 75]:3);
      WRITELN;
    END; (* FOR Index := 0 TO 24 *)
    READLN;
  END; (* DispRemainders *)
BEGIN
  RANDOMIZE;
  InitRemainders ( Freqs, 0);

  (* generate the values, and categorize the results *)
  FOR Index := 1 TO MaxTrials DO
  BEGIN
    Result := RANDOM ( MAXINT) MOD 100;
    (* E.g., if Result = 39, then increment Freqs [ 39] by 1 *)
    Freqs [ Result] := Freqs [ Result] + 1;
  END;

  DispRemainders ( Freqs);
END.
```

Remember that you first need to define the array type you intend to use in the **TYPE** definition statement:

```
TYPE Remainders = ARRAY [ 0 .. 99] OF INTEGER;
```

This statement describes a new type of variable, which will be named **Remainders**. The type is built out of familiar components. In particular, **Remainders** is defined as an **ARRAY**.

The syntax for such an array description is

<type identifier> ″= **ARRAY** [″ <bounds> ″] OF″
<base type>

Recall that an array's components are all of the same type. As part of the definition, you must specify this *base type*. For **Remainders**, the base type is **INTEGER.** This means that each cell of the array will be allocated two bytes and will contain an **INTEGER** value. Essentially, each cell is an **INTEGER** variable, except that it has been subsumed in a larger structure. As a variable, a cell can be used wherever a variable of that type is allowed.

You also need to specify a fixed size for the array. The information within square brackets (**[0 .. 99]**) represents the range of the indexes that should be associated with the array's cells. In this case, the definition says that the cells are to be named **0** through **99**, and indirectly tells the compiler that the array has 100 cells.

Once you've defined the new type, you can declare variables of that type. The first **VAR** declaration line shows how to do this. The format for such declarations is the same as for other types:

<Identifier> ″:″ <array type>

The first declaration will have the reserved word **VAR** before it.

Accessing Individual Array Cells

In the main **TestDigits** program, the value of one particular cell of the array is increased each time through the main program's **FOR** loop. The assignment statement that accomplishes this shows how to refer to specific cells.

To access the appropriate cell, specify the variable name (**Freqs**), followed by the cell's index enclosed in square brackets. The index can be any value, variable, or expression of the same type as the starting and ending indexes. In the program, the remainder from the **MOD** operation represents the index of the cell whose frequency count needs to be increased. Thus,

```
Freqs [ Result]
```

specifies the cell whose index corresponds to the current value of **Result**.

The right-hand side of the assignment statement increases the value of this cell by 1. Note that the 1 is outside the square brackets. The following statement accomplishes the same increment:

```
INC ( Freqs [ Result]);
```

Freqs[Result] is a memory location that contains an **INTEGER** value. As such, it is a valid argument for the **INC** procedure.

Cell Index Versus Cell Value   Don't confuse a cell's index with the value stored in the cell. The index is part of the cell's name. Thus, **Freqs[5]** represents a specific memory location (which contains an **INTEGER**).

Cell **Freqs[5]** has a value stored in it, which represents the frequency with which the random numbers ended in 05 (such as 3905, 105). Conversely, this value is stored at the location that corresponds to **Freqs[5]**.

To see more directly the difference between cell index and cell value, compare the two assignment statements in the following listing. Assume that **Freqs[5]** has the value 47 and **Freqs[6]** has the value 62.

```
(* Assume Freqs [ 5] = 47; Freqs [ 6] = 62 *)

Freqs [ 5] := Freqs [ 5] + 1;

Freqs [ 5] := Freqs [ 5 + 1];
```

After the first assignment, the value of **Freqs[5]** will be 48—that is, 1 more than before the assignment. After the second assignment, **Freqs[5]** will have the value 62—that is, the same value as **Freqs[6]**.

CAUTION Don't confuse a cell's index and its value. The index identifies the cell by its position in the array. The cell's value represents the contents of the memory location allocated for the cell.

Arrays as Parameters

The **TestDigits** program shows that you can pass array variables as arguments to procedures and functions. These arguments can be passed by value (for example, in **DispRemainders**) or by reference (for example, in **InitRemainders**).

Inside the called routine, the cells of the array are accessed using the same index values as in the calling routine, but using the local name for the array (**Vals** in both **InitRemainders** and **DispRemainders**).

Procedure **DispRemainders** displays the contents of the array, four cells per line. Note the indexing being done in **DispRemainders**. The values written on a particular line are those that belong to cells with indexes X, X + 25, X + 50, and X + 75.

The following listing shows sample results from the program:

```
[  0]:  48    [ 25]:  61    [ 50]:   33    [ 75]:  54
[  1]:  44    [ 26]:  46    [ 51]:   39    [ 76]:  48
[  2]:  50    [ 27]:  56    [ 52]:   56    [ 77]:  36
[  3]:  52    [ 28]:  36    [ 53]:   61    [ 78]:  48
[  4]:  49    [ 29]:  39    [ 54]:   43    [ 79]:  49
[  5]:  46    [ 30]:  56    [ 55]:   56    [ 80]:  61
```

[6]:	33	[31]:	53	[56]:	46	[81]:	53
[7]:	36	[32]:	40	[57]:	56	[82]:	35
[8]:	51	[33]:	66	[58]:	57	[83]:	44
[9]:	45	[34]:	48	[59]:	56	[84]:	49
[10]:	34	[35]:	60	[60]:	59	[85]:	55
[11]:	49	[36]:	57	[61]:	42	[86]:	55
[12]:	61	[37]:	47	[62]:	38	[87]:	50
[13]:	45	[38]:	60	[63]:	51	[88]:	42
[14]:	53	[39]:	53	[64]:	49	[89]:	50
[15]:	55	[40]:	46	[65]:	47	[90]:	57
[16]:	41	[41]:	58	[66]:	57	[91]:	45
[17]:	40	[42]:	60	[67]:	51	[92]:	54
[18]:	53	[43]:	49	[68]:	55	[93]:	40
[19]:	42	[44]:	46	[69]:	56	[94]:	56
[20]:	57	[45]:	49	[70]:	43	[95]:	46
[21]:	55	[46]:	56	[71]:	52	[96]:	43
[22]:	58	[47]:	54	[72]:	61	[97]:	62
[23]:	49	[48]:	42	[73]:	51	[98]:	57
[24]:	48	[49]:	60	[74]:	52	[99]:	52

This output indicates, for example, that the value of cell **Freqs[74]** was 52 after the program finished executing. This means that the digit pair 74 ended 52 of the 5000 (**MaxTrials**) random values generated. Similarly, the value of **Freqs[93]** was 40. Notice that **Freqs[74]** is actually the 75th cell, since the first cell has index 0 in this example.

Representing an Array

When you declare an array variable, the compiler allocates enough memory to store as many values of the base type as there are cells in the array. Thus, **Freqs** is allocated 200 bytes of storage, as you'll see if you add the following statement to the main program of **TestDigits**:

```
WRITELN ( 'Freqs takes ', SIZEOF ( Freqs), ' bytes of storage');
```

In memory, the cells of an array are stored in consecutive storage areas. Each cell is allocated enough space to store a value of the array's base type. Figure 7-1 shows the layout of a **Remainders** array in memory.

Index	Value	Address
0	48	x
1	44	$x + 2$
2	50	$x + 4$
3	52	$x + 6$
. . .	. . .	
96	43	$x + 192$
97	62	$x + 194$
98	57	$x + 196$
99	52	$x + 198$

Figure 7-1. *Memory layout and contents for a sample 100-element array of integers*

The index values are not stored in memory. Rather, the compiler just uses them when computing the memory location for the cell. Only the frequency values (48, 44, 50, and so on) are stored in memory.

Rules for Arrays

An array consists of cells. The cells can contain just about any type of information, which is known as the array's base type. However, each cell in the array must have the same base type. An array's size is determined by the base type and the number of elements. This size cannot be larger than 64K. An array also cannot contain an array identical to itself as a component.

You can use any ordinal type (except **LONGINT**) to specify cell indexes. To indicate both the number of cells and the indexes to be associated with those cells, specify a starting index value and an ending index value, separated by double dots (..).

The ending index value must be greater than the starting value. The compiler assumes that the array contains as many cells as there are values between the starting and ending values (including the endpoints). For example, in the **TestDigits** program, there are 100 values between 0 and 99.

The following are all valid array definitions, using different types to specify index values:

```
TYPE MyOrdinalType = ( one, two, three, four, five, six,
                       seven, eight, nine, ten, eleven,
                       twelve, thirteen, fourteen);

    (* INTEGER indexes: array has 14 cells *)
    WordArray = ARRAY [ -5 .. 8 ] OF WORD;

    (* CHAR indexes: array has 20 cells *)
    CharIndexArray = ARRAY [ 'a' .. 't'] OF REAL;

    (* MyOrdinalType indexes: array has 14 cells *)
    MyTypeIndexArray = ARRAY [ one .. fourteen] OF CHAR;

    (* BOOLEAN indexes: array has 2 cells *)
    BoolIndexArray = ARRAY [ FALSE .. TRUE] OF MyOrdinalType;

    (* each "cell" is a string; array has 11 cells *)
    StringArray = ARRAY [ -5 .. 5] OF STRING;
```

Operations on Arrays

If you have two array variables of exactly the same type, you can make the two arrays identical with a single assignment statement. For example, suppose **Freqs1** and **Freqs2** are each variables of type **Remainders** (as in the **TestDigits** program). The following assignment is syntactically valid:

```
Freqs2 := Freqs1;
```

The effect of this assignment is equivalent to the following loop.

```
FOR Index := 0 TO 99 DO
  Freqs2 [ Index] := Freqs1 [ Index];
```

Beyond this total assignment operation, arrays are accessed and manipulated cell by cell. The operations that you can apply to individual cells depend on their base type.

One More Example

This additional example illustrates some similarities between arrays and the mathematical concept of a vector. A *vector* is an ordered collection of values. Generally these values represent information that is related.

For example, you would use a vector to represent a point in space. For each point, you would have a value representing the point's position in each of the three spatial dimensions (x, y, and z), as you can see in Figure 7-2.

To represent this information in an array, you might use a definition like the one shown in the following program:

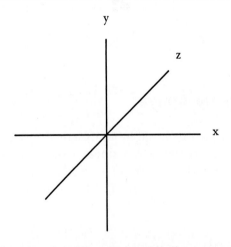

Figure 7-2.   *A three-dimensional (Cartesian) coordinate system*

```
P7-2      (* Program illustrating use of arrays as vectors *)

          PROGRAM DistanceDemo;

              (* Define a type to represent the three dimensions.
                 NOTE: the values are NOT equivalent to 'x,' 'y,' and 'z'
              *)
          TYPE Axes = ( x, y, z);
              (* A vector contains three values --
                 corresponding to the three dimensions.
              *)
              Vector = ARRAY [ x .. z] OF REAL;
          VAR PointA, PointB : Vector;
              Dist : REAL;

            PROCEDURE GetReal ( Message : STRING;
                                VAR Value : REAL);
            BEGIN
              WRITE ( Message, ' ');
              READLN ( Value);
            END; (* GetReal *)

            (* Get three coordinate values from the user *)
            PROCEDURE GetPoint ( VAR Pt : Vector);
            BEGIN
              GetReal ( 'x-value?', Pt [ x]);
              GetReal ( 'y-value?', Pt [ y]);
              GetReal ( 'z-value?', Pt [ z]);
            END; (* GetPoint *)

            (* Compute the distance between two points in space.
               Function uses the following formula:
               Dist := SQRT ( XDiff^2 + YDiff^2 + ZDiff^2),
               where XDiff := PtA[ x] - PtB [ x], etc.
            *)
            FUNCTION Distance3D ( PtA, PtB : Vector) : REAL;
            VAR Sum : REAL;
                Count : Axes;
            BEGIN
              Sum := 0.0;
              FOR Count := x TO z DO
                Sum := Sum + SQR ( PtA [ Count] - PtB [ Count]);
              Distance3D := SQRT ( Sum);
            END; (* FN Distance3D *)

          BEGIN
            WRITELN ( 'Enter point information.');
            WRITELN ( ' To STOP, make both points equal.');
```

```
  WRITELN;
  REPEAT
    WRITELN ( 'Point A:');
    GetPoint ( PointA);
    WRITELN ( 'Point B:');
    GetPoint ( PointB);
    Dist := Distance3D ( PointA, PointB);
    WRITELN ( 'Distance between points is ', Dist:10:3);
  (* termination condition doesn't test for strict
     equality to avoid differences due to rounding errors.
  *)
  UNTIL Dist <= 0.0;
  READLN;
END.
```

The program computes the distance between any two points that you specify. To specify a point, you need to provide *x*, *y*, and *z* coordinates.

Strings

In Chapter 3, "Turbo Pascal's Simple Data Types," you learned that a **STRING** is not a simple type, although you can often treat it as one. You also learned that an expression such as

```
MyString [ 6]
```

represents the sixth character in the string **MyString**.

It may be no surprise that Turbo Pascal's **STRING** type is represented as an array of **CHAR**. By default, this is an array of 255 elements. You can, however, specify a maximum length for a string. For example,

```
STRING [ 45]
```

specifies a string with at most 45 characters. (Actually, Turbo Pascal adds an extra cell, with index 0, when representing a string. This cell contains information about the length of the string.)

The following program shows how to use **STRING** variables and how to access and work with individual characters in the string. The program reads a string entered by the user and then sorts the characters in the string.

P7-3

```
(* Program to illustrate use of strings.
   Program sorts strings entered by the user.
*)

PROGRAM StringBubble;

CONST EmptyString = '';
VAR   CurrStr : STRING;
      Count : INTEGER;

  PROCEDURE GetString ( Message : STRING;
                             VAR Info : STRING);
  BEGIN
    WRITE ( Message, ' ');
    READLN ( Info);
  END; (* GetString *)

  (* Sort characters in a string by letting the "largest"
     remaining character work its way to the top of the
     array on each pass through the array.
  *)
  PROCEDURE StrBubbleSort ( VAR Info : String);
  VAR Temp : CHAR;
      Low, High, Top, Size : INTEGER;
  BEGIN
    Size := LENGTH ( Info);
    Top := Size + 1;
    WHILE ( Top > 1) DO
    BEGIN
      Low := 1;
      High := 2;
      WHILE High < Top DO
      BEGIN
        (* if lower string needs to move upward in the array *)
        IF Info [ Low] > Info [ High] THEN
        BEGIN
          Temp := Info [ Low];
          Info [ Low] := Info [ High];
          Info [ High] := Temp;
        END; (* If lower string needs to move upward *)
        Low := Low + 1;
        High := High + 1;
```

```
        END; (* WHILE High < Top *)
      Top := Top - 1;
    END; (* WHILE Top > 1 *)
  END;  (* StrBubbleSort *)

BEGIN
  (* Get the lines to be sorted *)
  Count := 0;
  WRITELN ( 'Enter your strings.');
  WRITELN ( ' To STOP, enter an empty string.');
  WRITELN;
  REPEAT
    GetString ( ':', CurrStr);
    Count := Count + 1;
    WRITELN ( CurrStr);
    StrBubbleSort ( CurrStr);
    WRITELN ( CurrStr);
  UNTIL CurrStr = EmptyString;
  WRITELN ( Count:3, ' lines read');
  READLN;
END.
```

The program uses a bubblesort algorithm to sort the letters in the strings entered by the user. Procedure **StrBubbleSort** is quite similar to **BubbleSort** in Chapter 2, "Pascal: An Overview." However, **StrBubbleSort** works with characters in individual strings.

The following listing shows some sample output from the program. Notice that blanks are sorted along with the alphabetic characters.

```
: aardvark
aardvark
aaadkrrv

: ant
ant
ant

: banana slug
banana slug
 aaabglnnsu

: wapiti
wapiti
aiiptw

: wolf
wolf
flow
```

```
: once upon a time, there was a very long sentence
once upon a time, there was a very long sentence
        ,aaacceeeeeeeghilmnnnnnoooprrssttuvwy

 7 lines read
```

Notice that you can declare **STRING** variables without first doing a **TYPE** definition. This is because the **STRING** type is predefined for you in Turbo Pascal.

Multidimensional Arrays

An array's base type can be almost any kind of information, including another array. For example, suppose you want to record the highest temperature during the day and the highest at night. Suppose that you also want to record this information for an entire month.

If you record this information by hand, you might organize it as shown in Figure 7-3.

This table of information has 62 different cells, grouped into 31 pairs. Each row of the table represents a pair of values. (The Date column represents the indexes and is not part of the array.)

Date	Day	Night
1		
2		
3		
4		
...		
29		
30		
31		

Figure 7-3. *Layout for recording two daily temperatures for a one-month period*

You can think of this data structure as 62 individual cells, or as 31 rows of two cells each. In the latter case, you can consider each row a two-element array.

There are actually several ways you can define such an array in Pascal, depending on whether you also want the component (two-element) array as a separate type. The following listing shows three different ways of defining the same kind of array:

```
(* make the 2-element array a separate, named data type *)
TYPE DailyTemps = ARRAY [ 1 .. 2] OF REAL;
     TempData1 = ARRAY [ 1 .. 31] OF DailyTemps;

     (* describe an array built of an anonymous array type *)
     TempData2 = ARRAY [ 1 .. 31] OF ARRAY [ 1 .. 2] OF REAL;

     TempData3 = ARRAY [ 1 .. 31, 1 .. 2] OF REAL;
```

A **TempData1** array consists of 31 cells of type **DailyTemps**. The preceding **TYPE** definition tells you that this **DailyTemps** is a two-cell array of **REAL**.

By providing a name for this component type, you've made it possible to declare variables of that type. For example, the following declaration is valid, given the preceding definitions:

```
VAR TodaysTemps : DailyTemps;
```

The definition for **TempData2** also specifies that it is a 31-element array whose cells are two-element arrays. In contrast to **TempData1**, however, this component type is anonymous. No name is provided for the type, which is described "on the fly." As a result, you can't declare any variables of this base type.

Finally, the definition for **TempData3** simply specifies that it's a two-dimensional array whose first dimension has 31 elements and whose second dimension has two elements.

Accessing Elements in Multidimensional Arrays

Figure 7-3 resembles a *matrix* in mathematics—a structure consisting of rows of values. Each row is a vector with one or more values; every row has the same number of elements. The rows are arranged vertically, so that the first element of every vector is in the first column of the matrix, the second elements are in the second column, and so forth.

If you think of Figure 7-3 as a matrix, it has 31 rows, each of which has two columns. This idea will help you see how to access individual elements in such an array.

Run the following program to see how such cells are accessed:

P7-4

```
(* Program to illustrate use of two-dimensional arrays *)

PROGRAM MatrixDemo;

TYPE Matrix = ARRAY [ 1 .. 5, 1 .. 3] OF INTEGER;
VAR SampleMatrix : Matrix;

  (* Put a value in each cell of Vals *)
  PROCEDURE FillMatrix ( VAR Vals : Matrix);
  VAR Row, Column : INTEGER;
  BEGIN
    FOR Row := 1 TO 5 DO
      FOR Column := 1 TO 3 DO
        (* To specify a single cell in a matrix, specify
           the row and column within the square brackets.
        *)
        Vals [ Row, Column] := 10 * Row + Column;
  END; (* FillMatrix *)

  (* Display the contents of Vals *)
  PROCEDURE DispMatrix ( Vals : Matrix);
  VAR Row, Column : INTEGER;
  BEGIN
    WRITELN ( 'Col 1':13, 'Col 2':8, 'Col 3':8);
    FOR Row := 1 TO 5 DO
    BEGIN
      WRITE ( 'Row ', Row);
      FOR Column := 1 TO 3 DO
        WRITE ( Vals [ Row][ Column]:8);
      WRITELN;
    END;
  END; (* DispMatrix *)

BEGIN  (* Main program *)
  FillMatrix ( SampleMatrix);
  DispMatrix ( SampleMatrix);
  READLN;
END.
```

The program defines a type named **Matrix**, which describes a two-dimensional array with five rows and three columns. Such an array has 15 (5 * 3) elements, each of which is an **INTEGER**.

The program uses two procedures — **FillMatrix** and **DispMatrix** — to do its work. Note that, like a one-dimensional array or a simple type, a two-dimensional array can be passed as a parameter.

The array is passed by reference to **FillMatrix**, since this procedure is supposed to put values in the cells. **DispMatrix**, on the other hand, does not change anything in the array, so a copy will do just as well. The parameter is passed by value in that case.

The program produces the following output:

```
        Col 1   Col 2   Col 3
Row 1      11      12      13
Row 2      21      22      23
Row 3      31      32      33
Row 4      41      42      43
Row 5      51      52      53
```

Procedure **FillMatrix** accesses the individual cells by using one **FOR** loop nested inside another. The outer loop, whose values change more slowly, represents the first (row) dimension; the inner loop represents the second (column) dimension.

The higher dimensions change more quickly. Thus, to visit each cell of a **Matrix**, you first visit each cell in row 1. That is, you visit columns 1 through 3 in row 1 (cells **[1,1]**, **[1,2]**, and **[1,3]**). Then you visit each successive row until you have visited all three columns in row 5.

The actual work in **FillMatrix** is done by the single statement in the inner **FOR** loop. This statement assigns a value to a particular cell. The rest of the loop's activity is administrative.

Notice how the cell is specified. To select a cell, indicate the row and then the column within square brackets. The two indexes are separated by commas. Thus, the statement

```
Vals [ 4, 2] := 10 * 4 + 2;
```

assigns the value 42 to the second cell in the fourth row.

Procedure **DispMatrix** shows a slightly different syntax for specifying a cell. Instead of putting both indexes within one set of brackets, you can use separate brackets for each index. Thus, the statement

```
Vals [ 4][ 2] := 10 * 4 + 2;
```

also assigns 42 to the second element in the fourth row. The comma syntax is easier and more common.

Accessing Component Arrays

In the **MatrixDemo** program, you accessed individual (**INTEGER**) cells of the array. However, remember that you can think of a two-dimensional array as one with arrays as elements.

Is there any way to access an entire row in the matrix? The following procedure shows how to assign values to a **Matrix** variable, an entire row at a time. The listing is not a stand-alone program, so don't try to compile it as such.

P7-5
```
(* Set entire rows of the matrix to new values.
    Row1 := Row5;   Row2 := Row4;   Row3 := Row3;
    Row4 := Row2;   Row5 := Row1;
*)
PROCEDURE ShuffleMatrix ( VAR Vals : Matrix);
VAR Row : INTEGER;
BEGIN
  FOR Row := 1 TO 5 DO
    (* To access an entire row, omit the column index *)
    Vals [ Row] := Vals [ 5 - Row + 1];
END; (* ShuffleMatrix *)
```

Procedure **ShuffleMatrix** assigns the array stored as row 5 to the array stored as row 1. Row 2 is assigned the contents of row 4, and so on. In each of these assignments, the three cells in a row are assigned values simultaneously.

To indicate how the assignment should work, include only the row dimension when specifying the variable. This tells the program to work with the base type for a row, which will be an array.

If you add the **ShuffleMatrix** procedure to the **MatrixDemo** program, and then add calls to **ShuffleMatrix** and **DispMatrix** at the end of the main program, you get the following output:

	Col 1	Col 2	Col 3
Row 1	11	12	13
Row 2	21	22	23
Row 3	31	32	33
Row 4	41	42	43
Row 5	51	52	53

	Col 1	Col 2	Col 3
Row 1	51	52	53
Row 2	41	42	43
Row 3	31	32	33
Row 4	41	42	43
Row 5	51	52	53

If you're not sure why the rows haven't simply been reversed, think about the contents of **Vals[2]** by the time this array is assigned to **Vals[4]**.

String Arrays

An array of **STRING** actually is another example of a two-dimensional array. The following program shows such an array:

P7-6

```
(* Program to illustrate use of string arrays *)

PROGRAM MenuDemo;

CONST MaxMenu = 20;
TYPE StrArray = ARRAY [ 1 .. MaxMenu] OF STRING [ 80];
VAR Menu : StrArray;

  (* Initialize the menu to the available choices.
     Cells for which no choices were provided are
     initialized as empty strings.
  *)
  PROCEDURE InitMenu ( VAR Menu : StrArray);
  VAR Index : INTEGER;
  BEGIN
    (* the first three cells get actual values in the example *)
    Menu [ 1] := 'Choice1';
    Menu [ 2] := 'Choice2';
    Menu [ 3] := 'Choice3';
    (* the remaining cells get null strings *)
    FOR Index := 4 TO MaxMenu DO
      Menu [ Index] := '';
  END;   (* InitMenu *)

  (* Display the contents of the menu array.
     NrChoices represents the number of Menu's cells
     that have choices (as opposed to empty strings)
  *)
  PROCEDURE ShowMenu ( VAR Menu : StrArray;
                           NrChoices : INTEGER);
```

```
      VAR Index : INTEGER;
      BEGIN
        (* To prevent procedure from reading past end of array *)
        IF NrChoices > MaxMenu THEN
          NrChoices := MaxMenu;
        FOR Index := 1 TO NrChoices DO
          WRITELN ( Menu [ Index]);
        WRITELN;
        WRITE ( 'Your Choice? (1 TO ', NrChoices, ') ');
      END; (* ShowMenu *)

BEGIN
  InitMenu ( Menu);
  ShowMenu ( Menu, 3);
  READLN;
END.
```

This program defines two procedures that will be useful later in the book. The procedures initialize and display a menu of choices for the user. In later programs, you'll use such menus to interact with the user.

Notice that only the row dimension is used when manipulating elements of the **Menu** array. This is because strings are generally treated as if they were a simple variable—that is, as a unit rather than as a sequence of individual characters.

You can still access individual character cells by specifying the second index as well as the row. For example, you would refer to the sixth character in the third string ('e') as:

```
Menu [ 3, 6]
```

Notice that **ShowMenu**'s first parameter is declared as a **VAR** parameter, even though the array's contents are not changed. This is common with arrays. If you pass an array by value, a copy of the entire array must be made for the called routine's local environment. For an array such as **Menu**, that copy takes up over 5000 bytes of storage—a significant amount of memory to lose (even temporarily) if you have a large program that uses lots of memory for other things.

When you pass **Menu** by reference, you don't need to copy the array to the routine's local environment. Rather, the routine assumes that the array is at the location of the argument specified in the call. This saves time and storage, both of which can make a difference in a large program. Of course, you must be careful not to change values inadvertently.

Note that **ShowMenu** first checks that **NrChoices** does not exceed the **StrArray**'s bounds. If you try to read past the end of a string (or any array), the program terminates with a run-time error.

CAUTION   Be careful not to access array elements beyond the bounds of an array. This will terminate your program with a run-time error.

Three-Dimensional Arrays   You learned how to define a matrix, an array of arrays. You can also define an array of matrices. That is, you can have arrays of three or more dimensions. For example, the following program shows how to define, declare, and use a three-dimensional array:

P7-7

```
(* Program to illustrate use of three-dimensional arrays *)

PROGRAM HyperMatrixDemo;

TYPE HyperMatrix = ARRAY [ 1 .. 3, 1 .. 4, 1 .. 5] OF INTEGER;
VAR Sample : HyperMatrix;

  (* Put a value in each cell of Vals *)
  PROCEDURE FillHyperMatrix ( VAR Vals : HyperMatrix);
  VAR Plane, Row, Column : INTEGER;
  BEGIN
    FOR Plane := 1 TO 3 DO
      FOR Row := 1 TO 4 DO
        FOR Column := 1 TO 5 DO
          (* To specify a single cell in a HyperMatrix, specify
             the row and column within the square brackets.
          *)
          Vals [ Plane, Row, Column] := 100 * Plane +
                                        10 * Row + Column;
  END; (* FillHyperMatrix *)

  (* Display the contents of Vals *)
  PROCEDURE DispHyperMatrix ( Vals : HyperMatrix);
  VAR Plane, Row, Column : INTEGER;
  BEGIN
    FOR Plane := 1 TO 3 DO
    BEGIN
      WRITELN ( 'Plane ':10, Plane);
      WRITELN ( 'Col 1':13, 'Col 2':8, 'Col 3':8,
                'Col 4':8, 'Col 5':8);
      FOR Row := 1 TO 4 DO
      BEGIN
        WRITE ( 'Row ', Row);
```

```
        FOR Column := 1 TO 5 DO
          WRITE ( Vals [ Plane][ Row][ Column]:8);
        WRITELN;
     END;  (* FOR Row *)
  END; (* FOR Plane *)
END; (* DispHyperMatrix *)

(* Set entire matrices of the hypermatrix to new values.
    Plane1 := Plane3;   Plane2 := Plane2;   Plane3 := Plane1;
*)
PROCEDURE ShuffleHyperMatrix ( VAR Vals : HyperMatrix);
VAR Plane : INTEGER;
BEGIN
  FOR Plane := 1 TO 3 DO
    (* To access an entire plane row,
       omit the row and column indexes
    *)
    Vals [ Plane] := Vals [ 3 - Plane + 1];
END; (* ShuffleHyperMatrix *)

BEGIN
  FillHyperMatrix ( Sample);
  DispHyperMatrix ( Sample);
  ShuffleHyperMatrix ( Sample);
  DispHyperMatrix ( Sample);
  READLN;
END.
```

This program does the same thing as **MatrixDemo**, but this version works with arrays of matrices. **FillHyperMatrix** shows one way of specifying individual (**INTEGER**) cells in the **HyperMatrix**; procedure **DispHyperMatrix** shows a second way.

Procedure **ShuffleHyperMatrix** shows how to assign an entire matrix of values at once—by leaving off the indexes for both rows and columns. To access an entire row of a matrix at once, omit only the column index.

Arrays: Miscellaneous Points

There are a few more things you should know about arrays. This section describes another way to specify an array's index values and explains how to define array constants.

The Subrange Type   Pascal has a simple type that was not discussed in Chapter 3. This type is simple in that each variable contains only a single value. The *subrange* type is actually derived from another simple type, and represents a limited range of values of the source type.

Because it is a derived type, a subrange type must be defined before you can declare a variable of that type. This is because the compiler needs to know the range of values included in the subrange type.

For example, suppose you want to use only single-digit integers—that is, values from 0 through 9. You could accomplish this as follows:

```
TYPE SingleDigit = 0 .. 9;
VAR DigitVal : SingleDigit;
```

The first statement specifies that variables of type **SingleDigit** can take on values from 0 to 9. Notice that there are no parentheses around the subrange specifiers. Parentheses are needed only when you tell the compiler about *new* values, as when you are specifying enumerated values. The compiler already knows about whole numbers, so it can interpret the **0 .. 9** properly.

Subrange types are most commonly used to specify array indexes, as in the following listing:

```
P7-8     TYPE SingleDigit = 0 .. 9;
              FaceValue = 2 .. 14;
              (* first define an enumerated type *)
              CardSuit = ( club, diamond, heart, spade);
              (* specify a subrange of that type *)
              RedSuit = diamond .. heart;

              SmallVal = ARRAY [ SingleDigit] OF REAL;
              (* arrays whose cells are TRUE if the card
                 is in the hand, FALSE otherwise.
              *)
              RedCards = ARRAY [ FaceValue, RedSuit] OF BOOLEAN;
              AnyCards = ARRAY [ FaceValue, CardSuit] OF BOOLEAN;

         VAR DigitData : SmallVal;
             RedHand : RedCards;
             Hand : AnyCards;
```

First, look at the definitions for **SingleDigit** and **SmallVal**. The subrange type is defined, as in the earlier listing. Once this is done, the compiler knows that **SingleDigit** is another way of saying **0 .. 9**. Thus, when it sees this identifier as the range specification between the square brackets, the compiler simply substitutes the **0 .. 9**. The result is that you've defined a ten-element array, with indexes ranging from 0 through 9.

The other array definitions are a bit more involved. Notice the enumerated type definition for **CardSuit**. This definition specifies that the type **CardSuit** can take on the values **club**, **diamond**, **heart**, and **spade**.

Once you've defined this type, you can specify subranges based on the **CardSuit**. For example, **RedSuit** specifies a subrange of **CardSuit** values — namely, the two middle values. Notice that the two dots (..) are used between the starting and ending values even if there is no intermediate value.

Notice also that there are parentheses around the original list of values when defining **CardSuit**. There are no parentheses around the subrange specification, since the compiler already knows what to do with the values.

After these definitions are two definitions for two-dimensional arrays. The first dimension in each case is the **FaceValue** subrange type. This type takes on values from 2 through 14.

The second dimension for the **RedCards** array is of type **RedSuit**. This means that the second dimension takes on two possible values. Thus, a variable of type **RedCards** will have 26 (13 * 2) cells.

The first cell in the **RedHand** array will be **RedHand[2][diamond]**, the second will be **RedHand[2][heart]**. The last two elements in the array will be **RedHand[14][diamond]** and **RedHand[14][heart]** — for the aces of diamonds and hearts, respectively. In other words, the different dimensions of an array don't have to be of the same type.

The **AnyCards** type definition is similar to that for **RedCards**. However, the second dimension for **AnyCards** spans the entire range of values that **CardSuit** can take on. This is allowed since, strictly speaking, the range of possible values is itself a subrange.

Although the compiler lets you define a subrange type, it only catches *explicit* attempts to assign values beyond that range. For example, if you try to assign the value **11** directly to a variable of type **SingleDigit**, the compiler complains that the constant is out of range.

On the other hand, if you first assign the **11** to an **INTEGER** variable and then assign this value to a **SingleDigit** variable, you won't get any error messages from the compiler. However, the program will crash at run time.

Array Constants   In Turbo Pascal, you can also define array constants. These constants have values specified at definition time that cannot be changed. The following listing shows two ways of defining array constants:

P7-9

```
(* Program to illustrate definition & use of array constants *)

PROGRAM ArrayConstDemo;

(* define an array constant named PowersOfThree;
   initialize its 6 cells by specifying the values
   within parentheses
*)
CONST PowersOfThree : ARRAY [ 1 .. 6] OF INTEGER =
                           ( 1, 3, 9, 27, 81, 243);
(* define a 5-element array of REAL *)
TYPE TestArray = ARRAY [ 1 .. 5] OF REAL;
(* define and initialize a constant of type TestArray *)
CONST SqrtArray : TestArray = ( 1, 1.414, 1.732, 2, 2.236);

VAR Count : INTEGER;
BEGIN
  FOR Count := 1 TO 6 DO
    WRITELN ( PowersOfThree [ Count]);
  FOR Count := 1 TO 5 DO
    WRITELN ( SqrtArray [ Count]);
  READLN;
END.
```

The first constant definition, for **PowersOfThree**, shows how to define and initialize such a constant in one step. This definition describes an anonymous array type containing six **INTEGER** values. The description is accomplished in the following part of the definition:

```
CONST PowersOfThree : ARRAY [ 1 .. 6] OF INTEGER
```

Once this type definition has been accomplished—even if on the fly, as here—you need to set the constant equal to the value it will have. To do this, include an equal sign, and then specify the value to be associated with the constant. In this case, the value actually consists of six individual values, which are specified within parentheses and separated by commas.

You should realize that you have *not* defined a new type in this process. That is, **PowersOfThree** is a constant, not a type. The array description tells the compiler what **PowersOfThree** looks like, but does not provide enough information to let you declare variables of this type. In particular, what's missing is a name for such a six-element array.

The main program shows that the individual cells of an array constant are accessed as are cells of other arrays.

The second constant definition (for **SqrtArray**) is done somewhat differently. A **TYPE** definition for a **TestArray** provides a name for the next array constant's type. Thus, to provide a description of the constant **SqrtArray**, you just need to specify the type name. When the compiler sees this, it will know that **SqrtArray** is a five-element array of **REAL**.

The constant is initialized to the square roots of the first five integers. The initialization is done as for **PowersOfThree**: values for each cell, separated by commas and surrounded by parentheses.

Notice that the second array constant is defined in a second **CONST** statement, after the **TYPE** definitions. This is allowed in Turbo Pascal but not in standard Pascal. In standard Pascal, all **CONST** definitions must precede the first **TYPE** definition, and you cannot have array constants.

Another type of array constant deserves mention, primarily because of the way it can be initialized. The following listing shows two ways of defining array constants whose base types are **CHAR**.

```
TYPE AlphArray = ARRAY [ 'a' .. 'z'] OF CHAR;
(* Define two array constants to illustrate two
   ways of initializing such an array constant.
*)
CONST Alfabet : AlphArray =
                ( 'a', 'b', 'c', 'd', 'e', 'f', 'g', 'h',
                  'i', 'j', 'k', 'l', 'm', 'n', 'o', 'p',
                  'q', 'r', 's', 't', 'u', 'v', 'w', 'x',
                  'y', 'z');
        Alphabet : AlphArray = 'abcdefghijklmnopqrstuvwxyz';
```

The first constant definition, for **Alfabet**, initializes the array by specifying each of the character values separately. This is tedious but valid.

The second definition, for **Alphabet**, shows a more compact and convenient way of initializing what is, essentially, a string. In the second case, the array is initialized by specifying a 26-character string and assigning this string to the array constant. Notice that no parentheses are used when setting the array constant equal to the string.

Multidimensional Array Constants   You can also define multidimensional array constants. Specifying the values can get a bit tricky, however, since each array's values are within a set of parentheses. For example, the following listing shows how to define two- and three-dimensional array constants:

```
TYPE TwoD = ARRAY [ 1 .. 3, 1 .. 2] OF INTEGER;
     ThreeD = ARRAY [ 1 .. 2, 1 .. 3, 1 .. 2 ] OF INTEGER;

CONST Twins : TwoD = ( ( 11, 12), ( 21, 22), ( 31, 32));
      Triplets : ThreeD =
                   ( ( ( 111, 112), ( 121, 122), ( 131, 132)),
                     ( ( 211, 212), ( 221, 222), ( 231, 232)));
```

Figure 7-4 shows the contents of **Twins**. Compare this layout to the definition. Notice that each row is enclosed in parentheses because each row represents a two-element array.

Figure 7-5 shows the contents of **Triplets**. In the definition for this constant array, each plane is within a set of parentheses. A plane consists of 6 (3 * 2) values. Within a plane—which is just a matrix—each row is enclosed within parentheses. For example, in Plane 1 the first row is specified in

(111, 112)

	Col 1	Col 2
Row 1	11	12
Row 2	21	22
Row 3	31	32

Figure 7-4.   *Contents and layout of a two-dimensional array constant*

Plane 1

	Col 1	Col 2
Row 1	111	112
Row 2	121	122
Row 3	131	132

Plane 2

	Col 1	Col 2
Row 1	211	212
Row 2	221	222
Row 3	231	232

Figure 7-5. *Contents and layout of a three-dimensional array constant*

The RECORD Type

Sometimes you'll want to group items of information that are not of the same type. For example, suppose you want to represent information about a country, including the country's name, its capital, population, and area. The name and capital will be strings; the population and area will be whole numbers.

You could represent each of these items as a separate variable. However, that would quickly get tedious and confusing, especially if you have many countries.

Pascal's **RECORD** type is ideal for creating such a variable. A record represents information containing multiple components, which need not be of the same type.

The following listing shows a **TYPE** definition for a variable to represent a country.

```
TYPE Country = RECORD
               Name, Capital : STRING[80];
               Pop, Area : LONGINT;
               END; (* RECORD Definition *)
```

This definition describes a data type with four components: two 80-character strings and two **LONGINT**s. The components are specified between the reserved word **RECORD** and the **END** that terminates the **RECORD** definition.

Within these bounds, the components are listed as in variable declarations: identifiers followed by a type (specified after a colon). These components are known as the *fields* of the record.

The general syntax for a record definition is

```
┌─────────────────────────────────────────────────────────────────┐
│      <type identifier> "=RECORD" <field list> "END"               │
└─────────────────────────────────────────────────────────────────┘
```

A record definition is one of three places in Pascal where you'll find an **END** without a corresponding **BEGIN**. (This also occurs in a **CASE** statement and in an object definition.)

Accessing Fields in a Record

The following program shows how to access the individual fields of a **Country**:

P7-10

```
(* Program to illustrate use of RECORD variables *)

PROGRAM RecordDemo;
```

```
TYPE Country = RECORD
                 Name, Capital : STRING[80];
                 Pop, Area : LONGINT;
               END; (* RECORD Definition *)
VAR Sample : Country;

  (* Assign the specified values to the appropriate
     fields of TheCountry.
  *)
  PROCEDURE InitCountry ( VAR TheCountry : Country;
                          CName, Capital : STRING;
                          Population, Size : LONGINT);
  BEGIN
    (* To specify a field:
       <variable name> "." <field name>
    *)
    TheCountry.Name := CName;
    TheCountry.Capital := Capital;
    TheCountry.Pop := Population;
    TheCountry.Area := Size;
  END; (* InitCountry *)

  (* Display the contents of the individual fields of
     TheCountry.
  *)
  PROCEDURE DispCountry ( TheCountry : Country);
  BEGIN
    WRITE ( 'NAME      : ', TheCountry.Name:20);
    WRITELN ( ';  CAPITAL: ', TheCountry.Capital:17);
    WRITE ( 'POPULATION: ', TheCountry.Pop:10, ' ':10);
    WRITELN ( ';  AREA    : ', TheCountry.Area:10, ' sq.mi.');
  END; (* DispCountry *)

BEGIN  (* Main program *)
  InitCountry ( Sample, 'Finland', 'Helsinki',
                4900000, 130119);
  DispCountry ( Sample);
  READLN;
END.
```

This program defines a **Country** type and then declares **Sample** as a variable of this type. The two procedures **InitCountry** and **DispCountry** do the program's work.

Once a particular **RECORD** type has been defined, declaring variables of that type is the same as declaring any other type of variable:

<identifier> ":" <type name>

The procedures **InitCountry** and **DispCountry** illustrate that you can pass records as parameters—either by value or by reference. The syntax for doing this is like the syntax for passing any other type of variable.

The syntax for accessing a particular field is as follows:

```
< variable name > "." < field name >
```

You can leave a space between the period and the identifiers on either side. Thus, the following statements are equivalent:

```
TheCountry.Area := Size;
TheCountry . Area := Size;
TheCountry .Area := Size;
TheCountry. Area := Size;
```

When **DispCountry** is called, the **Sample** record is copied and the copy is stored as **TheCountry**. The procedure produces the following output:

```
NAME     :            Finland; CAPITAL:        Helsinki
POPULATION:    4900000      ; AREA   :    130119 sq.mi.
```

A record variable such as **Sample** is stored in memory, as shown in Figure 7-6.

Structured Types as RECORD Fields

The **Country** record has two **STRING** fields. Recall that a **STRING** is an array of characters. As this indicates, you can have aggregate types as fields of a record.

Field	Value	Address
Name	Finland	*x*
Capital	Helsinki	*x* + 81
Pop	4900000	*x* + 162
Area	130119	*x* + 166

Figure 7-6. *Memory layout for the* **Sample** *record variable*

In fact, you can have any type as a record field—except for a file (discussed in Chapter 8, "Files") and another record of the same type. That is, you can't have any fields of type **Country** in the **Country** record. (You can have something called a *pointer* to a **Country** as a field, however, which leads to some powerful data structures. Pointers are discussed in Chapter 9, "Pointers.")

Thus, you can have an array of integers or an array of strings as fields. You can even have a record as a field for another record. The following listing shows examples of such record types, and includes variable declarations for the record types:

```
P7-11    TYPE FreqArray = ARRAY [ 0 .. 10] OF INTEGER;
              CoinTrials = RECORD
                                 Freqs : FreqArray;
                                 Probability : REAL;
                           END; (* CoinTrials RECORD *)

              Menu = ARRAY [ 1 .. 20] OF STRING;
              MenuRec = RECORD
                             Choices : Menu;
                             ShowExtendedMenu : BOOLEAN;
                        END; (* MenuRec RECORD *)

              MiscInfo = RECORD
                              Money : STRING[80];
                              Density, Literacy : REAL;
                         END; (* MiscInfo RECORD *)
```

```
          Country = RECORD
                      Name, Capital : STRING[80];
                      Pop, Area : LONGINT;
                    END; (* Country RECORD *)
          Nation = RECORD
                      Land : Country;
                      Data : MiscInfo;
                    END; (* Nation RECORD *)

   VAR Flips : CoinTrials;
       CurrMenu : MenuRec;
       SampleNation : Nation;
```

The **CoinTrials** structure has two fields. One of these fields is an array of type **FreqArray**, which contains 11 integers. The following procedure shows how to access each of the elements in a variable such as **Flips**:

```
P7-12    PROCEDURE InitCoinTrials ( VAR Vals : CoinTrials);
         VAR Index : INTEGER;
         BEGIN
           Vals.Probability := 0.5;
           (* To access the array: Vals.Freqs;
              to access a cell in the array: Vals.Freqs [ Index]
           *)
           FOR Index := 0 TO 10 DO
             Vals.Freqs [ Index] := 0;
         END; (* InitCoinTrials *)
```

The **MenuRec** structure also has two fields. However, one of them is a two-dimensional array. The access rules are a combination of the rules for accessing **Freqs** in a **CoinTrials** record and the rules for accessing a cell in a two-dimensional array.

To access a particular character in a string, first access the string, then specify the index for the character. For instance,

```
CurrMenu.Choices [ 3][ 4];
```

specifies the fourth character in the third string in the **Choices** field of **CurrMenu**.

To determine how to access fields that are records, extend the rules for accessing first-level fields. To access a field in a record variable, specify the variable name and the field name separated by a period.

If the field is a structured type, you may need to provide more information to get to the element you need. For example, you would use the following code to initialize **SampleNation**:

```
P7-13   (* Program to illustrate how to access record fields that are
            also structured types.
        *)

        PROGRAM MoreRecDemo;

        TYPE MiscInfo = RECORD
                          Money : STRING[80];
                          Density, Literacy : REAL;
                        END; (* MiscInfo RECORD *)

             Country = RECORD
                          Name, Capital : STRING[80];
                          Pop, Area : LONGINT;
                        END; (* Country RECORD *)
             Nation = RECORD
                          Land : Country;
                          Data : MiscInfo;
                        END; (* Nation RECORD *)

        VAR SampleNation : Nation;

          (* Assign the specified values to the appropriate
             fields of TheCountry.
          *)
          PROCEDURE InitCountry ( VAR TheCountry : Country;
                                      CName, Capital : STRING;
                                      Population, Size : LONGINT);
          BEGIN
            (* To specify a field:
               <variable name> "." <field name>
            *)
            TheCountry.Name := CName;
            TheCountry.Capital := Capital;
            TheCountry.Pop := Population;
            TheCountry.Area := Size;
          END; (* InitCountry *)

          (* Display the contents of the individual fields of
             TheCountry.
          *)
          PROCEDURE DispCountry ( TheCountry : Country);
          BEGIN
            WRITE ( 'NAME       : ', TheCountry.Name:20);
            WRITELN ( ';  CAPITAL: ', TheCountry.Capital:17);
```

```
    WRITE ( 'POPULATION: ', TheCountry.Pop:10, ' ':10);
    WRITELN ( ';   AREA   : ', TheCountry.Area:10, ' sq.mi.');
END; (* DispCountry *)

(* Display the contents of the individual fields of
   TheNation.
*)
PROCEDURE DispNation ( TheNation : Nation);
BEGIN
  DispCountry ( TheNation.Land);
  WRITELN ( 'Currency  = ', TheNation.Data.Money);
  WRITELN ( 'Density   = ', TheNation.Data.Density : 10:2,
            ' persons per sq mi');
  WRITELN ( 'Literacy  = ', TheNation.Data.Literacy : 10:2,
            '%');
END; (* DispNation *)

BEGIN  (* Main program *)
  InitCountry ( SampleNation.Land, 'Finland', 'Helsinki',
            4900000, 130119);
  SampleNation.Data.Money := 'Markka';
  SampleNation.Data.Density := 37.7;
  SampleNation.Data.Literacy := 100;
  DispNation ( SampleNation);
  READLN;
END.
```

Procedure **InitCountry** is from an earlier program. The call to this procedure shows how to pass a record as a parameter, even if this record is a field in a larger record. Thus, to initialize the components of **SampleNation**'s **Land** field, just call **InitCountry** with **Land** as the first argument.

Within the procedure, it makes no difference whether the record argument is stand-alone or part of another data structure. The local name is used to access components, so the true variable's full name never becomes an issue.

The rest of the program shows how to access a field within a field. First, access the **Data** field of **SampleNation**—that is, specify **Sample-Nation.Data**. This is just the name of a record. To access a field within this record, include a period and then the field name:

```
SampleNation.Data.Literacy
```

Using WITH to Shorten Field Names

You can have records as fields of other records to an arbitrarily deep level. To specify such deep fields, you simply extend the naming process used in the preceding example. The identifier up to the rightmost period must be a record name, and the identifier following the period must be a field. Beyond that, your name can have an unlimited number of periods, each indicating a record at another level.

Continuing this process can result in extremely long names, as in the following listing:

```
P7-14   (* Program to illustrate long field names *)

        PROGRAM LongFieldNameDemo;

        TYPE ShortStr = STRING[30];

             Education = RECORD
                            Major, Degree : ShortStr;
                            GPA : REAL;
                         END; (* Education RECORD *)

             Student = RECORD
                          Schooling : Education;
                          ID : ShortStr;
                          ClassOf : INTEGER;
                       END; (* Student RECORD *)

             Graduate = RECORD
                           FirstName, LastName : ShortStr;
                           Age : INTEGER;
                           Learning : Student;
                        END; (* Graduate RECORD *)

        VAR Grad : Graduate;

          (* Prompt user and read an INTEGER. *)
          PROCEDURE GetInteger ( Message : STRING;
                                 VAR Value : INTEGER);
          VAR TempStr : STRING;
          BEGIN
            WRITE ( Message, ' ');
            READLN ( Value);
          END; (* GetInteger *)
```

```
     PROCEDURE GetShortStr ( Message : STRING;
                             VAR Value : ShortStr);
     BEGIN
       Write ( Message, ' ');
       READLN ( Value);
     END; (* GetShortStr *)

     PROCEDURE GetReal ( Message : STRING;
                         VAR Value : REAL);
     BEGIN
       Write ( Message, ' ');
       READLN ( Value);
     END; (* GetReal *)

     PROCEDURE GetGraduateInfo ( VAR Info : Graduate);
     BEGIN
       GetShortStr ( 'First name?', Info.FirstName);
       GetShortStr ( 'Last name?', Info.LastName);
       GetInteger ( 'Age?', Info.Age);
       (* Get values for Learning fields *)
       GetShortStr ( 'ID?', Info.Learning.Id);
       GetInteger ( 'Class of?', Info.Learning.ClassOf);
       (* Get Info for Learning.Schooling Fields *)
       GetShortStr ( 'Major?', Info.Learning.Schooling.Major);
       GetShortStr ( 'Degree?', Info.Learning.Schooling.Degree);
       GetReal ( 'GPA?', Info.Learning.Schooling.GPA);
     END; (* GetGraduateInfo *)

     PROCEDURE DispGraduateInfo ( Info : Graduate);
     BEGIN
       WRITELN ( 'First name: ', Info.FirstName);
       WRITELN ( 'Last name : ', Info.LastName);
       WRITELN ( 'Age       : ', Info.Age);
       (* Display values for Learning fields *)
       WRITELN ( 'ID        : ', Info.Learning.Id);
       WRITELN ( 'Class of  : ', Info.Learning.ClassOf);
       (* Display values for Learning.Schooling fields *)
       WRITELN ( 'Major     : ', Info.Learning.Schooling.Major);
       WRITELN ( 'Degree    : ', Info.Learning.Schooling.Degree);
       WRITELN ( 'GPA       : ', Info.Learning.Schooling.GPA:5:2);
     END; (* DispGraduateInfo *)

BEGIN
  GetGraduateInfo ( Grad);
  DispGraduateInfo ( Grad);
  READLN;
END.
```

The first two records defined (**Education** and **Student**) are used as types for fields in other records. Thus, the field **Schooling** (in **Student**) is of type **Education**. In turn, the field **Learning** (in **Graduate**) is of type **Student**. As you can see from **GetGraduateInfo** and **DispGraduateInfo**, it can be tedious to write out such a long name each time.

Pascal's **WITH** statement helps you avoid such lengthy names. The following versions of the two procedures from **LongFieldNameDemo** show how:

P7-15
```
(* Get values for Graduate fields.
   Procedure shows how to use WITH statements to
   shorten field names.
*)
PROCEDURE WGetGraduateInfo ( VAR Info : Graduate);
BEGIN
  WITH Info DO
  BEGIN
    GetShortStr ( 'First name?', FirstName);
    GetShortStr ( 'Last name?', LastName);
    GetInteger ( 'Age?', Age);
    (* Get values for Learning fields *)
    WITH Learning DO
    BEGIN
      GetShortStr ( 'ID?', Id);
      GetInteger ( 'Class of?', ClassOf);
      (* Get Info for Learning.Schooling Fields *)
      WITH Schooling DO
      BEGIN
        GetShortStr ( 'Major?', Major);
        GetShortStr ( 'Degree?', Degree);
        GetReal ( 'GPA?', GPA);
      END; (* WITH (Info.Learning.)Schooling *)
    END; (* WITH (Info.)Learning *)
  END; (* WITH Info *)
END; (* WGetGraduateInfo *)

(* Display contents of a Graduate Record.
   Procedure also uses WITH statements to shorten field names.
*)
PROCEDURE WDispGraduateInfo ( Info : Graduate);
BEGIN
  WITH Info DO
  BEGIN
    WRITELN ( 'First name: ', FirstName);
    WRITELN ( 'Last name : ', LastName);
    WRITELN ( 'Age       : ', Info.Age);
  END; (* WITH Info *)
  (* Display values for Learning fields *)
  WITH Info.Learning DO
  BEGIN
```

```
      WRITELN ( 'ID         : ', Id);
      WRITELN ( 'Class of  : ', ClassOf);
   END; (* WITH Info.Learning *)
   (* Display values for Learning.Schooling fields *)
   WITH Info.Learning.Schooling DO
   BEGIN
      WRITELN ( 'Major      : ', Major);
      WRITELN ( 'Degree     : ', Degree);
      WRITELN ( 'GPA        : ', GPA:5:2);
   END; (* WITH (Info.Learning.)Schooling *)
END; (* WDispGraduateInfo *)
```

The syntax for a **WITH** statement is as follows:

"**WITH**" <record name> "**DO**"
  <simple or compound statement>

Independent WITH Statements The **WDispGraduateInfo** routine contains three independent **WITH** statements. The first one specifies that the record variable **Info** is meant whenever certain field names are used. This applies to the compound statement following the **WITH Info** specification. Thus, the **FirstName** in the procedure refers to the field **Info.FirstName**; similarly, **Age** refers to **Info.Age**.

If you specify **FirstName** in a statement that is not part of any **WITH** statement, the compiler looks only at ordinary variables, not at components of structured variables. Because of the **WITH** statement, however, the compiler first checks whether **Info** has a field named **FirstName**. If the record has no such field, the compiler looks through its local environment for a variable with this name.

Notice that **Info.Age** is used, instead of just **Age**. This shows that you can still use the full name for a record field, even within a **WITH** statement. In the example, both **Info.Age** and **Age** refer to the same memory location. It's not good programming practice to use two different names for the same variable in the same context. This was done here merely to illustrate a point.

The second **WITH** statement also specifies a record. This one is a nested record, however, whose full name is **Info.Learning**. In this case, the compiler first checks this variable for a field named **Id**. If it doesn't find one, it then checks the local environment.

The third **WITH** statement specifies an even more deeply nested record, namely, **Info.Learning.Schooling**. Because the three **WITH** statements are independent of each other, the shortened names apply only in the specified parts of the procedure. For example, you could not refer to **Id** inside the third **WITH** statement.

Nested WITH Statements
The **WITH** statements in **WGetGraduate-Info** are nested. This means that you can use shortened names when specifying records in the inner **WITH** statements. You can specify **Learning** as the record to use because **Info** is assumed, and you can specify **Schooling** because **Info.Learning** is assumed.

Nesting the **WITH** statements also changes the scope of the first two **WITH**s. The first **WITH** is within scope throughout the procedure, as you can see by the **END** that terminates its compound statement.

Using Names for Variables and for Fields
The following version of **WDispGraduateInfo** is identical to the previous one, but two lines have been added. The local variable **ClassOf** has been declared in the procedure and has been assigned the value 1538 outside the scope of any **WITH** statements.

```
P7-16   (* Display contents of a Graduate Record.
           Procedure also uses WITH statements to shorten field names.
        *)
        PROCEDURE WDispGraduateInfo ( Info : Graduate);
        VAR ClassOf : INTEGER;
        ClassOf := 1538;
        BEGIN
          WITH Info DO
          BEGIN
            WRITELN ( 'First name: ', FirstName);
            WRITELN ( 'Last name : ', LastName);
            WRITELN ( 'Age       : ', Info.Age);
          END; (* WITH Info *)
          (* Display values for Learning fields *)
          WITH Info.Learning DO
          BEGIN
            WRITELN ( 'ID        : ', Id);
            WRITELN ( 'Class of  : ', ClassOf);
          END; (* WITH Info.Learning *)
          (* Display values for Learning.Schooling fields *)
          WITH Info.Learning.Schooling DO
          BEGIN
```

```
        WRITELN ( 'Major      : ', Major);
        WRITELN ( 'Degree     : ', Degree);
        WRITELN ( 'GPA        : ', GPA:5:2);
      END; (* WITH (Info.Learning.)Schooling *)
  END; (* WDispGraduateInfo *)
```

What value do you think will be displayed when

```
WRITELN ( 'Class of  : ', ClassOf);
```

is called? If you run the program **LongFieldNameDemo** with the modified procedure, the value you entered for **Info.Learning.ClassOf** is displayed. This is because the call to **WRITELN** occurs within the scope of the second **WITH** statement. As a result, the expanded record field **(Info.Learning.)ClassOf** has greater visibility. (To avoid confusion, don't duplicate variable names in the first place.)

Arrays of Records

As you know, you can have records that contain arrays as fields. You learned that the base type of an array can be just about any type. Can you have a record as the base type for an array?

The following listing shows that you can define an array of records. It also shows how to access individual cells of the array and individual fields of a record (that is, of a cell).

P7-17
```
(*  Program to illustrate definition and use of
    Arrays of records.
*)

PROGRAM RecordTest;

CONST MaxVal = 26;
      MaxTrials = 1000;

TYPE Entry = RECORD
               Freq, Max, Min : INTEGER;
             END; (* Entry RECORD *)
     (* Each cell is an Entry RECORD *)
     IntArray = ARRAY [ 0 .. MaxVal] OF Entry;
```

```
VAR Data : IntArray;
    RawVal, Result, Count :INTEGER;

(* Initialize each cell of array to its appropriate values *)
PROCEDURE InitIntArray ( VAR Ints : IntArray);
VAR Index : INTEGER;
BEGIN
  FOR Index := 0 TO MaxVal DO
  BEGIN
    Ints [ Index].Freq := 0;
    Ints [ Index].Max := 0;
    Ints [ Index].Min := MAXINT;
  END; (* FOR Index := 0 TO MaxVal *)
END;  (* InitIntArray *)

(* Display the contents of each cell's fields *)
PROCEDURE DispIntArray ( VAR Ints : IntArray);
VAR Index : INTEGER;
BEGIN
  FOR Index := 0 TO MaxVal DO
  BEGIN
    WITH Ints [ Index] DO
      WRITE (Index:2, ':', Freq:3,
              ' (', Min:4, ')(', Max:5, ')  ');
    IF (Index MOD 3 = 2) THEN
      WRITELN;
  END;
  WRITELN;
END;  (* DispIntArray *)

BEGIN (* Main *)
  Randomize;
  InitIntArray ( Data);
  (* Fill array cells with random values *)
  FOR Count := 1 TO MaxTrials DO
  BEGIN
    RawVal := RANDOM ( MAXINT);
    Result := RawVal MOD ( MaxVal + 1);
    (* increment Freq field of cell whose
       index corresponds to Result
    *)
    INC ( Data [ Result].Freq);
    (* update Min and Max fields of same cell *)
    IF RawVal > Data [ Result].Max THEN
      Data [ Result].Max := RawVal;
    IF RawVal < Data [ Result].Min THEN
      Data [ Result].Min := RawVal;
  END; (* FOR Count := 1 TO MaxTrials *)
  DispIntArray ( Data);
  READLN;
END.
```

The main data structure for this program is a 27-element array. The individual cells of this array are actually records, each of which has three **INTEGER** fields. Figure 7-7 shows the layout of such an array.

For a sample run, the preceding program produced the following output:

```
 0: 35 (  162)(31698)    1: 24 (2053)(30025)    2: 35 (  677)(32672)
 3: 40 (1029)(32538)     4: 34 (  436)(31837)    5: 36 (  545)(32648)
 6: 39 (1734)(32028)     7: 34 (   34)(32677)    8: 44 (   35)(30599)
 9: 35 (2493)(31437)    10: 37 (  712)(32194)   11: 32 (1820)(30791)
12: 26 (1524)(32250)    13: 43 (  364)(32521)   14: 38 (  203)(30929)
15: 37 (  663)(32658)   16: 42 (1204)(32659)   17: 39 (1232)(32498)
18: 38 (1260)(31284)    19: 56 (1612)(32527)   20: 42 (  236)(32690)
21: 34 (  453)(32610)   22: 36 (1075)(31936)   23: 30 (  374)(29966)
24: 44 (   51)(32586)   25: 42 (  241)(31264)   26: 28 (3104)(31130)
```

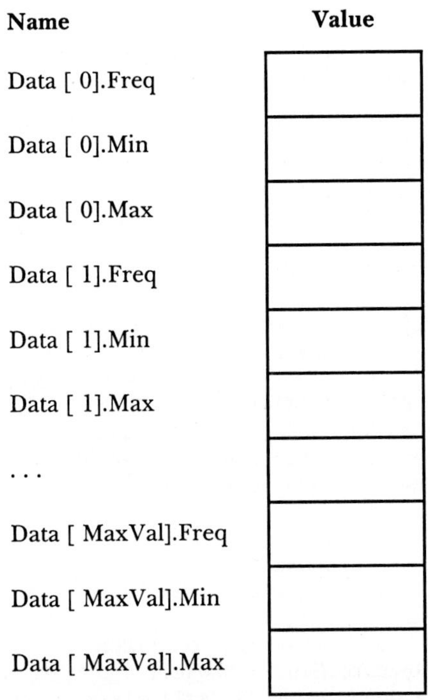

Name	Value
Data [0].Freq	
Data [0].Min	
Data [0].Max	
Data [1].Freq	
Data [1].Min	
Data [1].Max	
. . .	
Data [MaxVal].Freq	
Data [MaxVal].Min	
Data [MaxVal].Max	

Figure 7-7. *Layout for an array of records*

To produce such a run, this program:

■ Generates random integers and determines the remainder when divided by 27

■ Updates the array cell whose index corresponds to the remainder

In particular, the program increases the frequency count in the **Freq** field of the appropriate array cell. The program also checks (and updates, if necessary) the **Min** and **Max** fields, which contain the smallest and largest values that have produced the given remainder.

In the sample run, 35 of the 1000 values left a remainder of 0 when divided by 27. The smallest of these values was 162 and the largest was 31698.

Accessing Records in the Array   To access a particular cell, work through the task step by step. First, try to specify a record. In this case, the record is a cell of an array so the first step is to specify an array cell.

To specify an array cell, supply the variable name followed by the cell's index within square brackets. For example,

```
Data [ Result]
```

specifies the record whose index is the current value of **Result**. This object is a record.

Once you've specified the record, you need to specify the desired field. To do this, simply add a period and then the field identifier. For example,

```
Data [ Result].Max
```

specifies the **Max** field of the record with index value **Result**.

The WITH Statement Revisited   Remember, the **WITH** statement enables you to shorten record names. You can do this even if the record is an array cell, as shown in **DispIntArray** in the previous program. However, be careful of how and where you specify the **WITH** variable

under certain conditions. For example, consider the following version of
DispIntArray:

P7-18
```
(* INCORRECT routine to
    display the contents of each cell's fields.
    Routine is incorrect because of WITH statement location.
*)
PROCEDURE DispIntArray ( VAR Ints : IntArray);
VAR Index : INTEGER;
BEGIN
  Index := 0;
  (* This will always refer to the 0th cell *)
  WITH Ints [ Index] DO
  BEGIN
    WHILE Index <= MaxVal DO
    BEGIN
      WRITE (Index:2, ':', Freq:3,
             ' (', Min:4, ')(', Max:5, ')   ');
      IF (Index MOD 3 = 2) THEN
        WRITELN;
      INC ( Index);
    END; (* WHILE Index <= MaxVal *)
  END;
  WRITELN;
END;  (* DispIntArray *)
```

This procedure uses a **WHILE** loop to go through the array. There is
also a **WITH** statement; however, in this version, the loop is inside the
scope of the **WITH** statement.

To determine what cell is meant, **Index** must be evaluated. When the
procedure reaches the **WITH** statement, **Index** evaluates to 0. Once
inside the **WHILE** loop, the value of **Index** is never used again to
specifiy a new cell. As a result, the procedure always displays **Ints[0]**.

Operations on Records

You can assign the contents of an entire record to a variable of the same
type. This assignment requires only one statement. To assign an entire
record, an area of memory is copied at another location. The fact that
the two variables are of the same type assures that the memory areas will
be the same size. Besides this total assignment, operations on records
must be carried out on a component to component basis.

Variant Records

Suppose you need to keep information about individual persons who range from children through married adults. Much of the information you store will be the same for all of these age groups. For example, you may want to store first and last names, age, and sex for each person. However, there will also be a few items that are pertinent for one age group but not for others. For example, you may want income and marital status data for adults and possibly teenagers. Similarly, you might want to know whether a child is in preschool or school, and you may want to know a child's grade and school performance.

Pascal allows you to create a type definition for a *variant record*. In each instance of such a record you can store whichever collection of special information is relevant for that instance. The following listing shows such a variant record:

P7-19

```
(* Program to illustrate storage requirements of
   variant records, with tag field.
*)

PROGRAM VarRecDemo;

TYPE Sex = ( female, male);
     MaritalStatus = ( single, married, divorced, widowed);
     AgeGroup = ( infant, toddler, child, teenager, adult);
     Person = RECORD
                 First, Last : STRING;
                 Age : INTEGER;
                 Gender : Sex;
                 Weight, Height : REAL;
                 (* Variant part begins here;
                    variant used depends on value of WhichGroup.
                 *)
                 CASE WhichGroup : AgeGroup OF
                   (* if WhichGroup = infant, then
                      record has two REAL fields.
                   *)
                   infant : ( BirthWeight, BirthHeight : REAL);
                   toddler : ( InPreSchool, InDayCare : BOOLEAN);
                   child : ( Grade : INTEGER);
                   (* If WhichGroup = teenager, then
                      record has one INTEGER and two REAL fields.
                      Note that tGrade is used here, since Grade
                      has already been used, and cannot be used
```

```
                            for a field name twice. The same holds for
                            tIncome.
                        *)
                        teenager : ( GPA, tIncome : REAL;
                                        tGrade : INTEGER);

                        adult : ( Income : REAL;
                                    Status : MaritalStatus);
                    END; (* Person RECORD *)

VAR Nemo : Person;

BEGIN
  WRITELN ( 'Nemo requires ', SizeOf ( Nemo), ' bytes.');
  Nemo.Income := 39000.50;
  WRITELN ( Nemo.Income: 10: 2);
  READLN;
END.
```

Although this definition looks formidable, it's actually quite straightforward. The **Person** record has a fixed and a variant part. The syntax for the fixed part (fields **First** through **Height**) is like that for the record examples you've already seen.

The variant part begins with the **CASE WhichGroup** line. A particular **Person** record can store any of five different groups of fields—depending on the value of the record's **WhichGroup** field.

For example, if **Nemo.WhichGroup** is **teenager**, then the **Nemo** record is storing three items of variant information: **tGrade**, **GPA**, and **tIncome**. On the other hand, if **Nemo.WhichGroup** is **adult**, the record is storing **Status** and **Income** information. Since the value of the field **Nemo.WhichGroup** can, in principle, change during program execution, the program must be prepared to store any of the variant configurations.

To be able to store any of these configurations, a **Person** record must have enough room for the largest one. In the example, this amounts to 14 bytes to store the fields for a **teenager**. Running the **VarRecDemo** program shows that **Nemo** takes 542 bytes: 256 bytes for each of the strings, 2 bytes for **Age**, 6 bytes each for **Height** and **Weight**, 1 byte each for **Gender** and **WhichGroup**, and 14 bytes for the **teenager** variant configuration. Figure 7-8 shows how such a variant record would be laid out.

Field	Address	
Field	**Address**	
First	x	
Last	$x + 256$	
Age	$x + 512$	
Gender	$x + 514$	
Weight	$x + 515$	
Height	$x + 521$	
WhichGroup	$x + 527$	
		(End fixed record part) (Begin variant part) [**value of WhichGroup**]
BirthWeight	$x + 528$	[infant]
InPreSchool	$x + 528$	[toddler]
InDayCare	$x + 529$	[toddler]
Grade	$x + 528$	[child]
GPA	$x + 528$	[teenager]
Income	$x + 528$	[adult]
BirthHeight	$x + 534$	[infant]
tIncome	$x + 534$	[teenager]
Status	$x + 534$	[adult]
tGrade	$x + 540$	[teenager]
		(End of Record definition)

Figure 7-8. *Layout of a variant **Person** record*

At any given time, only one of the field configurations is the correct one, but you can access any configuration whenever you wish. To specify the fields for a particular configuration, you need to list them within parentheses. Within the parentheses, the list will have the same format as a variable declaration. The variant part of a record definition must follow the fixed part. The variant part always begins with **CASE**. The record definition ends with a single **END**, whether it's a variant or a fixed record.

Tagged and Untagged Variants

The **WhichGroup** field in the preceding definition is known as a *tag field*. This field acts as a filter, enabling you to check which of the variants to choose. Your program checks the value of this field to determine which variant configuration to read or write. A variant record such as **Person** is a *tagged variant* because it has a tag field.

In the preceding program, notice that you don't *have* to do anything with the **WhichGroup** field to use a specific variant. While it's not a syntactical error to access variants without going through **WhichGroup**, it can be dangerous, since your program will always need to remember the current configuration. The program could access garbage values by using the wrong configuration.

There is another way of specifying a record variant. You can omit the tag field and only specify the type whose values are used to specify the variants. The following listing shows a record definition in which the tag is omitted. **ZPerson** is identical to **Person** in the preceding program, but the **CASE** line is different.

P7-20
```
(* Program to illustrate storage requirements of
   variant records, without tag field.
*)

PROGRAM VarRecDemo2;

TYPE Sex = ( female, male);
     MaritalStatus = ( single, married, divorced, widowed);
     AgeGroup = ( infant, toddler, child, teenager, adult);
     ZPerson = RECORD
                  First, Last : STRING;
                  Age : INTEGER;
                  Gender : Sex;
```

```
                     Weight, Height : REAL;
                     (* Variant part begins here;
                        variant used depends on AgeGroup values
                     *)
                     CASE AgeGroup OF
                       infant : ( BirthWeight, BirthHeight : REAL);
                       toddler : ( InPreSchool, InDayCare : BOOLEAN);
                       child : ( Grade : INTEGER);
                       teenager : ( GPA, tIncome : REAL;
                                     tGrade : INTEGER);

                       adult : ( Income : REAL;
                                  Status : MaritalStatus);
                   END; (* Person RECORD *)

VAR ZNemo : ZPerson;

BEGIN
  WRITELN ( 'ZNemo requires ', SizeOf ( ZNemo), ' bytes.');
  ZNemo.Income := 39000.50;
  WRITELN ( ZNemo.Income: 10: 2);
  READLN;
END.
```

By omitting the tag, you also delete the **WhichGroup** field from the record definition. When you run the preceding program, **ZNemo** takes 541 bytes, one byte less than **Nemo**. This is because **ZNemo** doesn't have a **WhichGroup** field.

Using an untagged variant is equivalent to bypassing the **WhichGroup** field in the tagged version. It saves you a bit of storage, and can save you the accesses needed to update and check the tag field. However, you cannot check which variant is currently valid. If you need to use variant records, you're generally better off using tagged variants.

Record Constants

In Turbo Pascal, you can define record constants. That is, you can define a record structure and then specify a name to be associated with a particular combination of values for such a structure. The following listing shows how to define and initialize record constants.

P7-21

```
(* Program to illustrate record constants *)

PROGRAM RecConstantDemo;

TYPE DailyWeather = RECORD
                        HiTemp, LoTemp, Wind : REAL;
                        END; (* DailyWeather RECORD *)

     DaysData = ARRAY [ 1 .. 2] OF REAL;

     DaysWeather = RECORD
                        DaysHi, DaysLo, DaysWind : DaysData;
                        END; (* DaysWeather RECORD *)

CONST ExtremeWeather : DailyWeather =
          ( HiTemp : 115.6; LoTemp : -89.9; Wind : 183.2);
      ExtremeDays : DaysWeather =
          ( DaysHi : ( 101.6, 115.6); DaysLo : ( -89.9, -88.7);
            DaysWind : ( 183.2, 181.8));

BEGIN
  WITH ExtremeWeather DO
  BEGIN
    WRITELN ( 'HiTemp     = ', HiTemp : 12:2);
    WRITELN ( 'LoTemp     = ', LoTemp : 12:2);
    WRITELN ( 'Wind       = ', Wind : 12:2);
  END; (* WITH ExtremeWeather *)

  WITH ExtremeDays DO
  BEGIN
    WRITELN ( '<Data>             <Midnight>     <Noon>');
    WRITELN ( 'DaysHi     = ',
              DaysHi [ 1] : 12:2, DaysHi [ 2] : 12:2);
    WRITELN ( 'DaysLo     = ',
              DaysLo [ 1] : 12:2, DaysLo [ 2] : 12:2);
    WRITELN ( 'DaysWind = ',
              DaysWind [ 1] : 12:2, DaysWind [ 2] : 12:2);
  END; (* WITH ExtremeDays *)
  READLN;
END.
```

You define the constant by specifying an identifier, followed by a type and values for the record's fields.

<identifier> ":" <record type specifier>"= ("<values>")"

As with array constants, you specify the values for a record constant within parentheses. For a record, you specify the field identifier, a colon, and then a value, as here:

<field identifier> ":" <value>

You must specify the fields in the same order as in the original record definition, separating individual fields by semicolons. Thus, for the constant **ExtremeWeather**, the three fields are specified by name. Each of these is followed by a colon and a value. The first and second fields are followed by semicolons. The final field-value pair is followed by the right parenthesis that ends the value specification.

ExtremeDays is a record whose fields are arrays. The rules for initializing these arrays are a combination of the rules for initializing array and record constants. The field-value pairing is still in effect, as you can see by the **DaysHi :**, which is associated with (101.6, 115.6), and by the **DaysLo :**, which is associated with (−89.9, −88.7).

Because the values are for an entire array, they are specified within parentheses. The right parenthesis indicates the end of the array. The value specification is different than for **ExtremeWeather**, but the rest of the syntax is identical.

There's one other type of constant you could define: an array, each of whose cells is a record. Try defining and initializing such a constant.

Keep in mind the rules for initializing records and arrays, and remember to combine these rules in the appropriate way.

The OBJECT Type: A Preview

With Turbo Pascal, you can do *object-oriented programming* (OOP). This powerful programming technique will be discussed in Chapters 11, "Object-Oriented Programming in Turbo Pascal," and 12, "Virtual Methods in Object-Oriented Programming." An important concept in OOP is that of an object. This section briefly previews how objects are represented in Turbo Pascal.

An *object* includes a collection of features that characterize the object. (It may also include other components, which will be discussed in Chapter 11.) For example, a sphere might be characterized as an object that has a particular size, or radius, and that is either solid or hollow.

Once you have a description of an object, you can define new objects that are the same as the prototype object and have some additional characteristics. For example, you could describe a beach ball as something with the features of a sphere and an additional feature — namely, a design on the surface. Or you could describe a sports ball as a sphere that is either bouncy or not.

In Turbo Pascal, an object is represented much like a record. For example, the following describes a **Sphere** as an object with two features:

```
TYPE Sphere = OBJECT
            radius : REAL;
            solid : BOOLEAN;
        END;  (* OBJECT definition *)
```

Syntactically, the only difference between this and a record definition is the word **OBJECT** instead of **RECORD**. This difference has important consequences because you can define new objects that inherit the features of a **Sphere**. You could not do this if **Sphere** had been defined as a record.

OBJECT is a reserved word that is new in Turbo Pascal and that describes a new data type. Once you have such a type definition, you can declare variables of the new type. Such variables are known as *instances* of the object. The following listing shows how to declare an instance of a **Sphere**.

```
EuclideanSphere : Sphere;
```

Once you've defined an object, you can define variants on it. These variants will *inherit* the object's features and will have unique features of their own. For example, the following listing shows how to define such derivative objects as **BeachBall** and **SportsBall**, once **Sphere** has been defined. The listing is not a program, but is included on your disk in case you want to try building a program around such objects.

```
P7-22    TYPE Sphere = OBJECT
                         radius : REAL;
                         solid : BOOLEAN;
                      END;  (* OBJECT definition *)

         Design = ( solidcolor, patterns, pictures);

         BeachBall = OBJECT (Sphere)
                        Surface : Design;
                     END; (* OBJECT definition *)

         SportsBall = OBJECT ( Sphere)
                         Bouncy : BOOLEAN;
                      END; (* OBJECT definition *)

VAR MyBeachBall : BeachBall;
    Squashball, Basketball : SportsBall;
```

Objects that inherit features of another object are called *descendant objects*. In the example, **BeachBall** and **SportsBall** are descendant objects. Both have **Sphere** as their *ancestor object*.

To describe a descendant object, use an **OBJECT** definition. Next to the reserved word **OBJECT**, however, you need to specify the ancestor object within parentheses. This allows the new object to inherit the ancestor object's features. Thus, it makes available all the fields of the ancestor object—just as if they had been included explicitly in the definition of the descendant object.

The syntax for specifying an object and a descendant object is

---

<object name> "=**OBJECT**" <components> "**END**"
<descendant> "=**OBJECT** ("<ancestor>")"
          <components> " **END**"

The syntax for accessing an object's fields is the same as that for accessing a record's fields. For example, all of the following are valid statements:

```
Squashball.Solid := FALSE;
Squashball.Bouncy := TRUE;
MyBeachball.Radius := 12;
MyBeachball.Color := pictures;
```

You'll learn how to use objects in Chapter 11, which also describes a safer and more elegant way to access an object's components. This will involve routines associated with the object.

The SET Type

Sometimes it's useful to keep collections of values for comparison. For example, you might want to check whether a particular character descends below the line when printed—that is, whether the character is *g, j, p, q,* or *y.*

Or suppose you're keeping track of students' majors. In addition to determining the number of people in each major, you might count the number of students with science or humanities majors. To do this for a science major, you might check whether a student's major is math, physics, chemistry, biology, biochemistry, astronomy, or earth science.

In these situations, you not only need to work with individual values, you need to work with collections of values. Depending on the example, such collections may contain arbitrary combinations of values of the specified type. When you're working with such a collection, you're generally interested in whether or not a particular value is present. The actual value may not be of direct interest.

In mathematics, such a collection of values, or elements, is called a set. A *set* is an unordered collection of elements in which repetitions are discarded. That is, an element appears at most once per set. You can describe a set by listing the elements in the set. It doesn't matter how often you list an element; nor does the order matter.

For example, suppose you had the string 'sweeteners', and you wanted to represent its constituent letters in a set. This set would contain six elements: *s, w, e, t, n, r.* Notice that the *e* and *s* each appear only once in the set, although they are repeated in the word.

Pascal's **SET** type enables you to represent such collections. The following program shows how to define and initialize sets, but you won't see anything when you run it. Later, you may want to add instructions to display the contents of the sets.

P7-23   (* Program to illustrate use of SETs *)

PROGRAM SetDemo1;

```
      (* Define a type to represent a collection of characters *)
TYPE CharSet = SET OF CHAR;

      (* define a type whose values are majors *)
      Major = ( anthropology, art, astronomy, biochemistry,
               biology, chemistry, complit, earthsci,
               economics, english, literature, math, physics,
               politics, psychology);
      (* Define a type to represent a collection of majors *)
      MajorGroup = SET OF Major;

VAR AllMajors,Science : MajorGroup;
    WdSet : CharSet;

BEGIN
  (* Assign the entire collection of values to AllMajors *)
  AllMajors :=  [ anthropology .. psychology];
  (* Assign a list of majors to the set Science *)
  Science := [ physics, astronomy .. chemistry, earthsci];
  WdSet := [ 'b', 'd', 'f', 'h', 'k', 'l', 't'];
END.
```

As with the other structured types, you first need to describe the desired **SET** type with the following syntax:

< type identifier > " = **SET OF**" < ordinal base type >

There are restrictions on the base type, which are discussed shortly.

Once you've specified this set template, you can declare variables of the specified type. In the example program, the first type definition describes a **CharSet** as a set whose elements will be of type **CHAR**.

The **MajorGroup** type definition specifies a set whose base type is an enumerated type. Once the possible values of this enumerated type are listed, you can define types containing such values. Thus, the **Major-Group** definition is valid, as are the declarations for **Science** and **All-Majors**.

The main program shows how to assign a value to a set variable. You use an ordinary assignment operator, but you need to use the set constructor on the right-hand side of the assignment statement. The *set constructor*—[]—makes the element or elements it contains into a set.

Thus, the expression

```
[ anthropology .. psychology]
```

creates a set that contains all 15 possible values for a **Major**. To specify the contents of a set, you simply need to list the elements. Notice that you can use the double dots (..) to indicate a range of consecutive values.

The next assignment shows another way to specify a collection of values. In this case, a subrange of values is indicated by using double dots. In addition, two other majors are listed. Individual elements are separated by commas.

After this second assignment statement, **Science** will contain the following values: **astronomy, biochemistry, biology, chemistry, earth-sci**, and **physics**.

The fact that **physics** is listed first does not have any significance. Remember, a set is an *unordered* collection of elements. All that matters is whether or not a particular value is an element. For this reason, the following assignments will all produce the same set:

```
(* all four assignments make Science the same set *)
Science := [ physics, astronomy .. chemistry, earthsci];
Science := [ astronomy .. chemistry, earthsci, physics];
Science := [ astronomy .. chemistry, physics, earthsci];
Science := [ astronomy, biology, biochemistry, chemistry,
             physics, earthsci];
```

In the **SetDemo1** program, the third assignment builds a set containing several individual characters and assigns this set to **WdSet**. Can you guess what the characters included in **WdSet** have in common?

CAUTION   Be careful not to confuse the set constructor brackets with the brackets for specifying an array cell. The context in your program should make it clear which way the brackets are being used.

Set Features and Restrictions

The base type of a set must be an ordinal type, but not all ordinal types are allowed as set base types. The base type can have at most 256 possible values. Furthermore, the ordinal values of the set's base type cannot be less than 0 or greater than 255.

This means, for example, that you can't have a **SET OF INTEGER**. This type has too many possible values (more than 256), and the ordinal positions of these values lie outside the range of 0 to 255.

You also can't have a **SET OF SHORTINT**. Even though this type only has 256 possible values, their ordinal values range between −128 and 127. Finally, you can't have **LONGINT**s or **WORD**s as the base type for a set. If you create an enumerated type, it can't have more than 256 values if you want to use it for sets.

You can, however, have a set with a subrange type as its base type. For example, the following definitions create a set whose elements can be any value from 20 through 199:

```
P7-24    PROGRAM SubRangeSetDemo;

         TYPE MiddleNrs = 20 .. 199;
              MiddleSet = SET OF MiddleNrs;

         VAR MidVals : MiddleSet;
         BEGIN
           MidVals := [ 20, 199, 36];
         END.
```

The base type of the set in the example is an ordinal value (**Middle-Nrs**). This type has fewer than 256 values, and the ordinal values (20 .. 199) associated with its values are within the range 0 to 255. Therefore, **MiddleNrs** satisfies all the restrictions on set types.

REMEMBER   The base type of a set must be an ordinal type, subject to two restrictions:

■ The base type can have at most 256 possible values.

■ The ordinal positions of these values must be in the range 0 to 255.

Representation of Sets

In Turbo Pascal, a set is represented as an array of bits. Each bit corresponds to a possible value in the set. If the bit is 1, the value is an element in the set; if the bit is 0, the value is not an element.

This representation illustrates why order makes no difference when you specify elements in a set, and why repetitions have no effect. The order is irrelevant, since all that matters is whether a particular bit is 1 or 0. Repetitions are irrelevant because turning on a bit that is already on has no effect.

A Special Set

One set has a very special status: the set that contains no elements. Such a set is known as the *null set* or *empty set*. This set is similar to 0 in arithmetic—it is needed, but has no effect in many operations.

The null set is indicated by []. For example, the following program creates and declares a set type and then initializes this variable to an empty set:

P7-25
```
PROGRAM NullSetDemo;

TYPE CharSet = SET OF CHAR;

VAR WdSet : CharSet;

BEGIN
  (* After this assignment, WdSet has been initialized,
     but does not contain any elements.
   *)
  WdSet := [];
END.
```

You'll soon use the null set in expressions and find out what happens if you combine the null set with other sets.

Set Operators

What can you do with sets? You can add, select, and remove elements, and you can compare sets to determine whether they contain the same elements. You can also check whether a particular value is an element of a set.

Checking Whether an Element Is in a Set
You'll often want to check whether a specific value is an element in a set. In fact, it's essential to be able to do this to display the contents of a set.

Pascal's **IN** operator enables you to check whether a value is contained in a set. This binary operator takes two different types of values: an element of the set's base type and a set. The operator returns a **BOOLEAN**. If the element is contained in the set, the operator returns **TRUE**; otherwise, the operator returns **FALSE**.

The following listing shows how to use the **IN** operator:

P7-26
```
(* Program to illustrate use of IN operator *)

PROGRAM SetInDemo;

    (* Define a type to represent a collection of characters *)
TYPE CharSet = SET OF CHAR;

VAR WdSet : CharSet;

  (* Display any values between StartCh and EndCh, inclusive,
     that are elements in TheSet.
  *)
  PROCEDURE DispCharSet ( TheSet : CharSet;
                          StartCh, EndCh : CHAR);
  VAR IndexCh : CHAR;
      Count : INTEGER;
  BEGIN
    Count := 1;
    FOR IndexCh := StartCh TO EndCh DO
      (* Note that IN takes a CHAR and a CharSet
         as operands in this procedure
      *)
      IF IndexCh IN TheSet THEN
      BEGIN
        WRITE ( IndexCh:3);
        IF Count MOD 20 = 0 THEN
          WRITELN;
        INC ( Count);
      END;
  END; (* DispCharSet *)

BEGIN
  WdSet := [ 'A' .. 'z'];
```

```
     DispCharSet ( WdSet, 'A', 'z');
     READLN;
END.
```

Procedure **DispCharSet** displays the contents of the specified **Char-Set**. This procedure exemplifies a typical strategy for determining or displaying elements in a set:

- You loop through the specified range of base type values.

- You check whether each value is an element of the set.

You cannot read the contents of a set directly because there is no relationship between a bit in the set's representation and the value that the bit represents. Instead, you use the **IN** operator in such a procedure. For each value within the specified range (between *A* and *z* in the program), the procedure checks whether the value is an element of the specified set. If so, the procedure writes the element.

In addition to illustrating the **IN** operator, **DispCharSet** also shows how to pass a set parameter by value. To do this, simply specify the set's name as an argument. To declare a set parameter, provide an identifier and an appropriate type.

The program produces the following output:

```
A  B  C  D  E  F  G  H  I  J  K  L  M  N  O  P  Q  R  S  T
U  V  W  X  Y  Z  [  \  ]  ^  _  '  a  b  c  d  e  f  g  h
i  j  k  l  m  n  o  p  q  r  s  t  u  v  w  x  y  z
```

The ASCII table in Appendix A, "ASCII Codes," confirms that these are all the characters between *A* and *z.*

The precedence for the **IN** operator is low—it's the same as for the comparison operators (=, <=, and so forth).

The Set Union Operator   To add to a set, you need to use the *set union operator,* also called the *set addition operator* (+). The following listing shows how to do this:

P7-27   ```(* Program to illustrate use of set union operator *)```

```
PROGRAM SetUnionDemo;
```

```
      (* Define a type to represent a collection of characters *)
TYPE CharSet = SET OF CHAR;

VAR WdSet1, WdSet2 : CharSet;
    IndexCh : CHAR;

  (* Display any values between StartCh and EndCh, inclusive,
     that are elements in TheSet.
  *)
  PROCEDURE DispCharSet ( TheSet : CharSet;
                          StartCh, EndCh : CHAR);
  VAR IndexCh : CHAR;
      Count : INTEGER;
  BEGIN
    Count := 1;
    FOR IndexCh := StartCh TO EndCh DO
      (* Note that IN takes a CHAR and a CharSet
         as operands in this procedure
      *)
      IF IndexCh IN TheSet THEN
      BEGIN
        WRITE ( IndexCh:3);
        IF Count MOD 20 = 0 THEN
          WRITELN;
        INC ( Count);
      END;
  END; (* DispCharSet *)

BEGIN   (* Main program *)
  WdSet1 := [ 'b', 'd', 'f', 'h', 'k', 'l', 't'];
  (* Build WdSet by combining contents of two sets *)
  WdSet2 := WdSet1 + [ 'g', 'j', 'p', 'q', 'y'];
  WRITELN ( 'WdSet1:');
  DispCharSet ( WdSet1, 'a', 'z');
  WRITELN;
  WRITELN ( 'WdSet2:');
  DispCharSet ( WdSet2, 'a', 'z');
  READLN;
END.
```

This program builds **WdSet2** by combining the contents of two other sets. The set union operator takes two sets as operands and returns a third set as the result. This set is called the *union* of the two operand sets. The third (union) set contains all elements that are in either or both of the two operand sets.

Notice that no set constructor was used with **WdSet1** on the right-hand side of the assignment in the main program. This is because

WdSet1 already is a set. Writing

```
[WdSet1]
```

creates a set whose single element is itself a set. Such constructs are allowed in mathematics, but not in Pascal.

The program produces the following output:

```
WdSet1:
  b  d  f  h  k  l  t
WdSet2:
  b  d  f  g  h  j  k  l  p  q  t  y
```

Recall that repetitions are discarded in sets. This means that an element contained in both operand sets will only appear once in the resulting set. For example, the following assignment line does not create a different **WdSet2** than the program, even though the second and third sets have common elements:

```
WdSet2 := WdSet1 + ['g', 'j', 'p', 'q', 'y'] + ['g', 'y', 'y'];
```

The preceding statement also shows that you can list the same element twice in a set without causing a compiler error or repeating the element in the set. Listing an element twice has no effect.

REMEMBER   The union (+) of two sets is a set that contains all elements from either or both of the component sets. If an element is contained in both component sets, it appears only once in the union set. The union of two sets always contains at least as many elements as the larger of the two operand sets.

Set Unions Involving the Null Set   What do you think the following program will display?

P7-28
```
(* Program to illustrate unions involving null set *)

PROGRAM UnionDemo2;

TYPE CharSet = SET OF CHAR;

VAR WdSet : CharSet;

   (* Display any values between StartCh and EndCh, inclusive,
```

```
              that are elements in TheSet.
    *)
    PROCEDURE DispCharSet ( TheSet : CharSet;
                            StartCh, EndCh : CHAR);
    VAR IndexCh : CHAR;
        Count : INTEGER;
    BEGIN
      Count := 1;
      FOR IndexCh := StartCh TO EndCh DO
        (* Note that IN takes a CHAR and a CharSet
           as operands in this procedure
        *)
        IF IndexCh IN TheSet THEN
        BEGIN
          WRITE ( IndexCh:3);
          IF Count MOD 20 = 0 THEN
            WRITELN;
          INC ( Count);
        END;
    END; (* DispCharSet *)

BEGIN
  WdSet := ['g' .. 'k', 'k', 'z'];
  WdSet := WdSet + [];
  DispCharSet ( WdSet, 'a', 'z');
  READLN;
END.
```

The second assignment statement assigns the union of **WdSet** and another set to **WdSet**. The other set is the empty set, which contains no elements. If you combine a set with no elements with another set, the result is the other set. Thus, the assignment does not affect the value of **WdSet**.

REMEMBER The union of any set with the null set is the original set. In this context, the null set behaves like 0 in addition: it changes nothing.

The set union operator is essentially an additive operator, and has the same precedence as other additive operators. This precedence is below that for the multiplicative operators but above that for the comparison operators.

The Set Intersection Operator Whereas the set union operator creates a set made up of elements combined from two sets, the *set intersection* *operator* (*) creates a set of elements *selected* from other sets. This binary operator takes two set operands and returns a third set that contains only those elements that are contained in *both* of the operand sets. This resultant set is known as the *intersection* of the two operand sets and has *at most* as many elements as the smaller operand set.

The following program shows how to use the set intersection operator:

P7-29
```
(* Program to illustrate use of set intersection operator *)

PROGRAM IntersectionDemo;
CONST Smaller = 3;
      Larger = 4;
TYPE ByteSet = SET OF BYTE;
VAR BySmaller, ByLarger, Result : ByteSet;
    Count : INTEGER;

  (* Display any values between StartByte and EndByte,
     inclusive, that are elements in TheSet.
  *)
  PROCEDURE DispByteSet ( TheSet : ByteSet;
                          StartByte, EndByte : BYTE);
  VAR IndexByte : BYTE;
      Count : INTEGER;
  BEGIN
    Count := 1;
    FOR IndexByte := StartByte TO EndByte DO
      (* Note that IN takes a BYTE and a ByteSet
         as operands in this procedure
      *)
      IF IndexByte IN TheSet THEN
      BEGIN
        WRITE ( IndexByte:4);
        IF Count MOD 15 = 0 THEN
          WRITELN;
        INC ( Count);
      END;
  END; (* DispByteSet *)

  (* Display contents of the specified set. *)
  PROCEDURE ShowSetData ( TheSet : ByteSet;
                          Message : STRING);
  BEGIN
    WRITELN ( Message, ':');
    DispByteSet ( TheSet, 0, 255);
    WRITELN;
  END;  (* Show SetData *)
```

```
    (* Add the appropriate elements to TheSet:
       20 values, separated by Increment.
    *)
    PROCEDURE BuildSet ( VAR TheSet : ByteSet;
                             Increment : INTEGER);
    VAR Count, Val : INTEGER;
    BEGIN
      Val := 0;
      FOR Count := 1 TO 20 DO
      BEGIN
        INC ( Val, Increment);
        TheSet := TheSet + [ Val];
      END; (* FOR Count := 1 TO 20 *)
    END;  (* BuildSet *)

BEGIN
  (* Initialize both sets to null sets *)
  BySmaller := [];
  ByLarger := [];

  (* Build the two sets.
     BySmaller will contain 0, 3, 6, ..., 60;
     ByLarger will contain  0, 4, 8, ..., 80.
  *)
  BuildSet ( BySmaller, Smaller);
  BuildSet ( ByLarger, Larger);

  (* Display contents of the two sets *)
  ShowSetData ( BySmaller, 'BySmaller');
  ShowSetData ( ByLarger, 'ByLarger');

  (* Result is the intersection of BySmaller and ByLarger *)
  Result := BySmaller * ByLarger;
  (* Display contents of the intersection set *)
  ShowSetData ( Result, 'BySmaller * ByLarger');
  READLN;
END.
```

Don't be intimidated by the program; it's really not complicated. It uses the union operator to build two sets of values between 0 and 255, a subrange type. The sets are multiples of 3 and 4, respectively. This work is done in procedure **BuildSet**, which provides an example of a **SET** parameter passed by reference. As when passing by value, you just specify the name of the set to be passed. In this case, however, the program actually uses the storage allocated for the argument. As a result, the changes remain.

Procedure **ShowSetData** displays the contents of the specified set, along with a heading. After writing the heading, the procedure calls procedure **DispByteSet**, which has the same structure as **DispCharSet**.

The intersection operator is used in the assignment to **Result**. Just position the operator (∗) between two sets of the same type. If **BySmaller** consists of multiples of 3, and **ByLarger** consists of multiples of 4, **Result** consists of multiples of 3 *and* 4. Mathematically, this is equivalent to multiples of 12, as you can see when **Result**'s elements are displayed. The program produces the following output:

```
BySmaller:
   3    6    9   12   15   18   21   24   27   30   33   36   39   42   45
  48   51   54   57   60
ByLarger:
   4    8   12   16   20   24   28   32   36   40   44   48   52   56   60
  64   68   72   76   80
BySmaller * ByLarger:
  12   24   36   48   60
```

In the preceding example, the intersection set has very few elements compared to the operand sets. In the extreme, there may be no overlap between two sets and the intersection set will contain no elements. (Recall that such a set is known as the null set.) Two sets are called *disjoint* if their intersection is the null set.

In the following program, sets **SingleDigit** and **DoubleDigit** are disjoint:

P7-30

```
(* Program to illustrate disjoint sets *)

PROGRAM DisjointDemo;

TYPE ByteSet = SET OF BYTE;
VAR SingleDigit, DoubleDigit, Overlap : ByteSet;
    Count, NrIntersects : INTEGER;

BEGIN
  NrIntersects := 0;
  SingleDigit := [ 0 .. 9];
  DoubleDigit := [ 10 .. 99];
  Overlap := SingleDigit * DoubleDigit;
  WRITELN ( 'Overlap:');
  (* Display and count all common values.
     DispByteSet not used so NrIntersects could
     be used.
  *)
  FOR Count := 0 TO 255 DO
  BEGIN
    IF Count IN Overlap THEN
```

```
    BEGIN
      WRITE ( Count:4);
      INC ( NrIntersects);
    END; (* IF Count IN Overlap *)
  END; (* FOR Count ... *)
  WRITELN;
  WRITELN ( NrIntersects, ' common values');
  READLN;
END.
```

The intersection set, **Overlap**, contains no elements. Therefore, no values will be displayed. The value of **NrIntersects** is displayed to show that no common values were found.

As you've seen, the intersection of disjoint sets is the null set, by definition. What about the intersection of a null set with another set? You should be able to deduce this result; think about the size of an intersection set compared with its operand sets.

REMEMBER The intersection of any set with the null set is always the null set itself. This is similar to multiplication by 0, which always yields 0.

The set intersection operator is a multiplicative operator, and has the same precedence as the multiplicative arithmetic and logical operators.

The Set Difference Operator Suppose that you want to check whether a student has taken all the required courses. You could check each required course against the student's list of courses taken. If any course on the required list is not on the student's list, the student is missing a required course.

Pascal's *set difference operator* (−) enables you to determine whether any required courses are outstanding. This binary operator takes two sets (of the same type), and returns another set.

In the courses example, you would take the following set difference, in which **RequiredCourses** and **StudentsCourses** are both sets whose base types are course values:

```
RequiredCourses - StudentsCourses
```

If the result is anything but the null set, there are still required courses the student has not taken.

The following program shows how to use the set difference operator:

P7-31

```
(* Program to illustrate set difference operator *)

PROGRAM DifferenceDemo;
CONST Smaller = 6;
      Larger = 8;
TYPE ByteSet = SET OF BYTE;
VAR BySmaller, ByLarger, Result : ByteSet;
    Count : INTEGER;

  (* Display any values between StartByte and EndByte,
     inclusive, that are elements in TheSet.
  *)
  PROCEDURE DispByteSet ( TheSet : ByteSet;
                          StartByte, EndByte : BYTE);
  VAR IndexByte : BYTE;
      Count : INTEGER;
  BEGIN
    Count := 1;
    FOR IndexByte := StartByte TO EndByte DO
      (* Note that IN takes a BYTE and a ByteSet
         as operands in this procedure
      *)
      IF IndexByte IN TheSet THEN
      BEGIN
        WRITE ( IndexByte:4);
        IF Count MOD 15 = 0 THEN
          WRITELN;
        INC ( Count);
      END;
  END; (* DispByteSet *)

  (* Display contents of the specified set. *)
  PROCEDURE ShowSetData ( TheSet : ByteSet;
                          Message : STRING);
  BEGIN
    WRITELN ( Message, ':');
    DispByteSet ( TheSet, 0, 255);
    WRITELN;
  END;  (* Show SetData *)

  (* Add the appropriate elements to TheSet:
     20 values, separated by Increment.
  *)
  PROCEDURE BuildSet ( VAR TheSet : ByteSet;
                       Increment : INTEGER);
  VAR Count, Val : INTEGER;
```

```
    BEGIN
      Val := 0;
      FOR Count := 1 TO 20 DO
      BEGIN
        INC ( Val, Increment);
        TheSet := TheSet + [ Val];
      END; (* FOR Count := 0 TO 20 *)
    END;  (* BuildSet *)

BEGIN
  (* Initialize both sets to null sets *)
  BySmaller := [];
  ByLarger := [];

  (* Build the two sets.
     BySmaller will contain 0, 6, 12, ..., 120;
     ByLarger will contain  0, 8, 16, ..., 160.
  *)
  BuildSet ( BySmaller, Smaller);
  BuildSet ( ByLarger, Larger);

  (* Display contents of the two sets *)
  ShowSetData ( BySmaller, 'BySmaller');
  ShowSetData ( ByLarger, 'ByLarger');

  (* Result is the difference between BySmaller and ByLarger.
     That is, result contains those multiples of 6 that are
     NOT multiples of 8.
  *)
  Result := BySmaller - ByLarger;
  (* Display contents of the intersection set *)
  ShowSetData ( Result, 'BySmaller - ByLarger');
  READLN;
END.
```

The program first builds two sets, one containing multiples of 6 and the other containing multiples of 8. After displaying the contents of these two sets, the program removes the multiples of 8 from the set containing the multiples of 6. Thus, multiples of both 6 and 8 are removed from **BySmaller**.

This program is very similar to **IntersectionDemo**. The major difference is in the operator used when creating a value for **Result**, and the new values for **Smaller** and **Larger**.

The program produces the following output:

```
BySmaller:
  6  12  18  24  30  36  42  48  54  60  66  72  78  84  90
 96 102 108 114 120
```

```
ByLarger:
   8  16  24  32  40  48  56  64  72  80  88  96 104 112 120
 128 136 144 152 160
BySmaller - ByLarger:
   6  12  18  30  36  42  54  60  66  78  84  90 102 108 114
```

Notice that the difference set does not contain any multiples of 8. Essentially, the set difference operator removes from **BySmaller** any values that are also contained in **ByLarger**. The resulting set contains only elements unique to **BySmaller**.

If the two operands for a set difference operator are disjoint, the set from which you're trying to remove elements is unchanged.

The following program shows how to remove a specified element from a set. The first part of the program removes two specific characters from the set. In the second part, you can remove whatever characters you wish.

P7-32
```
(* Program to show how to remove single elements
     from a set.
*)

PROGRAM DiffDemo;

TYPE CharSet = SET OF CHAR;
VAR WdSet : CharSet;
    TheCh : CHAR;

  (* Display any values between StartCh and EndCh, inclusive,
     that are elements in TheSet.
  *)
  PROCEDURE DispCharSet ( TheSet : CharSet;
                          StartCh, EndCh : CHAR);
  VAR IndexCh : CHAR;
      Count : INTEGER;
  BEGIN
    Count := 1;
    FOR IndexCh := StartCh TO EndCh DO
      (* Note that IN takes a CHAR and a CharSet
         as operands in this procedure
      *)
      IF IndexCh IN TheSet THEN
      BEGIN
        WRITE ( IndexCh:3);
        IF Count MOD 20 = 0 THEN
          WRITELN;
        INC ( Count);
```

```
      END;
    WRITELN;
  END; (* DispCharSet *)

  (* Prompt user and read a character *)
  PROCEDURE GetChar ( Message : STRING;
                         VAR Value : CHAR);
  BEGIN
    WRITE ( Message, ' ');
    READLN ( Value);
  END; (* GetChar *)

BEGIN  (* Main program *)
  WdSet := [ 'a', 'c' .. 'x', 'z'];
  DispCharSet ( WdSet, 'a', 'z');
  (* Remove 'a' from the set; this is done *)
  WdSet := WdSet - [ 'a'];
  (* Note how to write a single quote: include two quotes *)
  WRITELN ( 'After removing ''a''');
  DispCharSet ( WdSet, 'a', 'z');
  (* Remove 'b' from the set; nothing happens,
      since 'b' is not in the set.
  *)
  WdSet := WdSet - [ 'b'];
  WRITELN ( 'After removing ''b''');
  DispCharSet ( WdSet, 'a', 'z');
  GetChar ( 'Remove what char? (! to stop)', TheCh);
  WHILE TheCh <> '!' DO
  BEGIN
    WdSet := WdSet - [ TheCh];
    WRITELN ( 'After removing ''', TheCh, '''');
    DispCharSet ( WdSet, 'a', 'z');
    GetChar ( 'Remove what char? (! to stop)', TheCh);
  END; (* WHILE TheCh <> '!' *)
END.
```

After building **WdSet**, the program removes two characters, *a* and *b*. It does this by using the set constructor to create a set consisting of the single character, and then using the set difference operator to "subtract" this set's contents from **WdSet**.

Notice how to represent single quotes in the two "After removing" lines. To include a single quote within a string, you need to write *two* single quotes. Thus, the quote before the letter is written as two quotes. The quote after the letter is also written as two quotes, and is then followed by a third quote, which actually terminates the string argument.

This program produces the following output for the first part.

```
a  c  d  e  f  g  h  i  j  k  l  m  n  o  p  q  r  s  t  u
v  w  x  z
After removing 'a'
c  d  e  f  g  h  i  j  k  l  m  n  o  p  q  r  s  t  u  v
w  x  z
After removing 'b'
c  d  e  f  g  h  i  j  k  l  m  n  o  p  q  r  s  t  u  v
w  x  z
```

Notice that there is no difference between the second and third versions of **WdSet**. Removing *b* from **WdSet** has no effect, since the letter was not an element of the set to begin with.

The precedence for the set difference operator is the same as for the set union operator, since both are additive operators.

Comparing Sets

Turbo Pascal has four operators for comparing sets. Comparisons between sets are based on the elements contained in each set rather than on the number of elements in the sets. For example, you can compare two sets to determine whether they have exactly the same collection of values as members. If so, the two sets are said to be *equal*. You also can test whether one set (A) contains all the elements in the other set (B). If so, A is said to be a *superset* of B, and B is said to be a *subset* of A.

Like other comparisons, these end up as true or false questions. The result of such comparisons is, not surprisingly, a **BOOLEAN** value. The operands for such comparisons are sets of the same type.

REMEMBER Set comparison operators take two sets (of the same type) as arguments and return a **BOOLEAN** value.

The Set Equality and Inequality Operators Pascal's *set equality operator* (=) enables you to test whether its two operand sets contain exactly the same elements. If so, the operator returns a **TRUE**; otherwise, the Boolean expression is **FALSE**. Note that the sets must contain the same elements, not just the same number of elements.

For example, suppose you have the following two sets:

```
Set1 := [ 'a', 'c' .. 'm', 'p']

Set2 := [ 'a' .. 'm', 'p' .. 's']
```

With these values, the following **IF** statement evaluates to **FALSE**:

```
IF Set1 = Set2 THEN
   ...
```

The *set inequality operator* (<>) enables you to test whether two sets are different.

The Subset Operator   In the previous example, all of **Set1**'s elements are also in **Set2**. This means that **Set1** is a subset of **Set2**. In Pascal, you use the *subset operator* for sets (<=) to indicate this relationship between the two sets. The following **IF** statement shows how to test whether **Set1** is a subset of **Set2**:

```
IF Set1 <= Set2 THEN
   ...
```

The Boolean expression in this case evaluates to **TRUE** for the example values.

The Superset Operator   Saying that **Set1** is a subset of **Set2** is equivalent to saying that **Set2** is a superset of **Set1**. In Pascal, the *superset operator* for sets (>=) enables you to test such an assertion. The following statement is equivalent to the one that used the subset operator:

```
IF Set2 >= Set1 THEN
   ...
```

REMEMBER   Pascal has four comparison operators for sets: equality (=), inequality (<>), subset (<=), and superset (>=).

According to the definition of a subset, two equal sets must be subsets of each other. For example, in the following program, all three **IF** clauses will be **TRUE** when **Set1** and **Set2** have the same elements.

```
P7-33    (* Program to illustrate use of set comparison operators
            with equal sets.
         *)

         PROGRAM SetComparisonOpDemo;

         TYPE CharSet = SET OF CHAR;

         VAR Set1, Set2, Alphabet : CharSet;

         BEGIN
           Alphabet := [ 'a' .. 'z'];
           Set1 := [ 'a' .. 'l', 'o' .. 'z'];
           (* a very roundabout way of making
              Set2 equal to Set1.
              Alphabet - Set1 = [ 'm', 'n'], so
              Alphabet - [ 'm', 'n'] = Set1.
           *)
           Set2 := Alphabet - (Alphabet - Set1);
           IF Set1 = Set2 THEN
             WRITELN ( 'Set1 = Set2');
           IF Set1 <= Set2 THEN
             WRITELN ( 'Set1 is a subset of Set2');
           IF Set1 >= Set2 THEN
             WRITELN ( 'Set1 is a superset of Set2');
           READLN;
         END.
```

The program uses each of the set comparison operators to compare **Set1** and **Set2**. The statement that assigns a value to **Set2** is just an obscure way of making **Set1** and **Set2** contain the same element. If you're not sure how the assignment works, add **DispCharSet** to the program and display the intermediate values.

There are no set comparison operators that correspond to less than (<) and greater than (>). Table 7-1 summarizes the set operators.

Set Constants and Anonymous Sets

In Turbo Pascal, you can define **SET** constants. The following listing shows how to define and initialize such a constant. Once initialized, you

Operator	Left Operand	Right Operand	Result
IN	value	set	**BOOLEAN**
Union (+)	set	set	set
Intersection (*)	set	set	set
Difference (−)	set	set	set
Equality (=)	set	set	**BOOLEAN**
Inequality (<>)	set	set	**BOOLEAN**
Subset (<=)	set	set	**BOOLEAN**
Superset (>=)	set	set	**BOOLEAN**

Table 7-1. *Pascal's Set Operators*

can refer to the set by name but can't perform any operations that would change the contents of the named set.

P7-34
```
(* Program to illustrate use of set constants *)

PROGRAM SetConstantDemo;

TYPE CharSet = SET OF CHAR;
(* Define a CharSet constant, and initialize it *)
CONST SmallLetters : CharSet =
                    [ 'a', 'c', 'e', 'i', 'm' .. 'o',
                      'r', 's', 'u' .. 'x', 'z'];
      (* Define a set constant that will contain BYTEs.
         Note that this is not a named type, so you can't
         declare any variables of this type.
      *)
      SingleDigitSet : SET OF BYTE = [ 0 .. 9];
      DoubleDigitSet : SET OF 0 .. 99 = [ 10 .. 99];
VAR Count, NrCounted : INTEGER;

   (* Display any values between StartCh and EndCh, inclusive,
      that are elements in TheSet.
   *)
   PROCEDURE DispCharSet ( TheSet : CharSet;
                           StartCh, EndCh : CHAR);
   VAR IndexCh : CHAR;
       Count : INTEGER;
   BEGIN
     Count := 1;
     FOR IndexCh := StartCh TO EndCh DO
       (* Note that IN takes a CHAR and a CharSet
          as operands in this procedure
       *)
```

```
      IF IndexCh IN TheSet THEN
      BEGIN
        WRITE ( IndexCh:3);
        IF Count MOD 20 = 0 THEN
          WRITELN;
        INC ( Count);
      END;
  END; (* DispCharSet *)
BEGIN
  NrCounted := 0;
  WRITELN ( 'SmallLetters:');
  DispCharSet ( SmallLetters, 'a', 'z');
  WRITELN;
  WRITELN ( 'DoubleDigitSet:');
  (* You can't write a Disp... procedure, since
     the set type only has a description (SET OF 0 .. 99),
     but has no name.
  *)
  FOR Count := 0 TO 100 DO
  BEGIN
    IF Count IN DoubleDigitSet THEN
    BEGIN
      WRITE ( Count:3);
      INC ( NrCounted);
      IF NrCounted MOD 20 = 0 THEN
        WRITELN;
    END; (* IF Count ... *)
  END; (* FOR Count ... *)
  READLN;
END.
```

The program defines three set constants. The first, **SmallLetters,** is
defined as a constant of a named type (**CharSet**). After specifying the
set's type, you initialize it by including an equal sign (=) and then listing the set's contents within a set constructor—that is, within square
brackets.

The other two set constants are described and then initialized. The
base types for **SingleDigitSet** and **DoubleDigitSet** are described, but not
named. That's why there isn't a procedure to display the contents of
DoubleDigitSet—as there is with **DispCharSet**.

Sometimes it is convenient to specify a collection of values at a
particular point in a program. For example, suppose you're looking for
input from the user. In particular, suppose you're looking for any
character whose name has a long *e* sound (as in keep). This means you're
looking for one of the following characters: *b, c, d, e, g, p, t, v, z.*

The following listing shows how to specify such a collection of values as an anonymous set:

```
IF UsersChar IN [ 'b' .. 'e', 'g', 'p', 't', 'v', 'z'] THEN
  ...
```

To specify such an anonymous set, put a set constructor around the values you need. You can then put this set within a Boolean expression involving an **IN** operator, as in the example.

In this chapter, you learned about Pascal's three structured types: arrays, records, and sets. These types provide building blocks that you can combine and extend to suit the information in your program. The chapter also previewed objects, which will be discussed in Chapter 11, "Object-Oriented Programming in Turbo Pascal." In the next chapter, you'll learn about files.

8 *Files*

So far, the programs you've built have involved the standard input (keyboard) and output (screen). Such programs get the information they need by reading what the user types in response to prompts. The programs then display their results on the screen. These displays disappear when new information is displayed or when another program starts running.

Sometimes it's convenient to have a more permanent representation of the information that needs to be input or that will be displayed. In such a case, Pascal files will come in handy. A *file* is essentially a way for a program to look at material from a disk in a logical manner—independent of the way the information may be laid out on the disk. For example, under DOS a file's contents may be located at various physical sites on a disk.

As far as your program is concerned, however, the file's contents are arranged in a neat, sequential manner. After the program reads an element from your file, it assumes that it can read the next element without any problem—as long as there are elements remaining in the file. This is possible because of low-level resources (*drivers*) provided with DOS and with your Turbo Pascal environment. These resources take care of chores such as finding the next file element on the physical disk and making this next element available to your program's routines.

A file name will be associated with these contents. This name is used when you need to refer to the file at the DOS command line. For example, under DOS, you could give the following command to get directory information about a file named DISKFILE.NAM:

```
dir diskfile.nam
```

If such a file exists in your current directory, DOS will tell you its size, the date when it was last modified, and so forth.

This chapter explains how to use files in your Turbo Pascal programs. In particular, you'll learn how to create, open, and close files. You'll also learn how to read and write files. In the text all uppercase is used to specify file names; in your listings you can use lowercase, uppercase, or mixed case.

Text Files

A file is actually a logical concept, which says nothing about the type of information contained in the file. In most cases, however, you'll want to store various kinds of textual material in your files. This might include strings or it might be numerical values. Such a *text file* contains ASCII information. You can read a text file with your text editor or with the DOS TYPE command. This is in contrast to a *binary file,* which is stored in a format that is unreadable for most text editors. As you'll see, the predefined procedures **WRITE, WRITELN, READ,** and **READLN** enable you to perform input and output with text files.

In Pascal, **TEXT** is a predefined type used to represent a text file. The following listing shows how you would declare a text file variable:

```
VAR FileVal : Text;
```

Actions on Files

There aren't many things that you can do with a file. However, unless you open and close files properly, nothing else will work.

To open (or create) a file in Turbo Pascal, you need to associate your file variable (which is declared in the program and which does not exist beyond the program) with a file name (which is known to the operating system). This step makes a disk file accessible to your program. Once you have made this association, the operating system's drivers take over the interactions with the file on disk.

The next step is to open the file for use in your programs. (In some implementations, these two actions are carried out as one step.) To carry out actions on files you can use predefined procedures. Similarly, there is a predefined procedure for closing a file — thereby saving its contents on disk.

Associating a Program and a Disk File

The **ASSIGN** procedure lets you associate a name with your file variable. For example, the following statement associates the name ZQZQ.QZQ with the **TEXT** variable **SampleFile**:

```
ASSIGN ( SampleFile, 'ZQZQ.QZQ' );
```

The listing assumes that you have already made the following variable declaration, and that the call to **ASSIGN** is within the scope of the declaration:

```
VAR SampleFile : Text;
```

Notice that the file name is specified as a string, whereas the file variable is represented by an identifier of type **TEXT**. The file variable and the file name are used in two different contexts. Use the variable when you want to refer to the file within your program. For example, the following statement would write the number 395.7 to **SampleFile**:

```
WRITELN ( SampleFile, 395.7);
```

You'll learn more about such statements in the next section.

The file name is not used within your program. Rather, it is used to specify your file outside the program — for example on a DOS command line. The following command would be valid if you were at the DOS command line and had a file named ZQZQ.QZQ that was in your current directory:

```
type zqzq.qzq
```

This instruction would display the contents of the file named ZQZQ.QZQ on the screen. DOS understands ZQZQ.QZQ, interpreting it as a reference to the file with that name stored on the disk.

On the other hand, DOS would not understand the file variable identifier (**Sample File**) used in the program since the variable identifier disappears when your program stops executing. By associating the file name with the file variable through the **ASSIGN** call in your program, you provide a way of referring to your **TEXT** variable outside the program. Naturally, it's assumed that you actually saved the file to disk by giving the appropriate command in your program.

Once you've linked the file to the environment outside your program, you still need to make the file usable within the program. Procedures **RESET** and **REWRITE** enable you to accomplish this. (In standard Pascal and some other Pascal implementations, the calls to **ASSIGN** and to either **REWRITE** or **RESET** are combined into a single call to either **REWRITE** or **RESET**.)

Creating a New File

REWRITE creates a new file; **RESET** opens a file that already exists on disk. You'll build a new file by writing to it, and you can read from an existing file. Turbo Pascal also enables you to add to an existing file.

Call up and run the following program, which shows how to create a new text file and how to write a single value into the file twice:

P8-1
```
(* Program to illustrate use of REWRITE procedure; program will
   create a file named FileName, and will write a value into
   the file twice. In its current form, the file will be empty
   when the program finishes. Can you guess why?
*)
```

```
PROGRAM CreateDemo1;

CONST FileName = 'zwzw.wzw';
VAR SampleFile : Text;

BEGIN
  (* Associate the file variable (SampleFile) with a string,
     representing the file's name.
  *)
  ASSIGN ( SampleFile, FileName);
  (* Create a new file, which will be named FileName.
     Within the program, the file will be created using
     the next statement.
  *)
  REWRITE ( SampleFile);
  WRITELN ( SampleFile, 397.5);
  WRITELN ( SampleFile, 397.5 : 10 : 3);
  WRITELN ( 'Done.');
  READLN;
END.
```

To write material in the file variable **SampleFile**, you can use the predefined **WRITE** and **WRITELN** procedures. When dealing with files, however, these procedures need a file variable as their first argument. The information to be written is specified in subsequent arguments. For example, the next to last call to **WRITELN** in the preceding program writes the value 397.5 to the file **SampleFile**.

If you do a directory listing after running this program, you'll find an entry for ZWZW.WZW, which will be 0 bytes long. If you look at this file with your editor, you'll see that it is empty. What happened to the 397.5's that you wrote to the file?

REMEMBER When using **WRITE** or **WRITELN** to output information to text files, you must specify a file variable as the first argument.

In order to save the contents of the entire file, you need to close the file explicitly. The predefined procedure **CLOSE** accomplishes this. Compare the contents of ZWZW.WZW after running the preceding version of the program with the outcome after running the following program:

```
P8-2   (* Program to illustrate use of REWRITE procedure; program will
          create a file named FileName, and will write a single value
          in the file.
       *)
```

```
PROGRAM CreateDemo2;
CONST FileName = 'zwzw.wzw';
VAR SampleFile : Text;

BEGIN
  (* Associate the file variable (SampleFile) with a string,
     representing the file's name on disk.
  *)
  ASSIGN ( SampleFile, FileName);
  (* Create a new file, which will be named FileName.
     Within the program, the file will be created using
     the next statement.
  *)
  REWRITE ( SampleFile);
  WRITELN ( SampleFile, 397.5);
  WRITELN ( SampleFile, 397.5 : 10 : 3);
  (* close file, thereby saving contents *)
  CLOSE ( SampleFile);
  WRITELN ( 'Done.');
  READLN;
END.
```

Now look at ZWZW.WZW with your editor. The number 397.5 (in exponential form and formatted) is in the file. By calling **CLOSE**, you ensure that the buffer for the file is saved before the file is closed.

The variable declaration in the **CreateDemo2** program tells the compiler to allocate storage for a variable of type **TEXT**. This variable is stored internally as a record that contains various information about the file. The record also contains a buffer into which you can write information, and from which the information is transferred to the file. This buffer is emptied into the disk file. The size of the file can actually change during the course of the program.

Once declared, you can use **SampleFile** wherever a variable of type **TEXT** is allowed. This occurs in several places in the main program.

The **ASSIGN** statement associates the value of **FileName** with the **SampleFile** variable. In the call to **ASSIGN**, notice that the file argument comes first, followed by the name. Once you've associated a file name with your file variable, the predefined procedure **REWRITE** lets you create and open a new file. **REWRITE** takes one argument, a file variable. When called, **REWRITE** opens the disk file associated with your file variable—with **SampleFile** in the program. This happens to be the file named ZWZW.WZW. In this particular case, the program actually creates a new file—regardless of whether a file named ZWZW.WZW already existed.

CAUTION **REWRITE** always creates a new file. If you already have a file with the specified name, it is lost and is replaced by a new, empty file.

Once the new file is opened, you can start writing to it. The pre-defined I/O routines (such as **WRITE** and **WRITELN**) are available—they take the same syntax used in earlier programs. However, the first argument always needs to be a file variable. Subsequent arguments specify what should be written—just as when you're writing to the standard output (the screen). The calls to **WRITELN** in the program illustrate how to write a value to a file.

After you've written what you want to the file, you need to call **CLOSE** to save your material. This call empties the buffer associated with the file by writing the contents to the file. The procedure then closes the file to save it permanently on disk.

The *file buffer* is an array of a particular size (128 bytes for a text file in Turbo Pascal). Material intended for the file will be stored in this buffer. Once the buffer is full, the contents are emptied into the file and the buffer is once again ready to receive information.

An Example

The following example program writes 125 random values to a file:

```
(* Program to illustrate file creation and use. Program:
      creates a file,  and writes 125 random values;
   The file's name will be the current value of FileName.
*)

PROGRAM CreateDemo3;

CONST MaxTrials = 125;
      MaxPerLine = 5;
      FileName = 'zwzw.wzw';
VAR SampleFile : Text;
    Index : INTEGER;

BEGIN
  RANDOMIZE;
  (* Associate the file variable (SampleFile) with a string,
     representing the file's name on disk.
  *)
  ASSIGN ( SampleFile, FileName);
```

P8-3

```
   (* Create a new file, which will be named FileName. *)
   REWRITE ( SampleFile);
   FOR Index := 1 TO MaxTrials DO
   BEGIN
     (* write a value to the file *)
     WRITE ( SampleFile, RANDOM : 10 : 5);
     (* Every MaxPerLine values,
        move to a new line in the file
     *)
     IF Index MOD MaxPerLine = 0 THEN
        WRITELN ( SampleFile);
   END; (* FOR Index ... *)

   (* close file, thereby saving contents *)
   CLOSE ( SampleFile);
   WRITELN ( 'Done.');
   READLN;
END.
```

Although the resulting file is much larger than for the previous program, **CreateDemo3** doesn't do anything new or different when compared with **CreateDemo2**, for example.

The last call to **WRITELN** in the **FOR** loop might seem a bit unusual since it has only one argument: a file name. This is the file equivalent of simply calling **WRITELN** with no arguments when not dealing with files. The call moves to the next line in the file.

The following listing shows the contents of ZWZW.WZW after a sample run:

```
0.93334    0.96816    0.74464    0.61578    0.04921
0.52520    0.30014    0.65408    0.59069    0.21203
0.77887    0.00790    0.84718    0.36403    0.04982
0.73287    0.40029    0.15667    0.07704    0.83261
0.93488    0.09791    0.56901    0.44299    0.84783
0.50981    0.57426    0.74785    0.51411    0.29629
0.50770    0.04801    0.31945    0.54393    0.34193
0.65551    0.81893    0.75256    0.94805    0.53492
0.63102    0.74275    0.82015    0.86355    0.92624
0.53678    0.66809    0.93254    0.61998    0.76024
0.61267    0.06060    0.62882    0.36092    0.96787
0.44235    0.79961    0.69204    0.84428    0.10309
0.37089    0.25657    0.05818    0.38187    0.07582
0.65952    0.08076    0.61482    0.24613    0.56522
0.01165    0.94049    0.52645    0.70622    0.81129
0.39913    0.05826    0.24096    0.27647    0.74785
0.24309    0.00685    0.49338    0.66344    0.44405
0.46574    0.75258    0.25472    0.23534    0.38874
```

```
0.16027    0.05641    0.05889    0.57706    0.43026
0.92629    0.39765    0.16590    0.59088    0.51753
0.82485    0.30825    0.59140    0.24811    0.53858
0.28542    0.04220    0.93922    0.24117    0.34119
0.57310    0.54441    0.47260    0.78651    0.54425
0.64149    0.75740    0.17154    0.09390    0.60896
0.17443    0.57196    0.75748    0.65895    0.20885
```

Checking the Outcome of Your File Operation

The preceding programs crashes if, for some reason, a file cannot be created. For example, suppose you have no more space on your disk, so a new file cannot be created. Fortunately, Turbo Pascal checks all calls to procedures such as **REWRITE**. If the procedure is unable to create the file, an error is detected. By default, the program terminates with a run-time error and displays a message about the error.

This automatic checking and termination feature protects you from certain kinds of errors that could cause problems. However, the automatic termination has disadvantages too. For example, it makes your programs less robust, since they will automatically crash if anything goes wrong in a call to a procedure involving files.

Turbo Pascal has compiler directives for turning automatic checking off and on. Thus, you can check the outcome of procedure calls yourself, avoiding automatic termination in the case of an error. The {$I-} directive turns automatic checking off. When this feature is off, the program does not crash if an I/O operation (such as creating a file) is unsuccessful. An error result is still returned, however.

You can check this value yourself by using the predefined function **IOResult**. This function returns a **WORD**, which represents the outcome of the last I/O operation. If the operation was successful, the function returns a 0; otherwise, some type of error occurred. (For the details of the error codes, consult the on-line help.) **IOResult** returns a meaningful result only if automatic checking is off. If an error has occurred while automatic checking is off, you must call **IOResult** before the program will respond to any more I/O operations.

To turn automatic checking (also known as *I/O checking*) back on, use {$I+}. The following program illustrates how to use these compiler directives to do your own I/O checking. Note that this program will not crash—whether or not the file creation was successful.

```
P8-4        (* Program to illustrate use of IOResult,
               and of compiler directives.
            *)

            PROGRAM IODemo;

            CONST FileName = 'qqqq';
            VAR Source : Text;

               (* Wait until user presses ENTER, so output will stay
                  on the screen.
               *)
               PROCEDURE AwaitUser;
               VAR Ch : CHAR;
               BEGIN
                 WRITE ( 'Press ENTER to continue. ');
                 READLN;
               END; (* AwaitUser *)


            BEGIN  (* Main Program *)
              ASSIGN ( Source, FileName);
              {$I-}                        (* Turn I/O checking off *)
              REWRITE ( Source);
              (*$I+*)                      (* Turn I/O checking back on *)
              IF IOResult = 0 THEN
                WRITELN ( 'Successful')
              ELSE
                WRITELN ( 'Could not create file ', FileName, '!');
              AwaitUser;
            END.
```

This program illustrates the general strategy for turning I/O checking on and off. Turn checking off before you call **REWRITE, RESET**, and other procedures available for handling files. After the call, you should generally turn automatic checking back on with the **{$I+}** directive. Notice that you can also write such a directive using (* and *) as delimiters.

A Safe File Creation Procedure   The sequence of statements and directives in the preceding listing is very common if your programs work with files. If you do much file manipulation, routines like this one will come in handy:

```
P8-5      (* Create a new file, doing all necessary and warranted
            checking, and taking all precautions.
              Returns TRUE if file was created; FALSE otherwise.
          *)
          FUNCTION FMade ( VAR TheFile : Text;
                               FName : STRING) : BOOLEAN;
          BEGIN
            ASSIGN ( TheFile, FName);
            (*$I-*)
            REWRITE ( TheFile);
            (*$I+*)
            IF IOResult = 0 THEN
              FMade := TRUE
            ELSE
              FMade := FALSE;
          END; (* FN FMade *)
```

By calling this function when you need to create a file, you simplify
your source code: You need only one line instead of over half a dozen.
You also make your program more robust and flexible. In case of an
error, your program can take suitable actions instead of just crashing.

Notice how to specify a text file as a parameter to a routine. The
format is the same as for any other type of parameter:

<identifier> ":" <type specifier>

File parameters must be passed by reference, however. That is, the
routine can never be expected to make a copy of the file because there
is no way of knowing how large the file will be. The file could easily be
too large to fit into available memory.

You can put the function **FMade** in a separate file. That way, you'll
be able to copy it easily into other programs that will use it. This chapter
includes similar routines for doing other I/O operations safely and for
carrying out the same operations with different kinds of files.

REMEMBER   File parameters must be **VAR** parameters. You cannot
pass a file by value.

Opening an Existing File

You should call **RESET** instead of **REWRITE** if you already have a file with the specified name and you want to keep the existing file rather than replace it with an empty one. The **RESET** procedure opens the file specified in its single argument. Unlike **REWRITE**, however, **RESET** assumes that the specified file already exists and is being opened for reading.

The following program reads the contents of file ZWZW.WZW and analyzes the values:

P8-6
```
(* Program to illustrate file opening and use. Program opens an
   existing file, and reads 125 random values contained in file.
   Each column of values is summed in a different array cell.
*)

PROGRAM ReadDemo1;

CONST MaxTrials = 125;
      MaxPerLine = 5;
      FileName = 'zwzw.wzw';
TYPE Stats = ARRAY [ 0 .. 4] OF REAL;
VAR SampleFile : Text;
    Index, WhichCell : INTEGER;
    Vals : Stats;  (* to store sums of columns *)
    Result : REAL;

  (* Open an existing file, doing all necessary
     and warranted checking, and taking all
     precautions.
     Returns TRUE if file was opened; FALSE otherwise.
  *)
  FUNCTION FOpened ( VAR TheFile : Text;
                     FName : STRING) : BOOLEAN;
  BEGIN
    ASSIGN ( TheFile, FName);
    (*$I-*)
    RESET ( TheFile);
    (*$I+*)
    IF IOResult = 0 THEN
      FOpened := TRUE
    ELSE
      FOpened := FALSE;
  END; (* FN FOpened *)

  (* Initalize each cell of the Vals array to 0.0 *)
  PROCEDURE InitStats ( VAR Vals : Stats);
  VAR Index : INTEGER;
```

```
        BEGIN
          FOR Index := 0 TO 4 DO
            Vals [ Index] := 0.0;
        END; (* InitStats *)


        (* Display the results for each column separately. *)
        PROCEDURE DisplayMeans ( Vals : Stats;
                                    ValsPerCell : INTEGER);
        VAR Index : INTEGER;
        BEGIN
          (* Display results for first four columns *)
          FOR Index := 1 TO 4 DO
            WRITELN ( Index, ': ',
                       Vals [ Index] / ValsPerCell : 10 : 5);
          (* Display results for last column,
             the one corresponding to cell 0.
           *)
            WRITELN ( 5, ': ', Vals [ 0] / ValsPerCell : 10 : 5);
        END; (* DisplayMeans *)


        (* Wait until user presses ENTER, so output will stay
           on the screen.
         *)
        PROCEDURE AwaitUser;
        VAR Ch : CHAR;
        BEGIN
          WRITE ( 'Press ENTER to continue. ');
          READLN;
        END; (* AwaitUser *)

    BEGIN
      RANDOMIZE;
      InitStats ( Vals);
      IF FOpened ( SampleFile, FileName) = TRUE THEN
      BEGIN
        FOR Index := 1 TO MaxTrials DO
        BEGIN
          (* read a value from the file *)
          READ ( SampleFile, Result);
          (* Determine the column from which the current value
             was read.
           *)
          WhichCell := Index MOD MaxPerLine;
          (* Increment the appropriate cell by Result *)
          Vals [ WhichCell] := Vals [ WhichCell] +  Result;

          (* display current total in cell *)
          WRITE ( Vals [ WhichCell] : 10 : 5);
          IF Index MOD MaxPerLine = 0 THEN
            WRITELN;
        END; (* FOR Index ... *)
```

```
      DisplayMeans ( Vals, MaxTrials DIV MaxPerLine);

      CLOSE ( SampleFile);
    END (* IF File could be opened *)
    ELSE
      WRITELN ( 'Could not open file ', FileName);
    AwaitUser;
  END.
```

The program reads all the values in ZWZW.WZW. These values must be read sequentially. That is, the second value in the file must be read after the first, the third after the second, and so forth. This sequential method is the only way you can access information in text files. For this reason, text files are sometimes known as *sequential-access structures*. This is in contrast to random-access structures (such as arrays, or even typed files — which you'll see later in the chapter).

Each column of values is added separately. These sums are stored in a five-element array of **REAL**. While reading its information, the program displays the intermediate cell totals. The program computes averages for each column. (These averages, or means, should be around 0.5, since **RANDOM** without an argument produces pseudorandom **REAL** values between 0.0 and 1.0.)

In **ReadDemo1**, all file activity takes place in the main program and in **FOpened**. The two procedures are for initializing and displaying results on the screen. Notice the call to **RESET** in function **FOpened**. This call ensures that the existing file is used, instead of a new ZWZW.WZW being created for the run.

REMEMBER   Files opened using **RESET** are input files and are for reading only; files opened using **REWRITE** are output files, and are for writing only.

The call to **READ** in the main program shows how to get information from a text file. The predefined **READ** and **READLN** procedures are available. As with the output procedures, these routines work as they do when you're reading from the standard input. The only difference is that the file variable needs to be the first argument to **READ** and to **READLN**.

When **READ** is expecting an **INTEGER**, it skips over any intervening blanks and then reads until it encounters a nonnumerical character. The procedure stops reading at that point. The next call to **READ** will continue from that position.

If the procedure encounters an end-of-line character (that is, if function **EOLN (SampleFile)** becomes **TRUE**), the procedure simply moves to the next line in the file. Subsequent values will be read beginning on the new line. If the procedure tries to read past the end of the file (that is, when **EOF**(< *FileName* >) is **TRUE**), the result is 0.

EOF is a predefined function. When used in connection with files, it takes one argument: a file variable. **EOF** returns a **BOOLEAN** that is **TRUE** if the end of the file has been reached, and **FALSE** otherwise.

For the file generated by **CreateDemo3**, the program produces the following results:

```
 0.93334   0.96816   0.74464   0.61578   0.04921
 1.45854   1.26830   1.39872   1.20647   0.26124
 2.23741   1.27620   2.24590   1.57050   0.31106
 2.97028   1.67649   2.40257   1.64754   1.14367
 3.90516   1.77440   2.97158   2.09053   1.99150
 4.41497   2.34866   3.71943   2.60464   2.28779
 4.92267   2.39667   4.03888   3.14857   2.62972
 5.57818   3.21560   4.79144   4.09662   3.16464
 6.20920   3.95835   5.61159   4.96017   4.09088
 6.74598   4.62644   6.54413   5.58015   4.85112
 7.35865   4.68704   7.17295   5.94107   5.81899
 7.80100   5.48665   7.86499   6.78535   5.92208
 8.17189   5.74322   7.92317   7.16722   5.99790
 8.83141   5.82398   8.53799   7.41335   6.56312
 8.84306   6.76447   9.06444   8.11957   7.37441
 9.24219   6.82273   9.30540   8.39604   8.12226
 9.48528   6.82958   9.79878   9.05948   8.56631
 9.95102   7.58216  10.05350   9.29482   8.95505
10.11129   7.63857  10.11239   9.87188   9.38531
11.03758   8.03622  10.27829  10.46276   9.90284
11.86243   8.34447  10.86969  10.71087  10.44142
12.14785   8.38667  11.80891  10.95204  10.78261
12.72095   8.93108  12.28151  11.73855  11.32686
13.36244   9.68848  12.45305  11.83245  11.93582
13.53687  10.26044  13.21053  12.49140  12.14467
1:    0.54147
2:    0.41042
3:    0.52842
4:    0.49966
5:    0.48579
```

CAUTION   If a file specified as a parameter does not exist, **RESET** causes a run-time error.

READ Versus READLN   When dealing with files the following program is identical to **ReadDemo1** except that **ReadDemo2** uses **READLN** instead of **READ** in the main program's **FOR** loop:

P8-7

```
(* Program to illustrate file opening and use.
   Program opens an existing file--named ZWZW.WZW on disk --
   and reads 125 random values contained in the file.
   Each column of values is summed in a different array cell.
   Program shows dangers of using READLN when you have
   multiple values on a line.
*)

PROGRAM ReadDemo2;

CONST MaxTrials = 125;
      MaxPerLine = 5;
      FileName = 'zwzw.wzw';
TYPE Stats = ARRAY [ 0 .. 4] OF REAL;
VAR SampleFile : Text;
    Index, WhichCell : INTEGER;
    Vals : Stats;  (* to store summs of columns *)
    Result : REAL;

  (* Open an existing file, doing all necessary
     and warranted checking, and taking all
     precautions.
     Returns TRUE if file was opened; FALSE otherwise.
  *)
  FUNCTION FOpened ( VAR TheFile : Text;
                        FName : STRING) : BOOLEAN;
  BEGIN
    ASSIGN ( TheFile, FName);
    (*$I-*)
    RESET ( TheFile);
    (*$I+*)
    IF IOResult = 0 THEN
      FOpened := TRUE
    ELSE
      FOpened := FALSE;
  END; (* FN FOpened *)

  (* Initalize each cell of the array to 0.0 *)
  PROCEDURE InitStats ( VAR Vals : Stats);
  VAR Index : INTEGER;
  BEGIN
    FOR Index := 0 TO 4 DO
      Vals [ Index] := 0.0;
  END; (* InitStats *)
```

```
      (* Display the results for each column separately. *)
      PROCEDURE DisplayMeans ( Vals : Stats;
                               ValsPerCell : INTEGER);
    VAR Index : INTEGER;
    BEGIN
      (* Display results for first four columns *)
      FOR Index := 1 TO 4 DO
        WRITELN ( Index, ': ',
                  Vals [ Index] / ValsPerCell : 10 : 5);
      (* Display results for last column,
         the one corresponding to cell 0.
      *)
      WRITELN ( 5, ': ', Vals [ 0] / ValsPerCell : 10 : 5);
    END; (* DisplayMeans *)

  (* Wait until user presses ENTER, so output will stay
     on the screen.
  *)
  PROCEDURE AwaitUser;
  VAR Ch : CHAR;
  BEGIN
    WRITE ( 'Press ENTER to continue. ');
    READLN;
  END; (* AwaitUser *)

BEGIN  (* Main program *)
  RANDOMIZE;
  InitStats ( Vals);

  IF FOpened ( SampleFile, FileName) = TRUE THEN
  BEGIN
    FOR Index := 1 TO MaxTrials DO
    BEGIN
      (* read a value from the file, then move to next line *)
      READLN ( SampleFile, Result);
      (* Determine the column from which the current value
         was read.
      *)
      WhichCell := Index MOD MaxPerLine;
      (* Increment the appropriate cell by Result *)
      Vals [ WhichCell] := Vals [ WhichCell] + Result;
      (* display current total in cell *)
      WRITE ( Vals [ WhichCell] : 10 : 5);
      IF Index MOD MaxPerLine = 0 THEN
        WRITELN;
    END; (* FOR Index ... *)

    DisplayMeans ( Vals, MaxTrials DIV MaxPerLine);

    CLOSE ( SampleFile);
  END; (* IF File exists *)
  AwaitUser;
END.
```

What do you think will happen in this program? Think about how **READLN** differs from **READ**.

Unlike **READ**, a call to **READLN** moves to the next line in the file after each value is read. Thus, only one of the five values on each line is read. In other words, after 25 calls to **READLN**, the program will be at the end of the file (which contains only 25 lines). From then on, the program will be at the end of the file, the calls to **READLN** will always return 0, and the array cells won't change. For instance, if you run this program, you'll get a listing such as the following:

```
0.93334   0.52520   0.77887   0.73287   0.93488
1.44315   1.03290   1.43438   1.36389   1.47166
2.05582   1.47525   1.80527   2.02341   1.48331
2.45495   1.71834   2.27101   2.18368   2.40960
3.27980   2.00376   2.84411   2.82517   2.58403
3.27980   2.00376   2.84411   2.82517   2.58403
3.27980   2.00376   2.84411   2.82517   2.58403
3.27980   2.00376   2.84411   2.82517   2.58403
3.27980   2.00376   2.84411   2.82517   2.58403
3.27980   2.00376   2.84411   2.82517   2.58403
3.27980   2.00376   2.84411   2.82517   2.58403
3.27980   2.00376   2.84411   2.82517   2.58403
3.27980   2.00376   2.84411   2.82517   2.58403
3.27980   2.00376   2.84411   2.82517   2.58403
3.27980   2.00376   2.84411   2.82517   2.58403
3.27980   2.00376   2.84411   2.82517   2.58403
3.27980   2.00376   2.84411   2.82517   2.58403
3.27980   2.00376   2.84411   2.82517   2.58403
3.27980   2.00376   2.84411   2.82517   2.58403
3.27980   2.00376   2.84411   2.82517   2.58403
3.27980   2.00376   2.84411   2.82517   2.58403
3.27980   2.00376   2.84411   2.82517   2.58403
3.27980   2.00376   2.84411   2.82517   2.58403
3.27980   2.00376   2.84411   2.82517   2.58403
3.27980   2.00376   2.84411   2.82517   2.58403
1:      0.13119
2:      0.08015
3:      0.11376
4:      0.11301
5:      0.10336
```

The fifth line of values is repeated for 20 more lines. Each of these last 100 values represents an attempt to read past the end of your file.

CAUTION It may make a big difference whether you use **READ** or **READLN** to get information from a file. If you use **READLN** to read from a file with multiple values per line, you'll lose all but one of the values on each line.

Example: Removing TABs
from a File

The following program copies each line of a file to another file. While moving the line, it replaces each TAB character (ASCII 9) with an appropriate number of spaces. The program also shows the behavior of **READ** when single characters are being read.

P8-8
```
(* Program to remove TAB characters from a file *)

PROGRAM DeTab;

CONST SmallCycle = 50;
      LargeCycle = 2500;
VAR Source, Log : Text;
    NrChRead : LONGINT;
    SName, LName : STRING;

  (* Create a new file, doing all necessary
     and warranted checking, and taking all
     precautions.
     Returns TRUE if file was created; FALSE otherwise.
  *)
  FUNCTION FMade ( VAR TheFile : Text;
                   FName : STRING) : BOOLEAN;
  BEGIN
    ASSIGN ( TheFile, FName);
    (*$I-*)
    REWRITE ( TheFile);
    (*$I+*)
    IF IOResult = 0 THEN
      FMade := TRUE
    ELSE
      FMade := FALSE;
  END; (* FN FMade *)

  (* Open an existing file, doing all necessary
     and warranted checking, and taking all
     precautions.
     Returns TRUE if file was opened; FALSE otherwise.
```

```
*)
FUNCTION FOpened ( VAR TheFile : Text;
                       FName : STRING) : BOOLEAN;
BEGIN
  ASSIGN ( TheFile, FName);
  (*$I-*)
  RESET ( TheFile);
  (*$I+*)
  IF IOResult = 0 THEN
    FOpened := TRUE
  ELSE
    FOpened := FALSE;
END; (* FN FOpened *)

(* Prompt user for a string *)
PROCEDURE GetString ( Message : STRING;
                          VAR Value : STRING);
BEGIN
  WRITE ( Message, ' ');
  READLN ( Value);
END; (* GetString *)

(* Write '.' periodically, to let the user know that
     the program is doing something.
     Val is the counter being tested;
     Small is the cycle for a '.'
     Large is the cycle for a WRITELN
*)
PROCEDURE ShowProgress ( Val, Small, Large : LONGINT);
CONST MarkerCh = '.';
BEGIN
  IF ( Val MOD Small = ( Small - 1)) THEN
    WRITE ( MarkerCh);
  IF ( Val MOD Large = ( Large - 1)) THEN
    WRITELN;
END; (* ShowProgress *)

(* Read InFile, and write it to OutFile.
     In the process, all TAB characters are replaced by an
     appropriate number of spaces.
     The procedure counts the number of characters processed.
*)
PROCEDURE DeTabFile ( VAR InFile, OutFile : Text;
                      VAR Count : LONGINT);
(* Give meaningful names to the characters that need special
     treatment.
     CtrlZ is the value returned when EOF is true.
*)
CONST TAB = #9;
      CR = #13;
      LF = #10;
      CtrlZ = #26;
```

```
           TabSkip = 8;
     VAR Ch : CHAR;
         (* Index is used to test whether you're at a tabstop *)
         Index : INTEGER;

   BEGIN  (* DeTabFile *)
     Index := 1;
     Count := 0;
     WHILE NOT EOF ( InFile) DO
     BEGIN
       (* Read a single character from InFile.
          This character can be any of the following:
          TAB, CR, LF, CtrlZ ( EOF), or anything else.
        *)
       READ ( InFile, Ch);
       CASE Ch OF
         TAB :      (* A TAB was read *)
           REPEAT
             WRITE ( OutFile, ' ');
             INC ( Index);
           UNTIL ( Index MOD TabSkip = 1);
         CR, LF :  (* either a CR or a LF was read *)
           BEGIN
             WRITE ( OutFile, Ch);
             Index := 1;
           END; (* CASE OF CR, LF *)
         CtrlZ : ; (* End of file has been reached; do nothing *)
         (* For anything else, just write the character to Log *)
         ELSE
           BEGIN
             WRITE ( OutFile, Ch);
             INC ( Index);
           END; (* CASE OF ELSE *)
       END; (* CASE OF Ch *)
       INC ( Count);
       ShowProgress ( Count, SmallCycle, LargeCycle);
     END; (* WHILE NOT EOF *)
   END; (* DeTabFile *)

   (* Wait until user presses ENTER, so output will stay
      on the screen.
    *)
   PROCEDURE AwaitUser;
   VAR Ch : CHAR;
   BEGIN
     WRITE ( 'Press ENTER to continue. ');
     READLN;
   END; (* AwaitUser *)

BEGIN (* Main *)
  GetString ( 'Source File Name?', SName);
  GetString ( 'Log File Name?', LName);
```

```
  IF ( FOpened ( Source, SName) = TRUE) AND
     ( FMade ( Log, LName) = TRUE) THEN
  BEGIN
    DeTabFile ( Source, Log, NrChRead);
    WRITELN;
    WRITELN ( NrChRead, ' chars read');
    CLOSE ( Source);
    CLOSE ( Log);
  END; (* IF both files were opened *)
  AwaitUser;
END.
```

The preceding program needs two file names. The first name refers to an existing file—presumably one that contains TAB characters. The contents of this file are read, character by character. Any required modifications are made to the material from the source file (**InFile**). The modified material is written to **OutFile**, which is associated with the second file name you provide for the program.

The program's work is carried out by procedure **DeTabFile**. This routine reads each character from the file associated with **InFile**. If the character is a TAB, the procedure replaces it with the number of spaces needed to get to the next tab stop. The tab stops are eight spaces apart. The value of **Index** is used to determine when a tab stop has been reached. If the character is a carriage return (CR) or a linefeed (LF), it is simply written to the target file. The tab stop counter is reset to 1, however, since the current file position is being changed to the leftmost column on a new line.

Most other characters are simply passed through unchanged. One exception is the CTRL-Z character (ASCII 26), which is returned when the end of the file is reached. CTRL-Z is also used by some text editors to pad out a file—for example, to make the file a particular size.

The **ShowProgress** procedure shows the user that the program is working. If a program is doing a long task, it may produce no output for some time. This can be disconcerting to the user, since there is no way of knowing whether the program is working or has hung up somewhere. In the program, **ShowProgress** writes a dot after every 50 characters read from **InFile** and moves to a new line after every 2500 characters.

DeTabFile counts the number of characters read from the old file. This value is used as the first parameter for **ShowProgress**. Notice that the files are passed to **DeTabFile** just like any other argument would be.

The procedure definition shows how to specify **TEXT** parameters. Note that these two parameters are **VAR** parameters, as required.

Reading Single Characters from a File

The **DeTab** program reads information from a file, character by character, using the predefined **READ** procedure. In the program, **READ** reads a single character from the specified file. The character read is returned in the second argument. For most values of this character, the procedure is executed. A few characters (for example, carriage return) require special treatment, however.

When the character is read, the outcome depends on whether either **EOLN** or **EOF** is **TRUE**—that is, whether you are at the end of a line in the file and whether you are at the end of the file itself. If **EOF(InFile)** is **TRUE**, a CTRL-Z is returned in the second parameter. If **EOLN(InFile)** is **TRUE**, a carriage return (ASCII 13) is returned and the program moves to the start of the next line in the file.

Notice that **EOLN** and **EOF** can take a file argument. By default, these functions apply to the standard input. However, just like many other predefined routines, **EOLN** and **EOF** can both take an additional parameter. This argument must be a file variable.

Adding to an Existing File

As you know, **RESET** lets you open an existing file for reading, and **REWRITE** lets you create a new file for writing. You can't write to a text file that was opened with **RESET**; similarly, you can't read from a text file that was created with **REWRITE**.

Sometimes, however, you may want to open an existing file and append new material to it. The **APPEND** procedure enables you to do this. This procedure takes a single argument, of type **TEXT**. It opens the file specified in the argument and moves the current file position to the end of the file. If the file does not exist, the procedure call results in a run-time error. If the file is already open, **APPEND** closes and then reopens the file. It's not good programming practice to call **APPEND** for an open file.

The following program adds 125 more random values to ZWZW.WZW. It calls **APPEND** to open the file for writing.

P8-9
```
(* Program to illustrate use of APPEND procedure.
   Program opens a file--named ZWZW.WZW on disk --
   and adds 125 random values  (5 values per line) to
   the end of this file.
*)

PROGRAM AppendDemo1;

CONST MaxTrials = 125;
      MaxPerLine = 5;
      FileName = 'zwzw.wzw';
VAR SampleFile : Text;
    Index : INTEGER;

   (* Open an existing file, doing all necessary
      and warranted checking, and taking all precautions.
      After the file is opened, the current file position is set
      to the end  of the file--so you can add more values.
      Returns TRUE if file was opened; FALSE otherwise.
   *)
   FUNCTION FAppended ( VAR TheFile : Text;
                           FName : STRING) : BOOLEAN;
   BEGIN
     ASSIGN ( TheFile, FName);
     (*$I-*)
     APPEND ( TheFile);
     (*$I+*)
     IF IOResult = 0 THEN
       FAppended := TRUE
     ELSE
       FAppended := FALSE;
   END; (* FN FAppended *)

   (* Wait until user presses ENTER, so output will stay
      on the screen.
   *)
   PROCEDURE AwaitUser;
   VAR Ch : CHAR;
   BEGIN
     WRITE ( 'Press ENTER to continue. ');
     READLN ;
   END; (* AwaitUser *)
```

```
BEGIN
  RANDOMIZE;
  IF FAppended ( SampleFile, FileName) = TRUE THEN
  BEGIN
    FOR Index := 1 TO MaxTrials DO
    BEGIN
      (* write a value to the file *)
      WRITE ( SampleFile, RANDOM : 10 : 5);
      (* Every MaxPerLine values,
         move to a new line in the file
      *)
      IF Index MOD MaxPerLine = 0 THEN
        WRITELN ( SampleFile);
    END; (* FOR Index ... *)

    CLOSE ( SampleFile);
  END
  ELSE  (* if call to APPEND was not successful *)
    WRITELN ( 'File ', FileName, ' could not be opened.');
  AwaitUser;
END.
```

Run the program; then look at file ZWZW.WZW. It now has 50 rows of values instead of 25. The call to **APPEND** (instead of **RESET**) enabled you to open and write to an existing file.

Operations on Text Files

You can do the following things with text files:

■ You can use **ASSIGN** to associate a variable of type **TEXT** with a file on disk. You do this by specifying the disk file's name as the second argument to **ASSIGN**, with a **TEXT** variable as the first argument.

■ You can use **REWRITE** to create a new file. If you already have a file with the same name as the new file, the existing file will be replaced by the new file. Files created with **REWRITE** are for writing only.

■ You can use **RESET** to open an existing file for reading. This file must exist, otherwise the program will crash with a run-time error (unless you have I/O checking turned off).

■ You can use **APPEND** to open an existing file, for adding to the end of the file. A file opened with this procedure is for writing. When the file is opened, the current file position is the end of the file.

■ You can use **CLOSE** to close a file you've been working on. The call to this procedure adds any material remaining in the file's buffer to the actual file and then closes the file to keep its contents on the disk.

■ You can use **READ** and **READLN** to read material from the text file. This material can be of any simple type except enumerated types and **BOOLEAN**s. You can also read strings from the file.

■ You can use **WRITE** and **WRITELN** to write material to the file. This material can be of any simple type except enumerated types. You can also write strings to the file.

■ You can use function **IOResult** to check the outcome of an I/O operation. Call this function only when I/O checking is off. Depending on the value returned by **IOResult** (0 if the operation was successful), you can take the appropriate actions in your program.

■ You can use the function **EOF** to determine whether your program has reached the end of the current file.

■ You can use **EOLN** to determine whether you are at the end of the current line in a file.

This list summarizes what you can do with text files. The list is small, but with these capabilities you can do just about anything you'll need to do with a text file.

The major restriction on text files is that you must access the elements in your file sequentially. That is, you must read the first ten lines of the file before you can get to the eleventh line. The main reason for this is that the lines may not all be the same length. As a result, the program has no way of knowing where the eleventh line starts—other than by reading the first ten in order to skip them. The next section teaches you how to define files that can be accessed randomly.

Typed Files

Turbo Pascal supports two kinds of nontext files: typed and untyped. In a *typed file,* each element is of the same type, which has a fixed size. The

following program demonstrates how to work with typed files. The
following pages discuss the program in greater detail, to show how it
works.

P8-10

```
(* Program to illustrate use of a typed file --
   in this case, a File of INTEGER.
*)

PROGRAM TypedDemo;

CONST FileName = 'qqqq.int';
      MaxTrials = 50;
(* Describe the type of file you want to use *)
TYPE IFile = FILE OF INTEGER;

(* Declare a variable of the appropriate type *)
VAR SampleFile : IFile;

  (* Create a new IFile, doing all necessary and warranted
     checking, and taking all precautions.
     Returns TRUE if file was created; FALSE otherwise.
  *)
  FUNCTION iFMade ( VAR TheFile : IFile;
                        FName : STRING) : BOOLEAN;
  BEGIN
    ASSIGN ( TheFile, FName);
    (*$I-*)
    REWRITE ( TheFile);
    (*$I+*)
    IF IOResult = 0 THEN
      iFMade := TRUE
    ELSE
      iFMade := FALSE;
  END; (* FN iFMade *)


  (* Open an existing IFile, doing all necessary and warranted
     checking, and taking all precautions.
     Returns TRUE if file was opened; FALSE otherwise.
  *)
  FUNCTION iFOpened ( VAR TheFile : IFile;
                          FName : STRING) : BOOLEAN;
  BEGIN
    ASSIGN ( TheFile, FName);
    (*$I-*)
    RESET ( TheFile);
    (*$I+*)
    IF IOResult = 0 THEN
      iFOpened := TRUE
```

```
          ELSE
            iFOpened := FALSE;
       END; (* FN iFOpened *)


       (* Display integer values, in a specified # of columns,
          and displaying a specified # of values per line.
       *)
       PROCEDURE DispInts ( Value, Precision,
                            Count, NrPerLine : INTEGER);
       BEGIN
         WRITE ( Value : Precision);
         IF Count MOD NrPerLine = 0 THEN
           WRITELN;
       END;   (* DispInts *)


       (* Generate random integers, and store them in TheFile;
          call DispInts to show the values to the user as well.
       *)
       PROCEDURE GenerateInts ( VAR TheFile : IFile;
                                Nr : INTEGER);
       VAR Count, Result : INTEGER;
       BEGIN
         FOR Count := 1 TO Nr DO
         BEGIN
           Result := RANDOM ( MAXINT);
           WRITE ( TheFile, Result);
           DispInts ( Result, 10, Count, 5);
         END; (* FOR Count ... *)
       END; (* GenerateInts *)


       (* Read all the values stored in the specified IFile,
          and show them to the user.
       *)
       PROCEDURE FReadInts ( VAR TheFile : IFile);
       VAR Count, Result : INTEGER;
       BEGIN
         Count := 0;
         WHILE NOT EOF ( TheFile) DO
         BEGIN
           READ ( TheFile, Result);
           INC ( Count);
           DispInts ( Result, 10, Count, 5);
         END; (* WHILE NOT EOF ... *)
       END; (* FReadInts *)

       (* Draw a line of a specified length,
          and using a specified symbol.
       *)
       PROCEDURE DrawLine ( Length : INTEGER;
                            Element : CHAR);
```

```
       VAR Count : INTEGER;
       BEGIN
         FOR Count := 1 TO Length DO
           WRITE ( Element);
         WRITELN;
       END; (* DrawLine *)

       (* Wait until user presses ENTER, so output will stay
          on the screen.
       *)
       PROCEDURE AwaitUser;
       VAR Ch : CHAR;
       BEGIN
         WRITE ( 'Press ENTER to continue. ');
         READLN;
       END; (* AwaitUser *)


     BEGIN (* Main Program *)
       RANDOMIZE;

       (* If the IFile was created, continue... *)
       IF iFMade ( SampleFile, FileName) THEN
       BEGIN
         GenerateInts ( SampleFile, MaxTrials);
         CLOSE ( SampleFile);  (* save the file's contents *)

         DrawLine ( 50, '-');

         (* If the file exists, read and display its contents. *)
         IF iFOpened ( SampleFile, FileName) THEN
         BEGIN
           FReadInts ( SampleFile);
           CLOSE ( SampleFile);
         END (* IF iFOpened *)
         ELSE
           WRITELN ( 'Could not open ', FileName);
       END
       ELSE
         WRITELN ( 'Could not create ', FileName);
       AwaitUser;
     END.
```

First, call up the program and run it. Before you press ENTER, you'll see two copies of the same 50 values, separated by a dotted line. The program generates and writes 50 pseudorandom **INTEGER**s to the specified file and to the screen. It then reads each value from the file and displays the value. The file created by the program is 100 bytes long — 50 variables, each requiring two bytes.

After the program has finished running, try looking at QQQQ.INT. Press F3 to call up the Open File Box, and then type

```
qqqq.int
```

to load this file into the Turbo Pascal editor. You'll see gibberish because the file is not a text file. Rather, the contents are encoded in the format the program uses to store binary information. Since a typed file is not in ASCII format, you can't simply edit it.

There are advantages to typed files that might outweigh such a drawback. First, however, look at the program to see how typed files are used. Don't be intimidated by the program's length. It is fairly straightforward, and you should have little difficulty following the discussion.

Defining a Typed File

If you want to use a **FILE OF INTEGER** in your program, you first have to describe this file type. That is, you need a type definition before you can declare variables of that type. The syntax for such a definition is

---

< type identifier > " = **FILE OF**" < base type >

The base type can be anything except a file type or a data structure that contains a file type as a component. For example, the definitions that follow are all valid. The comments indicate the size of each element in the file (in bytes). You'll find example programs that use some of these types later in the chapter.

```
    (* 64 bytes : 31 bytes per string + 2 for INTEGER *)
TYPE Person = RECORD
              First, Last : STRING[ 30];
              Age : INTEGER;
            END; (* Person *)
```

```
        (* 40 bytes : 4 bytes per element *)
        LIStats = ARRAY [ 1 .. 10] OF LONGINT;

        (* 60 bytes : 6 bytes per element *)
        RStats = ARRAY [ 1 .. 10] OF REAL;

        (* 32 bytes : required to store 256 bits *)
        CharSet = SET OF CHAR;

(* Now define files containing elements of these types. *)
        PersFile = FILE OF Person;
        LIFile = FILE OF LIStats;
        RFile = FILE OF RStats;
        SetFile = FILE OF CharSet;
        IFile = FILE OF INTEGER;
```

Declaring a Typed File Variable   Once you've described the type of file you'll be using, you can declare variables of that type. In the program, the following line accomplishes this:

```
VAR SampleFile : IFile;
```

Creating and Opening Typed Files

Procedures **iFMade** and **iFOpened**, respectively, create a new **IFile** and open an existing one. The procedure definitions are almost identical to the definitions for **FMade** and **FOpened**, which were defined for handling text files. The first parameter indicates that you must handle typed files in the same manner as text files. That is, you first need to associate the file variable with an external file. After that, you need to open the file.

Similarly, the **CLOSE** procedure works the same way for typed files as it does for text files. To save the contents of a typed file, you need to close it.

Writing to Typed Files

Look at the main program for **TypedDemo**. Once the new **IFile** has been created in the program **TypedDemo**, the main program calls **GenerateInts**. The **GenerateInts** procedure generates the desired number of pseudorandom **INTEGER** values and writes each of these values to the specified **IFile**. Notice that the information is written using the predefined **WRITE** procedure, as in the following statement from the program:

```
WRITE ( TheFile, Result);
```

This call has the same syntax as for writing to text files. In Turbo Pascal, you can also use this procedure to write information to typed files. The system takes care of converting the information into the required form for the file.

While **WRITE** can be used with typed files, **WRITELN** cannot. This is because **WRITELN** adds a CRLF to the end of its output—a character combination that is meaningless in a typed file. Including such characters in a **FILE OF INTEGER** would corrupt the file. As a result, **WRITELN** is not allowed for typed files.

CAUTION   You cannot use **WRITELN** to output values to typed files; you can, however, use **WRITE** with typed values.

Turbo Pascal's use of **WRITE** when outputting to typed files differs from standard Pascal. In standard Pascal, writing information to a typed file is a more involved process and is beyond the scope of this book. However, you'll probably need to handle typed files differently if you switch from Turbo Pascal to a different Pascal compiler.

Procedure **DispInts** checks that the information is formatted properly and displays the current value on the screen. The third parameter, **Count**, represents the number of values that have already been written. The procedure writes the **Value** passed as the first argument. Depending on whether **Count** is divisible by **NrPerLine**, the procedure may also call **WRITELN** to move to the next line on the screen.

Reading from Typed Files

After the specified number of values have been generated and written to the **IFile** by **GenerateInts**, **SampleFile** is closed. The file is reopened for reading by calling **iFOpened**. The actual reading is done in procedure **FReadInfo**. This procedure keeps reading values until it has read the last value in the file—at which point **EOF (TheFile)** becomes **TRUE** and the **WHILE** loop terminates. The **READ** procedure gets the value from the file.

The format for **READ** calls is the same whether you use text or typed files. When working with typed files, however, the second and later parameters must always be variables of the file's base type. Each call to **READ** with **TheFile** as the first argument gets exactly one **INTEGER** value from **TheFile**. You cannot use **READLN** to get information from a typed file.

Turbo Pascal also differs from standard Pascal in how values are read from a typed file. You cannot use **READ** to do this in standard Pascal. As with outputting to typed files, Turbo Pascal's approach is simpler than standard Pascal's.

As each value is read from **TheFile**, it is displayed on the screen using **DispInts**.

As you can see, the syntax for handling typed files is very similar to the syntax for dealing with text files. The contents of the files are in very different formats, however, as you should have noticed when you looked at QQQQ.INT.

Random Access to Typed Files

There is one very important difference between text and typed files. Text files are strictly sequential: you must read from the beginning of the file and read each line in order. When you have a typed file, in contrast, the program knows exactly how long each element is. Since there are no other characters (such as CRLF) in a typed file, the program can move to any random element in the file simply by computing an offset from the start of the file and moving the current file position to the location corresponding to this offset. In this context, an element is a value of the file's base type.

The predefined **SEEK** procedure enables you to move to an arbitrary element in a typed file. This procedure takes two arguments:

■ The typed file in which to seek

■ The number corresponding to the element's position in the file

In a typed file, elements are numbered beginning with 0. If a file had 1000 elements, they would be numbered 0 through 999. To move to the tenth element in a typed file—that is, the element at position 9—you would use a call such as:

```
SEEK ( MyTypedFile, 9);
```

The following program shows how to use **SEEK**. It writes a large number of pseudorandom **REAL**s to a file. After saving the file, the program reopens the file in order to read selected elements from it. The elements are specified by giving the position of the **REAL** in the file. All the elements displayed are from among the last 100 in the file—that is, elements with positions 1900 .. 1999. This restriction will make the advantages of random access very clear when compared to a file whose elements must be accessed sequentially.

P8-11

```
(* Program to illustrate use of SEEK procedure. Program:
    writes MaxItems random values between 0.0 and 1.0
    to an RFile;
    reopens the file for reading; and
    reads 10 selected values from the file.
*)

PROGRAM SeekDemo;

CONST MaxItems = 2000;
      FileName = 'qqqq.see';
TYPE RFile = FILE OF REAL;

VAR RF : RFile;
    Count : INTEGER;
    WhichElem : LONGINT; (* SEEK takes a LONGINT parameter *)
    CurrVal : REAL;

  PROCEDURE AwaitUser;
  VAR Ch : CHAR;
  BEGIN
    WRITE ( 'Press ENTER to continue.');
    READLN;
  END; (* AwaitUser *)

  (* Create a new RFile, doing all necessary and warranted
     checking, and taking all precautions.
     Returns TRUE if file was created; FALSE otherwise.
```

```
*)
FUNCTION rFMade (VAR TheFile : RFile;
                  FName : STRING) : BOOLEAN;
BEGIN
  ASSIGN ( TheFile, FName);
  (*$I-*)
  REWRITE ( TheFile);
  (*$I+*)
  IF IOResult = 0 THEN
    rFMade := TRUE
  ELSE
    rFMade := FALSE;
END; (* FN rFMade *)

(* Open an existing RFile, doing all necessary and warranted
   checking, and taking all precautions.
   Returns TRUE if file was opened; FALSE otherwise.
*)
FUNCTION rFOpened ( VAR TheFile : RFile;
                  FName : STRING) : BOOLEAN;
BEGIN
  ASSIGN ( TheFile, FName);
  (*$I-*)
  RESET ( TheFile);
  (*$I+*)
  IF IOResult = 0 THEN
    rFOpened := TRUE
  ELSE
    rFOpened := FALSE;
END; (* FN rFOpened *)

BEGIN
  RANDOMIZE;

  IF rFMade ( RF, FileName) THEN
  BEGIN
    (* Put values into the file *)
    FOR Count := 1 TO MaxItems DO
    BEGIN
      CurrVal := RANDOM;
      WRITE ( RF, CurrVal);
    END;
    CLOSE ( RF);
    WRITELN ( 'Done');
    (* open the file again, to read from it *)
    IF rFOpened ( RF, FileName) THEN
    BEGIN
      FOR Count := 1 TO 10 DO
      BEGIN
        (* Select an element to get; this element will be among
           the last 100 in the file (1900 .. 1999);
        *)
```

```
                WhichElem := RANDOM ( 100) + 1900;
                (* Move current file position to the desired element *)
                SEEK ( RF, WhichElem);
                (* read the desired element *)
                READ ( RF, CurrVal);
                WRITELN ( WhichElem:5, ': ', CurrVal : 10 : 5);
            END;
            CLOSE ( RF);
        END (* IF rFOpened *)
        ELSE
            WRITELN ( 'Could not open ', FileName);
      END
      ELSE
        WRITELN ( 'Could not create ', FileName);
      AwaitUser;
    END.
```

Run the program. Notice that it takes much longer to create the file than to get the elements. Once the file is filled, it takes almost no time to move to and read a specified element in a typed file.

Notice how **SEEK** is used. After selecting an element, the value corresponding to this element's position in the file is passed as the second argument to **SEEK**. This call puts the current cursor position at the desired element. This means that the next value read from the file will be the desired element.

The seeking is always done from the beginning of the file, not from the current cursor position, so you don't need to close the file after each seek.

To compare this method to searching for the 1950th element (for example) in a text file, try running the following program. This program also writes a large number of values to a file, and then reads selected values from the file. This time, however, the file is of type **TEXT**. Such files are strictly sequential-access files. In order to read the 1975th element, the program first needs to go through the preceding 1974 elements. This takes time, as you'll see when you run the program.

```
P8-12    (* Program to illustrate how long it takes to
            move through a file sequentially.
         *)

         PROGRAM TextSeekDemo;

         CONST MaxItems = 2000;
               FileName = 'qqqq.xxx';
```

```
VAR RF : Text;
    Count, Index : INTEGER;
    WhichElem : INTEGER;
    CurrVal : REAL;

  PROCEDURE AwaitUser;
  VAR Ch : CHAR;
  BEGIN
    WRITE ( 'Press ENTER to continue.');
    READLN;
  END; (* AwaitUser *)

  (* Create a new text file, doing all necessary and warranted
     checking, and taking all precautions.
     Returns TRUE if file was created; FALSE otherwise.
  *)
  FUNCTION FMade ( VAR TheFile : Text;
                      FName : STRING) : BOOLEAN;
  BEGIN
    ASSIGN ( TheFile, FName);
    (*$I-*)
    REWRITE ( TheFile);
    (*$I+*)
    IF IOResult = 0 THEN
      FMade := TRUE
    ELSE
      FMade := FALSE;
  END; (* FN FMade *)

  (* Open an existing text file, doing all necessary and
     warranted checking, and taking all precautions.
     Returns TRUE if file was opened; FALSE otherwise.
  *)
  FUNCTION FOpened ( VAR TheFile : Text;
                        FName : STRING) : BOOLEAN;
  BEGIN
    ASSIGN ( TheFile, FName);
    (*$I-*)
    RESET ( TheFile);
    (*$I+*)
    IF IOResult = 0 THEN
      FOpened := TRUE
    ELSE
      FOpened := FALSE;
  END; (* FN FOpened *)

  (* Display REAL values, in a specified # of columns,
     and displaying a specified # of values per line.
  *)
  PROCEDURE DispReals ( Value : REAL;
                        Width, Precision,
                        Count, NrPerLine : INTEGER);
```

```
    BEGIN
      WRITE ( Value : Width : Precision);
      IF Count MOD NrPerLine = 0 THEN
        WRITELN;
    END;  (* DispReals *)


  BEGIN
    RANDOMIZE;
    IF FMade ( RF, FileName) THEN
    BEGIN
      (* Fill the file with random values. *)
      FOR Count := 1 TO MaxItems DO
      BEGIN
        CurrVal := RANDOM;
        WRITELN ( RF, CurrVal : 10 : 5);
      END;
      CLOSE ( RF);
      WRITELN ( 'Done');
      (* Read 10 specified elements from the file.
         All elements read are among the last 100 in the file.
         Note that the file must be closed and reopened each
         time. This is because calls to READ or READLN always
         move forward in the file.
      *)
      FOR Count := 1 TO 10 DO
      BEGIN
        IF FOpened ( RF, FileName) THEN
        BEGIN
          WhichElem := RANDOM ( 100) + 1900;
          (* Move through the file by reading each value *)
          FOR Index := 1 TO WhichElem DO
            READLN ( RF, CurrVal);
          WRITELN ( WhichElem : 5, ': ', CurrVal : 10 : 5);
          CLOSE ( RF);
        END  (* IF Fopened *)
        ELSE
          WRITELN ( 'Could not open ', FileName);
      END; (* FOR Count ... *)
    END
    ELSE
      WRITELN ( 'Could not create ', FileName);
    AwaitUser;
  END.
```

Notice that the text file needs to be reopened for each value that you want to read. This is because you can only go forward in a text file. Once you've read the 1950th element, you can't read the 1949th one without starting again at the beginning of the file. To get to the beginning of a text file, you need to close the file and use **RESET** to reopen it. The current file position will then be at the start of the file. The time required to close and reopen the file is negligible in comparison with the time required to move through the file. In short, it takes much longer to plow through 1949 values to get to the 1950th than it takes to move to the location of the 1950th element and read the element.

More Typed-File Examples

The programs in this section show some additional examples of typed files. They will give you experience with a range of types, making it easier for you to write your own programs. The example programs also show you that you can write information (such as enumerated-type values) to typed files that you cannot write to text files. These examples also illustrate more about handling files.

Example: A File Containing Arrays   The following program shows how to define a file whose elements are 20-element arrays of **REAL**. This means that each element takes 120 (20 * 6) bytes.

```
P8-13    (* Program to ilustrate use of files containing arrays. Program:
            writes MaxArrays arrays of random REAL values;
            reopens the typed file; and
            reads and displays the values in each array.
         *)

         PROGRAM ArrayTypedDemo;

         CONST MaxArrays = 3;
               ArrSize = 20;
               FileName = 'qqqq.rea';

         (* Define an array type that will be the file's element *)
         TYPE RStats = ARRAY [ 1 .. ArrSize] OF REAL;
                 (* Define a typed file containing RStats elements *)
                 RFile = FILE OF RStats;

         VAR RF : RFile;
             RData : RStats;
             ArrCount, Count : INTEGER;
             NrElements : LONGINT;

           PROCEDURE AwaitUser;
```

```
VAR Ch : CHAR;
BEGIN
  WRITE ( 'Press ENTER to continue.');
  READLN;
END; (* AwaitUser *)


(* Create a new RFile, doing all necessary and warranted
   checking, and taking all precautions.
   Returns TRUE if file was created; FALSE otherwise.
*)
FUNCTION rFMade ( VAR TheFile : RFile;
                     FName : STRING) : BOOLEAN;
BEGIN
  ASSIGN ( TheFile, FName);
  (*$I-*)
  REWRITE ( TheFile);
  (*$I+*)
  IF IOResult = 0 THEN
    rFMade := TRUE
  ELSE
    rFMade := FALSE;
END; (* FN rFMade *)


(* Open an existing RFile, doing all necessary and warranted
   checking, and taking all precautions.
   Returns TRUE if file was opened; FALSE otherwise.
*)
FUNCTION rFOpened ( VAR TheFile : RFile;
                      FName : STRING) : BOOLEAN;
BEGIN
  ASSIGN ( TheFile, FName);
  (*$I-*)
  RESET ( TheFile);
  (*$I+*)
  IF IOResult = 0 THEN
    rFOpened := TRUE
  ELSE
    rFOpened := FALSE;
END; (* FN rFOpened *)


(* Display REAL values, in a specified # of columns,
   and displaying a specified # of values per line.
*)
PROCEDURE DispReals ( Value : REAL;
                      Width, Precision,
                      Count, NrPerLine : INTEGER);
BEGIN
  WRITE ( Value : Width : Precision);
  IF Count MOD NrPerLine = 0 THEN
    WRITELN;
END;  (* DispReals *)
```

```
(* Draw a line of a specified length,
   and using a specified symbol.
*)
PROCEDURE DrawLine ( Length : INTEGER;
                        Element : CHAR);
VAR Count : INTEGER;
BEGIN
  FOR Count := 1 TO Length DO
    WRITE ( Element);
  WRITELN;
END; (* DrawLine *)

BEGIN   (* Main program *)
 RANDOMIZE;
 (* Show the size of an RStats variable *)
 WRITELN ( 'RStats take ', SIZEOF ( RStats), ' bytes each');

 IF rFMade ( RF, FileName) THEN
 BEGIN
   WRITELN ( 'Writing arrays ...');
   FOR Count := 1 TO MaxArrays DO
   BEGIN
     (* Fill the array cells one by one ... *)
     FOR ArrCount := 1 TO ArrSize DO
       RData [ ArrCount] := RANDOM;
     (* ... but write the entire array to the file at once *)
     WRITE ( RF, RData);
   END;
   CLOSE ( RF);
   WRITELN ( 'Done writing.');

   (* reopen the file for reading *)
   IF rFOpened ( RF, FileName) THEN
   BEGIN
     WHILE NOT EOF ( RF) DO
     BEGIN
       DrawLine ( 50, '-');
       (* read an entire array at a time *)
       READ ( RF, RData);
       INC ( ArrCount);
       (* dislpay the array elements, one by one *)
       FOR ArrCount := 1 TO ArrSize DO
         DispReals ( RData [ ArrCount], 10, 5, ArrCount, 5);
     END;
     DrawLine ( 50, '-');
   END   (* IF rFOpened *)
   ELSE
     WRITELN ( 'Could not open ', FileName);
   (* Display information about the # of elements in file *)
   NrElements := FileSize ( RF);
   WRITELN ( FileName, ' contains ', NrElements,
             ' elements (arrays).');
```

```
      CLOSE ( RF);
      AwaitUser;
    END   (* IF rFMade *)
    ELSE
      WRITELN ( 'Could not create ', FileName);
  END.
```

After the definition for **RStats**, the file description is completely straightforward. The **rFMade** and **rFOpened** procedures are similar to routines you've seen in earlier programs, except for the first parameters.

You've already seen the other routines—**DrawLine, DispReals**, and **AwaitUser**. They should not interfere with your overview of the program. Note how the file elements and the file are used in the main program. Remember, each element actually contains 20 smaller components. Before you can write an element to the **RFile** you need to initialize the array—that is, the element itself.

This means initializing the 20 cells, which requires a **FOR** loop. Once the 20 iterations have been completed, the entire array (all 120 bytes) is written to the typed file. This process is repeated: the second array is initialized and written to the file.

Notice that the calls to **WRITE** and **READ** are no different than for simpler base types. However, multiple items of information can be transferred at once because they are all part of a single, structured type—the *file's* base type. If the file were of type **TEXT**, you would not be able to do this. Similarly, an entire **RFile** array is read at once from the typed file. Once the array has been read into the program, its individual cells must be displayed one by one.

Finally, the last part of the outer **IF** clause introduces a new predefined function: **FileSize**. This function takes a typed file argument and returns the number of elements (not bytes) in the file. In the example program, this value is 3 since the file only contains three (**RStats**) arrays—although it actually contains 60 values.

Example: Record and Set Types as File Components   You can have typed files with more exotic types as their components. The following program uses a record as the basic component. One field of this record is a **CharSet**—a **SET OF CHAR**. Run the program to see storage information about **CharSet** and **ChRec** and to determine the number of elements in the typed file. You'll also see the random **CharSets** generated by the program.

```
P8-14     (* Program to ilustrate use of records containing sets
             as a component type for a typed file. The program:
             displays information about the size of a ChRec;
             creates a file to contain ChRec values;
             determines maximum # of elements for current set;
             generates MaxTrials sets of random CHAR values;
             writes each of these sets to the typed file;
             reopens the typed file for reading;
             reads the contents of the file one element
             (that is, ChRec) at a time;
             displays the contents of each ChRec;
          *)

          PROGRAM ChRecTypedDemo;

          CONST MaxTrials = 10;
                FileName = 'qqqq.crc';
          TYPE CharSet = SET OF CHAR;

                ChRec = RECORD
                          SetInfo : CharSet;
                          MaxItems : INTEGER;
                        END;

                ChRecFile = FILE OF ChRec;

          VAR ChRF : ChRecFile;
              ChRecData : ChRec;
              SetCount, NrTimes, ArrCount, Count : INTEGER;
              ChIndex : CHAR;

            PROCEDURE AwaitUser;
            VAR Ch : CHAR;
            BEGIN
              WRITE ( 'Press ENTER to continue.');
              READLN;
            END; (* AwaitUser *)

            (* Draw a line of a specified length,
               and using a specified symbol.
            *)
            PROCEDURE DrawLine ( Length : INTEGER;
                                 Element : CHAR);
            VAR Count : INTEGER;
            BEGIN
              FOR Count := 1 TO Length DO
                WRITE ( Element);
              WRITELN;
            END; (* DrawLine *)

            (* Create a new ChRecFile, doing all necessary and warranted
               checking, and taking all precautions.
```

```
          Returns TRUE if file was created; FALSE otherwise.
 *)
FUNCTION chrFMade ( VAR TheFile : ChRecFile;
                         FName : STRING) : BOOLEAN;
BEGIN
  ASSIGN ( TheFile, FName);
  (*$I-*)
  REWRITE ( TheFile);
  (*$I+*)
  IF IOResult = 0 THEN
    chrFMade := TRUE
  ELSE
    chrFMade := FALSE;
END; (* FN chrFMade *)

 (* Open an existing ChRecFile, doing all necessary and
    warranted checking, and taking all precautions.
    Returns TRUE if file was opened; FALSE otherwise.
 *)
FUNCTION chrFOpened ( VAR TheFile : ChRecFile;
                          FName : STRING) : BOOLEAN;
BEGIN
  ASSIGN ( TheFile, FName);
  (*$I-*)
  RESET ( TheFile);
  (*$I+*)
  IF IOResult = 0 THEN
    chrFOpened := TRUE
  ELSE
    chrFOpened := FALSE;
  END; (* FN chrFOpened *)

BEGIN  (* Main program *)
  RANDOMIZE;
  (* display information about storage requirements *)
  WRITELN ( 'CharSets take ', SIZEOF ( CharSet), ' bytes');
  WRITELN ( 'ChRecs take ', SIZEOF ( ChRec), ' bytes');

  IF chrFMade ( ChRF, FileName) THEN
  BEGIN
    (* build 10 sets, and write each to ChRF *)
    FOR Count := 1 TO MaxTrials DO
    BEGIN
      (* Determine the # of candidate elements for the set *)
      NrTimes := RANDOM ( 27);
      ChRecData.SetInfo := [];   (* initialize to empty set *)
      ChRecData.MaxItems := NrTimes;
      (* generate NrTimes random letters; try to add to set *)
      FOR SetCount := 1 TO NrTimes DO
      (* the right hand side ensures that only
      'a' .. 'z' are used.
      *)
```

```
            WITH ChRecData DO
               SetInfo := SetInfo + [ CHR ( RANDOM ( 26) + 97)];
            (* after building the set component element-by-element,
               write the entire record at once.
            *)
            WRITE ( ChRF, ChRecData);
         END;
         CLOSE ( ChRF);

         DrawLine ( 50, '-');

         IF chrFOpened ( ChRF, FileName) THEN
         BEGIN
            WHILE NOT EOF ( ChRF) DO
            BEGIN
               (* Read an entire ChRec at a time *)
               READ ( ChRF, ChRecData);
               WRITE ( 'Max = ', ChRecData.MaxItems, ' : ');
               (* Write each set element *)
               FOR ChIndex := 'a' TO 'z' DO
               BEGIN
                  IF ChIndex IN ChRecData.SetInfo THEN
                     WRITE ( ChIndex, ' ');
               END;
               WRITELN;
            END;  (* WHILE NOT EOF *)
            DrawLine ( 50, '-');
            WRITELN ( FileName, ' contains ', FileSize ( ChRF),
                        ' elements (ChRecs)');
            AwaitUser;
         END    (* IF chrFOpened *)
         ELSE
            WRITELN ( 'Could not open ', FileName);
      END    (* IF chrFMade *)
      ELSE
         WRITELN ( 'Could not create ', FileName);
   END.
```

Once you've defined all your types and have declared the appropriate variables, the syntax for file handling is identical in all the examples. This means that you only need to change the details of routines such as **FMade** and **FOpened** to create the appropriate versions.

You may also need to change the details of how the file components get their values. For example, assigning values to a **ChRec** is much more involved than assigning values to an **INTEGER**. Nevertheless, once the variables have their values you'll use the same simple procedure calls to write the information to a typed file.

Example: Files Containing Enumerated Types You can even define files whose base type is an enumerated type. Recall that you could not write the values of enumerated types directly. This is true if you're trying to write to the screen or to a text file. On the other hand, if you want to write to a typed file, you can store values for enumerated types. This is because the ordinal values are simply stored. If you want to display these values on the screen, you'll still have to make the appropriate substitutions.

The following program shows an example involving typed files. Since the file handling aspects of the program are like those in earlier programs, the program is presented without comment. You may, however, want to experiment with the program. For example, try appending more values to the file. You'll need to define a procedure for calling **APPEND** (which works for typed files) in the appropriate manner.

P8-15
```
(* Program to illustrate files with enumerated types
    as components.
*)

PROGRAM EnTypeDemo;

CONST FileName = 'qqqq.clr';
TYPE Color = ( red, green, blue, yellow, white, black);
     CFile = FILE OF Color;
VAR CF : CFile;
    CurrColor : Color;


  PROCEDURE AwaitUser;
  VAR Ch : CHAR;
  BEGIN
    WRITE ( 'Press ENTER to continue.');
    READLN;
  END; (* AwaitUser *)

  (* Draw a line of a specified length,
     and using a specified symbol.
  *)
  PROCEDURE DrawLine ( Length : INTEGER;
                       Element : CHAR);
  VAR Count : INTEGER;
  BEGIN
    FOR Count := 1 TO Length DO
      WRITE ( Element);
    WRITELN;
  END; (* DrawLine *)
```

```
(* Create a new CFile, doing all necessary and warranted
   checking, and taking all precautions.
   Returns TRUE if file was created; FALSE otherwise.
*)
FUNCTION cFMade ( VAR TheFile : CFile;
                      FName : STRING) : BOOLEAN;
BEGIN
  ASSIGN ( TheFile, FName);
  (*$I-*)
  REWRITE ( TheFile);
  (*$I+*)
  IF IOResult = 0 THEN
    cFMade := TRUE
  ELSE
    cFMade := FALSE;
END; (* FN cFMade *)

(* Open an existing CFile, doing all necessary and
   warranted checking, and taking all precautions.
   Returns TRUE if file was opened; FALSE otherwise.
*)
FUNCTION cFOpened ( VAR TheFile : CFile;
                        FName : STRING) : BOOLEAN;
BEGIN
  ASSIGN ( TheFile, FName);
  (*$I-*)
  RESET ( TheFile);
  (*$I+*)
  IF IOResult = 0 THEN
    cFOpened := TRUE
  ELSE
    cFOpened := FALSE;
END; (* FN cFOpened *)

BEGIN  (* Main Program *)
  IF cFMade ( CF, FileName) THEN
  BEGIN
    (* CurrColor actually is assigned an ordinal value *)
    CurrColor := red;
    (* Write this ordinal value to CF *)
    WRITE ( CF, CurrColor);
    CurrColor := black;
    WRITE ( CF, CurrColor);
    CurrColor := green;
    WRITE ( CF, CurrColor);
    CurrColor := white;
    WRITE ( CF, CurrColor);
    CurrColor := blue;
    WRITE ( CF, CurrColor);
    CurrColor := yellow;
    WRITE ( CF, CurrColor);
    CLOSE ( CF);
```

```
    IF cFOpened ( CF, FileName) THEN
    BEGIN
      WHILE NOT EOF ( CF) DO
      BEGIN
        (* Read an ordinal value from CF *)
        READ ( CF, CurrColor);
        (* Display the string appropriate to the
           ordinal value.
        *)
        CASE CurrColor OF
          red : WRITELN ( 'red');
          green : WRITELN ( 'green');
          blue : WRITELN ( 'blue');
          yellow : WRITELN ( 'yellow');
          white : WRITELN ( 'white');
          black : WRITELN ( 'black');
        END; (* CASE of CurrColor *)
      END; (* WHILE NOT EOF *)
      CLOSE ( CF);
      AwaitUser;
    END    (* IF cFOpened *)
    ELSE
      WRITELN ( 'Could not open ' , FileName);
  END    (* IF cFMade *)
  ELSE
    WRITELN ( 'Could not create ' , FileName);
END.
```

Untyped Files

Recall that Turbo Pascal also supports *untyped files*. To declare an untyped file, simply specify **FILE** as the variable's type. An untyped file is essentially a stream of bytes. Your program transfers chunks of information between program and file. The chunks are of a fixed size, which you specify when you create or open the file. To write information into an untyped file, your program simply transfers the appropriate number of bytes to the file. Similarly, when reading from the file, the program transfers bytes from the file. The bytes are interpreted in the program.

WRITE and **READ** will not work for untyped files, however. Instead, you need to use two other procedures: **BlockRead** and **BlockWrite**. These are discussed briefly after the following program, which illustrates the use of untyped files. The program generates a few random

REALs and writes their bit patterns to an untyped file. The information is transferred six bytes at a time, since that's the size of a **REAL**. After the file has been written and saved, the program reads information back from the file and displays the values on the screen. Run the program to see how it works.

P8-16
```
(* Program to ilustrate use of untyped files
   Program generates random REALs, and writes these
   to an untyped file. The information is transferred
   6 bytes at a time, since that's the size of a REAL.
   NOTE that input and output is done with BlockRead and
   BlockWrite.
*)

PROGRAM UntypedDemo;

CONST MaxTrials = 10;
      FileName = 'qqqq.unt';
VAR UT : FILE;
    Count : INTEGER;
    Val : REAL;

  PROCEDURE AwaitUser;
  VAR Ch : CHAR;
  BEGIN
    WRITE ( 'Press ENTER to continue.');
    READLN;
  END; (* AwaitUser *)

  (* Draw a line of a specified length,
     and using a specified symbol.
  *)
  PROCEDURE DrawLine ( Length : INTEGER;
                       Element : CHAR);
  VAR Count : INTEGER;
  BEGIN
    FOR Count := 1 TO Length DO
      WRITE ( Element);
    WRITELN;
  END; (* DrawLine *)

  (* Create a new ChRecFile, doing all necessary and warranted
     checking, and taking all precautions.
     Returns TRUE if file was created; FALSE otherwise.
  *)
  FUNCTION utFMade ( VAR TheFile : FILE;
                     FName : STRING;
                     ChunkSize : WORD) : BOOLEAN;
```

```
   BEGIN
     ASSIGN ( TheFile, FName);
     (*$I-*)
     REWRITE ( TheFile, ChunkSize);
     (*$I+*)
     IF IOResult = 0 THEN
       utFMade := TRUE
     ELSE
       utFMade := FALSE;
   END; (* FN utFMade *)


   (* Open an existing ChRecFile, doing all necessary and
      warranted checking, and taking all precautions.
      Returns TRUE if file was opened; FALSE otherwise.
   *)
   FUNCTION utFOpened ( VAR TheFile : FILE;
                            FName : STRING;
                            ChunkSize : WORD) : BOOLEAN;
   BEGIN
     ASSIGN ( TheFile, FName);
     (*$I-*)
     RESET ( TheFile, ChunkSize);
     (*$I+*)
     IF IOResult = 0 THEN
       utFOpened := TRUE
     ELSE
       utFOpened := FALSE;
   END; (* FN utFOpened *)


   (* Display REAL values, in a specified # of columns,
      and displaying a specified # of values per line.
   *)
   PROCEDURE DispReals ( Value : REAL;
                         Width, Precision,
                         Count, NrPerLine : INTEGER);
   BEGIN
     WRITE ( Value : Width : Precision);
     IF Count MOD NrPerLine = 0 THEN
       WRITELN;
   END;   (* DispReals *)

BEGIN   (* Main program *)
  RANDOMIZE;

  (* Will write REALs *)
  IF utFMade ( UT, FileName, 6) THEN
  BEGIN
    (* generate random, and write each to utF *)
    FOR Count := 1 TO MaxTrials DO
    BEGIN
```

```
        Val := RANDOM;
        (* This write l 6-byte chunk to UT.
           Parameters: File, Buffer (Variable),
                       # of chunks being transferred.
        *)
        BlockWrite ( UT, Val, 1);
        DispReals ( Val, 10, 5, Count, 5);
      END;
      CLOSE ( UT);

      DrawLine ( 50, '-');

      IF utFOpened ( UT, FileName, 6) THEN
      BEGIN
        WHILE NOT EOF ( UT) DO
        BEGIN
          (* Read one 6-byte chunk from the file *)
          BlockRead ( UT, Val, 1);
          INC ( Count);
          DispReals ( Val, 10, 5, Count, 5);
        END;  (* WHILE NOT EOF *)
        DrawLine ( 50, '-');
        AwaitUser;
        CLOSE ( UT);
      END   (* IF chrFOpened *)
      ELSE
        WRITELN ( 'Could not open ', FileName);
    END   (* IF chrFMade *)
    ELSE
      WRITELN ( 'Could not create ', FileName);
END.
```

Before studying the main program, look at functions **utFMade** and **utFOpened**. These routines have one parameter more than their counterparts for typed files. This third parameter specifies the number of bytes to be treated as a single record, or chunk, when transferring information to and from the file.

For example, in the program, this argument is 6 when these procedures are called. This value allows you to transfer an entire **REAL** at a time, between program and file. The default chunk size is 128 bytes. However, you should select your chunk size on the basis of the type of information that you actually have in the file. If you have **INTEGER** values, it makes sense to transfer two bytes at a time. On the other hand, if your file contains a mixture of types, your safest strategy is to transfer the smallest unit—one byte at a time. Your program would then have to combine bytes in order to build the types of values it needed.

The **ChunkSize** parameter is used in the calls to **RESET** and **RE-WRITE** in **utFOpened** and **utFMade,** respectively. The calls to **RESET** and **REWRITE** have one parameter more than they did for text and typed files.

To write information to an untyped file, you need to use the **Block-Write** procedure. This routine takes three arguments and may take a fourth if you wish.

■ The first argument is an untyped file variable.

■ The second argument can be any variable, and represents a memory location. The procedure interprets this as the starting location of a buffer whose size is determined by the third parameter. This buffer parameter is passed by reference.

■ The third argument is a **WORD**, and specifies the number of chunks to read at a time. A chunk's size depends on the data type involved. For example, if this value were 2 in the program, each call to **BlockWrite** would transfer 12 bytes to the untyped file. This parameter is passed by value.

■ You may include a fourth parameter (also a **WORD**), which provides information about the number of chunks actually written. After procedure **BlockWrite** has finished its work, the value of this parameter will represent the number of chunks written. This number will be less than or equal to the number of chunks you specified as the third argument to **BlockWrite**.

For example, the disk may become full before **BlockWrite** has transferred all of the elements you specified in the third parameter. If so, fewer chunks than you specified will have been transferred. To determine how many were transferred, you have to check the value of the fourth parameter. (Naturally, you need to specify a variable as your fourth parameter when calling the procedure.)

When **BlockWrite** does its work, the current file position is updated accordingly. Essentially, the current file position will always be at the end of the file, since new material is always added to the end of a file.

Procedure **BlockRead** has the same parameter structure as does **BlockWrite.** This procedure reads the specified number of chunks from the untyped file and stores these bytes at the memory location specified by the second parameter, which can be any variable. For these procedures to work, the untyped file must be open.

Miscellaneous File-Handling Routines

There are other procedures and functions that can take file arguments. For example, there are procedures for renaming or deleting files, for checking the current directory on a specified drive, for checking the current position in a nontext file, and so forth.

The situations in which you might use such routines are beyond the scope of this book. In fact, some of the actions (such as erasing a file) can get you into real trouble if you're not careful. If you're interested in such topics, consult the documentation for the official Turbo Pascal compiler. Table 8-1 summarizes the procedures and functions covered in this chapter and indicates the types of files for which these routines work.

Routine	Text	Typed	Untyped	Notes
ASSIGN	✓	✓	✓	
RESET	✓	✓	✓	File must exist
REWRITE	✓	✓	✓	
CLOSE	✓	✓	✓	
APPEND	✓			File must exist
WRITE	✓	✓		File must be open
WRITELN	✓			File must be open
READ	✓	✓		File must be open
READLN	✓			File must be open
BlockWrite			✓	File must be open
BlockRead			✓	File must be open
SEEK		✓	✓	File must be open
FileSize		✓	✓	File must be open
EOF	✓	✓	✓	File must be open
EOLN	✓			File must be open
IOResult	✓	✓	✓	{$I-} required

Table 8-1. *Turbo Pascal's File-Handling Routines*

In this chapter, you learned how to work with files in Pascal. Most commonly, you'll use text files. Sometimes, however, you may want to work with typed or even untyped files. Nontext files are random access, which makes them useful if you need to access lots of data.

In the next chapter, "Pointers," you'll learn about Pascal's pointer types.

9 *Pointers*

In this chapter, you'll learn about Pascal's pointer data type. This type is generally used to access storage that is allocated when your program is executing, rather than in advance. Being able to allocate storage at run time rather than at compile time enables you to do things that would otherwise be difficult or impossible to do efficiently. For example, by allocating storage at run time, you can handle tasks for which you don't know in advance how many values you'll have to process.

Static Memory Allocation

When you declare variables in a Pascal program, the compiler knows exactly how much storage they require. The compiler allocates storage for global variables and constants in the form of a *data segment*—an area of contiguous memory whose size is determined by the number and types of global variables declared in the program.

Storage for local variables and parameters is allocated as needed during program execution. However, the compiler sets aside a chunk of memory (the *stack segment*) to be used for such allocations. The size of the stack segment is fixed, and is determined at compile time. The {$M} compiler directive lets you specify a stack size at compile time. Otherwise, a default size is used. The amount of the stack segment actually in use at any one time depends on what procedures are suspended and what is currently executing.

Both the data and stack segments are examples of *static memory allocation*. The term "static" is used because the amount of memory allocated is determined at compile time (before the program executes) and also because the amount of this storage is fixed, once determined.

Drawbacks of Static Memory Allocation

Sometimes, however, you may not be able to allocate storage statically. For example, suppose you need to write a program to rank numerical data. The program will get its data from the user, but the number of values to be sorted is not fixed.

For such a task, two approaches are possible:

■ Declare an array with as many cells as possible and accept at most that many values. This is a static memory allocation strategy.

■ Use a dynamic memory allocation strategy. Such a strategy involves pointers, as described in this chapter.

Dynamic Memory Allocation

In *dynamic memory allocation*, storage is not set aside until your program requests it while running. When storage is requested at run time, the system allocates and makes available to the program the desired amount of contiguous storage.

This storage is allocated from a pool of available memory, known as the heap. The *heap* encompasses the area of memory available after the program's code, data, and stack segments have been loaded.

Program Layout

Figure 9-1 is a rough sketch of the way memory is laid out when a Turbo Pascal program is about to execute. The figure shows the major components that occupy storage when a typical program runs. Specific programs may have different memory layouts because of special features (such as overlays, which enable you to load your program into memory in pieces).

The memory available to DOS must be used to store all sorts of things. Whenever you're running under DOS, a portion of the operating system is stored in memory. You may also have other programs (such as SideKick Plus) loaded into memory. These are stored in the lower DOS memory locations. When you run your program in the IDE, this environment is also loaded in the miscellaneous part of memory.

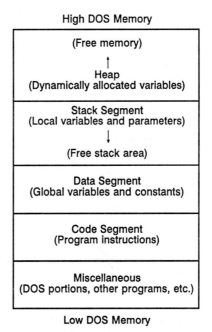

Figure 9-1. *Memory layout for a Turbo Pascal program*

Program Segments   After such programs and components have been accounted for, your Turbo Pascal program's code segment occupies the next portion of memory. This is followed by the data segment and the stack segment—both of which are of fixed size for your program.

The amount of the stack segment in use in the program depends on the parameters and local environments of routines that are active and suspended. The stack "grows" downward from the highest to the lowest address of the stack segment (indicated by the downward arrow in the figure).

When a routine finishes executing, any parts of the stack used for the routine's local environment are returned for reuse. If your program needs more memory for the stack than is available in the stack segment, it will crash with a stack overflow error. The consequences of such an error depend on whether the *stack-checking* compiler option **{$S}** is on or off.

If stack checking is on, the program checks whether there is enough stack space for a routine before that routine begins executing. If not, the program stops with a run-time error. If stack checking is off, the program doesn't check before loading the routine's environment. In this case, not only will the program still crash, it may cause the entire system to crash so that you'll have to reboot.

By default, stack checking is on. If you need to change this setting, you can add the appropriate line to your program:

```
{$S+}   (* turn stack checking on  *)

{$S-}   (* turn stack checking off *)
```

The Program Heap   The heap comprises whatever memory remains after the program's segments have been loaded. If your program is small, has little global data, and if there are no extraneous programs loaded into memory, the heap can be quite large. The following program shows how to use two predefined functions that provide information about the heap:

```
P9-1    (* Program to illustrate use of
           MEMAVAIL and MAXAVAIL  functions
        *)
```

```
PROGRAM HeapTest;

BEGIN
  (* Determine how much memory is available
     in the entire heap.
  *)
  WRITE ( 'MEMAVAIL = ', MEMAVAIL : 7, ' bytes; ');

  (* Determine the size of the largest area of
     contiguous storage in the entire heap.
  *)
  WRITELN ( 'MAXAVAIL = ', MAXAVAIL : 7, ' bytes');
  READLN;
END.
```

The **MEMAVAIL** function returns a **LONGINT** representing the number of bytes of storage available in the heap. These bytes are not necessarily contiguous.

MAXAVAIL returns a **LONGINT** that represents the size of the largest chunk of available contiguous memory. This may change, along with the total amount of available heap, as you read new values into a program that uses dynamic memory allocation.

The heap is administered by a component of the Turbo Pascal run-time library called the Heap Manager. The *Heap Manager* maintains a list that contains the status of all available storage in the heap.

Pointers

What happens when your program requests dynamic storage? To learn about this process, you need to understand pointers. A pointer is a data type that "points to," or *references*, a particular location in memory. A pointer variable contains an address as its value. This address corresponds to a memory location. This memory location is available for use in your program, and is accessible through the pointer. The size of the memory location depends on the type of information to be stored there. Such memory is generally allocated dynamically, when your program requests it. The following program illustrates how to define and declare pointers and how to get memory referenced by pointers.

P9-2

```
(* Program to illustrate how to define and declare pointers,
   and how to get memory referenced by pointers.
*)

PROGRAM PtrDemo;

(* Define two pointers: pointer to REAL; pointer to INTEGER *)
TYPE IntPtr = ^INTEGER;
     RealPtr = ^REAL;

(* Declare two pointer variables *)
VAR IP : IntPtr;
    RP : RealPtr;
    ISize, RSize : INTEGER;

BEGIN
  (* Determine how much memory is available
     in the entire heap.
  *)
  WRITE ( 'MEMAVAIL = ', MEMAVAIL : 7, ' bytes; ');

  (* Determine the size of the largest area of
     contiguous storage in the entire heap.
  *)
  WRITELN ( 'MAXAVAIL = ', MAXAVAIL : 7, ' bytes');

  (* Allocate storage for a REAL; RP will point to it *)
  NEW ( RP);

  (* RP^ is the area of memory to which RP points *)
  RSize := SIZEOF ( RP^);
  WRITELN ( 'After allocating ', RSize : 7, ' bytes:');
  WRITE ( 'MEMAVAIL = ', MEMAVAIL : 7, ' bytes; ');
  WRITELN ( 'MAXAVAIL = ', MAXAVAIL : 7, ' bytes');

  (* Allocate storage for an INTEGER; IP will point to it *)
  NEW ( IP);

  ISize := SIZEOF ( IP^);
  WRITELN ( 'After allocating ', ISize : 7, ' bytes:');
  WRITE ( 'MEMAVAIL = ', MEMAVAIL : 7, ' bytes; ');
  WRITELN ( 'MAXAVAIL = ', MAXAVAIL : 7, ' bytes');
  READLN;
END.
```

The following sections explain how this program uses pointers and their targets. (*Target* refers to the memory location that corresponds to the value of a pointer. Thus, a pointer's contents represent the address of the pointer's target.)

Defining Pointer Types

Program **PtrDemo** contains two type definitions. The first,

```
IntPtr = ^INTEGER;
```

defines an **IntPtr** as a *pointer to* **INTEGER**. That is, an address stored in a variable of type **IntPtr** will be interpreted as the starting location of a two-byte chunk of memory, whose contents will be interpreted as an **INTEGER**.

Similarly, the program defines **RealPtr** as a *pointer to* **REAL**. This means that an address stored in a **RealPtr** variable will be interpreted as the starting address of a six-byte chunk, whose contents will be interpreted as a **REAL**.

Note the syntax for a pointer definition:

> <pointer type name> " = ^ "<target's base type>

The caret (^) symbol before the base type specifier indicates that you're defining a pointer and not just a synonym for an existing type. The base type can be a simple or a structured type. In fact, it can even be a pointer type.

When defining a pointer type, you always specify the base type of the pointer's target so the program knows how much memory it should access at a pointer's target location.

Declaring Pointer Variables

Once you've specified what kinds of pointers your program will use, you can declare variables of these pointer types. Such declarations have the same syntax as other declarations.

```
<identifier> ":" <pointer type name>
```

In the program, **IP** and **RP** are declared as variables of type **IntPtr** and **RealPtr**, respectively. Since they are declared in the main program, these are global variables and the storage allocated for them is in the data segment. Thus, the storage for the pointer variables **IP** and **RP** is statically allocated. The storage corresponding to their targets, however, will be dynamically allocated.

REMEMBER   A pointer variable is generally a static variable. The pointer's target, on the other hand, will usually be allocated dynamically.

Allocating Dynamic Storage

The calls to the predefined procedure **NEW** in **PtrDemo1** allocate storage at run time. The call

```
NEW ( RP);
```

is a request for dynamic memory allocation. The argument passed to **NEW** must be a pointer variable. The base type of the argument's target variable determines the amount of storage being requested. Any storage returned will be on the heap.

When **NEW** is called with **RP** as its argument:

■ The program asks the Heap Manager for six bytes of contiguous memory, enough to store a **REAL**.

■ The Heap Manager finds such a chunk of memory in the heap. (This chunk of the heap is removed from the Heap Manager's list of available memory locations.)

■ The location of this chunk of memory is stored in **RP**. (Thus, **RP** is assigned a value when **NEW** is called.)

Prior to the call to **NEW**, **RP** was uninitialized. With the call to **NEW**, **RP** gets a value. Now there also should be fewer available bytes on the heap. Run the program again. The heap size will have decreased by six bytes after the call — exactly the amount allocated for **RP**'s target.

The heap size decreases by two more bytes when you allocate storage for **IP**'s target by calling **NEW** with **IP** as the argument. If the Heap Manager cannot allocate the desired amount of storage, the program will crash with a run-time error. One way to avoid such an error is to check whether there is enough storage available before allocating it. The following code excerpt shows an example of how to do this:

```
(* Assume the following declarations:

   TYPE RealArray = ARRAY [ 1 .. 500] OF REAL;
        RAPtr = ^RealArray;
   VAR RAP : RAPtr;
*)

...
IF MAXAVAIL > SIZEOF ( RealArray) THEN
  ...
```

For you to be able to allocate storage for a new dynamic variable, the largest chunk of available heap must be at least as large as the storage required for a **RealArray** in the example. If this is not the case — that is, if the heap has no more room — the **IF** part of the loop is bypassed.

Accessing a Target Variable

The following statement shows how to refer to a pointer's target variable:

```
RSize := SIZEOF ( RP^);
```

RP^ is the target variable whose address is stored in **RP**. Essentially, **RP^** means, "the variable referenced (or pointed to) by **RP**." The target variable has no name of its own; rather, it is identified in terms of the pointer that references it.

Such a reference—through the pointer—is known as an *indirect reference*. This is in contrast to a *direct reference,* in which you specify the variable by name. Indirect reference essentially places a named variable (the pointer) between you and the storage that you actually want to manipulate (in other words, the target variable).

The preceding assignment statement says to do the following:

■ Determine the amount of storage allocated for variable **RP^**.

■ Assign this value to **RSize**.

Assigning Values to Target Variables

The following program shows how to assign values to target variables:

```
P9-3    (* Program to illustrate how to assign values to
            target variables
        *)

        PROGRAM PtrDemo2;

        (* Define two pointers: pointer to REAL; pointer to INTEGER *)
        TYPE IntPtr = ^INTEGER;
             RealPtr = ^REAL;

        (* Declare two pointer variables *)
        VAR IP : IntPtr;
            RP : RealPtr;

        BEGIN
          RANDOMIZE;
          WRITELN ( 'MEMAVAIL = ', MEMAVAIL : 10, ' bytes');
          (* Allocate storage for a REAL; RP will point to it *)
          NEW ( RP);
          (* Allocate storage for an INTEGER; IP will point to it *)
          NEW ( IP);

          REPEAT
            (* Assign a random value to RP's target *)
            RP^ := RANDOM;
            (* Assign a random value between 0 and 499 to IP's target *)
            IP^ := RANDOM ( 500);
```

```
    WRITELN ( 'RP^ = ', RP^ : 10 : 5, '; IP^ = ', IP^ : 5);
  UNTIL ( RP^ < 0.5) AND ( IP^ < 250);

  WRITELN ( 'MEMAVAIL = ', MEMAVAIL : 10, ' bytes');
  READLN;
END.
```

The assignment statements in the **REPEAT** loop store numerical values at two locations on the heap. Note that you will assign **REAL** values to **RP^** and **INTEGER** values to **IP^**. The target variables are just variables of specific types. But unlike ordinary variables, dynamically allocated variables can only be accessed indirectly—that is, through their pointers.

Note that the program uses only eight bytes of heap, although the **REPEAT** loop may execute multiple times. No storage is allocated within the loop. **RP^** and **IP^** are simply assigned new values. This program allocates storage for targets only once, outside the **REPEAT** loop.

Don't Confuse Pointer and Target

You must be clear about what is stored where when you're working with pointers. You can only assign addresses to pointer variables. You cannot assign a pointer variable, such as **RP** in **PtrDemo2**, an ordinary numerical value. Thus, the following assignment is invalid:

```
(* Assume RP is a RealPtr -- that is, ^REAL *)

(* invalid call, since RP is not of type REAL *)
RP := 23.5;
```

RP is *not* of type **REAL**; rather, it is a *pointer to* **REAL**.

It's just as important to avoid mistaking **RP^** for a pointer variable. For example, you can't do something like this:

```
NEW ( RP^);
```

NEW requires a pointer argument, whereas **RP^** is of type **REAL**.

Pointer Assignments

You can assign the contents of one pointer variable to another pointer variable if both pointers are of the same type (that is, both pointers must point to the same type of value). The following program shows how to assign the contents of one pointer variable to another:

P9-4

```
(* Program to illustrate how to assign values to
    pointer variables
*)

PROGRAM PtrDemo3;

(* Define two pointer types: pointer to REAL and to INTEGER *)
TYPE IntPtr = ^INTEGER;
     RealPtr = ^REAL;

(* Declare four pointer variables *)
VAR IP, IP2 : IntPtr;
    RP, RP2 : RealPtr;

BEGIN
  WRITELN ( 'MEMAVAIL = ', MEMAVAIL : 10, ' bytes');
  (* Allocate storage for a REAL; RP will point to it *)
  NEW ( RP);
  (* Assign 23.5 to RP's target variable *)
  RP^ := 23.5;

  (* Assign the address stored in RP to RP2.
     After that, both will have the same target variable.
     This target variable will have 2 names: RP^ and RP2^
  *)
  RP2 := RP;
  WRITELN ( 'RP^ = ', RP^ : 10 : 5, '; RP2^ = ', RP2^ : 10 : 5);

  (* Allocate storage for an INTEGER; IP will point to it *)
  NEW ( IP);
  (* Assign 23 to IP's target variable *)
  IP^ := 23;
  WRITELN ( 'RP^ = ', RP^ : 10 : 5, '; IP^ = ', IP^ : 5);

  WRITELN ( 'MEMAVAIL = ', MEMAVAIL : 10, ' bytes');
  READLN;
END.
```

Remember that the pointer variables are stored in the data or stack segment (depending on whether these variables are global or local), while the target variables are stored on the heap. Although there are four pointers in this program, there are only two target values—indicated by the fact that the program only uses eight bytes of heap storage.

Once both pointers have the same value, you'll have two names for the same area of memory: **RP^** and **RP2^**. This is known as *aliasing,* and can cause problems if you're not careful.

Because a particular area of memory has multiple names associated with it, your program has various ways to change the value stored at this location. This makes it more difficult to trace errors that might involve the value stored at such a location. For example, run the following program. Enter a large value and then enter a small value (between 0 and 1). Look at the source code to see how **RP^** changes. To see the changes from another perspective, use **RP^** and **RPL^** as watch variables (CTRL-F7) in the IDE and then trace through the program as it executes.

P9-5
```
(* Program to illustrate how to change a value by using
   an alias.
*)

PROGRAM AliasDemo;

TYPE RealPtr = ^REAL;
VAR RP, RP2 : RealPtr;

  PROCEDURE GetReal ( Message : STRING;
                            VAR Value : REAL);
  BEGIN
    WRITE ( Message, ' ');
    READLN ( Value);
  END; (* GetReal *)

  (* Change ThePtr's target value:
     small values (between 0 and 1) become large;
     other values become small.
  *)
  PROCEDURE Transform ( VAR ThePtr : RealPtr);
  CONST MultFactor = 1000.0;
  BEGIN
    IF ( ThePtr^ >= 0) AND ( ThePtr^ < 1.0) THEN
      ThePtr^ := MultFactor * ThePtr^
    ELSE
      ThePtr^ := 1 / ThePtr^;
  END; (* Transform *)

BEGIN
  (* Allocate storage for a REAL; RP will point to it *)
  NEW ( RP);
  REPEAT
```

```
    GetReal ( 'Value? (< 0 to stop)', RP^);
    (* Make RP2 point to the same location, so that this
       location now has two names: RP^ and RP2^
    *)
    RP2 := RP;
    WRITELN ( 'RP^ = ', RP^ : 10 : 5);

    (* Change a target value;
       note that no mention is made of RP.
    *)
    Transform ( RP2);

    (* Although it was never used explicitly,
       RP^ has a new value.
    *)
    WRITELN ( 'After Transform:');
    WRITELN ( 'RP^ = ', RP^ : 10 : 5);
  UNTIL ( RP^ < 0);
  READLN;
END.
```

This program essentially converts large values to small ones, and vice versa. The user enters a value, which is stored at **RP^**. **RP^** is used only in the call to **GetString** and in two calls to **WRITELN**; nonetheless, its value is changed. The program is interesting because of how this is accomplished.

After assigning a value to **RP^**, the program makes a second pointer refer to the same memory location by assigning the address stored in **RP** to **RP2**. At this point, both **RP** and **RP2** contain the same address.

The call to **Transform** involves only the pointer **RP2** explicitly. No mention is made of a target variable. However, a pointer almost always has a target variable associated with it. If you can determine the pointer's contents (to find out the address stored there), you can change the value stored at the pointer's target. In this case, however, the target's location also has another name in the main program: **RP^**. Thus, when you change **ThePtr^** in **Transform**, you're also changing **RP^**.

Notice that **Transform** has a **VAR** parameter. Notice also that the procedure doesn't really change the value of **RP2**. In other words, this could be a value parameter and you would still get the same results. Remove the **VAR** from the interface for **Transform** and then run the program again. For the same input values, you'll get the same results.

To see why this is the case, you will work with a simplified concept of an address. Assume that memory addresses are simply integer values within a given range. (The address stored in a pointer variable actually consists of two two-byte portions — one represents a segment in memory and the other represents an offset from the start of that segment.)

Suppose that the address stored in **RP2** (and **RP**) is 5000. Now suppose that the program calls **Transform** and passes **RP2** by value. The contents of **RP2** will be copied and passed into the procedure. Within **Transform** the value 5000 would still be interpreted as an address. Thus **ThePtr^** would be interpreted as the value stored at location 5000. If this value is changed, it will still be changed when the procedure finishes executing. The value stored at **RP2** is not accessible, even if the target associated with this value is. Thus, when you pass a pointer by value, you can change the contents of the pointer's target, but not of the pointer itself.

Assigning Addresses to Pointers

So far, you have initialized pointers by calling **NEW** or by assigning the contents of another pointer variable to the pointer. Turbo Pascal also allows you to assign the address of a specific variable to a pointer — even if that variable is statically defined.

The Address Operator   Turbo Pascal provides an operator (**@**) and a function (**ADDR**) for determining an address. The *address operator* (**@**) produces the location of its argument, which must be a variable, a parameter, or a routine. Thus, **@** takes an argument that has a memory location and returns the location of this object. **@** is a unary operator and has the highest precedence.

CAUTION   The at sign (**@**) used for the address operator is used in many Pascal implementations as an alternative to the caret (^) for specifying a pointer. You'll need to make changes if you use this operator in Turbo Pascal and then move your programs to different Pascal environments.

The ADDR Function   The **ADDR** function takes a variable identifier or the name of a procedure or function — that is, the name of an object with an associated memory location—and returns the location of that object. Because it returns a memory location, **ADDR** is said to return a pointer. The result from **ADDR** is compatible with all pointer types and can thus be assigned to any pointer variable.

The following program shows how to use **@** and **ADDR** to get an address:

P9-6
```
(* Program to illustrate use of @ and ADDR for specifying
   an address.
*)

PROGRAM AddressOpDemo;

TYPE RealPtr = ^REAL;
VAR RP1, RP2 : RealPtr;
    RVall, RVal2 : REAL;

BEGIN
  RVall := 100.0;
  RVal2 := 200.0;

  (* Assign the address of RVall to RP1 *)
  RP1 := @RVall;
  (* Assign the address of RVall to RP2 *)
  RP2 := ADDR ( RVall);

  IF RP1 = RP2 THEN
    WRITELN ( 'Pointers contain the same address')
  ELSE
    WRITELN ( 'Pointers contain DIFFERENT addresses');

  WRITELN ( 'RP1^ = ', RP1^ : 10 : 5,
            '; RP2^ = ', RP2^ : 10 : 5);

  READLN;
END.
```

Using GETMEM to Allocate Dynamic Storage

In addition to **NEW**, Turbo Pascal has another procedure for dynamic storage allocation. Procedure **GETMEM** takes two arguments: a pointer variable, and a **WORD** value that represents the number of bytes of storage to allocate. For example, the following statement allocates six bytes of storage and assigns the location of these bytes to **PtrVar**:

```
GETMEM ( PtrVar, SIZEOF ( REAL));
```

It's your responsibility to ask for an appropriate amount of storage. For example, the preceding listing assumes that **PtrVar** is a pointer to **REAL**. However, the compiler will dutifully instruct the program to allocate whatever storage you ask for and to make the first argument point to this storage. Allocating too little storage may cause problems during program execution.

To see what can happen if you allocate too little storage, compare the output from the following two programs. Each program has two pointers to **REAL** and allocates storage for both variables. In the first program, **RP1** is assigned the address of a six-byte chunk of memory and **RP2** is assigned the address of a five-byte chunk of memory. Then a value is assigned to each of the targets, **RP1^** and **RP2^**. Trace through this program after setting **RP1**, **RP2**, **RP1^**, and **RP2^** as watch variables. Pointer contents are written in two parts. The second, offset values, should differ by 6.

P9-7
```
(* Program to illustrate use of GETMEM procedure.
   One of the calls to GETMEM allocates too little storage.
   Although this does not cause an error in the current program,
   it is very likely to do so in other circumstances -- such as
   in the program BadGetMemDemo.
   WARNING!!!! Even though this program works, do
   not allocate memory in this way.
*)

PROGRAM GetMemDemo;

TYPE RealPtr = ^REAL;
VAR  RP1, RP2 : RealPtr;

BEGIN
  WRITELN ( 'MEMAVAIL = ', MEMAVAIL : 10, ' bytes');
  GETMEM ( RP1, SIZEOF ( REAL));
  WRITELN ( 'After allocating for RP1^');
  WRITELN ( 'MEMAVAIL = ', MEMAVAIL : 10, ' bytes');
  RP1^ := 111.11;

  (* this call allocates too little storage for a REAL *)
  GETMEM ( RP2, 5);
```

```
      WRITELN ( 'After allocating for RP2^');
      (* Note that only 5 bytes have been used *)
      WRITELN ( 'MEMAVAIL = ', MEMAVAIL : 10, ' bytes');
      RP2^ := 222.22;
      (* Value of RP2^ will be correct, but purely by chance. *)
      WRITELN ( 'RP1^ = ', RP1^ : 10 : 5,
                '; RP2^ = ', RP2^ : 10 : 5);
      READLN;
   END.
```

When the program assigns **222.22** to **RP2^**, it uses six bytes to represent the value. The program is actually using an unallocated byte, since the Heap Manager assumes that only five bytes have been allocated at the location. Similarly, when the program is asked to display a **REAL** (such as **RP2^**), it reads six bytes, beginning at the variable's starting location. In the first program, this works out, since nothing has been written in heap locations after **RP2^**.

In the second program, the same actions are carried out. This time, however, the *first* pointer is allocated a five-byte chunk. This means that the second pointer's target will begin at a location that is only five bytes from the location of **RP1^**. Notice what happens when the program runs.

P9-8
```
(* Program to illustrate use of GETMEM procedure.
   Program also illustrates what can happen if you
   don't allocate the correct amount of storage.
   WARNING!!!! Do not allocate memory in this way.
*)

PROGRAM BadGetMemDemo;

TYPE RealPtr = ^REAL;
VAR  RP1, RP2 : RealPtr;

BEGIN
   WRITELN ( 'MEMAVAIL = ', MEMAVAIL : 10, ' bytes');
   (* this call allocates too little storage for a REAL *)
   GETMEM ( RP1, 5);
   WRITELN ( 'After allocating for RP1^');
   (* Note that only 5 bytes have been used *)
   WRITELN ( 'MEMAVAIL = ', MEMAVAIL : 10, ' bytes');
   RP1^ := 111.11;

   GETMEM ( RP2, SIZEOF ( REAL));
   WRITELN ( 'After allocating for RP2^');
   WRITELN ( 'MEMAVAIL = ', MEMAVAIL : 10, ' bytes');
   RP2^ := 222.22;
```

```
(* Value of RP1^ will be incorrect, because part of
   the value will be taken from the bit pattern for RP2^.
*)
WRITELN ( 'RP1^ = ', RP1^ : 10 : 5,
          '; RP2^ = ', RP2^ : 10 : 5);
READLN;
END.
```

When this program displays the value of **RP1ˆ**, it again reads and displays six bytes. This time, however, the sixth byte actually corresponds to the first byte of **RP2ˆ**. Consequently, the value of **RP1ˆ** is incorrect.

If you trace through this program as you did the previous one, you'll note that the addresses stored in **RP1** and **RP2** differ by only 5, and that the value of **RP1ˆ** changes as soon as **RP2ˆ** is assigned a value.

CAUTION   It's your responsibility to allocate the appropriate amount of storage when you call **GETMEM**.

Pointer Pitfalls

Pointers are a powerful programming aid. This power has its price, however, and if you're not careful, you can get yourself into a great deal of trouble. This section looks at a problem that can arise when you use pointers.

Reusing a Pointer

As you've seen, pointers generally get their target variables from the program's heap—through dynamic memory allocation. But what happens if you reuse a pointer already associated with a memory location? As an example, the following program shows what happens if you call **NEW** several times, with the same pointer as an argument each time:

P9-9
```
(* Program to illustrate how to reuse a pointer,
   and also what happens when you do so.
*)
```

```
PROGRAM ReUseDemo;

CONST MaxTimes = 20;
TYPE RealPtr = ^REAL;
VAR RP : RealPtr;
    Count : INTEGER;

  (* Allocate storage for a REAL, generate a random value
     and assign the value to newly allocated storage.
     NOTE that this procedure has a VAR parameter.
  *)
  PROCEDURE GetVal ( VAR ThePtr : RealPtr;
                         Count : INTEGER);
  BEGIN
    NEW ( ThePtr);
    ThePtr^ := RANDOM;
    WRITELN ( Count : 2, ': ThePtr^ = ', ThePtr^ : 10 : 5);
  END; (* GetVal *)

BEGIN
  RANDOMIZE;
  WRITELN ( 'MEMAVAIL = ', MEMAVAIL : 10, ' bytes');
  FOR Count := 1 TO MaxTimes DO
    GetVal ( RP, Count);
  WRITELN ( '      RP^     = ', RP^ : 10 : 5);
  (* Note that MaxTimes * 6 bytes of storage have been used *)
  WRITELN ( 'MEMAVAIL = ', MEMAVAIL : 10, ' bytes');
  READLN;
END.
```

This program calls a procedure multiple times. Each time, this procedure allocates storage for a **REAL**, and makes **ThePtr** reference this variable. (Here **ThePtr** corresponds to the global **RP**.) After doing this the required number of times, the program checks on the available heap storage.

Notice that the program has lost 120 bytes of heap. At the end of the program, however, there is only one **RP^**. The other 19 have been lost. With each call to **NEW**, the contents of **ThePtr** are changed. By writing over an address, the program loses access to the memory location stored there. This inability to reuse pointers is a severe handicap. Fortunately, there is a very elegant way around this obstacle. The solution enables you to create some very powerful data structures, such as linked lists. You'll learn about such methods later in the section "Linking Self-Referential Structures."

Returning Storage to the Heap

You can return storage to the heap. This process is also known as *deallocation,* and makes the storage available for reuse. The predefined **DISPOSE** procedure enables you to return storage that had been allocated with **NEW**. The procedure takes a pointer as its parameter and returns the storage allocated for the pointer's target variable to the heap for reuse. Run the following program and compare its output to that for **ReUseDemo**:

P9-10
```
(* Program to illustrate how to return storage to the
     heap for reuse.
*)

PROGRAM ReturnDemo;

CONST MaxTimes = 20;
TYPE RealPtr = ^REAL;
VAR RP : RealPtr;
    Count : INTEGER;

   (* Allocate storage for a REAL, generate a random value
      and assign the value to newly allocated storage.
      NOTE that this procedure has a VAR parameter.
      NOTE also that the procedure first gives back some storage.
   *)
   PROCEDURE GetVal ( VAR ThePtr : RealPtr;
                          Count : INTEGER);
   BEGIN
     DISPOSE ( ThePtr);
     NEW ( ThePtr);
     ThePtr^ := RANDOM;
     WRITELN ( Count : 2, ': ThePtr^ = ', ThePtr^ : 10 : 5);
   END; (* GetVal *)

BEGIN
  RANDOMIZE;
  WRITELN ( 'MEMAVAIL = ', MEMAVAIL : 10, ' bytes');
  (* Necessary because GetVal calls DISPOSE *)
  NEW ( RP);
  FOR Count := 1 TO MaxTimes DO
    GetVal ( RP, Count);
  WRITELN ( '    RP^    = ', RP^ : 10 : 5);
  (* Note that only 6 bytes of storage have been used *)
  WRITELN ( 'MEMAVAIL = ', MEMAVAIL : 10, ' bytes');
  READLN;
END.
```

The major difference between the two programs is that the preceding program uses only six bytes of heap, whereas **ReUseDemo** uses 120 bytes. This is because the pointer's target variable is returned to the heap before a new location is stored in **ThePtr**.

DISPOSE causes a run-time error if its pointer argument has no associated target variable. The call to **NEW** in the main program is needed to avoid such an error. You can only use **DISPOSE** with pointers that have been assigned values with **NEW**.

Using FREEMEM to Return Allocated Storage

To return storage allocated with **GETMEM**, Turbo Pascal provides the **FREEMEM** procedure. This procedure takes two arguments: a pointer type and a **WORD** that represents the number of bytes to return to the heap.

The following program shows how to use the **FREEMEM** procedure:

P9-11
```
(* Program to illustrate use of GETMEM and FREEMEM *)

PROGRAM FreeMemDemo;

TYPE RealArray = ARRAY [ 1 .. 500] OF REAL;
     RAPtr = ^RealArray;
     RealPtr = ^REAL;
     LongIntPtr = ^LONGINT;

VAR RA1 : RAPtr;
    RP1 : RealPtr;
    LP1 : LongIntPtr;

BEGIN
  WRITE ( 'MEMAVAIL = ', MEMAVAIL : 10, ' bytes');
  WRITELN ( '; MAXAVAIL = ', MAXAVAIL : 10, ' bytes');
  GetMem ( RA1, SIZEOF ( RealArray));
  GetMem ( RP1, SIZEOF ( REAL));
  GetMem ( LP1, SIZEOF ( LONGINT));
  WRITELN ( 'After allocating RA1^, RP1^, and LP1^');
  WRITE ( 'MEMAVAIL = ', MEMAVAIL : 10, ' bytes');
  WRITELN ( '; MAXAVAIL = ', MAXAVAIL : 10, ' bytes');
  WRITELN ( '------------');
  WRITELN ( '------------');
```

```
     (* A deallocation must be for EXACTLY the same
        amount of storage as the original allocation.
     *)
     FreeMem ( RA1, SIZEOF ( RealArray));
     FreeMem ( RP1, SIZEOF ( REAL));
     FreeMem ( LP1, SIZEOF ( LONGINT));
     WRITELN ( 'After freeing RA1^, RP1^, and LP1^');
     WRITE ( 'MEMAVAIL = ', MEMAVAIL : 10, ' bytes');
     WRITELN ( '; MAXAVAIL = ', MAXAVAIL : 10, ' bytes');
     READLN;
END.
```

You can only use **FREEMEM** to deallocate storage that was allocated with **GETMEM**. Moreover, you must deallocate *exactly* the same number of bytes that you originally allocated with the call to **GETMEM**.

NIL: A Predefined Value for Pointers

There's another way to avoid calling **DISPOSE** when its pointer argument is undefined. You can use a special address, **NIL**, that is predefined for use with pointers. **NIL** represents a special location that is assigned to pointers to give them an initial value. A pointer whose value is **NIL** does not have a target. However, the contents indicate that the pointer has been initialized — a fact that you can use to control program execution. The following program accomplishes the same thing as program **ReturnDemo**. However, it does not call **NEW** in the main program. Instead, it initializes **RP** to **NIL**.

```
P9-12  (* Program to illustrate how to return storage to the
          heap for reuse.
       *)

       PROGRAM NILDemo;

       CONST MaxTimes = 20;
       TYPE RealPtr = ^REAL;
       VAR RP : RealPtr;
           Count : INTEGER;

          (* Allocate storage for a REAL, generate a random value
             and assign the value to newly allocated storage.
             NOTE that this procedure has a VAR parameter.
             NOTE also that the procedure first gives back some storage.
```

```
*)
PROCEDURE GetVal ( VAR ThePtr : RealPtr;
                       Count : INTEGER);
BEGIN
  IF ThePtr <> NIL THEN
    DISPOSE ( ThePtr);
  NEW ( ThePtr);
  ThePtr^ := RANDOM;
  WRITELN ( Count : 2, ': ThePtr^ = ', ThePtr^ : 10 : 5);
END; (* GetVal *)

BEGIN
  RANDOMIZE;
  WRITELN ( 'MEMAVAIL = ', MEMAVAIL : 10, ' bytes');
  (* Necessary because GetVal calls DISPOSE *)
  RP := NIL;
  FOR Count := 1 TO MaxTimes DO
    GetVal ( RP, Count);
  WRITELN ( '    RP^      = ', RP^ : 10 : 5);
  (* Note that MaxTimes * 6 bytes of storage have been used *)
  WRITELN ( 'MEMAVAIL = ', MEMAVAIL : 10, ' bytes');
  READLN;
END.
```

In this version, **GetVal** simply tests whether **ThePtr** has been initialized to **NIL**. If so, **DISPOSE** is *not* called. It's always a good idea to initialize any pointers that you have by assigning **NIL** to them, as in **NILDemo**.

Self-Referential Structures

So far, you may have gotten the impression that pointers are more trouble than they're worth. This section describes a task for which dynamic memory allocation and the use of pointers are extremely well suited.

Often, a program will use multiple elements of the same type, with the number of elements undetermined until run time. For example, suppose you want to alphabetize the words read from a file, but you don't know in advance the number of words. You should use a dynamic storage allocation strategy for such a task—to allocate the storage for each element as necessary.

The basic data elements in such a program will almost always be some sort of record. In Chapter 7, "Turbo Pascal's Structured Data Types," you learned that a record cannot have itself as a field, but that it *can* have a pointer to another record like itself as a field. For example, consider the following excerpt from a declaration section:

```
TYPE LNodePtr = ^LNode;
     LNode = RECORD
               Info : REAL;
               Next : LNodePtr;
             END; (* LNode RECORD *)

VAR Root : LNodePtr;
```

This listing describes a record called **LNode** that has two fields. The **Info** field stores an item of numerical information. The **Next** field is a pointer to another element of the same type—that is, to another **LNode**. Thus, an **LNode** is a special kind of structure. It contains not only numerical information but the information needed to access another **LNode**. Figure 9-2 shows what an **LNode** might look like.

Linking Self-Referential Structures

If each **LNode** can reference, or point to, another **LNode**, it should be clear that you can build arbitrarily long chains of such structures, linked to one another by their **Next** fields. A *linked list* is a chain of elements, where each element is linked to the next one. (There are other types of chains, such as *trees*.) The individual elements in such a chain are often called *nodes*. The term node is a general one that refers to components in various types of sequences. In the example programs, **LNode** specifies a node for a linked list.

Figure 9-2. *Structure of an LNode*

The first **LNode** in a linked list is often referenced by a pointer to **LNode**—that is, by an ordinary pointer, *not* an **LNode** or **LNode** field. Thus, the **Root** variable declared in the previous listing is an **LNodePtr**, not an **LNode**. The **Next** field of the first **LNode** may, in turn, reference another **LNode**. The list may contain as many **LNodes** as your program can fit in the available heap memory. The value of the **Next** field of the last **LNode** in the list should be **NIL**, to indicate that there are no more nodes.

Figure 9-3 shows a simple linked list that contains three elements. Note again that **Root** is *not* an **LNode** but is rather a pointer to an **LNode** (in other words, a ˆ**LNode**).

Building Linked Lists

A linked list is a dynamic data structure in that its size is not determined until run time. This is different from an array, for which you specify the size and the base type in advance.

You must build a linked list node by node. To add a node to an existing list:

1. Get storage for the node via a call to **NEW** with the appropriate argument.

2. Store your information in the **LNode**.

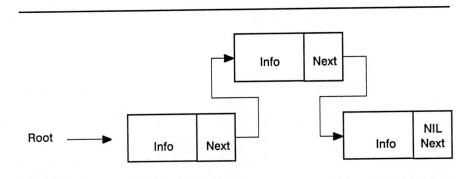

Figure 9-3. *Linked list containing three LNodes*

3. Connect the new node to the existing linked list by making the appropriate pointer from the linked list reference your new node. During this process, the program may also make the **Next** field of the new **LNode** point to an **LNode** already in the list.

Adding at the Front of a Linked List

You can build a linked list in which each new node is added at the front of the list, as shown in the following program:

P9-13
```
(* Program for building a linked list,
     by adding elements to the FRONT of the list.
*)

PROGRAM LListDemo;

TYPE LNodePtr = ^LNode;

     LNode = RECORD
                 Info : REAL;
                 (* a pointer to another record of this type *)
                 Next : LNodePtr;
             END;

VAR Root, Temp : LNodePtr;

   PROCEDURE GetReal ( Message : STRING;
                       VAR Value : REAL);
   BEGIN
     WRITE ( Message, ' ');
     READLN ( Value);
   END; (* GetReal *)

   (* Write the info from each node in a linked list *)
   PROCEDURE WriteList ( VAR TheNode : LNodePtr);
   BEGIN
     WRITELN ( TheNode^.Info : 10 : 5);
     IF ( TheNode^.Next <> NIL) THEN
       WriteList ( TheNode^.Next);
   END; (* WriteList *)

   (* get space for and initialize a linked list node *)
   PROCEDURE InitLNode ( VAR TheNode : LNodePtr);
```

```
BEGIN
  NEW ( TheNode);
  TheNode^.Info := 0.0;
  TheNode^.Next := NIL;
END; (* InitLNode *)

(* insert new node (ToAdd) at the front
   of a linked list (WhereToAdd)
*)
PROCEDURE LLAtFront ( ToAdd : LNodePtr;
                      VAR WheretoAdd : LNodePtr);
BEGIN
  ToAdd^.Next := WhereToAdd;
  WhereToAdd := ToAdd;
END; (* LLAtFront  *)

BEGIN (* Main *)

  (* Initialize the pointers *)
  Root := NIL;
  Temp := NIL;
  REPEAT
    (* Get storage for an LNode, and initialize it *)
    InitLNode ( Temp);
    GetReal ( 'Value (< 0 to stop)', Temp^.Info);
    (* Add new LNode to the front of the existing list *)
    LLAtFront ( Temp, Root);
  UNTIL Temp^.Info < 0.0;
  (* Display contents of the linked list, in order *)
  WriteList ( Root);
  READLN;
END.
```

The program works with **Root** and **Temp**, two pointers to **LNode**. **Root** serves as the permanent anchor for the linked list to be built. Thus, **Root** always points to the first node in the list, although the first node changes as the program executes. You need to go through **Root** to access any element in the list.

Temp "holds" new nodes while they are being initialized and before they are added to the list. The program makes **Temp** point to the storage for each new node and attaches this node to the list. **Temp** is then free to reference the next new **LNode**. By attaching the **LNode** to a list, you keep the storage accessible while freeing **Temp** for another **LNode**. Note that this use of **Temp** actually takes advantage of aliasing.

InitLNode   Procedure **InitLNode** gets the storage required for a new **LNode** and returns a pointer to this storage. As in earlier examples, **NEW** is called for the storage. The argument to **NEW** requests enough new space to store an **LNode**. If the program is unable to allocate storage, a run-time error occurs. Earlier you learned how to avoid this problem.

Make sure that the **Next** field of every new node is initialized to a **NIL** pointer (that is, a pointer whose value is **NIL**). Many list-handling routines look for such a value to determine whether they have reached the end of a list. If you don't initialize these pointers, the last node may not contain a **NIL** pointer, even though it should. The program may then try to read past the end of the list and cause the program to crash.

Notice the syntax for specifying a field in a target variable that also happens to be a record: **TheNode^.Info**, rather than **TheNode.Info^**. The syntax for specifying a target variable is to use the variable's identifier followed by a caret (^). In procedure **InitLNode**, the pointer variable's name is **TheNode**. Once you've specified the target variable, you can access individual fields by using a period followed by the field name.

LLAtFront   After the storage is allocated, the **Info** field of the **LNode** is assigned a value. Then procedure **LLAtFront** is called to insert the new node at the beginning of the existing linked list. Figure 9-4 shows this process for the second node. Notice that, for one statement, both **WhereToAdd** and **ToAdd^.Next** (or **Root** and **Temp^.Next**, respectively, in the main program) point to the same **LNode**.

The basic strategy is first to make the **Next** field of **ToAdd^** reference the current first node. Then the **WhereToAdd** pointer (that is, **Root**) is made to point to the new node. The order of these steps is important. Recall that the only way to access nodes in a list is through the pointer that references the first node. This is because the list anchor is the only statically allocated variable in the linked list and is, thus, the only variable in the list that is directly accessible.

If you first made **WhereToAdd** point to the new node, you would lose access to the rest of the existing list since the assignment would remove the only available access to the first element in the original list (**WhereToAdd^**). Figure 9-5 shows how this might happen. In Part A, the list is properly linked, and the new node is waiting to be added. The

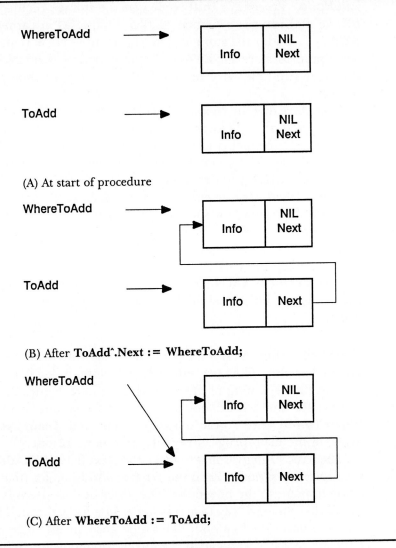

WhereToAdd

ToAdd

(A) At start of procedure

WhereToAdd

ToAdd

(B) After **ToAdd^.Next := WhereToAdd;**

WhereToAdd

ToAdd

(C) After **WhereToAdd := ToAdd;**

Figure 9-4. *Adding a node to the front of a linked list*

list is accessed through **WhereToAdd** (or **Root**, as it's called in the main program).

In Part B, the list anchor points to the new node immediately. You lose the original list since its first element is no longer accessible through the list anchor. To avoid this, you first need to make the **Next** field of

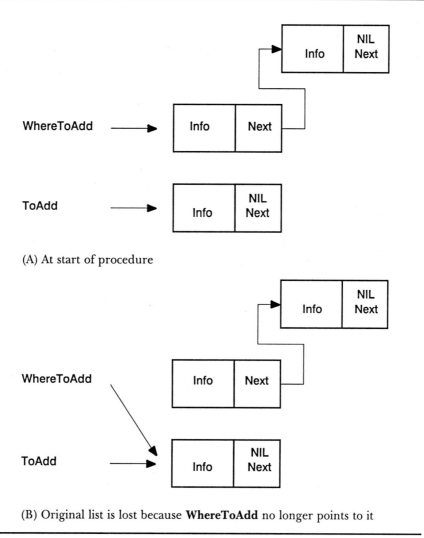

(A) At start of procedure

(B) Original list is lost because **WhereToAdd** no longer points to it

Figure 9-5. *Consequences of mixing up steps when adding to a linked list*

the new node point to the start of the list; only then can you safely "disconnect" the list from its anchor, as in Figure 9-4. Note that this works because **ToAdd** is also accessible through a statically allocated variable.

WriteList This procedure displays the contents of the individual nodes in the linked list, in the order in which they are encountered by the routine. Notice that **WriteList** is recursive. The procedure displays the **Info** field of the current **LNode** and calls a version of itself to handle the next **LNode** in the list. Eventually, the recursive call will be unnecessary because the routine will reach the last node in the list—the one whose **Next** field has the value **NIL**.

Because the instruction to display the **Info** field precedes the recursive call, the nodes are written from first to last. If you position the **WRITELN** call after the recursive call, you can have **WriteList** write the nodes from last to first.

REMEMBER   To access any element in a linked list, you need to start with the pointer to the first element in the list (**Root**, in the main program of several examples).

Adding Elsewhere in a Linked List

You can also build a linked list by adding each new element to the end of the current list, as in the following procedure. To see how **LLAtBack** works, add the procedure definition to the declaration section of the **LListDemo** program. You'll also need to change the call in the main program from **LLAtFront** to **LLAtBack**.

P9-14
```
(* insert a new node (ToAdd) at the back
    of an existing linked list (WhereToAdd)
*)
PROCEDURE LLAtBack ( ToAdd : LNodePtr;
                     VAR WhereToAdd : LNodePtr);
BEGIN
  (* if at the end of the list, can add *)
  IF ( WhereToAdd = NIL) THEN
    WhereToAdd := ToAdd
  ELSE (* if not at the end, keep looking *)
    LLAtBack ( ToAdd, WhereToAdd^.Next);
END; (* LLAtBack *)
```

This procedure adds the new node to the end of the current list. The strategy is to *traverse*, or move through the list until you reach the

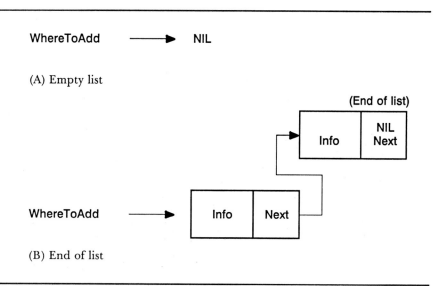

WhereToAdd ———➤ NIL

(A) Empty list

(End of list)

| | NIL |
| Info | Next |

WhereToAdd ———➤ | Info | Next |

(B) End of list

Figure 9-6. *Two places in a linked list with a **NIL** value*

end—where you'll find a pointer with **NIL** as its value. (This is guaranteed because **InitLNode** initializes the **Next** field of each allocated **LNode** to **NIL**.) Figure 9-6 shows the two places in a list where you will find a pointer with a **NIL** value.

If the procedure reaches such a point in the list, the new node is simply added and the modified list is passed back to the calling routine. If there is a node at the current position, the **LLAtBack** procedure calls a version of itself with the **Next** field of the current node (**WhereToAdd^.Next**) as the new argument. When the end of the list is finally reached, the last call to **LLAtBack** returns a list containing the new node to its calling routine. Thus, this outer list will be changed and will pass on this change to its calling routine. At the outermost part of this calling sequence, the list referenced by **Root** will have been changed, which is exactly what you want.

Figure 9-7 shows the logic that controls **LLAtBack**. In the figure, dotted lines indicate the same procedure call. In the first instance, the parameter names are those of the calling routine; in the second instance, the parameter names are those in the procedure itself.

Ordering a Linked List   Sometimes you'll want to order the elements in your list in some way. For example, you might want to order the nodes

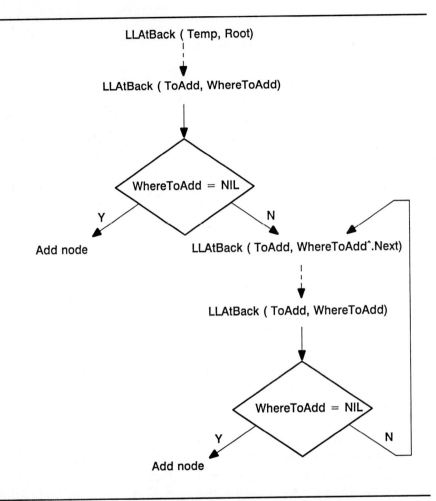

Figure 9-7. *Logic controlling procedure* **LLAtBack( )**

on the basis of numerical value. The following procedure lets you build such an ordered list, putting the node with the lowest value for **Info** at the front of the list. To see how the procedure works, add its source code to **LLListDemo** and change the call in the main program from **LLAtBack** to **LLInMiddle**.

```
P9-15    (* insert new node (ToAdd) in lexicographic position in a
           linked list (WhereToAdd)
         *)
```

```
PROCEDURE LLInMiddle ( ToAdd : LNodePtr;
                       VAR WhereToAdd : LNodePtr);
BEGIN
  (* if at the end, (and not yet added,) add the node *)
  IF ( WhereToAdd = NIL) THEN
    WhereToAdd := ToAdd
  (* if the node should be added at the current spot *)
  ELSE IF ( WhereToAdd^.Info >= ToAdd^.Info) THEN
  BEGIN
    ToAdd^.Next := WhereToAdd;
    WhereToAdd := ToAdd;
  END
  ELSE (* if still not able to add node *)
    LLInMiddle ( ToAdd, WhereToAdd^.Next);
END; (* LLInMiddle *)
```

This procedure resembles each of the other two list-building routines. It moves through the list, comparing the appropriate values of the new node and of the current node in the list. (The current node is the one referenced by the **WhereToAdd** parameter in the function — that is, **WhereToAdd^**.)

If the list is empty or the end of the list has been reached, the new node is simply added, as in **LLAtBack**. If the list value is larger than the value in the node being added, the new node is added before the current node in the list. This process is identical to adding an element at the front of a list. In fact, you are actually adding the new node to the front of a sublist containing only nodes with values greater than the value in the new node. What corresponds to **Root** in this case? If the list value is still smaller than the value in the new node, the program moves to the next node in the list. This should have a larger value, since the list is ordered after each node is added.

Eventually, the new node is added to a list and the modified list is passed back through the calling sequence, until the main program gets the modified list. Figure 9-8 shows the logic controlling **LLInMiddle**.

Example: Sorting Lines from a File

Suppose you want to read the contents of a file and write them to another file — but in alphabetical order. The following program shows how to do this with linked lists. Don't be intimidated — much of the source code is auxiliary routines (such as **ShowProgress** and **FOpened**). The code involving linked lists is actually quite short.

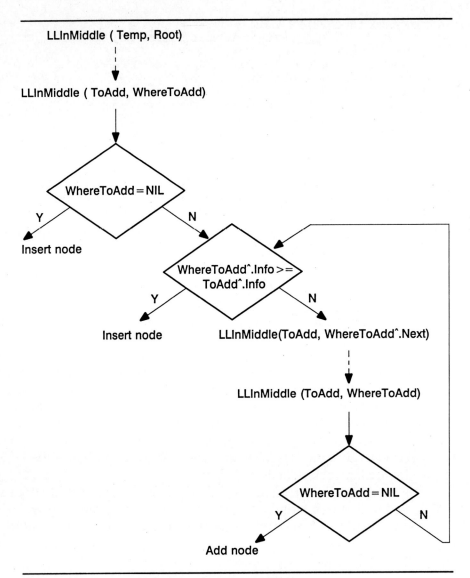

Figure 9-8. *Logic controlling procedure LLInMiddle( )*

P9-16

```
(* Program for sorting lines read from a file,
     and writing them to a new file.
*)

PROGRAM SortLines;

TYPE RegStr = STRING[80];
```

```
            LNodePtr = ^LNode;
            LNode = RECORD
                        Info : RegStr;
                        (* a pointer to another record of this type *)
                        Next : LNodePtr;
                    END;

    VAR Root, Temp : LNodePtr;
        Source, Log : Text;
        SName, LName : STRING;
        NrLines : INTEGER;

    (* ******************                    *************** *)
    (* ****************** Auxiliary Routines *************** *)
    (* ******************                    *************** *)

      (* Open an existing file, doing all necessary
         and warranted checking, and taking all
         precautions.
         Returns TRUE if file was opened; FALSE otherwise.
      *)
      FUNCTION FOpened ( VAR TheFile : Text;
                             FName : STRING) : BOOLEAN;
      BEGIN
        ASSIGN ( TheFile, FName);
        (*$I-*)
        RESET ( TheFile);
        (*$I+*)
        IF IOResult = 0 THEN
          FOpened := TRUE
        ELSE
          FOpened := FALSE;
      END; (* FN FOpened *)


      (* Create a new file, doing all necessary
         and warranted checking, and taking all
         precautions.
         Returns TRUE if file was created; FALSE otherwise.
      *)
      FUNCTION FMade ( VAR TheFile : Text;
                           FName : STRING) : BOOLEAN;
      BEGIN
        ASSIGN ( TheFile, FName);
        (*$I-*)
        REWRITE ( TheFile);
        (*$I+*)
        IF IOResult = 0 THEN
          FMade := TRUE
        ELSE
          FMade := FALSE;
      END; (* FN FMade *)
```

```
      PROCEDURE GetString ( Message : STRING;
                            VAR Value : STRING);
    BEGIN
      WRITE ( Message, ' ');
      READLN ( Value);
    END; (* GetString *)

    (* Write '.' periodically, to let the user know that
       the program is doing something.
       Val is the counter being tested;
       Small is the cycle for a '.'
       Large is the cycle for a WRITELN
    *)
    PROCEDURE ShowProgress ( Val, Small, Large : LONGINT);
    CONST MarkerCh = '.';
    BEGIN
      IF ( Val MOD Small = ( Small - 1)) THEN
        WRITE ( MarkerCh);
      IF ( Val MOD Large = ( Large - 1)) THEN
        WRITELN;
    END; (* ShowProgress *)

(* *****************                       *************** *)
(* ***************** Linked List Routines *************** *)
(* *****************                       *************** *)

    (* get space for and initialize a linked list node *)
    PROCEDURE InitLNode ( VAR TheNode : LNodePtr);
    BEGIN
      NEW ( TheNode);
      TheNode^.Info := '';
      TheNode^.Next := NIL;
    END; (* InitLNode *)

    (* insert new node (ToAdd) in lexicographic position in a
       linked list (WhereToAdd)
    *)
    PROCEDURE LLInMiddle ( ToAdd : LNodePtr;
                           VAR WhereToAdd : LNodePtr);
    BEGIN
      (* if at the end, (and not yet added,) add the node *)
      IF ( WhereToAdd = NIL) THEN
        WhereToAdd := ToAdd
      ELSE (* if the node should be added at the current spot *)
        IF ( WhereToAdd^.Info >= ToAdd^.Info) THEN
        BEGIN
          ToAdd^.Next := WhereToAdd;
          WhereToAdd := ToAdd;
        END
        ELSE (* if still not able to add node *)
          LLInMiddle ( ToAdd, WhereToAdd^.Next);
    END; (* LLInMiddle *)
```

```
    (* Write the info from each node in a linked list.
       Note that this is an iterative routine.
    *)
    PROCEDURE IterFWriteList ( VAR TheFile : Text;
                                   TheNode : LNodePtr);
    BEGIN
      (* Write as long as there's still something to write *)
      WHILE TheNode <> NIL DO
      BEGIN
        WRITELN ( TheFile, TheNode^.Info);
        TheNode := TheNode^.Next;
      END;
    END; (* IterFWriteList *)


BEGIN (* Main *)
  (* Initialize the pointers *)
  Root := NIL;
  Temp := NIL;
  NrLines := 0;
  WRITELN ( 'MEMAVAIL = ', MEMAVAIL : 10, ' bytes');
  GetString ( 'Source file?', SName);
  GetString ( 'Log file?', LName);

  IF FOpened ( Source, SName) AND FMade ( Log, LName) THEN
  BEGIN
    WHILE ( NOT EOF ( Source)) AND
          ( MAXAVAIL > SIZEOF ( LNode)) DO
    BEGIN
      (* Get storage for an LNode, and initialize it *)
      InitLNode ( Temp);
      READLN ( Source, Temp^.Info);
      INC ( NrLines);
      ShowProgress ( NrLines, 5, 250);
      (* Add new line to linked list, which is always sorted *)
      LLInMiddle ( Temp, Root);
    END;  (* WHILE NOT EOF and still heap available *)
    IF NOT EOF ( Source) THEN
      WRITELN ( 'Terminated early; not enough memory.');
    (* Display contents of the linked list, in order *)
    IterFWriteList ( Log, Root);
    CLOSE ( Log);
    CLOSE ( Source);
    WRITELN;
    WRITELN ( NrLines : 5, ' lines processed');
    WRITELN ( 'MEMAVAIL = ', MEMAVAIL : 10, ' bytes');
  END  (* IF FOpened and FMade *)
  ELSE
    WRITELN ( 'File error.');
  READLN;
END.
```

This program reads lines from **Source**, and adds them to a linked list. The nodes in the list are ordered on the basis of the strings (the **Info** fields) in each node. The program then writes the contents of this linked list, in order, to a log file.

Note that the definition of **LNode** in this program differs from the definition in earlier programs. This time, the **Info** field is a **STRING** type rather than a **REAL**. In particular, it is a string with at most 80 characters. By using a limited string size, you can fit many more nodes on the heap.

■ The list-handling routines are called in the main program's **WHILE** loop and in the first statement after this loop. As you saw, the program gets storage for each new line by using **InitLNode**, as in earlier programs.

■ The new storage is added to the existing list by the procedure **LLInMiddle**. This routine is identical to the version in earlier programs. The power of such routines becomes clearer when you consider that the eight or nine lines that make up the procedure body are actually sorting a collection of strings.

■ Finally, the sorted lines are written to a log file by using procedure **IterFWriteList**. This procedure is *not* recursive. A recursive version of this routine can easily exceed the stack limits when there are lots of nodes in the list.

Since the routine is iterative, the local environment only needs to be loaded onto the stack once. The strategy is to move **TheNode** through the list. At each stopping point, the procedure writes the **Info** field, and is ready to proceed.

Notice that the argument passed as the second parameter to procedure **IterFWriteList** is the linked list, anchored by **Root**. This argument is passed by value, which means that a copy of the address stored in **Root** is passed to the procedure. This is why it's safe to change the value of **TheNode** within **IterFWriteList**. Had this been a **VAR** parameter, you would lose your list by using an iterative loop like the one in the procedure.

Notice the continuation condition for the **WHILE** loop in the main program. This condition essentially says that the loop should continue as long as there is something to read from the file and there is heap storage available for the material from the file.

Example: Using More Complex Nodes

The complexity of the nodes that you can create depends on your needs and your imagination. You can accomplish quite a bit by modifying the basic template for an **LNode** that was described earlier. The **LNode** type that you've used in several programs is the basis for building *singly linked lists*. This means that each node in the list points to at most one node in the list. In fact, all nodes except the last point to exactly one node.

You can also create *doubly linked lists*, in which each node points to at most two other nodes. In a common doubly linked list, each node points to the next and preceding nodes in the list. The following listing shows the definitions for a node to be used in a doubly linked list and for a pointer to such a node.

```
TYPE DLLPtr = ^DList;
     DList = RECORD
                 Info : REAL;
                 Next, Preceding : DLLPtr;
             END; (* END DList RECORD *)
```

Doubly linked lists are convenient, since you can traverse the list in both directions instead of having to start at the beginning each time. Having two pointers in the record gives you considerable flexibility. For example, you could use the two pointers to build two different lists— perhaps based on two different items of information. In such a case, each pointer would be used for a different purpose.

For example, this section contains a program that lets you go through a file and count the number of times each word appears in the file. The words are read into a sorted linked list. A frequency is associated with each word and represents the number of times the word appears in the file. Thus, the record structure for such a node will have at least the following three fields: a **STRING** field for the word, an **INTEGER** field for frequency, and a pointer field. In fact, you'll use two pointer fields. One will be used to build a sorted list of words; the second pointer will be used to build a sorted list based on word frequencies. The program will use the following declarations:

```
TYPE ShortStr = STRING [ 30];
     DLNodePtr = ^DLNode;
     (* describe a node for a double linked list *)
```

```
DLNode = RECORD
            Wd : ShortStr;
            (* frequency with which Wd appears *)
            Freq : INTEGER;
            StrNext, FreqNext : DLNodePtr;
         END;  (* DLNode RECORD *)
```

As usual, nodes are represented as records. This time the record has four fields instead of two, however. Essentially, two records share the same structure. The first subrecord is involved in building the word list, and consists of the **Wd** and **StrNext** fields. The other subrecord is used to build the frequency list, and consists of **Freq** and **FreqNext**.

The **FileStats** program in the next listing does the following:

■ Reads from a source file line by line.

■ Adds individual words from each line to a sorted list of words. A **DLNode** is allocated for each word. If a word is already in the list, the program increases the **Freq** field for the word's node in the list. If the word is not yet in the list, the program adds the word at the appropriate place in the list.

■ After the entire source file has been processed, the program builds a second list, based on word frequencies.

Again, don't be intimidated by the program. Well over half of the code performs auxiliary tasks.

P9-17
```
(* Program to read contents of a file, and to analyze word
   frequencies for the file. Program counts the number of times
   each word found in the file appears. After building a sorted
   list based on the word ordering, the program builds a second
   linked list, based on frequencies.
*)

PROGRAM FileStats;

CONST EmptyString = '';
TYPE CharSet = SET OF CHAR;
     ShortStr = STRING[30];

     DLNodePtr = ^DLNode;
     (* describe a node for a double linked list *)
```

```
         DLNode = RECORD
                    Wd : ShortStr;
                    (* frequency with which Wd appears *)
                    Freq : INTEGER;
                    StrNext, FreqNext : DLNodePtr;
                 END;  (* DLNode RECORD *)

(* Note that there are separate anchors for the
   word and frequency lists.
*)
VAR FreqRoot, Root, Temp : DLNodePtr;
    CurrStr, CurrWd : STRING;
    Source, Log : Text;
    SName, LName : STRING;
    NrWds, NrUnique : LONGINT;
    Choice : INTEGER;


(* ******************                     *************** *)
(* ***************** Auxiliary Routines *************** *)
(* ******************                     *************** *)

  (* Remove the first word from a string;
     a word is separated from the next by 1 or more blanks
  *)
  PROCEDURE RemoveWd ( VAR Wd, Sentence : STRING);
  CONST Blank = ' ';
  VAR Where : INTEGER;
  BEGIN
    (* Remove all leading blanks *)
    WHILE POS ( Blank, Sentence) = 1 DO
      DELETE ( Sentence, 1, 1);
    (* Find the next blank in Sentence.
       This will separate the first two words.
    *)
    Where := POS ( Blank, Sentence);
    IF Where > 0 THEN
    BEGIN
      (* Get the first word, but leave the blank *)
      Wd := COPY ( Sentence, 1, Where - 1);
      (* Remove the first word (and blank) from Sentence *)
      DELETE ( Sentence, 1, Where);
    END
    ELSE  (* If no more blanks -- so only 1 word left *)
    BEGIN
      Wd := Sentence;
      (* Close out the sentence *)
      Sentence := EmptyString;
    END;  (* if Sentence contains no more blanks *)
  END;  (* RemoveWd *)


  (* Open an existing file, doing all necessary
     and warranted checking, and taking all
```

```
        precautions.
      Returns TRUE if file was opened; FALSE otherwise.
*)
FUNCTION FOpened ( VAR TheFile : Text;
                      FName : STRING) : BOOLEAN;
BEGIN
  ASSIGN ( TheFile, FName);
  (*$I-*)
  RESET ( TheFile);
  (*$I+*)
  IF IOResult = 0 THEN
    FOpened := TRUE
  ELSE
    FOpened := FALSE;
END; (* FN FOpened *)

(* Create a new file, doing all necessary
    and warranted checking, and taking all
    precautions.
    Returns TRUE if file was created; FALSE otherwise.
*)
FUNCTION FMade ( VAR TheFile : Text;
                    FName : STRING) : BOOLEAN;
BEGIN
  ASSIGN ( TheFile, FName);
  (*$I-*)
  REWRITE ( TheFile);
  (*$I+*)
  IF IOResult = 0 THEN
    FMade := TRUE
  ELSE
    FMade := FALSE;
END; (* FN FMade *)

PROCEDURE GetString ( Message : STRING;
                          VAR Value : STRING);
BEGIN
  WRITE ( Message, ' ');
  READLN ( Value);
END; (* GetString *)

(* Write '.' periodically, to let the user know that
    the program is doing something.
    Val is the counter being tested;
    Small is the cycle for a '.'
    Large is the cycle for a WRITELN
*)
PROCEDURE ShowProgress ( Val, Small, Large : LONGINT);
CONST MarkerCh = '.';
BEGIN
  IF ( Val MOD Small = ( Small - 1)) THEN
    WRITE ( MarkerCh);
```

```
    IF ( Val MOD Large = ( Large - 1)) THEN
      WRITELN;
END; (* ShowProgress *)


(* Convert characters in TheStr to lower case, if
   necessary.
*)
PROCEDURE MakeStrLower ( VAR TheStr : STRING);
CONST Offset = 32;
VAR Index, HowLong : INTEGER;
BEGIN
  HowLong := LENGTH ( TheStr);
  FOR Index := 1 TO HowLong DO
  BEGIN
    IF TheStr [ Index] IN [ 'A' .. 'Z'] THEN
      INC ( TheStr [ Index], Offset);

  END;  (* FOR Index := 1 TO HowLong *)
END;  (* MakeStrLower *)


(* Replace any characters other than those selected. *)
PROCEDURE CleanStr ( VAR TheStr : STRING;
                         TheSet : CharSet);
CONST Blank = ' ';
VAR Index, HowLong : INTEGER;
BEGIN
  HowLong := LENGTH ( TheStr);
  FOR Index := 1 TO HowLong DO
  BEGIN
    IF NOT ( TheStr [ Index] IN TheSet) THEN
      TheStr [ Index] := Blank;
  END;
END; (* Clean Str *)


(* Get an integer lying within the boundaries
   specified by MinVal and MaxVal
*)
PROCEDURE GetBoundedInt ( Message : STRING;
                            MinVal, MaxVal : INTEGER;
                            VAR Value : INTEGER);

  (* Fix boundary values if they are reversed --
     that is, if Small > Large.
  *)
  PROCEDURE AdjustVals ( VAR Small, Large : INTEGER);
  VAR Temp : INTEGER;
  BEGIN
    IF Small > Large THEN
    BEGIN
      Temp := Small;
      Small := Large;
      Large := Temp;
```

```
      END;
    END; (* AdjustVals *)


    (* Return TRUE if Small <= Val <= Large *)
    FUNCTION IsBetween ( Val, Small, Large : INTEGER) : BOOLEAN;
    BEGIN
      IsBetween := ( Small <= Val) AND ( Large >= Val);
    END;  (* FN IsBetween *)

  BEGIN
    AdjustVals ( MinVal, MaxVal);
    REPEAT
      WRITE ( Message, ' ');
      READLN ( Value);
    UNTIL IsBetween ( Value, MinVal, MaxVal);
  END; (* GetBoundedInt *)

(* ******************                  **************** *)
(* **************** Linked List Routines **************** *)
(* ******************                  **************** *)

  (* get space for and initialize a doubly linked list node *)
  PROCEDURE InitDLNode ( VAR TheNode : DLNodePtr);
  BEGIN
    NEW ( TheNode);
    TheNode^.Wd := EmptyString;
    TheNode^.Freq := 0;
    TheNode^.FreqNext := NIL;
    TheNode^.StrNext := NIL;
  END; (* InitDLNode *)

  PROCEDURE IterFWriteDList ( VAR TheFile : Text;
                                  TheNode : DLNodePtr);
  VAR Count : INTEGER;
  BEGIN
    Count := 0;
    WHILE TheNode <> NIL DO
    BEGIN
      WRITELN ( TheFile, TheNode^.Wd, ' : ', TheNode^.Freq);
      INC ( Count);
      TheNode := TheNode^.StrNext;
    END;
    WRITELN ( Count : 4, ' entries in word list');
  END; (* IterFWriteDList *)


  PROCEDURE iIterFWriteDList ( VAR TheFile : Text;
                                   TheNode : DLNodePtr);
  VAR Count : INTEGER;
  BEGIN
    Count := 0;
    WHILE TheNode <> NIL DO
    BEGIN
```

```
        WRITELN ( TheFile, TheNode^.Freq : 4, ' : ', TheNode^.Wd);
        INC ( Count);
        TheNode := TheNode^.FreqNext;
      END;
    WRITELN ( Count : 4, ' entries in frequency list');
  END; (* iIterFWriteDList *)


  (* insert new node (ToAdd) in lexicographic position in a
     linked list (WhereToAdd)
  *)
  PROCEDURE DLLInMiddle ( ToAdd : DLNodePtr;
                        VAR WhereToAdd : DLNodePtr);
  BEGIN
    (* if at the end, (and not yet added,) add the node *)
    IF ( WhereToAdd = NIL) THEN
      WhereToAdd := ToAdd
    (* else if the node should be added at the current spot *)
    ELSE IF ( WhereToAdd^.Wd > ToAdd^.Wd) THEN
    BEGIN
      ToAdd^.StrNext := WhereToAdd;
      WhereToAdd := ToAdd;
    END
    (* else if the word is already in the list,
       just increase the frequency field.
    *)
    ELSE IF ( WhereToAdd^.Wd = ToAdd^.Wd) THEN
    BEGIN
      INC ( WhereToAdd^.Freq);
    END
    ELSE (* if still not able to add node *)
      DLLInMiddle ( ToAdd, WhereToAdd^.StrNext);
  END; (* DLLInMiddle *)


  (* insert new node (ToAdd) in position in a
     linked list (WhereToAdd)
  *)
  PROCEDURE iDLLInMiddle ( ToAdd : DLNodePtr;
                         VAR WhereToAdd : DLNodePtr);
  BEGIN
    (* if at the end, (and not yet added,) add the node *)
    IF ( WhereToAdd = NIL) THEN
      WhereToAdd := ToAdd
    (* else if the node should be added at the current spot *)
    ELSE IF ( WhereToAdd^.Freq <= ToAdd^.Freq) THEN
    BEGIN
      ToAdd^.FreqNext := WhereToAdd;
      WhereToAdd := ToAdd;
    END
    ELSE (* if still not able to add node *)
      iDLLInMiddle ( ToAdd, WhereToAdd^.FreqNext);
  END; (* iDLLInMiddle *)
```

```
BEGIN   (* Main program *)
  WRITELN ( 'MEMAVAIL = ', MEMAVAIL : 10, ' bytes');
  WRITELN ( 'MAXAVAIL = ', MAXAVAIL : 10, ' bytes');
  Root := NIL;
  FreqRoot := NIL;
  Temp := NIL;
  NrWds := 0;
  NrUnique := 0;
  GetString ( 'Source file?', SName);
  GetString ( 'Log file?', LName);

  IF FOpened ( Source, SName) AND FMade ( Log, LName) THEN
  BEGIN
    WHILE ( NOT EOF ( Source)) AND
          ( MAXAVAIL > SIZEOF ( DLNode)) DO
    BEGIN
      (* Read the source file, line by line *)
      READLN ( Source, CurrStr);
      (* homogenize input by making everything lowercase *)
      MakeStrLower ( CurrStr);
      (* Replace any unusual characters with blanks;
         you may want to remove this line.
      *)
      CleanStr ( CurrStr, [ 'a' .. 'z', 'A' .. 'Z', '-', '''']);
      (* process each word on the line; add the word to the
         list, if warranted.
      *)
      REPEAT
        RemoveWd ( CurrWd, CurrStr);
        IF CurrWd <> EmptyString THEN
        BEGIN
          INC ( NrWds);
          ShowProgress ( NrWds, 5, 250);
          (* Allocate storage for the word *)
          InitDLNode ( Temp);
          Temp^.Wd := CurrWd;
          (* The word has appeared at least once *)
          Temp^.Freq := 1;
          (* Add the word to the list *)
          DLLInMiddle ( Temp, Root);
        END;
      UNTIL CurrStr = EmptyString;
    END;  (* WHILE NOT EOF ( Source) AND still heap available *)
    IF NOT EOF ( Source) THEN
      WRITELN ( 'Terminated early; not enough memory.');
    WRITELN;
    WRITELN ( NrWds : 10, ' words');

    (* Start at the front of the WORD list *)
    Temp := Root;
```

```
    (* While not every word has been processed *)
    WHILE Temp <> NIL DO
    BEGIN
       (* Build a sorted list using Frequency fields.
          NOTE use of FreqRoot, since this will be a
          second list -- distinct from the word list.
          Notice, however, that no storage is allocated
          for this second list. The frequency list shares
          the word list's storage.
       *)
       iDLLInMiddle ( Temp, FreqRoot);
       (* The word list will be used to provide the nodes,
          so Temp must follow the StrNext pointers.
       *)
       Temp := Temp ^.StrNext;
    END;

    (* Find out what information user wants to save. *)
    GetBoundedInt ( 'Save by 1) word;  2) frequency; 3) both',
                    1, 3, Choice);
    CASE Choice OF
      1 :
         IterFWriteDList ( Log, Root);
      2 :
         iIterFWriteDList ( Log, FreqRoot);
      3 :
         BEGIN
           IterFWriteDList ( Log, Root);
           WRITELN ( Log, '----------------------------------');
           iIterFWriteDList ( Log, FreqRoot);
         END; (* 3 *)
    END; (* CASE OF Choice *)

    WRITELN ( 'MEMAVAIL = ', MEMAVAIL : 10, ' bytes');
    WRITELN ( 'MAXAVAIL = ', MAXAVAIL : 10, ' bytes');
    CLOSE ( Source);
    CLOSE ( Log);
  END (* IF FOpened and FMade *)
  ELSE
    WRITELN ( 'File error');
  READLN;
END.
```

You can work through the list-building process for each list. The word list is built first. Storage for the nodes is allocated during this part. For each word that the program finds while reading **Source**, procedure **InitDLNode** is called.

After the necessary assignments and updating, the program adds the new word to the word list. This process involves **DLLInMiddle**. This procedure is similar to versions in other programs, but contains an extra **ELSE IF** clause. This clause handles the case where the new word is the same as one in the word list—that is, where

```
WhereToAdd^.Wd = ToAdd^.Wd
```

When this happens, the node is not added to the list. Instead, the value of the **Freq** field of **WhereToAdd^** is incremented by 1. Note that even though the node is not added to the list, the storage for the node is not reused in the example program. This storage will be lost when **InitDLNode** is called again. (You might want to try modifying the program so that you can give back unused storage. This will enable you to process a greater number of different words.)

The frequency list is anchored by **FreqRoot** and is built as follows:

■ The program traverses the word list to ensure that every node is added to the frequency list. **Temp** is used to loop through the word list.

■ The program adds to the frequency list each node in the word list, based on the value of the node's **Freq** field. Procedure **iDLLInMiddle** builds these lists.

Notice that **FreqRoot**, not **Root**, is the second parameter to procedure **iDLLInMiddle**. This is because the word and frequency lists must have different anchors. Even though both lists contain the same nodes, these won't be in the same order.

Notice also that there are no calls to **InitDLNode** in the second part of the **FileStats** program. All of the required nodes have already been allocated. The second part of the program takes advantage of the fact that a **DLNode** has two different pointer fields. This enables you to get "double mileage" out of the nodes. The program uses **IterFWriteList** and **iIterFWriteList**, respectively, to write the word and frequency lists. Both of these procedures are straightforward.

Other Methods for Handling Dynamic Storage: A Preview

When you learn about object-oriented programming in Chapters 11, "Object-Oriented Programming in Turbo Pascal," 12, "Virtual Methods in Object-Oriented Programming," and 13, "Introduction to Turbo Vision," you'll see some other ways to allocate storage dynamically and to initialize objects. This section covers these topics briefly, giving you a preview. You can skip this section if you'd rather wait until Chapter 11 for a more complete discussion.

In object-oriented Turbo Pascal, the syntax for procedures **NEW** and **DISPOSE** has been modified to make it easier to initialize and allocate heap storage for objects. You can call these procedures as you have been. But you can also call them with a second parameter—either a constructor or a destructor.

Constructors and *destructors* are routines, or methods, that are associated with a particular object. Syntactically, a method such as a constructor is similar to a procedure—it carries out some task relating to a particular object. For example, a constructor may initialize the fields of a particular object variable. This constructor can be used by other objects that are defined as special cases of the object with which the constructor was associated.

When using the extended syntax, you can allocate storage for an object variable and initialize this storage with a single call. For example, the following declaration section might appear in a program:

```
TYPE RegStr = STRING [ 80];
     AnimalPtr = ^Animal;
     Animal = OBJECT
                Name : RegStr;
                NrLegs : INTEGER;
                Wt : REAL;
                (* Init and Free are methods associated with
                   Animal. They can be used with any objects
                   that inherit the features of an Animal.
                *)
                CONSTRUCTOR Init ( Str : RegStr;
                                   Legs : INTEGER;
                                   Kg : REAL);
                DESTRUCTOR Free;
              END; (* Animal OBJECT *)

VAR AP1 : AnimalPtr;
```

This declaration defines three types: an 80-character string, a pointer to **Animal**, and an object named **Animal**. This object has three fields, and has two methods associated with it. (You'll learn more about methods in Chapter 11.)

The constructor **Init** presumably initializes the three fields of an **Animal** variable. (In a program, you would need a definition for the constructor.) With the preceding declarations, and with the necessary definitions for the **Init** and **Free** routines, the following would be a valid call to **NEW**:

```
NEW ( AP1, Init ( 'Human', 2, 70));
```

The preceding call

- Allocates enough storage on the heap to store a variable of type **Animal**

- Assigns the location of this chunk of memory to **AP1**

- Assigns the arguments passed to **Init** to the appropriate fields of **AP1^**

Similarly, the following call to **DISPOSE** would also be valid, provided that there had been a corresponding call to **NEW** with **AP1** as the first argument:

```
DISPOSE ( AP1, Free);
```

This would execute the code defined in the destructor, **Free**, associated with **Animal** and would then return the storage allocated for **AP1^**.

In Chapters 11 and 12, you'll learn more about using constructors and destructors to handle dynamic storage, and about using objects.

In this chapter, you learned about Pascal's pointer types. Pointers enable you to use the heap for some of your program's memory requirements. You can allocate and deallocate storage to suit the needs of your program. Pointers also enable you to define self-referential types, which you can use as components in building structures of indeterminate size. You learned how to build linked lists using this technique.

You might want to explore other data structures that involve pointers—for example, trees. If so, look at a more advanced book, such as a textbook used for data structures courses in computer science.

In the next chapter you'll learn about Turbo Pascal's predefined units.

10 *Turbo Pascal Units*

As you've seen, Turbo Pascal has dozens of predefined procedures and functions that you can call in your programs. These include routines for string handling (**INSERT, COPY,** and so on), for mathematical operations (**ARCTAN, FRAC,** and so on), and for miscellaneous tasks (**READ, WRITELN,** and so forth). These routines are incorporated into the Turbo Pascal run-time library (file TURBO.TPL). This library is already compiled and ready to use.

The Turbo Pascal compiler allows you to build your own collection of routines, which you can precompile and incorporate into your programs. Such a collection of routines is called a *unit*. The Turbo Pascal environment already includes several units that you can use in your programs. The following five units are built into the TURBO.TPL run-time library.

- The CRT unit contains definitions and routines for handling input and output and for managing the text screen.

- The DOS unit contains definitions and routines for dealing with the operating system and for accessing DOS services.

■ The OVERLAY unit contains definitions and routines for handling overlays (large program segments that are loaded into memory when needed during execution).

■ The PRINTER unit contains definitions to enable you to send output to a printer using **WRITE** and **WRITELN** commands.

■ The SYSTEM unit contains definitions and routines that are not part of standard Pascal and that are not included in other units.

In addition to these built-in units, Turbo Pascal includes a **GRAPH** unit which contains definitions and routines for managing the graphics screen. The **GRAPH3** and **TURBO3** units are provided for backward compatibility with earlier versions of Turbo Pascal.

Finally, version 6 of Turbo Pascal includes about a dozen additional units to support the language's object-oriented capabilities, especially Turbo Vision.

You'll learn how to create units of your own in Chapter 14, "Miscellaneous Topics." To call routines from these units, you need to include a **USES** statement, such as the following one, which indicates that you want to use routines from three units in your program.

```
USES CRT, DOS, GRAPH;
```

In this chapter, you'll learn a bit about some of the routines defined in several of the units included with Turbo Pascal: **DOS**, **CRT**, and **GRAPH**. Appendix B, "Turbo Pascal Procedures and Functions," contains a complete list of the routines available in these units.

The SYSTEM Unit

The run-time library actually contains a special unit (SYSTEM) designed to be accessible without a **USES** statement. This unit gives you access to the predefined routines described in Chapter 4, "Procedures and Functions," and elsewhere.

The CRT Unit

The routines in the **CRT** unit let you control output to the screen and input from the keyboard. For example, you can move to arbitrary positions on the screen, write with high-intensity characters, and even define windows. Similarly, you can detect when the user has pressed the ALT key or an arrow key on the numeric keypad. You can even check whether the user has pressed any key at all. **CRT** also contains several global variables that will be available to your program.

The routines in this unit provide very fast screen handling because they can bypass your computer's BIOS and access the memory allocated for the screen directly.

Routines for Configuring Your Screen

The **CRT** unit includes several routines that let you determine how your screen should look and where screen activity will take place. When you use the **CRT** module, your screen activity always takes place within a *window*. By default, this window is the entire screen; however, you can redefine the dimensions of your program's window.

The current window has two predefined variables associated with it. **WinMin** and **WinMax** are **WORD**s that represent the upper-left and lower-right corners of the current window. The *x* and *y* coordinates for those locations are stored in separate bytes of each **WORD**. Thus, the byte returned by **LO (WinMin)** contains the *x* coordinate of the upper-left corner of the window; **HI (WinMin)** contains the *y* coordinate. (Recall that **LO** returns the low-order byte of an **INTEGER** or **WORD** argument.) Similarly, the two bytes of **WinMax** contain the lower-right corner's coordinates.

TextMode (WhichMode : WORD)   The **TextMode** procedure lets you select the display mode for the screen you'll be using. This selection depends on your programs' hardware configuration. To select one of these modes, pass any of the following predefined (in **CRT**) constants when calling **TextMode**:

```
(* Text mode settings; NOTE: all are predefined in CRT.
   B/W = black and white.
*)
CONST BW40 = 0;        (* 40x25 B/W, color monitor *)
      CO40 = 1;        (* 40x25 color, color monitor *)
      BW80 = 2;        (* 80x25 B/W, color monitor *)
      CO80 = 3;        (* 80x25 color, color monitor *)
      Mono = 7;        (* 80x25 B/W, monochrome monitor *)
      Font8x8 = 256;   (* 80x43 or 50, EGA/VGA *)
      (* The following settings are *)
      (* for compatibility with Turbo Pascal v3.0 *)
      C40 = CO40;
      C80 = CO80;
```

Calling **TextMode** causes other actions and changes several predefined variables:

■ The default window is redefined as the entire screen.

■ The **BOOLEAN DirectVideo** is set to **TRUE**. This value tells **CRT** routines to use the screen memory directly, bypassing the BIOS and speeding up screen activity. If you don't want to do this, you must set **DirectVideo** to **FALSE** in your program—*after* you've called **TextMode**.

■ A predefined **WORD** variable, **LastMode**, is set to the video mode in effect when you called **TextMode**. By saving this value, your program can restore the screen to the mode that was active before the program started executing. This value is set automatically when your program starts running. It's good programming practice to restore the original mode when your program ends.

■ If you selected a color mode, the **BOOLEAN CheckSnow** is set to **TRUE**. This helps overcome an interference (snow) problem that can occur with CGA monitors.

■ Video intensity is set to normal (as opposed to high or low) intensity. You can also call the predefined procedure **NormVideo** to do this yourself.

See the on-line help for more information about constants and variables defined in the **CRT** unit.

You will sometimes see a call such as the following:

```
TextMode ( LO ( YourMode) + Font8x8);
```

Such a call does two things:

1. Selects the video mode specified in the low-order byte of **YourMode**

2. Switches to 43- or 50-line mode, if you have an EGA or a VGA monitor

To turn 43-line mode off, call

```
TextMode ( LO ( YourMode));
```

TextColor (WhatColor : BYTE)
TextBackGround (WhatColor : BYTE) These two procedures let you
specify the colors to use for the text and background being displayed in
the current window. If you have a monochrome monitor, you can
specify **Black** or **White**; other selections will either be mapped onto black
and white or distinguished by underlining.

For **TextColor**, you can have the following values:

```
CONST Black = 0;          DarkGray = 8;
      Blue = 1;           LightBlue = 9;
      Green = 2;          LightGreen = 10;
      Cyan = 3;           LightCyan = 11;
      Red = 4;            LightRed = 12;
      Magenta = 5;        LightMagenta = 13;
      Brown = 6;          Yellow = 14;
      LightGray = 7;      White = 15;
```

Note that the colors on the left (with values 0..7) have counterparts in the
range 8..15, which are light versions of the lower values.

For **TextBackGround**, the possible values range from **Black** through
LightGray. If you pass a value from the 8..15 range to **Text-
BackGround**, the program will simply substitute the counterpart from
the lower color range. For example, if you specify white as the background color, you'll actually get light gray.

To make characters blink, add 128 to your argument before calling
TextColor. The following call selects white for displaying text and specifies that the displayed material should blink:

```
TextColor ( White + 128);
```

When you call either **TextColor** or **TextBackGround**, you're actually changing the value of a global **BYTE** variable declared in **CRT**. This variable, **TextAttr**, contains three items of information:

■ Foreground (text) color (bits 0..3)

■ Background color (bits 4..6)

■ Blinking (bit 7)

Note that more bits are used for the text color than for the background color. This should not be surprising, since the valid range for background colors is 0..7 (3 bits) and for text colors is 0..15 (4 bits).

ClrScr   The **ClrScr** procedure clears the current window and moves the cursor to its upper-left corner. The procedure clears the window by writing a blank at each position, which makes the entire window the background color.

**Window (UpperLeftX, UpperLeftY, LowerRightX, LowerRightY :
BYTE)**   The **Window** procedure lets you designate an area of the screen to receive all input and output. Once you've specified a window, you can enter information just as if the entire screen were the window. When you reach the end of a "line," the program automatically moves to the beginning of the next line. Similarly, when you reach the bottom of the window, the contents scroll upward, just as when you're using the entire screen.

The following program uses the routines described so far to create several windows with different dimensions and locations. First, run the program to see the output. Note the **USES** statement at the start of the program.

P10-1

```
(* Program to illustrate use of selected routines
     from the CRT unit.
*)

PROGRAM WinDemo;
USES CRT;

    (* Define a window by specifying its boundaries;
       select text and background colors for the window;
       call ClrScr to make the entire window the background color.
    *)
```

```
    PROCEDURE SetWindow ( UX, UY, LX, LY : BYTE;
                             BackGr, ForeGr : BYTE);
    BEGIN
      Window ( UX, UY, LX, LY);
      Textbackground ( BackGr);
      TextColor ( ForeGr);
      ClrScr;
    END;

BEGIN
  SetWindow ( 1,1,80,25,Black,White);
  ClrScr;

  (* Create windows, each of which is smaller than its
     predecessor, and contained within it.
     Each window starts 1 row further down and ends 1 row
     further up than predecessor; column bounds for the
     successive windows also grow toward middle of screen.
     Note that text and background colors are reversed in
     successive windows.
  *)
  SetWindow ( 1, 1, 30, 20, White, Black);
  SetWindow ( 2, 2, 28, 19, Black, White);
  SetWindow ( 3, 3, 26, 18, White, Black);
  SetWindow ( 4, 4, 24, 17, Black, White);
  SetWindow ( 5, 5, 22, 16, White, Black);
  SetWindow ( 6, 6, 20, 15, Black, White);
  SetWindow ( 7, 7, 18, 14, White, Black);
  SetWindow ( 8, 8, 16, 13, Black, White);
  SetWindow ( 9, 9, 14, 12, White, Black);
  SetWindow ( 10, 10, 12, 11, Black, White);
  (* Write a message in the innermost window *)
  WRITE ( 'HI');

  SetWindow ( 41, 1, 70, 20, Black, White);
  SetWindow ( 43, 2, 69, 19, White, Black);
  SetWindow ( 45, 3, 68, 18, Black, White);
  SetWindow ( 47, 4, 67, 17, White, Black);
  SetWindow ( 49, 5, 66, 16, Black, White);
  SetWindow ( 51, 6, 65, 15, White, Black);
  SetWindow ( 53, 7, 64, 14, Black, White);
  SetWindow ( 55, 8, 63, 13, White, Black);
  SetWindow ( 57, 9, 62, 12, Black, White);
  SetWindow ( 59, 10, 61, 11, White, Black);
  WRITE ( 'BYE');
  READLN;
END.
```

The program is long but not complicated. The lines are all calls to the same procedure, with different parameter values each time. Look at the windows on the left half of the screen.

After creating a window of the entire screen, to provide a blank background, the program builds successively smaller windows. The first of these windows starts in the upper-left corner of the screen, which has screen coordinates 1,1. This window is 30 columns wide (from 1 through 30) and 20 rows deep (from 1 to 20). The background color is white and the text color is black. Once this window has been defined, the call to **ClrScr** in **SetWindow** makes the entire window white. This is followed immediately by another call to **SetWindow**. The program uses **Set-Window** instead of the predefined **Window** in order to specify the text and background colors at the same time.

The next window is smaller. It begins at position 2,2 and goes through row 19 and column 28 (the window is only 27 columns wide and 18 columns deep). This window contains white characters on a black background. Again, the call to **ClrScr** makes the entire window black. Note that this leaves the outer rim of the original window. This rim is one column by one row (except on the right side). To see what these two windows look like, insert a call to **READLN** immediately after the second call to **SetWindow** and run the program again. You can also see this by using F7 and F8 in the IDE to trace through the program, stepping over the details of the procedure calls. The right side of the window will shrink more quickly than the left, producing an overall asymmetry in the final window collection.

You create the windows on the right side of the screen in a similar manner, but their left boundary shrinks faster than the right. Notice that the message in the innermost window on the right scrolls out of the window when you press ENTER to end the program. The window is too small to contain the new line added when you press ENTER.

The following program is a more interesting version of **WinDemo**. It creates multiple windows but the windows on a given side change by different amounts on different runs of the program. The program pauses at several points—to let you examine the screen. To continue, just press ENTER.

P10-2
```
(* Program to illustrate use of selected routines from the CRT
   unit. Similar to WinDemo program, except that this program
   varies the design of the windows each time.
*)

PROGRAM WinDemo2;
USES CRT;
```

```
      (* Level represents the position of the window in its
         group; the outermost window is level 0.
      *)
  VAR Level, Index : INTEGER;
      (* UDeltal and LDeltal represent the amount of change
         in left and right column boundaries. U and L are
         used for consistency with the UX and LX parameters
         in the WinDemo program.
      *)
      UDeltal, UDelta2, LDeltal, LDelta2 : INTEGER;

  (* Determine the amount to change each column. *)
  PROCEDURE SetDeltas ( VAR UDeltal, LDeltal : INTEGER);
  BEGIN
    UDeltal := RANDOM ( 3);
    LDeltal := RANDOM ( 3);
  END; (* SetDeltas *)

  (* Define windows, but change the boundaries each time
     the routine is called. Level is used to keep track of
     how much to change the boundary.
  *)
  PROCEDURE FancySetWindow ( UX, UY, LX, LY : BYTE;
                             BackGr, ForeGr : BYTE;
                             VAR Level : INTEGER;
                             UDeltal, LDeltal : INTEGER);
  BEGIN
    Window ( UX + UDeltal * Level, UY + Level,
             LX - LDeltal * Level, LY - Level);
    Textbackground ( BackGr);
    TextColor ( ForeGr);
    ClrScr;
    INC ( Level);
  END;

BEGIN
  Level := 0;
  ClrScr;
  RANDOMIZE;
  SetDeltas (UDeltal, LDeltal);
  SetDeltas (UDelta2, LDelta2);
  WRITELN ( 'UDeltal = ', UDeltal, '; LDeltal = ', LDeltal,
            'UDelta2 = ', UDelta2, '; LDelta2 = ', LDelta2);
  READLN;
  (* Leave text mode in current setting *)
  TextMode ( LastMode);

  (* Create windows, each of which is smaller than its
     predecessor, and which is contained within it.
  *)
  FOR Index := 1 TO 5 DO
  BEGIN
```

```
      FancySetWindow ( 1, 1, 30, 20, White, Black, Level,
                       UDeltal, LDeltal);
      FancySetWindow ( 1, 1, 30, 20, Black, White, Level,
                       UDeltal, LDeltal);
  END;
  (* Write a message in the innermost window *)
  WRITE ( 'HI');
  READLN;

  Level := 0;    (* Need to reinitialize this counter *)
  FOR Index := 1 TO 5 DO
  BEGIN
    FancySetWindow ( 41, 1, 70, 20, Black, White, Level,
                     UDelta2, LDelta2);
    FancySetWindow ( 41, 1, 70, 20, White, Black, Level,
                     UDelta2, LDelta2);
  END;
  WRITE ( 'BYE');
  READLN;
END.
```

Procedure **SetDeltas** determines the amount by which the dimensions of successive windows differ from each other. The procedure can change a dimension by 0, one, or two columns (rows) each time a new window is defined.

Procedure **FancySetWindow** is essentially the same as **SetWindow**, except that it also sets the values for the last column and row in the window.

Pausing During Output: The Delay Procedure

The **CRT** unit includes a procedure that controls the pace at which material appears on the screen. The **Delay** procedure lets you specify the number of milliseconds the program should pause before executing the next statement. For example, the following call waits for ten seconds:

```
Delay ( 10000);
```

Add some calls to **Delay** in the **WinDemo** and **WinDemo2** programs. This will slow down the programs so you can see the individual windows being created.

Selecting Video Intensity

You can display characters at any of three levels of intensity, simply by calling one of three procedures.

HighVideo;
NormVideo;
LowVideo   **HighVideo** selects high-intensity video, which means that the characters appear much brighter than usual on the screen. **Norm-Video** selects the default intensity that you see when you're at the DOS command line, for example. Finally, **LowVideo** selects low-intensity characters.

These changes in video intensity are actually accomplished by switching to different versions of a color. For example, if you select a color in the range 0 through 7, calling **HighVideo** actually switches this to a value in the 8..15 range by adding 8 to your selection. Similarly, calling **LowVideo** subtracts 8 from colors in the 8..15 range. Colors already in the 0..7 range are left unchanged.

The following program lets you see what these levels look like. Try changing the color setting, and observe what happens when you select **HighVideo** and **LowVideo**. For example, if you have a color monitor, see what happens if you select light magenta (13) and call procedure **HighVideo**; then see what happens if you call **LowVideo**. Compare this to what happens if you select magenta (5) and ask for high and low intensity, respectively.

```
P10-3      (* Program to let user explore text and background
              color combinations
           *)

           PROGRAM IntensityDemo;
           USES CRT;
           VAR Fore, Back, Intensity : INTEGER;

             PROCEDURE GetInteger ( Message : STRING;
                                         VAR Value : INTEGER);
             BEGIN
               WRITE ( Message, ' ');
               READLN ( Value);
             END; (* GetInteger *)

             (* Display the names of the specified colors. *)
             PROCEDURE WriteColors ( Back, Fore : INTEGER);
```

```
   CONST Colors : ARRAY [ 0 .. 15] OF STRING [ 13] =
            ( 'black', 'blue', 'green', 'cyan', 'red', 'magenta',
              'brown', 'light gray', 'dark gray', 'light blue',
              'light green', 'light cyan', 'light red',
              'light magenta', 'yellow', 'white');
   BEGIN
     WRITELN ( 'Background color = ', Colors [ Back]);
     WRITELN ( 'Foreground color = ', Colors [ Fore]);
   END;

BEGIN
  REPEAT
    GetInteger ( 'Background color (-1 to stop)', Back);
    IF Back >= 0 THEN
    BEGIN
      GetInteger ( 'Foreground color', Fore);
      GetInteger ( '1) High or 2) Low intensity', Intensity);
      TextBackground ( Back);
      TextColor ( Fore);
      ClrScr;
      IF Intensity = 1 THEN
        HighVideo
      ELSE
        LowVideo;
      WriteColors ( Back, Fore);
    END;
  UNTIL  Back < 0;
END.
```

Moving in a Window

The **CRT** unit also has routines for checking where you are in a window and for moving to an arbitrary location in a window.

GoToXY (ColumnPos, RowPos : BYTE) The **GoToXY** procedure moves the cursor to the position specified by the two **BYTE** arguments. The first argument specifies the column (that is, the horizontal, or x, position); the second argument specifies the row (vertical, or y, position). The location is always relative to the current window, and must be a location in this window. If the coordinates are invalid, the program ignores the call to **GoToXY**.

The following program moves to random locations on the screen and writes the coordinates of that point. It then defines a smaller window and moves the cursor to random positions within this window.

P10-4

```
(* Program to illustrate use of GoToXY routine.
   Program defines a window and then writes coordinates
   of random characters in the window.
*)
PROGRAM GoToXYDemo;
USES CRT;

CONST MaxTrials = 6;
VAR Index, MaxRow, MaxCol, NewCol, NewRow : BYTE;

   (* Define a window by specifying its boundaries;
      select text and background colors for the window;
      call ClrScr to make the entire window the background color.
   *)
   PROCEDURE SetWindow ( UX, UY, LX, LY : BYTE;
                         BackGr, ForeGr : BYTE);
   BEGIN
     Window ( UX, UY, LX, LY);
     Textbackground ( BackGr);
     TextColor ( ForeGr);
     ClrScr;
   END;

   (* Select a random point to display *)
   PROCEDURE GetSpot ( VAR Col, Row : BYTE);
   BEGIN
     (* Use MaxCol-4 so there's room to write coordinates *)
     Col := RANDOM ( MaxCol-4) + 1;
     Row := RANDOM ( MaxRow) + 1;
   END; (* GetSpot *)

   (* display a collection of random dots in a window *)
   PROCEDURE ShowSpots ( NrTrials : BYTE);
   VAR Index : BYTE;
   BEGIN
     GoToXY ( 1,1);
     WRITE ( '*1,1');
     READLN;
     FOR Index := 1 TO NrTrials DO
     BEGIN
       GetSpot ( NewCol, NewRow);
       GoToXY ( NewCol, NewRow);
       WRITE ( '*', NewCol, ',', NewRow);
       READLN;
     END;
   END;  (* ShowSpots *)

BEGIN
  RANDOMIZE;
  SetWindow ( 1,1,80,25,Black,White);
  MaxRow := 24;
```

```
    MaxCol := 79;
    WRITELN ( 'Using entire screen. ');
    WRITELN ( 'During display, press ENTER to continue.');
    READLN;
    ClrScr;
    ShowSpots ( MaxTrials);
    ClrScr;
    GoToXY ( 1, 1);
    WRITELN ( 'Using smaller window.');
    SetWindow ( 11, 5, 60, 20 , White, Black);
    MaxCol := 50;
    MaxRow := 15;

    ShowSpots ( MaxTrials);
    READLN;
END.
```

If you run this program often enough, you'll get two points that almost overlap, so that one erases all or part of the information about the other. Modify the program to keep track of whether it has visited a point in the vicinity, so it will not overwrite points already visited.

WhereX : BYTE

WhereY : BYTE   The **WhereX** and **WhereY** functions return the current x and y coordinates relative to the current window. These coordinates are particularly useful if your program needs to respond to the arrow keys on the numeric keypad, as discussed in the next section.

The following listing shows how to call these functions:

```
(* Assume CurrXPos and CurrYPos are of type BYTE *)

CurrXPos := WhereX;
CurrYPos := WhereY;
```

Reading Input

The **READ** and **READLN** procedures enable you to read input from the user or from a file. The **ReadKey** function defined in **CRT** also enables you to get input from the user. **ReadKey** gets a character from the keyboard but does not echo this key. If you want to display the key, you need to do so explicitly in your program.

Unlike **READLN**, the **ReadKey** routine can distinguish special keys, such as function keys, combinations involving ALT, and also keys from the numeric keypad. Each key has a special code associated with it, known as the key's *scan code*. When you type an ordinary character, the resulting scan code is simply the character's ASCII code. When you type a special key, **ReadKey** returns an *extended scan code* for the key. The first part of an extended scan code is always **#0**. This is essentially the prefix for a special key code, and tells your program to look at the next scan code.

This additional scan code is already present as part of your previous key press. Thus, you don't need to press two keys to get these two codes; you do need to call **ReadKey** again. For example, if you press the LEFT ARROW on the numeric keypad, function **ReadKey** returns an extended scan code. The first part will be **#0**. The second code (which you get by calling **ReadKey** again in your program) will be **#75** to indicate the LEFT ARROW key.

CAUTION   Don't confuse a scan code for an ordinary character and an extended scan code for a special character.

The following loop shows how you would look for special keys:

```
(* Assume Ch has been declared as a CHAR *)

Ch := ReadKey;
IF Ch = #0 THEN
BEGIN
  (* Call ReadKey again, but do NOT press another key. *)
  Ch := ReadKey;
  (* some sort of CASE statement to consider all the
     scan values of interest.
  *)
END
ELSE
  WRITE ( Ch);
```

The following program lets you explore your keyboard. When you run the program, you can press the function keys (as well as all these keys in combination with SHIFT), keys on the numeric keypad, and so forth. When you press such a key, the program displays the extended scan code and enables you to provide a description. You can type a string that explains the code. The program continues when you press

ENTER. The extended scan code and your explanations are written to a file, which you can use for reference.

P10-5
```
(* Program to illustrate how to check for special keys.
   Program lets user press a special key, write the
   extended scan code to a file, and write a description
   of the key to a file.
*)

PROGRAM ScanDemo;
USES CRT;

CONST StopChar = '!';
(* Scan codes and descriptions will be written to Log *)
VAR Log : Text;
    LName, KeyName : STRING;
    Ch : CHAR;

  PROCEDURE GetString ( Message : STRING;
                        VAR Value : STRING);
  BEGIN
    WRITE ( Message, ' ');
    READLN ( Value);
  END; (* GetString *)

  PROCEDURE Introduction;
  BEGIN
    WRITELN ( 'Press various keys, including special keys.');
    WRITELN ( 'When you get a scan code prompt, enter a');
    WRITELN ( ' label for the special key you pressed.');
    WRITELN ( StopChar, ', to stop.');
    GoToXY ( WhereX, WhereY + 2);
  END; (* Introduction *)

BEGIN
  (* Don't respond to CTRL-C as a request to end the program. *)
  CheckBreak := FALSE;
  TextMode ( LastMode);
  Introduction;

  GetString ( 'Log file name?', LName);
  ASSIGN ( Log, LName);
  REWRITE ( Log);

  REPEAT
    (* get a key press *)
    Ch := ReadKey;
    (* if it's a special key, process further *)
    IF Ch = #0 THEN
    BEGIN
      (* this information is already there; user need not
         press another key to be read here.
```

```
            *)
            Ch := ReadKey;
            (* Write the scan code to Log *)
            WRITE ( Log, ORD ( Ch), ': ');
            WRITE ( ORD ( Ch), ': ');
            (* Wait for user to enter a description of the key. *)
            READLN ( KeyName);
            WRITELN ( Log, KeyName);
          END
          ELSE
            WRITELN ( ORD ( Ch), ': ', Ch);
      UNTIL  Ch = StopChar;
      CLOSE ( Log);
END.
```

If you run this program, you can create a list of scan codes associated with the special keys. For example, the following listing shows some codes that you might write to a file, using the program.

```
71: Home
72: Up
73: PgUp
75: Left
77: Right
79: End
80: Down
81: PgDn
82: Ins
83: Del
```

These values represent the extended scan codes for the keys on the numeric keypad. The scan codes are valid only if NUMLOCK is off; if it is on, pressing the LEFT ARROW key, for example, sends the digit 4, which has a different scan code.

The extended scan values have no intrinsic meaning and do not cause any actions on their own. For example, if you press the RIGHT ARROW key—that is, if your program reads an extended scan code of 77—the cursor does not move. You need to use **GoToXY** to move the cursor over one column to the right, as in the following program:

```
P10-6   (* Program to exercise various CRT routines.
            Program also lets user use arrow keys.
            After user presses ESC, program waits 3.5 seconds,
            then terminates.
        *)

        PROGRAM GoToXYDemo2;
        USES CRT;
```

```
    VAR LastCol, LastRow : BYTE;
        OrigMode : WORD;

    (* Make a window with the specified upper left and lower
       right corners; set the background and text color;
       and set the last row and column for the window.
    *)
    PROCEDURE MakeWindow ( UX, UY, LX, LY : BYTE;
                           BackColor, ForeColor : BYTE;
                           VAR LastRow, LastCol : BYTE);
    BEGIN
      WINDOW ( UX, UY, LX, LY);
      TextBackground ( BackColor);
      TextColor ( ForeColor);
      ClrScr;
      LastCol := LX - UX + 1;
      LastRow := LY - UY + 1;
    END; (* MakeWindow *)

    (* Let user type in the window, or move around using the
       arrow keys. User presses ESC to end the program.
    *)
    PROCEDURE Draw;
    VAR Done : BOOLEAN;
        Ch : CHAR;
        CurrX, CurrY : BYTE;

    BEGIN  (* Draw *)
      Done := FALSE;

      (* read user's key presses until  user presses ESC *)
      REPEAT
        Ch := ReadKey;
        CASE Ch OF
          (* if user pressed a special key, check which one *)
          #0 :
            BEGIN
              (* get the extended part of the scan code *)
              Ch := ReadKey;
              CASE Ch OF
                #72 : GoToXY ( WhereX, WhereY - 1);  (* Up *)
                #75 : GoToXY ( WhereX - 1, WhereY);  (* Left *)
                #77 : GoToXY ( WhereX + 1, WhereY);  (* Right *)
                #80 : GoToXY ( WhereX, WhereY + 1);  (* Down *)
                ELSE ; (* do nothing *)
              END; (* CASE OF Special Ch *)
            END; (* #0 value -- i.e. a special key *)
          (* if user presses enter move to start of next line *)
          #13 : GoToXY ( 1, WhereY + 1);
          (* if user presses ESC, return to main program. *)
          #27 : Done := TRUE;
```

```
                  (* if not a special key or ENTER or ESC *)
                ELSE  WRITE ( Ch);
            END; (* CASE OF Ch *)
        UNTIL Done = TRUE;
      END;    (* Draw *)

      PROCEDURE Introduction;
      BEGIN
        WRITELN ( 'Type anything you want in the window below.');
        WRITELN ( 'Use arrow keys to move around in window.');
        WRITE ( 'Press ESC to end the program.');
      END; (* Introduction *)

BEGIN
   OrigMode := LastMode;
   TextMode ( LastMode);

   MakeWindow ( 1, 1, 50, 3, Black, White, LastRow, LastCol);
   Introduction;

   (* Make 2 windows, one nested in the other. By reversing the
      background and text colors for the inner window, you get a
      border around the window in which the user will work.
   *)
   MakeWindow ( 15, 5, 60, 20, White, Black, LastRow, LastCol);
   MakeWindow ( 16, 6, 59, 19, Black, White, LastRow, LastCol);

   Draw;

   GoToXY ( 1, LastRow);
   Textbackground ( White);
   TextColor ( Black);
   WRITE ( 'Done. Program will end in 3.5 seconds.');

   (* Wait 3.5 seconds, then terminate *)
   DELAY ( 3500);
   TextMode ( OrigMode);
END.
```

Run the program, typing whatever you wish in the window. To move to the next line, press ENTER. To change something in an earlier line, use the arrow keys to move to the desired spot. If you type new material, note that the old contents of the window are simply overwritten. When you're finished, press ESC. The program waits 3.5 seconds because of the call to **Delay** and then terminates.

Procedure **MakeWindow** does the administrative work needed to define and configure a window. This procedure is an expanded version of **SetWindow** from earlier programs. The procedure creates the boundary around the window by defining two windows—one inside the other. The outer window has a white background and is larger than the inner one, which has a black background. The boundary is possible because **ClrScr** only clears the current window. Thus, when **ClrScr** is called to clear the inner window, it clears only columns 16 through 59 and rows 6 through 19.

Procedure **Draw** reads the user's input, echoing the ordinary characters and carrying out the desired cursor movement when you type a special character. When **ReadKey** reads a special character, the first scan code returned is **#0**. With this result, there will always be another scan code available for the function—this second scan code represents the special key. The **Draw** procedure is set to handle the four arrow keys.

Note that the last output line in **Introduction** uses **WRITE** rather than **WRITELN**. Since the window is only three lines deep the top line would scroll out of the window if you called **WRITELN** here.

KeyPressed : BOOLEAN The **CRT** unit also contains a function that checks whether a key has been pressed. If so, this function returns **TRUE**; it returns **FALSE** otherwise. The **KeyPressed** function is most useful when you need to check periodically whether the user has pressed a key or when you want to prompt the user if no key has been pressed within a particular amount of time.

Inserting and Deleting Text in a Window

The **CRT** unit also contains routines for deleting part or all of a line in your window and a routine for inserting a blank line in the window.

ClrEol
DelLine Procedure **ClrEol** deletes the contents of the current line from the column in which the cursor is located to the end of the line. This procedure replaces these columns with blanks, so that the deleted part of the line becomes the background color.

Procedure **DelLine** deletes the entire line on which the cursor is located. If there are any lines below the deleted one, these lines are moved up to fill in for the newly deleted line.

InsLine   The **InsLine** procedure inserts a blank line at the cursor. The entire current line is moved downward, regardless of the cursor's position on the line. The new line contains blanks, so it is the background color. Any lines below the insertion point (including the current line) are pushed down. If the window is already filled, the bottom line scrolls off the window.

The following listing shows how you can modify procedures **Draw** and **Introduction** in program **GoToXYDemo2** to let the user delete or insert lines. The middle line of **Introduction** has been changed to list the three new keys. Similarly, three new values have been added to the nested **CASE** statement to handle scan codes 82, 83, and 118.

```
(* Let user type in the window, or move around using the
   arrow keys. User presses ESC to end the program.
*)
PROCEDURE Draw;
VAR Done : BOOLEAN;
    Ch : CHAR;
    CurrX, CurrY : BYTE;

BEGIN  (* Draw *)
  Done := FALSE;

  (* read user's key presses until  user presses ESC *)
  REPEAT
    Ch := ReadKey;
    CASE Ch OF
      (* if user pressed a special key, check which one *)
      #0 :
        BEGIN
          (* get the extended part of the scan code *)
          Ch := ReadKey;
          CASE Ch OF
            #72 : GoToXY ( WhereX, WhereY - 1);  (* Up *)
            #75 : GoToXY ( WhereX - 1, WhereY);  (* Left *)
            #77 : GoToXY ( WhereX + 1, WhereY);  (* Right *)
            #80 : GoToXY ( WhereX, WhereY + 1);  (* Down *)
(* NEW LINES *)
            #82 : InsLine;
            #83 : DelLine;
            #132 : ClrEol;
(* END New Lines *)
          ELSE ; (* do nothing *)
          END; (* CASE OF Special Ch *)
```

```
        END; (* #0 value -- i.e. a special key *)
      (* if user presses enter move to start of next line *)
      #13 : GoToXY ( 1, WhereY + 1);
      (* if user presses ESC, return to main program. *)
      #27 : Done := TRUE;
      (* if not a special key or ENTER or ESC *)
      ELSE   WRITE ( Ch);
    END; (* CASE OF Ch *)
  UNTIL Done = TRUE;
END;    (* Draw *)

PROCEDURE Introduction;
BEGIN
  WRITELN ( 'Type anything you want in the window below.');
  (* The next line has been modified. *)
  WRITELN ( 'Use arrow keys, Ins, Del and CTRL-PgUp.');
  WRITE ( 'Press ESC to end the program.');
END;
```

Make the changes in **GoToXYDemo2** and run the program again to see what happens when you insert and delete lines.

Making Sound on Your Computer

Your computer has an internal speaker that can make sounds of various pitches. You can use this capability in your programs.

Sound (Frq : WORD)

NoSound   The **Sound** procedure takes one argument: a **WORD** that specifies the frequency of the sound, in hertz (Hz). The higher the frequency, the higher pitched the sound. Once you call this procedure, the sound continues until you call **NoSound** to turn it off. The following listing shows a common way to use the sound routines. Procedure **DoTones** contains the sounds and silences in the program—by calling **Sound** for **OnTime** milliseconds and then letting silence persist for **OffTime** milliseconds.

P10-7   (* Program to illustrate use of sound *)

```
PROGRAM SoundDemo;
USES CRT;

VAR Freq, Start, Finish, Increment : WORD;

  (* Make a sound having Freq as its frequency;
     the sound will continue for OnTime milliseconds,
     and will be followed by OffTime milliseconds.
  *)
  PROCEDURE DoTone ( Freq, OnTime, OffTime : WORD);
  BEGIN
    Sound ( Freq);
    Delay ( OnTime);
    NoSound;

    Delay ( OffTime);
  END; (* DoTone *)

BEGIN
  Start := 250;
  Finish := 5000;
  Increment := 250;
  Freq := Start;
  WHILE Freq <= Finish DO
  BEGIN
    DoTone ( Freq, 25, 50);
    INC ( Freq, Increment);
  END;
  (* Change the tone slightly *)
  INC ( Freq, -Increment DIV 2);
  WHILE Freq > Start DO
  BEGIN
    DoTone ( Freq, 50, 100);
    INC ( Freq, -Increment);
  END;
END.
```

Run the program to determine what your computer sounds like. Then modify the program to determine the lowest and highest sounds you can hear on your computer.

You can use sounds to create a timer, which makes a sound every second or half second. The following program shows such a timer. Run it and test its accuracy by timing the output with your watch.

```
P10-8    (* Program to illustrate use of Sound as a timer *)

        PROGRAM TimerDemo;
        USES CRT;

          (* Every half second, this procedure makes a sound;
              on the half second, the sound is high pitched;
              on the full second, the sound is lower pitched.
          *)
          PROCEDURE Timer ( HalfSecs : INTEGER);
          VAR Count : INTEGER;
          BEGIN
            FOR Count := 1 TO HalfSecs DO
            BEGIN
              (* The sum of the 2 delays is 500 ms or .5 second *)
              Delay ( 475);
              IF ODD ( Count) THEN
                Sound (5000)
              ELSE
                Sound ( 500);
              Delay ( 25);
              NoSound;
            END;
          END; (* Timer *)

        BEGIN
          WRITELN ( 'Timing 5 seconds');
          Timer ( 10);
          WRITE ( 'Press ENTER to continue.');
          READLN;
          WRITELN ( 'Timing 10 seconds');
          Timer ( 20);
          WRITE ( 'Press ENTER to end program.');
          READLN;
        END.
```

The DOS Unit

The **DOS** unit contains routines for handling files and for accessing various operating system information and services. These routines enable you to get or set the date and time, do a directory listing, check the values of various environment variables, and access low-level operating system services (such as reading the system clock), among other things.

Getting Information from the Operating System

The **DOS** unit contains several routines for getting various items of information from the operating system. This section briefly summarizes these routines.

DiskFree (DRIVE : BYTE) : LONGINT
DiskSize (DRIVE : BYTE) : LONGINT

The **DiskFree** function returns the number of bytes of available storage on the disk in a specified drive. The **DiskSize** function returns the total capacity (in bytes) of the disk in a specified drive. The drive is specified as a **WORD** argument. Drive A is 1; drive B is 2; and so forth. For example, the following program lets you check the available storage and disk capacity in the specified drive:

```
P10-9    (* Program to illustrate DiskFree and DiskSize functions *)

PROGRAM DiskDemo;
USES DOS;

CONST Offset = 65;    (* to get to uppercase 'A' *)
VAR FreeSpace, MaxSpace : LONGINT;
    DriveStr : CHAR;
    DriveNr : INTEGER;

  PROCEDURE GetUCString ( Message : STRING;
                          VAR Value : CHAR);
  BEGIN
    WRITE ( Message, ' ');
    READLN ( Value);
    Value := UPCASE ( Value);
  END; (* GetUCString *)

BEGIN
  REPEAT
    GetUCString ( 'Check what drive? (A -- K)', DriveStr);
  UNTIL ( DriveStr >= 'A') AND ( DriveStr <= 'K')
  (* Build argument for the function calls *)
  DriveNr := ORD ( DriveStr) - Offset + 1;
  FreeSpace := DiskFree ( DriveNr);
  MaxSpace := DiskSize ( DriveNr);
  WRITELN ( 'Drive ', DriveStr, ' has ', FreeSpace,
            ' free bytes;');
  WRITELN ( ' total capacity = ', MaxSpace, ' bytes');
  WRITE ( 'Press ENTER to end the program.');
```

```
    READLN;
END.
```

Run this program and try the following procedures.

■ If you have a hard disk, check the available and maximum storage.

■ Check floppy drives A and B. (If these are high-density drives, try this with different density disks. For example, if you have a 1.2MB drive, try the program with 360K and a 1.2MB disk in the drive.)

■ Check for capacity and free space on a nonexistent drive (such as J) or a drive containing no disk.

Compare the results from the preceding program with the outcomes when you run the DOS utility program, **CHKDSK**. (If you don't have **CHKDSK** installed on your hard disk or system disk, you can get some of this information by doing a directory listing of the diskette.)

EnvCount : INTEGER
EnvStr (WhichStr : INTEGER) : STRING   Under DOS, you can specify various *environment variables*. These enable you to store information about where to find a program or a group of files. For example, DOS has a PATH environment variable, with which to specify alternative directories to search for a program.

For example, suppose you've specified the following PATH statement in an AUTOEXEC.BAT or at the command line. (If you're not sure how to set a path, see your DOS documentation.)

```
PATH=c:\;a:\bin;c:\tptutor;
```

When you ask DOS to execute a program, it first checks the current directory for the program. If the program is not found, DOS then checks the directories specified in the PATH variable. In this case, DOS checks the root directory of drive C (C:\), the BIN directory of drive A (A:\bin), and finally the TPTUTOR directory of drive C (C:\tptutor). If the program is not found in any of these, you'll get the following DOS error message:

```
Bad command or file name
```

Function **EnvCount** returns the number of environment variables you have defined. For example, the following statement stores this number in **NrOfEnvs**:

```
NrOfEnvs := EnvCount;
```

Each of these variables is a string that contains the environment's name (such as PATH) and its definition, separated from the name by an equal sign. Function **EnvStr** returns a specified string from this collection of environments. This function takes an integer argument and returns an integer. The following statement displays the contents of the third environment string (provided that there are at least three strings defined):

```
WRITELN ( EnvStr ( 3));
```

EnvStr can give you useful information if you know what index is associated with a particular environment variable. More likely, you will know the variable's name but not its location in the environment list. For example, you may want to check the value of the PATH variable.

GetEnv (WhichEnvVar : STRING) : STRING   Function **GetEnv** lets you specify the environment variable by name. For example, the following statement displays the definition of PATH:

```
WRITELN ( GetEnv ( 'PATH'));
```

You can specify the variable name in any case, but you may not include the equal sign in the name. If no such environment variable exists, the function returns an empty string.

The following program lets you explore your environment variables, and also shows how to do this using the **DOS** routines:

```
P10-10    PROGRAM EnvDemo;

          USES DOS;
          CONST MaxIndex = 15;
          VAR Index : INTEGER;
              EnvResult : STRING;

          BEGIN
            FOR Index := 1 TO EnvCount DO
              WRITELN ( EnvStr ( Index));
            EnvResult := GetEnv ( 'path');
            WRITELN;
```

```
   WRITELN ( 'Based on GetEnv, PATH variable has the value: ');
   WRITELN;
   WRITELN ( EnvResult);
   READLN;
END.
```

This program produced the following output for a sample run:

```
COMSPEC=C:\COMMAND.COM
PROMPT=$p$g
PATH=\;C:\BIN;D:\USRBIN;D:\TEX;D:\TP;C:\M2;D:\MACE;D:\PCTOOLS
INCLUDE=d:\tc\inc
LIB=d:\tc\lib
MACE = D:\MACE
TEXINPUTS=D:\TEX\INPUTS;MACS;..\MACS;C:\PBK\MACS;\M2\DOC\MACS;
TEXFORMATS=D:\TEX\FORMATS
TEXFONTS=D:\TEX\FONTS;\TEXTSET\PSFONTS
```

```
Based on GetEnv, the PATH variable has the value:
```

```
\;C:\BIN;D:\USRBIN;D:\TEX;D:\TP;C:\M2;D:\MACE;D:\PCTOOLS
```

When **GetEnv** reports the value of an environment variable, it includes only the material after the equal sign. Thus, the value of the third **EnvStr** differs from the last line of the listing in that the **EnvStr** includes the **PATH =** before the definition. See your DOS documentation or a reference book about DOS for more information on environment variables.

GetDate (VAR Yr, Mo, Day, DayOfWk : WORD);
GetTime (VAR Hr, Min, Sec, Hundredths : WORD)
These two procedures let you determine the current date and time settings on your system. While each of the parameters is of type **WORD**, certain arguments can have values only within a specific range.

Yr	1980..2099
Mo	1..12
Day	1..31
DayOfWk	0 (= Sunday)..6 (= Saturday)
Hr	0..23 (23 = 11 P.M.)
Min, Sec	0..59
Hundredths	0..99

The following program lets you check your system's current date and time:

P10-11

```
(* Program to determine system date and time *)

PROGRAM DateTimeDemo;

USES DOS;

VAR Yr, Mo, Day, DayOfWk : WORD;
    Hr, Min, Sec, Hundredths : WORD;

PROCEDURE WriteDay ( Index : WORD);
BEGIN
  CASE Index OF
    0 : WRITE ( 'Sunday ');
    1 : WRITE ( 'Monday ');
    2 : WRITE ( 'Tuesday ');
    3 : WRITE ( 'Wednesday ');
    4 : WRITE ( 'Thursday ');
    5 : WRITE ( 'Friday ');
    6 : WRITE ( 'Saturday ');
    ELSE WRITE ( 'Day unknown ');
  END;
END;

BEGIN
  GetDate ( Yr, Mo, Day, DayOfWk);
  GetTime ( Hr, Min, Sec, Hundredths);
  WriteDay ( DayOfWk);
  WRITELN ( Mo, '-', Day, '-', Yr);
  WRITELN ( 'Time = ', Hr, ':', Min, ':', Sec, ':',
            Hundredths);
  READLN;
END.
```

SetDate (Yr, Mo, Day : WORD);
SetTime (Hr, Min, Sec, Hundredths: WORD)   These two procedures enable you to change the settings for the system date and time. Again, both take **WORD** arguments. The values for these arguments must be within the ranges specified for **GetDate** and **GetTime**. If you pass values that are outside the allowable ranges, the call will be ignored.

The following program lets you change the date and time settings.

P10-12

```
(* Program to change system date and time *)

PROGRAM DateTimeDemo2;

USES DOS, CRT;

VAR Yr, Mo, Day, DayOfWk : WORD;
    Hr, Min, Sec, Hundredths : WORD;
    OldYr, OldMo, OldDay, OldDayOfWk : WORD;
    OldHr, OldMin, OldSec, OldHundredths : WORD;

  PROCEDURE WriteDay ( Index : WORD);
  BEGIN
    CASE Index OF
      0 : WRITE ( 'Sunday ');
      1 : WRITE ( 'Monday ');
      2 : WRITE ( 'Tuesday ');
      3 : WRITE ( 'Wednesday ');
      4 : WRITE ( 'Thursday ');
      5 : WRITE ( 'Friday ');
      6 : WRITE ( 'Saturday ');
      ELSE WRITE ( 'Day unknown ');
    END;
  END; (* WriteDay *)

BEGIN
  WRITELN ( 'Saving current date and time ...');
  GetDate ( OldYr, OldMo, OldDay, OldDayOfWk);
  GetTime ( OldHr, OldMin, OldSec, OldHundredths);
  Delay ( 2000);
  WRITELN ( 'Changing values for date and time ...');
  Yr := 2010;
  Mo := 12;
  Day := 31;
  Hr := 0;
  Min := OldMin;
  Sec := OldSec;
  Hundredths := OldHundredths;

  SetDate ( Yr, Mo, Day);
  SetTime ( Hr, Min, Sec, Hundredths);

  GetDate ( Yr, Mo, Day, DayOfWk);
  GetTime ( Hr, Min, Sec, Hundredths);
  WriteDay ( DayOfWk);
  WRITELN ( Mo, '-', Day, '-', Yr);
  WRITELN ( 'Time = ', Hr, ':', Min, ':', Sec, ':',
            Hundredths);
  WRITELN ( 'Press ENTER to restore original setting.');
  READLN;
```

```
   SetDate ( OldYr, OldMo, OldDay);
   SetTime ( OldHr, OldMin, OldSec, OldHundredths);
   WRITELN ( 'Original setting restored successfully.');
   READLN;
END.
```

DosVersion : WORD   The **DosVersion** function lets you determine what version of DOS is being used on your computer. This information is passed back in a **WORD**, and has two components. The first component (found in the low-order byte of the returned value) represents the major version number — such as 3 in version 3.2. The second component (found in the high-order byte) represents the minor version number — such as 2 in 3.2.

The following program lets you check the version of DOS on your machine:

P10-13

```
(* Program to determine version of DOS on the machine. *)

PROGRAM DOSVersionDemo;

USES DOS;

BEGIN
   (* Major version is in LO ( DosVersion);
      minor version is in HI ( DosVersion).
   *)
   WRITELN ( 'DOS version ', LO( DosVersion),
            '.', HI ( DosVersion));
   READLN;
END.
```

File-Handling Routines

The **DOS** unit also contains some routines for getting information about files. For example, you can do a directory listing by using the routines **FindFirst** and **FindNext** together. These routines use a **SearchRec** data type, which is defined in the **DOS** unit as follows:

```
TYPE SearchRec = RECORD
                   Fill : ARRAY [ 1 .. 21] OF BYTE;
                   Attr : BYTE;
                   Time, Size : LONGINT;
                   Name : STRING [ 12];
                 END;
```

The **Fill** field is reserved for DOS so don't modify it. The **Attr** field tells something about the file (that is, whether it is read-only, hidden, and so forth). The **Time** field specifies the date and time when the file was last modified. This information is packed into the four bytes allocated for a **LONGINT**. To get the individual components of **Time,** you need to call the predefined routine **Unpack. Size** specifies the file's size (in bytes) and **Name** contains the file's name, including extension.

CAUTION Never modify the **Fill** field of a **SearchRec**.

FindFirst (PathArg : STRING; Attr : WORD; VAR SRec : SearchRec);
FindNext (VAR SRec : SearchRec) Procedure **FindFirst** searches the current directory (or whatever directory is specified as part of **PathArg**). The routine searches for any matches to the specified file name (also part of **PathArg**). You can include wildcard characters in **PathArg**. A file matches if the file has an appropriate name and the same combination of attributes specified in the **Attr** argument. If the procedure finds a match, it returns information about this file in **SRec**. You can then access individual fields of this record in your program. If an error occurs, it is reported through the global variable **DosError** defined in the **DOS** unit. If no error occurs, this variable has the value **0**. The errors that might arise when **FindFirst** is executing include "Directory not found" (error 2) and "No more files" (18). See the on-line help for **DosError** for a list of all the codes. To see this list, type **DosError** in a program file, move the cursor to this word, and press CTRL-F1.

Procedure **FindNext** continues searching the directory specified in the **Path** argument for additional files that match. When such a file is found, its information is stored in **SRec**. This argument must refer to the same location in memory as the **SRec** argument for **FindFirst**. Only error 18 is possible with this routine.

The following program shows how to do a directory listing. Do a listing of your current directory and then use the program to list the directory that contains your Turbo Pascal compiler.

P10-14

```
(* Program to get a directory listing, using
   FindFirst and FindNext
*)

PROGRAM DirListDemo;
```

```
USES DOS;

VAR DirList : SEARCHREC;
    PathStr : STRING;

  PROCEDURE GetString ( Message : STRING;
                        VAR Value : STRING);
  BEGIN
    WRITE ( Message, ' ');
    READLN ( Value);
  END;  (* GetString *)
BEGIN
  GetString ( 'Path name (including file; ENTER to stop)',
            PathStr);
  WRITELN ( 'PathStr = ', PathStr);
  FindFirst ( PathStr, Archive, DirList);
  (* As long as there are files to search *)
  WHILE DosError = 0 DO
  BEGIN
    WRITELN ( DirList.Name);
    FindNext ( DirList);
  END;
  READLN;
END.
```

PathStr can contain any of the following. If an element is included, it must appear in the correct order in relation to other elements.

■ *A drive specifier (such as A: or C:)*   Must appear first if present.

■ *A complete path name to the directory you want to search*   For example, use \TP\EXAMPLES, if you want to search the contents of the EXAMPLES directory nested in the TP directory.

■ *The file specifier to control the search*   This will be a file name but may contain wildcard characters.

The last element in the list must be included in **PathStr**. The other two elements are optional. If these are not included, the current directory on the current drive is assumed.

Program **DirListDemo** displays only the file name. Modify the program to provide more extensive information about the file (such as its size and date information). For a real challenge, you may want to create a linked list structure whose nodes will include a **SearchRec** as well as some pointers. While your program is reading the directory, the entries should be added to the linked list. If you order by name, you'll be able to present a sorted directory listing.

Appendix B, "Turbo Pascal Procedures and Functions," contains more **DOS** routines. Chapter 14 also contains some **DOS** unit routines for accessing the low-level operating system services.

The GRAPH Unit

The Turbo Pascal **GRAPH** unit implements the Borland Graphics Interface (BGI) for Pascal. This interface is designed to provide a standard collection of graphics routines that will work in a similar way for the various Borland languages (such as Pascal, C, and C++). The **GRAPH** unit contains several dozen routines. This chapter can discuss only a small fraction of these. Appendix B contains a summary of all the routines.

Computer Graphics: General Issues

Graphics can be tricky work on computers. There are several considerations and conventions for doing graphics.

Graphics Drivers   First, graphics are much more hardware dependent than other aspects of a program. Monitors differ in their resolution, in whether they support color, and so forth. In order to deal with the many possibilities, you need separate drivers. A *driver* is a program that acts as an intermediary between the operating system or your program and the hardware on which the graphics will be done. For example, if you want to draw a line from one point on the screen to another, you will eventually need to translate this request into explicit instructions regarding each pixel to be turned on or left off.

Once you've initialized the graphics environment, your programs can simply assume that the required driver is available. You don't need to worry about the driver itself, since your instructions will be given at a higher level.

Turbo Pascal supports the following graphics adapters:

- CGA, MCGA
- EGA
- VGA
- Hercules
- AT&T 400 series
- IBM 3270 PC
- IBM 8514
- Adapters completely compatible with one of the preceding ones

Drivers for these adapters are contained in the .BGI files included with your Turbo Pascal environment.

Graphics Modes   Ordinarily, your programs run in *text mode*. In this mode, the program displays material by requesting that particular characters be placed at specified positions on the screen. In text mode, your program can only put characters within fixed grids on the screen. For example, each row has exactly 40 or 80 columns, and the screen can have 25, 43, or 50 rows, depending on the characters being used. You can't split a character over two columns—that is, you can't have half the character in each column.

With graphics, however, your program has to control what happens to every single pixel on the screen. To accomplish this, you need to put the screen into *graphics mode*. In this mode, the screen is no longer a matrix of 25 × 80 (for example) cells. Rather, it is a much larger matrix of approximately 200,000 pixels. A *pixel* refers to a point on the screen. This point has a location (expressed in column and row coordinates) and a color associated with it. A pixel can be on or off at a particular time.

When your program is finished, it must restore the screen to the mode in effect before the program started executing. To move into and out of graphics mode, your graphics programs will generally begin and end with calls to routines for changing modes. The routine for starting

graphics mode is also responsible for accessing the necessary driver for
your hardware.

Screens and Viewports   With the **CRT** unit, you saw that positions on
the screen were expressed in terms of coordinates. The coordinate
system used for most text modes has the location 1,1 at the upper-left
corner of the screen. The lower-right corner has coordinates 80,25 (on
most systems).

Similarly, the graphics screen's coordinate system starts in the upper-
left corner. However, this pixel has coordinates 0,0. The maximum
horizontal and vertical values will depend on the graphics adapter and
its resolution. Resolution is expressed in the form *horizontal × vertical*,
where the values substituted for *horizontal* and *vertical* represent the
number of pixels in that direction. For example, an EGA adapter can
support 640 × 350 resolution. This means that the screen will have 640
horizontal and 350 vertical dots on each line. For such an adapter, the
pixel in the lower-right corner will have coordinates 639,349. Similarly,
the Hercules adapter has a 720 × 348 pixel resolution, so its lower-right
corner has coordinates 719,347.

Some adapters can be used in different modes. Used in this context,
a *mode* determines the resolution, the number of available colors, and the
amount of memory allocated for graphics. Often, the trade-off is between resolution and number of colors or between resolution and memory. For example, you can use a CGA adapter in any of five different
modes. In this case, the trade-off is between resolution and number of
colors.

You can write your programs so as to make them independent of the
resolution of specific monitors. Instead of having to specify a fixed value
in advance, you can simply use a variable to store the maximum x and
y values for a particular program.

In text mode, the screen is really a default window—a self-contained
area of the screen on which your program imposes coordinates. Once
you define a specific window, only locations within its boundaries are
accessible to your program (at least until you define a different window).
Screen coordinates are always relative to the window's boundaries.

In graphics mode, you can define a *viewport* to accomplish the same
thing. Instead of using the entire screen, you can define a rectangular
portion of the screen and do your work within this viewport. As with
windows, only one viewport is active at any one time. The examples in
this chapter work with the entire screen; however, you should experiment with other viewports.

Drawing Figures

This book covers only a small portion of the graphics capabilities offered by the **GRAPH** unit. You'll learn about some of the routines Turbo Pascal offers for drawing various types of figures. To make it easier to introduce procedures and functions, this section discusses an example program, which illustrates how to use about 20 graphics routines.

First, however, here is a simpler example that demonstrates how to get into and out of graphics mode and introduces a few of the drawing routines:

P10-15
```
(* Program to illustrate how to put program into graphics mode,
   draw some simple figures, and how to restore the video
   setting to its preprogram value.
   NOTE!!! The third argument to InitGraph is the name of the
           directory in which your drivers (*.BGI files) are
           stored. You need to change this argument accordingly.
*)

PROGRAM GraphIntro;
USES Graph, CRT;
(* NOTE: You need to set this string to the drive and
         directory in which your .BGI files are located.
*)

CONST DriverDirectory = 'A:';
VAR Driver, Mode, Outcome : INTEGER;
    XPos, YPos : INTEGER;
    XRadius, YRadius : WORD;

  (* Describe program and its actions *)
  PROCEDURE Introduction;
  BEGIN
    WRITE ( 'This program draws ellipses. ');
    WRITELN ( 'Press any key to end program.');
    WRITELN ( 'This message will disappear by itself.');
    Delay ( 3000);
  END; (* Introduction *)

  (* Generate random values needed to control the drawing. *)
  PROCEDURE MakeArgs ( VAR XPos, YPos : INTEGER;
                       VAR XRadius, YRadius : WORD);
  BEGIN
    XPos := RANDOM ( GetMaxX - 200) + 100;
    YPos := RANDOM ( GetMaxY - 100) + 50;
    XRadius := RANDOM ( 50) + 20;
    YRadius := RANDOM ( 25) + 10;
  END; (* MakeArgs *)

BEGIN
```

```
(* The first 3 statements are executed while in text mode *)
RANDOMIZE;
ClrScr;
Introduction;

(* let the program check the hardware to determine what
   driver to load. DETECT is a predefined constant.
*)
Driver := DETECT;

(* Go into graphics mode. The third argument tells where
   the driver files are stored.
   !!!!! You need to specify the directory !!!!!
   !!!!! in which you have put these files !!!!!
*)
InitGraph ( Driver, Mode, DriverDirectory);

(* GraphResult returns an integer that tells whether
   everything went all right. If not, this function
   returns the error code.
*)
Outcome := GraphResult;

(* If there was an error, write a suitable message.
   This message is provided by calling GraphErrorMsg
*)
IF Outcome <> grOK THEN
  WRITELN ( 'Error. ', GraphErrorMsg ( Outcome))

ELSE
BEGIN
  REPEAT
    MakeArgs ( XPos, YPos, XRadius, YRadius);
    IF ODD ( RANDOM ( 1000)) THEN
      Ellipse ( XPos, YPos, 0, 360, XRadius, YRadius)
    ELSE
      FillEllipse ( XPos, YPos, XRadius, YRadius);
    Delay ( 300);
  UNTIL KeyPressed;
END;

(* Unload the graphics drivers and restore the video mode
   in effect before the program started.
*)
  CloseGraph;
END.
```

The program does the following:

■ Introduces itself

■ Switches to graphics mode after determining and loading the driver appropriate to your hardware

■ Draws either filled or hollow ellipses at random locations on the screen until you press a key

■ Restores the screen to the mode in effect before the graphics mode was instated

Three statements are involved in putting your screen in graphics mode. In the first of these, the value (0) of **DETECT** (a predefined constant that specifies no particular driver) is assigned to **Driver**. This is then passed as an argument to **InitGraph**. Check the on-line help for the **GRAPH** unit for more information about predefined constants and variables.

InitGraph checks the hardware to determine what kind of adapter is present, and sets **Driver** to the appropriate value. **Mode** represents how the graphics adapter is to be used. For example, graphics are handled differently if you decide to use a color monitor in black and white mode. In a sense, **Driver** sets the high-level graphics mode by determining the adapter, and **Mode** specifies how the adapter is to be used. The third argument to **InitGraph** specifies the directory in which the drivers included with your compiler are to be found. By default, this is assumed to be drive A, in the root directory of that disk. If you've set up your Turbo Pascal environment differently, you'll need to change the value of **DriverDirectory** at the start of the programs in this section.

After **InitGraph** has done its work, you need to test whether it was successful. Function **GraphResult** returns the error code for the last graphics operation performed. If everything went smoothly, this code will be **grOK**, a predefined value defined as 0. All error codes are values of less than 0. See the on-line help for a list of the error codes.

Welcome to graphics mode! While you're in this mode, operations are carried out at the level of individual dots on the screen (pixels). In graphics mode, the program generates random location and size parameters and calls either of two routines for drawing ellipses.

Ellipse (XPos, YPos : INTEGER; StartAngle, EndAngle, XRadius, YRadius : WORD); Procedure **Ellipse** draws the outline of an ellipse (or part of one) at a specified location on the screen. The procedure takes six arguments. **XPos** and **YPos** represent horizontal and vertical coordinates for the center point of the ellipse.

The range of valid values for these arguments depends on the driver being used. For example, for the Hercules driver on a particular machine, the first argument might range from 0 through 719 and the vertical position might range from 0 through 347. The second pair of arguments specifies how far around the ellipse is drawn. These arguments will have values from 0 through 360. 0° is at a position directly to the right of the focal point (that is, at three o'clock). Degrees are counted in a counterclockwise direction, with 90° being at twelve o'clock and 180° at nine o'clock. A complete ellipse is drawn if you specify 0 and 360 (which are the same location) as the starting and ending angles, respectively. Figure 10-1 shows some ellipses and the angles corresponding to their starting and ending points.

The other two arguments specify the shape of the ellipse that will be drawn. **RadiusX** specifies the horizontal size of the curve; **RadiusY** specifies the vertical size. When **RadiusX** is greater than **RadiusY**, the ellipse looks like an egg on its side. When the size relationship is reversed, the ellipse looks like an egg standing on end. When the two radius values are equal, the ellipse is a circle.

In the program, the middle two arguments are fixed at 0 and 360 so that the procedure always draws closed ellipses. Modify the program so

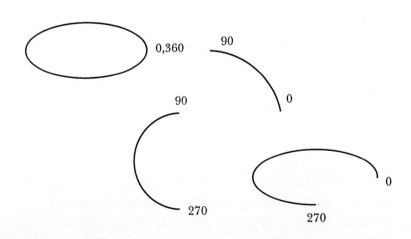

Figure 10-1.   *Ellipses drawn from various starting angles to other ending angles*

that it sometimes draws partial ellipses. (The cleanest way to do that is to add the statements for generating angle values to the **MakeArgs** procedure.)

FillEllipse (XPos, YPos : INTEGER; XRadius, YRadius : WORD)

The **FillEllipse** procedure always draws a complete ellipse (that is from 0° through 360°). The procedure fills the area within the curve. The arguments represent the same information as the corresponding arguments for **Ellipse**.

GetMaxX : INTEGER
GetMaxY : INTEGER

There are two other graphics routines used in the program. Procedure **MakeArgs** uses the **GetMaxX** and **GetMaxY** functions, which return the maximum horizontal and vertical pixel values, respectively, for the screen or viewport.

Figure Exploration:
A Longer Example

Program **GraphIntro** gave you a feel for how to use graphics. The next program (**GraphExplorer**) introduces you to a larger collection of graphics routines and techniques. Some of the routines are for drawing figures. These will have a format similar to the **Ellipse** and **FillEllipse** procedures in **GraphIntro**.

Other routines enable you to configure the graphics environment. For example, you can specify the format to be used when drawing a line. The program also contains routines for writing text while in graphics mode. **GraphExplorer** lets you select from a list of possible figures to draw. After you select a figure, the program gets the required argument values and then draws the figure. When you're ready to draw another one, just press ENTER. The menu reappears and you can select another figure, repeating the process. The program also uses nongraphics techniques that you may find useful in other programs. Run the program a few times, trying various inputs.

P10-16   (* Program to explore figure drawing. *)

```
PROGRAM GraphExplorer;
(*$V-*)   (* VAR-string checking is off, so can use SmStr *)
USES Graph, CRT;

CONST MaxMenu = 10;
      EmptyString = '';
      DriverDirectory = 'A:';
TYPE SmStr = STRING [ 30];
     StrArray = ARRAY [ 0 .. MaxMenu] OF STRING [ 80];
     SmStrArray = ARRAY [ 1 .. 10] OF SmStr;
     (* Stores unlabelled values, which will be used
        as arguments by drawing routines.
     *)
     ArgArray = ARRAY [ 0 .. 10] OF INTEGER;
     (* Adding a NrArgs field to the array info makes
        it easier to tell when to stop.
     *)
     ArgRec = RECORD
                Args : ArgArray;
                NrArgs : INTEGER;
              END; (* ArgRec *)
VAR Driver, Mode, Outcome, Choice : INTEGER;
    Labels : SmStrArray;
    Info : ArgRec;
    Menu : StrArray;

(* *************                          ************* *)
(* ************* General-Purpose Routines ************* *)
(* *************                          ************* *)

  (* Initialize the menu to the available choices.
     NOTE: This routine must be customized for each program.
  *)
  PROCEDURE InitMenu ( VAR Menu : StrArray);
  VAR Index : INTEGER;
  BEGIN
    Menu [ 0] := ' 0) QUIT';
    Menu [ 1] := ' 1) Arc';
    Menu [ 2] := ' 2) Circle';
    Menu [ 3] := ' 3) Ellipse';
    Menu [ 4] := ' 4) Line';
    Menu [ 5] := ' 5) Pixel';
    Menu [ 6] := ' 6) Rectangle';
    (* Space available for your routines. *)
    Menu [ 7] := ' 7) RESERVED';
    Menu [ 8] := ' 8) RESERVED';
    Menu [ 9] := ' 9) RESERVED';
    Menu [ 10] := '10) RESERVED';
  END;  (* InitMenu *)
```

```
(* Display the contents of the menu array.
   NrChoices represents the number of Menu's cells
   that have choices (as opposed to empty strings)
*)
PROCEDURE ShowMenu ( VAR Menu : StrArray;
                         NrChoices : INTEGER);
VAR Index : INTEGER;
BEGIN
   (* To prevent procedure from reading past end of array *)
   IF NrChoices > MaxMenu THEN
     NrChoices := MaxMenu;
   FOR Index := 0 TO NrChoices DO
     WRITELN ( Menu [ Index]);
   WRITELN;
   WRITE ( 'You Choice? (0 TO ', NrChoices, ') ');
END; (* ShowMenu *)

PROCEDURE GetInteger ( Message : STRING;
                           VAR Value : INTEGER);
BEGIN
   WRITE ( Message, ' ');
   READLN ( Value);
END; (* GetInteger *)

(* Get an integer lying within the boundaries
   specified by MinVal and MaxVal
*)
PROCEDURE GetBoundedInt ( MinVal, MaxVal : INTEGER;
                             VAR Value : INTEGER);

   (* Fix boundary values if they are reversed --
      that is, if Small > Large.
   *)
   PROCEDURE AdjustVals ( VAR Small, Large : INTEGER);
   VAR Temp : INTEGER;
   BEGIN
     IF Small > Large THEN
     BEGIN
       Temp := Small;
       Small := Large;
       Large := Temp;
     END;
   END; (* AdjustVals *)

   (* Return TRUE if Small <= Val <= Large *)
   FUNCTION IsBetween ( Val, Small, Large : INTEGER) : BOOLEAN;
   BEGIN
     IsBetween := ( Small <= Val) AND ( Large >= Val);
   END;   (* FN IsBetween *)

BEGIN (* GetBoundedInt *)
   AdjustVals ( MinVal, MaxVal);
```

```
    REPEAT
      READLN ( Value);
    UNTIL IsBetween ( Value, MinVal, MaxVal);
  END; (* GetBoundedInt *)


(* Remove the first word from a string;
    a word is separated from the next by 1 or more blanks
*)
PROCEDURE RemoveWd ( VAR Wd, Sentence : STRING);
CONST Blank = ' ';
VAR Where : INTEGER;
BEGIN
  (* Remove all leading blanks *)
  WHILE POS ( Blank, Sentence) = 1 DO
    DELETE ( Sentence, 1, 1);
  (* Find the next blank in Sentence.
      This will separate the first two words.
  *)
  Where := POS ( Blank, Sentence);
  IF Where > 0 THEN
  BEGIN
    (* Get the first word, but leave the blank *)
    Wd := COPY ( Sentence, 1, Where - 1);
    (* Remove the first word (and blank) from Sentence *)
    DELETE ( Sentence, 1, Where);
  END
  ELSE  (* If no more blanks -- so only 1 word left *)
  BEGIN
    Wd := Sentence;
    (* Close out the sentence *)
    Sentence := EmptyString;
  END;  (* if Sentence contains no more blanks *)
END;  (* RemoveWd *)


(* Define a window by specifying its boundaries;
    select text and background colors for the window;
    call ClrScr to make the entire window the background color.
*)
PROCEDURE SetWindow ( UX, UY, LX, LY : BYTE;
                      BackGr, ForeGr : BYTE);
BEGIN
  Window ( UX, UY, LX, LY);
  Textbackground ( BackGr);
  TextColor ( ForeGr);
  ClrScr;
END; (* SetWindow *)

(* *************                    ************* *)
(* ************* Program-Specific Routines ************* *)
(* *************                    ************* *)

  (* Does the busy work needed to enable GetArgs to work.
```

```
      Specifically : goes from graphics to text mode,
                     sets a window,
                     returns to graphics mode after GetArgs.
*)
PROCEDURE GetInfo ( VAR Data : ArgRec;
                    VAR Names : SmStrArray;
                    NrOfArgs : INTEGER);
VAR Index : INTEGER;
BEGIN
  RestoreCRTMode;
  SetWindow ( 1, 1, 50, 3, White, Black);
  GoToXY ( 1,1);
  Data.NrArgs := NrOfArgs;
  FOR Index := 1 TO NrOfArgs DO
    GetInteger ( Names [ Index], Data.Args [ Index]);
  SetGraphMode ( Mode);
END; (* GetInfo *)


(* Store individual words from TheStr in separate
   cells of Names. These values will be used as
   prompts in other routines.
*)
PROCEDURE MakeNames ( VAR Names : SmStrArray;
                      TheStr : STRING);
VAR Index : INTEGER;
BEGIN
  Index := 1;
  WHILE TheStr <> EmptyString DO
  BEGIN
    RemoveWd ( Names [ Index], TheStr);
    INC ( Index);
  END;
END; (* MakeNames *)


(* Display an introduction to the program and how it works. *)
PROCEDURE Introduction;
BEGIN
  SetWindow ( 10, 3, 60, 15, White, Black);
  WRITELN ( '  Welcome to the Figure Exploration program.');
  WRITELN ( '  With this program, you'll do the following');
  GoToXY ( 5, WhereY + 1);
  WRITELN ( '1) select a figure');
  GoToXY ( 5, WhereY);
  WRITELN ( '2) provide parameter values');
  GoToXY ( 5, WhereY);
  WRITELN ( '3) draw the figure');
  GoToXY ( 5, WhereY);
  WRITELN ( '4) repeat steps 1 .. 3, if you wish');
  GoToXY ( 15, WhereY + 1);
  WRITELN ( 'Press ENTER to continue.');
  READLN;
END; (* Introduction *)
```

```
(* Handles cases where an unimplemented routine
   is requested. Also shows how to write text
   while in graphics mode.
*)
PROCEDURE HandleNotAvailable;
BEGIN
  OutText ( 'Sorry, not implemented yet.');
  Delay ( 1000);
  ClearDevice;
  OutText ( ' Press ENTER to continue.');
END; (* HandleNotAvailable *)

(* Handle the details required to:
   1) get back to text mnode temporarily;
   2) get a selection from the user;
   3) return to graphics mode;
   4) specify parameters outputting text in graphics mode.
*)
PROCEDURE ToBusiness;
BEGIN
  RestoreCRTMode;
  SetWindow ( 1, 1, 50, 20, White, Black);
  ShowMenu ( Menu, MaxMenu + 1);
  GetBoundedInt ( 0, MaxMenu, Choice);
  ClrScr;
  SetGraphMode ( Mode);
  SetTextJustify ( LeftText, TopText);
  SetTextStyle ( DefaultFont, HorizDir, 2);
END; (* ToBusiness *)

(* *************                       ************* *)
(* ************* Figure-Drawing Routines ************* *)
(* *************                       ************* *)

(* Each of the following routines is specialized for a
   particular figure. Each of the routines does several things:
   1) Make labels for prompts;
   2) Get values for arguments needed to draw the figure;
   3) Mark the focal point (if relevent);
   4) Draw the figure.
*)

  PROCEDURE HandleArc;
  BEGIN
    MakeNames ( Labels,
               'CenterX CenterY StartAngle EndAngle Radius');
    GetInfo ( Info, Labels, 5);
    PutPixel ( Info.Args [ 1], Info.Args [ 2], White);
    Arc ( Info.Args [ 1], Info.Args [ 2], Info.Args [ 3],
          Info.Args [ 4], Info.Args [ 5]);
  END;   (* HandleArc *)
```

```
   PROCEDURE HandleCircle;
   BEGIN
     MakeNames ( Labels,
                 'CenterX CenterY Radius');
     GetInfo ( Info, Labels, 3);
     PutPixel ( Info.Args [ 1], Info.Args [ 2], White);
     Circle ( Info.Args [ 1], Info.Args [ 2], Info.Args [ 3]);
   END;   (* HandleCircle *)

   PROCEDURE HandleEllipse;
   VAR Temp : STRING;
   BEGIN
     Temp :=  'CenterX CenterY StartAngle EndAngle' +
              ' RadiusX RadiusY';
     MakeNames ( Labels, Temp);
     GetInfo ( Info, Labels, 6);
     PutPixel ( Info.Args [ 1], Info.Args [ 2], White);
     Ellipse ( Info.Args [ 1], Info.Args [ 2], Info.Args [ 3],
               Info.Args [ 4], Info.Args [ 5], Info.Args [ 6]);
   END;   (* HandleEllipse *)

   PROCEDURE HandleLine;
   BEGIN
     MakeNames ( Labels, 'X1 Y1 X2 Y2');
     GetInfo ( Info, Labels, 4);
     SetLineStyle ( DottedLn, 0, ThickWidth);
     Line ( Info.Args [ 1], Info.Args [ 2], Info.Args [ 3],
            Info.Args [ 4]);
   END;   (* HandleLine *)

   PROCEDURE HandlePixel;
   BEGIN
     MakeNames ( Labels, 'X Y');
     GetInfo ( Info, Labels, 2);
     PutPixel ( Info.Args [ 1], Info.Args [ 2], White);
   END;   (* HandlePixel *)

   PROCEDURE HandleRectangle;
   BEGIN
     MakeNames ( Labels, 'X1 Y1 X2 Y2');
     GetInfo ( Info, Labels, 4);
     Rectangle ( Info.Args [ 1], Info.Args [ 2], Info.Args [ 3],
                 Info.Args [ 4]);
   END;   (* HandleRectangle *)

BEGIN   (* Main program *)
  InitMenu ( Menu);
  ClrScr;
  Introduction;

  Driver := Detect;
```

```
InitGraph ( Driver, Mode, DriverDirectory);

Outcome := GraphResult;
IF Outcome <> grOK THEN
   WRITELN ( 'Error. ', GraphErrorMsg ( Outcome))
ELSE
BEGIN
  REPEAT
    ToBusiness; (* get choice from user *)

    CASE Choice OF
       0 : OutText ( 'Press ENTER to stop.');
       1 : HandleArc;
       2 : HandleCircle;
       3 : HandleEllipse;
       4 : HandleLine;
       5 : HandlePixel;
       6 : HandleRectangle;
       7 .. 10 : HandleNotAvailable;
    END; (* CASE OF Choice *)
    READLN;
    ClearDevice;
  UNTIL  Choice = 0;
  CloseGraph;
END;
END.
```

Before discussing individual graphics (and nongraphics) routines, this section examines the main program. The first few statements initialize the menu and introduce the program. The next several statements put the screen into graphics mode, as in program **GraphIntro**. If everything goes smoothly, the real work of the program can begin.

The heart of the program consists of the **REPEAT** loop in which the following steps are repeated:

- Display a menu for the user.
- Get a selection.
- Act on that selection.
- Clear the screen.

Procedure **ToBusiness** keeps the main program from being too cluttered. This procedure does the following:

1. Leaves graphics mode and restores text mode: The predefined (in **GRAPH**) procedure **RestoreCRTMode** restores the screen to the mode in effect before your program went into graphics mode. (Its counterpart for returning to graphics mode — **SetGraphMode** — is described later in this list.)

2. Defines a window for displaying the menu by using the **SetWindow** procedure defined in the discussion of the **CRT** unit.

3. Displays the menu and gets a selection: Procedure **ShowMenu**, defined in Chapter 7, "Turbo Pascal's Structured Data Types," is used to display the contents of **Menu**, a global array of strings. The procedure also prompts for a selection, which procedure **GetBoundedInt** reads. (This version of **GetBoundedInt** is a modified version of the procedure defined in Chapter 6, "Procedures and Functions Revisited.")

4. Restores graphics mode: This is accomplished by calling the predefined procedure **SetGraphMode**, which restores the screen to graphics mode and sets the resolution specified in **Mode**.

5. Initializes settings for writing text while in graphics mode: This is accomplished by using the two predefined procedures **SetTextJustify** and **SetTextStyle**, which are described next.

Depending on the driver, **Mode** can have any of several values. For example, for a CGA driver, five modes (with values 0..4) are possible. The higher the value, the greater the resolution. **SetGraphMode** returns an error code if you pass a mode value not supported by the adapter being used.

The predefined function **GetMaxMode** returns the largest mode value possible for the driver currently in use. For example, for a CGA driver, this function would return 4; for a Hercules driver, it would return 0, since this driver supports only one high-resolution mode. (The fact that more modes are possible with a CGA adapter does not mean the resolution is greater for this adapter.) If you always want to use the highest possible resolution, you can simply call procedures such as **SetGraphMode** with the value returned by **GetMaxMode**.

Graphics mode displays text by writing bit patterns at a particular location on the screen. The reference location is the current point (CP). Because graphics mode gives you control over individual pixels, you need to specify exactly where, in relation to the CP, the bit pattern should be written. For example, you might want to center the first letter over the CP or put the CP at the lower-left dot of the first letter.

Procedure **SetTextJustify** enables you to specify where the character is written. The procedure takes two arguments, both of type **WORD**. The first argument locates the character horizontally with respect to the CP. In the program, **LeftText** indicates that the CP should be at the left edge of the letter. Other possible values are **CenterText** and **RightText**. The second argument locates the character vertically with respect to the CP. In the program, **TopText** indicates that the CP should be at the top edge of the letter. Other possible values are **CenterText** and **Bottom-Text**.

Procedure **SetTextStyle** lets you:

■ Select a font in which to display the text. Generally, you'll use the **Default Font**, which draws characters in 8 × 8 grids. Other possible values here are **GothicFont, SansSerifFont, TriplexFont,** and **Small-Font**. Try these other fonts. The fonts are contained in the .CHR files on disk 2.

■ Specify whether to write horizontally or vertically. **HorizDir** writes from left to right and **VertDir** writes from bottom to top.

■ Specify the size of the characters. Ordinarily, the default font is size 1, which displays an 8 × 8 grid. At size 2, as in the program, the characters are written in a 16 × 16 grid. You can specify character sizes up to 10. Try using different fonts at various sizes.

After procedure **ToBusiness**, one of the routines specified in the **CASE** statement is executed. The first case, when selection is 0, shows how actually to write text in graphics mode.

OutText (TheStr : STRING)
OutTextXY (XPos, YPos : INTEGER; TheStr : STRING) Procedure **OutText** writes a string to the graphics screen, beginning at the CP. The string is written as specified by the calls to **SetTextJustify** and **Set-TextStyle**, subject to the following restrictions:

■ When using the default font, nothing is output if any part of a character would be off the screen. Try changing the justification settings in **GraphExplorer.** You'll see that these changes may result in no output.

■ When using another font, output is truncated at the edge of the screen or viewport.

■ This procedure updates the CP only if you're writing horizontally and the characters are left justified (that is, **LeftText** is in effect). If the CP is not updated, calling the procedure again after writing something will overwrite the original material.

A related graphics procedure, **OutTextXY**, lets you write a string wherever you want on a graphics screen. This procedure's first two arguments represent the horizontal and vertical coordinates to be used as a reference for writing the string.

OutTextXY uses the same information as **OutText** and works under the same restrictions—except that **OutTextXY** never updates the CP.

Figure Drawing Routines

The next six choices in the **CASE** statement all draw something—either a pixel, line, or figure. The **HandleX** routines all involve the same series of actions, each carried out slightly differently. The major actions for these routines are summarized in the program's comments, at the start of the section on figure-drawing routines.

Making Labels   First, you provide labels with which to prompt the user for argument values. These prompts are stored in separate cells of a string (actually, **SmStr**) array. This array will be accessible to the routine responsible for getting argument values.

Procedure **MakeNames** (not a graphics routine) does this. The procedure takes a **SmStrArray** and a **STRING** as its arguments. The string contains separate words, with each word corresponding to a prompt. The order in which the prompts are given is the order in which the words appear in the string.

MakeNames calls **RemoveWd** to get the first word of the string and then to shorten the string accordingly. This word is assigned to the appropriate cell in the string array. This process is repeated until all the prompts have been put into the array.

Getting Values Once the labels have been created, **GetInfo** gets the values for the required number of arguments. This procedure first needs to restore text mode and define a window. Then the routine calls procedure **GetInteger** the required number of times. Each time, the appropriate prompt from **Names** is used.

After the **FOR** loop, **Data.Args** will contain the required number of parameter values, which will be used by the drawing routine. Once **GetInfo** has gotten the values, it restores graphics mode by using the call to **SetGraphMode**, as you saw earlier.

PutPixel (XPos, YPos : INTEGER; Color : WORD) For some of the figure-drawing routines, it makes sense to speak of a center for the figure being drawn. For example, a circle is defined as the collection of points that are a fixed distance from its center. Similarly, to draw an arc, you need to specify a point and a distance from this point.

For such drawing routines, it can be helpful to see where the center point is. The predefined procedure **PutPixel** lets you write at a particular location, such as at a center point. This procedure takes three arguments. The first two represent the horizontal and vertical coordinates of the pixel. The third argument specifies the color of the pixel.

Actually Drawing After the preceding tasks (making labels, getting values, and possibly drawing the center point), the handler routines call an actual drawing procedure. These are discussed individually, except for **Ellipse**, which was covered in program **GraphIntro**.

Arc (XPos, YPos : INTEGER; StartAngle, EndAngle, Radius : WORD) The **Arc** procedure draws a circular arc, using the point at location **XPos**, **YPos** as the reference. The arc is drawn a distance **Radius** from this point. The length and orientation of the arc depend on the values of **StartAngle** and **EndAngle**. These values again range from 0 through 360 and follow the conventions described for **Ellipse** in program **GraphIntro**. If you use values of 0 and 360 for the angle parameters, the arc will be a complete circle.

Circle (XPos, YPos : INTEGER; Radius : WORD) The **Circle** procedure draws a circle with the point at location **XPos**, **YPos** as its center. The circle is drawn a distance **Radius** from this point.

Line (X1, Y1, X2, Y2 : INTEGER)
LineTo (XPos, YPos : INTEGER)
LineRel (XDist, YDist : INTEGER)   Procedure **Line** (the only one of the three used in the program) draws a line from the point at **X1, Y1** to the point at **X2, Y2**. This line's style will either use default settings or will use settings that you have specified.

Procedure **LineTo** draws a line from the current point to the point at **XPos, YPos**.

Procedure **LineRel** draws a line from the current point to a point at a distance determined by the two parameters. **XDist** specifies the horizontal distance and **YDist** specifies the vertical distance. The distances specified can be negative. For positive distances, the line goes to the right (positive **XDist**) and downward (positive **YDist**). For negative **XDist**, the line goes to the left, and for negative **YDist**, the line goes upward.

SetLineStyle (Style, Pattern, Thickness : WORD)   The source code for **HandleLine** in program **GraphExplorer** contains a call to **SetLineStyle**. This procedure lets you specify what your line should look like and how thick it should be.

The **Style** argument can take any of five values:

SolidLine	(= 0)
DottedLine	(= 1)
CenterLine	(= 2)
DashedLine	(= 3)
UserBitLine	(= 4), in which a pixel pattern you specify is used

The third parameter for **SetLineStyle** can have either of two values: **NormWidth** (= 1) or **ThickWidth** (= 3). In the latter case, three lines are drawn next to each other so that the line looks three times as thick. The **Pattern** parameter is used only if you've set **Style** to **UserBitLn**. In that case, you need to specify the bit pattern that should be used to draw the line. To do this, specify a hexadecimal value. The bit pattern corresponding to this value will be used when the line is drawn. For example, a dotted line is drawn with the following bit pattern:

```
1100110011001100    (* $CCCC *)
```

To specify such a line, set **Pattern** to **$CCCC**. (The bit pattern for hexadecimal C is 1100, and each hexadecimal digit represents four bits.)

Rectangle (X1, X2, Y1, Y2 : INTEGER)   This procedure draws a rectangle with **X1, Y1** as one corner and **X2, Y2** as the diagonally opposite corner.

More To Explore

There are many other things you can do with the Turbo Pascal graphics capabilities. In fact, entire books have been written about graphics. This section gave just a brief introduction to the topic. To explore other graphics routines, start with the information in Appendix B and the on-line help for the **GRAPH** unit and its routines.

In this chapter, you learned about some of the units provided with Turbo Pascal: **CRT, DOS**, and **GRAPH**.

In the next chapter, you'll learn about object-oriented programming.

Object-Oriented Programming and Language Extensions

Part Two

11 *Object-Oriented Programming in Turbo Pascal*

Object-oriented programming (OOP) enables you to take advantage of some important properties that often hold for the elements in a problem that your program is designed to solve. Many programmers regard OOP as the programming technique of the future. In this chapter and the next, you'll learn how to use object-oriented programming. OOP capabilities are relatively new to Turbo Pascal. You won't be able to compile programs in the next three chapters with other Pascal compilers or even with Turbo Pascal compilers earlier than version 5.5.

Traditional Versus Object-Oriented Programming

Traditional programming strategies are characterized succinctly in the title, *Algorithms + Data Structures = Programs* (Englewood Cliffs, N.J.: Prentice-Hall, 1976), of Niklaus Wirth's book on structured programming. In traditional programming, you design programs by determining what actions need to be performed and the most appropriate representation for the information to be transformed. The actions are systematized in algorithms and implemented in procedures and functions. These routines are then applied to the program's data structures.

Example: Cataloging Written Materials

Suppose you want to build a program to catalog written materials of various types. For example, you might want to keep track of the author, title, and other information for books, articles, and miscellaneous publications.

The following program shows the beginnings of a traditional approach to building such a program. It contains procedures for carrying out actions such as initializing, displaying, and extending information about specified items. The information is stored in records.

```
P11-1    PROGRAM PubDemo;
         TYPE MedStr = STRING [ 80];

              Document = RECORD
                           Author, Title, Code : MedStr;
                           Year : INTEGER;
                         END; (* Document *)

              Book = RECORD
                       Author, Title,
                       Code, Publisher : MedStr;
                       Year : INTEGER;
                       Price : REAL;
                     END; (* Book *)

              Article = RECORD
                          Author, Title, Code : MedStr;
                          Year : INTEGER;
                          Journal : MedStr;
                          Volume, Page : INTEGER;
                        END; (* Article *)


         (* ************************************************** *)

         PROCEDURE InitDocument ( VAR Pub : Document;
                                  Au, Ti : MedStr;
                                  Yr : INTEGER);
         BEGIN
```

```
    WITH Pub DO
    BEGIN
      Author := Au;
      Title := Ti;
      Year := Yr;
      Code := '';
    END;
END; (* InitDocument *)

PROCEDURE DescribeDocument ( Pub : Document);
BEGIN
  WITH Pub DO
    WRITELN ( Code, ': ', Author, ', ', Title,
              ' [', Year, ']');
END; (* DescribeDocument *)

PROCEDURE GetCode ( VAR TheCode : MedStr);
BEGIN
  WRITE ( 'Code? ');
  READLN ( TheCode);
END; (* GetCode *)

PROCEDURE CatalogDocument ( VAR Pub : Document);
BEGIN
  DescribeDocument ( Pub);
  GetCode ( Pub.Code);
END; (* CatalogDocument *)

PROCEDURE InitArticle ( VAR Art : Article;
                        Au, Ti, Jour : MedStr;
                        Yr, Vol, Pg : INTEGER);
BEGIN
  WITH Art DO
  BEGIN
    Author := Au;
    Title := Ti;
    Year := Yr;
    Code := '';
    Journal := Jour;
    Volume := Vol;
    Page := Pg;
  END;
END; (* InitArticle *)

PROCEDURE DescribeArticle ( Art : Article);
BEGIN
  WITH Art DO
  BEGIN
    WRITELN ( Code, ': ', Author, ', ', Title,
              ' [', Year, ']');
    WRITE ( Journal, ', ');
    WRITELN ( 'volume ', Volume, '; p. ', Page);
```

```
      END;
    END; (* DescribeArticle *)

    PROCEDURE CatalogArticle ( VAR Art : Article);
    BEGIN
      DescribeArticle ( Art);
      GetCode ( Art.Code);
    END; (* CatalogArticle *)

    PROCEDURE InitBook ( VAR TheBook : Book;
                         Au, Ti, Pub : MedStr;
                         Yr : INTEGER;
                         Pr : REAL);
    BEGIN
      WITH TheBook DO
      BEGIN
        Author := Au;
        Title := Ti;
        Code:= '';
        Year := Yr;
        Publisher := Pub;
        Price := Pr;
      END;
    END; (* InitBook *)

    PROCEDURE DescribeBook ( TheBook : Book);
    BEGIN
      WITH TheBook DO
      BEGIN
        WRITELN ( Code, ': ', Author, ', ', Title,
                  ' [', Year, ']');
        WRITELN ( '$', Price : 1 : 2, ', ', Publisher);
      END;
    END; (* DescribeBook *)

    PROCEDURE CatalogBook ( VAR TheBook : Book);
    BEGIN
      DescribeBook ( TheBook);
      GetCode ( TheBook.Code);
    END; (* CatalogBook *)

VAR MyBk : Book;
    MyArt : Article;
    MyPub : Document;

BEGIN (* main program *)
  InitDocument ( MyPub, 'Many Signers',
                 'Declaration of Independence', 1776);
  InitArticle ( MyArt, 'Mosteller, F.',
                'The Mystery of the Missing Corpus',
```

```
                'Psychometrika', 1958, 23, 279);
   InitBook  ( MyBk, 'Programming, O.O.', 'I, Object',
               'OOP Press', 1989, 22.95);
   WRITELN ( 'BOOK:');
   CatalogBook ( MyBk);
   DescribeBook ( MyBk);
   READLN;
END.
```

The program illustrates some things about traditional programming strategies and stands in contrast to object-oriented solutions that you'll develop during this and the next chapter.

First, look at the data structures used in the program. Three different record types are defined: **Document**, **Article**, and **Book**. These records are all similar but not identical. Most of the fields should be self-explanatory. In the **Code** field, you can identify the variable in an abbreviated form. For example, many books and magazines use the first few letters of the author's name and the year of publication within square brackets, as in the following:

```
Most[58]
```

For each of the record types, there are corresponding procedures to

- Initialize a variable of the given type
- Display the contents of such a variable
- Modify certain fields of such a variable

Another traditional approach uses a variant record to group all three kinds of documents within the same type definition. In that case, you would use a definition such as the following. Note that this variant record has an extra field:

```
TYPE MedStr = STRING [ 80];
     PubType = ( doc, article, book);

     Document = RECORD
       Author, Title, Code : MedStr;
       Year : INTEGER;
       CASE WhatKind : PubType OF
         doc : ();
```

```
      article : ( Journal : MedStr;
                  Volume, Page : INTEGER);
      book : ( Publisher : MedStr;
               Price : REAL);
  END; (* Document *)
```

With this approach, you could use the same **Describe** and **Catalog** routines, regardless of the variable. However, you need to add **CASE** statements to these routines to handle the variants. Moreover, you still need separate initialization routines for each of the variants, since the parameter list would contain too many unused arguments if you try to use the same routine for all the variants.

An Object-Oriented Approach

In OOP the approach is very different. Instead of focusing on the algorithms to be used and the data structures to which they should be applied, you first describe the entities involved in the program. The key in OOP is to find common features among entities, and to create data structures ("objects") that capture these common features. Other entities can then share these features.

Think about how you would organize information about written materials. At the minimum, you would want to store author, title, and year information. As part of your description of an object, you would also include information about how to use the object. All written documents have at least these three features; however, for certain types of documents, you would store additional information. Thus, a book is a special type of document; an article is also a type of document, but it differs from a book.

Object-oriented programming also lets you relate elements to each other. For example, in many problems and situations, related elements have features in common. These features may be derived (inherited) from a common element, which is more general (that is, has fewer features) than the elements being compared.

In OOP, you can use the fact that books and articles are special cases of a document. In essence, once you've defined a document, you can define a book as "a document with some additional information associated with it." In principle, you can extend your definitions as far as necessary. For example, you could distinguish novels and textbooks as special cases of books, which are a special case of document. You might further distinguish introductory and advanced textbooks, and so forth.

Similarly, poker, blackjack, and rummy are all card games. As such, they all use a deck, deal a fixed number of cards to each player, and so forth. These are some of the features that the three games might acquire from the more general category of card game. The three games differ in the way the cards are used by the players.

You can place such games in a hierarchy, with card games being a superordinate category under which you find the three types of card games. If you wish, you can even extend this hierarchy, both upward and downward. For example, card games are a specific example of games in general. Similarly, you can distinguish different types of poker games: five-card draw, seven-card stud, baseball, and so forth. Figure 11-1 shows a hierarchy involving card games.

Object-oriented programming lets you take advantage of the fact that elements in your programs can often be related in such a hierarchical fashion, with elements lower in the hierarchy having the features of elements higher in the hierarchy, as well as some features of their own. The data structures defined to represent such elements are known as *object types,* or *classes.*

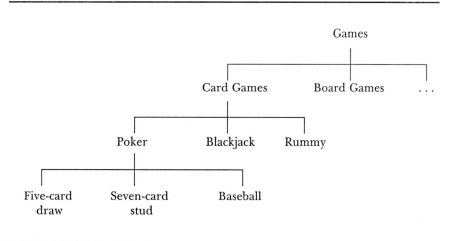

Figure 11-1.   *Hierarchical relationships among different types of games*

An element below another in the hierarchy is said to be a *descendant* of the higher element. For example, a book and an article are both descendants of a document; blackjack is a descendant of card games. Conversely, an element above another in the hierarchy is said to be an *ancestor* of the lower element. Thus, a document is an ancestor of an article and of a book. A descendant element is a special case of an ancestor, and has all the features of its ancestor, as well as additional features.

Inheritance

In object-oriented programming, you can build such acquired features directly into your object type definitions by using a property known as inheritance. Inheritance enables a descendant object type to have the features of its ancestor types. This capability makes certain programming tasks much easier and more convenient. You don't have to describe each feature explicitly for each element, since elements can inherit features from each other.

For example, suppose you're trying to represent information about animals. You may want to represent information about different types of animals—perhaps you want to differentiate among mammals, birds, and insects. These types represent subgroupings under the more general category of animals. For each of these groupings, you'll have unique information to record; however, each also has more general characteristics that apply to all animals. Thus, mammals, birds, and insects share those features that characterize animals.

You may also want to differentiate within groupings. For example, you may want to store different information about primates (humans and apes) and cats, or about flies and ants. These subgroupings will have unique features, but will share more general features of their common ancestor groupings. Thus, both cats and primates are mammals. Consequently, they share the attributes associated with mammals. Since mammals are animals, cats and primates will also have those features.

A lower-level (that is, more specific) element is said to inherit features of more general elements. In addition, lower-level elements also have unique features. Thus, primates inherit the characteristics of a mammal and of an animal; humans are primates, which are mammals, which are animals. In the earlier example, poker, blackjack, and rummy are all card games; these, in turn, are a special case of a more general category: games.

Look at one more example. Suppose you want to represent information about geometric shapes. At the most general level, a shape may have a name, and may have some specified number of dimensions (two dimensions for shapes that lie on a surface and three dimensions for shapes in space). You might divide shapes into categories such as triangles, four-sided figures (quadrilaterals), and round figures. Beyond this division, you might distinguish rectangles, parallelograms, and trapezoids within quadrilaterals. In such a system, the subgroupings would each have their own characteristics, but would also have any features of quadrilaterals and of shapes in general.

This subdivision process can continue for as many levels as you need. For instance, you could distinguish between squares and nonsquares within rectangles. These "subsubgroupings" have all the features of more general elements. A square is a rectangle, which is a quadrilateral, which is a shape.

Standard Pascal has no suitable way of representing inheritance that spans multiple levels. Variant records are the most likely approach for representing such relationships. However, these are limited to one level of inheritance, since you can only have one variant part in a record. In a variant record you could, for example, include both mammals and insects as variants within an animal record. You could not further distinguish primates and cats under mammals, however, without resorting to programming tricks to fool the system.

Turbo Pascal's object-oriented extensions enable you to represent such inheritance in a very clean way. You can define a high-level (general) element (such as animal). Once you've done this, you can define a lower-level element (such as insect) that is a special case of animal. By specifying an insect as a special case, you immediately associate an animal's features with this subdivision.

Associating Actions with Object Types

Standard programs are quite adequate for representing the features of problem elements. However, in real problems, elements often have actions associated directly with the elements. For example, each card game in the earlier example would have a dealing technique associated with it. The details of this routine will differ from game to game, however.

In object-oriented programming, such actions are included as part of an object type's definition. The actions are known as methods when associated with an object type. You'll see how to specify, define, and use methods after you learn how to define object types in Turbo Pascal.

Representing Objects

Suppose you want to use an object-oriented program to catalog written materials. You might first define a data type to represent a document—the minimal information you expect to store about any kind of written material.

Representing a Document

In Turbo Pascal, you can represent such an item by using the **OBJECT** type just introduced in the most recent version of Turbo Pascal. The following listing shows how to define a **Document** type:

```
TYPE MedStr = STRING [ 80];

    Document = OBJECT
       Author, Title, Code : MedStr;
       Year : INTEGER;
    END; (* Document *)
```

Notice that, except for the reserved word **OBJECT**, the syntax for the definition of **Document** is almost identical to a record definition. As you'll soon see, however, there are major differences between a record and an object type.

An **OBJECT** definition is the third place you can have an **END** without a corresponding **BEGIN**. (The other two are in a record definition and a **CASE** statement.)

Representing a Shape

As another example, suppose you want to create a program that uses geometric shapes. You might want first to define a data type to represent such a shape. The following listing shows how to define a **Shape**, how to declare a variable of this type, and how to refer to a field within this variable. Before you run the program, try to predict its output. In particular, determine the amount of storage allocated to **MyShape** and to a particular field within this variable.

```
P11-2    (* Program showing how to define an object type,
            how to declare an object variable, and how to
            refer to a field within an object.
         *)
         PROGRAM ObjDemo;
         TYPE SmStr = STRING [ 30];

            (* Define a shape as an object type with two features.
               Note how similar this syntax is to that for a record.
            *)
            Shape = OBJECT
                    Name : SmStr;
                    NrDimensions : INTEGER;
                  END; (* Shape OBJECT *)

         VAR MyShape : Shape;

         BEGIN
            WRITELN ( 'MyShape       requires ', SIZEOF ( MyShape),
                    ' bytes.');
            WRITELN ( 'MyShape.Name requires ', SIZEOF ( MyShape.Name),
                    ' bytes.');
            READLN;
         END.
```

If you predicted that a **Shape** requires 32 bytes, you probably forgot that Turbo Pascal adds an extra cell to a **STRING** variable. This cell contains the string's length.

Once you've defined an object type, you can declare variables of that type. These variables are known as instances of the object, or simply as objects. Thus, the variable **MyShape** is an instance of a **Shape**. The syntax for declaring an object variable is the same as for any other type.

To access an object's fields, use the same technique as for records. In other words, to refer to a field, specify the variable's identifier, followed by a period, followed by the field name.

Representing Inheritance

An object type's fields can be inherited by other, more specialized object types. Thus, once you've defined a **Shape**, you can define different types of shapes. For example, you can define shapes with three sides (triangles), four sides (squares, diamonds, and so on), and round shapes (circles, ellipses). Each of these special shapes inherits all the features of a **Shape**, and each has some unique fields.

REMEMBER   Only object types can inherit features from other object types. Inheritance is not possible for other Pascal data structures (such as records).

The following listing shows how to define descendant objects. **Shape** is the ancestor object type for the other three classes, which are all descendant object types. Again, try to predict the size of each variable before running the program.

```
P11-3    * Program to illustrate how to define and use
            descendant objects.
         *)

         PROGRAM ObjDemo2;

         TYPE SmStr = STRING [ 30];

               (* Define a shape as an object type with two features.
                  Note how similar this syntax is to that for a record.
               *)
               Shape = OBJECT
                       Name : SmStr;
                       NrDimensions : INTEGER;
                     END; (* Shape OBJECT *)
```

```
                (* Define a triangle as a shape with 2 additional features.
                   Note that a Shape's fields are not mentioned;
                   the identifier Shape is used, however.
                *)
                Triangle = OBJECT ( Shape)
                             Angle1, Angle2 : REAL;
                           END; (* Triangle OBJECT *)

                (* Define a quadrilateral as a shape with 3 additional
                   features. Both this and triangle are more specialized
                   instances of a Shape.
                *)
                Quadrilateral = OBJECT ( Shape)
                                  Angle1, Angle2, Angle3 : REAL;
                                END; (* Quadrilateral OBJECT *)

                (* Define a Round as a shape with only one additional
                   feature.
                *)
                Round = OBJECT ( Shape)
                          MinRadius : REAL;
                        END; (* Round OBJECT *)

        VAR MyShape : Shape;
            MyTri : Triangle;
            MyQuad : Quadrilateral;
            MyRound : Round;

          (* Display information about the storage required for
             the type specified by Name. Note that the size must
             be passed into the procedure; it is not determined here.
          *)
          PROCEDURE DispSize ( Name : STRING;
                               Size : INTEGER);
          BEGIN
            WRITELN ( Name : 20, ' requires ', Size : 3, ' bytes.');
          END; (* DispSize *)

        BEGIN
          DispSize ( 'MyShape', SIZEOF ( MyShape));
          DispSize ( 'MyShape.Name', SIZEOF ( MyShape.Name));
          WRITELN;

          DispSize ( 'MyTri', SIZEOF ( MyTri));
          DispSize ( 'MyTri.Name', SIZEOF ( MyTri.Name));
          WRITELN;

          DispSize ( 'MyQuad', SIZEOF ( MyQuad));
          DispSize ( 'MyQuad.Name', SIZEOF ( MyQuad.Name));
          WRITELN;

          DispSize ( 'MyRound', SIZEOF ( MyRound));
```

```
     DispSize ( 'MyRound.Name', SIZEOF ( MyRound.Name));
     WRITELN;

     READLN;
END.
```

Similarly, the following definitions let you describe books and articles as special types of documents. In the listing, **Book** and **Article** are descendants of **Document**, which is their ancestor.

```
PROGRAM DocDemo;

TYPE MedStr = STRING [ 80];

     Document = OBJECT
                   Author, Title, Code : MedStr;
                   Year : INTEGER;
                 END; (* Document *)

     Book = OBJECT (Document)
              Publisher : MedStr;
              Price : REAL;
            END; (* Book *)

     Article = OBJECT (Document)
                 Journal : MedStr;
                 Volume, Page : INTEGER;
               END; (* Article *)

VAR MyDoc : Document;
    MyBk : Book;
    NyArt : Article;

BEGIN
  (* Code will eventually be included here *)
END.
```

The syntax of the definitions for **Book** and **Article** differs slightly from the definition for **Document**. Both **Book** and **Article** have the word **Document** in parentheses after the word **OBJECT**. In the listing, **Book** inherits features from **Document**, as does **Article**.

To define a descendant object type, such as a **Book**, simply include the name of the ancestor type within parentheses after the reserved word **OBJECT**. The fields to be associated with a **Book** are specified after this—just as in a record or in **Document**.

The following illustration shows the syntax for an object type definition. The material within parentheses is included only if the object type is descended from an existing object type.

```
<type name> = "OBJECT" {"("<ancestor name>")"}
                <field list>
            "END"
```

When you specify **Book** as a descendant of the **Document** type, you're describing a book as having four fields more than its definition would suggest. Although the fields are never mentioned explicitly in the definition of a **Book**, this type will have one **INTEGER** and three **MedStr** fields, in addition to its **Publisher** and **Price** fields.

Thus, you can specify **MyBk.Author** as a field for a **Book** variable, even though this field was not included explicitly in the **Book** definition. The syntax for specifying a field from an object type's ancestor indicates that **Document** is not nested within **Book**. Rather, a **Document**'s fields are part of the definition of a **Book**.

Figure 11-2 shows how storage for a **Book** might be laid out and shows all six fields for a **Book**.

You can carry inheritance to further levels of descendants. For example, you could define a **Novel**, as in the following listing:

```
(* Define an object type that inherits the features of a Book
   which, in turn, inherits features of a Document.
   A novel variable will have seven fields:
   Author, Title, Code, Year (from Document);
   Publisher, Price (from Book); and
   Genre (unique to Novel).
*)
TYPE Novel = OBJECT (Book)
                Genre : MedStr;
             END; (* Novel *)
```

This definition says that a **Novel** has one explicit field: **Genre**. In addition, however, this type has all the fields of a **Book**. As a **Book**, a

Novel is a **Document** with several additional fields. Thus, **Novel** has inherited fields from two other object types: directly from **Book** and indirectly (through **Book**) from **Document**.

Again, such inherited fields are all represented at the same level. For example, if **MyNovel** is of type **Novel**, then all of the following are valid fields:

```
MyNovel.Year;
MyNovel.Price;
MyNovel.Code;
MyNovel.Genre;
MyNovel.Author;
```

Inheritance can make your programming tasks easier, because you can create your objects incrementally. That is, you can define a general object type, and use it as part of more specific objects without explicitly specifying all the individual fields again. This is especially useful if you want to create new objects to use in your program, as you will see in Chapter 12, "Virtual Methods in Object-Oriented Programming."

REMEMBER   When you specify that an object type is a descendant of

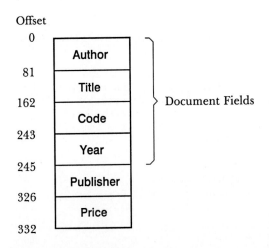

Figure 11-2.   *Storage layout for a Book object type*

another type, the descendant class inherits all the features of the ancestor class, as well as of any classes inherited by the ancestor type or *its* ancestors.

Methods

Another feature of object-oriented programming is the ability to specify methods when defining an object. A *method* is a routine associated with a particular object type. This routine is available to any objects and descendant objects. The method is *not* available for use with non-objects. In a sense, a method is part of an object type's definition.

REMEMBER A method is a procedure or function that is associated with an object type. You cannot associate methods with other Pascal data types (such as records).

The following listing expands the definition of a **Document** and shows how to specify methods as part of an object type's definition:

```
TYPE MedStr = STRING [ 80];

     Document = OBJECT
       Author, Title, Code : MedStr;
       Year : INTEGER;
       (* Specify four methods associated with a Document *)
       PROCEDURE Init ( Au, Ti : MedStr;
                        Yr : INTEGER);
       PROCEDURE Describe;
       PROCEDURE GetCode;
       PROCEDURE Catalog;
     END; (* Document *)
```

This extended version of **Document** has several new components. The headings for four procedures are specified as part of **Document**'s definition. These methods are part of the definition of the object type within which they are specified. Thus, an element's features and actions are included within the definition of the type. This combination of features and methods within the same object type is known as *encapsulation*. Here, the four procedures are encapsulated within **Document**.

The procedure headings indicate that **Init** takes three arguments to do its work, while the other methods don't need any specific values when called. (Notice that the **Init** method actually changes four fields of a **Document**, but initializes one of them — **Code** — to a default value. This field is changed to a desired value by using one of the other methods.)

The implementations (that is, heading plus body) for these procedures appear outside the type definition — generally in the section in which ordinary routines are defined. The implementations for the encapsulated methods indicate just how closely methods are associated with their objects. Notice the names of the procedures in the implementation.

```
(* Initialize fields of a Document to the specified values.
   Note that Init knows the names of Document's fields.
*)
PROCEDURE Document.Init ( Au, Ti : MedStr;
                          Yr : INTEGER);
BEGIN
  Author := Au;
  Title := Ti;
  Year := Yr;
  Code := '';   (* initialize to a default value *)
END; (* Document.Init *)

(* Display values of a Document's fields. *)
PROCEDURE Document.Describe;
BEGIN
  WRITELN ( Code, ': ', Author, ', ', Title, ' [', Year, ']');
END; (* Document.Describe *)

(* Get a value for the Code field from the user *)
PROCEDURE Document.GetCode;
BEGIN
  WRITE ( 'Code? ');
  READLN ( Code);
END; (* Document.GetCode *)

(* Catalog a particular element by getting a code for it.
   Note that the calls are to Describe and GetCode,
   rather than to Document.Describe, etc.
*)
PROCEDURE Document.Catalog;
BEGIN
  Describe;
```

```
    GetCode;
  END; (* Document.Catalog *)
```

To indicate that the routines are a part of a **Document**'s definition, the method's name includes the name of the object type. In other words, the action is specified as if it were a field in the object type.

Document.Init assigns specified or default values to the object type's fields. **Document.Describe** displays the values of these fields. The method **Document.GetCode** gets a value for a specific field of a **Document**. Finally, **Document.Catalog** displays information about the object type and then gets a value from the user.

A method automatically has direct access to the fields of its encapsulating object type. You don't need to use parameters to specify the actual fields within the object. Because an object's field names are known to a method associated with the object, you can't use the same identifiers in the method's parameter list. Doing so would be like using the same identifiers for parameters in the procedure heading and for local variables when defining a procedure.

REMEMBER A method has access to the fields of its encapsulating object type and to any fields accessible to this type through inheritance.

Also, notice how the arguments passed to **Document.Init** are used. Values are assigned directly to **Author, Title**, and so forth. You don't have to specify the type name before the field. In fact, it is an error to do so.

Once you have defined these methods, you just need to call them with a suitable object as the variable whose fields are to be assigned values. The object used should be of the same type as the one in the definition, but can also be a descendant of that type.

If you make the method part of the object type's definition, it becomes accessible to any instance of the object type. The next program shows how to refer to such an object. To call the **Init** method for your program's object variables, just specify the name of the **Document** variable you want to initialize. This name will be part of the call to **Init** in the program.

The following program lets you initialize a document variable as often as you want and displays the values each time. Look at the definitions and the calls to methods associated with **Document**.

P11-4

```
(* Program to illustrate how to specify, define and use
   methods.
*)

(*$V-*)

PROGRAM MethodDemo;
TYPE MedStr = STRING [ 80];

     Document = OBJECT
       Author, Title, Code : MedStr;
       Year : INTEGER;
       PROCEDURE Init ( Au, Ti : MedStr;
                        Yr : INTEGER);
       PROCEDURE Describe;
       PROCEDURE GetCode;
       PROCEDURE Catalog;
     END; (* Document *)

(* ************** Methods ************** *)

  PROCEDURE Document.Init ( Au, Ti : MedStr;
                            Yr : INTEGER);
  BEGIN
    Author := Au;
    Title := Ti;
    Year := Yr;
    Code := '';
  END; (* Document.Init *)

  PROCEDURE Document.Describe;
  BEGIN
    WRITELN ( Code, ': ', Author, ', ', Title, ' [', Year, ']');
  END; (* Document.Describe *)

  PROCEDURE Document.GetCode;
  BEGIN
    WRITE ( 'Code? ');
    READLN ( Code);
  END; (* Document.GetCode *)

  PROCEDURE Document.Catalog;
  BEGIN
    Describe;
    GetCode;
  END; (* Document.Catalog *)

(* ************** General-Purpose Routines ************** *)

  PROCEDURE GetString ( Message : STRING;
                        VAR Value : STRING);
```

```
    BEGIN
      WRITE ( Message, ' ');
      READLN ( Value);
    END; (* GetString *)

    PROCEDURE GetInteger ( Message : STRING;
                           VAR Value : INTEGER);
    BEGIN
      WRITE ( Message, ' ');
      READLN ( Value);
    END; (* GetInteger *)

VAR MyDoc : Document;
    Writer, Name : MedStr;
    Year : INTEGER;

BEGIN
  REPEAT
    GetString ( 'Author? (ENTER to stop)', Writer);
    IF Writer <> '' THEN
    BEGIN
      GetString ( 'Title', Name);
      GetInteger ( 'Year', Year);
      MyDoc.Init ( Writer, Name, Year);
      MyDoc.Catalog;
      MyDoc.Describe;
    END;
  UNTIL Writer = '';
END.
```

Note that the program calls **MyDoc.Init,** even though the procedure definition was for **Document.Init**. When you actually call an object type's method, it will be to initialize an *instance* of the object. The **MyDoc** in the call indicates that initialization and display are to involve the fields of this particular document. The definition of **Document.Init** serves as a generic template for calls involving specific documents.

The **MedStr** fields of a **Document** are 80-character strings. The **GetString** procedure in program **MethodDemo** will get and return a full (255-character) string. If the compiler is doing strict **VAR**-string checking (as described in Chapter 3, "Turbo Pascal's Simple Data Types"), you will get a compiler error indicating a type mismatch.

To convince the compiler to let you get a **SmStr** with the **GetString** procedure, use the **$V-** compiler directive (remember, this relaxes the **VAR**-string checking).

Overriding Methods

When you define descendant object types, these types also inherit any methods associated with the ancestor type. Thus, **Book** and **Article** would both inherit **Init** and **Describe** methods from **Document**.

However, these inherited methods may be insufficient when working with descendant types, which have more fields. In object-oriented programming, you can override an existing method by defining another one with the same name and associating this method with the descendant object.

The following program shows how to specify and use methods for descendant object types. The program lets you enter information to describe a **Document, Book,** or **Article**. After you describe the instance, the program initializes and then displays the values of the instance's fields.

P11-5
```
(* Program to illustrate how to specify methods to
     override methods inherited from ancestor object types.
*)
(*$V-*)
PROGRAM OverrideDemo;

TYPE MedStr = STRING [ 80];

     Document = OBJECT
               Author, Title, Code : MedStr;
               Year : INTEGER;
               PROCEDURE Init ( Au, Ti : MedStr;
                                      Yr : INTEGER);
               PROCEDURE Describe;
               PROCEDURE GetCode;
               PROCEDURE Catalog;
             END; (* Document *)

     Book = OBJECT (Document)
            Publisher : MedStr;
            Price : REAL;
            PROCEDURE Init ( Au, Ti, Pub : MedStr;
                                   Yr : INTEGER;
                                   Pr : REAL);
            PROCEDURE Describe;
            PROCEDURE Catalog;
          END; (* Book *)
```

```
    Article = OBJECT (Document)
                Journal : MedStr;
                Volume, Page : INTEGER;
                PROCEDURE Init ( Au, Ti, Jour : MedStr;
                                   Yr, Vol, Pg : INTEGER);
                PROCEDURE Describe;
                PROCEDURE Catalog;
              END; (* Article *)


(* *************** Methods *************** *)

  PROCEDURE Document.Init ( Au, Ti : MedStr;
                              Yr : INTEGER);
  BEGIN
    Author := Au;
    Title := Ti;
    Year := Yr;
    Code := '';
  END; (* Document.Init *)


  PROCEDURE Document.Describe;
  BEGIN
    WRITELN ( Code, ': ', Author, ', ', Title, ' [', Year, ']');
  END; (* Document.Describe *)


  PROCEDURE Document.GetCode;
  BEGIN
    WRITE ( 'Code? ');
    READLN ( Code);
  END; (* Document.GetCode *)


  PROCEDURE Document.Catalog;
  BEGIN
    Describe;
    GetCode;
  END; (* Document.Catalog *)

  PROCEDURE Article.Init ( Au, Ti, Jour : MedStr;
                             Yr, Vol, Pg : INTEGER);
  BEGIN
    Document.Init ( Au, Ti, Yr);
    Journal := Jour;
    Volume := Vol;
    Page := Pg;
  END; (* Article.Init *)

  PROCEDURE Article.Describe;
  BEGIN
```

```
    Document.Describe;
    WRITE ( Journal, ', ');
    WRITELN ( 'volume ', Volume, '; p. ', Page);
  END; (* Article.Describe *)

  PROCEDURE Article.Catalog;
  BEGIN
    Describe;
    GetCode;
  END; (* Article.Catalog *)

  PROCEDURE Book.Init ( Au, Ti, Pub : MedStr;
                        Yr : INTEGER;
                        Pr : REAL);
  BEGIN
    Document.Init ( Au, Ti, Yr);
    Publisher := Pub;
    Price := Pr;
  END; (* Book.Init *)

  PROCEDURE Book.Describe;
  BEGIN
    Document.Describe;
    WRITELN ( '$', Price : 1 : 2, ', ', Publisher);
  END; (* Book.Describe *)

  PROCEDURE Book.Catalog;
  BEGIN
    Describe;
    GetCode;
  END; (* Book.Catalog *)

(* ************** General-Purpose Routines ************** *)

  PROCEDURE GetString ( Message : STRING;
                        VAR Value : STRING);
  BEGIN
    WRITE ( Message, ' ');
    READLN ( Value);
  END; (* GetString *)

  PROCEDURE GetInteger ( Message : STRING;
                         VAR Value : INTEGER);
  BEGIN
    WRITE ( Message, ' ');
    READLN ( Value);
  END; (* GetInteger *)

  PROCEDURE GetReal ( Message : STRING;
                      VAR Value : REAL);
```

```
      BEGIN
        WRITE ( Message, ' ');
        READLN ( Value);
      END; (* GetReal *)


VAR MyDoc : Document;
    MyBk : Book;
    MyArt : Article;
    Writer, Name, Pub, Jour : MedStr;
    Choice, Year, Vol, Pg : INTEGER;
    Price : REAL;


BEGIN
  GetInteger ( '0) Quit; 1) Doc; 2) Book; 3) Article', Choice);
  WHILE Choice <> 0 DO
  BEGIN
    GetString ( 'Author?', Writer);
    GetString ( 'Title', Name);
    GetInteger ( 'Year', Year);
    CASE Choice OF
      1 :
        BEGIN
          MyDoc.Init ( Writer, Name, Year);
          MyDoc.Catalog;
          MyDoc.Describe;
        END;
      2 :
        BEGIN
          GetString ( 'Publisher', Pub);
          GetReal ( 'Price', Price);
          MyBk.Init ( Writer, Name, Pub, Year, Price);
          MyBk.Catalog;
          MyBk.Describe;
        END;
      3 :
        BEGIN
          GetString ( 'Journal', Jour);
          GetInteger ( 'Volume', Vol);
          GetInteger ( 'Page', Pg);
          MyArt.Init ( Writer, Name, Jour, Year, Vol, Pg);
          MyArt.Catalog;
          MyArt.Describe;
        END;
    END;
    GetInteger ('0) Quit; 1) Doc; 2) Book; 3) Article', Choice);
  END; (* WHILE Loop *)
END.
```

As descendants of **Document**, the **Book** and **Article** types inherit **Document.Init** and **Document.Describe**. However, when you specify new **Init** and **Describe** methods within **Book** and **Article**, these override the ones inherited from **Document**. Thus, when the main program calls **MyArt.Init**, the method associated with **Article** is used rather than one associated with **Document**.

Notice that **Book.Init** actually calls **Document.Init** to initialize the fields inherited from that ancestor object type. This is considered better programming practice than initializing **Author**, **Title**, and **Year** explicitly in **Book.Init**.

When **Document.Init** is called in this way, the program knows what variable is meant. This is because the call to **Book.Init** has already specified a variable. Within the context of this method, all activity is assumed to apply to the instance specified in the call.

In the program, note that **Book.Init** and **Document.Init** take a different number of arguments. The number and types of arguments passed when a method is called must match the interface for the method that will be executed. Thus, the compiler will not allow you to call **Book.Init** with only three parameters.

You can specify methods for descendants of descendants, and so forth. Each method that has the same name as a method already defined in an ancestor object type will override the method of the same name in the more general object type. For instance, when the program encounters a call to a method, it searches the local environment of the object specified in the call. If a method with that name is found, this method is executed. If no such method is associated directly with the object, the program checks the ancestor object for such a method. This process continues until a method with the specified name is found. The first matching method is executed—provided that the call has the appropriate number and types of parameters.

In this particular example, each object type has its own methods. If you had not specified methods for **Book** (that is, if the definition for **Book** did not specify an **Init** method), a call to **MyBk.Init** would activate **Document.Init**. However, only the four fields in that object type would be initialized in that case. The values for the other fields in **MyBk** would be undefined.

Assignments Between Different Object Types

Recall from Chapter 7, "Turbo Pascal's Structured Data Types," that you can assign an entire record variable to another, provided that both variables have exactly the same type. When you're dealing with objects, you can actually assign one object to another even if these are not exactly the same type. There are restrictions, however.

You can assign an instance of a descendant object to an instance of an ancestor object. For example, if you have a **Document** and a **Book** variable, you can assign the latter to the former in a single assignment statement. The converse (assigning a **Document** instance to a **Book** variable) is not allowed.

REMEMBER   You can assign an instance of a descendant object to a variable of the ancestor's type, but you cannot assign an ancestor instance to a variable of the descendant's type.

Similarly, you could assign a variable of type **Triangle** to one of type **Shape**, but you can't assign the ancestor object to a variable of a descendant type, as shown in the following program:

P11-6
```
(* Program to illustrate how to assign instances of
    different, but related object types in a single statement.
*)
{$V-}

PROGRAM AssignmentDemo;

CONST EmptyString = '';
TYPE SmStr = STRING [ 30];

        (* Define a Shape as an object type with two features
            and with two associated methods.
        *)
        Shape = OBJECT
                Name : SmStr;
                NrDimensions : INTEGER;
                PROCEDURE Init ( NewName : SmStr;
                                 Dims : INTEGER);
```

```
                    PROCEDURE Disp;
                END; (** Shape OBJECT *)


     (* Define a Triangle as a descendant of a Shape.
        The Init and Disp methods specified for Triangle
        will override the ones inherited from Shape.
     *)
     Triangle = OBJECT ( Shape)
                    Angle1, Angle2 : REAL;
                    PROCEDURE Init ( NewName : SmStr;
                                     Dims : INTEGER;
                                     A1, A2 : REAL);
                    PROCEDURE Disp;
                END; (* Triangle OBJECT *)

VAR MyShape : Shape;
    MyTri : Triangle;
    StrVal : SmStr;
    AngleVal1, AngleVal2 : REAL;
    DimVal : INTEGER;

  (* Initialize the fields of a Shape variable with the
     values passed in NewName and Dims.
     The variable will be the one whose name replaces
     Shape when the method is called.
  *)
PROCEDURE Shape.Init ( NewName : SmStr;
                       Dims : INTEGER);
BEGIN
  Name := NewName;
  NrDimensions := Dims;
END; (* Shape.Init *)

(* Display the fields of a Shape. *)
PROCEDURE Shape.Disp;
BEGIN
  WRITELN ( Name, ': ', NrDimensions, ' dimensions');
END; (* Shape.Disp *)

(* Initialize the fields of a Triangle. This method takes four
   arguments: the first two initialize the "Shape" fields, and
   the last two initialize fields unique to a Triangle.
   NOTE that the method actually calls the method Triangle.Init
   is overriding.
*)
PROCEDURE Triangle.Init ( NewName : SmStr;
                          Dims : INTEGER;
                          A1, A2 : REAL);
BEGIN
  (* Call the ancestor method to initialize the ancestor's
     fields.
  *)
  Shape.Init ( NewName, Dims);
```

```
        Angle1 := A1;
        Angle2 := A2;
    END;  (* Triangle.Init *)

    (* Display the contents of a Triangle variable.
       Note that Shape.Disp is called.
    *)
    PROCEDURE Triangle.Disp;
    BEGIN
      Shape.Disp;
      WRITELN ( 'ANGLES: 1 = ', Angle1 : 5 : 2,
                '; 2 = ', Angle2 : 5 : 2,
                '; 3 = ', 180 - Angle1 - Angle2 : 5 : 2,
                ' deg');
    END;    (* Triangle.Disp *)

    PROCEDURE GetString ( Message : STRING;
                          VAR Value : STRING);
    BEGIN
      WRITE ( Message, ' ');
      READLN ( Value);
    END; (* GetString *)

    PROCEDURE GetReal ( Message : STRING;
                        VAR Value : REAL);
    BEGIN
      WRITE ( Message, ' ');
      READLN ( Value);
    END; (* GetReal *)

BEGIN  (* Main Program *)
  GetString ( 'Shape Name? (ENTER to quit)', StrVal);
  WHILE ( StrVal <> EmptyString) DO
  BEGIN
    GetReal ( 'Angle 1', AngleVal1);
    GetReal ( 'Angle 2', AngleVal2);
    (* To initialize a Triangle, use the method
       appropriate to this descendant type.
    *)
    MyTri.Init ( StrVal, 2, AngleVal1, AngleVal2);
    MyTri.Disp;
    WRITELN;
    WRITELN ( 'Assigning MyTri to MyShape:');
    MyShape := MyTri;
    MyShape.Disp;
    WRITELN ( '*********************************************');
    GetString ( 'Shape Name? (ENTER to quit)', StrVal);
  END;
END.
```

In this program, **MyTri** is assigned to **MyShape**. The compiler does not complain about this assignment. On the other hand, if you reversed the two variables—assigning **MyShape** to **MyTri**—the compiler would respond with a type mismatch error.

Look carefully at what's going on here. First, note that a **Triangle** is actually larger (requires more storage) than a **Shape**. So how can the compiler make this assignment? In fact, the extra components are simply discarded and only the fields that are part of **MyShape** are assigned.

Why can't you assign a smaller variable to a larger one in this case? If you assigned **MyShape** to **MyTri**, only some of the fields in **MyTri** would be assigned values, leaving the remaining components uninitialized. Since you can get into lots of trouble if you have an uninitialized variable in a program, such an action is not allowed.

The Invisible Self Parameter

Look back at the **OverrideDemo** program. This program presents an apparent discrepancy. Notice that there are three versions of **Init**, **Describe**, and **Catalog**—one for each of the three object types used in the program. There is only one copy of **GetCode**, however.

Look at the definitions for **Document.Catalog**, **Article.Catalog**, and **Book.Catalog**. Each of these methods has exactly the same body. If you can get by with only one **GetCode** method, why are three "identical" versions of the **Catalog** method required? Because of the way the system decides what object you're working with, when you call a method, an invisible parameter, **Self**, is passed to the method. This parameter represents the object instance involved in the procedure call. For example, if you call **MyBk.Describe**, the **Self** parameter would refer to **MyBk**. Similarly, when there is a call to **Describe** in the body of **Book.Catalog**, this is actually interpreted as a call to **Self.Describe**, which is interpreted as **Book.Describe** in that instance.

If no such method is found, the system begins searching ancestor objects for a method called **Describe**. In the example, the method would be found associated with **Document**. That version of **Describe** would be executed. (Note that the ancestor's method could be used because a descendant is compatible with an ancestor, as you saw in the preceding section.)

However, if **Document.Describe** executes, it will display only the fields associated with the **Document** object, and will not display the additional fields that are part of **Book**, because the **Describe** method for **Document** doesn't know about them.

For this reason, each of the objects needs its own **Catalog** routine in the **OverrideDemo** program. It would be nice to be able to define just one general method for cataloging any of the object types. This is possible, as you'll see in the next chapter. However, before you can do that, you must learn several other features of OOP—which you'll do in the next chapter.

You don't need separate **GetCode** methods because this routine modifies a field (**Code**) that is inherited from the **Document** type. If the **Code** field were found in **Book** but not in **Document**, you would need a **GetCode** method for **Book** but not for the other object types.

Finally, the **Self** parameter also explains why you need to call procedure **Document.Init** in **Book.Init** and **Article.Init**. If the latter two routines simply called **Init**, this would be interpreted as a recursive call, which is not what you want.

This chapter introduced the major features of objects and object-oriented programming. You learned about the ability to associate objects and methods within an object definition, and the ability to inherit features from ancestor objects.

In the next chapter, you'll learn about some other advantages of object-oriented programming. These features enable you to build on and add to existing objects, even if you can't access the source code for the original objects. Moreover, object-oriented programming lets you design your objects and methods so that they are easy to extend at a later point.

12 Virtual Methods in Object-Oriented Programming

In the last chapter, you learned about the major features of object-oriented programming. In particular, you learned how to define object types and how to declare methods within these types. You also learned how to use object variables and methods. The principles of inheritance, encapsulation, and overriding all help to differentiate an object-oriented approach from traditional programming. In OOP, you can pass on features from one object type to another. The descendant type (which inherits the features) can also access any methods defined for or accessible to the ancestor type.

The ability to override methods, in order to apply methods better suited to a descendant type, enables you to create a family of methods for accomplishing the same type of task with different objects. Overriding permits you to create as many methods as you need to accomplish your tasks, and to carry out the same kinds of actions on the objects you've declared. As you saw in Chapter 11, "Object-Oriented Programming in Turbo Pascal," however, you may need to create multiple routines that all contain the same instructions. In the previous chapter, you had to create **Book.Catalog** and **Article.Catalog**, although each of these routines was identical to **Document.Catalog**. The reason is that the calls to **Describe** in **Document.Catalog** were interpreted as referring to **Document.Describe** because of the way the compiler builds the program file.

Binding

When the compiler processes your source file, it creates a code file that contains the program's routines in a code segment, and variables and constants in a data segment. Thus, both routines and variables have addresses associated with them.

When either a procedure or the program calls another routine, the location of the called routine must be provided to the caller. This process is called *binding*. Generally, binding occurs when the program is compiled and linked. This is known as early binding. Standard Pascal, and most other programming languages (such as C, Modula-2, and BASIC) use early binding.

In the example in Chapter 11, early binding means that the address of procedure **Document.Describe** is provided during compilation for the call to **Describe** in **Document.Catalog**. Thus, the method being called is determined before the program ever executes.

However, you can delay the binding until run time. This is known as *late binding*. In late binding, the program need not decide what routine to call until the program is actually executing.

Essentially, early binding says, "when you execute, carry out the instructions contained in this specific routine." In contrast, late binding says, "when you execute, you'll be told exactly which routine's instructions to carry out." In late binding, you can decide which **Describe** routine to execute just before you need to execute the routine.

This means that your program can use **Document.Catalog** for any descendant objects that don't have their own **Catalog** methods. When **Document.Catalog** is called, the system determines what object's **Describe** method is called. In order to do this, however, you need to define virtual methods.

Virtual Methods

Turbo Pascal implements late binding by means of *virtual methods*, where a method (such as **Describe**) is made to represent any of several methods—all of which have the same name, and each of which is associated with a different object type.

The **OverrideDemo** program in Chapter 11 had three **Describe** procedures. You will turn these into virtual methods later in the chapter.

Polymorphism

Such a collection of virtual methods illustrates what is generally known as *polymorphism,* when the same action (such as describing) can take different forms. With respect to the program, it also means that a single method name (such as **Describe**) can be instantiated in any of several ways.

Example: Cataloging Documents with Virtual Methods

The following program shows how to use virtual methods in the document cataloging program (**OverrideDemo**). The program does the same things as **OverrideDemo**, but uses virtual methods. Run the program, examine the source code, and then compare it to the source code for **OverrideDemo**.

P12-1
```
PROGRAM VirtualDemo;
(*$V-*)
TYPE MedStr = STRING [ 80];

     Document = OBJECT
               Author, Title, Code : MedStr;
               Year : INTEGER;
               CONSTRUCTOR Init ( Au, Ti : MedStr;
                                  Yr : INTEGER);
               PROCEDURE Describe;    VIRTUAL;
               PROCEDURE GetCode;
               PROCEDURE Catalog;     VIRTUAL;
            END; (* Document *)

    Book = OBJECT (Document)
           Publisher : MedStr;
           Price : REAL;
```

```
                CONSTRUCTOR Init ( Au, Ti, Pub : MedStr;
                                   Yr : INTEGER;
                                   Pr : REAL);
                PROCEDURE Describe;  VIRTUAL;
              END; (* Book *)

   Article = OBJECT (Document)
              Journal : MedStr;
              Volume, Page : INTEGER;
              CONSTRUCTOR Init ( Au, Ti, Jour : MedStr;
                                 Yr, Vol, Pg : INTEGER);
              PROCEDURE Describe;   VIRTUAL;
            END; (* Article *)

(* *************** Methods *************** *)

  CONSTRUCTOR Document.Init ( Au, Ti : MedStr;
                             Yr : INTEGER);
  BEGIN
    Author := Au;
    Title := Ti;
    Year := Yr;
    Code := '';
  END; (* Document.Init *)

  PROCEDURE Document.Describe;
  BEGIN
    WRITELN ( Code, ': ', Author, ', ', Title, ' [', Year, ']');
  END; (* Document.Describe *)

  PROCEDURE Document.GetCode;
  BEGIN
    WRITE ( 'Code? ');
    READLN ( Code);
  END; (* Document.GetCode *)

  PROCEDURE Document.Catalog;
  BEGIN
    Describe;
    GetCode;
  END; (* Document.Catalog *)

  CONSTRUCTOR Article.Init ( Au, Ti, Jour : MedStr;
                            Yr, Vol, Pg : INTEGER);
  BEGIN
    Document.Init ( Au, Ti, Yr);
    Journal := Jour;
    Volume := Vol;
    Page := Pg;
  END; (* Article.Init *)
```

```
   PROCEDURE Article.Describe;
   BEGIN
     Document.Describe;
     WRITE ( Journal, ', ');
     WRITELN ( 'volume ', Volume, '; p. ', Page);
   END; (* Article.Describe *)

   (* Look, Ma, no Article.Catalog!!! *)

   CONSTRUCTOR Book.Init ( Au, Ti, Pub : MedStr;
                           Yr : INTEGER;
                           Pr : REAL);
   BEGIN
     Document.Init ( Au, Ti, Yr);
     Publisher := Pub;
     Price := Pr;
   END; (* Book.Init *)

   PROCEDURE Book.Describe;
   BEGIN
     Document.Describe;
     WRITELN ( '$', Price : 1 : 2, ', ', Publisher);
   END; (* Book.Describe *)

   (* Look, Ma, no Book.Catalog!!! *)

(* ************** General-Purpose Routines ************** *)

   PROCEDURE GetString ( Message : STRING;
                         VAR Value : STRING);
   BEGIN
     WRITE ( Message, ' ');
     READLN ( Value);
   END; (* GetString *)

   PROCEDURE GetInteger ( Message : STRING;
                          VAR Value : INTEGER);
   BEGIN
     WRITE ( Message, ' ');
     READLN ( Value);
   END; (* GetInteger *)

   PROCEDURE GetReal ( Message : STRING;
                       VAR Value : REAL);
   BEGIN
     WRITE ( Message, ' ');
     READLN ( Value);
   END; (* GetReal *)

VAR MyDoc : Document;
    MyBk : Book;
    MyArt : Article;
    Writer, Name, Pub, Jour : MedStr;
```

```
      Choice, Year, Vol, Pg : INTEGER;
      Price : REAL;

BEGIN
   GetInteger ( '0) Quit; 1) Doc; 2) Book; 3) Article', Choice);
   WHILE Choice <> 0 DO
   BEGIN
     GetString ( 'Author', Writer);
     GetString ( 'Title', Name);
     GetInteger ( 'Year', Year);
     CASE Choice OF
       1 :
         BEGIN
           MyDoc.Init ( Writer, Name, Year);
           MyDoc.Catalog;
           MyDoc.Describe;
         END;
       2 :
         BEGIN
           GetString ( 'Publisher', Pub);
           GetReal ( 'Price', Price);
           MyBk.Init ( Writer, Name, Pub, Year, Price);
           MyBk.Catalog;
           MyBk.Describe;
         END;
       3 :
         BEGIN
           GetString ( 'Journal', Jour);
           GetInteger ( 'Volume', Vol);
           GetInteger ( 'Page', Pg);
           MyArt.Init ( Writer, Name, Jour, Year, Vol, Pg);
           MyArt.Catalog;
           MyArt.Describe;
         END;
     END;
     GetInteger ('0) Quit; 1) Doc; 2) Book; 3) Article', Choice);
   END; (* WHILE Loop *)
END.
```

To take advantage of polymorphism for a particular method, just put the reserved word **VIRTUAL** after the method declarations. The **VIRTUAL** specifier tells the program to use late binding instead of early binding.

In order for virtual methods to be usable, you must initialize each instance of an object with a constructor. A constructor is a method for setting up the tables and internal structures required for virtual methods. These are known as *virtual method tables*, or VMTs. From the programming standpoint, a constructor is similar to a procedure method.

Thus, the constructors **Document.Init**, **Book.Init**, and **Article.Init** all have the same statements as the procedures with these names defined in program **OverrideDemo** in the previous chapter. By labeling the method as a constructor, however, you tell the program to do some additional initializing so that late binding is possible. A constructor is never virtual, but enables your other methods to be virtual methods.

REMEMBER   To create a virtual method, just put the reserved word **VIRTUAL** after the heading for the method in the object type definition. Before you do anything with an object that has virtual methods, you must call the object's constructor to initialize the object's environment properly.

Recall that you can assign the contents of one object to another (provided compatibility restrictions are satisfied). You cannot, however, assign an object with virtual methods to another. You must first initialize each object separately with its own constructor. After that, you can assign elements from one object to another.

In the **VirtualDemo** program, the **Describe** routines are virtual. This means that the binding for the call to **Describe** in **Document.Catalog** need not be determined until the program is executing. As a result, you don't need **Book.Catalog** or **Article.Catalog** in this version. By making **Describe** a virtual method, you make it responsible for delivering the correct code at run time. Depending on the value of **Choice**, any of three object types can be used when calling **Catalog**.

What Should Be a Virtual Method?

Describe was converted to a virtual method because **Document.Catalog** needs to be able to call any of **Document.Describe**, **Book.Describe**, or **Article.Describe**, depending on what object is passed to **Catalog**. That is, the **Describe** method will need to take many forms, depending on the object with which it is called.

GetCode, on the other hand, is used in exactly the same way by its associated object type and by any descendant types. There is no need to make this a virtual method since the routine never changes.

What about **Catalog**? This has been made a virtual method, even though only one version of the method is used. A virtual method makes it easier (and, in some cases, possible) to extend the object types and methods to handle new problems. In fact, by using virtual methods you can do this whether or not you have access to the source code for the object definitions and implementations.

For example, suppose you want to add a new object type to the **VirtualDemo** program. This type, **Novel**, will be descended from **Book**. In addition to the object type definition, you need to create two methods: **Novel.Init** and **Novel.Describe**. **Novel.Init** will be a constructor, like all the other methods with that name in the current program.

Once you've defined the new object type and its methods, you need to declare any variables for the main program. For example, in the following program, a variable, **MyNovel**, has been added, along with a change to the prompt in the main program and a new **CASE** value:

```
P12-2    PROGRAM ExtendedVirtualDemo;
         (*$V-*)
         TYPE MedStr = STRING [ 80];

                 Document = OBJECT
                              Author, Title, Code : MedStr;
                              Year : INTEGER;
                              CONSTRUCTOR Init ( Au, Ti : MedStr;
                                                 Yr : INTEGER);
                              PROCEDURE Describe; VIRTUAL;
                              PROCEDURE GetCode;
                              PROCEDURE Catalog; VIRTUAL;
                            END; (* Document *)

                 Book = OBJECT (Document)
                          Publisher : MedStr;
                          Price : REAL;
                          CONSTRUCTOR Init ( Au, Ti, Pub : MedStr;
                                             Yr : INTEGER;
                                             Pr : REAL);
                          PROCEDURE Describe; VIRTUAL;
                        END; (* Book *)

                 Article = OBJECT (Document)
                             Journal : MedStr;
                             Volume, Page : INTEGER;
                             CONSTRUCTOR Init ( Au, Ti, Jour : MedStr;
                                                Yr, Vol, Pg : INTEGER);
                             PROCEDURE Describe;   VIRTUAL;
                           END; (* Article *)
```

```
    Novel = OBJECT (Book)
              Genre : MedStr;
              CONSTRUCTOR Init ( Au, Ti, Pub, NovelType:MedStr;
                                  Yr : INTEGER;
                                  Pr : REAL);
              PROCEDURE Describe; VIRTUAL;
            END; (* Novel *)

(* *************** Methods *************** *)

  CONSTRUCTOR Document.Init ( Au, Ti : MedStr;
                              Yr : INTEGER);
  BEGIN
    Author := Au;
    Title := Ti;
    Year := Yr;
    Code := '';
  END; (* Document.Init *)

  PROCEDURE Document.Describe;
  BEGIN
    WRITELN ( Code, ': ', Author, ', ', Title, ' [', Year, ']');
  END; (* Document.Describe *)

  PROCEDURE Document.GetCode;
  BEGIN
    WRITE ( 'Code? ');
    READLN ( Code);
  END; (* Document.GetCode *)

  PROCEDURE Document.Catalog;
  BEGIN
    Describe;
    GetCode;
  END; (* Document.Catalog *)

  CONSTRUCTOR Article.Init ( Au, Ti, Jour : MedStr;
                             Yr, Vol, Pg : INTEGER);
  BEGIN
    Document.Init ( Au, Ti, Yr);
    Journal := Jour;
    Volume := Vol;
    Page := Pg;
  END; (* Article.Init *)

  PROCEDURE Article.Describe;
  BEGIN
    Document.Describe;
    WRITE ( Journal, ', ');
    WRITELN ( 'volume ', Volume, '; p. ', Page);
  END; (* Article.Describe *)
```

```
CONSTRUCTOR Book.Init ( Au, Ti, Pub : MedStr;
                              Yr : INTEGER;
                              Pr : REAL);
BEGIN
  Document.Init ( Au, Ti, Yr);
  Publisher := Pub;
  Price := Pr;
END; (* Book.Init *)

PROCEDURE Book.Describe;
BEGIN
  Document.Describe;
  WRITELN ( '$', Price : 1 : 2, ', ', Publisher);
END; (* Book.Describe *)

CONSTRUCTOR Novel.Init ( Au, Ti, Pub, NovelType : MedStr;
                              Yr : INTEGER;
                              Pr : REAL);
BEGIN
  Book.Init ( Au, Ti, Pub, Yr, Pr);
  Genre := NovelType;
END; (* Novel.Init *)

PROCEDURE Novel.Describe;
BEGIN
  Document.Describe;
  WRITELN ( '$', Price : 1 : 2, ', ', Publisher,
             ' (', Genre, ')');
END; (* Novel.Describe *)

(* ************** General-Purpose Routines ************** *)

  PROCEDURE GetString ( Message : STRING;
                        VAR Value : STRING);
  BEGIN
    WRITE ( Message, ' ');
    READLN ( Value);
  END; (* GetString *)

  PROCEDURE GetInteger ( Message : STRING;
                         VAR Value : INTEGER);
  BEGIN
    WRITE ( Message, ' ');
    READLN ( Value);
  END; (* GetInteger *)

  PROCEDURE GetReal ( Message : STRING;
                      VAR Value : REAL);
  BEGIN
    WRITE ( Message, ' ');
    READLN ( Value);
  END; (* GetReal *)
```

```
VAR MyDoc : Document;
    MyBk : Book;
    MyNovel : Novel;
    MyArt : Article;
    Writer, Name, Pub, Jour, Genre : MedStr;
    Choice, Year, Vol, Pg : INTEGER;
    Price : REAL;


BEGIN
  GetInteger ( '0) Quit; 1) Doc; 2) Book; 3) Article; 4) Novel',
              Choice);
  WHILE Choice <> 0 DO
  BEGIN
    GetString ( 'Author', Writer);
    GetString ( 'Title', Name);
    GetInteger ( 'Year', Year);
    CASE Choice OF
      1 :
        BEGIN
          MyDoc.Init ( Writer, Name, Year);
          MyDoc.Catalog;
          MyDoc.Describe;
        END;
       2 :
        BEGIN
          GetString ( 'Publisher', Pub);
          GetReal ( 'Price', Price);
          MyBk.Init ( Writer, Name, Pub, Year, Price);
          MyBk.Catalog;
          MyBk.Describe;
        END;
       3 :
        BEGIN
          GetString ( 'Journal', Jour);
          GetInteger ( 'Volume', Vol);
          GetInteger ( 'Page', Pg);
          MyArt.Init ( Writer, Name, Jour, Year, Vol, Pg);
          MyArt.Catalog;
          MyArt.Describe;
        END;
       4 :
        BEGIN
          GetString ( 'Publisher', Pub);
          GetReal ( 'Price', Price);
          GetString ( 'Genre', Genre);
          MyNovel.Init ( Writer, Name, Pub, Genre, Year, Price);
          MyNovel.Catalog;
          MyNovel.Describe;
        END;
    END;
```

```
    GetInteger('0) Quit; 1) Doc; 2) Book; 3) Article; 4) Novel',
            Choice);
  END; (* WHILE Loop *)
END.
```

Little has changed from **VirtualDemo** to **ExtendedVirtualDemo**. The new methods are **Novel.Describe** and **Novel.Init**. Notice that this program lets you call **MyNovel.Catalog**, which executes the virtual method **MyNovel.Describe** in the appropriate circumstances. Thus, **Document.Catalog** can call a routine that did not exist when **Document.Catalog** was created.

This ability to apply existing methods to new objects is called *extensibility*, and is another advantage of OOP. With virtual methods, you can add new object types and methods to an existing hierarchy even if you just have a precompiled unit containing the other object types.

Example: Anagrams

The following, rather long program is included for your amusement, although there are some interesting points about it. Look at the method lists within the object type definitions. You'll find a new type of method—a *destructor*—which is discussed after the listing.

VirtualAnagrams presents anagrams for solution. The program reads its pool of anagrams from a file and then selects at random from the pool. The file for the version presented here is called ANAG.DAT, and is assumed to be in the same directory as the **VirtualAnagrams** program. The example file contains capital cities. You can create your own data file and substitute it for ANAG.DAT.

The program works with one, two, or three players. If there are two or more players, the player who presses a certain key most quickly gets to solve the problem.

Compile and run the program to see how it works. It is set up for three players. If you don't have another person to play, just take the part of each player in turn or at random to see how the program works.

To change to two players or to a solo game, change the argument list for the call to **Init** and change the type specifier for **MyPlay**. For two players, the type specifier should be **Twosome** and for one player it should be **Loner**. You don't need to change any of the other calls in the program. The virtual methods ensure that the appropriate versions of all methods are called.

When decreasing the number of players, remove the parameters (to **Init**) that relate to the keys the program will accept. For two players, it's most convenient to remove the *B* — that is, the fourth parameter to **Init**. The remaining parameters indicate that player 1 must type **A** to respond and player 2 must type **L**. The player who responds first tries to solve the anagram.

For a single player, pass in whatever character you wish (for example *A* in the current version). With only one player, you can just start typing the answer. You don't need to press a key first, since the program knows which player is responding.

P12-3
```
(* Program to play an "anagrams" game with 1 -- 3 players.
    Program represents another example involving virtual methods.
*)

PROGRAM VirtualAnagrams;
(*$V-*)
USES CRT;
CONST MaxData = 100;      (* maximum # items in pool *)
TYPE MedStr = STRING [ 80];
     (* used to store a collection of words for anagrams *)
     DatArray = ARRAY [ 1 .. MaxData] OF MedStr;
     (* used to record whether a word has been used *)
     LedgerArray = ARRAY [ 1 .. MaxData] OF BOOLEAN;
     CharSet = SET OF CHAR;

     Anagram = OBJECT
               Data : Datarray;
               Ledger : LedgerArray;
               NrData : INTEGER;   (* # of actual values *)
               (* the encrypted word, the original word *)
               TheAnagram, TheWd : MedStr;
               FName : MedStr;
               FIsOpen : BOOLEAN;
               DataFile : Text;   (* contains the words *)
               (* initialize object and prepare environment
                  for virtual methods.
               *)
               CONSTRUCTOR Init ( FileName : MedStr;
                                  NrVals : INTEGER);
               PROCEDURE OpenFile; VIRTUAL;
               PROCEDURE BuildData; VIRTUAL;
               PROCEDURE Describe; VIRTUAL;
               FUNCTION SelectPuzzle : INTEGER;
               FUNCTION OKToPlay : BOOLEAN; VIRTUAL;
               PROCEDURE Startup; VIRTUAL;
               PROCEDURE Encrypt ( Which : INTEGER); VIRTUAL;
```

```
                    PROCEDURE ShowPuzzle ( Which : INTEGER); VIRTUAL;
                    PROCEDURE ShowAnswer; VIRTUAL;
                    DESTRUCTOR Done; VIRTUAL;
                 END;  (* Anagram *)

    Loner = OBJECT ( Anagram)
                 (* used to keep track of performance *)
                 Right1, Wrong1, Player : INTEGER;
                 (* Key1 : key to which program responds;
                      for one player, any key works.
                      PressedKey is what used typed/
                 *)
                 Key1, PressedKey : CHAR;
                 Response : MedStr;  (* player's response *)
                 (* did player answer correctly? *)
                 RightAnswer : BOOLEAN;
                 CONSTRUCTOR Init ( FileName : MedStr;
                                    KeyA : CHAR;
                                    NrVals : INTEGER);
                 PROCEDURE Describe; VIRTUAL;
                 PROCEDURE ReadResponse; VIRTUAL;
                 PROCEDURE DeterminePlayer; VIRTUAL;
                 PROCEDURE Evaluate; VIRTUAL;
                 PROCEDURE AdjustScore (Which : INTEGER); VIRTUAL;
                 PROCEDURE DispScore (Which : INTEGER); VIRTUAL;
                 PROCEDURE Play ( PuzzleNr : INTEGER); VIRTUAL;
                 DESTRUCTOR Done; VIRTUAL;
              END;       (* Loner *)

    TwoSome = OBJECT ( Loner)
                 (* track player 2's performance *)
                 Right2, Wrong2 : INTEGER;
                 (* Key program expects from player 2 *)
                 Key2 : CHAR;
                 CONSTRUCTOR Init ( FileName : MedStr;
                                    KeyA, KeyB : CHAR;
                                    NrVals : INTEGER);
                 PROCEDURE Describe; VIRTUAL;
                 PROCEDURE DeterminePlayer; VIRTUAL;
                 PROCEDURE ReadResponse; VIRTUAL;
                 FUNCTION ShowPlayerNr : INTEGER;
                 PROCEDURE AdjustScore (Which : INTEGER); VIRTUAL;
                 PROCEDURE DispScore (Which : INTEGER); VIRTUAL;
                 DESTRUCTOR Done; VIRTUAL;
               END; (* Twosome *)

    Trio = OBJECT ( TwoSome)
              Right3, Wrong3 : INTEGER;
              Key3 : CHAR;
              CONSTRUCTOR Init ( FileName : MedStr;
                                 KeyA, KeyB, KeyC : CHAR;
                                 NrVals : INTEGER);
```

```
            PROCEDURE Describe; VIRTUAL;
            PROCEDURE DeterminePlayer; VIRTUAL;
            PROCEDURE AdjustScore (Which : INTEGER); VIRTUAL;
            PROCEDURE DispScore (Which : INTEGER); VIRTUAL;
            DESTRUCTOR Done; VIRTUAL;
          END; (* Trio *)

(* *************** General-Purpose Routines *************** *)

  (* Use bubblesort algorithm to sort characters in a string *)
  PROCEDURE StrBubbleSort ( VAR Info : String);
  VAR Temp : CHAR;
      Low, High, Top, Size : INTEGER;
  BEGIN
    Size := LENGTH ( Info);
    Top := Size + 1;
    WHILE ( Top > 1) DO
    BEGIN
      Low := 1;
      High := 2;
      WHILE High < Top DO
      BEGIN
        (* if lower string needs to move upward in the array *)
        IF Info [ Low] > Info [ High] THEN
        BEGIN
          Temp := Info [ Low];
          Info [ Low] := Info [ High];
          Info [ High] := Temp;
        END; (* If lower string needs to move upward *)
        Low := Low + 1;
        High := High + 1;
      END; (* WHILE High < Top *)
      Top := Top - 1;
    END; (* WHILE Top > 1 *)
  END;  (* StrBubbleSort *)

  (* Convert a string to uppercase *)
  PROCEDURE MakeStrUpper ( VAR TheStr : STRING);
  VAR Index, HowLong : INTEGER;
  BEGIN
    HowLong := LENGTH ( TheStr);
    FOR Index := 1 TO HowLong DO
      TheStr [ Index] := UPCASE ( TheStr [ Index]);
  END; (* MakeStrUpper *)

(* *************** Methods *************** *)

  CONSTRUCTOR Anagram.Init ( FileName : MedStr;
                             NrVals : INTEGER);
  VAR Index, MaxItems : INTEGER;
  BEGIN
    FName := FileName;
```

```
    FIsOpen := False;
    NrData := 0;
    TheAnagram := '';
    TheWd := '';
    FOR Index := 1 TO NrVals DO
      Data [ Index] := '';
    FOR Index := 1 TO NrVals DO
      Ledger [ Index] := FALSE;
END; (* Anagram.Init *)


(* Describe the general features of the game *)
PROCEDURE Anagram.Describe;
BEGIN
  ClrScr;
  WRITELN ( 'Welcome to the Anagram Game.');
  WRITELN ( 'You'll be presented with jumbled words.');
  WRITELN ( 'Type the word that you think is represented, ');
  WRITELN ( 'and press ENTER.');
  WRITELN ( 'Press ENTER to start, when you're ready.');
  WRITELN;
END; (* Anagram.Describe *)


(* Open the source file from which to read words *)
PROCEDURE Anagram.OpenFile;
BEGIN
  ASSIGN ( DataFile, FName);
  (*$I-*)
  RESET ( DataFile);
  IF IOResult = 0 THEN
    FIsOpen := TRUE
  ELSE
    FIsOpen := FALSE;
  (*$I+*)
END; (* Anagram.OpenFile *)


(* Read words from file to the data array *)
PROCEDURE Anagram.BuildData;
VAR Index : INTEGER;
BEGIN
  IF FIsOpen THEN
  BEGIN
    READLN ( DataFile, NrData);
    FOR Index := 1 TO NrData DO
    BEGIN
      IF NOT EOF ( DataFile) THEN
        READLN ( DataFile, Data [ Index]);
    END;
  END
  ELSE
    WRITELN ( 'ERROR. Source file is not open.');
```

```
END; (* Anagram.BuildData *)
(* Select a puzzle that hasn't been shown already *)
FUNCTION Anagram.SelectPuzzle : INTEGER;
VAR  TheVal : INTEGER;
BEGIN
  REPEAT
    TheVal := RANDOM ( NrData) + 1;
  UNTIL Ledger [ TheVal] = FALSE;
  Ledger [ TheVal] := TRUE;
  SelectPuzzle := TheVal;
END; (* Anagram.SelectPuzzle *)

FUNCTION Anagram.OKToPLay : BOOLEAN;
BEGIN
  OKToPlay := FIsOpen;
END; (* Anagram.OKToPlay *)

(* Jumble (alphabetize) the letters of the word *)
PROCEDURE Anagram.Encrypt ( Which : INTEGER);
BEGIN
  TheAnagram := Data [ Which];
  MakeStrUpper ( TheAnagram);
  TheWd := TheAnagram;
  StrBubbleSort ( TheAnagram);
END; (* Anagram.Encrypt *)

(* Display the puzzle at a specific location. *)
PROCEDURE Anagram.ShowPuzzle ( Which : INTEGER);
BEGIN
  GoToXY ( 30, 5);
  ClrEOL;
  GoToXY ( 30, 3);
  ClrEOL;
  WRITE ( TheAnagram);
END; (* Anagram.ShowPuzzle *)

(* Display the solution at a specific location. *)
PROCEDURE Anagram.ShowAnswer;
BEGIN
  GoToXY ( 30, 5);
  WRITE ( 'The answer is: ', TheWd);
  READLN;
END; (* Anagram.ShowAnswer *)

(* Clean up after playing the game *)
DESTRUCTOR Anagram.Done;
BEGIN
  Close ( DataFile);
END; (* Anagram.Done *)

(* Carry out the tasks needed to start the game. *)
PROCEDURE Anagram.Startup;
```

```
BEGIN
  Describe;   (* a virtual method *)
  OpenFile;
  BuildData;
  READLN;
  ClrScr;
END; (* Anagram.Startup *)

CONSTRUCTOR Loner.Init ( FileName : MedStr;
                         KeyA : CHAR;
                         NrVals : INTEGER);
VAR Index, MaxItems : INTEGER;
BEGIN
  Anagram.Init ( FileName, NrVals);
  Key1 := KeyA;
  PressedKey := ' ';
  Right1 := 0;
  Wrong1 := 0;
  Player := 1;
  RightAnswer := FALSE;
END; (* Loner.Init *)

(* Describe the game for a single player *)
PROCEDURE Loner.Describe;
BEGIN
  Anagram.Describe;
END; (* Loner.Describe *)

(* Select which player pressed the key first.
   With one player, this is always player 1.
*)
PROCEDURE Loner.DeterminePlayer;
BEGIN
  Player := 1;
  GoToXY ( 5, 10 + Right1 + Wrong1);
END; (* Loner.DeterminePlayer *)

(* Read player's answer *)
PROCEDURE Loner.ReadResponse;
BEGIN
  READLN ( Response);
END; (* Loner.ReadResponse *)

(* Determine whether player's answer is correct *)
PROCEDURE Loner.Evaluate;
BEGIN
  MakeStrUpper ( Response);
  IF Response = TheWd THEN
    RightAnswer := TRUE
  ELSE RightAnswer := FALSE;
END;    (* Loner.Evaluate *)
```

```
(* Change the player's score, depending on outcome *)
PROCEDURE Loner.AdjustScore;
BEGIN
  IF RightAnswer = TRUE THEN
    INC ( Right1)
  ELSE
    INC ( Wrong1);
END; (* Loner.AdjustScore *)

(* Display the player's score *)
PROCEDURE Loner.DispScore;
BEGIN
  WRITE ( Right1, ' correct, ', Wrong1, ' wrong ');
  WRITELN ( '(', 100 * Right1 / (Right1 + Wrong1) : 1 : 2,
            '%)');
END; (* Loner.DispScore *)

(* perform the tasks needed to play a round of the game *)
PROCEDURE Loner.Play ( PuzzleNr : INTEGER);
BEGIN
  (* select a word, and make it into a puzzle *)
  PuzzleNr := SelectPuzzle;
  Encrypt ( PuzzleNr);
  (* Display the puzzle *)
  ShowPuzzle ( PuzzleNr);
  (* Process the player's answer *)
  ReadResponse;
  Evaluate;
  AdjustScore ( Player);
  ShowAnswer;
END; (* Loner.Play *)

(* Clean up and summarize the scores *)
DESTRUCTOR Loner.Done;
BEGIN
  CLOSE ( DataFile);
  GoToXY ( 5, 3);
  ClrEOL;
  GoToXY ( 5, 5);
  ClrEOL;
  GoToXY ( 5, 3);
  WRITE ( 'Player 1: ');
  DispScore ( 1);
END; (* Loner.Done *)

CONSTRUCTOR Twosome.Init ( FileName : MedStr;
                           KeyA, KeyB : CHAR;
                           NrVals : INTEGER);
VAR Index, MaxItems : INTEGER;
BEGIN
  Loner.Init ( FileName, KeyA, NrVals);
  Key2 := KeyB;
```

```
    Right2 := 0;
    Wrong2 := 0;
END; (* Twosome.Init *)

PROCEDURE Twosome.Describe;
BEGIN
  Loner.Describe;
  WRITELN ( 'The first player to press her or his key');
  WRITELN ( 'will take the turn, and will get to answer');
  WRITELN ( 'Player 1, press A to take the turn.');
  WRITELN ( 'Player 2, press L to take the turn.');
END; (* Twosome.Describe *)

(* Check the key pressed, to see which player's key it is.
   Player 1 presses A, player 2 presses L.
   If any other key is pressed, the routine beeps,
   and waits for someone to press a valid key.
*)
PROCEDURE Twosome.DeterminePlayer;
CONST Beep = #7;
BEGIN
  IF UPCASE ( PressedKey) = Key1 THEN
  BEGIN
    Player := 1;
    GoToXY ( 5, 10 + Right1 + Wrong1);
  END
  ELSE IF UPCASE ( PressedKey) = Key2 THEN
  BEGIN
    Player := 2;
    GoToXY ( 30, 10 + Right2 + Wrong2);
  END
  ELSE
  BEGIN
    Player := 0;
    WRITE ( Beep);
  END;
END; (* Twosome.DeterminePlayer *)

(* Check whether anyone has an answer,
   determine who it is, and read their answer.
*)
PROCEDURE Twosome.ReadResponse;
BEGIN
  REPEAT
    PressedKey := ReadKey;
    DeterminePlayer;
  UNTIL Player > 0;
  READLN ( Response);
END; (* TwoSome.ReadResponse *)

(* Return the number of the player who responded first. *)
FUNCTION Twosome.ShowPlayerNr : INTEGER;
```

```
BEGIN
  ShowPlayerNr := Player;
END;  (* TwoSome.ShowPlayerNr *)

(* Adjust the score of the player who answered *)
PROCEDURE Twosome.AdjustScore;
BEGIN
  CASE Player OF
    1 :
      BEGIN
        IF RightAnswer = TRUE THEN
          INC ( Right1)
        ELSE
          INC ( Wrong1);
      END;
    2 :
      BEGIN
        IF RightAnswer = TRUE THEN
          INC ( Right2)
        ELSE
          INC ( Wrong2);
      END;
  END; (* CASE *)
END; (* Twosome.AdjustScore *)

(* Display the scores of the specified player. *)
PROCEDURE Twosome.DispScore ( Which : INTEGER);
BEGIN
  CASE Which OF
    1 :
      BEGIN
        WRITE ( Right1, ' correct, ', Wrong1, ' wrong ');
        WRITELN ( '(', 100 * Right1 / (Right1 + Wrong1) :1:2,
                  '%)');
      END;
    2 :
      BEGIN
        WRITE ( Right2, ' correct, ', Wrong2, ' wrong ');
        WRITELN ( '(', 100 * Right2 / (Right2 + Wrong2) :1:2,
                  '%)');
      END;
  END; (* CASE *)
END; (* Twosome.DispScore *)

(* Clean up after a 2-player game. Note that Loner.Done
   does most of the work.
*)
DESTRUCTOR Twosome.Done;
BEGIN
  Loner.Done;
  GoToXY ( 5, 5);
  WRITE ( 'Player 2: ');
```

```
    DispScore ( 2);
END; (* Twosome.Done *)


CONSTRUCTOR Trio.Init ( FileName : MedStr;
                        KeyA, KeyB, KeyC : CHAR;
                        NrVals : INTEGER);
VAR Index, MaxItems : INTEGER;
BEGIN
  Twosome.Init ( FileName, KeyA, KeyB, NrVals);
  Key3 := KeyC;
  Right3 := 0;
  Wrong3 := 0;
END; (* Trio.Init *)


PROCEDURE Trio.Describe;
BEGIN
  Twosome.Describe;
  WRITELN ( 'Player 3, press B to take the turn.');
END; (* Trio.Describe *)


(* Determine which of 3 players responded first.
   Accepts only the values specified in Key1, Key2, and Key3.
   These are A, L, and B, respectively.
*)
PROCEDURE Trio.DeterminePlayer;
CONST Beep = #7;
BEGIN
  IF UPCASE ( PressedKey) = Key1 THEN
  BEGIN
    Player := 1;
    GoToXY ( 5, 10 + Right1 + Wrong1);
  END
  ELSE IF UPCASE ( PressedKey) = Key2 THEN
  BEGIN
    Player := 2;
    GoToXY ( 30, 10 + Right2 + Wrong2);
  END
  ELSE IF UPCASE ( PressedKey) = Key3 THEN
  BEGIN
    Player := 3;
    GoToXY ( 55, 10 + Right3 + Wrong3);
  END
  ELSE
  BEGIN
    Player := 0;
    WRITE ( Beep);
  END;
END; (* Trio.DeterminePlayer *)


PROCEDURE Trio.AdjustScore;
BEGIN
  CASE Player OF
```

```
     1 :
       BEGIN
         IF RightAnswer = TRUE THEN
           INC ( Right1)
         ELSE
           INC ( Wrong1);
       END;
     2 :
       BEGIN
         IF RightAnswer = TRUE THEN
           INC ( Right2)
         ELSE
           INC ( Wrong2);
       END;
     3 :
       BEGIN
         IF RightAnswer = TRUE THEN
           INC ( Right3)
         ELSE
           INC ( Wrong3);
       END;
   END; (* CASE *)
END; (* Trio.AdjustScore *)

PROCEDURE Trio.DispScore ( Which : INTEGER);
BEGIN
  CASE Which OF
    1 :
      BEGIN
        WRITE ( Right1, ' correct, ', Wrong1, ' wrong ');
        WRITELN ( '(', 100 * Right1 / (Right1 + Wrong1) :1:2,
                  '%)');
      END;
    2 :
      BEGIN
        WRITE ( Right2, ' correct, ', Wrong2, ' wrong ');
        WRITELN ( '(', 100 * Right2 / (Right2 + Wrong2) :1:2,
                  '%)');
      END;
    3 :
      BEGIN
        WRITE ( Right3, ' correct, ', Wrong3, ' wrong ');
        WRITELN ( '(', 100 * Right3 / (Right3 + Wrong3) :1:2,
                  '%)');
      END;
  END; (* CASE *)
END; (* Trio.DispScore *)

DESTRUCTOR Trio.Done;
BEGIN
  Twosome.Done;
  GoToXY ( 5, 7);
```

```
      WRITE ( 'Player 3: ');
      DispScore ( 3);
    END; (* Trio.Done *)

VAR MyPlay : Trio;
    Index, PuzzleNr : INTEGER;

BEGIN
  RANDOMIZE;
  (* Set up for a game. NOTE: this call must be
     changed, depending on the number of players.
     All other routines can remain unchanged.
  *)
  MyPlay.Init ( 'anag.dat', 'A', 'L', 'B', MaxData);
  MyPlay.Startup;
  IF MyPlay.OKToPlay THEN
  BEGIN
    FOR Index := 1 TO 10 DO
      MyPlay.Play ( PuzzleNr);
    MyPlay.Done;
  END
  ELSE
    WRITELN ( 'ERROR. Could not open puzzle file.');
  WRITE ( 'Press ENTER to end program.');
  READLN;
END.
```

The logic for the main program is not difficult. After setting a seed for the random number generator, the core of the program begins. The calls to **MyPlay.Init** and **MyPlay.Startup** set the environment and introduce the game to the player.

The actual game takes place within the **FOR** loop, in which method **MyPlay.Play** is called each time. Finally, when the specified number of puzzles have been presented, the program finishes up by calling **MyPlay.Done**.

Finding the Method That Will Execute

To see the details of the method calls, you need to look at the definitions for these methods. To find the appropriate version of a method for a particular part of the program, start with the most specific object whose method could be used. For example, if you have three players, start with **Trio**; if you have two players, start with **Twosome**, and so forth.

If you don't find the method associated with that object, move upward in the hierarchy until you find an ancestor object type that has the method. This is the version that will be executed when the program runs.

For example, there is only one version of **Startup**, and it is defined for **Anagram**. Notice that this procedure calls several other methods. Because the methods in this program are almost all defined as virtual methods, resolution of the calls made in **Startup** follows the same sequence as **Startup** itself. That is, determine the most specific object type that has a method with the specified name. This is the one that will execute when called. For example, all four object types in the hierarchy have a **Describe** method. In other words, **Trio.Describe** will execute when you have three players.

Only **Anagram** has **OpenFile** and **BuildData** methods associated with it. Thus, when **MyPlay.Startup** calls **OpenFile**, **Anagram.OpenFile** will execute. Note that **OpenFile** and **BuildData** have both been defined as virtual methods, even though no other object type has such methods associated with it. Making these virtual methods ensures extensibility. You can create new objects (for example, different types of games) that use some of the same methods but work with different types of data.

For example, suppose you want to program a trivia question-and-answer game. For such a game, questions and answers will be distinct—unlike the anagrams, in which the answer is identical to the original word. To program this game, you might need to read a question file and an answer file (and you might need to store information in two data arrays). Similarly, if you program a trivia game with multiple categories for questions, you also need to work with multiple files. In such cases, you need different versions of **OpenFiles** and **BuildData**. If you define these as virtual methods, **Anagram.Startup** can handle the new versions with no modifications.

Look at the definition for **Play** (defined only for **Loner**). This method also calls a variety of methods, some of which have multiple forms and some of which are defined for only one object type. Note that a method need not be defined in the most general ancestor object. You can introduce a method anywhere in the hierarchy—wherever the method is first needed. All descendants will be able to use this method; ancestors, however, will not. Thus, **Twosome** and **Trio** can call **Play**, but **Anagram** cannot.

Destructors: Methods That Clean Up After You

When you use virtual methods, you must define a constructor to initialize the object instances and set up the required tables. The reserved word **CONSTRUCTOR** identifies the method as one that will set up this environment. Not surprisingly, Turbo Pascal has a counterpart for dismantling the virtual method environment when you're done with it. A method identified as a **DESTRUCTOR** will perform such a clean-up task. By using a constructor for each object variable at the start of your program, you ensure that you'll be able to use virtual methods in your program. By calling a destructor when you're finished working with each object, you make sure that the program environment retains no "garbage."

Modifications and Extensions of the Program

You can modify the **VirtualAnagram** program in many ways. The current version displays a fixed number of puzzles. You might have the program play until one player reaches a particular score. You might also set a time limit on the game—presenting as many puzzles as possible within the specified amount of time. (The next chapter presents routines for timing things in programs.)

You might also limit the amount of time players have to respond. For example, after presenting a puzzle, players might get five or ten seconds to respond. If no one finds the correct answer, the program moves to the next puzzle. Finally, you might turn the puzzle into a speed event, in which a player must solve all of the puzzles presented in as short a time as possible. You can even combine these variants. For example, you might pose a puzzle for all players. The player to respond first might then get a limited amount of time to solve as many puzzles as possible—thereby scoring points.

All of these modifications work with variants of the object types in the current program. Generally, such variants are described as new, descendant objects. A different type of modification would define more drastic variants. For example, you can create a question-and-answer game in which players could select from various categories or various levels of difficulty.

Dynamic Objects

Even though you've been using virtual methods in this chapter, all the variables used have been statically allocated. That is, these variables have been declared at the start of the program or routine, so that the program sets aside storage for them in the data segment or on the stack.

You can also work with dynamically allocated objects. That is, you can declare pointers to object types, and can then allocate storage for specific object instances as required in the program. The predefined **NEW** and **DISPOSE** routines have been modified in Turbo Pascal, so you can call these routines in coordination with constructors for the object types. The following program shows how to define and use pointers to object types:

P12-4
```
(* Dynamic, stripped-down version of VirtualDemo.
   Program shows how to define, declare, and use a
   pointer to an object type; also shows the modified
   syntax for NEW and DISPOSE.
*)

PROGRAM DynamicVirtualDemo;
(*$V-*)
(* Miscellaneous collection of authors and titles for the
   program to use.
*)
CONST Names : ARRAY [ 0 .. 5] OF STRING [ 20] =
                  ( 'Shakespeare', 'Cole Porter',
                    'Charles Dickens', 'Mary Shelley',
                    'Thomas Pynchon', 'Gilbert & Sullivan');
        Titles : ARRAY [ 0 .. 5] OF STRING [ 20] =
                  ('Othello', 'Anything Goes', 'Pickwick Papers',
                   'Frankenstein', 'V', 'Pirates of Penzance');
TYPE MedStr = STRING [ 80];

     DocPtr = ^Document;
     Document = OBJECT
                  Author, Title, Code : MedStr;
                  Year : INTEGER;
                  CONSTRUCTOR Init ( Au, Ti : MedStr;
                                     Yr : INTEGER);
                  PROCEDURE Describe; VIRTUAL;
                  PROCEDURE GetCode;
                  PROCEDURE Catalog; VIRTUAL;
                  DESTRUCTOR Done; VIRTUAL;
                END; (* Document *)
```

```
(* *************** Methods *************** *)

  CONSTRUCTOR Document.Init ( Au, Ti : MedStr;
                              Yr : INTEGER);
  BEGIN
    Author := Au;
    Title := Ti;
    Year := Yr;
    Code := '';
  END; (* Document.Init *)

  PROCEDURE Document.Describe;
  BEGIN
    WRITELN ( Code, ': ', Author, ', ', Title, ' [', Year, ']');
  END; (* Document.Describe *)

  PROCEDURE Document.GetCode;
  BEGIN
    WRITE ( 'Code? ');
    READLN ( Code);
  END; (* Document.GetCode *)

  PROCEDURE Document.Catalog;
  BEGIN
    Describe;
    GetCode;
  END; (* Document.Catalog *)

  (* Close up shop for the performer. NOTE: This routine is
     often used as an argument to DISPOSE, as in this program.
  *)
  DESTRUCTOR Document.Done;
  BEGIN
    WRITELN ( 'Done with: ');
    Describe;
  END; (* Document.Done *)

(* *************** General-Purpose Routines *************** *)

  (* Display the amount of heap storage available. *)
  PROCEDURE ShowHeap ( Message : STRING);
  BEGIN
    WRITELN ( Message, ': ', MEMAVAIL, ' bytes available');
  END; (* ShowHeap *)

VAR MyDocPtr : DocPtr;
    Writer, Name : MedStr;
    StartingHeap : LONGINT;
    NameIdx, TitleIdx, Count, Year : INTEGER;
```

```
BEGIN
  RANDOMIZE;
  Count := 0;
  ShowHeap ( 'Start of program');
  StartingHeap := MEMAVAIL;
  REPEAT
    INC ( Count);
    (* Select author and title at random *)
    NameIdx := RANDOM ( 6);
    TitleIdx := RANDOM ( 6);
    (* Allocate storage for a new Document instance,
       to be named MyDocPtr^
    *)
    NEW ( MyDocPtr, Init ( Names [ NameIdx],
                               Titles [ TitleIdx], Count));
    MyDocPtr^.Describe;
    ShowHeap ( 'After allocating storage for a Document');
  UNTIL MEMAVAIL < StartingHeap - 1000;
  DISPOSE ( MyDocPtr, Done);
  ShowHeap ( 'End of program');
  READLN;
  WRITE ( 'Press ENTER to end program.');
END.
```

This program allocates storage for a **Document** instance, selects some values at random, and displays information about the instance.

Look at the syntax in this program. First, notice the definition of a **DocPtr** as a **^Document**. This is just like the pointer definitions you used in Chapter 9, "Pointers." **MyDocPtr**'s contents will be an address—namely, the location of an anonymous **Document** variable. This variable's name will be **MyDocPtr^**.

Recall from Chapter 9 that the **NEW** procedure allocates storage for a variable of the type specified (indirectly) by the pointer argument. When you work with objects, the first argument will also be a pointer to an object—either a specific pointer variable (such as **MyDocPtr**) or a type specifier (such as **DocPtr**).

To facilitate working with dynamic object variables, Borland has extended the syntax for **NEW** (and for **DISPOSE**). These two routines can now take a second argument. This argument will be a constructor, which you can use to initialize the target object as you allocate storage for it. Thus, with one call to **NEW** you can allocate storage, assign values to the target object's fields, and set the environment for using virtual methods. This is all accomplished in the call to **NEW** in program **DynamicVirtualDemo**.

The first argument is a pointer variable—in this case, a pointer to a **Document** object. This target object will be initialized to the value of **Names[NameIdx]** for the author, **Titles[TitleIdx]** for the title, and so forth.

The call to **Describe** has the format you've seen in earlier programs. This time, however, the name of the object the program describes is given indirectly by referring to **MyDocPtr^**. Notice that the program restores storage for only one object at the end—even though storage for multiple objects is allocated and each of these objects is initialized. Obviously, this is not good programming practice. It has been done to demonstrate how memory changes as dynamic objects are allocated, and also to show that the **DISPOSE** process handles single objects.

The call to **DISPOSE** also represents a new syntax. The first argument is a pointer, as in the syntax from Chapter 9. The second argument is a destructor, which cleans up the object-oriented aspects—particularly the virtual methods environment.

In the current program, there is only one type of target object: a **Document**. Other programs may have descendant object instances as well. When you dispose of a pointer's target, the program needs to know how much storage this target used. The call to the destructor **Done** ensures that the right amount of storage is deallocated by **DISPOSE**. The version of **Done** required for the target object is executed and returns information about the object's storage requirements to the **DISPOSE** procedure, which then deallocates the appropriate amount of storage.

NEW as a Function

Under versions of Turbo Pascal that support object-oriented programming, **NEW** can also be a function that returns a pointer. In this case, the argument for the function call specifies the type of pointer you want returned. For example, the following call allocates storage for a **DocPtr** variable and assigns the location of this storage to **MyDocPtr**:

```
MyDocPtr := NEW ( DocPtr, Init ( Names [ NameIdx],
                                 Title [ TitleIdx], Count));
```

You can also use **NEW** as a function to return pointers to ordinary (that is, non-object) variables. On the other hand, you can only use the two-parameter, procedure version of **NEW** (described earlier) with pointer to objects.

Building a Linked List of Objects

This section explains how to build linked lists (similar to those in Chapter 9) whose nodes provide access to object instances. The following listing shows the data types the program uses. Look at these data structures carefully before you go on to the actual program.

```
TYPE MedStr = STRING [ 80];

    DocPtr = ^Document;
    Document = OBJECT
                Author, Title, Code : MedStr;
                Year : INTEGER;
                CONSTRUCTOR Init ( Au, Ti : MedStr;
                                    Yr : INTEGER);
                PROCEDURE Describe; VIRTUAL;
                PROCEDURE GetCode;
                PROCEDURE Catalog; VIRTUAL;
                DESTRUCTOR Done; VIRTUAL;
              END; (* Document *)

    BkPtr = ^Book;
    Book = OBJECT (Document)
            Publisher : MedStr;
            Price : REAL;
            CONSTRUCTOR Init ( Au, Ti, Pub : MedStr;
                                Yr : INTEGER;
                                Pr : REAL);
            PROCEDURE Describe; VIRTUAL;
            DESTRUCTOR Done; VIRTUAL;
          END; (* Book *)

    LNodePtr = ^LNode;
    LNode = RECORD
                Info : DocPtr;
                Next : LNodePtr;
```

```
                END; (* LNode *)

    List = OBJECT
             LNP : LNodePtr;
             CONSTRUCTOR Init;
             PROCEDURE Add ( Info : DocPtr); VIRTUAL;
             PROCEDURE ShowList; VIRTUAL;
             DESTRUCTOR Done; VIRTUAL;
           END;   (* List *)

VAR MyDocPtr : DocPtr;
    MyBkPtr : BkPtr;
    MyList : List;
```

The **Document** and **Book** types are familiar from earlier programs, as is **DocPtr**. **BkPtr** should also present no problems. A **List** is an object that provides access to a collection of nodes. The single field of a **List** instance is a pointer to an **LNode**. An **LNode**, in turn, is the basic component of the list.

Ultimately, you want the list to provide information about documents and books. The **LNode** elements in the list make this possible. The **LNode** record (*not* object) is similar to the record used in Chapter 9. It contains an information field and a pointer to another **LNode**. In this case, however, the **Info** field is a pointer to the real information, rather than the information itself. Why is this type of data structure used?

Building a Mixed List

Ideally, any list you build should be able to store both **Document** and **Book** information. However, a document and its descendant types require different amounts of storage. On the one hand, it's important to keep the list structure as simple as possible. The simplest structure for a list element is an ordinary record, with no variants. To satisfy this criterion, while also satisfying the "heterogeneous information" criterion, put the complications outside the list itself. That is, make the list a homogeneous collection of elements, but make these nodes provide access to what may be different objects. By using a pointer to **Document** as the information field of an **LNode**, you move any discrepancies in size, and so forth, outside the list itself. All **LNodes** are still exactly the same size, regardless of the information stored at the target location.

Assignment compatibility makes it easy to keep size differences outside the list structure itself. Remember from Chapter 11 that you can assign a variable of a descendant type to an ancestor variable. In that case, any extra fields in the descendant object are simply ignored. All pointers, in contrast, are the same size. Therefore, when you assign a ^**Book** variable to a **DocPtr** variable, the starting location of the book information is assigned. This means that the entire **Book** variable is accessible if there is some way of identifying the object as a **Book** rather than a **Document**.

The **Self** parameter (described in Chapter 11) makes it possible to identify the object as a book. This parameter identifies the instance as being a particular object type. Thus, by defining an **LNode** as in the preceding listing, you can access either book or document information. By using virtual methods, you can work with a **Document** or with a descendant object type without changing the code. You'll see this in the program **VirtualListDemo**.

The program shown over the next few pages uses **MyList** as the anchor for the list. This is a static variable, not a pointer. Storage for **MyList** is allocated in the data segment. Storage for the list's nodes is allocated dynamically, as the program executes. The program also allocates storage dynamically for the target instances (that is, for **MyDoc^** and **MyBk^**).

The linked-list program is shown in the following pages. The program generates values for a book or a document variable, and adds to the list a node representing this variable. This process continues until more than **MemToUse** bytes of heap storage have been used. The value chosen for this constant (1500) is arbitrary, and you can change it if you wish. After the list has been generated, the program displays the list's information. Finally, the program returns to the heap the storage used.

Compile the program and run it a few times. Notice that sometimes the program puts six elements in the list and at other times only five. Why do you think this happens? To study the program more closely, trace through it, or execute it by stopping at selected breakpoints to see what it looks like. To answer the question, you might try evaluating **SIZEOF (Book)** and **SIZEOF(Document)** and comparing the results. To do this, press CTRL-F4 while stopped at a breakpoint or tracing through the program. Then type

```
SIZEOF( Book)
```

in the first box and press ENTER. Then repeat these steps for **Document**.

P12-5   (* Program to build a linked list of object nodes. *)

```
PROGRAM VirtualListDemo;
(*$V-*)
(* Miscellaneous collection of authors, titles, and
   publishers for the program to use.
*)
CONST Names : ARRAY [ 0 .. 5] OF STRING [ 20] =
                ( 'Shakespeare', 'Porter', 'Dickens',
                  'Lem', 'Pynchon', 'Gilbert & Sullivan');
      Titles : ARRAY [ 0 .. 5] OF STRING [ 20] =
                ('Othello', 'Anything Goes', 'Pickwick Papers',
                 'Solaris', 'V', 'Pirates of Penzance');
      Pubs : ARRAY [ 0 .. 5] OF STRING [ 20] =
                ( 'SpeedyPress', 'SpeedierPress', 'ImPress',
                  'ComPress', 'BenchPress', 'ExPress');
      MemToUse = 1500; (* amount of storage to use for lists *)
TYPE MedStr = STRING [ 80];

     DocPtr = ^Document;
     Document = OBJECT
                    Author, Title, Code : MedStr;
                    Year : INTEGER;
                    CONSTRUCTOR Init ( Au, Ti : MedStr;
                                       Yr : INTEGER);
                    PROCEDURE Describe; VIRTUAL;
                    PROCEDURE GetCode;
                    PROCEDURE Catalog; VIRTUAL;
                    DESTRUCTOR Done; VIRTUAL;
                END; (* Document *)

     BkPtr = ^Book;
     Book = OBJECT (Document)
                Publisher : MedStr;
                Price : REAL;
                CONSTRUCTOR Init ( Au, Ti, Pub : MedStr;
                                   Yr : INTEGER;
                                   Pr : REAL);
                PROCEDURE Describe; VIRTUAL;
                DESTRUCTOR Done; VIRTUAL;
            END; (* Book *)

     (* An LNode is the basic element of a linked list *)
     LNodePtr = ^LNode;
     LNode = RECORD
                (* a pointer to document (or book) information *)
                Info : DocPtr;
                (* a pointer to the next node *)
                Next : LNodePtr;
```

```
                       END; (* LNode *)

        (* A List variable is the beginning of a
           collection of LNode elements.
        *)
        ListPtr = ^List;
        List = OBJECT
                 LNP : LNodePtr;
                 CONSTRUCTOR Init;
                 PROCEDURE Add ( Info : DocPtr); VIRTUAL;
                 PROCEDURE ShowList;  VIRTUAL;
                 DESTRUCTOR Done; VIRTUAL;
               END;    (* List *)

VAR MyDocPtr : DocPtr;
    MyBkPtr : BkPtr;
    MyList : List;
    StartingHeap : LONGINT;
    PubIdx, NameIdx, TitleIdx, Count : INTEGER;

(* ************** Methods ************** *)

  CONSTRUCTOR Document.Init ( Au, Ti : MedStr;
                              Yr : INTEGER);
  BEGIN
    Author := Au;
    Title := Ti;
    Year := Yr;
    Code := '';
  END; (* Document.Init *)

  PROCEDURE Document.Describe;
  BEGIN
    WRITELN ( Code, ': ', Author, ', ', Title, ' [', Year, ']');
  END; (* Document.Describe *)

  PROCEDURE Document.GetCode;
  BEGIN
    WRITE ( 'Code? ');
    READLN ( Code);
  END; (* Document.GetCode *)

  PROCEDURE Document.Catalog;
  BEGIN
    Describe;
    GetCode;
  END; (* Document.Catalog *)

  (* Close up shop for the performer. NOTE: This routine is
     often used as an argument to DISPOSE, as in this program.
  *)
  DESTRUCTOR Document.Done;
```

```
BEGIN
  WRITELN ( 'Disposing of another DOCUMENT.');
END; (* Document.Done *)

CONSTRUCTOR Book.Init ( Au, Ti, Pub : MedStr;
                        Yr : INTEGER;
                        Pr : REAL);
BEGIN
  Document.Init ( Au, Ti, Yr);
  Publisher := Pub;
  Price := Pr;
END; (* Book.Init *)

PROCEDURE Book.Describe;
BEGIN
  Document.Describe;
  WRITELN ( '$', Price : 1 : 2, ', ', Publisher);
END; (* Book.Describe *)

DESTRUCTOR Book.Done;
BEGIN
  WRITELN ( 'Disposing of another BOOK.');
END; (* Book.Done *)

(* Initialize the list by setting its LNode pointer to NIL *)
CONSTRUCTOR List.Init;
BEGIN
  LNP := NIL;
END; (* List.Init *)

(* Add a node to the front of the list. The parameter provides
   access to document info, not to an LNodePtr.
*)
PROCEDURE List.Add ( Info : DocPtr);
VAR Temp : LNodePtr;
BEGIN
  (* allocate storage for a new LNodePtr, which will
     point to the new Document or Book.
  *)
  NEW ( Temp);
  (* Make the Info field point to the new Document or Book *)
  Temp^.Info := Info;
  (* Make the new node point to current start of the list *)
  Temp^.Next := LNP;
  (* Make the list point to the new first node. *)
  LNP := Temp;
END;  (* List.Add *)

(* Display the contents of a linked list. *)
PROCEDURE List.ShowList;
VAR Curr : LNodePtr;
BEGIN
```

```
        Curr := LNP;
        WHILE Curr <> NIL DO
        BEGIN
          (* This is a call to a virtual method. Sometimes
             Document.Describe will execute and sometimes
             Book.Describe will.
          *)
          Curr^.Info^.Describe;
          Curr := Curr^.Next;
        END;
      END;   (* List.ShowList *)

  (* Clean up after the list has been built.
      NOTE: storage for the object target is deallocated
      first, and then storage is deallocated for the node
      through which the object was accessed.
  *)
  DESTRUCTOR List.Done;
  VAR TheNode : LNodePtr;
  BEGIN
     WHILE LNP <> NIL DO
     BEGIN
       TheNode := LNP;
       (* Dispose of the object's storage *)
       DISPOSE ( TheNode^.Info, Done);
       LNP := TheNode^.Next;
       (* Dispose of the LNode's storage *)
       DISPOSE ( TheNode);
     END;
  END; (* List.Done *)

(* *************** General-Purpose Routines *************** *)

  (* Display the amount of heap storage available. *)
  PROCEDURE ShowHeap ( Message : STRING);
  BEGIN
     WRITE ( Message, ': ', MEMAVAIL, ' bytes available');
  END; (* ShowHeap *)

BEGIN
  RANDOMIZE;
  Count := 0;
  ShowHeap ( 'Start of program');
  StartingHeap := MEMAVAIL;
  (* Initialize the list -- to NIL *)
  MyList.Init;

  REPEAT
    INC ( Count);
    (* Select author and title at random *)
    NameIdx := RANDOM ( 6);
    TitleIdx := RANDOM ( 6);
```

```
   IF ODD ( NameIdx) THEN
   BEGIN
     (* #10#13 send a LineFeed and Carriage Return *)
     WRITE ( #10#13'BOOK    : ');
     PubIdx := RANDOM ( 6);
     (* Allocate storage for a BkPtr, and initialize it.
        Notice the use of the function version of NEW.
     *)
     MyBkPtr := NEW ( BkPtr, Init ( Names [ NameIdx],
                                    Titles [ TitleIdx],
                                    Pubs [ PubIdx],
                                    Count + 1970, 29.95));
     (* Add a new node to the list. This node's Info field
        will point to a Book target variable.
     *)
     MyList.Add ( MyBkPtr);
     ShowHeap ( 'After allocating for a BOOK     ');
   END
   ELSE
   BEGIN
     WRITE ( #10#13'DOCUMENT: ');
     (* Allocate storage for a DocPtr, and initialize it.
        Notice the use of the function version of NEW.
     *)
     MyDocPtr :=  NEW ( DocPtr, Init ( Names [ NameIdx],
                                      Titles [ TitleIdx],
                                      Count + 1980));
     (* Add a new node to the list. This node's Info field
        will point to a Document target variable.
     *)
     MyList.Add ( MyDocPtr);
     ShowHeap ( 'After allocating for a DOCUMENT');
   END;
 UNTIL MEMAVAIL < StartingHeap - MemToUse;

 WRITELN;
 (* Display list's elements *)
 MyList.ShowList;
 (* Return the list's storage to the heap *)
 MyList.Done;
 ShowHeap ( 'End of program');
 WRITE ( 'Press ENTER to end program.');
 READLN;
END.
```

The definitions for the **Book** and **Document** related methods are the same as in earlier programs. However, two methods have been added to these objects: the destructors **Document.Done** and **Book.Done**.

You might have noticed that the program displays six items if more than three of them are documents, but only five items if most of the items are books. This is because documents require less storage than books. As a result, you can add more items to the list if they're small enough.

The Program's Execution

The program has three main parts:

■ Startup, in which variables are initialized and the **List.Init** constructor is called. Note that this call does *not* allocate any new storage. It just stores a value in existing storage (namely, in the field of **MyList**).

■ List building, in which as many items as possible are added to the list. This part is executed in the **REPEAT** loop. Storage for the document (or book) target variables is allocated during this loop.

■ Cleaning up, in which the contents of the list are displayed and used storage is returned to the heap.

The startup process simply sets the **LNP** field of **MyList** to **NIL** through the call to **List.Init**.

Adding To a List of Objects

The heart of the program is procedure **List.Add**. This routine is examined in detail, since it provides much important information about objects and pointers.

The interface for this method says that **List.Add** takes a **DocPtr** argument. After **Add** has finished its work, a new node at the front of the list points to the same location as the **DocPtr** argument.

The argument is generated with the function version of **NEW**. The arguments to this function are

■ A pointer type, which indicates whether a **DocPtr** or a **BkPtr** is to be assigned a value

■ The **Init** constructor for the appropriate object type

Note that **List.Add** doesn't care about the initial values being stored in the pointer's target. Nor does the **Add** routine care whether storage for a document or book is being generated, because of the assignment compatibility between **BkPtr** and **DocPtr** variables. Once a pointer variable has been returned by the call to **NEW**, this pointer is passed as the argument to **MyList.Add** in the program.

Suppose that a **DocPtr** is generated the first time through the loop. Before you add this to the list, the situation looks like Figure 12-1. The document variable referenced by **MyDocPtr** is anonymous, but its starting location is known to **MyList.Add** through the **Info** parameter.

In the Body of List.Add   Once a pointer has been returned from the call to **NEW**, the main body of the **Add** constructor is ready to begin

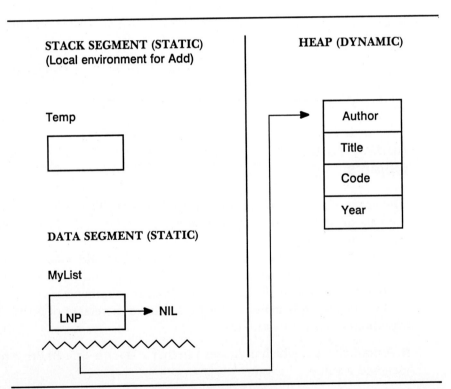

Figure 12-1.   *Memory usage at start of MyList.Add*

executing. The first instruction in this method allocates storage for an **LNode** and makes **Temp** point to this storage. This is shown in Figure 12-2.

After allocating storage, the fields for the target **LNode** are assigned values. In particular, the **Info** field is made to point to the same location as the parameter passed to **MyList.Add**. After this assignment, the object is connected to a node, as shown in Figure 12-3. The node is not yet connected to the list, however.

The next assignment,

```
Temp^.Next := LNP;
```

makes the **Next** field of the new node point to the same place as the list anchor—namely, to the current start of the list. The first time **Add** is

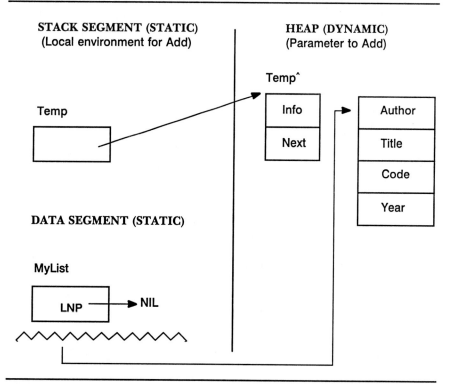

Figure 12-2. *Memory usage after allocating storage for a NodePtr in MyList.Add*

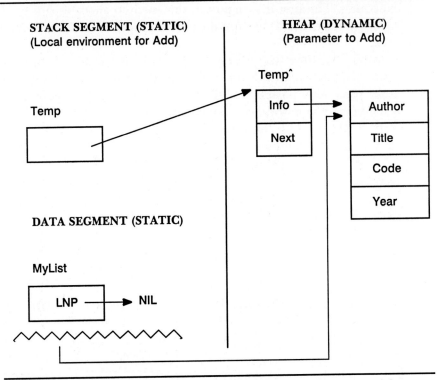

Figure 12-3.   *Memory usage after making **Temp^.Info** point to the location of the parameter to **MyList. Add***

called, the list will be empty and **LNP** will still be **NIL** (from the call to **MyList.Init**). Finally, **LNP** is made to point to the new node — that is, to the *new* first element. This is shown in Figure 12-4. After the first call to **Add**, this list will contain one node.

The next call repeats this process with a few variations. First, the **DocPtr** passed as argument this time might be pointing to a **Book**. This makes no difference to **Add**, however. A more important difference from the first time through the loop is when the new **LNode** is made to point to the same location as **LNP**'s target. This time, **LNP** will point to a node rather than to **NIL**. The situation, just before making **Temp^.Next** point to the same place as **LNP**, is shown in Figure 12-5.

After the assignment, **LNP** will point to the new node and the new node will point to the previous new node, as in Figure 12-6. After all the

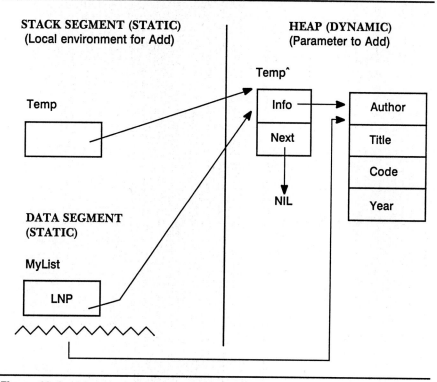

Figure 12-4. *Memory usage after making the start of the list (LNP) point to the new element*

work has been done, the list will look something like the one in Figure 12-7.

The list's contents are displayed by the **List.ShowList** method. This method simply moves from node to node in the list, and then calls **Describe** to display information about the target object for the current node (**Curr^.Info^**).

```
(* Display the contents of a linked list. *)
PROCEDURE List.ShowList;
VAR Curr : LNodePtr;
BEGIN
  Curr := LNP;
  WHILE Curr <> NIL DO
  BEGIN
```

```
     (* This is a call to a virtual method. Sometimes
        Document.Describe will execute and sometimes
        Book.Describe will.
     *)
     Curr^.Info^.Describe;
     Curr := Curr^.Next;
  END;
END;    (* List.ShowList *)
```

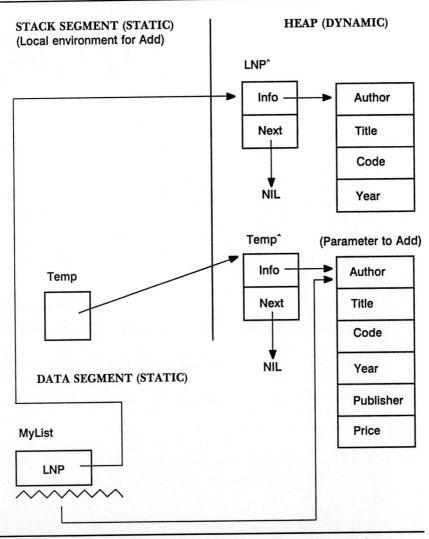

STACK SEGMENT (STATIC)
(Local environment for Add)

HEAP (DYNAMIC)

LNP^

Info	→	Author
Next		Title
		Code
NIL		Year

Temp^   (Parameter to Add)

Temp

Info	→	Author
Next		Title
		Code
NIL		Year
		Publisher
		Price

DATA SEGMENT (STATIC)

MyList

| LNP |

Figure 12-5. *Memory usage before making the new node point to the start of a nonempty list*

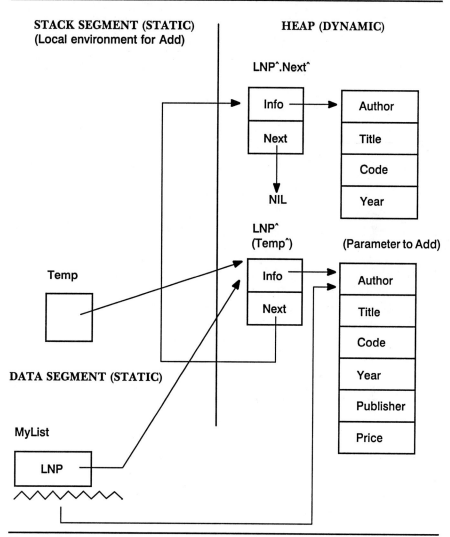

Figure 12-6. *Memory usage after making the start of the list point to the new first node*

Because **Describe** is a virtual method, this statement will call either **Book.Describe** or **Document.Describe**, depending on the type of object at the target location.

Finally, the **List.Done** destructor cleans up the list. Study this routine carefully. Notice that there are two different calls to **DISPOSE**. To see what these calls are disposing, look at Figure 12-7 to determine how

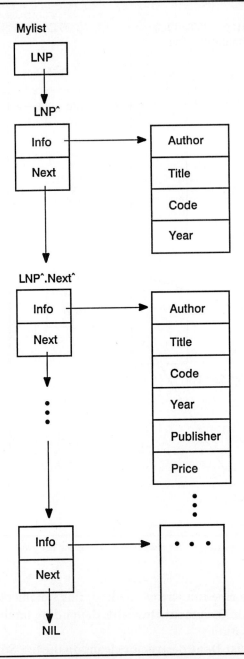

Figure 12-7.   *Memory layout after a linked list has been built*

many dynamically allocated areas of storage there are for each node. If you found both the **LNode** and the object, you're right.

```
(* Clean up after the list has been built.
   NOTE: storage for the object target is deallocated
   first, and then storage is deallocated for the node
   through which the object was accessed.
*)
DESTRUCTOR List.Done;
VAR TheNode : LNodePtr;
BEGIN
  WHILE LNP <> NIL DO
  BEGIN
    TheNode := LNP;
    (* Dispose of the object's storage *)
    DISPOSE ( TheNode^.Info, Done);
    LNP := TheNode^.Next;
    (* Dispose of the LNode's storage *)
    DISPOSE ( TheNode);
  END;
END; (* List.Done *)
```

The first call to **DISPOSE** deallocates the storage for the target object. Because **Document.Done** and **Book.Done** are virtual methods, this call deallocates the appropriate amount of storage. The storage is referenced through the **Info** field of the current node.

After the storage "hanging off" the **LNode** has been deallocated, you can also return the storage for the **LNode** itself. This is done in the second call to **DISPOSE**. Notice that this call does not involve an object so no destructor call is included.

Note also that **List.Done** first assigns **TheNode^.Next** to the list anchor. This prevents the list from being lost when the storage for the first element is deallocated. In essence, this assignment removes the first element from the list. The call to **DISPOSE** then returns the element's storage to the heap. This process continues until the list is empty again.

A List as a Dynamic Object

Congratulations, you have just worked your way through some very difficult concepts. If you need to create such lists, the techniques described in the preceding pages will work. There is another way of doing this, which is described briefly in this section. If you haven't gotten your fill of object lists, read on. Otherwise, you can skip to the next section.

In the **VirtualListDemo** program, the list was declared as a static variable. You could just as well have defined a **ListPtr** and then allocated storage for a list anchor dynamically. In that case, the calls to **MyList.Init** and **MyList.Done** would have to be made within the context of calls to **NEW** and **DISPOSE**, respectively.

The following program shows the changes needed in the main program. You don't have to change any of the methods. Note that the program assumes that **MyList** is now a **ListPtr** rather than a **List**.

```
(* Main program when MyList is a ListPtr (^List).
   Changed lines are marked.
*)
BEGIN
  RANDOMIZE;
  Count := 0;
  ShowHeap ( 'Start of program');
  StartingHeap := MEMAVAIL;
  NEW ( MyList, Init);                              (* CHANGED *)

  REPEAT
    INC ( Count);
    (* Select author and title at random *)
    NameIdx := RANDOM ( 6);
    TitleIdx := RANDOM ( 6);
    IF ODD ( MEMAVAIL) THEN
    BEGIN
      WRITELN ( #10#13'Building Book');
      PubIdx := RANDOM ( 6);
                                                     (* CHANGED *)
      MyList^.Add ( NEW ( BkPtr, Init ( Names [ NameIdx],
                                        Titles [ TitleIdx],
                                        Pubs [ PubIdx],
                                        Count + 1970, 29.95)));
    END
    ELSE
    BEGIN
      WRITELN ( #10#13'Building Document');
      (* Allocate storage for a new Document instance,
         to be named MyDocPtr^
      *)
                                                     (* CHANGED *)
```

```
      MyList^.Add ( NEW ( DocPtr, Init ( Names [ NameIdx],
                                         Titles [ TitleIdx],
                                         Count + 1980)));
    END;
    ShowHeap ( 'After allocating storage for a Document');
  UNTIL MEMAVAIL < StartingHeap - 1000;
  WRITELN;
  (* Display list's elements *)
  MyList^.ShowList;                                      (* CHANGED *)
  (* Return the list's storage to the heap *)
  DISPOSE (MyList, Done);                                (* CHANGED *)
  ShowHeap ( 'End of program');
  READLN;
END.
```

Extensions and Modifications

There's more to learn about objects and object-oriented programming, but you now have enough information to extend your understanding on your own. For example, you can modify existing programs to see how different things work and to become more proficient at using objects and pointers. You might want to extend the linked-list program by including routines for adding to the front and middle of the list. Keep in mind that these will be methods, just like **Add**. To add to the middle of the list, you must decide which field to use as the key for the comparison; for example, you could order by author, title, code, or year. (To order by code, however, you first need to assign values to the code field.)

You can also define more objects as descendants of **Book**. For example, you might add the **Article** type to the program so you can include such items in the list. To do this, you need to add a **Done** destructor for **Article** and expand the list-building part of the program.

In this and the previous chapter, you learned about object-oriented programming. You've seen the power of this approach, especially in the use of virtual methods. The spirit of Pascal programming is quite likely to change as object-oriented features become more widely available.

In the next chapter, you'll learn about the Turbo Vision object tools provided with version 6 of Turbo Pascal.

13 *Introduction to Turbo Vision*

With version 6, Borland has provided a major addition to the Turbo Pascal environment: Turbo Vision. With Turbo Vision you can use windows, menus, dialog boxes, and so forth in your programs. Turbo Vision provides you with the resources you need to create and use such entities. These capabilities come in the form of a collection of objects, along with other data structures and routines.

What Is Turbo Vision?

Turbo Vision is the interface for the underlying mechanisms that Borland used to write the Integrated Development Environment (IDE) for Turbo Pascal version 6. By giving you access to these mechanisms, Borland has allowed you to develop software that has the look and feel of the IDE.

Turbo Vision is extremely flexible. A side effect of this flexibility is that Turbo Vision is also fairly complicated. It contains hundreds of new types, objects, procedures, and methods.

In fact, Turbo Vision contains definitions for over 40 objects, arranged in a hierarchy with **TObject** at the top level. This hierarchy

605

includes object definitions for such program elements as windows, menu bars and menu boxes, dialog boxes, and so forth. Figure 13-1 shows this hierarchy. Object types used in the example program are shown white on black. Note that, if an object is used in a program, methods and fields from any ancestor objects may also be used.

In addition to the object hierarchy, over 130 other data types, procedures, and functions are defined. Some of the data structures serve as fields in object definitions; however, many of these can be used as data structures in their own right—that is, independently of any object. Even though Turbo Vision includes both object-oriented and more traditional program elements, if you want to use Turbo Vision's capabilities you'll need to be serious about object-oriented programming. In fact, Turbo Vision is almost entirely built around the concepts of polymorphism and inheritance.

A major benefit of Turbo Vision is that it provides a huge collection of reusable software. The next time you need to create a menu, for example, you'll simply define an object variable of type **TMenuBox** and insert the menu items into the object. If **TMenuBox** doesn't quite handle a specific capability, you can create a new object type that inherits all the functionality of **TMenuBox** but adds the new capability.

Since one could easily write a book about Turbo Vision, it's impossible to provide you with a complete account here. Instead, you'll find a discussion of a few of the major capabilities afforded by Turbo Vision. As you'll see, you can do quite a lot with the features to be described.

This chapter breaks Turbo Vision into meaningful portions, then covers those portions in enough detail so that you can write very complex programs. The chapter goes through the development of one complete example, so each section flows into the next.

Learning Turbo Vision

The details of Turbo Vision are quite overwhelming and learning to use Turbo Vision will take time. In fact, even after you've become familiar with Turbo Vision, and have written several programs, you'll probably still find yourself copying examples without any clear idea of why you're doing certain things. As you know, much of life seems to work that way—so don't get overwhelmed. You'll find that your understanding

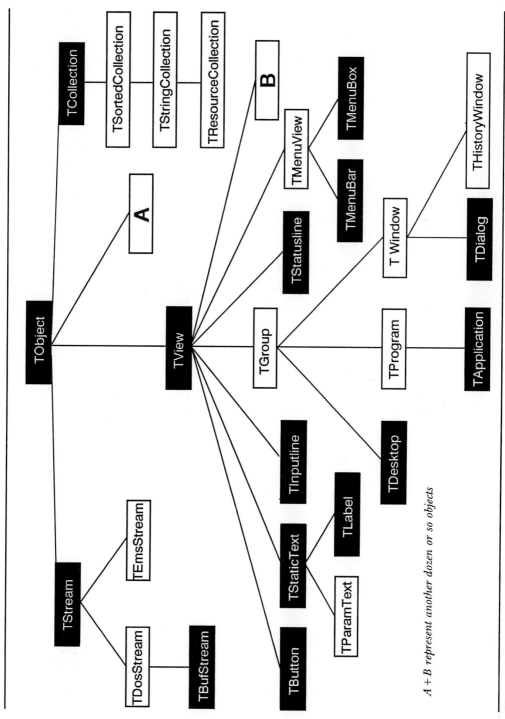

Figure 13-1. Turbo Vision's object hierarchy. Objects shown white on black are used in the example program.

A + B represent another dozen or so objects

will improve, and the details will gradually become clearer, as you gain an overview of the Turbo Vision system.

As you're learning, you'll find example programs such as the one developed in this chapter and the ones included with the Turbo Pascal software to be among your most useful resources.

Creating and Using a Game Program

Throughout this chapter you'll follow the development of a single application. Each example listing will therefore have some context, making it easier to understand.

The application to be developed is a program that lets you play word games. The program reads a list of words or phrases (from a text or binary file), and presents them as puzzles to the player in a fixed or random order.

In the anagram game that has been implemented, a scrambled version of the word is presented, and your task is to find the word as quickly as possible. The program records the amount of time it takes you to solve each puzzle.

As with all Turbo Vision programs, this application has the same look and feel as the Turbo Pascal environment. Figure 13-2 shows a sample screen from the running program.

The program can build a puzzle collection by reading a list of words from an ordinary text file or by reading entire puzzle objects from a binary file. The program can save such a collection of puzzles to a binary file. The examples disk contains three text files with sample puzzle words.

Writing Applications with Turbo Vision

Turbo Vision programs work by "executing" an application. This means that methods associated with an object based on Turbo Vision's **TApplication** type are invoked. As you'll see, it's very easy to execute an application—because Turbo Vision knows so much about how an application behaves when it is executing.

When running the program, you will select commands from menus or use shortcut keys to give the commands. In a Turbo Vision program, you'll need to specify the contents of the menus—that is, the wording of the menu entries, the keystrokes associated with the menu selection or with shortcuts, and so forth. Fortunately, all the details of creating and displaying such menus are provided in Turbo Vision. All you need to do is supply the specific values.

As part of this application, objects will be created and manipulated. For example, in the program developed here, puzzle objects will be built, modified, and displayed. Information about these objects will be read from or displayed in dialog boxes and windows—just as in the IDE. You may need to scroll the contents of a window or dialog box. Objects and methods for doing this are provided in Turbo Vision. Objects can also be grouped into collections of the basic object type. You can also do file I/O using Turbo Vision.

The rest of this chapter takes you step by step through the development of the example program. You'll see that many of the Turbo Vision

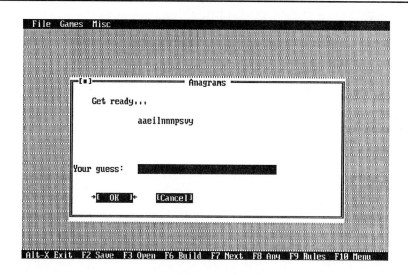

Figure 13-2. *Example screen from the Turbo Vision word game program*

elements just touched upon are used in the program. This example will
help you to create your own programs using Turbo Vision.

Creating an Application Object

When you first decide to tackle a large programming effort, you will
probably find it difficult to determine a starting place. Often, if you start
by prototyping your user interface, you can iron out the functionality of
your application. Turbo Vision makes it easy for you to start this way. It
allows you to see the results of your efforts almost immediately—by
creating a skeleton for the main program and the menus for the user
interface.

All Turbo Vision programs work with applications. Therefore, the
first step in creating a Turbo Vision application is to create a descendant
of the **TApplication** object type. You can start by creating a simple
descendant, with no new data fields and no overridden virtual methods.
As you progress, you'll add fields and methods to this template.

In the simplest applications, the main program consists of three calls
to methods inherited from or through **TApplication**. The following
listing shows such a skeleton program.

P13-1
```
(* Skeleton for Turbo Vision-based game program *)

PROGRAM TVGameApp;

USES App;      (* Unit that contains TApplication, etc *)

(* TGame is an identical descendant of TApplication
   ... for now.
*)
TYPE TGame = OBJECT ( TApplication)
     END;

VAR  MyGame : TGame;

BEGIN  (* MAIN Program *)
   MyGame.Init;    (* set up internals for Turbo Vision *)
   MyGame.Run;     (* run a session with the application *)
   MyGame.Done;    (* clean up *)
END.
```

After "describing" the new object type, the skeleton program creates a variable of that type and calls three inherited methods: **Init**, **Run**, and **Done**. To run any Turbo Vision application, you must call these three methods.

The **Init** method initializes all the internal structures required by Turbo Vision. You may choose to override this to include your own initializations. If you do, be sure to call the parent method, **TApplication.Init**. The **Run** method executes the application based on the way you set it up. Finally, **Done** cleans everything up.

Figure 13-3 shows the screen displayed when you run this simple program. Although you've created no code of your own yet, the program already displays three main screen components of almost all IDE programs:

- A line at the top, used for menus, and known as the *menu bar*.

- A wide open area in the middle of the screen, on which the program activity will generally take place. This area is known as the *desktop*.

- A line at the bottom that is used to provide information on available

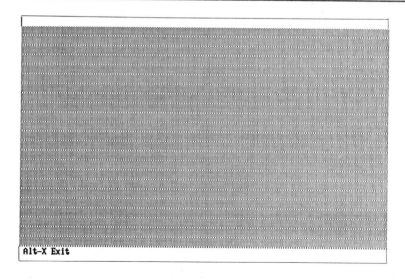

Figure 13-3. *Default screen for a running Turbo Vision application*

actions. This is the *status line*. Note that there is already a command available—ALT-X—which lets you end the program.

Creating Event Commands

The **Run** method in a Turbo Vision program essentially keeps processing events until there are no more, at which point the program ends. An *event* is a program element to which your program must respond.

A Turbo Vision program classifies an event and then passes the event on to the intended program element for a response. This processing is done by an *event handler*. You'll write such a handler for your program.

There is a predefined method, **HandleEvent**, that is available even to your skeleton program. This handler processes the ALT-X command and sends it to the appropriate program element for processing. The **HandleEvent** method is inherited by your application from **TApplication**, which inherited the method from **TProgram**.

One of your tasks is to specify the commands that will be available in your program. Certain commands are already available, as part of Turbo Vision. For example, pressing ALT-X in the skeleton program corresponds to the command **cmQuit**. When this event occurs, the program ends. Other predefined commands include **cmOK** and **cmCancel** (for the OK and Cancel buttons, respectively, in a dialog box).

By convention, event commands should be defined as constants and should start with the letters *cm*. Turbo Vision reserves all constants from 0 to 99 and from 256 to 999. This leaves you with the values 100 to 255 and 1000 to 65535 for your own commands. (There is a difference between commands with values below 256 and commands with larger values; this difference relates to context sensitivity for the commands, and won't concern us in this chapter.)

The vast majority of the reserved commands are handled internally by Turbo Vision, so you need not be concerned about them. The few exceptions are covered in later discussions.

For the word game program, the following commands are defined. If you decide to expand the game, you may add other commands at a later point.

```
CONST
(* valid event commands *)
  cmFileOpen   = 201;     (* open a specified puzzle file *)
```

```
cmFileSave  = 202;      (* save puzzle list to file *)
cmAnag      = 211;      (* play anagrams *)
cmHang      = 212;      (* play hangman *)
cmTriv      = 213;      (* play a trivia game *)
cmBuild     = 221;      (* build a list of puzzles *)
cmNext      = 222;      (* display next puzzle from list *)
cmAny       = 223;      (* display a random puzzle *)
cmRules     = 224;      (* display game rules *)
```

The numbering scheme used for these commands reflects the menu structure that will support the commands. You can use any nonreserved values you wish.

Creating a Menu Bar

You can use Turbo Vision to create menus in two forms: horizontal and vertical. Their associated object types are **TMenuBar** and **TMenuBox**, respectively. Turbo Vision creates a global variable, **MenuBar**, for the menu bar associated with the main application. To assign menu items to this global variable, you must override the virtual method called **TApplication.InitMenuBar**.

For the example program, the following listing defines the menu structure that is defined.

```
PROCEDURE TGame.InitMenuBar;
VAR R : TRect;
BEGIN
  GetExtent(R);
  R.B.Y := 1;
  MenuBar := NEW (PMenuBar, Init (R, NewMenu(
      NewSubMenu ('~F~ile', hcNoContext, NewMenu (
        NewItem ('~O~pen', 'F3', kbF3, cmFileOpen, hcNoContext,
        NewItem ('~S~ave', 'F2', kbF2, cmFileSave, hcNoContext,
        NewItem ('~Q~uit', 'Alt-X', kbAltX, cmQuit, hcNoContext,
        Nil)))),
      NewSubMenu ('~G~ames', hcNoContext, NewMenu (
        NewItem ('~A~nagrams', 'Alt-A', kbAltA, cmAnag, hcNoContext,
        NewItem ('~H~angman', 'Alt-H', kbAltH, cmHang, hcNoContext,
        NewItem ('~T~rivia', 'Alt-T', kbAltT, cmTriv, hcNoContext,
        Nil)))),
      NewSubMenu ('~C~ommands', hcNoContext, NewMenu(
        NewItem ('~B~uild List', 'F6', kbF6, cmBuild, hcNoContext,
        NewItem ('~N~ext Puzzle', 'F7', kbF7, cmNext, hcNoContext,
```

```
                NewItem ('~A~ny Puzzle', 'F8', kbF8, cmAny, hcNoContext,
                NewItem ('~R~ules', 'F9', kbF9, cmRules, hcNoContext,
                Nil))))),
            Nil))))));
END;
```

The first step in creating a menu is to define its physical dimensions. This is done in terms of a rectangle. As a data type, a rectangle is a record with two record fields: **A** and **B**. These correspond to the upper-left and lower-right corners, respectively. **A** and **B** are records of type **TPoint** and have two fields, **X** and **Y**. These correspond to the horizontal and vertical coordinates, respectively, of the point.

To define the physical dimensions of the menu bar, call method **GetExtent** for the application object. All dimension rectangles include (0,0) as their upper-left corner. Since the menu bar takes only one line, you should set the bottom line to 1. In the program, setting **R.B.Y** (the *y* coordinate for the lower-right corner) to 1 accomplishes this. Note that a menu's dimensions are for the main part of the menu only, not for any of its submenus.

The global variable **MenuBar** is actually a pointer to a menu, so it must be assigned a value using the procedure **NEW**. Using the extended form of this procedure, the second parameter to **NEW** is a call to **TMenuBar.Init**. **Init** is a fairly complex constructor because it must handle menus of any size. It requires the dimension rectangle and the menu items as parameters.

When you define the menu items, you are actually inserting them into a linked list. The functions **NewMenu**, **NewSubMenu**, and **NewItem** are required to define the list. The last parameter in each of these functions is a pointer to the next menu item (or submenu item), which will be **NIL** for the last item.

Thus, this procedure defines three submenus: File, Game, and Command. The File and Game menus each have three entries. For Game, these are Anagram, Hangman, and Trivia. The Command submenu has four entries.

In the source code, each menu entry has five parts:

■ Name of the entry

■ Name of a shortcut key for that entry (if applicable)

■ Key code for the shortcut key

- Command to be executed
- Help context key

The entry name can include a character enclosed by tilde (~) characters; this defines the letter that will be highlighted and that can be pressed to access that menu entry. For now, set all help context keys to the global constant **hcNoContext**, which defines no related help. The key codes are all defined as constants in the **Drivers** unit, and all start with the letters *kb*.

Creating a Status Line

Defining the status line is similar to defining menus. The **InitStatusLine** method, which is shown in the following listing, accomplishes this.

```
PROCEDURE TGame.InitStatusLine;
VAR  R : TRect;
BEGIN
  GetExtent(R);
  R.A.Y := R.B.Y - 1;
  StatusLine := NEW (PStatusLine, Init (R,
    NewStatusDef (0, $FFFF,
      NewStatusKey ('~Alt-X~ Exit', kbAltX, cmQuit,
      NewStatusKey ('~F2~ Save', kbF2, cmFileSave,
      NewStatusKey ('~F3~ Open', kbF3, cmFileOpen,
      NewStatusKey ('~F6~ Build', kbF6, cmBuild,
      NewStatusKey ('~F7~ Next', kbF7, cmNext,
      NewStatusKey ('~F8~ Any', kbF8, cmAny,
      NewStatusKey ('~F9~ Rules', kbF9, cmRules,
      NewStatusKey ('~F10~ Menu', kbF10, cmMenu,
      Nil)))))))),
    Nil)));
END;
```

As with the menu bar, this method starts by assigning a rectangle to the desired dimensions of the status line (at the bottom of the screen, this time). By default such a rectangle takes the entire screen. By assigning a value to **R.A.Y**, you specify the vertical location of the rectangle's upper-left corner. This value is set to one line above the vertical coordinate at the bottom of the screen.

After creating the appropriate rectangle for the status line, the method initializes the pointer **StatusLine** with a call to **Init**. This call requires a list of status key items.

Each status key has three parts:

■ The string entry that normally includes the key name and the command name

■ The code for the hot key

■ The command to be executed when the appropriate key is pressed

The key name is normally enclosed in tilde characters, so it appears in a highlighted color.

Creating the Event Handler

The final piece in the outer layer of each application object is the event handler. You create an event handler by overriding the method **TProgram.HandleEvent**.

Any event handler must first call its ancestor's event handler so your program can handle internal events. The rest of the structure is easier to copy as a template than to understand. The following listing shows the event handler you'll be building for this program.

```
PROCEDURE TGame.HandleEvent(Var Event: TEvent);
BEGIN
  TApplication.HandleEvent(Event);
  IF Event.What = evCommand THEN
  BEGIN
    CASE Event.Command Of
      cmFileOpen  : OpenFile ( MyList);
      cmFileSave  : SaveFile ( MyList);
      cmAnag    : AnagramGame ( MyPuzz);
      cmHang : PlayHang;
      cmTriv : PlayTriv;
      cmBuild :
      BEGIN
        GetInfo ( SrcName, 'Source file name? ');
        BuildList ( MyList, SrcName);
      END;
```

```
          cmNext :
          BEGIN
            PPtr := MyList.NextPuzz;
            AnagramGame ( PPtr^);
          END;
          cmAny :
          BEGIN
            PPtr := MyList.AnyPuzz;
            AnagramGame ( PPtr^);
          END;
          cmRules   : ShowRules;
          ELSE  Exit;
       END;
       ClearEvent(Event);
    END;
END;
```

All event handlers should have the same **CASE** statement nested inside the **IF** statement. The options for the case statement are the application's commands.

Notice that when a command is received, the event handler simply calls a procedure to process the command. For prototyping purposes, you might consider making null stubs for each command processor. Here are the stubs for the game program commands, as taken from the event handler. These routines will have to be defined for the program. You'll learn about these procedures and about the data types involved later in the chapter.

```
(* get a puzzle collection from a file *)
PROCEDURE OpenFile ( Var NewList : TPuzzList);
BEGIN
END;

(* save a puzzle collection in a file *)
PROCEDURE SaveFile ( Var TheList : TPuzzList);
BEGIN
END;

(* play a round of anagrams with the player. *)
PROCEDURE AnagramGame ( VAR Puzz : TPuzzle);
BEGIN
END;

(* play a round of hangman with the player. *)
PROCEDURE PlayHang;
BEGIN
END;

(* play a round of trivia with the player *)
```

```
PROCEDURE PlayTriv;
BEGIN
END;

(* get a string value *)
PROCEDURE GetInfo ( VAR TheInfo : STRING; Message : STRING);
BEGIN
END;

(* build a collection of puzzles by reading information
   from a file.
*)
PROCEDURE BuildList ( VAR TheList : TPuzzList; TheName : STRING);
BEGIN
END;

(* get the next puzzle in a collection *)
FUNCTION MyList.NextPuzz : PPuzzle;
BEGIN
END;

(* get a random puzzle from a collection *)
FUNCTION MyList.AnyPuzz : PPuzzle;
BEGIN
END;

(* display information about how to play the game. *)
PROCEDURE ShowRules;
BEGIN
END;
```

Although nonfunctional now, you can implement and test these procedures one at a time. Note that two of the routines are actually methods.

Given the three application-based methods just defined, you can create the final definition of the **TGame** object:

```
TYPE TGame = OBJECT ( TApplication)
        PROCEDURE InitMenuBar; VIRTUAL;
        PROCEDURE InitStatusLine; VIRTUAL;
        PROCEDURE HandleEvent ( VAR Event : TEvent); VIRTUAL;
     END;
```

Almost every application you write will override these three methods. You may also choose to override **TApplication.Init** to include program initialization code, although it's usually better to keep them separate.

As you develop this application, you'll put certain parts of the program into include files and other parts into separate units. The three **TGame** methods — **TGameInitMenuBar**, **TGame.InitStatusLine**, and **TGame.HandleEvents** — will be stored in the include file TVGAMES .PAS. The other routines — currently defined just as stubs — will be collected in the include file TVGPROCS.PAS. This file's contents will be fleshed out later.

Creating a Simple Dialog Box

In their present form, the procedure stubs do little to support program development. A much more effective way to show that a particular section of code has yet to be developed is to tell that to the user. This can be done in Turbo Vision by using a dialog box.

Being familiar with the Turbo Pascal environment from the user's point of view, you already know how dialog boxes operate and what types of I/O can be represented. Creating your own dialog box is a matter of initializing an empty box and then inserting the pieces you want.

To ease you into the methods of dialog box design, consider the creation of a very simple box. This box will have one button on it. When the box is displayed on the screen, a user must press that button in order to continue.

Study the code for the procedure that creates this simple dialog box:

```
PROCEDURE SimpleBox(Name : String);
VAR Dialog : PDialog;
    R : TRect;
    Control : Word;
BEGIN
  (* define the boundaries of the dialog box *)
  R.Assign(20, 9, 55, 15);
  (* Allocate storage for the box *)
  Dialog := NEW ( PDialog, Init(R, Name));
  WITH Dialog^ DO
  BEGIN
    (* create a smaller view within the dialog box *)
    R.Assign(4, 2, 29, 4);
    Insert(NEW(PButton, Init(R, '(not implemented yet)',
        cmOK, bfDefault)));
```

```
  END;
  (* execute the dialog box, to display the information *)
  Control := DeskTop^.ExecView(Dialog);
END;
```

The first step in creating a dialog box is to specify the area of the screen where the box will appear. For this you use **R.Assign**, just as you did for menus and status lines. Then you allocate memory to a dialog pointer, using **NEW**. This creates a blank dialog box with the title taken from a parameter.

The next step is to insert one or more standard objects. In this case a button was chosen. After you assign a rectangular area for the button, **Insert** is called with an initialization of the button. This initialization includes the text that will appear and the event that will be generated when the button is pressed.

When you've completely defined the dialog box, you make a call to **ExecView**. This function displays the dialog box and accepts no commands other than the ones defined by the box itself. This exclusiveness makes this dialog box a modal view. (The *modal* view is the one in which the next user response will be handled.) Later in this chapter, you will see how to make nonmodal dialog boxes.

Procedure **SimpleBox** lets you display a dialog box with a message when the user tries to invoke a command that has not yet been implemented. Figure 13-4 illustrates a sample call to this procedure, within procedure **PlayTriv**. You'll learn more about dialog boxes later in this chapter.

Writing Support Code

Until now you've watched the development of an application prototype that can support any Turbo Vision program. Once you are satisfied with the design and the interface, you must start on the implementation of the "meat" of the program. In this section, you will see the lowest level of the word game application, an object that represents a single puzzle. The next sections build on this object until the application is complete.

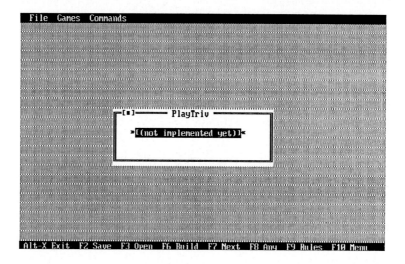

Figure 13-4. *Dialog box displayed when procedure **SimpleBox** is called*

In the spirit of OOP, the rest of the design revolves around two objects: **TPuzzle**, which models a single puzzle, and **TPuzzList**, which represents a group of puzzles.

Implementing a Puzzle

Each of these two objects is implemented in a separate unit. The following listing shows the source code for the **tpz** unit (TPZ.PAS on the examples disk), which implements the **TPuzzle** type.

```
(* TPuzzle Unit *)

UNIT TPZ;

INTERFACE

USES Objects, TVMISC;
```

```
TYPE PPuzzle = ^TPuzzle;
     TPuzzle = OBJECT ( TObject)
         CONSTRUCTOR Init;
         (* Stream methods *)
         CONSTRUCTOR Load ( VAR S : TStream);
         PROCEDURE Store ( VAR S : TStream);

         FUNCTION GetAnswer : STRING;
         PROCEDURE SetAnswer (TheAnswer : STRING);
         FUNCTION GetClue : STRING;
         PROCEDURE SetClue (TheClue : STRING);
         FUNCTION GetIndex : INTEGER;
         PROCEDURE SetIndex ( IndexVal : INTEGER);

         PROCEDURE BuildClue; VIRTUAL;
     PRIVATE
         Answer, Clue : STRING;
         Index : INTEGER;
     END;

IMPLEMENTATION

CONSTRUCTOR TPuzzle.Init;
BEGIN
  Answer := '';
  Clue := '';
  Index := -1;
END;

FUNCTION TPuzzle.GetAnswer : STRING;
BEGIN
  GetAnswer := Answer;
END;

FUNCTION TPuzzle.GetClue : STRING;
BEGIN
  GetClue := Clue;
END;

PROCEDURE TPuzzle.SetAnswer ( TheAnswer : STRING);
BEGIN
  Answer := TheAnswer;
END;

PROCEDURE TPuzzle.SetClue ( TheClue : STRING);
BEGIN
  Clue := TheClue;
END;

FUNCTION TPuzzle.GetIndex : INTEGER;
BEGIN
  GetIndex := Index;
```

```
END;

PROCEDURE TPuzzle.SetIndex ( IndexVal : INTEGER);
BEGIN
  Index := IndexVal;
END;

(* Generate a value for the puzzle clue;
   current version assumes anagrams,
   jumbles by sorting the letters.
*)
PROCEDURE TPuzzle.BuildClue;
VAR Where : INTEGER;
BEGIN
  Clue := Answer;
  (* delete any blanks from the word *)
  Where := POS ( ' ', Clue);
  WHILE Where > 0 DO
  BEGIN
    DELETE ( Clue, Where, 1);
    Where := POS ( ' ', Clue);
  END;

  (* sort the letters to "jumble" them up *)
  StrBubbleSort ( Clue);
END;

(* Read a puzzle from a stream *)
CONSTRUCTOR TPuzzle.Load ( VAR S : TStream);
BEGIN
  S.Read ( Index, SIZEOF ( Index));
  S.Read ( Answer, SIZEOF ( Answer));
  S.Read ( Clue, SIZEOF ( Clue));
END;

(* Write a puzzle to a stream *)
PROCEDURE TPuzzle.Store ( VAR S : TStream);
BEGIN
  S.Write ( Index, SIZEOF ( Index));
  S.Write ( Answer, SIZEOF ( Answer));
  S.Write ( Clue, SIZEOF ( Clue));
END;

BEGIN
END.
```

The implementation of **TPuzzle** is straightforward. A **TPuzzle** has three fields and several methods defined for it. The **Answer** and **Clue** fields represent the word puzzle itself. **Index** provides a way of identifying puzzles in a collection.

Note that these three fields are defined as **PRIVATE**. Earlier, you learned that it's considered good programming practice to access object fields through methods, rather than directly. **PRIVATE** is a predefined identifier that enables you to enforce this restriction. By declaring a field as **PRIVATE** you make it invisible to anything outside the object. Thus, you can only access these fields through methods.

The **PRIVATE** identifier is new to version 6, and applies only to objects. You cannot make record fields private.

The **Load** and **Store** methods are used for dealing with streams associated with a puzzle collection. The **BuildClue** method is used to create a clue from the answer. Note that **tpz** uses the unit **tvmisc**. This unit is defined later in the chapter, and includes the definition of **StrBubbleSort** (used by **BuildClue**).

Implementing a Puzzle Collection

How many times have you written code to support arrays or linked lists? Every time you create a new record structure, you find yourself writing more code to support collections of that structure. With Turbo Vision, you may never have to write array support software again.

Turbo Vision includes an object type called a **TCollection**, as well as a few descendant object types. These collection objects are independent of the user interface software, so they can be used easily in any application. Even more advantageous is that collections are polymorphic—used properly, they can store different objects in the same set. If you want the collection to stay sorted at all times, use **TSortedCollection**.

A Turbo Vision collection is a list of pointers. Therefore, to use a collection object, you do not need to create a descendant object type. For proper encapsulation, however, you will often create descendants anyway, to refine the functionality of the object type.

To make this clearer, look at the definition of the **TPuzzList** object in the **tpzlist** unit (TPZLIST.PAS on your examples disk). This object definition provides complete functionality for a collection of word puzzles.

The **Load** and **Store** methods are used for working with streams. **NewPuzz**, **ReplacePuzz**, and **RemovePuzz** are used to create the puzzle collection. **NextPuzz** and **AnyPuzz** are used to select puzzles form the collection.

```
(* TPuzzList unit *)

UNIT TPZList;

INTERFACE

USES Objects, TPZ;

TYPE PPuzzList = ^TPuzzList;
     TPuzzList = OBJECT (TCollection)
       CONSTRUCTOR Init;
       CONSTRUCTOR Load ( VAR S : TStream);
       PROCEDURE Store ( VAR S : TStream);
       FUNCTION NewPuzz : PPuzzle;
       FUNCTION NextPuzz : PPuzzle;
       FUNCTION AnyPuzz : PPuzzle;
       PROCEDURE ReplacePuzz ( PP : PPuzzle);
       PROCEDURE RemovePuzz ( PP : PPuzzle);
     PRIVATE
       PuzzNr : INTEGER;
     END;

IMPLEMENTATION

CONSTRUCTOR TPuzzList.Load ( VAR S : TStream);
BEGIN
  TCollection.Load ( S);
  PuzzNr := -1;
  Randomize;
END;


PROCEDURE TPuzzList.Store ( VAR S : TStream);
BEGIN
  TCollection.Store ( S);
END;


CONSTRUCTOR TPuzzList.Init;
BEGIN
  TCollection.Init ( 10, 5);
  PuzzNr := -1;
  Randomize;
END;

(* Add storage for a puzzle to the collection *)
FUNCTION TPuzzList.NewPuzz : PPuzzle;
VAR PP : PPuzzle;
BEGIN
  NEW ( PP, Init);
  TCollection.Insert ( PP);
  PP^.SetIndex ( Count);
  NewPuzz := PP;
END;
```

```
(* get the next puzzle in the collection *)
FUNCTION TPuzzList.NextPuzz : PPuzzle;
VAR PP : PPuzzle;
BEGIN
  PuzzNr := PuzzNr + 1;
  IF PuzzNr = Count THEN
    PuzzNr := 0;
  PP := TCollection.At ( PuzzNr);
  PP^.SetIndex ( PuzzNr + 1);
  NextPuzz := PP;
END;

(* get a random puzzle from the collection *)
FUNCTION TPuzzList.AnyPuzz : PPuzzle;
VAR PP : PPuzzle;
BEGIN
  PuzzNr := RANDOM(Count);
  PP := TCollection.At ( PuzzNr);
  PP^.SetIndex ( PuzzNr + 1);
  AnyPuzz := PP;
END;

(* substitute a puzzle for one already in the collection *)
PROCEDURE TPuzzList.ReplacePuzz ( PP : PPuzzle);
BEGIN
  TCollection.AtPut ( PP^.GetIndex - 1, PP);
END;

(* remove a specified puzzle from the collection *)
PROCEDURE TPuzzList.RemovePuzz ( PP : PPuzzle);
BEGIN
  TCollection.AtDelete ( PP^.GetIndex - 1);
END;


BEGIN
END.
```

The initialization for a **TPuzzList** object is done primarily through a call to **TCollection.Init**. This method takes two arguments: the initial size of the collection and the amount the collection will grow when the initial size is exceeded. The growth process takes a relatively long time when the collections get large, so choose these numbers carefully. The call to **Randomize** is to support the ability to select puzzles from the collection at random.

Normally, when you want to add an object to a collection, you enter the data and then insert the pointer into the collection. From an object-oriented sense, however, the method for adding puzzles works more as follows:

- Get a new puzzle template

- Fill in the information

- Replace the template in the collection

This is done with the **NewPuzz** method.

Collections number their entries from 0 to *N-1*, just like most computer science applications. However, most of us are used to numbering things starting from 1. You can see such number-shifting in the **ReplacePuzz** and **RemovePuzz** methods.

Notice that both **NextPuzz** and **AnyPuzz** set the number of a puzzle, even though the number is stored in the collection. The reason is that, when the collection deletes an object, it doesn't know anything about numbering of the objects, so it can't make any updates. Therefore, the puzzle numbers stored in the collection are not necessarily correct.

Filling in Program Details

Until now, you've seen the skeleton user interface and the internal mechanisms for the word game application. You've also seen the implementations for the program's main objects. In this section, you'll see how to put everything together to create a working program. Most of the commands involve the use of dialog boxes, so you'll be able to see more examples of dialog box entries.

To see the general features of a dialog box routine, let's look at the **GetInfo** procedure.

```
(* Get a string value *)
PROCEDURE GetInfo ( VAR TheInfo : STRING; Message : STRING);
TYPE SRec = RECORD
        StrVal : STRING;
      END;
VAR Dialog :PDialog;
    R : TRect;
    Control : WORD;
    G : PView;
    Info : SRec;

BEGIN
  Info.StrVal := '';
```

```
   R.Assign ( 1, 3, 40, 13);
   Dialog := NEW ( PDialog, Init ( R, ''));

   WITH Dialog^ DO
   BEGIN
     (* insert the Ok command as a button *)
     R.Assign(3, 7, 9, 9);
     Insert(NEW(PButton, Init(R, '~O~K', cmOK, bfDefault)));

     (* insert the Cancel command as a button *)
     R.Assign(13, 7, 24, 9);
     Insert(NEW(PButton, Init(R, 'Cancel', cmCancel, bfNormal)));

     (* display prompt message *)
     R.Assign ( 2, 2, 36, 3);
     G := NEW ( PStaticText, Init ( R, Message));
     Insert ( G);

     (* prepare for player's response *)
     R.Assign ( 4, 5, 20, 6);
     G := NEW( PInputLine, INIT( R, 60));
     INSERT (G);
   END;   (* WITH Dialog^ *)

   Dialog^.SetData ( Info);
   Control := DeskTop^.ExecView ( Dialog);

   IF Control <> cmCancel THEN
   BEGIN
     Dialog^.GetData( Info);
     TheInfo := Info.StrVal;
   END
   ELSE
     TheInfo := ' ';
   Dispose ( Dialog, Done);
END;   (* GetInfo *)
```

This procedure starts by initializing a record field. Once you define a dialog box that requires data entry, you must assign initial values to entry areas. The **SRec** record will be used to store values for and from the dialog box. After you assign values to the field in this record, a call to the **SetData** method stores the data in the internal structures of the dialog box.

GetInfo creates the dialog box (with the first call to **NEW**), and then adds several elements to the box. The first two objects actually go near the bottom of the dialog box. These are the command buttons for OK and Cancel. The procedure also displays some static text—namely, the prompt message.

The last object added is the default item. This object consists of a **TInputLine**, used to enter data. The other object in the box is a message to the player.

The **ExecView** method is called after the data values are set. This method does all of the I/O for the dialog box. It terminates only when the user presses one of the two buttons. The value of the button pressed is returned as the value of the function.

If the user presses the OK button, the **GetData** method is called to retrieve the value entered for the **TInputLine**. That value is then passed back to the program through the **TheInfo** parameter.

Other Program Routines

The following listing shows the contents of an include file, TVG-PROCS.PAS. This file contains various routines that are called in the word game program. In particular, this listing contains fleshed out versions of several of the routines called by the event handler.

```
(* display a simple "not implemented" message *)
PROCEDURE SimpleBox ( Name : String);
VAR Dialog : PDialog;
    R : TRect;
    Control : Word;
BEGIN
  (* define the boundaries of the dialog box *)
  R.Assign(20, 9, 55, 15);
  (* Allocate storage for the box *)
  Dialog := NEW(PDialog, Init(R, Name));
  WITH Dialog^ DO
  BEGIN
    (* create a smaller view within the dialog box *)
    R.Assign(4, 2, 29, 4);
    Insert(NEW(PButton, Init(R, '(not implemented yet)',
        cmOK, bfDefault)));
  END;
  (* execute the dialog box, to display the information *)
  Control := DeskTop^.ExecView(Dialog);
END;  (* SimpleBox *)


(* Begin timing player's response to a puzzle *)
PROCEDURE StartTime;
BEGIN
  Start := GetTime;
```

```
  END;  (* StartTime *)


(* Stop timing player's response to a puzzle;
   add elapszed time to player's time to that point.
*)
PROCEDURE EndTime;
BEGIN
  Finish := GetTime;
  PzTime := HowLong ( Start, Finish);
  CumTime := CumTime + PzTime;
END; (* EndTime *)


(* Report player's cumulative time for the specified
   # of puzzles.
*)
PROCEDURE ReportTime;
VAR Dialog :PDialog;
    R : TRect;
    Control : WORD;
    G : PView;
    PzNrStr, TimeStr, PzTimeStr : STRING;
BEGIN
  STR ( PzCount, PzNrStr);
  STR ( CumTime:5:2, TimeStr);
  STR ( PzTime:5:2, PzTimeStr);

  R.Assign ( 41, 3, 75, 13);
  Dialog := NEW ( PDialog, Init ( R, ''));

  WITH Dialog^ DO
  BEGIN
    (* insert the Ok command as a button *)
    R.Assign(3, 7, 9, 9);
    Insert(NEW(PButton, Init(R, '~O~K', cmOK, bfDefault)));

    R.Assign ( 1, 1, 32, 2);
    G := NEW ( PStaticText, Init ( R, 'Puzzles: ' + PzNrStr));
    Insert ( G);

    R.Assign ( 2, 3, 33, 4);
    G := NEW ( PStaticText, Init ( R, 'This puzzle: ' +
                                      PzTimeStr + ' seconds.'));
    Insert ( G);

    R.Assign ( 2, 5, 33, 6);
    G := NEW ( PStaticText, Init ( R, 'Total time:  ' +
                                      TimeStr + ' seconds.'));
    Insert ( G);
  END;  (* WITH Dialog^ *)

  Control := DeskTop^.ExecView ( Dialog);
  Dispose ( Dialog, Done);
```

```
END;  (* ReportTime *)


(* Report outcome from an event *)
PROCEDURE ReportOutcome ( DlgName, Message : STRING);
VAR Dialog :PDialog;
    R : TRect;
    Control : WORD;
    G : PView;
BEGIN
  R.Assign ( 41, 3, 70, 13);
  Dialog := NEW ( PDialog, Init ( R,  DlgName));

  WITH Dialog^ DO
  BEGIN
    (* insert the Ok command as a button *)
    R.Assign(3, 7, 9, 9);
    Insert(NEW(PButton, Init(R, '~O~K', cmOK, bfDefault)));

    R.Assign ( 2, 2, 36, 3);
    G := NEW ( PStaticText, Init ( R, Message));
    Insert ( G);
  END;  (* WITH Dialog^ *)

  Control := DeskTop^.ExecView ( Dialog);
  Dispose ( Dialog, Done);
  (* ************* *)
  (* NOTE::::
     To make the dialog box displayed here non-modal, substitute
     the following statement for the preceding TWO statements--
     i.e., for Control ... and Dispose ...
   *)
  (* DeskTop^.Insert ( Dialog); *)
END;  (* ReportOutcome *)


(* Play one round of anagrams with the player. *)
PROCEDURE AnagramGame ( VAR Puzz : TPuzzle);
TYPE DataRec = RECORD
       drGuess : STRING;
     END;
VAR Dialog :PDialog;
    R : TRect;
    Control : WORD;
    G : PView;
    Correct : BOOLEAN;
    Info : DataRec;
BEGIN
  Correct := FALSE;
  StartTime;                (* Start timing *)

  R.Assign ( 10, 5, 70, 20);
  Dialog := NEW ( PDialog, Init ( R, 'Anagrams'));
```

```
WITH Dialog^ DO
BEGIN
   (* insert the Ok command as a button *)
   R.Assign(5, 12, 15, 14);
   Insert(NEW(PButton, Init(R, '~O~K', cmOK, bfDefault)));

   (* insert the Cancel command as a button *)
   R.Assign(18, 12, 28, 14);
   Insert(NEW(PButton, Init(R, 'Cancel', cmCancel, bfNormal)));

   (* insert the clue *)
   R.Assign ( 15, 4, 45, 5);
   G := NEW ( PStaticText, Init ( R, Puzz.GetClue));
   Insert ( G);

   (* set up the input line with a prompt *)
   R.Assign ( 15, 9, 45, 10);
   G := NEW( PInputLine, INIT( R, 60));
   INSERT (G);
   R.Assign ( 1, 9, 14, 10);
   G := NEW( PStaticText, INIT( R, 'Your guess? '));
   INSERT ( G);
END;  (* WITH Dialog^ *)

REPEAT
   Info.drGuess := '';    (* Clear guess value *)
   (* write the current date to the dialog box *)
   Dialog^.SetData ( Info);
   (* make the dialog box the modal one *)
   Control := DeskTop^.ExecView ( Dialog);

   (* If user says OK, get the input value, and check it *)
   IF Control <> cmCancel THEN
   BEGIN
      (* save the information entered *)
      Dialog^.GetData( Info);
      (* check player's guess *)
      Correct := Info.drGuess = Puzz.GetAnswer;
      IF Correct THEN   (* BEEP if correct *)
         WRITE ( CHR(7));
   END;
   UNTIL ( Control = cmCancel) OR Correct;
   IF Correct  THEN  (* Count and report only correct answers *)
   BEGIN
      PzCount := PzCount + 1;    (* another puzzle solved *)
      EndTime;                   (* stop timing *)
      ReportTime;                (* Report information *)
   END;
   Dispose ( Dialog, Done);
END; (* AnagramGame *)


(* play a round of hangman with the player *)
```

```
PROCEDURE PlayHang;
BEGIN
  SimpleBox ( 'PlayHang');
END;  (* PlayHang *)


(* play a round of trivia with the player *)
PROCEDURE PlayTriv;
BEGIN
  SimpleBox ( 'PlayTriv');
END; (* PlayTriv *)

(* Get a string value *)
PROCEDURE GetInfo ( VAR TheInfo : STRING; Message : STRING);
TYPE SRec = RECORD
       StrVal : STRING;
     END;
VAR Dialog :PDialog;
    R : TRect;
    Control : WORD;
    G : PView;
    Info : SRec;
BEGIN
  Info.StrVal := '';

  R.Assign ( 1, 3, 40, 13);
  Dialog := NEW ( PDialog, Init ( R, ''));

  WITH Dialog^ DO
  BEGIN
    (* insert the Ok command as a button *)
    R.Assign(3, 7, 9, 9);
    Insert(NEW(PButton, Init(R, '~O~K', cmOK, bfDefault)));

    (* insert the Cancel command as a button *)
    R.Assign(13, 7, 24, 9);
    Insert(NEW(PButton, Init(R, 'Cancel', cmCancel, bfNormal)));

    (* display prompt message *)
    R.Assign ( 2, 2, 36, 3);
    G := NEW ( PStaticText, Init ( R, Message));
    Insert ( G);

    (* prepare for player's response *)
    R.Assign ( 4, 5, 20, 6);
    G := NEW( PInputLine, INIT( R, 60));
    INSERT (G);
  END;  (* WITH Dialog^ *)

  Dialog^.SetData ( Info);
  Control := DeskTop^.ExecView ( Dialog);

  IF Control <> cmCancel THEN
```

```
    BEGIN
      Dialog^.GetData( Info);
      TheInfo := Info.StrVal;
    END
    ELSE
      TheInfo := ' ';
    Dispose ( Dialog, Done);
END;  (* GetInfo *)


(* Build a collection of puzzles by reading information
   from a file.
*)
PROCEDURE BuildList ( VAR TheList : TPuzzList; TheName : STRING);
VAR Src :Text;        (* file to read *)
    WdVal : STRING;
    PP : PPuzzle;
    CountStr : STRING;
BEGIN
  IF FOpened ( Src, TheName) THEN
  BEGIN
    WHILE NOT EOF ( Src) DO
    BEGIN
      READLN ( Src, WdVal);   (* read puzzle *)
      NEW ( PP, Init);  (* allocate storage for a puzzle *)
      PP := TheList.NewPuzz; (* add puzzle to collection *)
      (* fill in puzzle's fields *)
      PP^.SetAnswer ( WdVal);
      PP^.BuildClue;
      TheList.ReplacePuzz ( PP);
    END;
    STR ( TheList.Count, CountStr);
    ReportOutcome ('PuzzleBuilder', CountStr + ' puzzles built');
  END (* If File was opened *)
  ELSE
    ReportOutcome ( 'PuzzleBuilder', 'ERROR building puzzles');
END;  (* BuildList *)


(* Display information about how to play the game. *)
PROCEDURE ShowRules;
VAR Dialog :PDialog;
    R : TRect;
    Control : WORD;
    G : PView;
BEGIN
  R.Assign ( 1, 3, 70, 23);
  Dialog := NEW ( PDialog, Init ( R, 'Game Rules'));

  WITH Dialog^ DO
  BEGIN
    (* insert the Ok command as a button *)
    R.Assign(3, 17, 9, 19);
    Insert(NEW(PButton, Init(R, '~O~K', cmOK, bfDefault)));
```

```
      (* insert a message, then the clue *)
      R.Assign ( 2, 2, 66, 3);
      G := NEW ( PStaticText, Init ( R, 'Guess the word that ' +
                                         'appears in jumbled ' +
                                         'form at the top of the'));

      Insert ( G);

      R.Assign ( 2, 3, 66, 4);
      G := NEW ( PStaticText, Init ( R, 'screen in the ' +
                                         'dialog box.'));

      Insert ( G);

      R.Assign ( 2, 6, 66, 7);
      G := NEW ( PStaticText, Init ( R, 'Solve as quickly ' +
                                         'as possible.'));

      Insert ( G);

      R.Assign ( 2, 8, 36, 9);
      G := NEW ( PStaticText, Init ( R, 'A BEEP means you ' +
                                         'guessed corectly.'));

      Insert ( G);
   END;  (* WITH Dialog^ *)

   Control := DeskTop^.ExecView ( Dialog);
   Dispose ( Dialog, Done);
END;  (* ShowRules *)
```

SimpleBox   You have already looked at this procedure in an earlier section.

StartTime, EndTime, ReportTime   These procedures are called by **AnagramGame** to time a round of play. The procedures use global variables. Note the use of the **STR** procedure in **ReportTime** to convert integer and real number values to strings before displaying the values in a dialog box.

ReportOutcome   The **ReportOutcome** procedure enables certain events to provide feedback—for example, about success or failure. In particular, the procedure is called by **BuildList**. If successful, that routine reports how many puzzles were built; otherwise, the routine reports failure.

    This dialog box is purely information, so there is nothing the user can do but acknowledge. As a result, this box has only an OK button.

So far, all the routines for dialog boxes have used the function, **Desktop^.ExecView**. This makes the dialog box being defined the modal one, so that the next response will be handled within this dialog box.

To see how to display a nonmodal dialog box and to see how such a box behaves, makes the substitution suggested at the end of **Report-Outcome**. Then compile and run the program.

AnagramGame   This procedure plays a round of anagrams with the player. That is, the procedure displays the specified puzzle clue and reads a response from the player. If the player's guess matches the answer, the round ends, and the program reports how long it took.

PlayHang, PlayTriv   These procedures would be used to play a round of hangman or trivia, respectively. You may want to implement one or both of these games. If you do implement these games, you'll probably want to define objects derived from a **TPuzzle**, so you can define the appropriate **BuildClue** methods.

BuildList   This procedure reads puzzle words from a file and adds the puzzles created with these words to a puzzle collection. Three such files are included on your disk: STATES, GEO, and MUSIC. After opening the source file, the procedure does the following for each line read from the file.

1. Allocates storage for a puzzle variable (**NEW**)

2. Adds the newly acquired storage to the puzzle collection (**TheList .NewPuzz**)

3. Fills in the details for the puzzle (**PP^.SetAnswer** and **PP^.BuildClue**)

4. Replaces the placeholder in the puzzle collection with the completed puzzle (**TheList.ReplacePuzz**)

This routine reads from an ordinary text file, *not* a binary stream, as discussed in a later section. You must call this procedure before you play an anagram game.

GetInfo   You've already looked at this procedure.

ShowRules   This procedure displays some instructions on how to play the anagram game. The use of the dialog box does not present any new features.

A Unit of Miscellaneous Routines

The game program uses several general purpose routines that have been defined in earlier chapters. In particular, four such routines have been gathered in a separate unit, **tvmisc** (TVMISC.PAS on your examples disk). The code for this unit is shown in the following listing.

```
(* General utilities unit for Turbo Vision Game program *)

UNIT TVMISC;

INTERFACE

USES DOS;

PROCEDURE StrBubbleSort ( VAR Info : String);
FUNCTION FOpened ( VAR TheFile : Text;
                      FName : STRING) : BOOLEAN;
FUNCTION GetTime : REAL;
FUNCTION HowLong ( Start, Finish : REAL) : REAL;


IMPLEMENTATION

(* Sort characters in a string by letting the "largest"
   remaining character work its way to the top of the
   array on each pass through the array.
*)
PROCEDURE StrBubbleSort ( VAR Info : String);
VAR Temp : CHAR;
    Low, High, Top, Size : INTEGER;
BEGIN
  Size := LENGTH ( Info);
  Top := Size + 1;
  WHILE ( Top > 1) DO
  BEGIN
    Low := 1;
    High := 2;
    WHILE High < Top DO
    BEGIN
      (* if lower string needs to move upward in the array *)
```

```
      IF Info [ Low] > Info [ High] THEN
      BEGIN
        Temp := Info [ Low];
        Info [ Low] := Info [ High];
        Info [ High] := Temp;
      END; (* If lower string needs to move upward *)
      Low := Low + 1;
      High := High + 1;
    END; (* WHILE High < Top *)
    Top := Top - 1;
  END; (* WHILE Top > 1 *)
END;  (* StrBubbleSort *)


(* Open an existing file, doing all necessary
   and warranted checking, and taking all
   precautions.
   Returns TRUE if file was opened; FALSE otherwise.
*)
FUNCTION FOpened ( VAR TheFile : Text;
                      FName : STRING) : BOOLEAN;
BEGIN
  ASSIGN ( TheFile, FName);
(*$I-*)
  RESET ( TheFile);
(*$I+*)
  IF IOResult = 0 THEN
    FOpened := TRUE
  ELSE
    FOpened := FALSE;
END; (* FN FOpened *)


(* Function to get the number of seconds elapsed since
   midnight on the system clock.
*)
FUNCTION GetTime : REAL;
VAR  Hrs, Mins, Secs, Hundredths : WORD;
     MyRegs : Registers;

BEGIN
  (* Request DOS service $2C *)
  MyRegs.Ah := $2C;

  (* Call interrupt $21 with the appropriate unions *)
  MSDOS ( MyRegs);

  Hrs := MyRegs.CH;       (* hours elapsed returned in CH *)
  Mins := MyRegs.CL;      (* minutes elapsed returned in CL *)
  Secs := MyRegs.DH;      (* seconds elapsed returned in DH *)
```

```
   Hundredths := MyRegs.DL; (* 1/100's secs returned in DL *)

   (* Total elapsed time (in seconds) =
      3600 (secs / hr)  * hrs +
      60 ( secs / min) * mins +
      1 ( secs / sec) * secs +
      .01 ( secs per 1/100th sec) * hundredths.
   *)
   GetTime :=   Hrs * 3600.0 + Mins * 60.0 +
                Secs + Hundredths / 100.0;
END; (* FN GetTime *)

(* Function to compute the number of seconds elapsed between
   start and finish
*)
FUNCTION  HowLong ( Start, Finish : REAL) : REAL;
CONST FullDay = 86400.0;  (* seconds in a 24 hr day *)

BEGIN
  (* start = first elapsed time measurement;
     finish = second elapsed time measurement.
     If start > finish then the time must have passed midnight
     between start and finish of process.
     In that case, a formula adjustment is necessary.
  *)
  IF Start > Finish THEN
    HowLong := FullDay - Start + Finish
  ELSE
    HowLong := Finish - Start;
END; (* HowLong *)

BEGIN
END.
```

The **StrBubbleSort** procedure sorts the individual characters in a string. This is used in the **BuildClue** method. The other three routines in **tvmisc** are all functions:

■ **FOpened** returns **TRUE** if the specified file was opened successfully.

■ **GetTime** returns the time elapsed since midnight.

■ **HowLong** returns the amount of time elapsed between two calls to **GetTime**.

Take heart, you've almost got the whole program done! The next section discusses the remaining component—streams.

Using Streams

The major commands remaining are those that save puzzles to a file and reload them. Turbo Vision provides an extremely powerful object, called a stream, to support this. A *stream* is a path that an object can follow to or from another location. The primary support for streams is for DOS files and EMS memory. Streams are as polymorphic as collections, allowing you to use the same stream for different object types.

The word game application uses a buffered DOS file stream. This object type is called **TBufStream**. In order to use this stream in objects you create, you must register the objects into Turbo Vision. The first step in registration is to define a registration record.

Here are the records for registering a puzzle (a **TPuzzle** type) and a puzzle collection (a **TPuzzList** type):

```
(* A registration record for a puzzle stream *)
CONST RPuzzle : TStreamRec =
      (
        ObjType : 1111;    (* arbitrary but unique ID value *)
        VmtLink : Ofs ( TYPEOF ( TPuzzle)^);
        Load : @TPuzzle.Load;
        Store : @TPuzzle.Store
      );

      RPuzzList : TStreamRec =
      (
        ObjType : 2222;
        VmtLink : Ofs ( TYPEOF ( TPuzzList)^);
        Load : @TPuzzList.Load;
        Store : @TPuzzList.Store
      );
```

Note the record names: **RPuzzle** and **RPuzzList**. By convention, registration records for objects are given the same name as the corresponding objects, except that the leading *T* is replaced by *R*.

A registration record has the following information components:

■ The first field of the registration record is a unique object ID. The valid values go from 1000 to 65535.

■ The second field points to the VMT (virtual method table) for the object.

■ The third and fourth fields are the addresses of the methods that handle streams for this object type. The methods whose addresses are to be provided here are defined along with the other methods for the base object types. In this example, these types are **TPuzzle** and **TPuzzList**, respectively.

There is actually another information component, which is used internally to manage a linked list of registration records. You don't need to concern yourself about this field.

The **Load** and **Store** methods for a **TPuzzle** object work by calling the methods **TStream.Read** and **TStream.Write** (as appropriate) for each data field in the object type. If the object is a descendant of another object, these overridden methods must call the respective procedures of their ancestors. The following listing shows the **TPuzzle.Load** and **TPuzzle.Store** methods. Recall that these methods are part of the **tpz** unit.

```
(* Read a puzzle from a stream *)
CONSTRUCTOR TPuzzle.Load ( VAR S : TStream);
BEGIN
  S.Read ( Index, SIZEOF ( Index));
  S.Read ( Answer, SIZEOF ( Answer));
  S.Read ( Clue, SIZEOF ( Clue));
END;

(* Write a puzzle to a stream *)
PROCEDURE TPuzzle.Store ( VAR S : TStream);
BEGIN
  S.Write ( Index, SIZEOF ( Index));
  S.Write ( Answer, SIZEOF ( Answer));
  S.Write ( Clue, SIZEOF ( Clue));
END;
```

Registering Streams

Once you've set up each object in your application hierarchy, you must register the streams. This is often done in a single procedure at the start of the application. All object types that will be used in the stream must be registered.

Abstract object types (such as **TObject**) don't need to be registered, since such an object will never be written to a stream. Descendants of this object (such as **TPuzzle**) will be written, and so must be registered. In particular, for the word game program, you need to register the following types: **TPuzzle**, **TPuzzList**, and **TCollection**. For the word game program, this is accomplished by procedure **RegisterStreams**, whose definition is shown in the following listing. The listing shows the **tvstrm** unit (TVSTRM.PAS on your examples disk).

```
(* Streams-based unit for Turbo Vision game program *)

UNIT TVStrm;

INTERFACE

USES tpz, tpzlist, App, Objects, StdDlg, Views, DOS;

CONST
  RPuzzle : TStreamRec =
  (
    ObjType : 1111;
    VmtLink : Ofs ( TYPEOF ( TPuzzle)^);
    Load : @TPuzzle.Load;
    Store : @TPuzzle.Store
  );

  RPuzzList : TStreamRec =
  (
    ObjType : 2222;
    VmtLink : Ofs ( TYPEOF ( TPuzzList)^);
    Load : @TPuzzList.Load;
    Store : @TPuzzList.Store
  );

PROCEDURE RegisterStreams;
PROCEDURE SaveFile ( Var TheList : TPuzzList);
PROCEDURE OpenFile ( Var NewList : TPuzzList);

IMPLEMENTATION

PROCEDURE RegisterStreams;
BEGIN
  RegisterType (RCollection);
  RegisterType (RPuzzle);
  RegisterType (RPuzzList);
END;
```

```
(* save a puzzle collection to a file *)
PROCEDURE SaveFile ( Var TheList : TPuzzList);
VAR SaveBox : PFileDialog;
    PLStream : TBufStream;
    Control : Word;
    TheFileNAme : PathStr;
BEGIN
  (* use the standard Save File dialog box *)
  NEW( SaveBox, Init( '*.dat', 'Save File As',
      'Save File Name', fdOkButton, 1));
  Control := DeskTop^.ExecView ( SaveBox);
  IF Control <> cmCancel THEN
  BEGIN
    (* save the set using a buffered stream *)
    SaveBox^.GetFileName ( TheFileName);
    PLStream.Init ( TheFileName, stCreate, 512);
    PLStream.Put ( @TheList);
    PLStream.Done;
  END;
END;


(* get a puzzle collection from a file *)
PROCEDURE OpenFile ( Var NewList : TPuzzList);
VAR OpenBox : PFileDialog;
    PLStream : TBufStream;
    Control : Word;
    PPL : PPuzzList;
    TheFileNAme : PathStr;
BEGIN
  (* use the standard Open File dialog box *)
  NEW( OpenBox, Init( '*.dat', 'Open File', 'Puzzle File Name',
      fdOkButton + fdOpenButton, 1));
  Control := DeskTop^.ExecView ( OpenBox);
  IF Control <> cmCancel THEN
  BEGIN
    (* read the file as a buffered stream *)
    OpenBox^.GetFileName ( TheFileName);
    PLStream.Init ( TheFileName, stOpenRead, 512);
    PPL := PPuzzList ( PLStream.Get);
    NewList := PPL^;
    PLStream.Done;
  END;
END;

BEGIN
END.
```

In the word game program, streams are used for the Save File and Open File commands. Only files that were saved using the application can be read into the application directly.

To create a binary version of a puzzle text file, you need to do two things when using the program:

1. Build a list of puzzles (F6), using one of the text files provided or a text file of your own.

2. Save the built list to a binary file (F2). You'll see that a disk file is much longer than the text file.

Turbo Vision provides the entire dialog box (the **TFileDialog** object type) used for file handling in the IDE for use in your own program. Procedure **SaveFile** uses such a dialog box.

The **SaveFile** procedure starts by creating the dialog box through a call to **NEW**. Required parameters for this initialization are the default file name, the title of the dialog box, a label for the file name, a list of buttons to be used, and a history list ID. The dialog box is then executed, and it returns an event based on the button pressed by the user.

Assuming the user wants to save the puzzle collection to the stream, the procedure gets the name of the file, opens the file as a stream, and calls **TBufStream.Put** with the address of the puzzle list. The **Put** method calls the **Store** method for the **TPuzzList** object type, which in turn calls the **Store** method for each puzzle.

Loading data from the stream follows a very similar process. First a dialog box obtains the file name. Second, a stream is created based on the file name. Finally, the data is loaded from the stream.

Building the Game Program

Congratulations! You're finally ready to put together all the elements for the program. The following files and units are needed for this program:

■ Main program file (shown in the following listing)

■ Include file TVGAMES.PAS

■ Include file TVGPROCS.PAS

■ Four units: **tpz**, **tpzlist**, **tvmisc**, and **tvstrm**

You've seen the source code for each of these components. (The TVGAMES.PAS include file contains the **TGame** definitions and methods — specifically, the **InitMenuBar**, **InitStatusLine**, and **HandleEvents** methods.

If you haven't already done so, you need to compile the units created for this program.

The following listing shows the complete main program, with all the variables used.

```
P13-2   (* Turbo Vision-based word game program *)
        PROGRAM TVGameProg;

        USES Objects, Drivers, Views, Menus, Dialogs, App, Stddlg, Dos,
             (* remaining UNITS were built for this program. *)
             TVSTRM, TVMISC, TPZ, TPZLIST;

        CONST
        (* valid event commands *)
          cmFileOpen   = 201;      (* open a specified puzzle file *)
          cmFileSave   = 202;      (* save puzzle list to file *)
          cmAnag       = 211;      (* play anagrams *)
          cmHang       = 212;      (* play hangman *)
          cmTriv       = 213;      (* play a trivia game *)
          cmBuild      = 221;      (* build a list of puzzles *)
          cmNext       = 222;      (* display next puzzle from list *)
          cmAny        = 223;      (* display a random puzzle *)
          cmRules      = 224;      (* display game rules *)

        TYPE PGame = ^TGame;
             TGame = OBJECT ( TApplication)
                PROCEDURE InitMenuBar; VIRTUAL;
                PROCEDURE InitStatusLine; VIRTUAL;
                PROCEDURE HandleEvent ( VAR Event : TEvent); VIRTUAL;
             END;

        VAR  MyGame : TGame;
             MyPuzz : TPuzzle;
             MyList : TPuzzList;
             PPtr : PPuzzle;
             SrcName : STRING;    (* name of source file *)
             Index : INTEGER;
             PzCount : INTEGER;   (* number of puzzles solved *)
            ·Start, Finish,
             PzTime,              (* time to solve last puzzle *)
             CumTime : REAL;      (* time to solve all puzzles so far *)

        (*$I TVGProcs *)
```

```
(*$I TVGames *)          (* Methods for TGame *)

BEGIN  (* MAIN Program *)
  (* Initialize counters and timers *)
  PzCount := 0;
  PzTime := 0.0;
  CumTime := 0.0;

  (* initialize the data types *)
  MyPuzz.Init;
  MyList.Init;
  RegisterStreams;
  MyGame.Init;
  MyGame.Run;
  MyGame.Done;
END.
```

More About Turbo Vision

There are many capabilities and features of Turbo Vision that have not even been addressed through this example program. Depending on the application, your program may need to deal with very different situations.

For example, when you want to display a large amount of text or allow the user to enter a large amount of text, you should create a descendant of the **TWindow** type. Windows are special cases of Turbo Vision entities called groups — they are enclosed in a frame, numbered, and often have scroll bars for use with a mouse.

If the information in the window will not all fit on the screen at once, a view object of type **TScroller** must be inserted into the window. The physical scroll bars are type **TScrollBar**. For an example of a scrollable window, study the TVGUID08.PAS program included as an example with Turbo Pascal version 6.

A resource is a special case of a buffered DOS stream. It is used to store and retrieve user-interface objects such as menus and dialog boxes. You can place the code that creates these objects into a separate program that also writes the objects to a resource file. Your main application program would then simply read the objects from the resource file. This makes your programs more modular and also decreases the size of your main executable program.

There are also other Turbo Vision capabilities to explore. For example, you can

■ Move or resize windows and dialog boxes

■ Create context-sensitive Help and status lines

■ Explore the use of color and the use of a mouse for your Turbo Vision applications

Program Extensions

You can explore some of Turbo Vision's other capabilities if you extend the example program. The following list mentions just a few of the possibilities for extending the program.

■ Add a command to show an answer if the player requests it.

■ Modify the program to handle multiple players—along the lines of the Anagrams program in Chapter 12, "Virtual Methods in Object-Oriented Programming."

■ Implement the Hangman and Trivia commands. For this, you would probably want to define descendant object types. You would need different **BuildClue** methods and would also need to develop different ways to build puzzle collections (specifically, different **BuildList** routines).

■ Give the program a more flexible way to create a clue—for example, shuffling the letters, rather than sorting them.

In this chapter, you learned a bit about Borland's Turbo Vision programming tools. The next chapter discusses miscellaneous topics, which are too specialized for earlier chapters.

14 Miscellaneous Topics

This chapter discusses miscellaneous topics that have not been covered elsewhere. Some of these features are Turbo Pascal extensions to standard Pascal; others are specialized capabilities that may not be of general interest.

Bit Handling

As you know, in Turbo Pascal numerical values are stored as sequences of bits. For whole number types (**BYTE, INTEGER, LONGINT,** and so forth), Turbo Pascal provides operators that let you work with individual bits of such representations. These operators take one or two whole number operands and produce a result of the same type. You denote the operators themselves by using the same words you use for the logical operators.

Bitwise Negation: The NOT Operator

The *arithmetic* negation operator reverses the sign of a number. For example, 35 becomes −35; −59 becomes +59 (−−59 = +59), and so on. Turbo Pascal's *bitwise negation* operator reverses the value of each bit in a number's representation. You denote this operator by using the reserved word **NOT**.

The bitwise **NOT** is a unary operator that takes a whole number operand and returns another number. If a particular bit in the original number were 1, this bit would be 0 in the resulting number; conversely, if the original bit were 0, the corresponding bit in the new value would be 1.

Although this operator has the same notation as the logical negation operator, the two operators are quite different and their operands cannot be substituted for each other. The logical negation operator changes a **TRUE** to a **FALSE** and vice versa; the bitwise negation operator changes 0 to 1 and vice versa, throughout the representation of a number.

The following program illustrates the bitwise **NOT** operator and compares it to the arithmetic negation operator. Don't worry about the **IntBits** function for now. It simply provides a clean way of determining the bit pattern for a whole number.

P14-1
```
(* Program to illustrate use of bitwise NOT operator *)

PROGRAM BitNotDemo;
(*R$-*)
VAR Val : INTEGER;

  PROCEDURE GetInteger ( Message : STRING;
                         VAR Value : INTEGER);
  BEGIN
    WRITE ( Message, ' ');
    READLN ( Value);
  END; (* GetInteger *)

  (* Determine and return bit pattern for specified value. *)
  FUNCTION IntBits ( Value : WORD) : STRING;
  CONST Patterns : ARRAY [ 0 .. 15] OF STRING [ 4] =
          ( '0000', '0001', '0010', '0011', '0100', '0101',
            '0110', '0111', '1000', '1001', '1010', '1011',
            '1100', '1101', '1110', '1111');
```

```
                  (* Used to get individual hexadecimal digits *)
                  Mask1 = $F;           Mask2 = $F0;
                  Mask3 = $F00;         Mask4 = $F000;
        VAR Temp, Piece : STRING;
        BEGIN   (* IntBits *)
          Temp := '';

          Piece := Patterns [ Value AND Mask4 SHR 12];
          Temp := Temp + Piece + ' ';
          Piece := Patterns [ Value AND Mask3 SHR 8];
          Temp := Temp + Piece + ' ';
          Piece := Patterns [ Value AND Mask2 SHR 4];
          Temp := Temp + Piece + ' ';
          Piece := Patterns [ Value AND Mask1];
          Temp := Temp + Piece;

          IntBits := Temp;
        END; (* FN IntBits *)
BEGIN
  REPEAT
    GetInteger ( 'Value? (0 to stop)', Val);
    WRITELN ( Val : 10, IntBits ( Val) : 20);
    WRITELN ( 'NOT ', Val : 6, IntBits ( NOT Val) : 20,
              '(' : 4, NOT Val : 6, ')');
    WRITELN ( -Val : 10, IntBits ( -Val) : 20);
  UNTIL Val = 0;
  READLN;
END.
```

Run the program using the following values on successive times through the loop. The values are grouped to indicate comparisons you might find informative:

■ A small and a large positive number

■ A small and a large negative number

■ Two consecutive positive values

■ The same two consecutive negative values

■ **MaxInt** and **MaxInt** + 1

■ Any other values that you're curious about

The program displays bit patterns for the original value, its bitwise negation, and its arithmetic negation. Next to the bitwise negation is the numerical value corresponding to the bit pattern.

Notice the relationship between the bit patterns and the values of the bitwise and arithmetic negation. The arithmetic negation is simply the bitwise negation + 1. If you wonder why, you should learn about one's and two's complement representations for numbers. (Books on discrete mathematics and computer science textbooks will cover these representations.)

The bitwise **NOT** operator has the same order of precedence as the logical **NOT** and other unary operators.

Bitwise Multiplication: The Bitwise AND Operator

There are several binary bitwise operators. These combine corresponding bits of two whole number operands to produce a bit for the resulting number. For example, the bitwise **AND** operator multiplies corresponding bits from its two operands and returns the product (0 or 1) as a bit value for the number being built.

The following program shows how to use the bitwise **AND** operator. Run the program for different combinations of values. In particular, try two positive numbers, two negative numbers, and two numbers of opposite sign. What is the sign of the result in each instance?

P14-2   `(* Program to illustrate use of bitwise AND operator *)`

```
PROGRAM BitAndDemo;
(*$R-*)
VAR Val1, Val2, Result : INTEGER;

  PROCEDURE GetInteger ( Message : STRING;
                         VAR Value : INTEGER);
  BEGIN
    WRITE ( Message, ' ');
    READLN ( Value);
  END; (* GetInteger *)

  (* Determine and return bit pattern for specified value. *)
  FUNCTION IntBits ( Value : WORD) : STRING;
  CONST Patterns : ARRAY [ 0 .. 15] OF STRING [ 4] =
```

```
                  ( '0000', '0001', '0010', '0011', '0100', '0101',
                    '0110', '0111', '1000', '1001', '1010', '1011',
                    '1100', '1101', '1110', '1111');

              (* Used to get individual hexadecimal digits *)
              Mask1 = $F;            Mask2 = $F0;
              Mask3 = $F00;          Mask4 = $F000;

    VAR Temp, Piece : STRING;
    BEGIN  (* IntBits *)
      Temp := '';

      Piece := Patterns [ Value AND Mask4 SHR 12];
      Temp := Temp + Piece + ' ';
      Piece := Patterns [ Value AND Mask3 SHR 8];
      Temp := Temp + Piece + ' ';
      Piece := Patterns [ Value AND Mask2 SHR 4];
      Temp := Temp + Piece + ' ';
      Piece := Patterns [ Value AND Mask1];
      Temp := Temp + Piece;

      IntBits := Temp;
    END; (* FN IntBits *)


    (* Draw a line of a specified length on the screen.
       The line will be built of TheCh.
    *)
    PROCEDURE DrawLine ( Size : INTEGER;
                         TheCh : CHAR);
    VAR Index : INTEGER;
    BEGIN
      FOR Index := 1 TO Size DO
        WRITE ( TheCh);
      WRITELN;
    END; (* DrawLine *)

BEGIN
  REPEAT
    GetInteger ( 'Value 1? (0 to stop)', Val1);
    IF Val1 <> 0 THEN
    BEGIN
      GetInteger ( 'Value 2?', Val2);
      Result := Val1 AND Val2;
      WRITELN ( ' ':6, IntBits (Val1) :16, ' (', Val1 : 6, ')');
      WRITELN ( 'AND   ', IntBits ( Val2) : 16, ' (',
              Val2 : 6, ')');
      DrawLine ( 25, '=');
      WRITELN (IntBits (Result) :16, ' (',Result : 6, ')');
    END;
```

```
   UNTIL Val1 = 0;
END.
```

Notice that the bitwise **AND** yields a 1 only if the bits from both operands are 1. That is, 1 * 1 is the only product of 0 and 1 that equals 1.

Masks   The bitwise **AND** operator excludes bits from the result. Not surprisingly, this operator is often used to convert a 16-bit value to an 8-bit one or, more commonly, to remove particular portions of a number's bit pattern.

The process of removing certain bits in a number is called *masking*. The easiest way to mask is to apply the bitwise **AND** operator, using an appropriate bit pattern as the mask. The *mask* is a bit pattern that has a 0 at every position that you want to remove from your number and a 1 everywhere else.

For example, to get an 8-bit value (between 0 and 255) from an integer, you could use the following mask (but without the spaces, which are included for clarity):

```
0000 0000 1111 1111
```

By applying the bitwise **AND** operator to your original value and this mask, you'll get a result that has 1's only in the rightmost byte. No matter what bit pattern your number has in the left byte, the mask ensures that the resulting bits are all 0. Note that the mask value is **255**, or **$FF**, in hexadecimal. Note also that you're actually getting back an integer — that is, a 16-bit value — which just happens to be an integer with all 0's in its left byte.

Function **Mask** in the following listing lets you carry out such modifications. The parameters and return type are of type **WORD** instead of **INTEGER** so you can use masks that involve the leftmost bit without having to worry about signs.

```
FUNCTION Mask ( Value, MaskPattern : WORD) : WORD;
BEGIN
  Mask := Value AND MaskPattern;
END; (* FN Mask *)
```

Specifying a Mask The mask you'll want to use in a particular situation will have a specific bit pattern; however, the **MaskPattern** parameter to the function is a **WORD**. You may find it easier to specify your mask value in hexadecimal form.

To determine the hexadecimal form of the mask you want,

1. Determine the binary representation your mask should have.

2. Group the digits from this representation into groups of four bits.

3. For each group of bits, determine the hexadecimal digit that corresponds to the bit pattern. (You can use the **Pattern** array defined in function **IntBits** to determine the digit that corresponds to a particular bit pattern.)

The resulting value for each group of bits will be a hexadecimal digit — 0..9 or A..F.

Each **INTEGER** mask will have up to four hexadecimal digits. (A mask will have fewer than four if any leading hexadecimal digits are 0.) A mask for a **LONGINT** would have eight hexadecimal digits, since 32 bits are used to represent such a value.

For example, suppose you want to generate a random value between 0 and 64. You could generate a random integer and then mask out everything but six consecutive bits somewhere within the number. You can then use the value of those six bits as your random number. For example, the following bit pattern would get digits 5 through 10:

```
0000 0011 1111 0000
```

The hexadecimal digits for this bit pattern are: 0, 3, F (15), and 0. Thus, the mask would be $3F0. This is much easier to determine than 1008, the decimal value corresponding to this bit pattern. To use just the six bits desired, you would drop the 0 digit and use just the 3 and the F.

The following program lets you generate random integers and mask these values in two different ways. Run the program and see whether you notice any pattern in the results.

```
P14-3    (* Program to illustrate use of masks *)

PROGRAM RandomAndDemo;

CONST OnOff = $AAAA;
```

```
        OffOn = $5555;
VAR Index, NrTrials, Value : INTEGER;

  (* Return the result when all but the bits in MaskPattern
     are removed from Value.
  *)
  FUNCTION Mask ( Value, MaskPattern : WORD) : WORD;
  BEGIN
    Mask := Value AND MaskPattern;
  END; (* FN Mask *)

  PROCEDURE GetInteger ( Message : STRING;
                          VAR Value : INTEGER);
  BEGIN
    WRITE ( Message, ' ');
    READLN ( Value);
  END; (* GetInteger *)

BEGIN
  RANDOMIZE;
  GetInteger ( '# of Trials?', NrTrials);
  FOR Index := 1 TO NrTrials DO
  BEGIN
    Value := RANDOM ( MAXINT);
    WRITELN ( Value : 5, ': ', Mask ( Value, OnOff) : 5, ' + ',
              Mask ( Value, OffOn) : 5);
  END;
  READLN;
END.
```

This program produced the following output for a sample run:

```
# of Trials? 15
 9676:  8328 +  1348
25162:  8714 + 16448
18097:   672 + 17425
12514:  8354 +  4160
18849:  2208 + 16641
26203:  8714 + 17489
28461: 10792 + 17669
24289:  2720 + 21569
 6960:  2592 +  4368
30914: 10370 + 20544
 5113:   680 +  4433
30076:  8232 + 21844
 8987:  8714 +   273
18326:   642 + 17684
27186: 10786 + 16400
```

Notice that the mask results add up to the original number in this case. To see why this should be the case, just add the bit patterns for **OnOff** and **OffOn**.

Bitwise Addition: The OR Operator

The bitwise **OR** operator also takes two whole number operands and returns a value of the same type. The returned value's bit pattern contains a 1 wherever corresponding bits for either operand or for both operands are 1, and a 0 when both operands have a 0 at that position. Since a 1 in either operand is enough for a 1 in the result, the bitwise **OR** operator is useful for turning bits *on*. For example, you might use this operator to add elements to a collection.

The following program uses the bitwise **OR** operator to classify different animals into the appropriate groups. Think about how you would write this program using sets.

P14-4
```
(* Program to illustrate use of bitwise OR operator
    for building collections.
*)

PROGRAM OrDemo;

TYPE SmStr = STRING [ 30];
CONST MaxNames = 15;
      MaxBits = 16;
      CRLF = #13#10;

(* Predefine some codes for animals. Note that the codes all
   have unique digits, because each is a different power of 2.
*)
      Possum   = $1;    Wolf     = $20;    Lynx    = $400;
      Wombat   = $2;    Fox      = $40;    Ocelot  = $800;
      Koala    = $4;    Whale    = $80;    Jaguar  = $1000;
      Numbat   = $8;    Porpoise = $100;   Cheetah = $2000;
      Dog      = $10;   Narwhal  = $200;   Lion    = $4000;

      Names : ARRAY [ 1 .. MaxNames] OF SmStr =
        ( 'possum', 'wombat', 'koala', 'numbat',
          'dog', 'wolf', 'fox', 'whale', 'porpoise', 'narwhal',
          'lynx', 'ocelot', 'jaguar', 'cheetah', 'lion');
```

```
VAR Marsupial, Canine,
    Feline, Cetacean,
    Carnivore, Mammal,
    Large, Small : INTEGER;

 (* Display the members of the specified class *)
 PROCEDURE DispMembers ( ClassName : SmStr;
                          Members : INTEGER);
 VAR Index, Count : INTEGER;
 BEGIN
   Index := 1;
   Count := 1;

   WRITELN ( CRLF, ClassName, ':');
   WHILE ( Index <= Lion) AND ( Count < MaxBits) DO
   BEGIN
     IF ( Members AND Index <> 0) THEN
       WRITELN ( Names [ Count]);
     Index := Index * 2;
     INC ( Count);
   END; (* WHILE loop *)
 END; (* DispMembers *)

BEGIN (* Main Program *)
 (* Assign animals to the classes.
    Note how the bitwise OR operator is used.
 *)
 Marsupial := Possum OR Wombat OR Koala OR Numbat;
 Canine := Dog OR Wolf OR Fox;
 Cetacean := Whale OR Porpoise OR Narwhal;
 Feline := Lynx OR Ocelot OR Jaguar OR Cheetah OR Lion;
 Carnivore := Canine OR Feline;
 Mammal := Carnivore OR Marsupial OR Cetacean;
 Large := Cetacean OR Feline OR Wombat OR Wolf;
 Small := Mammal AND NOT Large;

 DispMembers ( 'MARSUPIALS', Marsupial);
 DispMembers ( 'CETACEANS', Cetacean);
 READLN;
 DispMembers ( 'CANINES', Canine);
 DispMembers ( 'FELINES', Feline);
 READLN;
 DispMembers ( 'CARNIVORES', Carnivore);
 READLN;
 DispMembers ( 'MAMMALS', Mammal);
 READLN;
 DispMembers ( 'LARGE MAMMALS', large);
 DispMembers ( 'SMALL MAMMALS', small);
 READLN;
END.
```

The program is easy to follow, despite its length. The constants are defined to make particular bit patterns available. Notice that the patterns are successive powers of 2. More important, all the constants have 1 in unique places—that is, the 1's in the constants' values don't overlap.

To create a grouping, such as **Marsupial**, the program uses the bitwise **OR** operator to turn on the bits corresponding to the appropriate constants: **Possum**, **Wombat**, **Koala**, and **Numbat**. Work through the calculations involved in assigning a value to **Feline** to test your understanding of the bitwise **OR** operator.

To understand how **Small** is assigned a value, first notice that **Mammal** consists of all the groups, as you can see from the following calculations. This collection will be used as a reference set from which **Large** animals will be excluded to leave **Small**. (The leftmost bit is not used in the examples, since there are only 15 animals. If the bit were used, you would need to work with **WORD** or **LONGINT** values.)

```
(* Build Mammal *)

   0000 0000 0111 0000 (Canine)
OR 0111 1100 0000 0000 (Feline)
--------------------------------
   0111 1100 0111 0000 (Carnivore)

   0111 1100 0111 0000 (Carnivore)
OR 0000 0000 0000 1111 (Marsupial)
OR 0000 0011 1000 0000 (Cetacean)
--------------------------------
   0111 1111 1111 1111 (Mammal)
```

Similarly, the following calculations yield the bit pattern for **NOT Large**:

```
   0000 0011 1000 0000 (Cetacean)
OR 0111 1100 0000 0000 (Feline)
OR 0000 0000 0000 0010 (Wombat)
OR 0000 0000 0010 0000 (Wolf)
--------------------------------
   0111 1111 1010 0010 (Large)

   1000 0000 0101 1101 (NOT Large)
```

The only animals that will be included in **Small** are those that are 1 in **NOT Large**.

Order of Precedence for the Bitwise Operators

The statement in which **Small** is assigned a value has two bitwise operators in succession. How do you know the order in which these should be applied?

The bitwise negation operator is unary. It has a high precedence, at the same level as the other unary operators. The bitwise **AND** operator has a higher precedence than the bitwise **OR** operator. Recall that the logical counterparts of these operators were compared to multiplication and addition, respectively. Seen in this light, these operators again show the precedence of multiplication over addition.

Bitwise Exclusion: The XOR Operator

The preceding section demonstrated how to use the bitwise **OR** operator to build groups of values. You also saw how to use the bitwise **AND** and the bitwise negation operators to help build such groups.

The bitwise **XOR** operator yields a 1 if exactly one of the corresponding operand bits is 1. That is, **XOR** yields 1 if either the left or the right bit is 1, but *not* if both bits are 1.

Toggling

The bitwise **XOR** operator is particularly useful for *toggling* bits—that is, for turning a bit on when it is off, and turning it off when it is on. Toggling always changes the current value. For example, suppose that you decided on the basis of new information that a koala should be considered a large animal. The easiest way to accomplish the desired change is to toggle the **Koala** bit in both **Large** and **Small**. The **Koala** bit is the one with value **$4**, which means the third bit from the right is involved.

In the current groupings, this bit will be 1 in **Small** and 0 in **Large**. The following two assignments would change both of these values, thereby reclassifying a koala as large:

```
Large := Large XOR Koala;
Small := Small  XOR Koala;
```

If you decided to return to the original grouping, you could simply repeat the preceding statements by toggling the appropriate variables again.

You can toggle any bit pattern, whether it contains a single 1 bit or multiple bits that will each be toggled simultaneously.

The precedence of the bitwise **XOR** operator is the same as for the bitwise **OR** and other additive operators.

Shift Operators

Pascal also has operators for shifting a sequence of bits to the left or right by a specified number of positions. For example, when you shift to the left, the bits being vacated at the right end are filled with 0's. The bits at the left end simply drop off the variable and are discarded. Bits are not carried over into the next word.

The Left Shift Operator

The *left shift operator* (**SHL**) lets you move bits to the left. The operator takes two operands: an integral value whose bits will be shifted and a number specifying the number of places to shift—in other words, the number of places to be vacated at the right.

The following program lets you specify a left shift and then carries
out this shift one position at a time. The program displays the new value
resulting from each left shift, until the desired number of places have
been shifted.

P14-5   `(* Program to illustrate the left shift operator *)`

```
PROGRAM SHLDemo;
(*$R-*)
VAR Index : INTEGER;
    ValToShift, NrPlaces, ShiftedVal : INTEGER;
    BinStr1, BinStr2 : STRING;

  PROCEDURE GetInteger ( Message : STRING;
                          VAR Value : INTEGER);
  BEGIN
    WRITE ( Message, ' ');
    READLN ( Value);
  END; (* GetInteger *)

  (* Determine and return bit pattern for specified value. *)
  FUNCTION IntBits ( Value : WORD) : STRING;
  CONST Patterns : ARRAY [ 0 .. 15] OF STRING [ 4] =
          ( '0000', '0001', '0010', '0011', '0100', '0101',
            '0110', '0111', '1000', '1001', '1010', '1011',
            '1100', '1101', '1110', '1111');

          (* Used to get individual hexadecimal digits *)
          Mask1 = $F;          Mask2 = $F0;
          Mask3 = $F00;        Mask4 = $F000;

  VAR Temp, Piece : STRING;
  BEGIN  (* IntBits *)
    Temp := '';

    Piece := Patterns [ Value AND Mask4 SHR 12];
    Temp := Temp + Piece + ' ';
    Piece := Patterns [ Value AND Mask3 SHR 8];
    Temp := Temp + Piece + ' ';
    Piece := Patterns [ Value AND Mask2 SHR 4];
    Temp := Temp + Piece + ' ';
    Piece := Patterns [ Value AND Mask1];
    Temp := Temp + Piece;

    IntBits := Temp;
  END; (* FN IntBits *)
```

```
BEGIN
  WRITELN ( 'Left Shift demo program.');
  GetInteger ( 'Shift what value?', ValToShift);
  GetInteger ( '# places to shift?', NrPlaces);
  BinStr1 := IntBits ( ValToShift);
  WRITELN ( ValToShift : 5, ' : ', BinStr1);
  ShiftedVal := ValToShift;
  (* Shift bit by bit, displaying after each shift *)
  FOR Index := 1 TO NrPlaces DO
  BEGIN
    ShiftedVal := ShiftedVal SHL 1;
    BinStr2 := IntBits ( ShiftedVal);
    WRITELN ( 'Value SHL ', Index : 2, ' = ', ShiftedVal : 7,
              ' : ', BinStr2);
  END; (* FOR Index ... *)
  READLN;
END.
```

For **255** as the starting value and **10** as the number of places to shift, the program produces the following output:

```
Left Shift demo program.
Shift what value? 255
# places to shift? 10
  255 : 0000000011111111
Value SHL  1 =     510 : 0000000111111110
Value SHL  2 =    1020 : 0000001111111100
Value SHL  3 =    2040 : 0000011111111000
Value SHL  4 =    4080 : 0000111111110000
Value SHL  5 =    8160 : 0001111111100000
Value SHL  6 =   16320 : 0011111111000000
Value SHL  7 =   32640 : 0111111110000000
Value SHL  8 =    -256 : 1111111100000000
Value SHL  9 =    -512 : 1111111000000000
Value SHL 10 =   -1024 : 1111110000000000
```

You can literally see the bits marching across the word. Notice that the bits on the right are always filled in with 0's for each shift. Notice also that each new value is twice the starting value—at least until you start dropping bits off the edge of the word. Shifting to the left by one position means multiplying by 2, just as adding a 0 at the end of a decimal value means multiplying by 10.

Finally, notice what happens when the 1's reach the end of the word: they simply disappear. The function always returns a whole number value after carrying out the desired shift. If the bit pattern for this value has a 1 in the leftmost (sign) bit, the value will be negative, as you see for left shifts of 8 and more. To avoid this problem of negative values, use **WORD** variables instead. Modify the program so that you are shifting bits in a **WORD**, which has no negative values. What values do you find for the last few digits when you use **WORD** variables?

The Right Shift Operator

There is also a *right shift operator* (**SHR**), which shifts bits towards the right side of the number. Bits at the right end drop off the word and are discarded as bits are shifted from the left. Turbo Pascal fills the left bits with 0's as the shift moves to the right. Right shift operations are not handled in this way by all implementations or in all programming languages. The two common strategies are logical shift and arithmetic shift:

■ In a *logical shift,* vacated bits for **INTEGER** values are always replaced by 0. Turbo Pascal uses a logical shift.

■ In an *arithmetic shift,* vacated bits are filled with 1 if the sign bit was 1; otherwise, they are filled with 0.

The following program shows the right shift operator at work:

```
P14-6    (* Program to illustrate right shift operator *)

PROGRAM SHLDemo;
(*$R-*)
VAR Index : INTEGER;
    ValToShift, NrPlaces, ShiftedVal : INTEGER;
    BinStr1, BinStr2 : STRING;

    PROCEDURE GetInteger ( Message : STRING;
                           VAR Value : INTEGER);
    BEGIN
      WRITE ( Message, ' ');
      READLN ( Value);
    END; (* GetInteger *)

    (* Determine and return bit pattern for specified value. *)
    FUNCTION IntBits ( Value : WORD) : STRING;
    CONST Patterns : ARRAY [ 0 .. 15] OF STRING [ 4] =
```

```
            ( '0000', '0001', '0010', '0011', '0100', '0101',
              '0110', '0111', '1000', '1001', '1010', '1011',
              '1100', '1101', '1110', '1111');

        (* Used to get individual hexadecimal digits *)
        Mask1 = $F;          Mask2 = $F0;
        Mask3 = $F00;        Mask4 = $F000;

    VAR Temp, Piece : STRING;
    BEGIN  (* IntBits *)
      Temp := '';

      Piece := Patterns [ Value AND Mask4 SHR 12];
      Temp := Temp + Piece + ' ';
      Piece := Patterns [ Value AND Mask3 SHR 8];
      Temp := Temp + Piece + ' ';
      Piece := Patterns [ Value AND Mask2 SHR 4];
      Temp := Temp + Piece + ' ';
      Piece := Patterns [ Value AND Mask1];
      Temp := Temp + Piece;

      IntBits := Temp;
    END; (* FN IntBits *)

BEGIN
  WRITELN ( 'Right Shift demo program.');
  GetInteger ( 'Shift what value?', ValToShift);
  GetInteger ( '# places to shift?', NrPlaces);
  BinStr1 := IntBits ( ValToShift);
  WRITELN ( ValToShift : 5, ' : ', BinStr1);
  ShiftedVal := ValToShift;
  (* Shift bit by bit; display bit pattern after each shift *)
  FOR Index := 1 TO NrPlaces DO
  BEGIN
    ShiftedVal := ShiftedVal SHR 1;
    BinStr2 := IntBits ( ShiftedVal);
    WRITELN ( 'Value SHR ', Index : 2, ' = ', ShiftedVal : 7,
              ' : ', BinStr2);
  END; (* FOR Index ... *)
  READLN;
END.
```

Right Shifts and Powers of Two   You saw that shifting a bit pattern to the left amounts to multiplying by 2. Shifting to the right is essentially dividing by 2 — at least in logical shifts — as shown by the output from the preceding program. If you haven't run the program, do so now.

IntBits (Value : INTEGER) : STRING   Now that you've learned about
the right shift operator, you can finally look at function **IntBits** to see
how it accomplishes its task:

```
(* Determine and return bit pattern for specified value. *)
FUNCTION IntBits ( Value : WORD) : STRING;
CONST Patterns : ARRAY [ 0 .. 15] OF STRING [ 4] =
        ( '0000', '0001', '0010', '0011', '0100', '0101',
          '0110', '0111', '1000', '1001', '1010', '1011',
          '1100', '1101', '1110', '1111');

          (* Used to get individual hexadecimal digits *)
      Mask1 = $F;          Mask2 = $F0;
      Mask3 = $F00;        Mask4 = $F000;

VAR Temp, Piece : STRING;
BEGIN  (* IntBits *)
  Temp := '';

  Piece := Patterns [ Value AND Mask4 SHR 12];
  Temp := Temp + Piece + ' ';
  Piece := Patterns [ Value AND Mask3 SHR 8];
  Temp := Temp + Piece + ' ';
  Piece := Patterns [ Value AND Mask2 SHR 4];
  Temp := Temp + Piece + ' ';
  Piece := Patterns [ Value AND Mask1];
  Temp := Temp + Piece;

  IntBits := Temp;
END; (* FN IntBits *)
```

The function builds the string **Temp** by adding successive values of
Piece to the end of the string. **Piece** is assigned a value by getting a value
between 0 and 15—the range covered by four bits—and determining
the bit pattern associated with that hexadecimal value. The bit pattern
is stored in the appropriate cell of **Patterns**.

To get the values, **IntBits** uses four masks. Each mask takes one of
the hexadecimal digits in an **INTEGER** representation. Thus, **Mask4**
gets the leftmost hexadecimal digit of the value.

The result from this masking will be a very large value because it will
have three trailing zeros. Obviously, there is no **Pattern** cell corresponding to an index of over 4000. To bring the leftmost hexadecimal digit
within range, it is shifted to the right by 12 places. This removes the
trailing zeros. The **Pattern** cell corresponding to this shifted value will
then start the bit pattern string.

Similarly, **Mask3** is shifted, but only 8 bits because it has only two trailing zeros. This sequence is repeated for each mask until each digit's bit pattern has been added to the string. The spaces are added to make it easier to group bits.

Precedence of the Shift Operators Since they produce the same effect as multiplication and division, these shift operators have the same precedence as other multiplicative operators.

Accessing DOS Services
Through Interrupts

Under DOS, low-level communications between the program and the operating system are effected by means of *interrupts*. In this and the following sections, you'll learn something about software interrupts. You'll also find routines that use some of the more common functions and services provided by DOS and the ROM-BIOS for your PC. Before learning about DOS, however, you need some background and context.

Registers

Machines based on the Intel 8086 family of processors (including the 8088, 80286, and 80386) do much of their work in machine registers of various sorts. These registers are 16 bits wide, and store various pieces of information when a program is running. When a program is executing, much of the action either takes place in these registers or is controlled by values currently stored in certain registers.

Machines based on the 8086 have 14 registers. Four are general-purpose registers—known as AX, BX, CX, and DX—and are used by the interrupt functions you'll learn about. The AX register is generally known as the *accumulator,* since input, output, and arithmetic operations use this register. The BX, or *base,* register often stores the base address of tables or address offsets. The CX register is often a counter for loops, and is called the *count* register. Finally, the DX, or *data*, register stores data used in computations.

Several other registers are used for some of the interrupts. The FLAGS register signals errors or other special occurrences. Although this is a 16-bit register, individual bits in it indicate particular states or outcomes (such as overflow, zero result, and so forth). In the following functions, the FLAGS register might be checked to determine whether it is zero (no error) or nonzero (error). If there was an error, other registers will contain details or a code for this error.

You may also use two other registers, the *index* registers, when you're accessing the operating system services. These registers generally store addresses during other activities, but may also be used to store intermediate results during computations. The two index registers are DI (destination index) and SI (source index). For example, the DI register is used in a DOS service for renaming a file. The location of the new name string is stored in the DI register.

You can access an entire register at once, or you can access the high- and low-order bytes of the register separately. When you access the entire register, you refer to AX, and so on. When you access individual bytes, you refer to the AH (high-order) and AL (low-order) bytes of AX, for example.

The Turbo Pascal **DOS** unit includes a predefined variant record type called **Registers**. (In the official compiler, this type is defined in the **DOS** unit.) You can use variables of this type to access individual machine registers. **Registers** variables are used when you want to call DOS or the BIOS (Basic Input/Output System) to perform a particular task. The following listing shows the definition of the **Registers** type:

```
TYPE Registers = RECORD
            CASE INTEGER OF
              0 : ( AX, BX, CX, DX, BP,
                    SI, DI, DS, ES, Flags : WORD);
              1 : ( AL, AH, BL, BH,
                    CL, CH, DL, DH : BYTE);
          END; (* Registers RECORD *)
```

One variant of the record has several **WORD** fields. These represent the registers used when interacting with the operating system. The other variant lets you access the individual **BYTE**s of a register. This variant has fields for the high- and low-order bytes of the four general-purpose registers—that is, AH, AL, BH, BL, CH, CL, DH, and DL.

Figure 13-1 shows a diagram of this record. The one-cell variables (such as **AL, BH**, and **DL**) are of type **BYTE**; two-cell variables (such as **AX, DX**, and **SI**) are of type **WORD**. In the figure, identifiers in parentheses are fields of the second variant; the remaining identifiers are fields of the first (**WORD**) variant.

In addition to this **Registers** definition, the **DOS** unit contains procedures that you need to access the registers. This chapter explains how to use these functions to interact with DOS or the BIOS at a low level.

Interrupts

An interrupt is essentially a signal from the program or elsewhere to the CPU. When an interrupt is made, the current activity stops temporarily while the desired task is carried out. Each interrupt has a numerical code associated with it. This code identifies the interrupt for the hardware, which then finds the code required to carry out the task specified by the interrupt.

There are two ways of interrupting DOS via software. The first way uses a function call to pass an interrupt number directly to the operating system or the BIOS. The number passed corresponds to the interrupt requested. For example, software interrupt $25 is a request to do an absolute disk read—that is, to read a particular sector of the disk, whether or not this sector is part of a file. The **DOS** unit includes a procedure, **Intr**, to call and execute interrupts directly.

The other way to interrupt DOS is to call a special software interrupt, $21, that provides access to additional DOS services. This interrupt is sometimes known as the *function dispatcher,* since its job is to access the appropriate DOS service. To use interrupt $21, you need to pass another value, which corresponds to the DOS service you want. For example, DOS service $36 tells you the amount of free disk space, service $30 returns the DOS version number, and so forth. You must place the requested service number in a particular field of a **Registers** variable before you call interrupt $21. This call is generally accomplished by using the **MSDOS** procedure that is predefined in the **DOS** unit.

**Offset
(Bytes)**

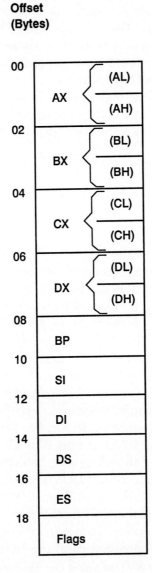

Figure 14-1.   *Storage layout for **Registers** Record Variant (Fields in the longer list represent fields for Record Variant 0; fields in parentheses are for Variant 1.)*

Most discussions of DOS interrupts represent the codes in hexadecimal form. Thus, it's very common to see references to interrupt $21 (or 21H, for 21 *hex*), rather than to 33 (the decimal value corresponding to $21). This discussion uses hexadecimal representations.

This book only reviews a few of the many services available via the function dispatcher or directly through interrupts. For more information on DOS interrupts and DOS services, you might want to consult more specialized books, such as Kris Jamsa's *DOS: The Complete Reference, Second Edition* (Berkeley, CA: Osborne/McGraw-Hill, 1990) or the second edition of Ray Duncan's *Advanced MS DOS* (Redmond, WA: Microsoft Press, 1988).

Cautions When Using DOS Interrupts

Be very careful when using DOS interrupts, especially if you're using interrupts or services that will actually change something on the disk. Before you use services that will reset the current date or write to particular parts of a disk, make certain that you understand exactly how the interrupt or service works and that you know exactly what values you want to change as well as the replacement values. You can get yourself into lots of trouble if you are sloppy here.

CAUTION Interrupts can give you access to very privileged and critical areas of your disk, such as the directory area, or internal settings. If you are not careful, you can easily change something inadvertently, damaging crucial files. Before you experiment with interrupts that will actually write or change information, back up your system. Also, make sure that you are sending the correct values *and* that the values are stored in the appropriate registers. You should get into the habit of doing as much error checking as possible when working with interrupts.

Interrupting DOS Through the Function Dispatcher

There are two ways of accessing the DOS or BIOS services: through the function dispatcher and by interrupting directly. Using the function dispatcher is safer. By calling interrupts this way, you can be confident that your routines will work in the same way on different machines running DOS. This is because the function dispatcher "protects" your routines from hardware differences that may affect the way your machine actually does its work.

One drawback to the function dispatcher is speed. Indirect calls through interrupt $21 are slower than sending the interrupt directly to DOS or the BIOS. Certain services are also unavailable through the dispatcher. To access those services (such as certain video functions) you need to interrupt directly.

First, you'll learn how to use the predefined procedure **MSDOS** to access operating system services through the function dispatcher. In the programs, the **USES DOS** statements indicate that you are calling routines that are ordinarily included in separate units.

The **MSDOS** procedure takes one **VAR** parameter: a variable of type **Registers**. This procedure calls the function dispatcher (interrupt $21) to perform the service specified by a value stored in one of the argument's fields. You must put this value in the appropriate field. The number of the service being requested is always stored in AH, the high-order byte of AX. Depending on the service you're requesting, you may need to store additional values in other fields. You'll see examples of this in the next few pages.

The **MSDOS** procedure returns its results in registers, whose values are passed back in the **Registers** parameter. The particular registers used depend on the service you requested. Some examples follow.

Reading a Character from the Keyboard

DOS service function $1 gets a character from the input (usually the keyboard) buffer, and echoes this character on the screen. This service function simply waits until you type something into the keyboard buffer.

The following program shows how to call DOS service function $1. The program lets you type input for as long as you like and ends when you type CTRL-D.

```
P14-7    (* Program to illustrate use of MSDOS for service function $1
            -- read and echo a character from the keyboard.
         *)

         PROGRAM MSDOS1HDemo;
         USES DOS;

         VAR MyRegs : Registers;  (* A record type defined in DOS unit *)
             Result : INTEGER;

         BEGIN
           WRITELN ( 'Type your message, press Ctrl-D when done.');
           REPEAT
             (* Specify the DOS service you want *)
             MyRegs.AH := $1;
             (* Call MSDOS with $1 in MyRegs.AH *)
             MSDOS ( MyRegs);
             (* result comes back in MyRegs.AL *)
             Result := MyRegs.AL;
             If Result = 13 THEN    (* if user typed return *)
               WRITELN ( #13);      (* need to send carriage return *)
           UNTIL Result = $4;
           WRITE ( #10#13'Press ENTER to end program.');
           READLN;
         END.
```

To call this service, you need to request it by number. Store the service number in the AH byte of the AX register. The program shows one way of doing this: by assigning the value directly to AH. This implicitly tells the program to work with the second variant of the **Registers** type definition.

The DOS service is accessed as part of the call to **MSDOS**. This call accomplishes the following things:

■ Calls DOS function dispatcher ($21) for the service function specified in **MyRegs.AH** (in this case, $1).

■ Invokes the desired service function. This service carries out its task, which, in the present example, is to read and display a character.

■ Returns the result of its actions in the AL byte of **MyRegs** after the service has completed its work and returned control to **MSDOS**.

The character typed has already been echoed by the time **MSDOS** returns. The echoing was done automatically by the DOS service. The main program then checks whether a CTRL-D (ASCII 4) has been typed, and stops when this happens. CTRL-D is echoed to the screen as a diamond.

The following three steps were involved in calling DOS service $1:

1. Store the DOS service number in the AH byte of **MyRegs**.

2. Call **MSDOS** with **MyRegs** as the argument.

3. Check the appropriate fields of **MyRegs** for the results from the service's actions.

These steps will be involved in any service request that uses the **MSDOS** procedure. Services differ in the amount of information needed in the **Registers** argument before the call and in the amount that is returned.

Writing a Character to the Screen

DOS service function $2 writes a specified character to the standard output, which is generally the screen. The character you want to write is assigned to the DL byte of the **Registers** argument you pass to **MSDOS**. The following program shows how to write "Hello there, duckies" using DOS service function $2:

P14-8
```
(* Program to illustrate use of MSDOS for service function $2
     -- write a character to the screen.
*)

PROGRAM MSDOS2HDemo;
USES DOS, CRT;

VAR MyRegs : Registers;  (* A record type defined in DOS unit *)
    Index, HowLong : INTEGER;
    Message : STRING;

BEGIN
  WRITE ( 'The following messags is written using');
  WRITELN ( ' DOS service $2:');
  WRITELN;
```

```
    Message := 'Hello there, duckies!';
    HowLong := LENGTH ( Message);
    FOR Index := 1 TO HowLong DO
    BEGIN
      (* Specify the DOS service you want *)
      MyRegs.AH := $2;
      (* Assign the character you want to write *)
      MyRegs.DL := ORD ( Message [ Index]);
      (* Call MSDOS with $2 in MyRegs.AH *)
      MSDOS ( MyRegs);
      DELAY ( 50);  (* wait 50 milliseconds *)
    END;
    READLN;
END.
```

Each time through the loop, the character to be written is assigned to **MyRegs.DL**. Note that **MyRegs.AH** is also given a value each time. In this particular case, you could have initialized it once outside the loop and used it from then on because service function $2 does not change this byte. Nevertheless, it's safer to initialize the byte each time—at a cost in speed, however.

Procedure **DELAY** (from the CRT unit) is used to slow down the display.

Writing Strings

The services you've seen so far have all handled single characters. With service function $9, you can also use DOS to display an entire string. The string must end with a $ character because the service function displays until it finds this character. The following listing uses service function $9 to echo a string you type. Notice that the carriage return and linefeed are written separately after the string. This is accomplished by calling procedure **SendCRLF**, which calls DOS service function $2 twice.

Run the program. Notice the period at the beginning of the last line the program writes. Try to guess why this period is there as you read the following discussion.

```
P14-9    (* Program to illustrate use of MSDOS for service function $9
            -- write a string to the screen.
         *)

         PROGRAM MSDOS9HDemo;
         USES DOS;
```

```
VAR MyRegs : Registers;  (* A record type defined in DOS unit *)
    Index, HowLong : INTEGER;
    Message, Prompt : STRING;

  (* Use DOS service $2 to send a carriage return (#13, or $D)
     and a line feed (#10, or $A).
  *)
  PROCEDURE SendCRLF;
  VAR MyRegs : Registers;
  BEGIN
   MyRegs.AH := $2;
   MyRegs.DL := $D;
   MSDOS ( MyRegs);
   MyRegs.DL := $A;
   MSDOS ( MyRegs);
  END;

BEGIN
  Prompt := 'Press ENTER to quit. Note start of this line.';
  Prompt := Prompt + '$';
  WRITELN ( 'Type a string. Program will echo it.');
  READLN (Message);
  (* Terminate string with $ for service $9 *)
  Message := Message + '$';

  (* Specify the DOS service you want *)
  MyRegs.AX := $900;
  (* Specify segment and offset location of the
     first character of the string.
  *)
  MyRegs.DS := Seg ( Message [ 1]);
  MyRegs.DX := Ofs ( Message [ 1]);
  MSDOS ( MyRegs);
  SendCRLF;
  (* Specify the DOS service you want *)
  MyRegs.AX := $900;
  (* Specify segment and offset location of the
     start of the string.
  *)
  MyRegs.DS := Seg ( Prompt);
  MyRegs.DX := Ofs ( Prompt);
  MSDOS ( MyRegs);
  READLN;
END.
```

This program assigns a service number to the entire AX register, rather than assigning the value directly to the AH byte. This is done for consistency—since the assignments involving DS and DX assume the first variant of the **Registers** type.

By adding the two trailing 0's—that is, by writing **$900** instead of **$9**—you make the number large enough so that the high-order byte of AX actually gets the required value. Recall that each hexadecimal digit represents four bits. Thus, the two 0's move the value **9** to the left by 8 bits.

DOS service function $9 writes the string whose address is specified in the **DS** and **DX** fields. In DOS, an address is specified as a segment and an offset. Turbo Pascal has two predefined functions, **SEG** and **OFS**, that return the segment and offset, respectively, of the argument passed to them. These two functions can take any variable as their argument.

The DOS service function simply goes to the specified location and starts writing until the character to be written is a $, at which point the end of the string has been reached. Notice how the location of **Message** is specified: by determining the location of the first letter in the string. Compare this to how the location of **Prompt** is specified: by using the string's name as the argument.

Recall that Turbo Pascal adds a 0th cell to a string and stores the length of the string in this cell. Recall also that a variable's name is another way of referring to a specific memory location. Thus, **Prompt** refers to the starting location of the string with that name. This location is actually the same as the location of **Prompt[0]**.

Thus, when service function $9 goes to the location of **Prompt**, it will begin by writing the 0th character of this string. The length of **Prompt** (including the $) is 46 characters, which also happens to be the ASCII code for a period.

CAUTION   When specifying a string address to a DOS service, be sure to specify the location of the first actual character in the string. Do not specify the location of the length character, which is stored in cell 0 of the string array.

Getting Date and Time

The following program shows how to use two more DOS services and provides you with a few functions that you may find useful in other programs. The **GetDate** and **GetTime** routines use DOS services to determine the current date and the number of seconds that have elapsed since midnight on your system clock. **HowLong** computes the

34time elapsed between some starting point and a finishing point in your
program.

In its current form, the program selects a random value and then
times how long it takes to call **GetDate** that often. Run the program a few
times to get a sense of how quickly your computer works. Then modify
the program to call **GetDate** 1000, 5000, and 10000 times.

P14-10
```
(* Program to get current date and to time how long it takes
   to do this a random # of times. Program also illustrates use
   of DOS interrupts to time events.
*)

PROGRAM TimeDemo;
USES DOS;

VAR Start, Finish : REAL;
    NrTimes, Index, Month, Day, Year : WORD;


(* Get current date, and pass information back in three pieces :
   month, date, year. Notice that month and date are stored in
   bytes, whereas year is stored in a 16 bit register value.
*)
PROCEDURE GetDate ( VAR month, day, year : WORD);
VAR MyRegs : Registers;
BEGIN
  (* Ask for DOS service $2A *)
  MyRegs.AH := $2A;
  (* Call the DOS function handler *)
  MSDOS ( MyRegs);
  (* Results are returned in the following registers. *)
  Month := MyRegs.DH;   (* current month returned in DH *)
  Day := MyRegs.DL;     (* current day returned in DL *)
  Year := MyRegs.CX;    (* current year returned in CX *)
END; (* GetDate *)


(* Function to get the number of seconds elapsed since
   midnight on the system clock.
*)
FUNCTION GetTime : REAL;
VAR  Hrs, Mins, Secs, Hundredths : WORD;
     MyRegs : Registers;

BEGIN
  (* Request DOS service $2C *)
  MyRegs.Ah := $2C;
```

```
      (* Call interrupt $21 with the appropriate unions *)
      MSDOS ( MyRegs);

      Hrs := MyRegs.CH;        (* hours elapsed returned in CH *)
      Mins := MyRegs.CL;       (* minutes elapsed returned in CL *)
      Secs := MyRegs.DH;       (* seconds elapsed returned in DH *)
      Hundredths := MyRegs.DL; (* 1/100's secs returned in DL *)

      (* Total elapsed time (in seconds) =
         3600 (secs / hr)  * hrs +
         60 ( secs / min) * mins +
         1 ( secs / sec) * secs +
         .01 ( secs per 1/100th sec) * hundredths.
      *)
      GetTime :=   Hrs * 3600.0 + Mins * 60.0 +
                   Secs + Hundredths / 100.0;
END; (* FN GetTime *)


(* Function to compute the number of seconds elapsed between
   start and finish
*)
FUNCTION  HowLong ( Start, Finish : REAL) : REAL;
CONST FullDay = 86400.0;  (* seconds in a 24 hr day *)

BEGIN
   (* start = first elapsed time measurement;
      finish = second elapsed time measurement.
      If start > finish then the time must have passed midnight
      between start and finish of process.
      In that case, a formula adjustment is necessary.
   *)
   IF Start > Finish THEN
      HowLong := FullDay - Start + Finish
   ELSE
      HowLong := Finish - Start;
END; (* HowLong *)


BEGIN (* Main Program *)
   RANDOMIZE;
   WRITELN ( 'Timing. Please wait...');
   Start := GetTime;     (* start timing *)
   NrTimes := RANDOM ( 20000);
   For Index := 1 TO NrTimes DO
      GetDate ( Month, Day, Year);
   Finish := GetTime;    (* stop timing *)
   WRITELN ( Month, ' / ', Day, ' / ', Year);
   WRITELN ( NrTimes, ' times. ',
             HowLong ( Start, Finish) : 10 : 2,
             ' seconds elapsed');
END.
```

Procedure **GetDate** determines the current date on your machine. $2A is the DOS service function that provides this information. The service returns the information in three pieces, corresponding to month, day, and year. Notice that month and day are returned in bytes, whereas the year is returned in an entire 16-bit value. Actually, this service also returns the day of the week in numerical form. This information is returned in AL, with Sunday being 0, Monday being 1, and so on. Modify the procedure to provide this information to your program.

The **GetTime** function uses DOS service function $2C to get information about the amount of time elapsed on the system clock since midnight. This time is reported in units ranging from hours to hundredths of a second. Again, each of these values is returned in a different byte: hours in CH, minutes in CL, seconds in DH, and hundredths of a second in DL. (Actually, the clock is only updated about 18 times a second, so the accuracy will be about 1/20, rather than 1/100 of a second.)

To time something in your program, just call **GetTime** before starting the portion of the program that you want to time. This call assigns the amount of time elapsed between midnight and the time the portion to be timed begins. When the timed portion is finished, call **GetTime** again. The difference between the values returned by the second and first calls to **GetTime** represents the amount of time the program portion took—provided that you were not running this program around midnight.

If your first time reading is before midnight and your second reading is after midnight, the results will be incorrect if you simply subtract one value from the other, since elapsed time will start from 0 again at midnight. The **HowLong** function returns the amount of time elapsed between two calls to **GetTime** and corrects the computations when you cross the midnight boundary. Check the code to see how this is done.

Modify program **TimeDemo** to write a dot each time **GetDate** is called. Then set **NrTimes** to 5000 and run the program. Record the time it takes to write 5000 dots and call **GetTime** that many times. Then run the program again, this time letting the **CRT** unit handle the call to **WRITELN**. Don't forget that you need to add **CRT** to your **USES** statement. Notice the increase in speed—this is because the **CRT** unit does not go through the BIOS.

Interrupting Without a Dispatcher

So far, the service functions have all done their work in an orderly fashion, through the mediation of the DOS function dispatcher. In this section, you'll learn about some services you can use by directly interrupting the BIOS on your computer. To invoke these services, you need to use the **Intr** procedure, which is also defined in the **DOS** unit.

Software interrupts through the function dispatcher are more likely to work the same way on different hardware than are service calls that interrupt the BIOS directly. Some of the services available through BIOS interrupts will work as stated only on machines that are completely compatible with the IBM PC, XT, and AT series machines.

The **Intr** procedure gives you direct access to software interrupts, without going through the function dispatcher (interrupt $21), as **MSDOS** does. The **Intr** function takes two parameters: the interrupt's code number and a **Registers** argument. Here are a few simple examples.

Determining Equipment and Memory

BIOS interrupt $11 lets you determine the configuration of your machine. This interrupt has a very simple calling process: just call **Intr** with the appropriate parameters. You don't need to set any registers before calling this interrupt. Thus, the following line will call BIOS interrupt $11:

```
Intr ( $11, MyRegs);
```

All equipment information is returned in **MyRegs.AX**. The individual bits of this register contain the information about your configuration:

■ Bit 0 (rightmost bit): Set to 1 if you have any disk drives connected to your computer; set to 0 otherwise.

■ Bit 1: Set to 1 if your AT has an 80287 coprocessor. This bit is not used by non-AT's.

■ Bits 2 and 3: Specify the amount of memory on the system board in early IBM PC's. This information is not used by more recent machines.

■ Bits 4 and 5: Specify the video mode on your machine. Bit pattern 01 ($1) indicates a color graphics adapter in 40-column text mode; bit pattern 10 ($2) indicates a color graphics adapter in 80-column text mode; and bit pattern 11 ($3) indicates a monochrome adapter in 80-column text mode. Bit pattern 00 is unused.

■ Bits 6 and 7: Specify the number of disk drives in your configuration. Bit pattern 00 indicates one drive, and so forth, up to four drives for bit pattern 11. If bit 0 is 0—indicating that you have no drives attached— these two bits are ignored.

■ Bit 8: Specifies that a direct memory access chip is present on the PC*jr*. This bit is not used by other machines.

■ Bits 9 through 11: Specify the number of serial ports installed on your machine.

■ Bit 12: Set to 1 if a game adapter is attached.

■ Bit 13: Set to 1 on the PC*jr* if a serial printer is attached. This bit is not used by other machines.

■ Bits 14 and 15: Specify number of printers installed on your machine.

BIOS interrupt $12 lets you determine the amount of RAM installed on your machine. As with interrupt $11, you don't need to set any values before calling this interrupt. Again, the results are returned in the field **MyRegs.AX**. The value of the AX register represents the amount of RAM, in 1K units. For example, a value of 384 indicates that your machine has 384K of memory.

The following listing illustrates BIOS interrupts $11 and $12:

```
P14-11   (* Program to illustrate use of interrupts to determine
             hardware configuration and available memory.
         *)

         PROGRAM Intr12Demo;
         USES DOS;
```

```
VAR MyRegs : Registers;

   (* Determine and return bit pattern for specified value. *)
   FUNCTION IntBits ( Value : WORD) : STRING;
   CONST Patterns : ARRAY [ 0 .. 15] OF STRING [ 4] =
           ( '0000', '0001', '0010', '0011', '0100', '0101',
             '0110', '0111', '1000', '1001', '1010', '1011',
             '1100', '1101', '1110', '1111');

         (* Used to get individual hexadecimal digits *)
         Mask1 = $F;          Mask2 = $F0;
         Mask3 = $F00;        Mask4 = $F000;

   VAR Temp, Piece : STRING;
   BEGIN  (* IntBits *)
     Temp := '';

     Piece := Patterns [ Value AND Mask4 SHR 12];
     Temp := Temp + Piece + ' ';
     Piece := Patterns [ Value AND Mask3 SHR 8];
     Temp := Temp + Piece + ' ';
     Piece := Patterns [ Value AND Mask2 SHR 4];
     Temp := Temp + Piece + ' ';
     Piece := Patterns [ Value AND Mask1];
     Temp := Temp + Piece;

     IntBits := Temp;
   END; (* FN IntBits *)

BEGIN (* Main Program *)
  WRITELN ( 'BIOS Interrupt $11: ');
  (* Call the interrupt *)
  Intr ( $11, MyRegs);
  WRITELN ( 'AX register = ', IntBits (MyRegs.AX),
            ' (', MyRegs.AX, ')');
  Intr ( $12, MyRegs);
  WRITELN ( 'BIOS Interrupt $12: ');
  WRITELN ( 'AX register = ', MyRegs.AX,
            ' Kbytes available.');
  READLN;
END.
```

An Interrupt for Video Functions

BIOS interrupt $10 is particularly important because it gives you access to the video input and output. This interrupt actually provides access to over a dozen *function requests,* each of which lets you check or change some aspect of the video input or output.

CAUTION Don't confuse service functions (which are accessed through the function dispatcher) with function requests (which are accessed through BIOS interrupt $10). Function requests use the **Intr** procedure, whereas the function dispatcher is accessed through the **MSDOS** procedure.

Changing the Shape of the Cursor Function request $1 lets you change the shape of the cursor. The cursor is drawn with dots, just like any other character. With a color graphics adapter, characters are drawn by using eight rows, numbered 0 (top row) through 7 (bottom row); with a monochrome adapter, 14 rows are used (0 through 13). The default cursor uses the bottom two lines—6 and 7 for a CGA and 12 and 13 for a monochrome adapter.

The **NewCursor** procedure in the following program lets you redefine the cursor's shape and location. The first parameter specifies the top line to be turned on for the cursor. This value is put into the field **MyRegs.CH** before being passed to the function request. The second parameter specifies the bottom line, and is stored in **MyRegs.CL**. All lines between these two lines are also turned on. For example, calling **NewCursor** with 0 and 3 as the first two arguments would change the cursor so that it blinked in the top four lines of the character. To specify that you want function request $1, set **MyRegs.Alt** to that value.

P14-12
```
(* Program to illustrate how to use Intr
    to change cursor size
*)

PROGRAM VideoIntrDemo;
USES DOS;

CONST ColorMax = 7;
      MonoMax = 13;

VAR  CurrMode, Top, Bottom : INTEGER;
     Info : STRING;

  (* Change the cursor to its new design *)
  PROCEDURE NewCursor ( Top, Bottom, MaxVal : INTEGER);
  VAR MyRegs : Registers;
  BEGIN
    WITH MyRegs DO
    BEGIN
      (* Function request 1 *)
```

```
      AH := $01;
      (* bring out of range values within bounds *)
      IF ( Top < 0) OR ( Top > MaxVal) THEN
        Top := 0;;
      CH := Top;
      (* bring out of range values within bounds *)
      IF ( Bottom < 0) OR ( Bottom > MaxVal) THEN
        Bottom := MaxVal;
      CL := Bottom;
    END; (* WITH *)
    (* call video interrupt *)
    Intr ( $10, MyRegs);
END; (* NewCursor *)

PROCEDURE GetInteger ( Message : STRING;
                       VAR Value : INTEGER);
BEGIN
  WRITE ( Message, ' ');
  READLN ( Value);
END; (* GetInteger *)

BEGIN (* Main Program *)
  (* get coordinates for top and bottom of cursor *)
  GetInteger ( 'Top row of cursor?', Top);
  GetInteger ( 'Bottom row of cursor?', Bottom);

  NewCursor ( Top, Bottom, MonoMax);
  READLN;
END.
```

To restore the cursor to its default value, run the program again with 6 and 7 or 12 and 13 as your values—for color and monochrome monitors, respectively.

Moving and Locating the Cursor Function requests $2 and $3 let you set and read the cursor position, respectively. You can use request $2 to control where your programs write their output. To call this function request, you need to provide three values in addition to the request code. You must specify the row to which you want to move the cursor. The top row of the screen is row 0 and the bottom row is generally 24. This value is put into **MyRegs.DH**. The column number is placed in **MyRegs.DL**. This will be a value between 0 and 79 or between 0 and 39, depending on the text mode. Column 0 is the leftmost column.

Finally, you need to specify the video page number for which you are setting the cursor. This value will be stored in **MyRegs.BH**. The page number must be 0 in graphics mode. The following procedure shows how to move the cursor to an arbitrary location.

```
(* move the cursor to the position specified,
   using BIOS interrupt $10 (video) for access to
   function request $2.
*)
PROCEDURE MoveCursor ( Row, Column : INTEGER);
VAR MyRegs : Registers;
BEGIN
  MyRegs.AH := $2;           (* function request code *)
  MyRegs.DH := Row;          (* new row position *)
  MyRegs.DL := Column;       (* new column position *)
  MyRegs.BH := 0;            (* page 0 *)

  Intr ( $10, MyRegs);  (* BIOS interrupt *)
END;   (* MoveCursor *)
```

Function request $3 tells you not only the cursor location, but also its shape. After you specify the video page for which you want to know the cursor position, the function returns the column and row for the current cursor position on that page. The function also returns the top and bottom rows of the cursor's shape.

To specify the video page, set **MyRegs.BH** to the desired page number. To determine the current row, check the value of **MyRegs.DH**. This will be a value between 0 and 24, as for request $2. The current column coordinate will be stored in **MyRegs.DL** after the call to **Intr**. The top row of the cursor will be in **MyRegs.CH** and the bottom row will be in **MyRegs.CL**.

The following program writes points at random positions on the screen and then determines the location of the pointer after writing all the random points:

P14-13
```
(* Program to illustrate use of function requests
   to change and to determine cursor location
*)

PROGRAM CursorDemo;
USES DOS;

VAR Row, Column : INTEGER;

(* move the cursor to the position specified,
   using BIOS interrupt $10 (video) for access to
   function request $2.
*)
PROCEDURE MoveCursor ( Row, Column : INTEGER);
VAR MyRegs : Registers;
BEGIN
  MyRegs.AH := $2;             (* function request code *)
```

```
      MyRegs.DH := Row;        (* new row position *)
      MyRegs.DL := Column;     (* new column position *)
      MyRegs.BH := 0;          (* page 0 *)

   Intr ( $10, MyRegs);   (* BIOS interrupt *)
END;  (* MoveCursor *)

(* write a specified # of dots at random positions
   on the screen.
*)
PROCEDURE PlayWithCursor ( NrPoints : INTEGER);
CONST CharToWrite = '.';
VAR Index, Row, Col : INTEGER;
BEGIN
  (* select positions and write the character *)
  FOR Index := 1 TO NrPoints DO
  BEGIN
    Row := RANDOM ( MaxInt) MOD 25 + 1;
    Col := RANDOM ( MaxInt) MOD 80 + 1;
    MoveCursor ( Row, Col);
    WRITE ( CharToWrite);
  END;
END; (* PlayWithCursor *)

(* determine the current location of the cursor,
   using BIOS interrupt $10 (video) for access to
   function request $3.
*)
PROCEDURE LocateCursor ( VAR Row, Column : INTEGER);
VAR MyRegs : Registers;
BEGIN
  MyRegs.AH := $3;          (* function request code *)
  MyRegs.BH := 0;           (* using video page 0 *)

  Intr ( $10, MyRegs);      (* BIOS interrupt *)
  Row := MyRegs.DH;
  Column := MyRegs.DL;
END; (* LocateCursor *)

BEGIN (* Main Program *)
  RANDOMIZE;
  PlayWithCursor ( 1920);
  LocateCursor ( Row, Column);
  READLN;  (* wait before displaying cursor location. *)
  WRITELN ( 'Row ', Row, '; Column ', Column);
  READLN;
END.
```

For more information about DOS function requests and about how to access BIOS services, see the books by Jamsa or Duncan mentioned earlier in the chapter.

Creating Units

Earlier, you learned about the routines available through separate units in Turbo Pascal. In this section, you'll learn how to create such precompiled units of your own.

A Turbo Pascal unit consists of two parts: an interface and an implementation section. The *interface* contains any type definitions and variable declarations for the unit, as well as headers for the routines defined in the unit (and available to users of the unit). The *implementation* contains the actual definitions for the routines listed in the interface. The implementation part may also contain *initialization code* in which variables are initialized or actions needed by the unit are taken.

Example: A Small Utilities Unit

To understand these parts, let's look at a small example. The following listing shows a utilities unit that contains just two functions and defines two constants:

P14-14

```
(* Unit DemoUnit: Pascal utilities. *)

UNIT DemoUnit;

(* Specify type definitions and variable declarations;
   list procedure and function headings (interfaces).
*)
INTERFACE

CONST InvalidVal = -99999.99;
      Tolerance  =  1.0E-6;

(* Interfaces for routines available through the unit *)
FUNCTION NonZero ( Val : REAL) : BOOLEAN;
FUNCTION SafeDivision ( Numer, Denom : REAL) : REAL;
```

```
(* Define the routines listed in interface, as well as
   any others that are private to the unit.
*)
IMPLEMENTATION

(* Return TRUE if Val differs from zero by more
   than a predefined amount.
*)
FUNCTION NonZero ( Val : REAL) : BOOLEAN;
BEGIN
  IF ABS ( Val - 0.0) > Tolerance THEN
    NonZero := TRUE
  ELSE
    NonZero := FALSE;
END; (* FN NonZero *)

(* Divide num by denom, checking for division by zero
   before doing so. Return quotient or a default value
   ( InvalidVal) on division by zero.
*)
FUNCTION SafeDivision ( Numer, Denom : REAL) : REAL;
BEGIN
  IF NonZero ( Denom) THEN
    SafeDivision := Numer / Denom
  ELSE
    SafeDivision := InvalidVal;
END; (* SafeDivision *)

(* A routine available only within DemoUnit,
    NOT to any other program or unit.
*)
PROCEDURE APrivateProc;
BEGIN
  WRITELN ( 'Hello from Util unit.');
END; (* APrivateProc *)

(* Initialization code -- if any -- comes here *)
BEGIN
  APrivateProc;
END.
```

This example contains an interface, an implementation, and even some initialization code in the implementation. The syntax for the unit definition is as follows:

```
UNIT <Unit name>;
INTERFACE
{USES <list of other units used by the unit>}
  . .declarations and headers. .
IMPLEMENTATION
  . .procedure and function definitions. .
{BEGIN <initialization code>}
END.
```

The unit's name and the name of the file in which the unit is stored must be the same. Thus, **DemoUnit** must be stored in a file named DEMOUNIT.PAS. If you have an official compiler and you're going to build this unit, you need to rename or copy the file to DEMOUNIT.PAS.

The first part of the unit source file will contain the interface. In **DemoUnit**, two constants are defined and two functions are declared. Because these objects are specified in the interface, they are available to any programs that use the unit—just as if the constants had been defined in the main program and the routine headers had been included as a **FORWARD** declaration—so that the definition would come later. (The word **FORWARD** is not used in the unit's interface, however.)

The remainder of the file contains the implementation for the unit— that is, the procedure and function definitions.

There are several points to notice about the implementation:

■ Both the interface and the implementation include parameter lists for the functions. They are required in the interface because the compiler uses the information in the interface to evaluate the correctness of your calls to the unit's routines. The parameter lists are optional in the implementation. If you use them, however, the lists in the interface and the implementation must match exactly; otherwise, the compiler will respond with an error.

■ The implementation contains a third routine—**APrivateProc**. This routine is called in the initialization code. The procedure is not available to outside programs, since it was not declared in the interface. Such a routine is said to be *private* or *hidden*.

■ Initialization code is optional. The example includes a procedure call to show when the initialization code is executed. If your unit has initialization code, you must include **BEGIN** at the start of the initialization code section. This is followed by the actual code. The implementation part of every unit terminates with **END** followed by a period, whether or not there is initialization code.

Once you've written the code for the unit, you need to compile it to a .TPU file. This extension is used for a precompiled unit. The same commands apply as when you're compiling a program. The Turbo Pascal compiler will automatically create a .TPU file (instead of an .EXE file).

Once the .TPU file has been created, you can use the unit's routines in your other programs, as shown in the following listing:

P14-15
```
(* Program to illustrate use of DemoUnit *)

PROGRAM DemoTest;
USES DemoUnit;      (* include the DemoUnit routines *)

VAR One, Two : REAL;

BEGIN
  RANDOMIZE;
  One := RANDOM;
  Two := RANDOM;
  WRITELN ( One : 5 : 3,  ' / ', Two : 5 : 3, ' = ',
          SafeDivision ( One, Two) : 10 : 3);
  READLN;
END.
```

Command-Line Arguments

Under many operating systems, including DOS, you start a program simply by typing the program's name. For example, to start the Turbo Pascal compiler, you simply type **turbo**. When the compiler starts running after this command, it makes certain decisions about the current session. For example, if you start the IDE simply by typing the program's name, it puts you in an edit window. You can prevent the IDE

from making such decisions by typing a file name in addition to the
program name at the operating system prompt. For example, to edit a
file named DEMO.PAS, you could type

```
turbo demo
```

When you type something at the operating system prompt, you're
writing on the *command line*. The things you write—such as file names—
are *command-line arguments*. The following are all sample command lines;
all but the last two command lines have multiple arguments:

```
C:\TP> turbo demo

C:\TP\BK> tex ch13

C:\USRBIN> dir | sort > proglist

C:\TP\BK\TMP> copy *.* b: /v

C:\> chkdsk

C:\TP\BK> intrdemo
```

Look more closely at some of the sample command lines to see the
types of arguments that can appear on command lines.

Common Command-Line Arguments

The things you can specify on a command line are limited only by your
imagination. However, a few types of arguments account for the overwhelming majority of command-line elements. This section covers program and file names.

Program Names   The name of an executable program file is perhaps
the most common command-line argument under DOS. A line containing just a program name constitutes the minimal command line, and
executes the named program.

In the preceding list, the last two command lines just contain a program name: **Chkdsk** and **Intrdemo,** respectively. The first element in each of the other six command lines is also a program (or command) name. Certain of these elements—such as **dir** and **copy**—actually represent commands that are understood by the operating system's interpreter program. Such commands are included in this group because they are similar to program name commands.

File, Directory, and Drive Names Another large group of arguments consists of file or directory names, or references to a particular disk or logical drive (such as A, C, or D). For example, when you invoke the COPY command, you'll generally specify the name of the file to copy or a drive from which to copy files. You may also specify the destination to which the file or files will be copied—or you can let the current directory be the default destination. The fourth line of the preceding listing illustrates the use of such arguments, and also raises an important issue about file names—namely, how to specify multiple file names in a single name.

You may want to copy several or all of the files in a directory. This task would quickly become tedious if you had to copy each file separately. To overcome this problem to a certain extent, you can use *wildcard characters* in your file names. A wildcard character is one that can be replaced by one or more other characters in order to build a file name. DOS uses ? to represent any single character and * to represent any sequence of zero or more characters. For example, CH?.TEX would be matched by the first three names in the following list, but not the last two:

```
ch1.tex
cha.tex
ch8.tex
ch12.tex
chapt.tex
```

The non-matching names have more than one character to substitute for the question mark.

Only the first two of the following names would match CH*.T*:

```
chapter1.tex
ch.tex
(* the following names do not match *)
```

```
chapter1
ch
ch.pas
nomatch.pas
```

In each non-matching case, the names don't match because of the file's extension. See your operating system documentation for more information about wildcard characters.

Passing Arguments to Turbo Pascal Programs

This section contains a simple example of how to pass command-line arguments to your Turbo Pascal programs. The following program simply displays any command-line arguments you pass. Run the program. It will tell you that no arguments were passed. The discussion following the program explains how to pass such arguments.

P14-16
```pascal
(* Program to illustrate how to determine and
   display command line arguments.
*)

PROGRAM ArgDemo;
VAR Index, MaxArg : INTEGER;

BEGIN
  (* ParamCount returns the number of command-line
     arguments found
  *)
  MaxArg := ParamCount;
  (* ParamStr ( X) returns the Xth command-line argument *)
  FOR Index := 1 TO MaxArg DO
    WRITELN ( Index, ': ', ParamStr ( Index));
  WRITELN ( MaxArg, ' arguments passed.');
  READLN;
END.
```

Passing Arguments in the IDE

To pass command-line arguments in the IDE,

1. Press ALT-R to access the Run menu.

2. Move the cursor to the last item on the menu, and press ENTER to select Parameters from this menu.

3. In the resulting box, type a command-line argument sequence, such as the following, and then press ENTER:

```
Greetings from the command line!
```

4. Run the program.

Your program will produce the following output:

```
1: Greetings
2: from
3: the
4: command
5: line!
5 arguments passed.
```

If you've compiled the program to an executable file (for example, ARGDEMO.EXE), you can accomplish the same thing by typing the following at the DOS command-line prompt:

```
argdemo Greetings from the command line!
```

Note that you don't include the program name when specifying parameters in the IDE.

ParamCount
ParamStr (WhichParam : INTEGER) : STRING Turbo Pascal provides two functions for handling command-line arguments in programs. Function **ParamCount** returns the number of arguments found.

Function **ParamStr** returns a specified string, which represents the argument corresponding to the index passed as an argument when **ParamStr** is called. For example, the first command-line argument would have index 1 and the last would have index **ParamCount**. Command-line arguments are interpreted as strings by **ParamStr**, and each word is considered a separate argument. Thus, the five words in the previous example were each treated as separate command-line parameters.

Processing Numerical Command-Line Arguments

Command-line arguments are treated as strings in Turbo Pascal. If you want to interpret a particular argument as a number, for example, you'll need to build the number internally. The following **ArgCalc** program provides a very simple four-function calculator that can carry out one calculation on any given run. The program provides another example that uses command-line arguments, and introduces a predefined procedure for converting a string to a numerical value.

To use the program in the IDE, specify your command-line arguments by selecting Run Parameters, as described earlier. The arguments should consist of multiple elements. The first element must be one of the four operator symbols (+, −, *, /). The remaining arguments should be numbers.

Run the program a few times, trying the following:

■ Run the program with no command-line arguments.

■ Use an incorrect operator.

■ Use just an operator, but no values.

■ Use an operator and one value.

■ Use an operator and several values, including an invalid value (such as "hello").

■ Use an operator and just valid values.

```
P14-17    (* Program to illustrate how to pass numerical arguments to
             a Pascal program. Command line for the
             program has the following format:

                 <operator> <value> {<value>}

             elements within { } are optional, and can be repeated
             0 or more times.
          *)
```

```
PROGRAM ArgCalc;
USES DemoUnit;

CONST Beep = #7;      (* Beep character *)
VAR RunningTotal, Temp : REAL;
    Index, Outcome, NrArgs : INTEGER;
    OpStr : STRING;

  PROCEDURE Explain;
  BEGIN
    WRITELN;
    WRITELN;
    WRITELN ( 'Your arguments should have the following form:');
    WRITELN ( '                OP Nr Nr Nr ...');
    WRITELN ( 'Where OP is + - * or /, and Nr is any number.');
    WRITELN ( 'Press ENTER to continue.');
  END;  (* Explain *)

  PROCEDURE Calculations ( OpChar : CHAR);
  BEGIN
    (* convert argument to a number *)
    VAL ( ParamStr ( Index), Temp, Outcome);
    IF OutCome = 0 THEN
    BEGIN
      (* CASE depends on first character of ParamStr ( 1). *)
      CASE OpChar OF
        '+' : RunningTotal := RunningTotal + Temp;
        '-' :
          IF Index = 2 THEN
            RunningTotal := Temp
          ELSE
            RunningTotal := RunningTotal - Temp;
        '*' :
          IF Index = 2 THEN
            RunningTotal := Temp
          ELSE
            RunningTotal := RunningTotal * Temp;
        '/' :
          IF Index = 2 THEN
            RunningTotal := Temp
          ELSE
            RunningTotal := SafeDivision (RunningTotal, Temp);
        ELSE  WRITELN ( 'Invalid Operator?');
      END; (* CASE OF OpChar *)
    END (* IF Outcome = 0 *)
    ELSE
      WRITELN ( Beep, 'ERROR! Argument ',
                Index, ' is invalid!');
  END;  (* Calculations *)

BEGIN  (* Main program *)
```

```
    RunningTotal := 0.0;
    NrArgs := ParamCount;

    IF NrArgs > 1 THEN
    BEGIN
      WRITELN ( NrArgs, ' arguments.');
      (* The first character of the first argument
         specifies the operator.
      *)
      OpStr := ParamStr ( 1);
      (* process each string in the array *)
      FOR Index := 2 TO NrArgs DO
        Calculations ( OpStr [ 1]);
      WRITELN ( 'Sum = ', RunningTotal : 15 : 8);
    END  (* if NrArgs > 1 *)
    ELSE (* If 0 arguments *)
      Explain;
    READLN;
END.
```

The program checks the number of arguments. If there are fewer than two arguments, the program explains how to use the calculator. If there are enough arguments to warrant processing, the program gets the first argument (so it will be able to get an operator from it), and then processes the remaining operators within procedure **Calculations**.

The operator is specified in **OpStr[1]**, which must exist because **NrArgs** was greater than 0. Subsequent arguments are converted from strings to numerical values using the predefined **VAL** procedure.

VAL (TheStr : STRING; VAR TheVal; VAR ResultCode : INTEGER)

Turbo Pascal's **VAL** procedure converts the string passed as the first argument. The resulting numerical value is returned in **TheVal**. Note that no type was specified for this argument. Turbo Pascal allows you to have untyped **VAR** parameters in procedure definitions. Such parameters aren't discussed in any detail here. If you want to use untyped parameters in your own programs, check the documentation for the Turbo Pascal compiler.

In the case of **VAL**, the untyped argument can be any integer-type or real-type variable. If this argument is **REAL**, the numerical value will be returned as a **REAL**. The argument passed as **TheVal** must be a variable, however, since this is a **VAR** parameter.

In the program, **VAL** is called with **ParamStr(Index)** as the first argument and **Temp** as the second. The value stored in **Temp** when

VAL has finished will be the numerical form of the parameter string.

The third argument, **ResultCode**, is 0 if the conversion went smoothly. If an invalid character was encountered while processing the string, the index of this character is returned in **ResultCode**.

Units Revisited   Note that the **ArgCalc** program uses the **DemoUnit** unit. Before using this unit elsewhere, you'll want to remove the initialization code message and then recompile **DemoUnit**.

Happy programming!

Appendixes

Part Three

A ASCII Codes[*]

Table A-1 lists the ASCII codes for characters.

DEC	OCTAL	HEX	ASCII
0	000	00	NUL
1	001	01	SOH
2	002	02	STX
3	003	03	ETX
4	004	04	EOT
5	005	05	ENQ
6	006	06	ACK
7	007	07	BEL
8	010	08	BS
9	011	09	HT
10	012	0A	LF

Table A-1.   *ASCII Character Codes*

[*]Reprinted from *The C Library* by Kris Jamsa (Berkeley, CA: Osborne/McGraw-Hill, 1985).

DEC	OCTAL	HEX	ASCII
11	013	0B	VT
12	014	0C	FF
13	015	0D	CR
14	016	0E	SO
15	017	0F	SI
16	020	10	DLE
17	021	11	DC1
18	022	12	DC2
19	023	13	DC3
20	024	14	DC4
21	025	15	NAK
22	026	16	SYN
23	027	17	ETB
24	030	18	CAN
25	031	19	EM
26	032	1A	SUB
27	033	1B	ESC
28	034	1C	FS
29	035	1D	GS
30	036	1E	RS
31	037	1F	US
32	040	20	SPACE
33	041	21	!
34	042	22	"
35	043	23	#
36	044	24	$
37	045	25	%
38	046	26	&
39	047	27	'
40	050	28	(
41	051	29	)
42	052	2A	*
43	053	2B	+
44	054	2C	,
45	055	2D	-
46	056	2E	.
47	057	2F	/

Table A-1. *ASCII Character Codes* (continued)

DEC	OCTAL	HEX	ASCII
48	060	30	0
49	061	31	1
50	062	32	2
51	063	33	3
52	064	34	4
53	065	35	5
54	066	36	6
55	067	37	7
56	070	38	8
57	071	39	9
58	072	3A	:
59	073	3B	;
60	074	3C	<
61	075	3D	=
62	076	3E	>
63	077	3F	?
64	100	40	@
65	101	41	A
66	102	42	B
67	103	43	C
68	104	44	D
69	105	45	E
70	106	46	F
71	107	47	G
72	110	48	H
73	111	49	I
74	112	4A	J
75	113	4B	K
76	114	4C	L
77	115	4D	M
78	116	4E	N
79	117	4F	O
80	120	50	P
81	121	51	Q
82	122	52	R
83	123	53	S
84	124	54	T

Table A-1. *ASCII Character Codes* (continued)

DEC	OCTAL	HEX	ASCII
85	125	55	U
86	126	56	V
87	127	57	W
88	130	58	X
89	131	59	Y
90	132	5A	Z
91	133	5B	[
92	134	5C	\
93	135	5D	]
94	136	5E	^
95	137	5F	—
96	140	60	`
97	141	61	a
98	142	62	b
99	143	63	c
100	144	64	d
101	145	65	e
102	146	66	f
103	147	67	g
104	150	68	h
105	151	69	i
106	152	6A	j
107	153	6B	k
108	154	6C	l
109	155	6D	m
110	156	6E	n
111	157	6F	o
112	160	70	p
113	161	71	q
114	162	72	r
115	163	73	s
116	164	74	t
117	165	75	u
118	166	76	v
119	167	77	w
120	170	78	x
121	171	79	y

Table A-1. *ASCII Character Codes* (continued)

DEC	OCTAL	HEX	ASCII
122	172	7A	z
123	173	7B	{
124	174	7C	|
125	175	7D	}
126	176	7E	~
127	177	7F	DEL

Table A-1. *ASCII Character Codes* (continued)

B Turbo Pascal Procedures and Functions

This appendix contains a brief summary of the actions performed by the procedures and functions available in Turbo Pascal. These routines are either included in the run-time library or defined in units, and can be accessed by including the unit in your program. This appendix does not summarize the methods associated with the Turbo Vision objects. Example methods are used in Chapter 13, "Introduction to Turbo Vision."

Functions are identified by the reserved word **FUNCTION**. Routines that are defined in a unit are specified with the unit as the first part of the name. For example, **CRT.GoToXY** indicates that the routine is defined in the **CRT** unit. The list is alphabetical by the routine's name. Unit name and **FUNCTION** prefix are not used in the ordering. Thus, **CRT.GoToXY** comes after **DISPOSE**, since *G* comes later than the *D* in **DISPOSE**.

See the on-line help for more information and for examples. To do this, press F1 SHIFT-F1 to access the help index. Select the unit of interest, and press ENTER to request help about the unit. As part of the information provided about the unit, you'll find information about predefined identifiers.

FUNCTION ABS   Returns the absolute value of the argument.

FUNCTION ADDR   Returns the address of the entity specified as its argument.

APPEND   Opens an existing text file so you can add to the end of the file.

GRAPH.ARC   Draws a circular arc, centered on a specified point and with a specified radius. The arc covers a range specified by two angles.

FUNCTION ARCTAN   Returns the arctangent (in radians) of its argument.

ASSIGN   Associates the name of an external file with a file variable. If the name is an empty string, the file is associated with the standard input or standard output.

CRT.AssignCRT   Associates the specified file with the screen. This speeds up input and output.

GRAPH.BAR   Draws a filled rectangle at a specified location on a graphics screen.

GRAPH.BAR3D   Draws a filled three-dimensional rectangular shape at a specified location on a graphics screen.

BlockRead   Reads one or more values from a file into an untyped variable.

BlockWrite   Writes one or more values from an untyped variable to a file.

CHDIR   Changes the current directory to the one specified in an argument.

FUNCTION CHR   Returns the character corresponding to the ordinal value passed as argument. The argument must be an integer-type expression.

GRAPH.CIRCLE   Draws a circle with a specified radius and center.

GRAPH.ClearDevice   Clears the graphics screen and moves the cursor to the upper-left corner of the screen, ready for output.

GRAPH.ClearViewPort   Clears the current viewport, or perspective on the screen and moves the cursor to the upper-left corner of the screen.

CLOSE   Closes the file specified in the argument. The file can be of type **TEXT** or another file type. The file must have been opened using either **APPEND, RESET,** or **REWRITE.**

GRAPH.CloseGraph   Shuts down the graphics system and restores the screen to the mode in effect before graphics was initialized.

CRT.ClrEOL   Clears from the current cursor position to the end of the line.

CRT.ClrScr   Clears the entire screen or active window. Moves the cursor to the upper-left corner of the current window.

FUNCTION CONCAT   Creates a concatenated string consisting of the individual strings. The resulting string is truncated after the 255th character, if necessary.

FUNCTION COPY   Copies and returns a specified part of a string.

FUNCTION COS   Returns the cosine (in radians) of the specified angle.

FUNCTION CSeg   Returns the value of the CS register.

DEC   Decreases the value of a specified variable. If the procedure has only one argument, the argument is decreased by 1. If there are two arguments, the value is decreased by an amount specified in a second argument. Only ordinal variables can be changed using this procedure.

CRT.Delay   Waits a specified number of milliseconds.

DELETE   Deletes a specified portion of a string.

CRT.DelLine   Deletes the current line.

GRAPH.DetectGraph   Checks the hardware to determine which graphics driver and mode to use.

FUNCTION DOS.DiskFree   Returns the amount of available storage on the disk in the specified drive.

FUNCTION DOS.DiskSize   Returns the total storage capacity of the disk in the specified drive.

DISPOSE   Deallocates storage for a dynamic variable returning the storage to the heap. The argument must be a pointer. If the target variable is an object, you can provide a second argument: the destructor associated with the object.

FUNCTION DOS.DOSExitCode   Returns the exit code for a sub-program.

FUNCTION DOS.DOSVersion   Returns the major and minor DOS version numbers.

GRAPH.DrawPoly   Draws the outline of a polygon through the specified points.

FUNCTION DSeg   Returns the contents of the DS register.

GRAPH.ELLIPSE   Draws an elliptical arc with specified vertical and horizontal dimensions. The arc covers the distance between two specified angles.

FUNCTION DOS.EnvCount   Returns the number of strings defined in the DOS environment.

FUNCTION DOS.EnvStr   Returns the specified DOS environment string.

FUNCTION EOF   Returns **TRUE** if the end of the specified file has been reached. Returns **FALSE** otherwise. When called with a parameter, the function checks the file specified in the parameter. When called without a parameter, the function checks the standard input for an end-of-file character (usually either CTRL-D or CTRL-Z).

FUNCTION EOLN   Returns **TRUE** if the end of the current line has been reached; returns **FALSE** otherwise.

ERASE   Deletes the external file associated with the argument.

DOS.Exec   Executes the specified program. The program will operate with the command-line arguments specified in a second argument to **DOS.Exec**.

EXIT   Exits immediately from the currently executing block.

FUNCTION EXP   Returns the result of raising *e* to a specified power.

FUNCTION DOS.FExpand   Expands a file name to a name with complete path information.

FUNCTION FILEPOS   Returns the current position in the specified file. The file must be open, and cannot be of type **TEXT**.

FUNCTION FILESIZE   Returns the size of the specified file, which cannot be of type **TEXT**.

FILLCHAR   Initializes a specified area of memory with a specified value.

GRAPH.FillEllipse   Draws and fills an ellipse.

GRAPH.FillPoly   Draws a polygon through specified points and fills it.

DOS.FindFirst   Searches for the first file entry that matches a specified file name. This name string may include wildcard characters.

DOS.FindNext Searches for the next file entry that matches the name specified in a call to **DOS.FindFirst**.

GRAPH.FloodFill Fills a bounded region of the screen with the current fill pattern.

FLUSH Flushes the buffer associated with the specified text file. The file must be open for output—that is, must have been created by using **REWRITE** or **APPEND**.

FUNCTION FRAC Returns the fractional part of the real-type argument.

FREEMEM Disposes a specified number of bytes that had been allocated for the pointer argument. The storage must have been allocated by using **GetMem**.

FUNCTION DOS.FSearch Searches for a specified file in a list of directories. If the file is not found, the function returns an empty string.

DOS.FSplit Splits a file name into three components: drive and directory, file name, and file extensions.

GRAPH.Get ArcCoords Returns the parameter values for the last call to **GRAPH.Arc**.

GRAPH.Get AspectRatio Returns the resolution of the graphics screen in the horizontal and vertical directions.

FUNCTION GRAPH.GetBkColor Returns the index associated with the current background color in the current color palette.

DOS.GetCBreak If the value of the argument is **TRUE**, the program checks whether CTRL-BREAK has been called at every system call. When the parameter is false, the program checks only at certain points in the program.

FUNCTION GRAPH.GetColor Returns the color index passed to the last successful call to **SetColor**.

DOS.GetDate Returns information about the current date setting on your computer.

FUNCTION GRAPH.GetDefaultPalette Returns the record containing the palette settings set by the driver while executing **GRAPH.InitGraph**.

GetDir Returns the current directory on the specified drive.

FUNCTION GRAPH.GetDriverName Returns the name of the current graphics driver.

FUNCTION DOS.GetEnv Returns the value of the environment variable specified in the argument.

DOS.GetFAttr Returns the attributes (for example, hidden, read only, and so on) of the specified file.

GRAPH.GetFillPattern Returns the last fill pattern set (through a call to **GRAPH.SetFillPattern**).

GRAPH.GetFillSettings Returns the last fill pattern and color set (through a call to **GRAPH.SetFillPattern** or **GRAPH.SetFillStyle**).

DOS.GetFTime Returns the date and time the specified file was last modified. The file parameter can be any file type.

FUNCTION GRAPH.GetGraphMode Returns the current graphics mode, whose value depends on which driver is being used.

GRAPH.GetImage Saves, in a buffer, the bit pattern of a specified region of the graphics screen.

DOS.GetIntVec Returns the address stored in the vector associated with a specified interrupt.

GRAPH.GetLineSettings   Returns the current settings for line style, line pattern, and line thickness.

FUNCTION GRAPH.GetMaxColor   Returns the highest color code that can be passed to procedure **SetColor**.

FUNCTION GRAPH.GetMaxMode   Returns the highest graphics mode that can be used with the current graphics driver.

FUNCTION GRAPH.GetMaxX   Returns the rightmost pixel coordinate for the current graphics driver and mode.

FUNCTION GRAPH.GetMaxY   Returns the bottom pixel coordinate for the current graphics driver and mode.

GETMEM   Allocates a specified amount of storage and assigns the starting location of this block to a pointer variable.

FUNCTION GRAPH.GetModeName   Returns a string that represents the name of the specified graphics mode.

GRAPH.GetModeRange   Returns the codes for the lowest and highest graphics modes for the specified graphics driver.

GRAPH.GetPalette   Returns information about the current color palette.

FUNCTION GRAPH.GetPaletteSize   Returns the number of colors on the current palette in the current configuration.

FUNCTION GRAPH.GetPixel   Returns information about the pixel at a specified location.

GRAPH.GetTextSettings   Returns information about the current text font, size, and so on.

DOS.GetTime   Returns the current time on your system.

DOS.GetVerify   Returns the current setting of the DOS verify flag.

GRAPH.GetViewSettings   Returns settings information about the current viewport and about clipping.

FUNCTION GRAPH.GetX   Returns the *x* coordinate of the current position in graphics mode.

FUNCTION GRAPH.GetY   Returns the *y* coordinate of the current position in graphics mode.

CRT.GoToXY   Moves the cursor to the specified location on the screen.

GRAPH.GraphDefaults   Resets the graphics environment to the default settings.

FUNCTION GRAPH.GraphErrorMsg   Returns the error message string corresponding to a specified graphics error code.

FUNCTION GRAPH.GraphResult   Returns the error code for the most recent graphics operation.

HALT   Stops program execution and returns control to the operating systems.

FUNCTION HI   Returns the high-order byte of its argument.

CRT.HighVideo   Selects the high-intensity mode for screen display.

FUNCTION GRAPH.ImageSize   Returns the number of bytes needed to store a rectangular section of the screen.

INC   Increases the value of a specified variable. If the procedure has only one argument, the argument is increased by 1. If there are two arguments, the value is increased by an amount specified in a second argument. Only ordinal variables can be changed using this procedure.

GRAPH.InitGraph Initializes the graphics environment and switches the hardware to graphics mode.

INSERT Inserts one string into another, beginning at a specified position.

CRT.InsLine Inserts a blank line at the current cursor position. Lines below the new one are moved downward on the screen.

FUNCTION GRAPH.InstallUserDriver Lets you add a device driver to the BGI device driver table, so you can use the new driver in programs.

FUNCTION GRAPH.InstallUserFont Lets you add a new font to the BGI environment.

FUNCTION INT Returns the integer portion of the real-number argument.

DOS.Intr Executes a specified software interrupt.

FUNCTION IORESULT Returns information about the last I/O operation performed.

DOS.Keep Terminates the current program, but keeps it in memory for possible later reactivation.

FUNCTION CRT.KeyPressed Returns **TRUE** if a key has been pressed, and **FALSE** otherwise.

FUNCTION LENGTH Returns the length of the specified string.

GRAPH.Line Draws a line from a specified starting point to a specified ending point.

GRAPH.LineRel Draws a line to a point at a relative distance from the current location.

GRAPH.LineTo Draws a line from the current point to a specified ending point.

FUNCTION LN Returns the natural logarithm (that is, logarithm to the base e) of its argument.

FUNCTION LO Returns the low-order byte of its argument.

CRT.LowVideo Selects the low-intensity mode for screen display.

MARK Stores the current heap location in a pointer variable for later use.

FUNCTION MaxAvail Returns the size (in bytes) of the largest unused area of contiguous storage in the heap.

FUNCTION MemAvail Returns the amount (in bytes) of available storage in the heap.

MkDir Creates a specified directory.

MOVE Copies a specified number of consecutive bytes in memory from one location to another.

GRAPH.MoveRel In graphics mode, moves the current pointer to a location a relative distance from the starting location.

GRAPH.MoveTo In graphics mode, moves the current pointer to a specified location.

DOS.MSDOS Lets you access a DOS service by going through the function dispatcher (interrupt $21).

NEW Allocates storage dynamically and assigns the starting location of this storage to a pointer. The routine can also be used as a function that returns a pointer to the allocated location. When used with objects, **NEW** also enables you to initialize the object for virtual methods.

CRT.NormVideo   Selects the text attribute settings read at startup.

CRT.NoSound   Turns the internal speaker off.

FUNCTION ODD   Returns **TRUE** if the argument is an odd number, **FALSE** otherwise.

FUNCTION Ofs   Returns the offset of a specified data object.

FUNCTION ORD   Returns the ordinal number corresponding to a specified ordinal-type value.

GRAPH.OutText   In graphics mode, outputs a string at the current position.

GRAPH.OutTextXY   In graphics mode, outputs a string at a specified position.

OVERLAY.OvrClearBuf   Clears the overlay buffer. Not available in DiskTutor.

OVERLAY.OvrGetBuf   Returns the size of the overlay buffer. Not available in DiskTutor.

OVERLAY.OvrInit   Initializes the overlay manager and opens the overlay. Not available in DiskTutor.

OVERLAY.OvrInitEMS   Does the same thing as **OVERLAY.OvrInit**, but tries to load the overlay file into EMS. Not available in DiskTutor.

OVERLAY.OvrSetBuf   Lets you set the size of the overlay buffer. Not available in DiskTutor.

DOS.PackTime   Converts date and time information into a four-byte, packed format used by other routines.

FUNCTION ParamCount   Returns the number of command-line arguments passed to the program.

FUNCTION ParamStr   Returns a specified command-line argument.

FUNCTION PI   Returns the value of π.

GRAPH.PieSlice   Draws and fills a pie slice on the screen.

FUNCTION POS   Returns the position of a specified substring in another string.

FUNCTION PRED   Returns the predecessor of the argument.

FUNCTION PTR   Converts an address in segment:offset form to a pointer-type value.

GRAPH.PutImage   Puts a graphics image on the screen.

GRAPH.PutPixel   Puts a pixel at a specified location.

FUNCTION RANDOM   Returns a random integer or real number, depending on whether it's called with one or no arguments.

RANDOMIZE   Initializes the random-number generator with a random seed.

READ   Reads one or more values from a text file, and stores these values in the specified program variables. For typed files, this routine reads a single file component and stores this value in a specified variable.

FUNCTION CRT.ReadKey   Reads a character from the keyboard.

READLN   Does the same as **READ** for a text file, and then moves to the next line of the file.

GRAPH.Rectangle   Draws a rectangle at a specified location on the screen.

FUNCTION GRAPH.RegisterBGIDriver   Registers a new driver with the graphics system.

FUNCTION GRAPH.RegisterBGIFont   Registers a new font with the graphics system.

RELEASE   Returns the heap to an earlier state, which was recorded with **MARK**.

RENAME   Renames an external file.

RESET   Opens an existing file for reading.

GRAPH.RestoreCRTMode   Restores the screen from graphics mode to the state before graphics mode was initialized.

REWRITE   Creates and opens a new file for writing.

RMDIR   Removes the specified directory, provided that it is empty.

FUNCTION ROUND   Rounds a real-type value to an integer-type value.

RUNERROR   Stops program execution and indicates a run-time error.

GRAPH.Sector   Draws and fills an elliptical sector on a graphics screen.

SEEK   Moves the current file position to a specified component in the file.

FUNCTION SEEKEOF   Returns **TRUE** if the current position in a text file is at the end-of-file marker.

FUNCTION SEEKEOLN   Returns **TRUE** if the current position in a text file is at an end-of-line marker.

FUNCTION SEG   Returns the segment portion of the argument's location.

GRAPH.Set ActivePage   Makes a particular page active for graphics activity.

GRAPH.Set AllPalette   Changes palette colors as specified.

GRAPH.Set AspectRatio   Changes the default correction factor for aspect-ratio.

GRAPH.SetBkColor   Sets the current background color.

DOS.SetCBreak   Lets you specify whether to check for CTRL-BREAK at every opportunity.

GRAPH.SetColor   Sets the current color.

DOS.SetDate   Sets the current date on your system.

DOS.SetFAttr   Sets the attribute of a specified file.

GRAPH.SetFillPattern   Enables you to specify the pattern used when filling graphics figures.

GRAPH.SetFillStyle   Enables you to specify the pattern and color used when filling graphics figures.

DOS.SetFTime   Sets the date and time a file was last modified.

GRAPH.SetGraphBufSize   Lets you specify the size of the graphics buffer used for filling graphics figures.

GRAPH.SetGraphMode   Switches to graphics mode and clears the screen.

DOS.SetIntVec   Sets a specified interrupt vector to a specified location.

GRAPH.SetLineStyle   Sets the current line style and line width.

GRAPH.SetPalette   Changes a palette color to a new value.

GRAPH.SetRGBPalette Modifies palette entries for VGA and IBM 8514 graphics drivers.

SetTextBuf Assigns a buffer to a text file, for use in I/O related to the file.

GRAPH.SetTextJustify Lets you specify justification for text to be displayed in graphics mode.

GRAPH.SetTextStyle Lets you specify the current text font, style, and size for display on a graphics screen.

DOS.SetTime Sets the current time on your system.

GRAPH.SetUserCharSize Lets you specify the dimensions for certain fonts in graphics mode.

DOS.SetVerify Lets you set the value for the DOS verify flag.

GRAPH.SetViewPort Sets the current viewport or window for graphics output.

GRAPH.SetVisualPage Sets the graphics page number, if multiple pages are supported by your graphics card.

GRAPH.SetWriteMode Sets the writing mode used for drawing lines.

FUNCTION SIN Returns the sine (in radians) of the specified angle.

FUNCTION SIZEOF Returns the number of bytes required to store a variable of the type specified in the argument. The argument may be a specific variable or a general type specifier.

CRT.Sound Turns on an internal speaker at a specified frequency.

FUNCTION SPtr Returns the current value of the SP register.

FUNCTION SQR   Returns the square of the argument.

FUNCTION SQRT   Returns the square root of the argument, which must be nonnegative.

FUNCTION SSeg   Returns the current value of the SS register.

STR   Converts a numeric argument to a string representation.

FUNCTION SUCC   Returns the successor (in the ordered values for the type) of the argument.

FUNCTION SWAP   Swaps the high- and low-order bytes of the argument.

DOS.SwapVectors   Swaps interrupt vectors.

CRT.TextBackground   Sets the background color for text output.

CRT.TextColor   Sets the foreground color for text output.

GRAPH.TextHeight   Returns the height (in pixels) of a specified string in graphics mode.

CRT.TextMode   Selects a specific text mode for output.

GRAPH.TextWidth   Returns the width (in pixels) of a specified string in graphics mode.

FUNCTION TRUNC   Converts a real-type value to an integer-type value by truncating the number's fractional part.

TRUNCATE   Truncates the specified file at the current position in the file.

FUNCTION TYPEOF   Returns a pointer to the virtual method table of the object passed as an argument. This function can be used only with object parameters.

DOS.UnpackTime   Converts date and time information from a packed four-byte format to individual components.

FUNCTION UPCASE   Converts the character argument to uppercase.

VAL   Converts a specified string value to a numeric form.

FUNCTION CRT.WhereX   Returns the x coordinate of the current cursor position. The position is determined relative to the current window.

FUNCTION CRT.WhereY   Returns the y coordinate of the current cursor position. The position is determined relative to the current window.

CRT.Window   Defines a text window at the specified location on the screen.

WRITE   Writes one or more values to a text file or to the standard output. For typed files, writes one variable into a file component.

WRITELN   Writes one or more values to a text file or to the standard output, and then moves the cursor to the next line on the screen or writes an end-of-line marker to the file.

   Turbo Pascal also has numerous identifiers that are used to represent various kinds of information. These identifiers are not reserved, but they are used for particular purposes in Turbo Pascal. The most common of these identifiers are presented in this section.
   In addition to the identifiers summarized here, you can use the Help facility to get information about other identifiers associated with the various Turbo Pascal units.

CRT.CheckBreak : BOOLEAN   This variable enables and disables checking for CTRL-BREAK.

CRT.CheckEOF : BOOLEAN   This variable enables and disables generating an end-of-file character when the user presses CTRL-Z.

CRT.CheckSnow : BOOLEAN   This variable determines whether information will be written to direct video memory only at times when interference will be minimized.

CRT.CheckVideo : BOOLEAN   This variable determines whether information will be written directly to video memory or be written using BIOS calls.

DOS.DateTime   This record type is used to store information about dates and times.

DOS.DosError : INTEGER   This variable is used to store DOS error codes. Possible values are as follows:

0	No error
2	File not found
3	Path not found
5	Access denied
6	Invalid file handle
8	Not enough memory
10	Invalid environment
11	Invalid format
18	No more files

DOS.FileRec   This record type is used to represent information about typed and untyped files.

Input : Text   This variable represents the standard input for your program.

CRT.LastMode : WORD   This variable is used to store the current video mode when the program starts and each time procedure **TextMode** is called.

Printer.Lst : Text   This variable is associated with the LPT1 device (parallel printer) on your computer.

Output : Text   This variable represents the standard output for your program.

RandSeed : LONGINT   This value provides a seed for the random number generator.

DOS.Registers   This record type is used to store values from the hardware registers, as described in Chapter 14, "Miscellaneous Topics."

DOS.SearchRec   This record type is used to store information about directory entries.

DOS.TextBuf   This **ARRAY OF CHAR** provides a buffer associated with a particular text file.

DOS.TextRec   This record type is used to represent information about text files.

CRT.TextAttr : BYTE   This variable is used to store the current text attributes.

CTR.WindMax : WORD   This variable is used to store the cooordinates of the lower right-hand corner of the current window. *x* and *y* coordinates are stored in the low and high bytes, respectively, of the variable.

CTR.WindMin : WORD   This variable is used to store the coordinates of the upper left-hand corner of the current window. *x* and *y* coordinates are stored in the low and high bytes, respectively, of the variable.

C IDE Commands

This appendix summarizes the commands you can use in the IDE, including editor and menu commands. In many cases, more than one keystroke sequence can be used to invoke a command. Some commands are available directly (for example, through hot keys), others only through menu selections, and others directly and through menus.

Help Commands

The main Help command (F1) is always accessible, as is the help index (SHIFT-F1). Other help-related commands are accessible only under certain conditions.

F1	Get help about the current context—for example, the editor, a particular menu, and so on
SHIFT-F1	Display the help index
F1 F1	Call up help about help
ALT-F1	Display the most recently shown help screen
CTRL-F1	Display help about the Pascal language construct at the current cursor position (the cursor must be in the edit window and at a letter in such a construct)

Commands Available in the Help Window

PGDN	Move forward one screen in the help information
PGUP	Move backward one screen in the help information
ESC	Exit help
F1	Call up help about help
TAB or SHIFT-TAB	Move among highlighted items in a help screen
ENTER	Select a highlighted item to get more help about the item

Editor Commands

You can use the following commands in the edit window. Some of the commands modify your file; others modify the editing environment itself.

Cursor Movement Commands

CTRL-S or LEFT ARROW	Move one character to the left
CTRL-D or RIGHT ARROW	Move one character to the right
CTRL-A or CTRL-LEFT ARROW	Move left to the start of the current or preceding word
CTRL-F or CTRL-RIGHT ARROW	Move right to the start of the next word
CTRL-E or UP ARROW	Move up one line
CTRL-X or DOWN ARROW	Move down one line
CTRL-W	Scroll up one line
CTRL-Z	Scroll down one line
CTRL-R or PGUP	Page up
CTRL-C or PGDN	Page down

CTRL-Q S or HOME	Move to beginning of line
CTRL-Q D or END	Move to end of line
CTRL-Q B	Move to beginning of block
CTRL-Q K	Move to end of block
CTRL-Q W	Move to location of last error
CTRL-Q P	Move to cursor position before most recent command
CTRL-Q E or CTRL-HOME	Move to top of the current window
CTRL-Q X or CTRL-END	Move to end of the current window
CTRL-Q R or CTRL-PGUP	Move to start of the file
CTRL-Q C or CTRL-PGDN	Move to the end of the file
TAB or CTRL-I	Move cursor to next tab stop (all text from current cursor position is moved)

Insert and Delete Commands

CTRL-V or INS or ALT-O E E I	Toggle insert mode on and off
CTRL-N	Insert a blank line at current cursor position
CTRL-O O	Insert compiler options in source file
CTRL-Y	Delete current line
CTRL-Q Y	Delete from current cursor position to end of line
CTRL-K Y	Delete marked block
CTRL-H or BACKSPACE	Delete character to the left of the cursor
CTRL-G or DEL	Delete character at the current cursor position
CTRL-T	Delete rightwards from the current cursor position to the current or next word

Block Commands

CTRL-K B	Mark start of block
CTRL-K K	Mark end of block
CTRL-K T	Mark the current word (or the preceding one, if the cursor is between words)

CTRL-K Y or CTRL-DEL or ALT-E L	Clear marked block (delete marked block permanently)
CTRL-K C or CTRL-INS or ALT-E C	Copy marked block to clipboard, but leave original block in file
CTRL-K V or SHIFT-DEL or ALT-E T	Cut marked block from file (move marked block to clipboard)
SHIFT-INS or ALT-E P	Paste block from the clipboard to cursor location in current window (which may contain the clipboard)
SHIFT + Arrow keys	Define boundaries of text block being marked
CTRL-K R	Read block from disk
CTRL-K W	Write block to disk
CTRL-K H	Toggle between hiding and displaying the marked block
CTRL-K I	Indent block
CTRL-K U	Unindent block
CTRL-K P or ALT-F P	Print marked block

Miscellaneous Commands

ESC	Abort operation
CTRL-K S or F2	Save current file and return to edit window
F3	Load a new file into the edit window
CTRL-O T	Toggle between Tab mode on and off
CTRL-O F	Toggle between Fill mode on and off
CTRL-O I	Toggle between Autoindent mode on and off
CTRL-O U	Toggle between Unindent mode on and off
CTRL-Q L or ALT-E R	Restore current line to its state before your last action (only possible if no new command has been given)
CTRL-K n	Set place marker n
CTRL-Q n	Find place marker n
CTRL-Q [or CTRL-Q]	Find the matching delimiter
CTRL-P	Prefix for writing a control character

CTRL-U	Abort current operation
CTRL-Q W	Go to location of last error
CTRL-Q F or ALT-S F	Find text
CTRL-Q A or ALT-S R	Find and replace text
CTRL-L or ALT-S S	Repeat last find or replace operation
ALT-F N	Create a new file, making its edit window the active one
ALT-F O or F3	Open a file to be specified
ALT-X or ALT-F X	Exit IDE
ALT-O E E A	Set Autoindent mode (toggle)
ALT-O E E B	Enable BACKSPACE to indent current line to an indentation based on the previous line (toggle)
ALT-O E E C	Enable cursor to move through tab stops, one column at a time (toggle)
ALT-O E E F	Create backup (.BAK) file when saving a newly edited file (toggle)
ALT-O E E O	Replace blanks with optimal combination of blanks and tab characters (toggle)
ALT-O E E U	Use actual tab characters (instead of blanks) in file (toggle)

Function Key Commands

The following commands are associated with the function keys. Many of these commands are also listed in other sections.

F1	Get help about current context
ALT-F1	Display most recent help screen
CTRL-F1	Get help about selected language topic
F2	Save file
CTRL-F2	Reset program for execution from the beginning
F3	Open file
ALT-F3	Close active window
CTRL-F3	Display call stack during program execution
F4	Execute program and then stop at current cursor position

CTRL-F4	Evaluate expression, value, or function during program execution
F5	Toggle edit window between full and partial screen
ALT-F5	Toggle between program's output screen and edit window
F6	Move to next window in open window list
SHIFT-F6	Move to previous window in open window list
F7	Trace through program step by step
CTRL-F7	Add watch variable
F8	Step over procedure or function during program execution
CTRL-F8	Toggle breakpoint
F9	Make program by compiling all required files
ALT-F9	Compile file
CTRL-F9	Run program, compiling first if necessary
F10	Switch to menu line

Menu Commands

This section summarizes the commands accessible through the items on the menu list in the IDE.

The System Menu

ALT-SPACEBAR	Pull down the System menu
ALT-SPACEBAR A	Display version information about the IDE
ALT-SPACEBAR R	Refresh the display
ALT-SPACEBAR C	Clear the desktop

The File Menu

ALT-F	Pull down the File menu
ALT-F O or F3	Open a file whose name will be specified in a dialog box and make the edit window for this file the active one
ALT-F N	Create a new file and make the edit window for this file the active one
ALT-F S or F2	Save the file in the active edit window to disk
ALT-F A	Save the file in the active edit window under a name to be specified in a dialog box
ALT-F L	Save all currently open files
ALT-F C	Change to the directory to be specified in a dialog box
ALT-F P	Print contents of the active edit window
ALT-F G	Get information about the file in the active edit window
ALT-F D	Exit temporarily from the IDE, to a DOS shell
ALT-F X or ALT-X	Exit from the IDE

The Edit Menu

ALT-E	Pull down the Edit menu
ALT-E R	Restore a line to its state before the most recent action
ALT-E T or SHIFT-DEL	Cut the marked block of text from the active window and copy this block to the clipboard
ALT-E C or CTRL-INS	Copy the marked block of text from the active window to the clipboard, leaving the text in the original file
ALT-E P or SHIFT-INS	Paste text from the clipboard to the cursor position in the active window (which may contain the clipboard)

ALT-E E   Copy a predefined example—about a particular Pascal construct or routine—from the Help files to the clipboard. You must be in the Help window for this command to be valid

ALT-E L or CTRL-DEL   Clear the marked block of text from the active edit window. This deletion is permanent and cannot be undone

The Search Menu

ALT-S   Pull down the Search menu

ALT-S F   Find the text to be specified, using the search guidelines selected in the following dialog box

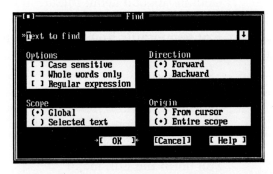

ALT-S R   Search for text to be specified in a dialog box, and replace this text with other text to be specified. The following dialog box shows the search and replace criteria you can specify with this command

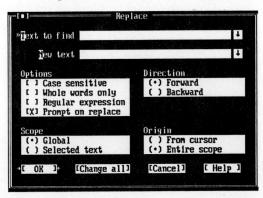

ALT-S S or CTRL-L	Repeat the last find or replace command
ALT-S G	Go to a line number to be specified in a dialog box
ALT-S P	Find the beginning of the procedure or function to be specified in a dialog box (valid only in debugging mode)
ALT-S E or ALT-F8	Find the source code location corresponding to a run-time error. The error's address is reported at run time, and is specified in a dialog box

The Run Menu

ALT-R	Pull down the Run menu
ALT-R R or CTRL-F9	Run the program in the active edit window—compiling first, if necessary
ALT-R P or CTRL-F2	Reset the program; that is, stop a debugging session, release any allocated memory, and close any files opened by the program
ALT-R G or F4	Execute the program, pausing execution at the command corresponding to the current cursor location
ALT-R T or F7	Execute the program in the active edit window by tracing the statements as they execute (the debugger traces execution into any procedures or functions called)
ALT-R S or F8	Execute the program in the active edit window by tracing the statements as they execute (the debugger skips over details of execution in any procedures or functions called)
ALT-R A	Pass command-line arguments for running the program in the active edit window

The Compile Menu

| ALT-C | Pull down the Compile menu |
| ALT-C C or ALT-F9 | Compile the file in the active edit window |

ALT-C M or F9	Make an executable version of the primary program file by compiling that file and any other modified files used in the program (the primary file is usually, but not always, the file in the active edit window)
ALT-C B	Make an executable version of the primary program file by compiling that file and any other files used in the program, regardless of whether the files have been modified since the last compilation (the primary file is usually, but not always, the file in the active edit window)
ALT-C D	Specify whether the executable version of a program is saved to memory or to disk (toggle)
ALT-C P	Specify the primary file for a program whose source code is found in multiple files

The Debug Menu

ALT-D	Pull down the Debug menu
ALT-D E or CTRL-F4	Evaluate or modify an expression to be specified in a dialog box
ALT-D W	Open a pop-up menu of commands relating to watchpoints
ALT-D W A or CTRL-F7	Add a watch expression to the Watches window
ALT-D W D	Delete the current expression in the Watches window
ALT-D W E	Edit the current expression in the Watches window
ALT-D W R	Remove all watch expressions from the Watches window
ALT-D T	Set or clear an unconditional breakpoint on the current line (toggle)
ALT-D B	Specify breakpoints and conditions for these in a dialog box

The Options Menu

ALT-O	Pull down the Options menu
ALT-O C	Specify options relating to the compilation process in the following dialog box

ALT-O M	Specify default memory sizes (for example, for the stack) for a program
ALT-O L	Specify options relating to the linking process in the following dialog box

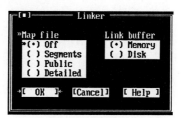

ALT-O B	Specify options relating to the integrated debugger in the following dialog box

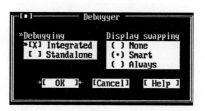

ALT-O D	Specify the directories in which various types of files (.EXE, .PAS, .TPU, and so forth) are to be found or written
ALT-O E	Open a pop-up menu through which to specify settings for the IDE
ALT-O E P	Specify preferences for IDE display and actions in the following dialog box

ALT-O E E	Specify configuration settings for the editing environment in the following dialog box

ALT-O E M	Specify settings for the mouse keys in the following dialog box

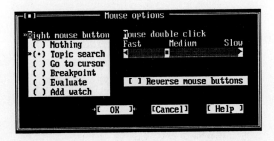

ALT-O E S   Specify configuration settings for starting up the
IDE in the following dialog box

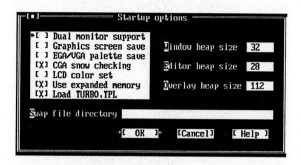

ALT-O E C   Specify the color combinations for the various IDE
windows in the following dialog box

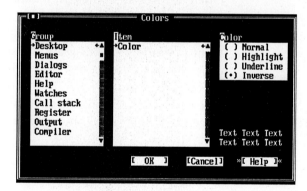

ALT-O S   Save configuration option settings to a file to be
specified in a dialog box

ALT-O R   Retrieve configuration option settings from a file
to be specified in a dialog box

The Window Menu

ALT-W   Pull down the Window menu

ALT-W S or CTRL-F5   Change the size or position of the active window,
using the arrow keys to move the window

ALT-W Z or F5	Zoom in or out, to set the window size to maximum or to default sizes (toggle)
ALT-W T	Tile all open edit windows; that is, reposition them so that none of the windows overlaps
ALT-W C	Cascade all open edit windows; that is, reposition them so that the windows overlap
ALT-W N or F6	Make the next window in the open window list the active one (this list is a circular one, so that the window after the last is the first window opened)
ALT-W P or SHIFT-F6	Make the previous window in the open window list the active one (this list is a circular one, so that the window before the first is the last window opened)
ALT-W C or ALT-F3	Close the active window
ALT-W W	Open the Watches window, making it the active one
ALT-W R	Open the Register window, making it the active one
ALT-W O	Open the Output window, making it the active one
ALT-W K	Open a window that displays the stack of procedures and functions currently called in an executing program
ALT-W U or ALT-F5	Open the User screen, which uses the entire screen to display program output

The Help Menu

ALT-H	Pull down the Help menu
ALT-H C	Open the Help window with a table of contents displayed
ALT-H I or SHIFT-F1	Open the Help window with an index of keywords for which help is available
ALT-H T or CTRL-F1	Open the Help window to information about the Pascal construct at the current cursor position

| ALT-H P or ALT-F1 | Open the Help window (if not already open) to the help screen displayed most recently |
| ALT-H H or F1 F1 | Open the Help window to a screen that provides help about the help system |

IDE Command-Line Options

You can also specify certain options on the command line, when you first invoke the IDE. Options can begin with a **/** or **-**. If options start with **-**, you must leave at least one space between consecutive options. (This is because **-** can also be a value for an option setting.)

The options themselves are all specified as one-letter codes and are not case sensitive. Depending on the option, you will need to provide an argument value, for example, a file name, a numerical value, a **+** or a **-** sign. Placing a **+** or a blank after an option turns that option on; placing a **-** after the option turns it off. Values must follow immediately after the option. For example, the first of the following command lines is valid, but the second is not:

```
turbo /E64 myfile
turbo /E 64 myfile
```

/Cfile name	Use the configuration file specified as the argument.
/D[+ or -]	Work in dual monitor mode (if the hardware is present).
/Enumber	Change the size of the editor heap to the specified size (in Kb). The argument must be a value between 28 (default) and 128.
/G[+ or -]	Enable (or disable) a full graphics save during debug mode (does not work on CGA systems).
/L[+ or -]	Specify if using the IDE on an LCD screen, such as on a laptop.
/N[+ or -]	Enable (or disable) snow checking on CGA monitors.

/O*number*	Change the size of the overlay heap to the specified size (in Kb). The argument must be a value between 64 and 256, with 112K being the default.
/P[+ or -]	Use to control palette swapping on EGA adapters.
/S*path*	Specify a fast swap area for the IDE's temporary files.
/T[+ or -]	Disable this option to tell the IDE *not* to load the **turbo.tpl** run-time library. If disabled, you must have the **system.tpu** unit available.
/W*number*	Change the size of the window heap to the specified size (in Kb). The argument must be a value between 24 and 64, with 32K being the default.
/X[+ or -]	Disable this option to tell the IDE *not* to use expanded memory (EMS).

D Command-Line Compiler Options

In addition to the IDE (TURBO.EXE), your Turbo Pascal package includes TPC.EXE, a command-line version of the Pascal compiler. You can use this version of the compiler to create executable programs directly from the command line—that is, without having to enter the IDE.

To control the code generated by the compiler and to specify the manner in which the compiler is to process your files, you can specify options on the **tpc** command line. Most of these options are equivalent to IDE commands, which would be specified through menus in the IDE.

Compiler options can appear before or after the file name on the command line. Each option must begin with a **/** or a **−**. This delimiter is followed by a single letter or by a dollar sign followed by a letter. The letter identifies the option and may be in upper- or lowercase. The option identifier may be followed by a value for the option. For most options, this will be a **+** or **−** or it will be a path specifier.

If the options begin with a **−**, there must be a blank between options, since **−** is also a valid setting for certain options. For example, the following two command lines are equivalent:

```
tpc /$B-/$I- /Imyinc myfile
tpc -$B- -$I- -Imyinc myfile
```

745

Compiler Directives

Many of the command-line options are actually compiler directives, which determine the type of code produced and the type of checking done by the compiler. For example, the **/$B** directive lets you specify whether Boolean expressions should be evaluated completely or whether the compiler can short-circuit the evaluation process by stopping as soon as a definitive value is found.

In Pascal, compiler directives begin with a dollar sign ($). This will be followed by a single letter, which identifies the directive. The directive will also get a value, indicated by a + or − immediately after the letter. Thus, the **$B** directive can take either of two forms: **$B+** and **$B−**. The **$M** directive requires more than + or − when used, as described below.

When a directive appears on the command line, the directive will, of course, be preceded by a **/** or **−**. However, if you have multiple directives on a single command line, you can save yourself some typing. Instead of beginning each directive with a **/$** or a **−$**, you can omit these leading characters if you separate directives with commas. You only need the **/$** or **−$** for the first directive. For example, the following two command lines are equivalent:

```
tpc /$B-/$I-/$V+/Imyinc myfile
tpc /$B-,I-,V+ /Imyinc myfile
```

Note that **/I**, which is not a directive, is not included in the comma-separated list on the second command line. The shortcut notation is allowed for all directives except **$M**, which requires three values. These values are themselves separated by commas.

When you include a directive as a command-line option, the directive is interpreted as if it had appeared at the start of the source file. When directives appear in a source file, they are included within comment markers. Multiple directives can be included within the same comment markers and require only one dollar sign at the start of the directory list, as in the following:

```
(*$I-,B+,V-*)
```

The directives all correspond to IDE commands. Since all but one of the directives have only two possible values, these commands toggle in the IDE. For example, the IDE menu command ALT-O C B (for **O**ptions **C**ompile complete **B**oolean evaluation) corresponds to either **$B +** or **$B −**, depending on how often the command is given. In the following **tpc** option summary, the corresponding menu command is given in parentheses.

/$A+	Align data on word boundaries in compiled file (ALT-O C W).
/$A−	Align data on byte boundaries in compiled file (ALT-O C W).
/$B+	Evaluate Boolean expressions completely (ALT-O C B).
/$B−	Short-circuit evaluation of Boolean expressions (ALT-O C B).
/$D+	Enable generation of debugging information for program (ALT-O C D).
/$D−	Disable generation of debugging information for program (ALT-O C D).
/$E+	Enable linking with a run-time library that emulates an 80x87 math coprocessor (ALT-O C E).
/$E−	Disable linking with a run-time library that emulates an 80x87 math coprocessor (ALT-O C E).
/$F+	Use far calls (calls with 32-bit addresses) for all procedures and functions in the generated code (ALT-O C F).
/$F−	Use far or near calls, as appropriate, for procedures and functions in the generated code (ALT-O C F).
/$G+	Enable generation of 80286 instructions (ALT-O C 2).
/$G−	Disable generation of 80286 instructions, so that only generic 8086 instructions are generated (ALT-O C 2).
/$I+	Turn I/O checking on (ALT-O C I).
/$I−	Turn I/O checking off (ALT-O C I).
/$L+	Enable generation of local symbol information for program files (ALT-O C L).
/$L−	Disable generation of local symbol information for program files (ALT-O C L).

/$M*stack,min,max*	Specify memory allocations for the stack and the minimum and maximum heap sizes (ALT-O M). The first argument (*stack*) must be a value between 1024 and 65520. The value *min* must be between 0 and 655360, and *max* must be a value between *min* and 655360.
/$N+	Generate code that uses the 80x87 coprocessor to do real number operations (ALT-O C 8).
/$N−	Generate code that uses software to do real number operations (ALT-O C 8).
/$O+	Enable generation of code for overlays (ALT-O C O).
/$O−	Disable generation of code for overlays (ALT-O C O).
/$R+	Enable range checking (ALT-O C R).
/$R−	Disable range checking (ALT-O C R).
/$S+	Enable stack overflow checking (ALT-O C S).
/$S−	Disable stack overflow checking (ALT-O C S).
/$V+	Enforce strict type checking on **VAR** string parameters (ALT-O C V).
/$V−	Do not enforce strict type checking on **VAR** string parameters, so that strings defined as having different lengths can be passed to routines (ALT-O C V).
/$X+	Enable the use of Turbo Pascal's extended syntax (ALT-O C X).
/$X−	Disable the use of Turbo Pascal's extended syntax (ALT-O C X).

Nondirective Options

The remaining **tpc** options determine how the compiler itself works, specify directories for various files, and control whether and what debugging information is saved. IDE menu commands corresponding to the **tpc** options are again given in parentheses.

/B	Build a program by recompiling all units and files used in the program (ALT-C B).

/D*symbols* Define conditional symbols that can be used to control the compilation process (ALT-O C C). This option is equivalent to the **$DEFINE***symbols* compiler directive. The option must be followed by one or more symbols separated by semicolons. For example, the following option defines two symbols, **debug** and **stackcheck**, which can be used in conjunction with the **$IFDEF** directive to control compilation.

```
/Ddebug;stackcheck
```

/E*path* Tell **tpc** where to write any .EXE and .TPU files created during compilation (ALT-O D E). The argument for the option must specify a valid path. By default, files are written to the current directory.

/F*seg:off* Find the location, in the source file, of a run-time error (ALT-S E). When a run-time error is reported, the error's location in the code file is provided as segment and offset values. To find the source code corresponding to this, you must enable the **$D** directive (to include debugging information), and then compile the program with the **/F** option. As arguments to the option, include the segment:offset information for the error you want to find.

/GD Tell **tpc** to generate a .MAP file that includes segment, publics, and line number information (ALT-O L D).

/GP Tell **tpc** to generate a .MAP file that includes segment and publics information (ALT-O L P).

/GS Tell **tpc** to generate a .MAP file that includes only segment information (ALT-O L S).

/I*path* Tell **tpc** where to look for include files, if these are not found in the current directory (ALT-O D I). This option is equivalent to the **$I***filename* compiler directive. The argument to this option must be one or more valid paths separated by semicolons. For example:

```
tpc myprog /Iincdir;c:\pascal\inc
```

/L	Disable use of memory to store linker information between the linker's two passes (ALT-O L I). (The default IDE setting is ALT-O L M, which buffers in memory.) When disabled, the information is reread from files for each pass. This is slower, but requires less memory.
/M	Build a program by recompiling only those files and units that have changed since the last compilation (ALT-C M). The **M** refers to a **make** utility, which is a (more or less) standard project maintenance tool.
/O*path*	Tell **tpc** where to search for .OBJ files that need to be linked into your program (ALT-O D O). This option is equivalent to the **$L***filename* compiler directive. The argument to this option must be one or more valid paths separated by semicolons. For example,

```
tpc myprog /Oobjdir;c:\pascal\obj
```

/Q	Suppress the display of file names and line numbers during compilation (no menu equivalent).
/T*path*	Tell **tpc** not to load TURBO.TPL (ALT-O E S T). When this option is used, SYSTEM.TPU must be available.
/U*path*	Tell **tpc** where to look for units, if not found as part of TURBO.TPL (ALT-O D U). The argument to this option must be one or more valid paths separated by semicolons. For example,

```
tpc myprog /Uunitdir;c:\pascal\units
```

/V	Tell **tpc** to append debugging information to the end of the created .EXE file (ALT-O B S).

Index

The manuscript for this book was prepared and submitted to Osborne/McGraw-Hill in electronic form. The acquisitions editor for this project was Jeffrey Pepper and the technical reviewer was Steven Nameroff.

Text design, by Marcela Hancik and Stefany Otis, uses Century Expanded for text body and Swiss for display.

Cover art by Graphic Eye, Inc. Cover supplier and color separation by Phoenix Color Corp. Screens produced with InSet from Inset Systems, Inc. Book printed and bound by R.R. Donnelley & Sons Company, Crawfordsville, Indiana.

Osborne McGraw-Hill

— Tear off for Bookmark

Computer
Books

(800) 227-0900

▼

You're important to us...

We'd like to know what you're interested in, what kinds of books you're looking for, and what you thought about this book in particular.

Please fill out the attached card and mail it in. We'll do our best to keep you informed about Osborne's newest books and special offers.

▶ *YES, SEND ME A FREE COLOR CATALOG*
of all Osborne/McGraw-Hill computer books.

Name:_____Title:_____

Company:_____

Address:_____

City:_____State:_____Zip:_____

I'M PARTICULARLY INTERESTED IN THE FOLLOWING(*Check all that apply*)

I use this software:
❏ Lotus 1-2-3
❏ Quattro
❏ dBASE
❏ WordPerfect
❏ Microsoft Word
❏ WordStar
❏ Others_____

I program in:
❏ C
❏ PASCAL
❏ BASIC
❏ Others_____

I chose this book because...
❏ Recognized author's name
❏ Osborne/McGraw-Hill's reputation
❏ Read book review
❏ Read Osborne catalog
❏ Saw advertisement in _____
❏ Found while browsing in store
❏ Found/recommended in library
❏ Required textbook
❏ Price
❏ Other_____

I use this operating system:
❏ DOS
❏ OS/2
❏ UNIX
❏ Macintosh
❏ Others_____

I rate this book:
❏ Excellent   ❏ Good   ❏ Poor

Comments_____
_____

Topics I would like to see covered in future books by Osborne/McGraw-Hill

include:_____
_____

Print **ISBN** from the back cover here: 0-07-881_ _ _ - _

Osborne McGraw-Hill

Computer Books

(800) 227-0900

No Postage
Necessary
If Mailed
in the
United States

BUSINESS REPLY MAIL

First Class   Permit NO. 3111 Berkeley, CA

Postage will be paid by addressee

 Osborne **McGraw·Hill**

2600 Tenth Street

Berkeley, California 94710–9938